C

SITTING IN JUDGMENT

The public image of judges has been stuck in a time warp; they are invariably depicted in the media—and derided in public bars up and down the country—as 'privately educated Oxbridge types', usually 'out-of-touch', and more often than not as 'old men'. These and other stereotypes—the judge as a pervert, the judge as a right-wing monster—have dogged the judiciary long since any of them ceased to have any basis in fact. Indeed the limited research that was permitted in the 1960s and 1970s tended to reinforce several of these stereotypes. Moreover, occasional high profile incidents in the courts, elaborated with the help of satirists such as *Private Eye* and *Monty Python*, have ensured that the 'old white Tory judge' caricature not only survives but has come to be viewed as incontestable.

Since the late 1980s the judiciary has changed, largely as a result of the introduction of training and new and more transparent methods of recruitment and appointment. But how much has it changed, and what are the courts like after decades of judicial reform? Given unprecedented access to the whole range of courts—from magistrates' courts to the Supreme Court—Penny Darbyshire spent seven years researching the judges, accompanying them in their daily work, listening to their conversations, observing their handling of cases and the people who come before them, and asking them frank and searching questions about their lives, careers and ambitions. What emerges is without doubt the most revealing and compelling picture of the modern judiciary in England and Wales ever seen. From it we learn that not only do the old stereotypes not hold, but that modern 'baby boomer' judges are more representative of the people they serve and that the reforms are working. But this new book also gives an unvarnished glimpse of the modern courtroom which shows a legal system under stress, lacking resources but facing an ever-increasing caseload. This book will be essential reading for anyone wishing to know about the experience of modern judging, the education, training and professional lives of judges, and the current state of the courts and judiciary in England and Wales.

Sitting in Judgment

The Working Lives of Judges

Penny Darbyshire

·HART·
PUBLISHING

OXFORD AND PORTLAND, OREGON
2011

Published in the United Kingdom by Hart Publishing Ltd
16C Worcester Place, Oxford, OX1 2JW
Telephone: +44 (0)1865 517530
Fax: +44 (0)1865 510710
E-mail: mail@hartpub.co.uk
Website: http://www.hartpub.co.uk

Published in North America (US and Canada) by
Hart Publishing
c/o International Specialized Book Services
920 NE 58th Avenue, Suite 300
Portland, OR 97213–3786
USA
Tel: +1 503 287 3093 or toll-free: (1) 800 944 6190
Fax: +1 503 280 8832
E-mail: orders@isbs.com
Website: http://www.isbs.com

British Library Cataloguing in Publication Data

Data Available

ISBN: 978-1-84946-239-6

Typeset by Columns Design XML Ltd, Reading
Printed and bound in Great Britain by
TJ International Ltd, Padstow, Cornwall

This book is for Igor Judge,
the epitome of kindness.

Foreword

By Lord Judge, Lord Chief Justice of England and Wales

This is an illuminating and intriguing study of the way in which judges throughout England and Wales actually work. It reveals the practical day to day realities, not the myths nor the theories nor the misconceptions. It tells us a great deal about the stresses and strains of judicial life and provides penetrating insights into the attitudes of judges to their responsibilities and the way in which they approach them.

Until recently research of this kind would not and did not happen. It was an essential feature of my personal willingness to offer my support for this proposed research that it should be approached with an open mind and without preconceptions. These were preconditions. On the other hand, if they were satisfied, then there would be no attempt to exert any form of editorial control. It was obvious from my first meeting with Dr Darbyshire that her objective was to discover and report the facts rather than seek to find material which would support any pre-existing prejudices, and that equally, she would not countenance any form of such control. Once the ground rules were established, as she explains, she was given unrestricted access to a vast body of judges. The 'absolute transparency' of which she speaks is perhaps best illustrated by the fact that she sat in with judges in the Court of Appeal and Supreme Court as they deliberated with each other.

The research method was direct observation. Dr Darbyshire spent long periods over several years, sitting in court with judges exercising their different jurisdictions in crime, civil and family work (but not the Tribunals) from the Supreme Court to district judges sitting in the County Court, trying civil cases, and the Magistrates' Courts, trying criminal cases. She did so in the context of discussions of the relevant issues with the judges, so that she could see for herself how the judicial mind was working. She recorded their responses, and the responses of their colleagues who she met, for example, at lunch, to broader issues affecting the judiciary and she saw for herself the problems which judges encounter. She noted, too, areas where she felt criticism was justified as well as concerns expressed by individual judges themselves about different aspects of the system in which they work.

The result of what I believe to be the first research of this kind, certainly in this country, is vividly, yet fairly described. It will be welcomed by anyone who wishes to be better informed about today's judges and the ways in which their responsibilities are discharged.

The Nuffield Foundation is an endowed charitable trust that aims to improve social well-being by means of research. It funds research and innovation in education and social policy and also works to build capacity in education, science and social science research. The Nuffield Foundation has funded this project, but the views expressed are those of the author and not necessarily those of the Foundation. More information is available at www.nuffieldfoundation.org.

Acknowledgements

Hearty thanks are due. Lord Judge, His Honour Judge Shaun Lyons, District Judge Michael Walker and Tim Workman gave hours of their time in helping to construct a broad sample and approaching the selected judges. Our hard-working Lord Chief Justice has read every draft. Professor Kate Malleson and Sir Stephen Sedley, project consultants, read almost as much and similarly provided useful suggestions. The project would not have started without the unwitting inspiration of two of the anonymous pilot study judges, with whom I had sat many years earlier. I would not have expanded this hobby into a project without a chance but very encouraging conversation with Sharon Witherspoon, Deputy Director of the Nuffield Foundation. I thank her and its trustees. Their patience and generosity never faltered through years of my grovelling apologies for taking so long. The independence and integrity of this research rest on the fact that it was sponsored by this invaluable charity. Nichola Hay efficiently typed almost all 80 lengthy interview schedules and Natasha Slabas helped footnote the family chapter. I am indebted to Hart's independent reviewer for his alarming comments. The swift, meticulous, prescriptive report by Emeritus Professor John Baldwin helped channel a panic-attack into a re-write. I am thrilled that Richard Hart, my first choice, published this book and his team, Mel Hamill, Jo Ledger and others, have provided a service that authors of other publishers would envy. Kingston University funded the three pilot studies and the review report. Above all, warm thanks to the hundreds of anonymous judges who contributed, especially the 80 who agreed to lengthy interviews and those who had me watching and questioning their every move for long days on end, sometimes from breakfast to bedtime.

Contents

1

Introduction

She's writing a little anthropology—a study of judges in their habitat

explained one High Court judge to another.

Anyone at any time could undertake observation of judicial behaviour. It is just rarely done.

Professor Dame Hazel Genn, 2008[1]

I WANTED TO find out what judges did, in and out of court, and what they were really like. It seemed to me there was a mismatch between the comedic and media folk-devil: the eccentric, sometimes malign, buffer, out-of-touch with the real world, and the senior judges I had met. They seemed unpretentious, quick-witted, perceptive, and encouragingly kind to my students. Far from clocking-off at four, they worked at weekends and evenings. I had spent time casually work-shadowing and interviewing circuit and district judges for eight years and watched judges since 1971. They seemed like lawyers in general. I resolved to work-shadow every type of judge in different aspects of their work, throughout the six court circuits of England and Wales. After three pilot studies, with district, circuit and High Court judges, I shadowed 40 judges for at least four days each and interviewed them and 37 others. I met hundreds of others.

The public know very little about judges. Most people never appear in court and, while old assize courts like Chester and Lincoln can accommodate hundreds of spectators, modern folk find *Judge John Deed* more entertaining. Academics have produced a sizeable literature on judges but almost all of it is on judgments, which form only part of judging. Genn, in 2009, said the concentration on appellate decisions reflects academics' preoccupation with the law, yet everyday judging is a much more reliable indicator of judicial attitudes. Very little research has been conducted in the UK, especially in the lower courts.[2] Even in the US, the eminent academic, Judge Richard A Posner, in *How Judges Think* said 'I am struck by how unrealistic are the conceptions of the judge held by most people, including practicing lawyers and eminent law professors … and even by some

---

[1]   H Genn, *Judging Civil Justice* (Cambridge, Cambridge University Press, 2009) 137.

[2]   ibid 131–36. As R Moorhead and D Cowan also said, introducing their collection, *Legal Studies*: 'Judgecraft: An Introduction' (2007) 16 (3) *Social and Legal Studies* 315–20. Posner's book is on *judgments*.

judges'.[3] My aim is to paint a portrait of all types of judge and judicial work, including the routine.[4] This book gives judges a voice, through extensive interviews and commentary on their working world. As Posner said, judges are not intellectual giants, oracles or calculating machines, they are human workers, responding to the conditions around them.[5] No-one had researched judges before by using this method of work-shadowing and no-one had researched such a variety of judges.[6]

AIMS

These were outlined in the research design and have not changed.

> To describe, by observational research, a sample of forty contemporary judges in their working lives . . .The following will be examined: career backgrounds and aspirations, relationships with other judges and other court actors; day to day work and workload and its effects; the job of judging; adequacy of support and training; opportunities to meet and observe other judges; membership of and attitudes towards judicial organisations; attitudes towards recent and proposed changes in procedure and how this has affected or will affect their lives; attitudes towards proposed changes to the trial structure and the judge's relationship with the jury.

The details are contained in the successful Nuffield Foundation funding application.[7]

METHOD

I repeated a method used in studying magistrates' clerks,[8] sitting beside the judge in and out of court, asking them to reflect aloud on their work and those they encountered. The pilot studies, in London, were funded by Kingston University. They were essential in formulating the detailed research design, interview schedules and Nuffield application.

Access and Funding

In 2003, a Court of Appeal judge told me a worrying story. In the 1990s, he had asked the Lord Chief Justice (LCJ) for permission to write a book about the judiciary, whilst on sabbatical leave and funded by a charity. The Judges' Council

---

[3] RA Posner, *How Judges Think* (Cambridge, Mass, Harvard University Press, 2008) 2.
[4] Not including tribunal judges.
[5] Posner, above n 3 at 7.
[6] This research was designed in 2002–03.
[7] An abridged version is on the author's web page at Kingston University.
[8] P Darbyshire, *The Magistrates' Clerk* (Winchester, Barry Rose, 1984).

refused. It was well known to UK academics[9] that judges had generally kept researchers away.[10] Malleson, the leading UK writer on judges, noted in her 1999 book[11] how little research there was, compared with other jurisdictions, especially the US.[12] This was *partly* caused by judicial hostility, noted by Harlow in 1986[13] and Abel-Smith and Stevens in 1968.[14] Harlow said that, by comparison, jurimetrics—the analysis of judicial decision-making—was well-established in the US by 1966.[15] Paterson, in his 1982 classic on the Law Lords,[16] noted five UK projects which were aborted because the judiciary or Bar withdrew co-operation. The 1970s story of the Bar's endeavours to block Baldwin and McConville's book on plea bargaining is infamous.[17] Ashworth's work on sentencing was terminated in 1981 by Lord Chief Justice Lane, despite its being funded by the Home Office. Judges were apparently offended by questions on membership of local organisations and travel to work. Lord Lane even gave a press conference.[18] Malleson listed two more: Hood's study on race and sentencing was stopped because although individual judges consented, managing judges instructed them to

[9] It has become textbook knowledge: J Baldwin, 'Research on the Criminal Courts' in RD King and E Wincup, *Doing Research on Crime and Justice*, 2nd edn (Oxford, Oxford University Press, 2008).

[10] Though S Shetreet, *Judges on Trial* (Amsterdam, North Holland, 1976) thought 'blame is not to be attached to the English judges but to the English scholars, who, unlike their American colleagues, have embarked quite late upon sociological research of the . . .machinery of justice, and instead of trying to interview judges have reiterated to themselves that judges are protected from scholarly inquiries' (at 196). Genn too blamed the lack of academic curiosity, at 135.

[11] K Malleson, *The New Judiciary: the effects of expansion and activism* (Aldershot, Dartmouth, 1999).

[12] ibid 196–97.

[13] 'Refurbishing the Judicial Service' in C Harlow (ed), *Public Law and Politics* (London, Sweet & Maxwell, 1986).

[14] B Abel-Smith and R Stevens, *In Search of Justice* (London, Penguin, 1968). See P Rock, *The Social World of an English Crown Court* (Oxford, Clarendon Press, 1993) 2–5; D Pannick, *Judges* (Oxford, Oxford University Press, 1987) 10 and J Baldwin, *Small Claims in the County Courts in England and Wales* (Oxford, Clarendon Press, 1997) 48 fn 7. See L Blom-Cooper and G Drewry, *Final Appeal* (Oxford, Clarendon Press, 1972) 3. There had been almost no attempt to analyse the functions of any British court, 'employing…methodological and statistical techniques … widely used in … other areas of social research'.

[15] Though Posner attributed the lack of understanding to the fact that most judges are 'cagey' about what they do and they deliberate in secret, 'professional mystification', Posner, above n 3 at 2–3. Literature on theories of judicial behaviour was ignored by most academics and virtually all judges, Posner, above n 3 at 7.

[16] A Paterson, *The Law Lords* (London, Macmillan, 1982).

[17] Baldwin, in King and Wincup, above n 9 at 388–90; J Baldwin and M McConville, *Negotiated Justice* (London, Martin Robertson, 1977).

[18] Information from Professor Ashworth and see A Ashworth et al, *Sentencing in the Crown Court, Report of an Exploratory Study*, Occasional Paper no 10, Oxford Centre for Criminological Research, cited by Harlow, above n 13 at 189 fn 29. The blocking of Ashworth's research stifled criminologists' court research, said P Rock, above n 14 at 4–5. The story became notorious: T Gifford, *Where's the Justice? A Manifesto for Law Reform* (London, Penguin, 1986) 31.

withdraw. Her own doctoral research in 1992–93 was affected. She resorted to interviewing retired judges, as the LCJ refused to allow sitting judges to partici-pate.[19]

There were exceptional successes. Paterson's book is rich with frank interview material from the Law Lords, independent of any hostile LCJ. He cited three preceding studies using interviews. Indeed, as can be seen from the UK Supreme Court chapter here, we know everything about the top court. In the UK, there have been some other studies using interviews and/or observation of specific groups of judges, such as Baldwin's work on small claims,[20] Baldwin and McConville's *Jury Trials,*[21] N Fielding's *Courting Violence,*[22] research with family judges, interviews with some senior judges by Peay in *Tribunals on Trial,*[23] interviews with trial judges in Zander's Crown Court Study[24] and interviews with appeal judges in Drewry, Blom-Cooper and Blake's 2007 book, *The Court of Appeal.*[25] Shetreet, in 1976, used interviews,[26] for a detailed and penetrating book on the appointment, discipline, removal and politics of judges, though he did not ask judges about themselves. There were studies commissioned by the Lord Chancellor's Department/Department of Constitutional Affairs that were dependent on judicial co-operation. Nevertheless, this handful of empirical projects[27] contrasts strongly with the US where, as Paterson noted, by 1978, there were over 100 studies on appellate judges, using interviews or questionnaires.[28]

During the times of casually sitting with judges, I noticed they were keen to have a companion and were forthcoming on just about everything. I assumed that I could continue to approach individuals and find enough research subjects but the first proposal to The Nuffield Foundation was referred back, asking me to secure 'official' permission, from the Lord Chancellor's Department. I was reluctant. Rejection would put an end to the plans and, because I considered it a breach of judicial independence that a civil servant could grant or withhold consent, I consulted Professors Baldwin and Ashworth. One of them advised that there was an official procedure and that I should approach the Senior Presiding

---

[19] Malleson, above n 11 at 197 fn 13.

[20] Examined in ch 11.

[21] J Baldwin and M McConville, *Jury Trials* (Oxford, Clarendon Press, 1979).

[22] N Fielding, *Courting Violence: Offences Against the Person Cases in Court* (Oxford, Oxford University Press, 2006).

[23] J Peay, *Tribunals on Trial* (Oxford, Clarendon Press, 1989) and Genn's interviews with tribunal judges in *Tribunals for Diverse Users,* DCA, Research Series 1/06, 2006.

[24] M Zander and P Henderson, *Crown Court Study,* for the Royal Commission on Criminal Justice, Research Study No 19 (London, HMSO, 1993).

[25] G Drewry, L Blom-Cooper and C Blake, *The Court of Appeal* (Oxford, Hart Publishing, 2007).

[26] Shetreet, above n 10 at xix. The book is mostly from published material. At 195, he said all contacted judges gave time generously and answered most questions.

[27] Moorhead and Cowan, above n 2 repeat a plea for 'a more serious research agenda on judges'.

[28] Paterson, above n 16 at 5 fn 26. But see Tamanaha, below n 56. US judges may not be as accessible as British researchers believe.

Judge. I sent the research design and draft questionnaire to Sir Igor Judge, who asked 'What procedure?' but after 45 minutes' cross-examination he offered to do all he could to help. This project owes its success to him and to all the other judges who gave days of their time. It was serendipitous that immediately prior to my commencing this project, I had done some work for Sir Robin Auld, on his *Criminal Courts Review 2001*. He had given that paper to various senior judges, including Judge LJ. I was in the right place at the right time.

This research also owes its success to the generosity of the Nuffield Foundation and the patient encouragement of Sharon Witherspoon. Past experience had taught me to seek non-governmental funding. In the 1970s, I showed my interview schedule for magistrates' clerks to a Home Office researcher, engaged in researching magistrates. Her interview schedule had contained some near-identical questions that had been removed by C2 Division of the Home Office and she envied my academic freedom. I also knew about academic research that had been blocked because the funding department or agency did not like the results. Most strikingly, this had just happened to my work.[29] During the fieldwork, I was repeatedly grateful to be funded by a charity, when the research judges had to explain to their fellows that I was not a 'departmental inspector'.

Sample

Observation over decades in different courts had indicated that each had a distinct culture. Clientele, case load and case speed differed according to size, culture, location and management[30] so the courts were selected to span as great a variety as possible. Nevertheless, this research found that, thanks to centralised training and management and electronic communications, courts and judges differ much less from each other nowadays.

The problem with previous writing, especially statistical surveys, is that it has concentrated on the senior judiciary and sees judges as homogeneous.[31] The core sample of 40 judges were selected to represent as broad a selection of experience, seniority and jurisdiction as possible. They comprised: six county court district

---

[29] The 2001 jury research paper was funded by the Criminal Courts Review. The Review team praised the work but explained that the department would not publish it 'because Government considers your findings sensitive'. I had exposed how easy it was to avoid jury service in London, because there was no budget for chasing non-attenders and I quoted a circuit judge who encouraged friends to evade service if they were reluctant. However, the team wanted to see it published so suggested it was uploaded onto the Kingston University website, adding a link from the Review site.

[30] In researching *The Magistrates' Clerk*, n 8 above. See RB Flemming, PF Nardulli and J Eisenstein, *The Craft of Justice* (Philadelphia, University of Pennsylvania Press, 1993) 1, 'State trial courts in America are highly diverse ... even courtrooms in the same courthouse may differ'.

[31] Explored later.

judges; three district judges (magistrates' courts); one High Court district judge,[32] 16 circuit judges (family, crime and civil), some of whom were managers, eight High Court judges, including one each from the Commercial Court, the Employment Appeal Tribunal, the Chancery and Family Divisions and some from the Administrative Court (some were circuit Presiding Judges, or equivalent), four Lords Justices of Appeal, with backgrounds in family, commercial and administrative law (some were managers), and two Law Lords/Supreme Court Justices.

I drew up a provisional grid of courts. Circuit judges were selected with the help of the Senior Presider and Judge Shaun Lyons, then Secretary of the Council of Circuit Judges, as they had access to background information on judges' career histories, responsibilities and courts. District Judge Michael Walker, then Secretary of the Association of District Judges,[33] helped in selecting the county court district judges. He added courts that were experimenting with new case management software. District judges (magistrates' courts) were selected with the help of Tim Workman, then Senior District Judge (Magistrates' Courts), though I included one who had been a court clerk in my PhD research sample 30 years earlier. I included one overtly gay judge, because he had written about this, more women and more solicitor circuit judges than were representative of the judicial population as a whole, and a High Court judge who had been a circuit judge, because I was interested in their experiences. Welsh judges were over-represented in the core sample: I selected one district, one High Court and two circuit judges, three of whom were Welsh speakers. Sometimes I chose judges out of curiosity, such as a High Court judge born two days after me.

Sir Igor Judge drafted a strongly supportive letter to district and circuit judges and he contacted my chosen High Court and Court of Appeal judges. The response rate was overwhelming. All but one district judge accepted. This meant the sample was bigger than intended. For example, I wrote to 16 circuit judges, in the hope of finding 12, but all 16 accepted.

I selected a supplementary sample of 37 interviewees, generally chosen opportunistically but again to provide variety. With district and circuit judges, I often approached the judge in the next room, provided they were sufficiently different from the core sample judge. If I were shadowing a young female, I would approach an experienced male. If I were shadowing the resident circuit judge, I would seek out the most newly appointed. These interviewees were given no notice of the request and did not have the benefit of examining the research design, just a verbal description and the interview schedule. Happily, at courts with only two judges, the second one always consented. Only one district judge and two circuit judges declined. The senior judge interviewees were again selected, with the help of Sir Igor, to provide a span of seniority, experience and

---

[32]   Added when I realised county court district judges did not know what High Court district judges did.

[33]   Now the Association of Her Majesty's District Judges.

jurisdiction and other than that, pin in list. In other words, this senior sub-sample was randomly selected from a stratified sample. The reason for these 'knocking on doors' and 'pin in list' methods was so that I could not be accused of allowing my judicial helpers to manipulate this sample.

At two Crown Courts, I was questioned about sampling criteria. At one, they suspected that 'Igor Judge' had 'fixed me up' with 'the softie'. They explained that 'There's a judge here who makes barristers cry in court' so I asked him for an interview and he readily consented.[34] On two circuits, I rapidly learned from the judges (and my own ex-students at the Bar) who the 'nutters' were, and noted that Sir Igor had steered me away from one of them (at a court on my provisional grid). They were indeed so notorious that they did not need me to report on them, as their homilies appeared weekly in the local press. At one London magistrates' court, the newly appointed core sample district judge said that all the district judges had discussed my work and concluded that had I shadowed one of the old judges with 'severe judgitis', I would have 'got much less out of them'. They suggested I should balance out with an interview with an older woman, so I did.

Why did Judges Want to be Researched?

Baby Boomer judges seem to understand social research and academic freedom and most trust academics not to behave like journalists. Six of the 77 had been academics (ex-academics are far more common on the bench than is generally known); several had spouses who were academics and others had postgraduate degrees (one in criminology). They had grown up with the Peter Cook/Rowan Atkinson/JAG Griffith image of the judiciary[35] and were daily bombarded with negative media coverage. They welcomed the opportunity to open up the judiciary to outside scrutiny. I entered their world at a time when judges had just equipped themselves with a press office and a website. Desperate to portray themselves as human and user-friendly, Lord Chief Justice Phillips was photographed holding a baby.[36]

As for the work-shadowing method, judges I met were familiar with the judicial work-shadowing scheme and before it, barristers accompanying them as marshals. They were used to entertaining work-experience children beside them,

---

[34] He appears in the Crown Court chapter: Judge EC (eats counsel).

[35] Explored in ch 2. Hammerslev said it could be useful not to see lawyers or judges as a coherent body, because they were defined by their relation to other participants in the field, 'How to Study Danish Judges' in R Banakar and M Travers, *Theory and Method in Socio-Legal Research* (Oxford, Hart Publishing, 2005).

[36] New generation judges welcome researchers. 24 attended the launch of the UCL Judicial Studies Institute in 2010.

or school groups in their courtrooms. Judging is a lonely business. Their enthusiastic replies to my letter, like these from circuit judges, usually came quickly:

> Your project sounds interesting and not a little intriguing. As one of those judges that complains bitterly about the media's misrepresentation of the judiciary in all its aspects, it would be a small opportunity to help inform and educate them as to our true role, responsibilities and capabilities.

> I would be only too pleased to help in any way I can. Your research sounds very interesting. I've always wanted to know something about judges!

The gay judge welcomed a researcher. He said it was important that people understood that the judiciary was made up of all types of people.

Reactions of Non-sample Judges

At the first court, I met a vociferous circuit judge who said he would not have permitted my research. 'You won't get co-operation from the senior judiciary.' I would find judges 'the same as anyone else' but there should be a divide between them and the rest of society, 'Just like your doctor … There's nothing wrong with judges'. He also opposed the research, as there was 'no editorial control'. I related this to a resident judge on another circuit. He said 'that would have been the majority reaction 20 years ago'. The judge in question has since retired.

I was normally given a warm reception in court dining rooms, with judges fussing over my comfort and serving me drinks and coffee. In three courts, my presence was an excuse for wine or champagne. In another, the judges repeatedly regretted that I could not stay for a retirement party. In another, the resident organised for me to be seated at lunch between a different pair of judges every day, to maximise my contact opportunities. On several occasions, though, I was given a stern warning not to report anything I heard and twice a research judge wanted to discover what I was like on the first day before deciding whether to allow me into the dining room. There was a general interest in what I was doing. I was often the main subject of discussion and routinely used as a foil for teasing other judges 'Look out! She'll put that in her book', such as a recorder, whose cases went short every day so he left early. Judges outside the research sample with a point to make sought to attract my attention, such as the Family Division High Court judges who complained of overwork and the judges who wanted to assert their non-traditional credentials, like the judge who told me three times: 'I failed the 11 plus and went to state school. Put *that* in your book'.

In the High Court, Court of Appeal and with the Law Lords, my work seemed to be instantly understood and no-one questioned my presence in deliberations. Only once was I excluded from watching a constitution of the Court of Appeal (Criminal Division). I was included in the general banter off-stage in the Royal Courts of Justice. With the Law Lords, I was a novelty. I spoke to most of them, in addition to the two in my research sample. I could have added dozens of judges to the sample. Judges often asked when it was their turn to be interviewed or observed, including appeal judges and the Law Lords. One Lord Justice was in the interview sample because he often asked if he could participate.

I met several judges repeatedly, as I travelled the circuits, including one High Court judge on three circuits. In magistrates' courts, I met people who had read my book on clerks. This almost backfired. At one court, my core sample district judge's fellows warned him 'She'll do another hatchet job'. I met two judges who had lectured at Kingston, two Kingston graduates, a judge who had lectured me and I unwittingly selected a judge who had graduated in law alongside me.

Research Ethics

The circuit judge's attack about lack of editorial control, noted above, made me reflect on ethics. For fear of inaccuracy and in the belief that this is a fair way to proceed, in treating judges as research subjects, not objects, I emailed the draft chapters to the judges who featured in them and asked for comments. This is a very unusual technique in social research and is very time-consuming but judges are highly intelligent research subjects and I thought this would help clarify my aims to them and enable them to correct and update the work. It would enhance the work's authenticity and credibility. I emailed draft chapters to non-sample judges too. For instance, in the Court of Appeal and Law Lords chapters, where examples from deliberation are included, and I described the behaviour of outsider judges, I emailed all those judges. I also sent successive versions of all draft chapters to Sir Igor Judge. This resulted in increased accuracy. No judge tried to censor my work. They did correct technical errors and added to some of the descriptions. For instance, asking two Supreme Court Justices, in addition to the sample Justices, to comment on a draft, helped to develop a richer picture of judgment-formation in the UK Supreme Court and alerted me to differences of opinion. I allowed draft chapters to be forwarded by the core sample judges to other interested parties. For instance, some High Court judges asked if they could send that chapter to colleagues. The High Court family judge asked to forward the Family chapter to the President of the Family Division. At three Crown Courts I visited outside the core sample, I permitted the resident judges to circulate the draft Crown Court chapter so about 30 Crown Court judges had access to it, in addition to those featured. The work has benefited from countless verbal and emailed comments on early drafts. Sir Igor Judge questioned the currency of the first draft of the Crown Court chapter so I added to the fieldwork. I presented six draft chapters as conference papers at the Socio Legal Studies Association and the Society of Legal Scholars, resulting in some feedback. I have tried to write in accessible English, for the sake of transparency and accountability to the research subjects, the charitable funders and readers. I asked judges to choose their own false names so that they could identify themselves when reading drafts.

There were three project consultants. Professor Kate Malleson and Sedley LJ (who gave his fee to charity) suggested helpful amendments to the interview schedule and made very intelligent comments on drafts. I am in their debt. I am deeply grateful for the incisive comments of the publisher's independent reader and for Emeritus Professor John Baldwin's suggested amendments.

Enviable Fieldwork

The amount of information gleaned over the years was overwhelming. I was granted unlimited access to the research judges and many others and everything that impinged on their work. There was absolute transparency. There was almost no activity from which I was debarred and no documentation denied.[37] I shadowed each core judge on sequential days or, where possible, separate days, in different courthouses, spanning anything up to three years, in a variety of their work. For example, I sat with a district judge (magistrates' courts) in three outer London courts and one in Inner London in the family proceedings court. With the High Court judges, I sat with them in the Royal Courts of Justice, in short hearings, trials and in the Court of Appeal. I accompanied each judge in and out of court (normally sitting on the bench)[38] during the full working day and I stayed in lodgings on circuit, accompanying each judge from breakfast until after dinner. Each core sample judge had read the research design and interview schedule. I encouraged them to think out loud, explaining and commenting on everything they did and that impinged on their work, such as buildings, resources, court users and workmates, including staff and fellow judges. Judges talked me through their paperwork and shared all correspondence and court documentation, such as skeleton arguments, Law Lords/UK Supreme Court printed cases, document bundles, confidential reports in sentencing and family cases, letters from defendants, witnesses and jurors, and prisoners' appeal petitions. They showed me how they wrote judgments and jury directions. The Court of Appeal and the Law Lords in the appeals committee allowed me to watch deliberations, thus giving me access to a phenomenon from which researchers are normally excluded. This is a prize beyond jewels. Apart from participant observation, a researcher could hardly have been closer to the subjects. One of the Nuffield Foundation independent referees suggested that I should select a smaller sample of judges and spend more time with them but the

---

[37]   As Baldwin said in 2008, 'Researchers who sit in court commonly realize, with a sense of unease, that the really important decisions in most cases are being taken elsewhere', above n 9 at 383.

[38]   In the CA there was no room, so I sat at the side or in the well, as with the Law Lords.

method used here did not result in any lack of trust or shortfall in information. As I said in the final Nuffield application:

> The first week of the pilot taught me that four days shadowing each judge is enough and that five days is exhausting, because the judge and I talked all the time out of court and, in court, both of us need to concentrate 100 per cent of the time … Judges … agree with me that four days should normally be adequate. I have not found judges to be at all inhibited in expressing their views to me, as soon as they meet me. Baldwin found district judges to be very candid and he shadowed them for much less than four days each.

As for the interviews, because of the sample size and the breadth of the research, questions were much more structured than those often used in elite interviewing. The schedule[39] was generated for district judges and modified as the research worked its way up the judiciary. The interview took about 1.5 hours, with a range of 42 minutes to three hours.

The depth of this study and my access to appellate deliberations is all the more remarkable, in the context of judges' previous general hostility to research. American judges Harry T Edwards and Posner, whose academic analyses of judging are enriched by their experiences, have both observed how handicapped academics are in writing about judging, because of lack of access to judicial deliberations.[40] I attended management and other meetings, such as court users' meetings and Judicial Studies Board training days. As I usually lunched with all of the judges in a courthouse, or with a judge in the Inns of Court, I met and spoke to hundreds of judges, court staff, judges' clerks and judges' friends and spouses or partners. Judges gave me lifts to courts and stations. The research judges and I sometimes took one other to social or academic events. The Law Lords/Justices invited me to the Anglo-Canadian judicial exchange and to a closed seminar on the UK Supreme Court's first anniversary in 2010. I went shopping with two women judges and to a Pilates class with another. One took me to his house for lunch and another took me home to stay with him and his wife, twice. As well as sitting with the core sample judges, I was able to sit with a number of judges in the interview sample and with some other judges in the same courthouse. For example, one judge asked me to sit with him in order to demonstrate how his approach in family cases differed from that of his workmate, in that he was far more proactive and interventionist. In the years since most of the fieldwork was completed, I have kept in touch with many of the judges and added more observation days every year with several of the core judges and with the resident judges of two London Crown Courts (outside the research sample). In establishing a rapport, it may have helped that I was in the same Baby Boomer generation as many of them. We shared not just a 1970s legal education, but by now the

---

[39] Available on the author's web page on the Kingston University website.
[40] Posner, n 3 above, and H Edwards in 'The Effects of Collegiality on Judicial Decision Making' (2003) 151 *University of Pennsylvania Law Review* 1639.

agonies of persuading teenage boys to work for their GCSEs (especially by remote control) and the pride of graduations. One judge and I played 'mother of the bride' on the same day.

Fieldwork Hazards

A non-sample judge reminded me of the Hawthorne effect, that by overtly observing, I was bound to affect behaviour. All such research is prone to this defect. Interested parties can measure the typicality of the courtroom accounts here by sitting at the back of courtrooms anonymously.

Potential interference in the observed activity was a bigger hazard. From Flood's descriptions of his research in 2005, one can see that sometimes the observer is drawn into participant observation by stealth. In this case it occurred whenever a judge walked out of court and asked 'what do *you* think?' This occurred on most days but I usually turned the question back. It occurred quite spectacularly in one case, as can be seen from the Court of Appeal chapter. My comments and questions sometimes affected judges. In the Commercial Court, I asked 'How is this bankrupt country to pay the $80 million the claimant wants?' and the judge returned to the courtroom and asked the claimant the same question. In the county court, I asked 'Why is this guy defending this pollution action when he's already been convicted in the magistrates' court?' and very soon, the judge persuaded him to concede, for that reason. With a Chancery judge, I asked why two simple cases with hopeless defences had been allocated four and two High Court days respectively and the judge truncated them both. In the Crown Court chapter, I describe a disagreement I had with a resident judge about the collapse of a very expensive trial due to a witness outburst which I considered predictable and he did not.

The research affected the subjects' behaviour in other ways. Two district judges were prompted to apply for recorderships by the interview question on promotion. In Wales, parties and their solicitors were all set for a Welsh-language hearing, as Welsh was the first language for all participants, but they conducted proceedings in English for my benefit. There was another danger that affected the court users. In the High Court, when I was sitting next to an ungowned judge, counsel kept addressing me. In any hearing, it was a natural hazard that disputing parents, litigants in person and frustrated jurors tried to catch my eye, especially when the judge was head down, taking notes.

THE NATURE AND PRIOR RESEARCH CONTEXT OF THIS WORK

I have not used any theoretical model. Models are often indispensible in analysing socio-legal research, or the history or current policy of the elements of a legal system[41] but no one model is helpful or comprehensive enough here. For example, in Posner's 2008 book he examines nine positive, descriptive models of judicial behaviour and finds them all wanting, because they fail to recognise that judges are 'all-too-human workers', a point already made by Baum, who said they all portrayed judges as Mr Spock.[42] In any event, all these models are about judgments, mainly appellate judgments, which is not what this book is about. Even Feeley and Rubin, for instance, who, in their article, 'Creating Legal Doctrine',[43] focused on phenomenology (that is, lived experiences) developed 'a theory of judicial law making'. This book is certainly phenomenological, but such a theory might help here in analysing only *part of* the Court of Appeal and UK Supreme Court chapters' findings, because those are the only law-making judges. All 'judging' models are rendered even less helpful by their context: the US, where judges' party politics are a predominant factor.

Judges would occasionally ask me 'What's your hypothesis?' or 'What angle are you taking?' As Flood has said, though, 'it is not always possible to set up prior theoretical frameworks in ethnography' and 'If social science had the confidence not to attempt to replicate the natural sciences, its impact on the world would be potentially greater'.[44] In its methodology (the science of method), this work is *not* 'scientific', meaning positivist. Most modern socio-legal research is, understandably, positivist, especially government-funded work designed to test piloted policy changes or to inform government consultations. Some positivists and some lawyers, apparently unfamiliar with different philosophies of social science, think collecting statistics or developing hypotheses are the *only* way of doing social science.[45] The approach taken in this book lays it open to their criticism. In chapter fifteen, I call Paterson's book a socio-legal masterpiece, yet Harlow, a lawyer, called it 'anecdotal' and 'impressionistic', in 1986. Nevertheless, by 2010, Paterson's work was widely regarded as unsurpassed, in providing an in-depth insight into the Law Lords. Harlow's remains a singular view. This book may similarly be regarded as anecdotal. It does, however, provide very wide, rich and frank insight into judges' everyday work, from a researcher privileged to have unprecedented access to a very wide sample of judges, their workplaces and the material to which only they have access. In getting so close to the judges, there is a necessary loss of objectivity but that is well-recognised in this field of phenomenological research and indeed in all anthropological research. This type of work

---

[41] Classics include M King, *The Framework of Criminal Justice* (London, Croom Helm, 1981), citing Packer's models and others, and P Parsloe, *Juvenile Justice in Britain and the United States* (London, Routledge and Kegan Paul, 1978).

[42] L Baum, *Judges and their audiences* (Princeton, Princeton University Press, 2006). Both focus on judicial psychology.

[43] M Feeley and E Rubin, 'Creating Legal Doctrine' 69 (1996) *Southern California Law Review* 1989.

[44] In Banakar and Travers, below, 2005, 47.

[45] See R Banakar and M Travers, *Theory and Method in Socio-Legal Research* (Oxford, Hart, 2005) 14–15.

cannot and does not pretend to be impeccably objective, scientifically pure and quantitatively rigorous, as if it were chemistry. As it happens, there are plentiful statistical studies on judges, providing simple demographic information. They normally fuel attacks on the composition of the judiciary, as too old, white and male. Such studies are invaluable, for those of us who have repeatedly criticised the pre-2006 judicial selection system and judicial composition as an international embarrassment,[46] but they are easy 'research' and have been done by journalists since the 1950s.

This research is heuristic (meaning fact-finding) and phenomenological, insofar as its primary but not exclusive focus is the study of the judges' conscious experience of their world.[47] It is nearest in execution to a socio-legal ethnography, like those described by Flood in 2005, but that is too grand a label and this study is too big. It is observational research.[48] Paterson used role analysis, in examining the Law Lords, but I have not. Courts lend themselves to cultural studies, especially because they used to have distinct cultures when I observed them in the 1970s, but differences have diminished. Nevertheless, as will be seen, different levels of the judiciary do see themselves as culturally distinct, to some extent.

There is one well-known ethnography of a single court, Rock's *The Social World of an English Crown Court*.[49] Ethnographers study every element of a social microcosm, over months, or years. This book is an examination of judges, not courts and it is on a very different scale. Although part of it examines what goes on in the courtroom, it has little in common with, say, Carlen's *Magistrates' Justice*, which is part of a school of ethnomethodological[50] and conversational-analytic portraits of the courtroom.[51]

What it *does* have in common with some of these studies is what Travers calls the 'practical character of everyday activities'. It responds to his criticism of them. He lists over a dozen ethnographies of lawyers and the courts but says they place over-reliance on interviews, or observations from the back of the courtroom,

---

[46] See P Darbyshire, *Darbyshire on the English Legal System*, 10th edn (London, Sweet & Maxwell, 2011).

[47] See Posner, above n 3 at 40: 'phenomonology studies first person consciousness—experience as it presents itself to the conscious mind. So we might ask what it *feels* like to make a judicial decision'.

[48] Like Baldwin's research of small claims but on a bigger scale.

[49] P Rock, *The Social World of an English Crown Court* (Oxford, Clarendon Press, 1993), referred to in ch 9.

[50] P Carlen, *Magistrates' Justice* (London, Martin Robertson, 1976). Coined by Garfinkel in the mid-1990s. See M Travers, *The Reality of Law: Work and Talk in a Firm of Criminal Lawyers* (Aldershot, Ashgate: Dartmouth, 1997) 19.

[51] See also J Maxwell Atkinson and P Drew, *Order in Court: The Organisation of Verbal Interactions in Judicial Settings* (London, Macmillan, 1979); M Lynch, 'Preliminary Notes on Judges' Work: The Judge as a Constituent of Courtroom "Hearings"' in M Travers and JF Manzo, *Law in Action—Ethnomethodological and Conversation Analytic Approaches to Law* (Aldershot, Ashgate/Dartmouth, 1997).

because 'they do not provided sufficient insight into what lawyers actually do'. Travers continues, 'even researchers who have spent weeks and months inside the courts and offices, still seem to provide little sense of what work means as a practical matter to the people doing it ... [especially those with] ... an unashamedly competitive stance towards common-sense knowledge, with the result that the ethnography becomes a vehicle to advance a particular theoretical view of the world'.[52] I have tried to be much more penetrating. I could hardly have got closer to the judges.[53]

Crucially, this is not a study in judicial decision-making, or sentencing. There are ample sentencing studies in the UK, which interview magistrates, the primary sentencers,[54] but very few on decision-making, except Paterson's socio-legal and Robertson's multivariate analysis work, reviewed in the UK Supreme Court chapter, plus analyses of Law Lords' judgments on specific subjects.[55] A useful review of the copious US literature on judicial decision-making is by Tamanaha in 1999.[56] '[O]wing to its prominence, an inordinate number of social scientific studies have been conducted on decision-making in the US Supreme Court.'[57] Most are behaviourist, identifying decision patterns and trying to link them to independent variables like politics but all US research must be read in the knowledge that 'law is shot through with [party] politics',[58] the opposite of this jurisdiction. I comment later that, such is the difference in the UK interpretation of judicial independence, every judge I met was impeccably apolitical in out-of-court conversations and most research judges had no prior party connections, unlike their predecessors a hundred years earlier.[59] Had I wanted even to ask judges in England and Wales about their politics, it would not have been permitted. The only question the judiciary censored from my interview schedule was a question on political backgrounds. Very importantly, Tamanaha complains

---

[52]   Travers, above n 50 at 7–8.

[53]   I think I fit this description: 'driven and motivated by an unlimited curiosity about social life...a threatened species': Banaker and Travers, above n 45 at 11. Flood (same book) at 34, said 'The research process for ethnography is different...multi-textured, open-ended and discursive. It starts from a point of learning and enquiry'.

[54]   Listed by Baldwin, above n 9 at 386.

[55]   One reason for the establishment of the UCL Judicial Institute was the lack of such research.

[56]   BZ Tamanaha, *Realistic Socio-legal Theory—Pragmatism and a Social Theory of Law* (Oxford, Oxford University Press, 1999) ch 7.

[57]   ibid 205.

[58]   Posner, above n 3 at 9. eg, Judge Edwards, above, was shocked to be asked 'I am a Liberal. Can I count on your vote?' when he joined the Court of Appeals. *The Craft of Justice*, above n 30, starts 'The characteristics of these relationships . . .were shaped by local political incidents'. See also L Epstein, *Courts and Judges* (Aldershot/Burlington, Ashgate, 2005), concentrating on voting behaviour in American appellate courts, and the politics of judicial selection, none of which is relevant here.

[59]   In the first half of the twentieth century, appointments were routinely awarded for lawyers' party political service: JAG Griffith, *The Politics of the Judiciary* (London, Fontana, 1977).

of the defects of studies of judges, caused by the *inaccessibility of US judges*, contrary to the impression given by some British writers, above:

> Most problematic [is] ... a central defect, one shared by the mass of existing studies on judicial decision-making: less than a handful have actually ever tested for the influence of judges' perceptions of their judicial role on their decision-making behaviour ... one reason for this gaping omission is that judges have traditionally been inaccessible.[60]

In other words, judicial decisions are analysed only against biographical data on US judges.[61] The punch-line of Tamanaha's review is that, while attitudes have had a dominant influence on the decisions of some US Supreme Court Justices, in most other cases, in the lower federal courts, 'the background and attitudes of judges do not have a determinative influence'.[62] As for the popular idea that judges' similar backgrounds (elite, white, middle-aged males) are what produce uniform decisions, he says it fails close inspection, and is indeed 'absurd' because it cannot account for the levels of disagreement in the US Supreme Court, and studies have shown that female judges do not significantly differ from males, nor black from white. They *do* share an indoctrination and institutional context and a belief that they are bound by the law and the law largely determines their decisions. While attitudes undoubtedly influence how judges interpret the law, in most cases, says Tamanaha, this is 'not extraordinarily much'.[63] I am not denying, though, that who judges matters.[64] This is not a piece of research about whether the law is working as intended. Government departments have become increasingly keen on and good at that type of work, especially since the 1990s.[65] Nevertheless, some chapters here do document and comment on legal processes against their stated aims, such as glaring disproportionality in some civil cases and the complete failure of electronic case handling, as aspired to by the Woolf reforms to civil procedure.

Other previous publications of all types, including research material, are referred to in the appropriate chapters. There are ample books and articles about and by judges in this jurisdiction and they are referred to throughout but very few are based on empirical research.

---

[60] Tamanaha, above n 56 at 211.

[61] Tamanaha considers it ironic that behaviourists think they discovered that judges make law, not realising that Holmes, Cardozo and Hart recognised this in the UK and the US, in the early twentieth century, ibid 204.

[62] ibid 221.

[63] ibid 222–24. His conclusions are in striking contrast to those of Harlow, a decade earlier.

[64] And see R Hunter, C McGlynn and E Rackley (eds), *Feminist Judgments* (Oxford, Hart Publishing, 2010).

[65] Harlow deplored the absence of a government justice department with a positive attitude to research. The Ministry of Justice, and predecessors is/were keen to pilot policy changes and monitor their efficacy before 'rolling them out'. See Baldwin in King and Wincup, above n 9 at 376, referring to governmental keenness on 'evidence-led' criminal justice policy. See further, Morgan and Hough, in the same book.

ORGANISATION OF THE BOOK

Chapter two examines public image, against which the description of real judges and their work is to be contrasted. Chapters three to six examine career backgrounds: motivations, recruitment as a part-timer, then full-timer, and training. Chapter seven examines working personality and characteristics. Chapters eight to fifteen are the 'working' chapters, the real core of the book, describing different types of judges in their working world, from district judges to the Law Lords (UK Supreme Court). The last two chapters examine general issues: judges' relationship with other levels of the judiciary and judges' tools for their trade.

2

Images of Judges

Ironically, the complaint that the judiciary is too libertarian and lenient is made most often and most loudly by people who, 20 years ago, denounced 'capitalist courts' and 'Tory laws'. It all goes to show that it is possible to swing from far left to indeterminate right and still remain stupid.

Roy Hattersley, on the 2005 Labour Cabinet[1]

A High Court judge did tell me that Judge John Deed's done a power of good for them. When they were in the big limo they used to get fingers up at them. Now they get whistles.

Circuit judge

I like the anonymity in cases where they bury witnesses but they're not appropriate here.

Commercial Court judge, on wigs

MOST PEOPLE HAVE never met a judge and if they did, they normally would not know, because judges tend not to admit it.[2] Of the few people who have to attend court, they are statistically far more likely to encounter a bench of lay magistrates than a judge. Courts used to be a source of free entertainment. Fabulous, evocative assize-courts can seat over 300 people, who, until 1971, were attracted by the spectacle of the monarch's judge parading into the assize-town, accompanied by his entourage and trumpeters and javelin-men.[3] In the 1970s, each magistrates' court had a regular audience. Casual spectators are gone now. Although courts provide free daily shows, magistrates and some Crown Courts have resorted, ironically, to 'open days', doing pretend justice, to try to attract people in. In 2009, magistrates complained that reporters seldom visited their courts.[4] Rare visitors are pulled towards

---

[1] In the *Guardian* article discussed below n 128, 17 October 2005.
[2] Like 56 of the 77 judges interviewed.
[3] The Crown Court replaced assizes and quarter sessions in 1972: Courts Act 1971.
[4] *The Media Show*, BBC Radio 4, April 2009. L Mulcahy recounts how courts have moved from public open spaces to dedicated rooms where the public can be restricted to galleries, 'the [2004] *Guide* now recommends the provision of just 25 seats in the public area of the standard court' in 'Architects of Justice: The Politics of Courtroom Design' (2007) 16 *Social and Legal Studies* 383.

tourist attractions like the Old Bailey. Proceedings are not televised.[5] As Pannick said, 'The English judge is not a public figure. He acts on the principle ... that the best judge [is] the man who [is] least known to the readers of the *Daily Mail*'.[6] The media are swift to foment outrage when judges fail to uphold expectations of neutrality (or punitiveness) and superhuman resistance to human frailty. Most people's only images of judges are fictional, or from news reports. As we shall see, they promulgate an overwhelmingly negative stereotype, constructing the folk-devil judge against which the portraits of the real judges depicted in this book must be contrasted.

ELEMENTS OF THE IMAGE

'They're just old men', 'fuddy old', 'very old', 'doddery old guy'; 'silly', 'pompous old weirdos', [in wigs], 'really outdated'.[7]

These were responses to Genn's question on what people 'felt about' judges.[8] The image of old, male (and white) is accurate, as can be seen from diversity statistics on the Judiciary website. Lawyers do not reach the bench until their forties or fifties. Women and non-whites are grossly under-represented among the senior judiciary and the circuit bench, the judges normally in the news. The fogey image is exacerbated by incidents such as 'Judge's snores prejudiced Dome raid jurors',[9] the judge who fell asleep in a 2001 rape trial,[10] and 'Judge so slow to rule "that he forgot evidence"'[11] on Harman J's 20-month delay in delivering a judgment. Genn's responses show that people have absorbed the negative images below.

The comedy or Clip-Art judge wears a full-bottomed wig, really only worn in ceremonies, complete with lace ruff, tights and buckle shoes. People do not realise that pictures of judges in ceremonial dress do not reflect judges' everyday wear. The UK Supreme Court Justices do not wear wigs and gowns; nor do civil or criminal district judges, or family judges. Civil judges no longer wear wigs. Short wigs are worn in the five per cent of criminal cases heard in the Crown Court but this is highly significant because the Crown Court judge is the public's archetype. It seemed to me that a wig added a decade to a male judge's appearance. Genn found 'very little support ... for wigs and gowns. It was felt that they accentuated

---

[5] A 2004–05 consultation and experiment have gone no further. See P Darbyshire, *Darbyshire on the English Legal System* 10th edn (London, Sweet and Maxwell, 2011). The issue is currently under review in 2011.

[6] D Pannick, *Judges* (Oxford, Oxford University Press, 1987) 169.

[7] H Genn, *Paths to Justice: what people do and think about going to law* (Oxford, Hart Publishing, 1999) 241 and 244.

[8] ibid 240.

[9] London *Evening Standard*, 21 January 2004.

[10] Lord Chancellor's Department Press Release 226/02.

[11] F Gibb, *The Times*, 2 December 1997.

age, distance and a degree of menace'.[12] Since the 1980s, senior judges like Lord Chief Justice Taylor have been trying to get rid of wigs because they think they damage judges' image. In 1999, Scott J said wigs depicted the law as 'antiquated and foolish'.[13] Lord Bingham said in 2002 'this traditional garb ... has an alienating effect on the ordinary citizen who gets into a courtroom and suddenly finds himself in a sort of eighteenth century pantomime'.[14] Lady Hale said in 2004 'It seems to be strange that lawyers and judges are so puzzled that the general public think of them as old men when they insist on dressing up as old men'.[15] Attacking the 'mysticism' of legal language and dress, Pannick said:

> Wigs and gowns, and other types of legal ceremony, encourage legal pomposity and distance courts from common standards and common sense. They imply ... that judges are not ordinary human beings... Judicial dress is ... a barrier to communication... It is scarcely surprising that judges are misunderstood, unfairly criticised.[16]

The Lord Chancellor's Department consulted on 'Court Dress' in 1992 but the reformers Lord Chancellor Mackay and Lord Taylor decided not to act because 67 per cent of the 520 respondents favoured retaining traditional dress. In 1993, 88 per cent of jurors surveyed agreed.[17] Lord Chancellor Irvine issued another consultation in 2003.[18] He was replaced by Lord Falconer, the first in 1,400 years to insist on being sworn-in without his wig and gown. Media carried pictures of him flanked by Lord Chief Justice Woolf and Lord Phillips MR, unrobed, smiling modernists.[19] While most respondents favoured the status quo, this did not reflect a 2002 public opinion survey, in which the minority supported wigs and gowns.[20] Regardless of the consultation's conservative outcome, Lord Chief

---

[12] Genn, above n 7 at 244.

[13] 'Wigs give law a bad name, says judge', *The Times*, 12 January 1999.

[14] Radio 4, *Inside the Judiciary*, 2002.

[15] F Gibb, '"Softline feminist" would do away with wigs and robes', *The Times*, 6 November 2003. Some lawyers share this revulsion: 'I have had an overwhelming sense of absurdity of wearing 18th century dress to do my work ... in the criminal courts of the 21st century... The wing collar and white bands indicate that the wearer is a member of a minor order of the Anglican clergy ... The black ... gown signifies ... that the Bar is still in mourning for Queen Anne.' M Sylvester, Letter to *The Times*, 8 August 2003.

[16] Pannick, above n 6 at 143–44.

[17] M Zander and P Henderson, *Crown Court Study, Research Study No 19* for the *Royal Commission on Criminal Justice* (London, HMSO, 1993) 221.

[18] *Court Working Dress in England and Wales*, CP 03/03.

[19] H Rumbelow, 'Lord Chancellor dresses down for his swearing-in', *The Times*, 19 June 2003.

[20] The responses to the 2003 paper were published in 2007: Ministry of Justice website, 'Court working dress in England and Wales: consultation response'. Respondents over-represented judges. One judge showed me the tactics he was using, asking friends and family (and me) to respond, opposing change.

Justice Phillips, impatient, commissioned the design[21] of new civil robes to be worn from 2008 without a wig, though traditional gear remains for criminal cases.[22]

Old Boy Network—An Educational Elite of Privileged Toffs

The selection system was widely criticised from the mid-twentieth century, until the Constitutional Reform Act 2005. Judges played a prominent part in selection and the watchdog Commission for Judicial Appointments stridently condemned systemic bias. Since 1956, academics and journalists have harvested easy statistics from *Who's Who*, demonstrating that the senior judiciary are mainly Oxbridge educated. In the UK, this is the basis for an attack. This is because many were also privately schooled, which is characterised as evidence of a class bias. This fixation is a product of acute class-consciousness in the UK, which Cannidine argues is, and is perceived abroad as, a peculiarly 'class-bound and class obsessed nation'.[23] Smith and Stevens noted that during 1955–65, public attitudes towards the law and judges changed and 'it became fashionable to note that judges came from a narrow social background'.[24] In 1956, *The Economist* reported 53 per cent of the superior (senior) judges as belonging to 'the best known clubs in London', including 26 per cent in the Athenaeum. They listed their recreations as hunting, shooting, fishing and sailing.[25] The 'privileged' image is perpetuated in headlines like 'Sex is better in Latin, says former judge'[26] 'Judge accused of sacking groom when she had baby'[27] and 'Judge Bread—free lodgings for High Court cost the taxpayer £5 million a year'.[28]

Class Biased/Politically Biased, Out of Touch and Pontificating on Ordinary People

The English judge, biased towards a fellow toff, was enacted in Peter Cook's parody of Cantley J's summing-up in the 1979 trial of Etonian Jeremy Thorpe,

---

[21] Provided free by Betty Jackson, fashion designer.

[22] 'Practice Direction Handed Down For Court Dress Working Reforms', 31 July 2008, with the Direction attached, Judiciary website. For a picture of Phillips LCJ in his new robes, see F Gibb, 'Model judge and his funky new gown', *The Times*, 13 May 2008.

[23] D Cannadine, *Class in Britain* (London, Penguin, 2000) 1. Modern examples include the Labour 2009 paper, *Unleashing Aspiration*, discussed below in ch 3.

[24] B Abel-Smith and R Stevens, *Lawyers and the Courts* (London, Heinemann, 1967) 299.

[25] Cited by Abel-Smith and Stevens, ibid 300.

[26] R Verkaik, the *Independent on Sunday*, 29 September 2002.

[27] H Johnstone, *The Times*, 6 January 1998.

[28] B Roberts, *Daily Mirror*, 20 October 2003.

former Liberal leader.[29] Thorpe was satirised as 'one of the prettiest ... most distinguished politicians', falsely accused of 'ludicrous charges' by a 'so-called hit-man ... a piece of *ordure*, unable to carry out a simple murder plot' and a 'scrounger, a bounder, a parasite, a worm'. Note that Cook, like Rowan Atkinson later, enhanced comedic effect with a full-bottomed wig. JAG Griffith said in *The Politics of the Judiciary*:

> The judiciary reflects the interests of its own class ... tenderness towards private property and dislike of trade unions, strong adherence to the maintenance of order, distaste for minority opinions, demonstrations and protests, support of governmental secrecy, concern for the preservation of the moral and social behaviour to which it is accustomed ... judges do not stand out as protectors of liberty, of the rights of man, of the unprivileged.[30]

Griffith's book was historically accurate, when last published in 1997[31] but it is still in print and thus a *current* image. A best-selling paperback, it may be the only book on judges that many intellectually curious non-lawyers have read. This is the received image of people interviewed by Genn: 'biased', 'narrow minded' and 'Most judges come from a very good background ... judges will have a less than objective view on cases brought before them'.[32] Nevertheless, this contradicts the modern stereotype of judges as upholding the human rights of unpopular minorities, which is the point Hattersley makes, above.

As for isolation, 'By 1963 even an ex-chairman of the Bar Council ... was ... pointing out that the life of a successful barrister or a judge involved living in a close professional society which had little contact "with the disagreeable world outside"'.[33] Genn found two thirds of interviewees agreed that most judges were out of touch with ordinary people's lives, with 'perceptions of remoteness based on social distance, inconsistency in sentencing, and examples of insensitive judicial comments reported in the media'.[34] One said 'most of them come from a privileged background, been to private school ... they've not had the life that the people that they are dealing with have had'.[35] While they believed that if judges were selected from a wider section of society, they would not be so narrow-minded, Griffith

---

[29] Entitled 'Entirely a Matter for You', performed at *The Secret Policement's Ball* on 29 June 1979: best viewed on *You Tube* in 'Peter Cook's Biased Judge Sketch and its Background', with narration by Dawn French and explanation and analysis by John Cleese, Terry Jones, Stephen Fry and Michael Palin.

[30] JAG Griffith, *The Politics of the Judiciary*, 5th edn (London, Fontana, 1997) 336 and 342.

[31] Other books made the same point, such as T Gifford's *Where's the Justice? A Manifesto for law Reform* (London, Penguin, 1986): 'a heartless and legalistic approach to the law' (on homelessness), at 35.

[32] Genn, above n 7 at 242–43.

[33] Abel-Smith and Stevens, above n 24 at 300.

[34] ibid 240.

[35] ibid 243.

disagreed. 'The years in practice and middle-aged affluence would remove any aberration in political outlook.'[36]

Comedy judges are stern, old buffoons, ignorant of modern life. Rowan Atkinson's 1980s judge on *Not the Nine O'Clock News* had to have 'digital watch' and 'video recorder' explained to him but was happy to explain that the 'luxury' inflatable doll was the one with the hair—supporting the 'hanky-panky' image, below. Judges unwittingly fuel this image. When judges and retired judges make radio comments, their accents and vocabulary betray their years at independent school and/or the Bar. They sound condescending. In 2006, Alice Miles commented:

> It is left to Sir Oliver Popplewell to speak for the judiciary. Sir Oliver, a retired judge … pops into the Today programme … and sounds like the jovial, posh old cove that judges are caricatured as being … Judges don't really do media.[37]

A judge talking about drinking laws on *Today* in 2005 was criticised by an emailer for using words like 'bellicose' and 'fisticuffs'. 'It showed he benefited from an education which defendants couldn't.'[38] A district judge, reviewing a circuit judge's autobiography in 2006, said 'Baker starts the book with justified criticism of those who enjoy stereotyping judges—though every time he uses the word "rugger" and tells us which clubs he belongs to, he undermines his case'.[39] Famously, Harman J asked who 'Gazza' was, when Paul Gascoigne played for England, and denied knowing who Kevin Keegan, or Bruce Springsteen, or Oasis were. Some felt this was an affectation. Popplewell J asked what Linford Christie's 'lunchbox' was but claimed this was a piece of 'light humour'.[40] Because journalists are vigilant for evidence of judges' ignorance, language can be misinterpreted. Openshaw J had been an avid laptop user for years, before saying in a cyber-terrorist trial, 'I don't really understand what a website is', apparently for the sake of the jury.[41] Judges commonly ask questions to which they know the answer, for the jury's sake, but this did lasting damage and was being referred to over a year later.

---

[36]   ibid 338. This was also the overwhelming message of Hazell's *The Bar on Trial*, published in the 1970s, when today's senior judges were at the Bar. See 'a cloistered profession', 28–92.

[37]   *The Times*, 14 June 2006, cited below in the row over 'soft' sentencing.

[38]   BBC Radio 4, 9 August 2005.

[39]   P Firth, review of J Baker, *Ballot Box to Jury Box- Life and Times of an English Crown Court Judge* (2006) 156 *New Law Journal* 1228.

[40]   Popplewell, 'Legal legend and the 'lunchbox' question', *The Times*, 20 May 2003.

[41]   F Gibb, 'Judge halts terror trial to ask: what's a website?', *The Times*, 18 May 2007 and 'Just a case of playing Devil's advocate for website judge', *The Times*, 19 May 2007.

Sexist, Racist, Homophobic and Prone to Insensitive Comments, or Rude and Caustic

In 1982, Judge Bertrand Richards fined a rapist, because his teenage victim had been 'guilty of a great deal of contributory negligence' by hitch-hiking home late at night. Although there was a media outcry and 50 Labour MPs signed a motion to have him dismissed, Sir Melford Stevenson, a former High Court judge, best known for calling the 1967 Act legalising adult homosexuality 'a buggers' charter', defended him, because girls who hitch-hiked alone at night were 'asking for it'.[42] This fostered a stereotype that is *still* current. When a 2008[43] panel of *Any Questions* were asked to comment about a High Court judge 'sounding off', Tim Smit, founder of the Eden Project, said 'They tend to sound off about sex crimes against women ... there is always some kind of comment about "they asked for it"'.

In 1983, Judge Brian Gibbens was reported to have said, of a man who had sex with a seven-year-old, that it was 'one of those kind of accidents that could almost happen to anyone'.[44] In 1990, a judge said in a rape trial, 'When a woman says no, she doesn't always mean it'.[45] In 1993, another achieved wide publicity by freeing a rapist and ordering him to pay £500 to his victim, 'for a good holiday to get over the trauma'. Another put a man on probation for assaulting an eight-year-old, who he said was 'not entirely an angel herself'.[46] In 1996, another stopped the trial of a police officer accused of grabbing the breasts of two constables, because he thought the officer should have had 'a sound ticking off'.[47] In 1997, one judge said to a 14-year-old in a rape trial, 'If you are going to sulk like a baby, we are not going to get very far' and another said, when a defendant handed in a medical note, 'I know people with duodenal ulcers who work like niggers'.[48] Another likened a woman's forced oral sex ordeal to a trip to the dentist and another said a tutor who had fondled a student had done nothing 'very serious'.[49] In 1998, Rougier J told a 14-year-old rape victim how to dilute her Pimms[50] and in 1999 he suggested an Asian assault victim who feared black people should move to the country.[51] Then a circuit judge told a racist, sexist,

---

[42]   Obituary: 'His Honour Bertrand Richards', *The Times*, 1 September 2000.

[43]   BBC Radio 4, 15 August 2008.

[44]   Unattributed, *The Times*, 18 December 1983. The judge complained he had been misreported but explained himself in open court in the same terms, 'It is one of the kind of accidents which happen in life to almost anyone', Pannick, above n 6 at 34.

[45]   S Boseley, 'Judge tells "rape" girl to dilute Pimms', *The Independent*, 21 January 1998.

[46]   Editorial, 'Judicial Discretion' (1994) 144 *New Law Journal* 889.

[47]   K Alderson and J Bale, 'Outcry as judge halts police sex assault case', *The Times*, 24 July 1996.

[48]   Boseley, above n 45.

[49]   F Gibb, 'Judge compares woman's sex ordeal to visit to the dentist', *The Times*, 14 November 1997.

[50]   Boseley, above n 45.

[51]   S Steiner, 'Move into the country, judge tells man who fears blacks', *The Times*, 19 February 1999.

homophobic joke in an after-dinner speech.[52] Judges continue to provoke negative headlines, such as 'Judge clears driver because "Chinese all look the same"', in 2006[53] and 'Judge lets paedophile go free and says: buy a bike to cheer up victim', in 2007.[54] In 2005, women's groups condemned a High Court judge for instructing a rape jury that 'drunken consent is still consent', misunderstanding the Sexual Offences Act 2003.[55] In 2007, Singer J made astonishing remarks about a sheikh in a divorce case, including that he could 'depart on his flying carpet' and that his evidence was 'a bit gelatinous ... like Turkish delight'.[56] Newspapers are vigilant for sentences they consider too low, especially when they appear to be caused by negative views of victims in sex offences, such as a case in the *Sun* and elsewhere in 2007, 'Judge lets off rapist of girl, 10...because she wore provocative frilly bra and thong'.[57]

Journalists collected the sayings of Sir Melford Stevenson, such as 'it was an anaemic rape, as rapes go' and Harman J, 'the kicking judge', who aimed at a taxi driver he mistook for a journalist.[58] A trio of convictions was quashed in 2004–05 because of the rudeness and intervention of a circuit judge, and these were widely publicised.[59]

Up to Hanky-panky, or Perversion, or Drunk; Getting off Lightly

The 2006 Old Bailey trial of a Brazilian cleaner accused of blackmailing two immigration and asylum judges with a sex video was a gift to the media. The trial involved allegations of home-made sex videos of the judges, emails from the judge, calling the cleaner 'really chilli hot stuff' and 'a lovely shag', and that the cleaner was being employed illegally by the judges. Immigration adjudicators had been renamed 'judges' two years earlier, in an undisguised attempt to manipulate the diversity statistics.[60] In 2007, a similar frenzy was provoked by the trial of a

---

[52]   F Gibb, 'Judge in dock as joke falls flat', *The Times*, 28 April 1999.

[53]   D Lister, *The Times*, 23 October 2006. In 2010, Judge Trigger 'received formal advice' from the LCJ, following a complaint about remarks on immigrants (OJC announcement 09/10).

[54]   D Kennedy, *The Times*, 3 February 2007.

[55]   F Gibb, 'Judge's Ruling Dubbed a Green Light for Rapists', *The Times*, 24 November 2005 and F Gibb, 'Rape case judges fail to abide by consent rule', *The Times*, 29 November 2007.

[56]   F Gibb, 'Divorce case judge tells sheikh to take off on his flying carpet', *The Times*, 16 November 2007.

[57]   25 June 2007.

[58]   See F Gibb, 'Retired judges rally to defence of Melford Stevenson', *The Times*, 1 November 1994 and F Gibb and K Knight, 'Fast exit for the slowest judge', *The Times*, 14 February 1998.

[59]   F Gibb, 'Convictions are quashed following trial judge's bad temper', *The Times*, 22 July 2005.

[60]   The *Evening Standard* headline for 22 September 2006 was 'Sex Case Judge Suicide Threat'. See also S Bird, 'Judge's mistress "feared hired hitman"', *The Times*, 26 September 2006 and 'Blackmail case judge was "lover's puppy"', 27 September 2006. See also D Pannick, 'Why a

Court of Appeal judge for indecent exposure. The reporting was much more neutral, although readers were titillated by sketches of the judge holding up his underpants as evidence,[61] and the reasoned verdict by a district judge and two magistrates was somewhat ambiguous: 'Senior judge cleared of flashing on train due to insufficient evidence—witness a model of composure'.[62] One inconclusive story ran intermittently from 2003–07: 'Wife "took in washing" as adulterous judge burnt to death in the garden shed'.[63] An investigation in 1993 of a conspiracy theory involving a 'gay' magic circle of Scottish judges, advocates, lawyers and criminals attracted more publicity, rather than dissipating it.[64] For sheer salaciousness though, these were all trumped by a 2010 *News of the World* 'exclusive' on a senior circuit judge who kept a rent-boy and even sat him on the bench.[65] Judges' bête noir is the *Daily Mail*, because of its constant right-wing complaints about their decisions. It also seems to be unique in reporting some extra-marital affairs. Examples are 'Judge's heartbreak over wife's affair with golf pal'[66] and articles alleging an affair between Gloster J and Sir Oliver Popplewell.[67]

Drunken 'judges' provide good copy[68] but these reports are a constant annoyance to real judges because the 'judge' involved is normally just a lawyer sitting part-time, such as 'Jail for judge who drove while five times over the limit',[69] 'Drunk judge caused chaotic night in cells'[70] and 'Drunken judge escorted from court after kissing a solicitor',[71] reported in the *Sun* as 'Sozzled judge in courtroom snog'. *Sun* readers were scandalised again in 2007, by 'Pig in a wig: Love rat judge', who 'ran off with a pal's wife while his own missus was

---

judicial inquiry into "real chilli-hot stuff" is not needed', *The Times*, 10 October 2006. The male judge died a day after retirement, in 2009. The female retired in ill health, in 2006: unattributed, *The Times*, 23 February 2011.

    [61]   F Gibb, 'Judge gets his briefs out to prove a point', *The Times*, 13 June 2007.
    [62]   F Gibb, *The Times*, 14 June 2007. See *The Times* on 12 June and 22 January 2007; O Koster, 'Judge flashed at me twice in eight days on rush-hour train', *Daily Mail*, 12 June 2007; O Koster, 'I can't be the flasher, says judge—check out my briefs', *The Mirror*, 13 June 2007; J Clothier, 'Flasher judge gets briefs out', *The Sun*, 13 June 2007; 'Appeal Court judge "flashed at me twice"', *The Telegraph*, 12 June 2007.
    [63]   S de Bruxelles, *The Times*, 9 October 2007 and 'Judge who died in garden shed fireball "was being blackmailed by his lover"', *The Times*, 12 October 2007.
    [64]   Unattributed, 'Not proven verdict on Scots judiciary' (1990) 140 *New Law Journal* 78 and 'Gay Scots judges; no magic circle' (1993) 143 *New Law Journal* 155.
    [65]   D Evans, 'Court in the Act', 21 June 2009 and links from the online version: 'M'LUDDY DISGRACE', 'Rent Boy Judge in Dry Dock', 'NO COURT FOR JUDGE IN RENT BOY SCANDAL', and 'Gay fling judge quits', 18 July 2010.
    [66]   20 May 2004.
    [67]   R Kay, 'Court out', 5 April 2004 and 'What reduced a top woman judge to tears', 22 June 2004. Allegations seem to have emanated from the cuckold or his supporters.
    [68]   Judge Bruce Macmillan resigned in 2009, before pleading guilty to drink driving: news media, 30 September 2009.
    [69]   F Gibb, *The Times*, 2 May 1997.
    [70]   A Norfolk, *The Times*, 24 September 2003.
    [71]   *The Mirror*, 14 January 2009.

PREGNANT'.[72] Another part-timer was featured in 'Judge's link to crime family'[73] and another was reported as 'Mum's "swinging" judge ... at the centre of alleged romps'.[74] The most extreme example of misreporting was the case of a recorder, not even on the lowest rung of the full-time judicial ladder, reported in 2008 as 'An eminent judge gets community service for harassing his ex-wife and her new lover'.[75]

A recurring theme is 'judge escapes punishment'. Angus Macarthur resigned as a circuit judge in 1997, before headlines such as 'Judge jailed for third drink-driving offence—"Broken man" starts his sentence as campaigners claim 28 day sentence is too lenient'.[76] In 1998, all media carried headlines such as 'Fraud case against judge abandoned',[77] on a circuit judge who had drawn £250,000 in salary since arrest and was reported as being on holiday with his wealthy wife. The Attorney General was condemned for stopping the prosecution, despite evidence that he was unfit for trial. Lady Butler-Sloss was criticised when she was offered re-training instead of being prosecuted for careless driving after a crash left a passenger with facial injuries.[78] There was moral outrage over the community sentence imposed on a paedophile, a former circuit judge. The *Daily Express* asked 'Was this paedophile let off with a soft sentence because he is a Crown Court judge?'[79] The *Daily Mail* reported 'Judge who kept child porn on his computer escapes jail (and he can still call himself His Honour)'and the *Sun* commented 'How perverse: child porn judge walks free ... yet other sickos are jailed'. The *Times* restrained itself to 'Sex register shame of child porn judge'.

Incompetent: Soft on Sentencing

The commonest criticism is that judges are 'soft on sentencing'. Genn found inconsistency a 'constant theme'.[80] Examples from the *Daily Mail*[81] include 'Let's

[72]   C Hartley, *The Sun*, 2 March 2007.
[73]   S Hughes, *The Sun*, 17 November 2006.
[74]   J Askill, *The Sun*, 3 Nov 2006.
[75]   V Soodin, 'Community rap for judge', 21 July 2008 and 'Stalker judge is let off jail again', 22 July 2008.
[76]   D McGrory, *The Times*, 13 November 1997.
[77]   F Gibb, *The Times*, 8 October 1998. The media were scandalised that he tried to claim costs and pension.
[78]   'Public figures and the law' (1998) 148 *New Law Journal* 1701.
[79]   14 July 2004.
[80]   Genn, above n 7 at 243. In 2007–08, 77 per cent of respondents felt that sentences were too lenient but many underestimated sentencing practice: Ministry of Justice, 'Public Confidence in the CJS: findings from the British Crime Survey 2002/3 to 2007/8', July 2010. A Lovegrove, (Australia), in 'Public Opinion, Sentencing and Lenience: An Empirical Study Involving Judges Consulting the Community' [2007] *Crim LR* 769 said this image is common to other jurisdictions. His experiment concluded that judges were not more lenient than the community and the community did not speak with one voice so he questioned the wisdom of increasing sentence severity to pander to the populist view. Harsh sentencers in the population

judge the judges', calling for an 'exposure',[82] 'Why don't our judges believe in punishment?',[83] 'Soft judges, derisory jail sentences and the subversion of justice',[84] 'Judge gives paedophile light sentence',[85] 'Justice is murdered by a judge',[86] criticising Lord Chief Justice Woolf's views on life sentences, and regretting the abolition of the death penalty, and 'Outrage after top judge calls for shorter sentences for murderers', castigating Lord Chief Justice Phillips.[87] There are dozens more but in 2008–09, the paper heralded comments by his successor, Lord Judge as 'a dramatic break' from policies pursued by his two predecessors, in 'Criminals must fear justice says new top judge as he calls for tougher sentencing'[88] and 'Your home IS your castle: Top judge says burglars must face stiff sentences'.[89]

The *Sun* similarly lambasts judges it perceives as being soft on sentencing, especially on sex offenders, such as 'Judge frees paedo over distress',[90] '"No risk" paedophile migrant to stay in UK'[91] and 'Soft judge lets paedo off twice'[92] and speeches by Lord Chief Justice Phillips, such as 'Top judge: let killers out of jail … crime victims were up in arms … Lord Phillips has taken leave of his senses'.[93] Judges thus become folk devils by association.[94] By contrast, Lord Judge's sentiments, above, were reported without comment.'[95]

Most other newspapers periodically join in, such as the *Mirror* with 'Paedophile OK to be naturist … can still be part of naturist clubs and go on naked trips

---

'complain more loudly', creating a false impression. Research reported by JV Roberts, M Hough, J Jacobson and N Moon, 'Public Attitudes to Sentencing Purposes and Sentencing Factors: An Empirical Analysis' [2009] *Crim LR* 771 counters 'the stereotypical view of the public as punitive sentencers', at 781. A classic example of a newspaper calling for populist sentencing is (unusually) in *The Times*' leading article on 21 January 2010, 'Judging the Judges', praising Lord Judge for reducing the sentence for a retaliatory attack on a burglar, yet criticising a nine-year sentence for a mother who mercifully murdered her son: 'If the judges are to safeguard an independent future, they must keep an eye on their reputation in the world outside'.

[81]   And *Mail on Sunday*.
[82]   3 February 2003.
[83]   M Phillips, *Daily* Mail, 15 May 2003.
[84]   M Phillips, *Daily Mail*, 12 May 2005.
[85]   22 February 2008.
[86]   27 June 2005.
[87]   S Doughty, *Daily Mail*, 9 March 2007.
[88]   S Doughty, *Daily Mail*, 6 November 2008.
[89]   M Hickley, *Daily Mail*, 17 January 2009.
[90]   K Lister and T Bonnici, *The Sun*, 30 September 2006.
[91]   C Spratt, *The Sun*, 7 June 2008, criticising Judge J Hall, who has been the subject of regular criticism by the *Sun*.
[92]   G O'Shea, *The Sun*, 30 November 2007.
[93]   G Pascoe-Watson, *The Sun*, 10 March 2007.
[94]   In the introduction to *Folk Devils and Moral Panics*, 3rd edn (London, Routledge, 2002), Stanley Cohen reviewed the literature on demonisation of paedophiles, noting that social workers became folk devils for failing to protect children. Reporting cited here show that judges are similarly demonised.
[95]   17 January 2009.

to theme parks … Det Insp "extremely disappointed".[96] The *Sun* and the *Mail* are the most vigilant judge-watchers. This turned to vigilantism in June 2006, when the *Sun* ran a three-day, front page 'CAMPAIGN' called 'JUDGES ON TRIAL: We demand an end to soft sentences', picturing individual judges, in their full-bottomed wigs, detailing their sentences, stamped 'GUILTY'.[97] Coverage spanned nine pages, with the entire front page on the second and third days given to 'rages' from the 'Dad of Paedophile victim, aged 3' and 'GUILTY AS CHARGED—SACK THE SOFTIE'. The judge had been required by practice to explain that an offender, Craig Sweeney, could be freed on parole after five years. He had imposed a compulsory 18-year life sentence but cut it by one third for a guilty plea, in accordance with the (Labour) Criminal Justice Act 2003 and the recommendations of the Sentencing Guidelines Council.[98] He explained that Sweeney was eligible for parole after six years, minus one year on remand. Labour Home Secretary John Reid publicly criticised the sentence as 'unduly lenient' and the *Sun* claimed Prime Minister Blair had 'added support' to their campaign.[99] When judges defended themselves, complaining they were constrained by complex sentencing law and policy developed by his government, most papers, like the *Metro* grasped the point that the 'Sentencing system is faulty' but the *Sun* was still thundering against judges, with 'Wimp M'Luds in rage', depicting the Lord Chief Justice in full-bottomed wig.[100] It was left to informed newspapers, such as the *Times*, to explain that 'Rules on guilty plea put judges in a straightjacket'[101] and retort, 'Get some policies, Mr Reid, and stop hiding behind an odious sex offender'.[102] They quoted expert David Thomas explaining that only around one in 500 Crown Court sentences was ruled by the Court of Appeal to be 'unduly lenient'. In the meantime, the Lord Chancellor's junior minister Vera Baird QC joined in to criticise the Sweeney sentence but was forced to publicly apologise after Lord Falconer rebuked her for breaching ministerial duty under the one-year-old (Labour) Constitutional Reform Act 2005 to uphold judicial independence. In the weeks following, the Lord Chief Justice and Council of Circuit judges defended the judiciary. The President of the Queen's Bench Division (QBD) appeared on *Question Time*.[103] Judges complained of the complexity of sentencing and the fact that their obligation to explain that parole would halve a sentence and tagging would halve it again invited a negative image. The sentencing guidelines were reviewed and amended.

---

[96] 16 January 2009.

[97] 12–14 June 2006.

[98] Created by the same Act.

[99] G Pasco-Watson and J Coles, 'OUT-RAGE', *The Sun*, 14 June 2006.

[100] 19 June 2006.

[101] F Gibb, *The Times*, 13 June 2006.

[102] A Miles, *The Times*, 14 June 2006.

[103] F Gibb, 'Chief Justice hits back in row over 'soft sentencing', *The Times*, 19 June 2006.

A similar attack was made in *Dispatches: Judges in the Dock* on Channel 4 in 2003.[104] With a trailer 'Who's protecting the public from incompetent judges?' the melodramatic introduction featured judges in full-bottomed wigs.

> They get a six-figure salary and a job for life. They're accountable to no-one yet nobody's bothered to check whether our judges are any good … *we* name and shame the judges making mistake after mistake, the men whose incompetent judgments screw up other people's lives … a scandal born of power without responsibility.

The programme named judges who had supposedly had a higher than average number of sentences corrected on appeal, with lawyers explaining that some were predictably harsh or soft sentencers, so justice was a lottery. Featured judges declined to participate. One wrote that he sentenced 200 offenders per year and two per cent of his decisions were overturned. The focus of this programme supports my thesis below that 'judges cannot win'. A judge under attack for having 58 over-harsh sentences overturned in seven years was said by a solicitor to think he was 'in line with the *Daily Mail*. He would say that the Court of Appeal was wrong, he was right *and the public would agree with him*' (my emphasis). The solicitor repeated this point about public approval but the fact that it contradicted the programme's message was apparently lost on the presenter, who was talking over him. Acknowledging the Court of Appeal's role in correcting sentences, it complained of lack of accountability: no statistics were kept of judges whose sentences were repeatedly overturned and they suffered no consequences.[105] A similar article appeared in the *Guardian* two days earlier.[106] 18 months later, the Attorney General published a list of judges who had given 'unduly lenient' sentences. The Judicial Communications Office tried a damage limitation exercise, explaining that these statistics should be set in context but it was the Attorney General who gained the headlines, such as '"Unduly lenient" judges outed'.[107]

This image has changed slightly since Lord Judge became Lord Chief Justice in 2008, because of his perceived tough views on sentencing. By January 2009, two of his statements advocating stiffer sentencing were very widely and favourably reported. The *Daily Express*, like other papers welcomed the 'Your home is your castle' judgment, quoting Ann Widdecombe ('excellent news') and another Tory MP ('music to my ears').[108] The *Sun* welcomed his appointment, as 'New judge to tackle knife crime'[109]

Reporting of 'soft' sentencing fuels some readers' appetite for vengefulness which should not be underestimated: public hangings were abolished at the Old

---

[104]   18 December 2003.

[105]   Pannick said such a judge should be answerable to a Commission, above n 6 at 101.

[106]   A Wade, 'When justice is caught napping', *The Guardian*, 16 December 2003.

[107]   June 2006. These statistics are greeted annually with adverse publicity now, such as 'Killers and rapists "getting off with soft sentences"', unattributed, *The Mail*, 29 August 2008.

[108]   J Chapman, 'Judge: your home is your castle', *The Daily Express*, 17 January 2009.

[109]   G Rolling, *The Sun*, 10 July 2008.

Bailey only because Queen Victoria considered the crowded spectacle distasteful. The *Sun* and others specialise in reporting paedophile sentencing. Readers' blogs in the *Mail*, the *Sun* and the *Express* in 2009–11 include calls for permission to kill burglars and the reintroduction of the treadmill and capital punishment. The blogs show that the image of 'soft on sentencing' is persistent and absorbed by readers, despite the fact that judges periodically point out that sentence tariffs have increased since the 1990s.[110] It is well-known to judges and academics that when members of the public take part in research sentencing exercises they 'impose' sentences in line with or less than real sentences.[111] The real meaning and length of a sentence is beyond the control of the judiciary. The media blame judges for lenient sentences but the Government invented early release as a response to prison overcrowding. This means a prisoner can be released before having served the minimum sentence. The judges will not alter the entire sentencing tariff system to take account of potential executive interference. In 2009, a circuit judge outside the research sample said he considered early release to be a fraud on the public. Sentencing should be transparent. A six-month sentence effectively meant six weeks.

Incompetent: Prosecution-minded and Responsible for Miscarriages of Justice

This is an old image, prominent until the 1980s and revived in 1989–91 with the quashing of multiple convictions of Irish defendants wrongly imprisoned for IRA crimes. Given the longevity of the images above, however, this characterisation is probably still current. The Birmingham Six were freed in 1991 after 16 years of wrongful imprisonment, three appeals and high-profile campaigning. Headlines attacked the Court of Appeal in general and trial judge Lord Bridge and Lord Chief Justice Lane in particular, for, respectively, the conduct of the trial and commenting sarcastically in an earlier appeal. The *Observer*, the *Independent* and other broadsheets carried double-page spreads headed 'How the judges got it wrong'[112] and 'Strong evidence against the Court of Appeal—Eighty years on, still in a psychological straightjacket'.[113] Lord Lane's judgment in rejecting an earlier appeal was quoted everywhere: 'As with many cases referred by the Home Secretary to the Court of Appeal, the longer this case has gone on, the more this court has been convinced that the jury was correct'. Within two days, 100 MPs had joined an all-party campaign to remove him and, on the day of the successful

---

[110]   F Gibb and R Ford, 'Law chief attacks longer sentences', *The Times*, 11 October 2006.

[111]   See above n 80 and JV Roberts and others, 'Public Attitudes to the Sentencing of Offences Involving Death by Driving' [2008] *Crim LR* 525 and the 'myth busting' section of the Judiciary website.

[112]   C Mullin, *The Observer*, 17 March 1991.

[113]   P Wynn Davies, *The Independent*, 15 March 1991.

appeal, the Royal Commission on Criminal Justice was established.[114] The judicial image was not helped by the most populist judge, Lord Denning, repeatedly saying that the Birmingham Six (and the Winchester Three) were really guilty.

Judges v Government

Judges are reported as being in conflict with government because they often are. The constitutional ramifications are the subject of academic analysis.[115] Battle recommenced with the appointment of Thatcher's reforming Lord Chancellor Mackay in the 1980s. Judges and government disagree over sentencing policy, court funding, asylum seekers, terrorist suspects, and so on. Governments see themselves as mandated by democratic election and the judges as unaccountable. Judges see themselves as upholders of the rule of law and the common law, of values that transcend ephemeral government. Examples from the pre-1997 Conservative era are:

— 'Lane [LCJ] rebukes LCD over judge shortage';[116]
— the 1989 dispute between Lord Mackay and the judiciary over powers to grant rights of audience to lawyers, featuring a judges' meeting described by media as a 'judges' strike', and the Master of the Rolls' comical outburst 'Get your tanks off my lawn';
— the heated parliamentary debate over the Crime (Sentences) Bill 1997 between the Government and an array of judges, 'Lord Chief Justice leads attack on sentencing plans';[117]
— Lord Woolf's attacks on Thatcher's Home Secretary ('Prison works!') Howard,[118] saying 'prison is degrading and expensive';[119]
— and by 1996 there were arguments about asylum seekers, with a 'scathing' attack by the Court of Appeal on the withdrawal of benefits as 'draconian'.

This led the *New Law Journal* to conclude that relations were at an 'all time low'[120] but argument descended when David Blunkett became Labour Home Secretary. In 2003, a judge determined that depriving asylum seekers of benefits breached the European Convention on Human Rights, causing headlines like 'Dictators in Wigs' and 'What have our judges got against Britain?'. Blunkett

---

[114] Its 1993 report resulted in an expansion of appellate powers and the establishment of the Criminal Cases Review Commission to investigate alleged miscarriages of justice, in the Criminal Appeal Act 1995.

[115] Notably the works of Stevens and Griffith.

[116] The Law Society's *Gazette*, 17 July 1991, reporting a speech at the Mansion House.

[117] F Gibb, *The Times*, 28 January 1997.

[118] Asserted at the 1993 Conservative conference but oft-repeated.

[119] Quoted in 'Politics and the judiciary' (1993) 143 *New Law Journal* 1486.

[120] Editorial, 'Mutterings in Whitehall' (1996) 146 *New Law Journal* 941.

complained judges were 'undermining democracy'. He was labelled 'whiner' by a retired judge and complained to a police audience that he was 'frankly fed up' of judges overturning policy and wanted '*judges that live in the same real world as the rest of us ... I just like judges who help us and help you to do the job*' (my emphasis). He complained that the Bar chairman had 'lost the plot'.[121] There swiftly followed an attack by the Lord Chief Justice on proposed tough minimum sentences, 'Woolf attacks political interference in the courts'.[122] The row continued into 2004. Two judicial speeches attacking the Asylum and Immigration Bill, which endeavoured to oust review by the courts, gained wide coverage.[123] While the popular press promoted Blunkett's story of himself as the champion of the victim and the police, the serious papers engaged intellectual heavyweights to explain concepts such as 'rule of law', 'civil liberties' and 'supremacy of Parliament' in the 'unwritten constitution' defended by an 'independent judiciary'.[124] A mass of coverage was attracted in December 2004 by the unrestrained language of the Law Lords in attacking Labour's post-'9/11' legislation permitting indefinite detention of terrorist suspects, as 'the stuff of nightmares ... associated with Soviet Russia in the Stalinist era' and a 'real threat to the life of the nation'.[125] Again, the judges were defended in the serious newspapers.[126] Blair backed his Home Secretary and in 2005 appealed to the judges to respond to public concern about suicide bombing but his wife, Cherie Booth QC, gained equal publicity in speeches urging the Government not to erode civil liberties. Lord Chief Justice Phillips took over from Lord Woolf, to tell the Prime Minister 'Don't push us around',[127] 'We are all trying to do our job.' The judiciary were defended on asylum seekers by another Labour Sheffielder, Roy Hattersley, cited at the top of this chapter. Attacking his own party, he said 'It is time for Charles Clarke to explain to his less intelligent colleagues that they make themselves ridiculous by attacking the judiciary for administering the law'.[128]

[121] S Tendler, R Ford and F Gibb, '"Whiner" Blunkett assaults judges in front of 1,000 PCs', *The Times*, 15 May 2003.

[122] F Gibb and G Hurst, *The Times*, 17 June 2003.

[123] Lord Woolf's Squire Centenary Lecture at Cambridge and a speech by Lord Steyn, both 3 March 2004.

[124] A Howard, 'Lord Woolf v the Home Secretary', *The Times*, 9 March 2004 rounded on 'loutish tabloids'; H Kennedy, 'A good brand: is that all the Lord Chancellor is?', *The Times*, 24 February 2004.

[125] *A (FC) and others v SS for the Home Department* [2004] UKHL 56, per Lords Scott and Hoffmann.

[126] A Sampson, 'As Parliament has failed to protect our democracy, we must turn to the judges', *The Independent*, 18 December 2004.

[127] A Travis, *The Guardian*, 12 October 2005.

[128] 'Borderline failure', *The Guardian*, 17 October 2005.

THE VAIN ATTEMPT TO CONTROL THE JUDGES' IMAGE

Look, the public doesn't want truth and justice. They want scandal and lies, the viler the better!

Inspector Frost[129]

In the last decades of the twentieth century, magistrates stopped berating miscreants with homilies designed to attract press attention[130] and judges, except Denning, Scarman and Pickles, stopped talking to the press. In 1955, Lord Chancellor Kilmuir forbade it because of 'the overriding importance of keeping the Judiciary of this country insulated from the controversies of the day'.[131] In turn, the media were expected not to criticise judges. Bernard Levin was threatened with prosecution for criticising Lord Goddard in 1958.[132] These 'Kilmuir Rules' were not abolished until 1987, by Lord Chancellor Mackay. His predecessor, Hailsham, discouraged judges from defending themselves and even now, most judges do not do so. None criticised on the 2003 Channel 4 programme accepted the invitation to appear. Curiously, although the senior judges' 'union', the Judges' Council, was created in 1873, expressly to harvest their collective opinions on 'defects' in the legal system, it fell into disuse and its legal obligation to meet was abolished in 1981.[133] It was not fully revived until 2002–03. In 1986, Lord Hailsham rebuked two appeal judges for criticising a Bill.[134] In 1987, Pannick deprecated the silencing of judges.[135] Journalists resorted to questioning retired judges.[136]

This period of judicial aloofness, from 1955, coincided exactly with emergent public critiques of judges. In the first half of the twentieth century, judges were inactive in law creation and British justice was accepted, as a mantra, as 'the finest in the world'. Judges thought they basked in this glory. Lord Hewart said at the 1936 Lord Mayor's banquet, 'His Majesty's judges are satisfied with the almost universal admiration in which they are held'[137] but Abel-Smith and Stevens report that 1955–65 was 'noticeable for vital changes in public attitudes towards both the judges and the law'. Like other institutions, they were 'pushed dramatically before the public eye'.[138] They were attacked for their narrow social

---

[129]   *A Touch of Frost*, 18 July 2009, ITV1.
[130]   Conclusion drawn from observation.
[131]   Cited by Pannick, above n 6 at 174.
[132]   ibid 122.
[133]   ibid 183.
[134]   ibid 185.
[135]   ibid 181.
[136]   Sir Melford Stevenson, Sir Frederick Lawton and HH James Pickles: M Berlins, *The Guardian*, 14 October 1990.
[137]   Cited by Canadian Justice Beverley McLachlin, 'The Role of Judges in Modern Commonwealth Society' (1994) 110 *LQR* 260. There are different versions of the wording.
[138]   Abel-Smith and Stevens, above n 24 at 299.

background; their outdated support of capital and corporal punishment,[139] inconsistent sentencing, morally conservative development of the criminal law, handling of civil liberties and trades unions, performance in handling political scandals and generally being reactionary. Judges have been criticised ever since, though their own attitudes and performance, the consequent criticism and the image have shifted.

As late as 1990, Rozenburg pointed out that judges were one of the few large groups without a press officer. He interviewed Peter Taylor LJ who advocated televising appeals and abolishing wigs and gowns.[140] On his appointment as Lord Chief in 1992, he called a press conference. He was the first of the series of Chiefs who tried to attract public attention. They all 'intend[ed] to show that the judiciary today is more deserving of public confidence than ever before'.[141] Taylor appeared on *Question Time* and gave lectures and statements on judges, calling novel press conferences. Judges, he said, were now more pleasant than their remote, brusque, arbitrary predecessors, yet criticism was rampant.[142] In 1996, he urged an audience of judges to comment on the legal system, answer criticism and explain policies, in the hope of dispelling the 'widely held belief' that they were out of touch.[143] Lord Bingham succeeded him in 1996, set to continue reforming. He too gave press conferences and favoured stripping away wigs and gowns, and televising appeals. He took his court to the people, sitting in the provinces. He never missed an opportunity to deliver a public lecture. The negative media stereotypes persisted. In 1997, the Lord Chancellor asked judges to provide media notes on their sentencing. In 1998, a British Crime Survey showed that 80 per cent of respondents thought judges were out of touch or too lenient. It reported very poor knowledge of sentencing, especially among tabloid readers. Judges contemplated a press office.[144]

Lord Woolf continued Bingham's high lecture and press-release output. At last, in 2005, he established a Judicial Communications Office.[145] Since then, judges have occasionally defended their sentences on the Judiciary website.[146] Next was Lord Phillips, who uploaded pictures of smiley judges in casual wear. By 2008, he banned wigs, at least in civil cases. In 2006, he posed in denims, subjecting

---

[139]   Lord Goddard LCJ, controversial defender of corporal and capital punishment, provoked 'a storm of public anger' over his role in the Craig and Bentley trial and Bentley's hanging in 1952–53: M Lewis, 'Lord God-damn', the Law Society's *Gazette*, 30 May 1990.

[140]   'Packaging the Judges', *The Guardian*, 14 October 1990.

[141]   Editorial, 'In defence of the judiciary' (1992) 142 *New Law Journal* 1673.

[142]   'What Do We Want From Our Judges?' 17th Leggatt lecture, University of Surrey, 1993.

[143]   (1996) 146 *New Law Journal* 542.

[144]   R Ford and F Gibb, 'PR campaign to polish judges' image', *The Times*, 6 January 1998.

[145]   Under the Constitutional Reform Act 2005.

[146]   The debate over whether judges should defend their decisions was raised again in 2008 when the editor of the *Daily Mail* criticised the 'arrogant and amoral' privacy judgments of Eady J: D Pannick, 'Should judges respond to criticism?', *The Times*, 27 November 2008. In this research, I found that some resident Crown Court judges were regularly in touch with local newspaper editors, in an attempt to influence reporting.

himself to community service, but his continual negative press in the *Mail* and the *Sun* showed that in the attempt to portray themselves as in touch, judges cannot win. The *Observer* published an interview with Lord Phillips but the *Daily Mail* editorial called it 'a naked piece of propaganda' on non-custodial sentences. Columnist Melanie Phillips called it 'a bizarre initiative' and 'improper meddling in politics'. Judges should 'depart from la-la land and come back to planet Earth'. Pannick retorted that newspapers that complain that judges are out of touch should be slow to condemn. As Pannick said, had Lord Phillips delivered a lecture calling for corporal punishment, the *Mail* would have praised his wisdom,[147] just as it praised his successor Lord Judge in 2008–09 for his advocacy of tougher sentencing. In 2007, the House of Lords Constitution Committee heavily criticised the 'systemic failure' in the relationship between judges and the Lord Chancellor, in reacting to ministerial criticism and media hysteria over the Sweeney sentence. They said senior judges should have acted more quickly to head off inflammatory press coverage. They urged the Judicial Communications Office to be more 'active and assertive' in its dealings with the media[148] so in 2007, Lord Phillips recruited five judges to train as media spokespeople.[149] In 2010, in introducing the new Sentencing Council, Leveson LJ said 'Addressing media coverage is one of the areas that the Council will be seeking to tackle in its work to increase public confidence in sentencing'.[150]

This and all the above attempts to control the judicial image will surely not work because a Lord Chief Justice cannot control the following:

— Individual sentencing: while low sentences can be corrected on appeal, the lasting and disproportionate damage is done by initial reporting and the consequent hysteria of victims, families and commentators.
— Remarks in and out of court: when judges continue making remarks like 'flying carpet', even though such lapses are extremely rare, all other judges' hearts sink, because these will become rooted for decades.
— While judges are sitting targets for criticism and lampooning, historically and internationally, wig-wearers are asking for trouble.

---

[147] 'Community service? The Chief Justice knows more than most', *The Times*, 24 October 2006.

[148] *Relations between the executive, the judiciary and Parliament*, HL 151, July 2007, Parliament website and see their follow-up report in October 2008.

[149] In his 2009 annual report, Lord Judge LCJ, said this 'small media panel of judges were trained to give interviews on issues where we feel it is important to enhance public understanding and confidence in the judiciary and justice system, and in particular the sentencing aspects of our work'.

[150] Opening remarks at the CBA conference, 18 May 2010. He said:

The Sentencing Council will ensure that it is working both to seek the views of the public on sentencing but also inform them about sentencing. Working with the media will be just one part of a wider strategy on confidence that we will put in place with the aim of providing better information to the public through a range of communication channels.

— Judges interviewed have irritating Bar/public school accents, reinforcing the privileged stereotype.
— Retired judges are even worse and they are out of the control of the Lord Chief.
— Selective reporting: Lord Judge may implore editors to stop damaging commentary[151] and the Judicial Communications Office can upload dozens of press releases onto its website but newspapers choose to ignore these. They report paedophile cases in disproportionately high numbers. They print pictures of judges in full-bottomed wigs, instead of downloading 'smiley Lord Chief Justice in denim'.
— Judges are not the only people under attack. They are a soft target in a trend of sloppy journalism. Lord Birt, former Director General of the BBC complained of the 'tabloidisation' of British intellectual life. He said the media had become too reliant on 'easy cruelty' and 'the desire to humiliate'.[152]
— Judges cannot win because they cannot please everybody. *Express* and *Sun* readers' blogs call for the reintroduction of the death penalty yet *Guardian* readers (and *Guardian* columnists like Polly Toynbee) hold the opposite view.

JUDGES' VIEWS OF THEIR IMAGE

The 77 judges interviewed were acutely aware of their collective image. Some were defensive in claiming they were not 'out of touch' or stereotypical and some thought that media portrayal was damaging to society in a sinister way.

toffee-nosed leisure workers. (HC judge)[153]

people said 'you look far too young to be a judge'. They had this image of a 77 year old man with a stick. (CA/UKSC)

They think I live in the lodgings. (CJ)

white, male, old and Oxbridge ... my father went to sea, my mother was a housewife. (Female Oxbridge CJ)

stuffy old farts and completely out of touch ... a bunch of idiots. (CJ)

Bizzare ... full-length wig, driven around in a limo and living in lodgings. (CJ)

judges are scapegoats ... obviously their purpose is to sell newspapers. (HC)

romanticised view of doctors and nurses and ... jaundiced view of judges. (HC)

---

[151] 'Heroes and villains', speech, 13 October 2003.
[152] O Gibson, 'Birt attacks "easy cruelty" of tabloid Britain', *The Guardian*, 27 August 2005.
[153] Key: DJ = county court district judge; DJMC = district judge (magistrates' court); CJ = circuit judge; HC = High Court judge; CA/UKSC = Lord Justice of Appeal or Justice of the UK Supreme Court.

We are trying to involve school pupils ... but they don't seem interested. (CJ)

out of touch ... as if we are removed from paying the mortgage and having kids at school. (CJ)

fogies with ... old fashioned social attitudes ... only work from ten to four. (CA/UKSC)

typical television programme will portray a judge of 30 years ago. (HC)

dig out the same six cases ... stupid old men giving stupidly low sentences in rape cases. (CA)

Reporting ... of what you say in court bears no resemblance to what you have said ... as though some idiot has taken it down. (CJ)

prancing about in silk stockings ... there is a real danger of politicians seriously undermining the role of judges in society. (CJ)

My mother was a farmer's daughter from Ireland ... My father was in the army. His mother had been a refugee from Hungary and his father had been a tailor. I didn't go to a public school.

The trouble is that the job of a judge has a magic ... you are just one under God ... the way that you can affect ... people's lives hardly bears thinking about but I wish the public could divorce the job from the people. (HC)

A judge who tries criminal cases is more in touch not only than the public but most members of the press as well ... going into very detailed evidence about people's private lives. (HC)

Many judges talk and express themselves in ways which are very unlike ordinary people ... so it makes [them] think that judges ... don't understand them. (DJ)

Stuffy ... white, middle class, arrogant, don't know who Kevin Keegan is ... Every time a judge says something a little bit silly, it seems to be prayed in aid of the fact that all judges are silly. I know who Kevin Keegan is. I know about modern stuff cos I've got a couple of teenagers at home. (DJ)

I come from a working class family ... I managed a betting shop. We are supposed to be sitting eating quails' eggs with our pumps on. (DJMC)

Judges in the family courts couldn't be more in the real world if they tried ... the people in my village are surprised to find you are actually a very normal person. (CJ)

old and doddery, deaf and out of touch ... promoted by ... the Daily Mail ... very sad and probably damaging to society. (HC)

The notion that we are out of touch is frankly absurd. I have vicariously had more experience of the brutal reality of life than the reporters in the press who denigrate us for being out of touch ... It's a Chinese torture ... to the detriment of our society and of our freedom. (CA/UKSC)

I asked whether they thought media portrayal had changed. Forty-nine thought it had, 30 mentioning a greater readiness to criticise. Many considered it part of a general trend of less deference to authority, which was no bad thing unless it involved misreporting. A typical response was:

> They are more critical and less careful. They have become far less deferential and that is not a bad thing. The media is for the most part unprofessional. If you have ever seen a report of anything you have been involved in it bears little relation.

Fourteen mentioned *Judge John Deed*. One thought the programme 'an insult to judges … gibberish' but a High Court judge said 'I think *Judge John Deed* has done marvels' and others said his sex appeal and individuality were positive characterisations. A circuit judge said 'I thought it was a good idea to have a judge who was screwing the prosecution counsel and driving a nice Audi'.

I asked the judges what they thought of wigs and gowns. 32 were in favour, 26 suggested abandoning them in civil cases and 15 wanted wigs or wigs and gowns abolished.[154] Responses bore no relationship to other characteristics. Judges who were otherwise viewed as very modern and/or radical were surprisingly traditionalist. Many defended wigs in criminal trials as embodying the office of judge, symbolically distancing the person from the office and practically, 'they operate as a variable disguise' (HC judge). Several felt wigs protected their security.

> I tried that chap who … killed ten people … the media circus descended … ten satellite vans … I passed sentence … I then … changed into a soft-collared shirt and an old raincoat. I walked out … there was a frenzy of these journalists interviewing each other … and none of them recognised me. It was a marvellous feeling … I had become me again and I was an individual who had nothing to do with the case. The person who had just done the job in court was a judge. (HC)

> I have stood in the queue in the Post Office next to a defendant I was trying and who did not recognise me. (CJ)

> People who bump into me in Tesco don't necessarily recognise me. (CJ)

> a wig is the disembodied face of justice … Once in Bristol on a bleak November Friday evening, after the jury acquitted a chap of … rape … (I had rather hoped … that he would be found guilty), he and I were the only people on the station but he hadn't the first idea of who I was. I was quite glad of that. (CA/UKSC)

> Divorcing the person from the job and all that authority and artificial hair. The wig is a very important symbol. You are no longer whoever you are … I don't feel like a judge unless I dress up … The number of times I have taken foreign lawyers to Westminster Abbey.[155] These are intelligent, cultured men and women … they are very impressed at this sort of dedication to the idea of the law … the job is such an impossible, absurd job for an individual to do. (HC, considered a radical)

---

[154] In hindsight, I should have asked for separate opinions on wigs and gowns. Several judges pointed out that they were unaware of any country that had no gowns.
[155] To the ceremonial opening of the legal year.

Sandra Berns has repeated the point that the wig and gown symbolically eradicate individual identity.[156] She reported that an Australian experiment in abandoning gowns in one court was stopped, because of the 'threat of repeated violence'. As the civil and criminal district judges in this research were swift to point out, however, they are the judges who have most contact with court users and they sit unrobed so even if judicial garb is, as she argues, a dehumanising protection, then it is not available here to the judges who most need it. Others considered court dress was a 'prop' necessary to assert 'the dignity of the court' or maintain order.

> the fragility of trials ... anything which assists the respect of the court helps trials and also possibly helps witnesses to tell the truth ... I sat in consistory courts ... I got too idle to [wear wig and robes] ... I rapidly found people thought it was a public meeting! (HC)

> it is very difficult to maintain respect and control ... often you are dealing with some pretty thuggish people who aren't used to doing what they are told. (CJ)

> maintains respect and good order. When I started at the Bar we would have two ushers, a clerk and at least one officer in uniform in every courtroom. Now I see sometimes only one usher, no clerk, no police officer and a dock officer who is a Group 4 ... who is falling asleep or reading a newspaper. (CJ)

Others defended wigs as part of tradition, 'eccentric and typical of the English to do something quite as barmy as that ... long live eccentricity' (CJ of foreign parentage). Those who opposed wigs entirely often did so in strong language:

> Codswallop! (CJ)

> how stupid it is, that they need to be disguised from their customers! (HC)

> attracts more bad publicity because it looks so out of date now. (DJ)

> bizarre bit of equipment ... you can chuck them around the room but still they will sit on your head like a little cap ... bloody expensive. (DJ)

> a load of nonsense ... absolutely stupid! ... All this stuff about the majesty of the court. It's a lot of crap; a lot of rubbish ... If you have to rely on wigs, gowns and oak panelling to give what you do some significance or majesty then you're in the wrong job, Pal! (DJ)

> just fuels this public perception ... makes us look perfectly ridiculous. (CA)

> If we can't keep order in court we shouldn't be on the bench ... [the wig] messes up my hairstyle. (Female CJ)

> absolutely absurd ... wearing an eighteenth century wig. (CJ)

> there is something incongruous in me sitting to decide a TCC[157] case involving a computer, with a bit of seventeenth century horsehair on my head. (CJ)

---

[156]   S Berns, *To Speak as a Judge* (Dartmouth, Ashgate, 1999) 30, 202 and 208.
[157]   Technology and Construction Court.

ARE THERE ANY POSITIVE VIEWS ON JUDGES?

Jurors normally gain a positive impression of the judge. Judges observed in this research were meticulously polite and considerate to jurors. Zander and Henderson's *Crown Court Study*[158] found that over 85 per cent of 8,000 jurors rated judges as doing their job very well, in controlling proceedings fairly and explaining things to the jury.[159] Matthews, Hancock and Briggs[160] found:

> In contrast to those decontextualised studies which claim that judges are 'out of touch' … our research found an overwhelming degree of support for the work judges carry out in managing and summarising cases … Jurors took particular offence at the denigration of judges and the ways in which they are sometimes represented in the mass media.

While conducting this research, I noticed that while academics generally share the media's and public's negative view of judges,[161] the few who have met judges are just as defensive as jurors.[162] Rock remarked on the

> conspicuous and courteous even-handedness with which judges treated witnesses and defendants: witnesses were always addressed by their proper title and always with politeness … Relations between judges and civilians were very largely ordered, calm, clear and exact … Prosecution witnesses acknowledged their impartiality … The prevailing epithet applied to the judiciary was that they were 'very nice'.[163]

Since 1983, *Ipsos MORI* has polled the public on which professionals they trust the most. Judges come near the top. In 2009, they ranked third equal, behind doctors and teachers.[164] *YouGov* asks the public 'How much do you trust the following to tell the truth?' Judges ranked fifth in 2010.[165] The incorruptibility of UK judges is taken for granted. Lord Phillips said in 2007, 'I am fortunate in coming from a jurisdiction where it is inconceivable that a litigant should even attempt to bribe a judge'.[166]

---

[158] Zander and Henderson, above n 17.

[159] See ch 7 below.

[160] *Jurors' perceptions, understanding, confidence and satisfaction in the jury system: a study in six courts* Home Office Online Report 05/04, at 30–31.

[161] Chapters here presented as conference papers sometimes provoked hostile/disbelieving reactions from academics.

[162] Genn describes civil judges as 'heroic', *Judging Civil Justice* (Cambridge, Cambridge University Press, 2009) 127.

[163] P Rock, *The Social World of an English Crown Court* (Oxford, Clarendon Press, 1993) 153–54 and he cited a similar research finding, by Raine and Smith.

[164] *Ipsos MORI* website.

[165] *YouGov* website. See also Genn, above n 162 at 144–45. Like Shetreet, she remarked on the English judiciary's global reputation for intellect and incorruptibility. As she said, trust in English law and English judges has facilitated the global importance of the Commercial Court.

[166] Speech, 'Judicial Independence', September 2007.

CONCLUSION

The media image of the judge is negative in the extreme—old, white and male, which is accurate—but also privileged, elitist, insensitive and out-of-touch. This is directly absorbed by the public because only exceptional people have access to any other source of image, such as encountering a judge in court, as a party or juror, or knowingly meeting a judge out of court. Jurors speak favourably of the judges with whom they have interacted, almost in reverse of the general image. Individual judges are acutely aware of this negative stereotype and seek to distance themselves by reference to their own ordinariness and humble backgrounds. Criticism started at the mid-point of the twentieth century. At the same time, judges were banned by the Kilmuir Rules from talking to the media in defence of themselves. This ban was lifted before 1990 but individual judges still do not normally defend themselves, preferring to keep a very low profile. By the early 1990s, Lords Chief Justice tried to improve the judges' public image, by calling press conferences and giving lectures and eventually developing a press office which now defends individual judges' decisions, depicts judges on its website as friendly, ordinary and approachable and tries to provide simple information in an easily navigable format. The current Lord Chief has pleaded with the media to present a fairer image and some judges have been media-trained.

Shedding this Dickensian image is an almost impossible goal, however, because the media are free to distort judges' image. The same newspapers that report *every* paedophile trial in lurid detail are the ones that latch onto and sometimes misreport judges' inappropriate comments. Straightforward trials by fair judges, dispensing suitable sentences are reported neutrally, with the judge's name seldom mentioned. The media, especially the red-tops, are free to indulge in cruel and lazy journalism, attacking a soft target, a perceived elite, in the full knowledge that this group will not defend themselves, unlike, for instance, the much more highly paid and privileged stars of sport and screen who are swift to protect themselves with superinjunctions and defamation and privacy laws. Media attacks worsened recently and became more frequent when minsters, forgetting judicial independence, joined in to criticise lenient sentences caused by their own policies.

In their turn, though, some judges, especially lawyers sitting part-time, do a disproportionate disservice to the full-time judiciary by their ill-advised comments in court and unbecoming out-of-court behaviour, which is doubtless why those lawyers never progressed to become full-time judges. These incidents are magnified and repeated by the media and become lodged in folk memory for decades. While judges throughout the world wear gowns, senior judges have long pointed out that judges in the UK do themselves no favours by conducting business with a lump of horsehair on their heads, in eighteenth century fashion. While wigs are now confined to Crown Court criminal cases, civil gowns are designer-wear and hundreds of judges wear neither wig nor gown, the public image is, of course, derived almost exclusively from fictional and comedy judges and from photographs of real judges on parade annually in knee-breeches and full-bottomed wigs. Some have realised that while judges continue to dress up like pantomime characters, they will be lampooned as 'a pampered and privileged elite'.[167] This, then, is the archaic media folk-devil against which the real judges depicted in their working world, in this book, are to be measured.

---

[167] Austin Mitchell MP, examining a witness before the Parliamentary Public Accounts Committee hearing on Crown Court Administration, 16 March 2009.

3

Where Do English and Welsh Judges Come From?

> There were two things as a girl I wanted to do. One was a postmistress and the other was a nun. Nuns wore black clothes and the other filled in forms and I was a bit of a busy body so I have sort of combined the two by being a district judge.

THIS CHAPTER EXAMINES the backgrounds of the 77 judges. The quotations allow them to speak for themselves, in an unprecedented manner, in contrast with articles based on statistics trawled from *Who's Who*.[1] These repetitive surveys of the senior judiciary, demonstrating that they are predominantly independently schooled and Oxbridge educated, are the only general information on judges available to the public so they feed the stereotype. They are easily done by journalists or pressure groups like the Sutton Trust, whose statistics have been used by the Labour Government in 2009, then the Coalition in 2010, to fuel discussion papers on social mobility. Since the 1950s they have been routinely used to attack the judiciary for lack of diversity. As we shall see here, though, these surveys are superficial and misleading. This chapter provides a more in-depth insight into judges' education and career backgrounds and what prompted them to study law.

DEMOGRAPHIC INFORMATION

Age, Ethnicity and Gender

The sample had a broad age-span. They were born in 1936–58 and aged 45–68 at the time of the research. The 40 core sample were white, although one of the three pilot judges was non-white. 14 were women (nine of the core sample) representing a greater proportion in the sample than there was in the population of judges at that time.

---

[1] An earlier version was published as [2007] *Cambridge Law Journal* Vol 66 (2) 365.

		%	Women as % of judges 2006	
District judges:[2]	5 of 19	26.3	22.42	130 of 580
Circuit judges:	6 of 32	18.9	11.39	73 of 641
High Court judges:	3 of 16	18.9	10.29	11 of 107
CA/UKSC	0 of 10	0	8.33	4 of 48

Three women were married to judges, two outranking their husbands.

SCHOOLING AND UNIVERSITY

Attention is generally drawn to senior judges' educational backgrounds, with the claim often being made that all judges are out of touch.[3] This is deeply misleading. For most people involved in a case, they will be dealt with by a district judge or bench of lay magistrates. Around 95 per cent of all criminal cases and many family cases are disposed of by magistrates. 30,000 are unpaid lay people. Only 143 are district judges (magistrates' courts) (DJMCs). Most civil and most remaining family cases are decided by the 448 civil district judges (DJs) in the county court. These DJs do not appear in *Who's Who*. Most are solicitors. They come from much more diverse backgrounds than the senior judiciary.

Forty of the 77 here were privately educated, with senior judges more likely to have attended independent schools. A number won free or subsidised places, such as the only Eton educated judge. Of the six DJMCs, none was privately educated. Five attended state grammars and one an 'awful' comprehensive. Of the 13 DJs, five were privately educated. Of the 32 circuit judges (CJs), half were privately educated, as were 11 of 16 High Court judges (HCJs) and eight of the eight Court of Appeal judges and two UK Supreme Court Justices (CA/UKSC). One DJ and two CJs failed their '11 plus' and went to secondary moderns. All remaining judges attended state grammars or direct grant schools. The judges graduated between 1959 and 1979. The public image of the judiciary is Oxbridge, again based on the senior judiciary. 35 of the 77 were Oxbridge, concentrated at the top of the pyramid.

---

[2] Including DJMCs and HC DJs.
[3] Surveys are published by Labour Research. In 2005, the Sutton Trust published a survey of 'top solicitors, barristers and judges': 75 per cent of the senior judiciary attended independent schools and 81 per cent were Oxbridge-educated (website). *The Economist* published a survey in 1956, cited in B Abel-Smith and R Stevens, *Lawyers and the Courts* (London, Hienemann, 1967) 299, finding 76 per cent and 76 per cent respectively.

	Oxbridge	Old Uni	New Uni	Poly	No Degree	Total
DJMCs	1 (16.7 %)	1	1	2	1	6
DJs	2 (15.4%)	4	1	3	3	13
CJs	11 (34.5%)	15	4	0	2	32
HCJs	12 (75%)	4	0	0	0	16
CA/UKSC	9 (90%)	1	0	0	0	10
Total	35 (45.5 %)	25	6	5	6	77

(Each of the six non-graduates had served five years as a solicitors' articled clerk).

The Criticism of Narrow Educational Backgrounds

I suggest that it should not be a surprise, or a subject of criticism, that judges in the highest courts are educated at elite universities. High Court judges spend their time in the Court of Appeal (CA), or handling extremely complex trials. The CA has a very heavy workload, requiring minds that can process masses of highly complex data very swiftly. This is the crucial court for establishing precedents—developing the law. UK Supreme Court Justices are confined to deciding points of law of general public importance. It would surely be a matter of concern if senior judges were *not* highly educated and exceptionally intelligent. An examination of senior judges elsewhere demonstrates that they too are an intellectual elite. In 2006, at the time of the research, six of the nine US Supreme Court Justices were Harvard educated, two were Yale graduates and two also had Oxford degrees. Sonia Sotomayor, appointed in 2009, is a Yale graduate and Elena Kagan, appointed in 2010, graduated from Princeton, Oxford and Harvard.[4] Canadian Supreme Court Justices were drawn from top Canadian universities and one was the first Canadian to be elected President of the Cambridge Union.[5] Bell, in his review of European judges,[6] explains the following: members of the French *Conseil D'Etat* have social standing as a *grand corps*, drawn from the elite of the *Ecole Nationale de l'Administration*, a *grand école*; the German judicial culture has traditionally been of an intellectual elite;[7] Swedish judicial selection in meritocratic competition emphasises educational achievement and law is taught at few Swedish universities. De Groot-Van Leeuwen explains that law is one of the

---

[4] USSC website.

[5] Canadian SC website.

[6] J Bell, *Judiciaries Within Europe—A Comparative Review* (Cambridge, Cambridge University Press, 2006).

[7] German lawyers in general are exceptionally highly educated.

most elite university studies in the Netherlands and the most recent survey of *all* judges showed that 60 per cent came from elite family backgrounds.[8]

The criticism of Oxbridge education and independent schooling needs further examination. Underlying it is the accusation that *buying* an education provided not only a superior schooling but also a greater chance of entering Oxbridge. This is a fair criticism but it should be directed at the UK education process itself. The problem is this: Oxford and Cambridge are the UK's elite universities but they do not and did not have a monopoly of the highly intelligent, especially when these judges were entering university. In that period, an even higher proportion of Oxbridge undergraduates came from independent schools than they do now.[9] In the 1960s, some Oxbridge colleges still had overt recruitment links with named independent schools, through 'closed scholarships'. Over-recruitment of Oxbridge graduates into the judiciary would, then, have resulted in its being skewed towards those with a privileged background and independent schooling and in turn, it excluded some highly intelligent lawyers who graduated from other universities. The problematic relationship between Oxbridge, independent schooling and social class results partly from the historic connection between them and partly from the UK's education system and cultural attitudes, where many of the middle classes consider it acceptable that a better school education can be bought than that which is generally provided by the state. This produces a class divisive education system which is incomprehensible to citizens of other European states such as Germany and France and Scandanavia, where middle class energy is expended in improving the state education system, rather than in paying privately for an alternative.[10]

My argument that criticism should be directed at the education system, not the judges, is supported by the fact that the educational elites are found in other powerful sections of the UK economy, such as the civil service and private enterprise, as demonstrated by regular surveys by the Sutton Trust, an educational charity promoting social mobility. For instance, a 2005 survey showed that a quarter of MPs were Oxbridge educated and that a large proportion of the Cabinet and Shadow Cabinet were Oxbridge and independently educated. Oxbridge graduates are over-represented even among the most famous comedians. The complex relationship between social mobility, access to the professions and background factors such as family, community, family income, parental aspirations and so on is explored in the Cabinet Office Report, *Unleashing Aspiration: The Final Report of the Panel on Fair Access to the Professions*, 2009. This shows that, while seven per cent of the UK population are privately

---

[8] 'Merit Selection and Diversity in the Dutch Judiciary' in K Malleson and PH Russell (eds), *Appointing Judges in an Age of Power* (Toronto, University of Toronto Press, 2006).

[9] In 2007, the Sutton Trust reported that 30 per cent of Oxbridge students came from 100 elite schools: *University admissions by individual schools*.

[10] *From Our Own Correspondent*, Radio 4, 31 July 2010 and J Vasagar, 'No league table, no inspections, no private schools', *The Guardian*, 6 December 2010.

educated, over half of most professionals were independently schooled. It should not be news that an independent schooling buys an employment advantage. The report yet again claims that 75 per cent of judges are independently schooled but does not say which judges. It is obviously the Sutton Trust 2005 statistic again.[11]

I have explained this at length because judges are acutely aware of this criticism. Some were apologetic about their privileged education and others defensive. One High Court judge wanted me to note that his single mother had worked 'damned hard' and impoverished herself to pay for his independent schooling. It was very clear that, whatever their birth-family background, the factor most had in common was parental expectations and involvement in education, which was identified and much discussed in 2009[12] as part of 'cultural capital', a major 'driver' behind educational attainment and entry to the professions.[13]

A second and much more valid criticism is made of Oxbridge judges, however: that the pre-2006 selection process[14] was dependent on the opinions of existing judges and thus open to nepotism, including a bias towards certain Oxbridge colleges. This criticism was revived and directed specifically at Lord Chancellor Falconer in 2005, when the Commission for Judicial Appointments accused him of favouring Oxbridge graduates over objectively selected candidates who were better qualified. This criticism is examined in the chapter on judicial selection.[15]

The attack on Oxbridge judges is often couched in misleading language that implies that *all* Oxbridge judges come from privileged backgrounds. This has not been the case since the mid-twentieth century, when some of the most eminent Oxbridge judges came from humble backgrounds, such as Lord Denning MR (son of a draper) and Lord Chancellor Elwyn-Jones (son of a tin-plate rollerman in a Welsh steelworks). Nor was it the case with all of the 77 judges here.[16] One QC failed his '11 plus', was sent to a secondary modern school and moved to a

---

[11]   On the Cabinet Office website, until the 2010 general election and now in the National Archives web archive. See especially chs 1 (with these statistics) and 2. Publications by Iain Duncan Smith's Centre for Social Justice use the same statistic. The 2010 Coalition Government carries a very similar document on their Cabinet Office website, with similar statistics on social mobility: *State of the nation report: poverty, worklessness and welfare dependency in the UK*, 3 June 2010.

[12]   Discussed in three August 2009 episodes of *Thinking Allowed*, BBC Radio 4 and generally discussed in the 2008–09 media commentary on *Unleashing Aspiration*.

[13]   *Unleashing Aspiration*, ch 2.

[14]   Selection by the Lord Chancellor was replaced in 2006 with by a Judicial Appointments Commission, as a result of the Constitutional Reform Act 2005, examined in P Darbyshire, *Darbyshire on the English Legal System*, 10th edn (London, Sweet & Maxwell, 2011).

[15]   In its 2004–05 Annual Report and in its review of the recorder competition (Midland Circuit), the independent watchdog, the CJA criticised two instances where the disagreement of the Lord Chancellor (LC) with officials led to an increase in the proportion of Oxbridge appointees. The LC overrode the choice of candidate for a specialist CJ in Cardiff: see news reports of 18 September 2005.

[16]   On reading this, as an article, a well-known CA/UKSC judge outside this research, who was brought up in a pub and worked as a lorry driver and in a bakery to fund his higher

state grammar when he 'showed promise'. The same applies to those who attended older universities. With two district judges educated at Russell Group universities,[17] one was born into a family living in a council house in 'the Black Country' and another had an unemployed father and lived in the East End of London. Another circuit judge and QC, born into a family living in a council house, was educated at a Russell Group university. Baby boomers[18] were and are highly socially mobile, compared with their predecessors and successors, because of the post-war growth in the professions and the desire for a more egalitarian society, reflected in the development of the welfare state.[19] Baby boomer judges, most judges serving in 2011, benefited from having their university tuition fees and often their professional qualifications funded by their local authorities, as well as generous maintenance grants for those of low means. Many judges were aware that this permitted them a social mobility that they felt was denied to the current generation, such as this East Ender who attended London University.

> I was very lucky because during the early 1970s…it was a great time for education for the working classes, because the barriers were being broken down. Whilst the posh barrister image was still there, it was starting to be broken.

Of the 71 graduates, 61 were law or law joint honours, 10 having postgraduate degrees, including three with doctorates. None of the DJs or DJMCs had postgraduate qualifications. For four of the law graduates, this was their second undergraduate degree. There was a *significant* difference in terms of educational achievements between the 26 senior judges and the 13 DJs. This DJ came from a family of solicitors but was not academic.

> My 'A' levels were appalling … two Ds and an E. I retook one A level and ended up with a lower grade…and went to … Polytechnic … I did a … law degree and spent a lot of time staring out of the window. I realised I was never going to be an academic and scraped through with a basic 2:2.

By contrast, at least 11 of the 26 senior judges had obtained double firsts at Oxbridge and/or scholarships from Oxbridge or the Bar (usually in multiples) and/or a PhD. I say 'at least' because some were too modest to list everything. As for the circuit judges, it was often said by judges that they were 'a mixture' in

---

education, including PhD, emailed, reminding me of his 'impeccable working class background, who failed his 11+ three times'.

[17] The UK's top 19 research universities.

[18] There are 7.6 million baby boomers, according to government statistics, born between 1945–57, with 'shadow boomers' born between 1958 and 1963: A Grice, 'Labour and Tories target the "baby boomers"', *The Independent*, 20 October 2006, 29. See also *Unleashing Aspiration*, above.

[19] *Unleashing Aspiration*, ch 1 at 17 reports:

> The end result was an unprecedented period of social mobility … For men, there was positive social mobility for every generation born after 1900 … highest for those born in the decades after the Second World War. For women, social mobility accelerated with the generations born in the 1940s and 1950s and later.

terms of ability. The 32 in this sample were no exception. Six listed outstanding achievements similar to the senior judiciary. Five had won competitive scholarships at their university or Inn of Court.

PROFESSIONAL QUALIFICATIONS

Eighteen were solicitors and the remainder barristers. As with the national pattern, solicitors were predominant among DJs. Twelve of the 13 were solicitors, as were two of the six DJMCs and five of the 16 CJs. (One of these had qualified as a barrister and then requalified as a solicitor.) None of the 26 senior judges was a solicitor. Nineteen of the barrister judges and one solicitor had taken a correspondence or part-time professional course, or were self-taught. Most of these 20 had supported themselves by working as schoolteachers or law lecturers. The others had taken the traditional full-time professional course. For some older judges, qualifying as a barrister in the 1960s was straightforward:

> I didn't attend any course ... I just read a few books at home and then came and squeaked through the exams. (CA/UKSC)

> It was all terribly simple. You went to Gibson and Weldon in Chancery Lane. I came down from Oxford in June. I took Part One crime in September and the Bar Finals in December ... and that was that. My professional education consisted ... of rather parrot-like learning. (CA/UKSC)

A number remarked on how their professional exams had required mechanical learning, pre-1979.[20]

> I hated the exam process. They were animal ... You just had to remember lots and lots of stuff and regurgitate it. (Solicitor)

A number of barristers had opted for the Bar exams because it was a swifter and easier option.[21] They spoke in disparaging terms:

> It was a farce really ... I didn't know anything about the law at all ... It was extremely undemanding and that is one of the reasons I did it to be honest. I was called to the Bar in 1963. (HC)

> The standard ... was somewhere between moderate and appalling. I think things have changed. I was called to the Bar in 1971. (CJ)

This DJ was typical of those solicitors who had not studied for a degree but had served five years' articles:

> I went straight from school ... I started off making tea and counting stamps. I did a part-time law course.

---

[20]   At that date, the professional courses were redesigned.
[21]   And cheaper: Abel-Smith and Stevens, above n 3 at 358.

WHY STUDY LAW?

When they completed school, barrister families, judicial dynasties and solicitors' practices handed down within a family were not uncommon so I expected a substantial number to have been influenced by relatives. However, I was surprised to find that this was not the case.[22] Only two had fathers who were judges. Another's father was a barrister and five (four solicitors) had solicitor fathers. Three more had relatives in the law. The remaining 66 had no lawyer-relatives. Like many, they were the first lawyers in their family, in an era of expanding legal education[23] and rapid growth of professions.[24] They had a variety of reasons for choosing law. For some, it seemed glamorous:

> I decided … I wanted to be a barrister … at the age of seven. I saw a programme … called Boyd QC … a very posh barrister and, being a very poor Jewish boy … I thought … I would love to be Anglo-Saxon and posh. I asked my father, who was a cab driver at the time, 'What do barristers do?' and he said 'They get paid for arguing' and I spent most of my life arguing with everybody. (DJ)

> When I was eleven I watched a Bogart movie and decided I was going to be a barrister and it became a fixation. I don't have any family in the law. They are all engineers, farmers or miners. (CJ)

> I was about fifteen or sixteen. I saw it on the telly and I just liked the romance of being an advocate. Pure vanity. (CJ)

> Perry Mason at school; I always enjoyed debates in class … and it also seemed to me to be terribly exciting. (CJ)

> Perry Mason on telly. (CJ)

> Glamorous. Plus you earned a lot of money. (DJ)

> Being paid to argue. (CJ)

> Gift of the gab. (CJ)

> Opinionated. Liked the sound of my own voice. (CJ)

Three were inspired by judicial biographies. Three had met real judges.

---

[22] L Blom-Cooper and G Drewry, *Final Appeal* (Oxford, Clarendon Press, 1972) found that, of 53 Law Lords, 18 had fathers with some legal background. At 158, they said:

> A tendency for law to be a family profession, coupled with the special financial burdens [of] the Bar, have tended to make the profession the preserve of the rich, and of the exceptionally gifted. Gradually this picture is changing.

[23] Abel-Smith and Stevens, above n 3 at ch XIII. Contrast this with modern French judges. Bell, above n 6, cited a 1993 survey which showed that one in 10 French judges was from a family of judges, one in five from a family of lawyers and 43.6 per cent were married to judges.

[24] *Unleashing Aspiration*, ch 1.

> There was a lecture at my school by [someone] who had just become a High Court judge ... very charismatic and exciting ... He became Lord Scarman. He was then one of the youngest High Court judges ever. (HC)

Three had been to watch a court, including one who had a salutary experience.

> I went to the magistrates' court ... and sitting there ... trying to mind my own business, was identified by a witness as being the young thug who had attacked him in the street. That took me by surprise and it led me to think that identification evidence wasn't always the most convincing. (CJ)

Several insisted on law in the face of parental opposition but others were given a talking to:

> I didn't decide. My Mum did, in the sixth form. (Female HC now tipped to be a future LCJ)

> My Dad kept pointing out I had no prospective means of support. (HC)

For some, the choice was an accident.

> I tore the margin off the [university] application form. It didn't seem to me, because of that, I was going to get in so I filled in whatever came to the top of my head and it was law. (CJ)

> I filled in the first set of UCCA [university] forms to do economics but changed my mind and decide to go and do a degree in law. (CJ)

Some had studied law 'as something to fall back on', then became enamoured with legal practice. This one wanted to be a theatre director but on his first day as a pupil barrister:

> Within an hour or two I was already hooked. It is a fascinating job. It is such a testing, complicated game of heavy chess. (CJ)

This one started off indifferently.

> I honestly can't say that I went with a burning sense of vocation ... It was just that I really couldn't think of anything else that seemed to fit ... Once I got to the Bar, after a year or two I certainly became completely addicted to it. (HC)

A number were influenced by friends and they made a change of course.

> Sixth form. All my friends were doing law. (DJ)

> I had dropped out of the first term of an economics degree. I knew one or two people who had gone to study law and ... they encouraged me. (DJ)

For six, including three bored scientists and a police officer, law was a career change. Other people's grass seemed greener, to this banker and taxi driver:

> I was walking home rather discontent one evening and met a friend who ... had just started his own practice ... and he described what life was like at the Bar and it was rather like St Paul on the road to Damascus. I just thought this is really what I want to do. (CA/UKSC)

[I decided] after having picked up some law students, as a taxi driver ... aged 20. I ... heard what they were doing; how they went off to London; how in the Inns of Court everyone got drunk and had a very good time. (CJ)

Seven judges seemed to be fulfilling a close relative's lost career or ambition. The first explained why she and her siblings had become lawyers. She was one of three judges from refugee or war-migrant families:

My Dad came here at the end of the war and worked in the coalmines, completely wasting any education that he had ... He came over here with the intention of earning some money and then going back to study at university in Austria. He had a place but he never went back and spent the rest of his life in a factory ... he had a lot of intellectual abilities ... (he spoke a number of languages), he really didn't do anything with his life, which is why I guess we did. (DJ)

When I was about fourteen, I was interested in a career in the law. It was prompted by discussions with my father, who was a teacher of modern languages. He had started after the war doing an external law degree. When I was born he gave it up and he probably mentioned that to me and it started my interest in the law. (HC)

My father had wanted to go to the Bar in the 1930s but for financial reasons hadn't been able to, so became an economist. He encouraged me to look at the Bar from early on, and certainly from the age of eleven or twelve he started steering me in that direction. I started reading books about the lives of lawyers and became quite interested. (CJ)

Two had fathers in the law who had died when they were young.

My father was a solicitor. He died when I was thirteen and I ... decided ... that I wanted to be a solicitor. I never thought of any other career from then on. (CJ)

In addition to the judges mentioned in this chapter with adverse family circumstances, an additional seven had suffered the death of a child, discussed in chapter seven.[25]

SOCIAL MOBILITY

None came from an aristocratic background but seven had fathers and three had brothers listed in *Who's Who* or *Who Was Who* for their outstanding achievements in industry, academia, the Church, medicine or the law.[26] For 21, entering the middle classes as a lawyer (let alone becoming a judge) represented significant

[25] In the context of judges in this sample, here and below, with adverse circumstances in their background, see 'The Entrepreneur's Wound', BBC Radio 4, 5 April 2010, a series of high achievers discussing how death of a parent or family displacement across borders prompted their work ethic and ambition. Professor Manfred Kets de Vries of the INSEAD Business School in Paris has established that a disproportionately high proportion of them had suffered adverse childhood circumstances but encouragement was also a factor. See INSEAD website.

[26] Reminiscent of Lord Denning MR, whose brothers were Lieutenant-General Sir Reginald Denning, KCVO, KBE and Vice-Admiral Sir Norman Denning KBE. They all attended Andover

upward mobility. These included the taxi driver, the taxi-driver's son, the coalminer's daughter, and four children from council estates. Some had been down a rocky road.

> My father was a solicitor's managing clerk. I had failed my 11 plus and my father would not agree to my remaining in education past school leaving age. The compromise was to do a secretarial course and then work in his office. Before this happened, he was killed in front of me. I had no money and no job. The very far-sighted head teacher at the local grammar school employed me as a junior secretary and allowed me to sit in on the 6th form classes. It was not an ideal situation ... so at 18, I went to North America, taking my secretarial skills over there. (CJ and QC)

> My father was unemployed when I started at the Bar. He had been ill and packed in work. I managed to get a couple of crisis loans ... and a couple of scholarships and I also did some teaching ... I failed my A levels first time round so I ... spent two years working as a betting shop manager so I was able to put more money aside. By the time I went to university at 21, but for the supplements, I don't think I could have done it, because we had literally no money coming into the house, apart from what I earned so I was really fortunate. (DJ)

> I left school at ... sixteen ... I had always wanted to go to the Bar but my parents couldn't have sent me to university for the five years it took so I went off to become an attorney first, then doing the university course at night. I did the BA lectures from five to ten o'clock every night ... But for the LLB [I studied] 7:30 to 8:15 am and then 5 to 7:30 pm so I ended up with a BA LLB from the University of Pretoria ... Then on a weekend cricket tour, we had a very entertaining weekend in Transvaal. Three of my team were arrested. We got them released then under marshal law. They were arrested outside the gates of Pretoria jail and given 90 days' detention. I thought I was likely to be next so I resurrected an ambition. By then at the age of 23, I had given up the choice to go to Cambridge, but they were foolish enough to accept my letter to say 'Please can I come?' (CA/UKSC)

This judge had turned his back on South Africa in the 1960s, as had a number of his compatriots then working at all levels of the judiciary in England and Wales. In the Bingham court, at the time of the initial interviews, three of the 12 Lords of Appeal in Ordinary were South African: Steyn, Scott and Hoffmann.

Social mobility in judges' backgrounds will increase in the immediate future, regardless of the Judicial Appointments Commission's statutory duty to diversify the judiciary under the Constitutional Reform Act 2005, because those born in the late 1950s and early 1960s were amongst the most socially mobile of working adults in current society.[27]

Grammar School but only the judge was educated beyond school: *Who's Who 2009 and Who Was Who* online.

[27] 'Those born in the 1950s and early 1960s were three times more likely to be a professional at age 35 than those born during or before the Second World War', *Unleashing Aspiration*, at 16.

CAREERS AS LAWYERS

Fifty-nine were barristers, all but three having been in private practice. During the 1960s and 1970s, when most were called to the Bar, obtaining a pupillage, or a tenancy in chambers, depended on who you knew. A worthy 'set' of chambers with a sound reputation was briefed by solicitors in important and lucrative cases. Many judges admitted that they were 'lucky'. Parentage helped this judge's son.

> I went straight into my father's old chambers, which nowadays people would be horrified by. Life was made, certainly for my generation, a Hell of a lot easier than it is for them now. (HC, called to the Bar in 1963)

Most had to find their own connections. Some were eased into the Bar by a supporter who had spotted a bright student, like these four, who modestly described themselves as 'lucky' but who indeed did very well at university or in the Bar exams, such as the taxi driver's son.

> Then, luckily, my pupil master, who had taught me at university, got me into ... Chambers. They were a big left-wing chambers doing just defence work. (DJMC, called in 1976)

And the printer's brilliant child:

> I was very lucky to get a pupillage with [by 2011, one of the most eminent CA judges]. Life is all about being in the right place at the right time and it so happened that one of the lecturers at [London University] knew I was interested and knew [him] ... it was before any sort of fair selection system or online applications for pupillage so you just tended to make your own arrangements. I rang him up ... and he just said 'Come along and have a chat with me and I'll see what we can do'. There wasn't any sort of structured interview at all ... He said he would offer me a pupillage and I started pupillage in January of 1976. (HC)

And in 1971, one child, born into a council flat, graduated from a Russell Group university and joined a chambers

> which was probably the principal criminal law set, servicing London and East Anglia. The head ... was [V] who went on to become Attorney General and Lord Chancellor. (CJ and QC)

This Essex grammar school boy (who now speaks with the distinctive patrician accent he received at the Bar) had done well in his Bar exams, in 1972.

> I took a bit of time to get pupillage, about six months ... I had no connections with the Bar ... In my local pub ... there was this old curmudgeon who happened to be a barrister. He said 'Come along and see me.' ... The head of chambers was [W, who later became Chancellor of the Exchequer] and he said 'I will have you as a pupil. There is a chap along the corridor who hasn't got a pupil' ... That was very lucky ... I then had to hang around a little bit to see if they wanted to take me on as a tenant ... Those were the days where ... there were about 150 applicants for decent chambers and about 60

got in … so I was lucky again. I was the first person from state education who was taken on in the days where everyone was Harrow or Eton and Oxbridge. How on earth I got in I don't really know and there were no women at that stage. (CJ)

Finding pupillage could be a matter of tenacity, such as this son of a foreign single mother, in 1970.

I wandered round the Temple not knowing anybody and I ended up in the last building bar one … I said to the clerk 'I am at my wits' end. What do I do?' and he said 'We don't take pupils here, although we have taken on a chap who has just got a double first at Oxford and he was a Minister's son' so it didn't look very promising but he said 'Try Mr … He hasn't had a pupil for years and years and years' … He turned up late from court and was told there was this wretched individual waiting to see him and I went into see him and he was an absolutely charming man and he said 'You can start on Monday'. (CJ)

Some middle class youngsters were helped by their parents' connections, like one doctor's son who 'had an introduction through a solicitor who my parents knew' but another public school boy (now CA/UKSC) whose father's *Who's Who* entry was breathtaking for his achievements in medicine, struggled to find a tenancy, despite all his promising connections.

I only knew one senior person at the Bar and he was the father of a friend. … In those days pupillages were done partly on the old boy network so he placed me as a pupil … [but] it was clear somebody else was going to be taken on … So I met … a husband of a friend of my wife's, who said come to his chambers … There were four pupils … One of the others got taken on … I then met another chap who I was at school with … I did [another] three months … and again I wasn't taken on. So I was getting virtually to the end of my tether and I had virtually run out of money I had saved … and the head of chambers had been talking to … another set of chambers … They … were looking to recruit so I went there … My chancery pupil master … begged me not to go there. He said it was inferior, county court, rubbishy work … but in the end I decided that beggars couldn't be choosers and this time the outcome was a happy one. If it hadn't been a happy one I think I would have left the Bar.

Entering the Bar as a tenant was only the first step, because all private practice barristers are self-employed and most drop out within the first 10 years, having failed to obtain sufficient work to support themselves. Many described a 'hand-to-mouth' existence. This senior judge's child, married to another barrister, did not seek parental support.

The pair of us were as poor as church mice. Whoever got paid that week bought the food shopping … I remember my first case. The book cost me more than my brief fee so I was down at the end of the day. (DJ)

For those in a weak set of chambers, the first few years at the Bar were a struggle, such as this northern grammar school child.

I started my pupillage in [X] so I could live at home, as I didn't have an income. I stayed … for a year after I had finished my pupillage. I then decided to move back to [Y]. I obtained a place in chambers there. I did some teaching at [the local university and polytechnic]. I wasn't quite sure I was going to end up at the Bar. I think I found the first few years extremely difficult because the chambers I joined was a bit of a disaster. (CJ)

Dependent on building up their career by getting lucrative or prominent cases, many described a 'lucky' break at this stage.

I had a few lucky breaks, including, for instance, a brief in a rape trial … in front of Mr Justice Melford Stephenson, who I managed to persuade to give me a suspended sentence if I twisted my client's arm to plead guilty. He described it as the most anaemic rape, as he gave my client a suspended sentence. (CJ)

I knew nobody. I was a complete stranger but an [Oxbridge] chum of mine had a contact … and they offered me a pupillage … I was not posh enough to stay there because I was a crude South African boy so I was chucked off into the second or even third division, where I was a common law hack. Gradually, because there was a degree of divorce work in the long vacation, when I was working and my head of chambers was away, I had to cover for him and picked up a brief in a huge Greek shipping divorce and began to do more and more of it so ended up in silk [as a Queen's Counsel], as a sort of family specialist. (CA/UKSC)

I got well in with [the] Local Authority because I was quite good with old ladies that tripped so they would give me rating cases to do, so it was quite off the wall. Because of working for them, I was involved in the [major disaster] Inquiry. (CJ)

I was very lucky. First of all the work suited me and secondly, it involved landlord and tenant work which sounds deeply boring and at the Bar was fairly sneered at because everybody thought they could do landlord and tenant, as it involved traipsing around country courts, but it was the most terrific training. It was lots of little cases, badly prepared, with judges who were not always the best judges so it really taught you how to think on your feet, how to be a good advocate, how to cross-examine the experts without any prior warning (CA/UKSC)

They acknowledged that they had benefited from being at the Bar during a time of expanding demand. Several told a story of entering small chambers that grew or went from being common law to specialist.

Within a few years they became a very specialised set of chambers, specialising in construction law because one of the senior members of chambers had written a book on the subject and it was at the time when that area of law exploded. So within no time at all I found myself doing this kind of work, although I never would have intended to do it and I wasn't actually hugely interested in technical things and never had been much good at them. Life takes strange turns and twists. (CA/UKSC)

He did not mention that, despite his professed disinterest, he became head of the Technology and Construction Court.

I joined a very small provincial chambers that are now the biggest set of chambers in [the region]. There were only eight of us when I joined and … we produced three of the great advocates of their generations and of course this is a big advantage for those who are associated with them. (DJMC)

Just when I took silk in 1986, building society law changed radically with a new Act of Parliament ... and that meant there was sudden expansion for the need for advice and sometimes representations for building societies ... and that influenced my career considerably as a young QC. (HC)

I joined ... predominantly a common law set of chambers that were leaning towards divorce. [X], who eventually became head of chambers, was a dedicated building contracts specialist, who wrote what is one of the now leading textbooks on construction law. Quite soon the chambers developed into a construction specialist. (HC)

The emphasis of chambers was changed considerably ... Historically, chambers had a pretty mixed practice but we moved towards commercial work ... and from the time I took silk, I was practising largely in international banking law. (HC)

Most had, however, orchestrated their careers into more lucrative work. Only eight of the 59 barristers specialised from the time they were called to the Bar, in commercial law, patents, competition, chancery (three), family and admiralty. The general pattern was to start in general practice and eventually specialise.

Everyone did everything to start with. So I traipsed round magistrates' courts, quarter sessions and so on. But the expectation was that people would eventually have a civil practice based on defendants' insurance company work. They were a very good set at the time. We had produced no fewer than five High Court judges from a set of chambers that had only 13 when I joined them. (CJ)

Early days were a lot of magistrates' court work and ... matrimonial, little stuff in the Crown Court ... the senior people were all mainly doing personal injury ... industrial accidents. I got into that with masses of Dunlop cases ... Gradually the ... practice ... dropped [crime] as the clerk of the chambers was devoted to looking after the interests of the solicitors who did the big insurance company work. (HC)

I started in common law chambers ... quite a lot of crime. I then decided to go into civil work, because I was advised that I had a much better chance of getting silk ... and rapidly developed a planning practice and parliamentary work ... I then moved into specialist planning chambers. I moved twice ... I took silk and I did seven or eight years. (CJ)

I had a very busy common law practice ... I loved advocacy, adored addressing a jury ... could persuade the hind legs off a donkey ... Then everybody said 'You really must stop doing that ... .specialise to make a decent living'. Crime wasn't paying; family ceased to pay. So I ended up doing an enormous amount of building ... and commercial work ... I didn't particularly enjoy doing that. (CJ)

Six had been full-time academics, three reaching professor status. The Bar proved more lucrative.

I was lecturing ... combining that with working at the Bar ... I realised that I could make more money in a week than I could make in three months. Although I'd been warned at university if you didn't have connections you would never succeed at the Bar … I found I was able to succeed and … and I quite enjoyed the work. (CJ)

Two sandwiched academia with the Bar, until they grew 'fed up' with academia. Two had served as legal advisers to non-governmental organisations and the others were private practice solicitors.

Generally, the private practice solicitors described their careers in very straightforward terms, such as this one: 'Articled clerk; assistant solicitor; partner; managing partner last three years.' None had stories of a struggle or a lucky break. Three entered their family firms but one was asked to leave by his father's partners when they realised he was gay. One broke up with his business partner who was irritated by his taking time out to sit as a part-time judge.

CAREER PROFILES

District Judges and District Judges (Magistrates' Courts)

The 13 DJs had had fairly unremarkable careers as solicitors for 17–25 years, except one barrister who was the first woman in her chambers, in 1977, and another who had been prominent in her local then the national Law Society. Four of the six DJMCs had been in private practice, two as barristers and two as solicitors, with 19–25 years' post-qualification experience. Magistrates' courts hear family cases but the bulk is criminal and two had developed their practices to concentrate on crime.

I really hated … doing civil work … I was a fish out of water. I hated the clients coming in every two minutes or phoning up … one day I decided I just want to do crime so I thought 'Right I am going to work from home'. I had built up enough connections … to enable me to do that … I did CPS prosecuting work and … lots of defence work too. (Solicitor)

My practice at the Bar was quite mixed. I was quite idle so I let the civil paperwork rest on my table for weeks on end and my room mate, who is now a circuit judge … said 'You ought to do it' and eventually he would take it and do it for me and I would get paid for it. I started to feel a bit guilty so I said 'You sort this and start to get paid for it yourself' so I palmed that off onto him because I was only ever interested in doing crime.

Two had been justices' clerks, magistrates' chief legal advisers. They became stipendiary magistrates, now DJMCs, after having served part-time, while employed as clerks.

Circuit Judges

The 32 CJs were a mixture. Some had career profiles similar to those of the High Court judges and one became a High Court judge during the research. Of the 27 barrister CJs, 10 had achieved QC status. Typical was the planning specialist, quoted above. He had written two practitioner textbooks and, before specialising, had become standing counsel to the Department of Trade and Industry (DTI) in criminal cases. One QC had been a professor. Three QCs and one non-QC had been counsel to, or appeared before, major public inquiries. Another seven non-QCs had something that enhanced their profile. Two had been standing counsel to the Inland Revenue, one had been on the Professional Conduct Committee of the Bar Council, one had been appointed to the Senate of the Inns of Court at a young age, one had been head of advocacy training and an active organiser in his circuit Bar, one had been sheriff and then deputy lieutenant of his county and another had been a young head of her chambers. One had not aspired to become a QC, being content to earn a lot of money doing 'very heavy' family cases.

Of the five solicitor CJs, one had become a partner in a city firm at the age of 33. Building up an international practice, she wrote articles in refereed and trade journals and gave lectures to promote her firm's business, explaining 'My brain grew'. Another was, by 25, head of litigation in a provincial firm which acted in a major disaster inquiry. He became head of his regional Law Society and a member of the Lord Chancellor's Advisory Committee on Legal Aid. Two had been solicitor advocates and one had been a county court registrar (DJ) before being promoted to the circuit bench.

The Senior Judiciary

All 26 were high achievers. If some of the CJs had glittering careers, then 11 of the seniors were *dazzling*. With four, most lawyers of their generation would recognise their faces from the press. All 26 were QCs, eminent in their fields, except three who served as First Junior Treasury Counsel,[28] who expected to be made High Court judges. Three others had been on the list of Treasury Counsel, two had been Attorney General for the Duchy of Lancaster, one had chaired a major inquiry and one had been counsel to such an inquiry. Four had been members of royal commissions, government advisory committees or court rule committees. Three had been academics, with a string of publications. Another five had written or contributed to major practitioner texts and a ninth had written widely. Five had chaired or founded a specialist Bar Association and/or were very active in the Bar Council. Each had 20–34 years' post-qualification experience.

---

[28] The first in a list of private practice barristers who represent the Government in major litigation.

EXPERIENCES OF MINORITIES IN THE LEGAL PROFESSION

Being a Woman

It would be dangerous to make any generalisations from such a tiny sample (14). In any event, race and gender discrimination in the legal profession since the 1960s has been examined in great depth[29] but I quote some of the women here, in order to give them a 'voice'. I did not ask any judge whether they had been the victim of gender discrimination as lawyers but those quoted below volunteered this information. I then telephoned some of the others to ask if they felt they had suffered any discrimination. They confirmed that they had not, some adding that being a woman had enhanced their career. These two felt that their gender had delayed progress at the start of their careers.

> I got pupillage after a struggle. It took me nearly a year ... because women found it quite difficult to get in then [1967]. (DJMC)

This CJ said that she had done pupillage in London in the days of 'real sex discrimination'.

> I was never going to be taken on in the chambers I was in ... They did take on a girl and my pupil master was livid. They had interviews and they didn't say anything to him, so they arranged for me to have an interview with the head of chambers. He just explained ... that places had been taken and I would be happy to know that I had much nicer legs than the woman they had taken on ... What I wanted to do was crime. Girls shouldn't really do crime at all because they can't possibly cross-examine police officers! ... Every time a boy pupil came into chambers and was taken on as a tenant, my practice would be given to him by the clerks and I always used to have to fight to get it back but I always did get it back. It was appalling in those days. There were numerous rows with the clerks about my practice but I always won in the end and ended up with a serious criminal practice as a junior. I applied for silk four or five times. My peers thought that I should have silk but I came from nowhere ... They'd see a guy as a potential silk and they groomed him for it. (Called to the Bar 1975)

This CJ did not complain of any handicap to her career but she found sexist attitudes at the Bar disgusted her, causing her to leave and requalify as a solicitor.

> I found it old fashioned ... in those days there were a very small number of women at the Bar and when one would go into a county court and a middle aged male would come up to you and if you were really unlucky he would put his arm round you but in any event he would say 'How are we today? I don't think I should have much difficulty today and women, women, women ... ' with his public school voice and *that* used to bring out the fighter in me and I thought 'I am going to wipe the floor with you today'.

---

[29] For instance, P Thomas, *Discriminating Lawyers* (London, Cavendish, 2000); C McGlynn, *The Woman Lawyer—Making the difference* (London, Butterworths, 1998) and material cited therein.

> I quite enjoyed the traditions, the dining in halls … but the manifestation of male public school I didn't enjoy. (Called to the Bar 1977)

These experiences should be placed in the astonishing context that race and gender discrimination were not outlawed at the Bar of England and Wales until the Courts and Legal Services Act 1990. The judge quoted below was prompted into her application to become a QC because of her concern over the low status of women lawyers but was pleasantly surprised. Her attitude typifies a problem that has long been identified: women's habit of devaluing themselves.

> I was so horrified at the shortage and lack of status of women … I would never in a million years have thought about applying for silk. I wouldn't have been good enough, but another female silk … said … there are so few women that if you don't … show you are willing there are going to continue being so few women … I got very wrong-footed because I got appointed first time.

Being a Gay Male

One judge spoke at length about being a gay solicitor and judge. His sexuality forced him to leave his father's firm.

> I was gay and my father knew … but my employers … didn't … I … spoke to the partner I was working with and the answer came … it wasn't a problem … It became a problem when [the others] found out … and they didn't react well. It was difficult because one … was my godfather. I knew all of them since I was a child and I was pretty much angry … I ended up with respect for one of them. He was very straightforward about the reasons—that he wasn't sure that it was good to have me working there with the same name as the firm etc … I hadn't got a future there. They were never going to offer me partnership.

Overtly gay judges were underrepresented in his generation. The early 1980s saw the prolongation of a policy of not appointing homosexuals to the judiciary.

Being a Solicitor

The arrogance of some barristers and the fact that Bar etiquette and practice rules are hierarchical and mark solicitors out as inferior are well-known irritants to solicitors. For instance, barristers traditionally referred to fellow barristers in court as 'my learned friend' but to solicitors as 'my friend';[30] solicitor advocates were not permitted to wear wigs in court until recently, despite repeated applications to Lord Chancellors; the Law Society recently opposed the retention of the rank of Queen's Counsel, a position not open to solicitors, historically. One

---

[30] J Boyle, 'When solicitors take the role of barristers', *The Times*, 12 December 1989; J Gordon, 'A solicitor born to suffer' (1995) 145 *New Law Journal* 1345; R Hazell (ed), *The Bar on Trial* (London, Quartet, 1978).

solicitor judge had a bitter experience as a solicitor advocate, told later in this book. The arrogance of barristers and the resentment this caused among solicitors, becomes a repeating theme in this book.

CONCLUSION

This is an unprecedented examination of the backgrounds of a broad sample of modern judges, which is much more representative than surveys of the senior judiciary, conducted from *Who's Who*. Its abbreviated biographies exclude civil district judges, with whom the public are much more likely to come into contact, and it excludes all who chose not to be included, like some of the research sample, who considered it a tool for snobbery and boasting.

As can be seen by letting judges speak for themselves, most modern judges do not come from judicial or even legal backgrounds and a surprising number grew up in poor households or on council estates. Regardless of background, they were generally prompted to study law as a 'safe' choice by their parents, or by watching *Perry Mason* on the TV as children, or because they had 'the gift of the gab' or argued a lot. For some, they simply switched to studying law at the last minute, or were influenced into a career change by a chance conversation. Reflecting national judicial statistics, the lower judiciary, especially district judges, are much more demographically diverse than top judges. Many more went to state school and a non-Oxbridge university. As with the national pattern, the DJs, especially civil DJs, are more likely to be solicitors and they are much more diverse, representing about 90 per cent of lawyers. Nevertheless, most of the research judges were barristers, and they joined the Bar at a time of significant expansion when this was far more easy than it is in 2011 but getting into chambers was again sometimes based on serendipity, chance conversation or tenaciousness. As the Bar grew, some said that they were lucky to be in an expanding set of chambers that became specialist and well known. Others had engineered their careers into more lucrative specialisations.

Again, contrary to the privileged image conveyed by the media, no judge came from the aristocracy, though 10 had high-achieving fathers or brothers. Like others of this generation, many were intensely socially mobile. For one third, becoming a lawyer, let alone a judge, represented social elevation in a manner unavailable to other generations and we can already see that the generally accepted image of privilege is unfair and inaccurate.

Most of the senior judiciary here, and generally, were independently schooled and attended Oxbridge. As seen in the previous chapter, this is used as a reason for attacking judges, in this peculiarly class-obsessed nation. However, judges in the world's *top* courts are recruited from the top universities. Half the circuit judges here were unusually high achievers and many of the senior judges had stellar legal backgrounds, being the best-known lawyers of their generations. Every jurisdiction needs the sharpest, most highly educated, hard-working and high-achieving lawyers to handle the intellectual challenges faced by the top courts. The problem of elitism lies rather in the UK's class-bound education system. Unlike other Europeans, to whom our habits are inexplicable, some middle-class people here choose to pay for their children's education. With smaller classes, better facilities and supportive parents, unsurprisingly, the independently schooled are more likely to enter Oxbridge, and in the 1960s, when some of these judges entered university, Oxbridge colleges indeed had recruitment ties to named independent schools. All this means criticism should be focused on the divisive education system.

This type of social mobility described by these judges will not be reflected in future generations of judges, because modern school-leavers will not be as mobile as the post-war generation. Thus for people from humble backgrounds to enter the top jobs, obviously some people from high-achieving families need to slide down the social scale, as sociologist Laurie Taylor pointed out in his *Thinking Allowed* programme, in 2009.

4

The First Step on the Ladder: Becoming a Part-time Judge

I did apply ... my old pupil master said wasn't it about time [in 1979]. It was regarded as quite a natural progression for people who were in chambers who saw their senior people becoming judges ... and, as it were, join the Apostolic succession ... I don't remember an interviewing process ... I just got a letter and I went off to sit as what we would call then a deputy circuit judge ... without any induction.

I walked home with tears in my eyes because I was so chuffed at being allowed to try a case. (CJ).

ALL 77 JUDGES HAD been 'tested' as part-timers, in accordance with policy since the 1970s. The last chapter examined what made them study law. In this chapter they were asked to describe what prompted them to apply to sit as a fee-paid judge, or how they experienced the 'tap on the shoulder' invitation. They were asked about their experience of the recruitment and selection procedure. Since the sample spanned those who had first sat part-time in the 1970s to the late 1990s (then been appointed full-time in 2004), this encompasses a *very* wide range of experiences. These are reflective of the progressive change in recruitment practice, described below. They were asked what it felt like to sit in judgment for the first time. Experiences provoked a range of emotions, from the 'exhilarating' for those in familiar surroundings to the terror of judges whose first experience of a jury trial was one they conducted.

THE SELECTION SYSTEM—A BACKGROUND OF CONTROVERSY

The pre-2006 selection system was so biased that criticisms of it have been the stuff of student textbooks since the 1970s. Decades before the Constitutional Reform Act 2005 regularised the system and created the Judicial Appointments Commission (JAC), criticisms were made in strong language. Foreign lawyers and judges and professional people, non-lawyers asked to scrutinise judicial recruitment, were incredulous. In 2007, Lord Chief Justice Phillips said:

The system demonstrably ensured that those who were appointed were good; it did not, however, demonstrably ensure that those who were good were appointed. It was criticised as being a system under which white Oxbridge males selected white Oxbridge males.[1]

Until 2007, eligibility was based on rights of audience,[2] and the more elite the advocate, the higher he was (and is) likely to enter and progress in the judiciary, despite four decades of criticism that the skill-set and temperament for a successful advocate does not guarantee those required of a judge. The judicial hierarchy reflects the hierarchical legal profession. Almost all senior judges and many circuit judges (CJs) are the elite 10 per cent of the Bar, Queen's Counsel. Most other CJs are recruited from the 90 per cent of barristers referred to as junior barristers. District judges (DJs) are mainly solicitors, who form about 90 per cent of practising lawyers.

Existing judges were 'consulted' about applicants. As recently as 2004, CJs showed me the lists of recorder applicants they received and explained how they selected candidates upon whom to comment. This system was criticised as detrimental to solicitors, who mostly do not have rights to appear in the higher courts, in front of circuit and senior judges,[3] and by those barristers who did not appear in front of the 'right' judges. The Law Society called these 'secret soundings'.[4] Like non-white and women barristers, who also found themselves outside judicial circles, they condemned this practice as an 'old-boy network'.[5] Research showed that many High Court judges were recruited from a small number of chambers.[6] Indeed, the previous chapter quotes many judges who said they were recruited from top chambers. Furthermore, appointments were made on the recommendation of one person—a politician—the Lord Chancellor. The nepotism and subjectivity dangers were obvious but the breach of the separation of powers in the Lord Chancellor's role was not acknowledged until 2003, when the Council of Europe told the UK Parliament it was embarrassing trying to

[1]   Judicial Studies Board Annual Lecture, March 2007, Judiciary website.
[2]   Until the Tribunals, Courts and Enforcement Act 2007 broadened the eligbility conditions. Since 2010, legal executives are able to apply for posts such as DJ and DJMC.
[3]   Solicitors became eligible to chair quarter sessions from 1938 and as stipendiaries from 1949: S Shetreet, *Judges on Trial* (Amsterdam, North Holland, 1976) 58, but were not eligible as recorders until 1972: Courts Act 1971. In 1977, the first five solicitor circuit judges joined 265 barrister CJs: Hazell, *The Bar on Trial* (London, Quartet, 1978) 25.
[4]   In 1991, the Law Society, representing solicitors, published a discussion paper, complaining: unattributed, 'Society Urges Lay Involvement in Appointments', Law Society's *Gazette*, 13 March 1991, at 6. They became progressively more strident.
[5]   See evidence to the House of Commons HA Committee in 1995–96, above.
[6]   Hayes found that in 1986–96, 28.8 per cent of HC appointees came from 1.8 per cent of chambers, all in London. The 2009 report by the JAC, referred to in the concluding chapter of this book, showed that barristers in Barmark chambers (43 of 690 chambers) were more likely to aspire to the judiciary.

explain the requirement for judicial independence to emergent Eastern European democracies in the face of the UK's bizarre set-up.[7]

Although Lord Hailsham LC listed his selection methods in 1980, and disclosed that 'files' were kept on potential candidates, the full criteria, job specifications and application forms were not published in newspapers and uploaded onto the then Lord Chancellor, Lord Mackay's website until 1994–95. Application forms had been available but the system was confusing and amateurish, as can be seen here. An application system for the High Court bench was introduced as late as 1998. Even after that, most of them and all other senior ranks were recruited by the 'tap on the shoulder', until 2006.

Although interviews were eventually established, this chapter gives graphic accounts of just how unprofessional the system was, reaffirming the outspoken attacks by the Commission for Judicial Appointments (CJA), a watchdog of outsiders from commerce and industry, accustomed to transparent and fair recruitment systems, who were scandalised by their findings. They considered judges' subjective comments about applicants to be symptomatic of 'wider systemic bias in the way that the judiciary and the legal profession operate, that affects the position of women, ethnic minority candidates and solicitors in relation to silk and judicial appointments'.[8] It was not until 2003, after years of mounting pressure from critics, including two Law Lords, that the Government announced they would dismantle the tripartite role of the Lord Chancellor and reform the judicial appointment system (as well as reforming the QC appointment system and replacing the Law Lords with the UK Supreme Court). They issued a set of consultation papers[9] and the eventual hard-fought compromise resulted in structures established in the 2005 Act.[10] The JAC has continued the endeavour to diversify the judiciary, started before its creation.[11] Nevertheless, its reformed system has been attacked by judges who still think their opinions on candidates ought to carry weight.

---

[7] The Council of Europe published a condemnatory report in April 2003. Embarrassment was expressed by its author, rapporteur Erik Jurgens, under examination before the House of Commons Committee on the Lord Chancellor's Department, in February 2003.

[8] Especially their 2003 and 2004 annual reports. In 2003, they said that in 20 years of experience, they had not come across such vague and subjective comments as those made by judges and lawyers in 'soundings'. The CJA was disbanded when the new appointment system was created.

[9] Department for Constitutional Affairs, *Constitutional Reform: A New Way of Appointing Judges, Constitutional Reform: a Supreme Court for the United Kingdom, Constitutional Reform: the future of Queen's Counsel* (2003), archived website.

[10] The current system is explained in textbooks and on the JAC website.

[11] For instance, by appointing fractional-time circuit judges, like Sylvia de Bertodano: 'I hope my new role will encourage others', *The Times*, 4 June 2009. See further, P Darbyshire, *Darbyshire on the English Legal System*, 10th edn (London, Sweet & Maxwell, 2011) ch 14.

WHAT PROMPTED THESE LAWYERS TO TRY JUDGING?

Given that most of the 150,000 or so practising lawyers in England and Wales will never sit in judgment, we need to know what or who prompted these people to apply.

County Court (Civil) District Judges

Twelve were solicitors who appeared regularly in front of county court registrars and knew exactly what the job entailed. For nine, a judge suggested it. Three had to wait some years to follow up the suggestion, on discovering they would not be accepted, under 35.

> The person [judging] was another local solicitor ... He told me he was a deputy registrar, which I didn't know existed ... I was quite interested and he said 'Well then, apply' so I did. (1981)

For the gay solicitor, a gay friend among the court staff suggested it:

> I suspect that both of us had an underlying thought that it might be nice to have someone gay doing it ... My first reaction was 'it is ridiculous' ... this is something you do ... in your fifties, old man stuff.

Two applied unprompted. 'I thought "I could do your job"'(1992). Five thought there was more to life than being a solicitor and one thought it would make him 'a better solicitor'. The High Court DJ saw her job advertised in *The Times*, in 1996. Another DJ had taken a career break to have children:

> Very few barristers were applying ... a girlfriend ... from the Bar had applied ... it sounded ideal. I thought 'That ... gets me back into work'.

District Judges (Magistrates' Courts)

All were very familiar with magistrates' courts, as advocates or magistrates' clerks (legal advisers). The two solicitors saw stipendiary magistrates ('stipes') at work (now DJMCs) when they came to London, and were inspired. Of the two barristers, one woman was encouraged by a female 'stipe' who became a well-known circuit judge and the other received a welcome suggestion from a stipe, when he was finding a career at the Bar 'horrible'. As we shall see in chapter eight, he craved the comfort of the magistrates' court, 'a law-free zone'.

> They were all very clever people at the Bar ... I had bad nerves. I managed to get away with a 22-year career without anybody discovering ... Because I am a comedian ... it was utter torture ... I gave the impression it was easy ... I would sit down for hours on end writing closing speeches, getting up at three in the morning changing words ... I hated law. I still do.

Given that he hated the Bar but adored his job as a judge, it can already be seen that the temperament and skills required of a judge are not the same as those required of an advocate.

THE CIRCUIT JUDGES

While all those above had had opportunities to observe their future judicial role, some did not. The 32 circuit judges had been appointed as assistant recorders (part-timers), or deputy circuit judges, as they used to be called, and were usually promoted to the status of recorder automatically, having proven themselves satisfactory.[12] Of the longest serving CJs, eight barristers were simply invited to sit part-time, in the early 1980s, often around the time they became Queen's Counsel. Their accounts are very similar to those of the senior judiciary, below. In 1979, Hazell remarked that because the judiciary had undergone a massive expansion and very few solicitors were appointed,

> any barrister of 15 years' call ... who is reasonably competent and who has not blotted his copybook ... can expect to become a Circuit judge ... it has been quite difficult to find suitable candidates.[13]

Little wonder then that the Lord Chancellor's Department (LCD) solicited barristers to sit part-time. These stories reflected the desperation to recruit lawyers and a system so casual that it is unimaginable to post-millenium applicants, where competition is fierce and the application process very complex.

> In 1984, I was 34 ... Three of us got the same letter in chambers. We were [trying to] find out what it meant ... It was along the lines that 'If we were going to invite you to some course, would you be prepared at some stage ... ?' It was a bizarre letter. It took the three of us to think 'They are asking us to be assistant recorders. Isn't that nice?' (QC 1993)

> I got a letter saying 'Would you like to come and see the circuit administrator?' (Late 1970s; QC 1983)

> I received a telephone call from the then Secretary of the Lord Chancellor's Department. He said 'Have you thought about becoming an assistant recorder?' and I said 'Not particularly' as I didn't do criminal work. (1986; QC 1981)

> One of the judges said I ought to have a crack at it. I was appointed the year I was 34. I did that for about six years and was made recorder ... I was very flattered to be asked, particularly if you are asked by a judge who you appear before. It is a mark that they think you are suitable for it. It is a step in ... one's career.

---

[12] Assistant recorder was an informal appointment, with no protection against removal and has since been abolished, because it breached the judicial independence guarantee in the European Convention on Human Rights, Art 6.
[13] Hazell, above n 3 at.25.

> In 1985, I got a letter from the LCD inviting me to become a recorder ... I phoned up and asked them 'Do you realise that I am only 35?' so they told me to come back in three years.

For five barristers, a circuit judge suggested they apply and for two solicitors who became deputy registrars, a full-timer suggested it. Another solicitor was 'very pleased' to be prompted to become one of the first solicitors to sit part-time on the circuit bench. It was simply a matter getting your name on a list of locums.

> The Courts Act [1971] was passed so solicitors were for the first time enabled to sit in the Crown Court and the county courts. I had close connections with members of the Bar and one of them ... encouraged me and put my name forward to become what was in those days called deputy circuit judge ... Your name was placed on a list and the administration would ... invite you to sit for a week or a fortnight.

The remaining 18 applied unprompted.

> I saw it as a useful step to help me towards silk.

> To broaden my experience and to invest in a possible future. (QC 1994)

> I quite fancied the idea of being a full-time judge and it was an inevitable step ... very much a status thing. If you don't apply, people wonder why.

> A lot of my mates were doing it.

> I felt I badly needed some sort of change and fresh impetus.

Three applied because they thought they could do a better job than the local part-timers. One 'thought it would be a good selling point' for his services as a barrister.

The Senior Judges

All 26 were appointed around the time they became QCs or Treasury Counsel. Partly because of the era (1970s and 1980s), and partly because these lawyers were more likely to have been identified as 'high fliers', destined for the High Court, more of them had been invited than the circuit judges. 20 had been invited to sit or apply, two as deputy High Court judges and the rest as assistant recorders, or deputy circuit judges. Some remembered an 'expectation', on their part or on the part of the LCD that they would serve part-time, both as a 'public duty' and to prepare them for a potential High Court post. There was and is no career judiciary in England and Wales. High Court judges are generally recruited from the Bar, not circuit judges. Hazell explained that in 1979, the High Court bench had doubled in 20 years and because it was the preserve of QCs, 'The opportunities for a barrister to step into a salaried judicial appointment towards the end of his or her career are therefore unusually high'.[14]

---

[14]   ibid 27.

Invited and then persuaded. I thought it was a sort of public duty. (Early 1980s)

I was told I was required to sit as an assistant recorder. (1974)

Everyone in my chambers seemed to become a recorder when they were in their late thirties or forties. I was urged to apply (1979)

I was telephoned out of the blue by Harry Woolf. They must have been short of people on the circuit ... I might have filled in a form but there was no interview. (Early 1980s)

All of us were invited—the six leading silks at the patent Bar. (Late 1980s)

I applied because I think it was expected of you ... It sounds frightfully pompous ... a sense of duty. (1987)

Soon after being appointed as Treasury Counsel I was invited. I simply received the application forms and took the hint. I appreciated it was expected of me. If you became Treasury Counsel you did it for about six years and then go on to the High Court bench. There was no guarantee and that was made quite clear when I was appointed but historically for the last century it has happened to all but one incumbent. (1982)

The Head of the Bar Association summoned three or four of us who had recently taken silk. He said that he would like people of our generation from the Chancery Bar to apply to be recorders to assist the career track of Chancery barristers because he thought that there was a feeling at the time that if you were in the Chancery Bar the only place to which you could ever go was the Chancery High Court [as opposed to the generalist Queen's Bench Division]. (1993)

Three were taken by surprise. The first below is a UK Supreme Court (UKSC) Justice.

I did actually, I am not joking, ring up the Lord Chancellor's Office and say 'Are you sure you don't mean [ABA] or [ABC]?' because there were two [ABs] apart from myself. (Early 1980s)

There was a letter from the circuit administrator ... There was no interview. It was all done on soundings. I think it was regarded then as a mark of success that you were regarded as a competent ... advocate so it was really like a brownie point. (Early 1980s)

For the six who applied unprompted, some again said it was seen as part of a 'natural' career progression. The very successful barrister was appointed a QC and in due course might become a High Court judge. For this, he needed some judging practice and in turn he provided a useful public service as an inexpensive, fee-paid part-timer, fulfilling the needs of the Department, with whom he thus had a symbiotic relationship.

I applied to further my career. I wanted to take silk the next year ... There is no reason of altruism. (1988)

I applied to become a QC and failed in 1986. My pupil master ... said 'Don't be discouraged. Most people fail first time but it might help if you apply to become an assistant recorder', basically saying that I had done nothing but work away at my career ... In those days they were very keen to get people. The course [was run by] Mr Justice

Ognall who ... opened by saying 'I just want to congratulate the five of you who sucked up to the Lord Chancellor's Department by applying to come on this course who succeeded in getting silk' and I was one of those.

Only two applied for the sake of the part-time job itself.

WHAT WERE THEIR SELECTION EXPERIENCES?

The system became progressively formalised. For those appointed in the 1970s, many asked to have their name added to a list, as above. By 1995, an annual competition was held. The process became tougher, with deputy DJ applicants, then recorder applicants eventually attending day-long assessment centres, from 2002.

Civil District Judges

Three solicitors, applying in the 1980s, were appointed without an interview. Five, applying before 1993, attended a short interview at the Department, conducted by the same person.

> On the train to London ... I couldn't breathe ... It then occurred to me that this is probably how people feel when they go into court for the first time ... I met Helen Baker, the lady at the LCD who then regarded district judges as her boys because she did all the interviewing.

From the mid-1990s, the process became more challenging.

> It was a question of filling in an application form, getting a couple of referees, ... from the local judiciary. Then I was interviewed by the senior district judge here, somebody from the LCD and a lay magistrate. The interviews weren't very structured. They are much more structured now ... The district judge fired a lot of questions at me about technical rules and then the lay magistrate asked a few more general questions, as did the person from the LCD and that was it. It lasted about half an hour and then I got a letter a few months later. (1996)

In the same year, the 'young mother' barrister who had taken a career break found the interview 'a nightmare' and complained to the LCD of its unfairness.

> The district judge who interviewed me just kept firing legal questions at me ... I kept saying I didn't know and I felt totally humiliated ... I looked up the terms of reference and it didn't say anything about being given specific questions so I got in touch with the LCD ... They said I could go on an induction course to learn about becoming a deputy DJ before I next applied ... I went on the course knowing I hadn't been appointed which was very embarrassing and then I applied again. I then got the appointment. (1997)

District Judges (Magistrates' Courts)

The longest serving had applied in the late 1970s, again in a process that lacked transparency.

> I expressed an interest in my early thirties ... I had to wait quite a while because it was just a letter and interview and no-one really knew what was happening. (1981)

> I think you had to get four referees. I was invited for a preliminary interview with ... the Chief Metropolitan Magistrate ... and then by someone in the LCD. It was just one person with a secretary taking notes but it was pretty clear that she was not just taking notes because there were meaningful glances and nods exchanged. (1987)

> I went down to London ... wearing my lucky suit [which he then scorched, while ironing]. I had to go into the interview with my trousers burnt. It was terrible. The interview was so relaxed: a note-taker and a man ... with the LCD. So I thought to myself 'I will just agree with everything he says' so he says ... 'Would you sit anywhere in England?' and I said 'Yes I'll sit anywhere and at any time' ... so the interview lasted about 10 or 15 minutes and I didn't have to say anything. (1994)

For this solicitor, applying in the late 1990s, the process had become strikingly tougher and intensely competitive, as many lawyers, threatened with cutbacks to legal aid, saw judging as an attractive career with a stable income. Because she was a solicitor, she was anxious about not having the right 'connections' to provide references. The preparation to apply took years. She secured a job as an immigration adjudicator and even qualified as an advocate in the Crown Court so as to become 'known' by circuit judges who could then write her reference. She remarked on how protracted the system was. In this respect, the circuit judges' stories are worse.

> Hard work. The form required a lot of attention. I did 10 drafts. It was extremely difficult to get the right calibre of referee because, as a solicitor, you don't have contact with High Court judges. You are very lucky if you have contact with Crown Court judges ... So although you could get perhaps a local magistrate or a local stipendiary it was quite difficult to get that application to be strong enough to beat the competition because those who are at the Bar have all this access to judges ... I *did* get rights of audience in the Crown Court two years before I applied for deputy and I did a few cases in the Crown Court. I absolutely hated it but I did it because I had to become known. A couple of the judges said some nice things and were pleased with what I had done ... I just sat there all day and did whatever I had to do and, make no bones about it, I *had* to make an impression. Then I said 'Will you now support this?' and they did ... Once you send off the form you hear nothing at all and the delay was intolerable ... You never even knew whether they had received the application, or if it had got lost in the post. Then out of the blue you get your letter requiring you to go for an interview.

The Circuit Judges

For the nine who were invited, in the 1970s or early 1980s, they were 'added to the circuit list', without interview. In 2010, Lord Mackay explained that all barristers of 10 years' standing and solicitors who had applied for appointment were considered for an assistant recordership. Of those who applied during that era, they completed a form but were not interviewed. Five barristers found the recruitment process opaque. Their stories illustrate how confusing and unfair it was, with astonishing delays, with one waiting *six years* for a reply, even in the 1990s. The last reads like a *Monty Python* sketch.

> I was rather put out that I wasn't made an assistant recorder … When I complained, I was told 'Well, you never applied!' (1979)

> Almost all my contemporaries in chambers had been invited, under the new system in the early 1980s and I was just too young. I eventually discovered, although it hadn't been published, that you had to apply.

> I applied to be a recorder twice, first in 1990 and in those days you just applied by sending a letter in and I heard nothing for about six years and I then I had an interview, when I again heard nothing.

> I applied … and was sidelined for two or three years … then one of the senior silks reminded the judges that I had applied and then I went for an interview.

> I didn't understand how the system worked. I wrote an informal letter to the LCD in 1989/1990 saying could they tell me how the system worked. I can't believe I had the brass neck to do so. They wrote back saying the requirement was for criminal barristers and I had clearly said that I wasn't a criminal practitioner. I then got a phone call asking me if I would be willing to take part in an experimental scheme to interview prospective applicants. Would I be a guinea pig for the interviewer but I wasn't to read anything into it? I went up to the House of Lords and there was a very nice civil servant and a judge for the northern circuit and we played at having an interview. They threw me because they said 'Of all the barristers we have spoken to, you have nothing in your file. You don't exist as far as we are concerned. Why is that?' He said 'It is not that bad a thing. It means nobody has complained about you.' So I went away thinking that was the end of that so I was … completely dumbstruck when I got a letter saying 'We have appointed you as an assistant recorder' and that was in early 1991. (QC 1993)

Three who applied in 1986 said they were interviewed by one person, at the LCD. This barrister was also concerned that he was not known by 'the right' judges.

> I was terrified from start to finish. I had to go and see a lady at the LCD who had two scribes with her and she was a judge's wife … a very intelligent lady. She asked me lots of questions and I was as nervous as a cat but that went reasonably alright. So I became an assistant recorder. [He was asked to provide referees] and that was very difficult. I had been before one High Court judge … and I wrote to him and said 'Would you mind being a referee?' to which he said he couldn't remember me but 'come and see me' and once I did, he remembered who I was. (1988)

Ten years later, when this barrister was appointed, the system was more professional.

It was a novel experience, filling in application forms, thinking about criteria that would make you suitable ... and then to be interviewed ... I thought that the procedure was transparent, fair and, frankly, properly conducted.

Turning to the five solicitor CJs, one had sat as a full-time DJ before applying to be an assistant recorder. One considered that sitting part-time would be impossible for a partner in a city law firm and so left the partnership before applying. Two felt like outsiders, among the normal barrister applicants. They too were anxious about not having the right judicial connections.

I was a solicitor from a small firm, so there was nobody who I can turn to, to ask what happens ... They did ask me for referees and I was able to give the Clerk to the Justices and one or two very senior magistrates. I wasn't able to give any judges because I don't think many circuit judges knew who I was. (1993)

This one below had sat as a deputy DJ. This new solicitor-judge related bitter experiences, elsewhere in this book, of discrimination he had suffered, both in his career as a solicitor advocate, suffering the snobbery of barristers, and as a judge. Despite the fact that district judge, at the bottom of the judicial ladder, was perceived as the normal career route to which the 'inferior' profession, the solicitors, could aspire, he maintained his ambition to be a Crown Court recorder, the 'natural' route for barristers. He felt he was sidelined at first and, even when his application was successful, he found solicitors like him were bizarrely branded as outsiders.

Several times I was offered a full-time [DJ] vacancy but it was not the job I wanted. I applied to become a recorder ... [in the] early 80s and I really did think in those days one only applied if they were well-known by the Law Society ... It was very hard unless you had the right connections ... then I rang up to say I hadn't heard anything and they said 'Oh we don't seem to have your application.' It was that sort of silliness but anyway I had another go at the end of the 80s to become a recorder. It was probably 1990 when I was interviewed and I went on the course in 1991. Even then, there were only three solicitors on the course and we were marked out by having an 'S' by our names. It was like the Star of David!

I did not ask the High Court judges, as most had been 'tapped on the shoulder', that is, invited.

WHAT DID IT FEEL LIKE TO SIT IN JUDGMENT?

I asked whether their part-time job matched up to expectations. Many were within their comfort zone and excited to be given the responsibility but some were entering such alien territory that they could have had no realistic expectations.

District Judges

Twelve solicitors practising county court advocacy had a clear idea of what to expect. Three said it was 'challenging'. One enjoyed it but found it difficult to fit in part-time sittings around his solicitor's practice. They experienced a range of emotions. Two were enthusiastic—one said it exceeded expectations and another felt it a 'home from home'. Four replied 'nerve-wracking'.[15]

> You think that you have sat as an advocate so you have … seen it all. However, when you are actually sitting there, you are dealing with the stuff of people's lives. It is not just a paper exercise, as you are making people bankrupt. You are taking their houses off them and you are taking their children away.

> I found it hard. These days … [as lawyers] we all specialise and the job [of judging] just covers such a wide area of law.

> You just apply yourself and you learn each time … I didn't have any inhibitions of finding other [judges and asking for advice] … You have just got to learn and very fast.

> My first reaction was 'Why I am putting myself through this?' … Pretty soon I relaxed and enjoyed it but it was damn hard work, frankly. As a deputy you know that you are reliant on the views of other people. There was the desire to do the job well and to get on. Secondly, there was the desire not to alienate yourself from anybody so, for example, at lunchtimes I would find offensive remarks being made about people who were gay. I would ignore them and bite my tongue … also you had to do as much work as you could. There were many days when I would sit there until six doing box work, then have to go back to the office and try and maintain a proper fee-earning profile [as a solicitor]. My partners were [unhappy].

His lunchtime silences, anxious not to alienate full-timers, on whose reports his full-time application might be dependent, were re-enacted by recorders I caught sight of during the research period. New recorders, unknown to a table of judges in a Crown Court dining room, would often eat in silence, head down, speaking only when addressed. Experienced recorders, who did not aspire to the bench were the judges' erstwhile colleagues and regaled their contemporaries with tales from the Bar.

---

[15] L Alpert, 'Learning About Trial Judging: The Socialization of State Trial Judges' in JA Cramer (ed), *Courts and Judges* (Beverly Hills, Sage, 1981) developed a model of five stages of socialisation, applied to Florida judges, but this did not work when applied by PB Wice to Philadelphia judges, in the same book. Neither piece of research is directly comparable here because those judges sat full-time straightaway and in Philadelphia 'all judges interviewed attested to the extreme politicization of the judicial selection process' and were elected for fixed terms. Some of Alpert's findings are relevant to this chapter and the next two. He talks of 'reality shock', self-education and learning by doing.

District Judges (Magistrates' Courts)

Deputies were generally sent to sit away from home. Although they did not mention it, they probably found the variety less daunting than some of the civil DJs above, because, uniquely to magistrates' courts, these part-timers had the benefit of an experienced legal adviser sitting in front of them. Four were immediately enthusiastic: 'Really interesting', 'immensely enjoyable', 'exhilarating'.

> It must be similar to playing at gigs. You become sharper. You become more aware of the dynamics of the court and I hope you become responsive to the needs of the public.

> Exhilarating ... I was this person making the decisions. I didn't have to wait hours for the lay magistrates to decide. I was in control. I also saw the downside of the job. It surprised me that the administration was so poor ... Some days I got the impression that they totally forgot that I was coming ... extremely frustrating ... They never seemed to overload the court sufficiently to take account of the fact that it was one person sitting instead of three [lay magistrates] ... I did more shopping than sitting ... I also saw the job for the mundane side ... the TV licensing ... fines ... the traffic courts that go on forever.

> It was lovely ... It was what I had been waiting for all my life ... undemanding and yet stimulating because there was a variety ... I have got ... the attention span of a gnat ... so this job was great because nothing took more than about three minutes, apart from the trials. It was not what I call real law. There was no summing up to jurors ... keeping it simple was the way to do it. The solicitors [advocates appearing in his court] were basically businessmen. They just wanted to get in and out.

One, like the DJ above, was in awe of the responsibility.

The Circuit Judges

Twenty-one of the 32 had practised criminal law at the Bar and so understood the job of sentencing and instructing juries. Nine mentioned how much they enjoyed it. It taught some of them the value of good advocacy.

> [S]uch good practice. Sometimes I would go ... with the family and we would all take a house ... The kids enjoyed it by the seaside.

> I began to relax and enjoy it ... to concentrate on one particular case or a small number of cases ... free from the additional stresses of practice ... wondering when your next brief was going to come ... also you could actually do things at your own pace and to the best of your ability.

> I knew immediately ... that the idea ... of being a judge was a good one ... I was doing things that nowadays [recorders] simply wouldn't be let near ... I was trusted with trying ... a grandfather with indecently assaulting his grandchildren, which you would probably need a rape-ticketed judge to get anywhere near nowadays ... I was sad at the end of the week ... It just fitted everything I had hoped it would.

> I enjoyed it enormously ... the first trial ... I had two of my contemporaries appearing in front of me. They behaved themselves ... It was a street robbery and the clerk ... came out afterwards and said ... 'I can't believe this is the first case you have ever tried'.

> It exceeded my expectations ... I kept a diary of my first week ... It was almost as if this had been what I had been waiting to do all my life ... There was no stress.

> The first thing I found was the great release of tension ... that I carried as an advocate ... You sat there listening to the submissions and you would make up your mind, give your judgment and that was it, done ... You also realise the value of the advocate ... even in a hopeless litigation, a good effort of a barrister and the sight of that poor wretch sitting there in the dock might incline me to shave three months off his sentence.

> It gave you a completely different view of the court and the trial process ... refreshing ... to be able to see every side of the case. It also taught me some things that you should never do as an advocate. After that I never leant on a podium.

Despite 17 years as a criminal advocate, one judge had a baptism of fire. He became an eminent circuit judge and pioneered radical improvements in training new part-timers by throwing them into a problematic mock trial that we shall see vividly described in the training chapter and this is why:

> A 13-year-old girl started ripping up her statement. She went hostile and you are thinking 'What am I going to do about this? I can't send her to prison—she is only 13'. It was in the middle of what I would now say was a two-a-penny trial but to me at that time it was terribly important and, I dare say, to other people. I think it was from that moment I realised what a challenge it was. That sounds very pompous I know ... It was quite frightening at times, quite harrowing.

Another experienced barrister said his first judgment was 'drivel'. Five had not practised criminal law for years and described judging as 'terrifying', 'scary' and 'nerve-wracking'.

The five solicitor circuit judges had different experiences in practice. Two had sat as county court registrars, one as a deputy and one full-time, so at least they had judicial experience, but one of these was surprised by 'the breadth of work a judge does', as an assistant county court registrar. His next job, sitting as an assistant recorder in the Crown Court, was 'exciting'.

> [A]ddressing a jury, when I had never addressed a jury as an advocate. It was good fun. It was a big buzz for me but also there was a big fear to get it right ... Keeping out of the arena is the biggest learning really, particularly when you get advocates who aren't asking obvious questions.

The second found the transition to unfamiliar criminal work a 'considerable strain ... [but] if you want to do further judicial jobs you have to do the criminal work'. The others had no prior judicial experience. Two had practised as advocates.

> solicitors who were busy didn't go the Crown Court very often ... The whole process in the court environment was quite novel.

I had not appreciated how different it is to be a judge from being an advocate. If you are an advocate you have lived with a case … you are in command of it … although you have to see what the opponent's case is … but as a judge you come to it much colder … and it is quite a different experience.

The solicitor below was allocated to sit as an assistant recorder in civil cases, having conducted litigation in similar cases and having sat behind barristers in court. The courtroom was familiar and her cases lived up to expectations but the working environment was a surprise—the loneliness of the solitary judge on the bench—and she felt like an outsider in the coterie of ex-barristers in the dining room.

I walked home with tears in my eyes because I was so chuffed at being allowed to try a case. It seemed like the accumulation of an incredible amount of aspirations. [My tutor judge] had repeatedly said … 'Remember you are in a goldfish bowl up there', which was a good image … I loved the buck stopping with me … Perhaps I wasn't as familiar with the procedure provisions as someone who had been at the Bar … I am very happy to sit down for the night with books and learn it as I go along … The only shock I had was just how lonely I felt. I had always worked with a team and I did get a shock being in this room with no-one … going in and out … also, having been a solicitor, there was the lunches. People [in the judges' dining room] talk about other people at the Bar and other judges and I wasn't party to the social chit chat so I felt a) lonely and b) slightly out of it and, stupidly, I hadn't thought of that.

The Senior Judges

Eight found themselves trying serious Crown Court cases, with no experience of criminal work. The first said the well-known, seemingly apocryphal words: 'The first summing up to a jury I ever heard was given by me'. Another said 'I had never been in a criminal court in my life'. They enjoyed the experience, however. Two mentioned that they were surprised how interesting it was, despite expectations of being bored, and one called the experience 'challenging—each day brought with it the unexpected'. Those below all had the benefit of an intensive training course in the 1980s or 1990s and so were not too intimidated.

quite a steep learning curve to work out how to conduct a criminal trial on a minute-by-minute basis.

Nine were criminal practitioners. Another four had some rusty experience. Five enjoyed sitting. One found it 'terrifying'.

The first time I had to pass a sentence that was a pretty awesome experience … and the full might of the law behind you!

One criminal practitioner found it intimidating.

> There was no teaching of how you should approach your summing-up or anything. My first sitting … the list all collapsed. I remember coming out of court at 11:15 am and I couldn't remember a thing about any case that I had just sat on.

Three were appointed within their civil expertise in chancery and patents but this one still found some surprises.

> There were things that I hadn't expected … for example … finding myself as the only lawyer in court where both parties were in person.

This remark is highly relevant to the 'working' chapters of this book (chapters eight to fifteen), which expose just how much time civil and family judges have to interface with litigants in person. Judges considered this one of the most challenging and straining parts of their job. There was, of course, one for whom the first day was a disaster:

> Terrifying … They were a perverse jury. They acquitted this lady of six counts and perversely convicted her of one general count, despite my best efforts to persuade them otherwise. The result was promptly appealed 'The learned assistant recorder had done his incompetent best but … ' I thought it was the end of my career.

CONCLUSION

All 77 judges were tested part-time. This chapter demonstrates a very wide range of experiences of recruitment and initiation, dependent on when they were appointed and to what rank, and dependent on whether they were solicitors or barristers and were familiar with the courts in which they would sit.

As most lawyers will never sit as judges, it is interesting to reflect on why these people applied part-time (though many were asked to apply). A number were encouraged by a full-timer, who experienced their advocacy, or a colleague who sat part-time. Most DJs and DJMCs had appeared in front of one type of judge in one type of court, and thought 'I could do your job' but one barrister was elated to escape the misery of Crown Court advocacy for the comfort of stress-free, summary proceedings in the magistrates' court where he would not be bothered by the law. Unlike all others, all six deputy district judges (magistrates' courts), or deputy 'stipes' knew they wanted to apply to be full-time judges before applying part-time.

The 1980s shortage of CJs caused the LCD to write to barristers inviting them to apply to become assistant recorders, in letters sometimes couched in mystifying language, to the hilarity of groups of young lawyers. There was a shortage of High Court judges so the high flyers, QCs and Treasury Counsel, were even more likely to have been pushed. Their interview responses were strikingly likely to contain the words 'expectation' and 'public duty'. Several of both groups were prompted to apply by a serving judge. The barrister, especially one destined for the High Court bench, internalised the idea that it was his duty to serve. This was a symbiotic relationship. Barristers provided the LCD with a cheap, instant, flexible system of locums, as a remedy for the judge shortage, whilst they experienced fee-paid judging, a 'natural progression' in the barrister's career, towards silk, and/or the full-time bench. Of the 18 CJs who applied unprompted, again they thought of it as career enhancing or assumed it was somehow expected of them and many copied their friends. Only six senior judges applied unprompted but for the same reasons. All 26 senior judges and many of the CJs had realised, sooner or later, around the time they became QCs or Treasury Counsel, that they were strongly expected to apply to sit part-time.

The experiences differed enormously and directly reflected the era in which they were recruited. From the 1970s, the appointment system was very heavily criticised as being extremely elitist, disadvantageous for most practising lawyers, rife with nepotism and operated by a single government minister under the heavy influence of existing judges. The interviews bring to life in vivid descriptions the criticisms that were repeatedly made by groups of excluded lawyers such as solicitors, women barristers and minority barristers. Those circuit and district judges appointed part-time in the 1970s and early 1980s simply 'let their names be added' to the list of lawyers prepared to do locum work. As the selection process became more formalised, in the 1980s, people were expected to apply and were interviewed but the application system remained unclear and confusing until job specifications and application forms were uploaded onto the Departmental website in 1994–95. Nevertheless, the stories show that even in the 1990s, lawyers would apply for a part-time job then might not receive a reply for anything up to *six* years. Even after interviews were introduced, the stories show that they were amateurish as late as the mid-1990s.

Much worse was the system of what Lord Chancellors defended as 'consultations' with serving judges, something the Law Society, representing solicitors, called 'secret soundings'. This system was heavily criticised by excluded groups of lawyers and appeared shocking, corrupt and anachronistic to outsiders used to proper recruitment systems, yet it was still going on during the research period, post-2003. The stories here put flesh on the bones of these criticisms. Repeatedly, we see just how anxious solicitors and others were to become 'known' to the 'right' judges, who would stand up for them in the 'soundings' system, or at least provide a reference. By 2004, the intensity of competition position was the reverse of the 1980s, with thousands of lawyers entering. The selection system had become progressively modern and transparent, with time-consuming forms and assessment centres. Barristers praised its fairness but solicitors still had the strain of getting to know 'the right' judges. Some prepared for years, gaining advocacy qualifications in order to appear in front of the right judges and serving in more minor judicial jobs. At the same time that barristers, who for no good reason consider themselves the superior profession, were being groomed for recorderships and the circuit bench, at least two solicitors here seemed to be steered down to the district bench, perceived as the natural home of solicitor judges, and had an uphill struggle aiming for the circuit bench that they ultimately joined.

The interviews expose something else, a hidden policy, unknown to the outside world and apparently some applicants, that a lawyer would not be considered for a part-time appointment until they were 35. Given that people usually graduate in law at about 21, then qualify as a solicitor or barrister at 23 or 24, this creates an 11-year gap before they could sit part-time, and then these 77 lawyers were tested part-time for at least five years, yet they would have been statutorily eligible for a *full-time* appointment at 33 or 34. In recent years, there have been repeated examinations of why our judiciary lacks diversity[16] and one of the factors exposed as a cause for the old age and maleness of the bench is the 15-year gap between qualifying as a lawyer and applying for a full-time appointment. The interviews quoted here, exposing this ban on the under-35s, identify the cause of this gap.

When they first sat, however familiar they were with their surroundings, these new part-timers were struck by their responsibility, which many found exhilarating and others found awesome or terrifying, as one DJ put it, 'dealing with the stuff of people's lives'. Deputy DJs, albeit comfortable in the county court, were challenged by the range of legal and factual decisions they faced and they still carried the strain of their full-time solicitor's workload and risked annoying their partners by taking time out. By contrast, all the deputy DJMCs instantly loved the job. Cases were swift and easy, summary procedure was relaxing and although they were sent away from home, they were very familiar with the magistrates' court. They were special and novel, the lone, visiting professional among the lay justices, and they had the unique luxury of a legal adviser, possibly a barrister or solicitor just like them, to keep them on track with the case throughout, to provide interpretation of the law, to lay before them the range of their sentencing powers, and generally to take the terror out of the job.

While 21 of the 32 CJs were familiar with the Crown Court, only nine said they enjoyed their initial experience, away from the strain of practice. Others were frightened through lack of training or because jury trials are generally unpredictable and sentencing is complex. One experienced criminal advocate had such a shocking experience with his first jury trial that, when he later became eminent in training judges, he ensured that all new recorders were put through a stressful 'baptism of fire' mock trial, as we shall see in the training chapter. His nasty experience thus prompted this intensely practical, skills-based recorder training, praised as 'ahead of its time' and still terrifying trainees. The solicitor circuit judges found the unfamiliar Crown Court extremely challenging and one, used to teamwork, was surprised by the loneliness of county court judging and of being in a dining room clique of older, male barrister judges.

---

[16]   DCA, Increasing *Diversity in the Judiciary*, 2004, CP 25/04, on the archived DCA website, in the consultation papers.

Although the senior judges were high-flying lawyers who thrived on successive challenges, and most enjoyed the novelty of this one, they again described a range of emotions. Eight were unfamiliar with the Crown Court criminal work they would do as recorders. Those who had received the scary mock-trial training found it made their first trial experience less horrific but, thanks to the unpredictability of juries, one had a nightmarish first trial. One chancery judge was shocked by cases where he was the only lawyer in court. By definition, advocates do not encounter the many cases where neither party is represented. In the next two chapters we shall see how the 77 judges described their training and we shall examine their path to the full-time judiciary.

5

Becoming Her Majesty's Judge

I'd 'ave liked to have been a judge but I never 'ad the Latin. I never 'ad sufficient Latin to
get through the rigorous judgin' exams. They're very rigorous, the judgin' exams. People
come staggerin' out sayin' 'Oh My God! What a rigorous exam!' So I became a miner
instead, a coal miner. They're not so rigorous, the minin' exams. They only ask you one
question. They say 'Who are you?' and I got 75 per cent for that.

Peter Cook as EL Whisty, *A Night at Her Majesty's,* 1976

WE NEED TO know how these 77 came to be full-time judges because
many lawyers progress no further than being part-time judges. They
are either deemed unsuitable, or they realise they do not like being a
judge, like the eminent Treasury Counsel who was asked to sit as a deputy High
Court judge and found he 'hated being in the limelight'.[1] An independent reader
of this chapter commented on the interviews below, challenging 'the claim by so
many of the senior judges that they had never thought about promotion to the
upper courts'. He considered it 'a collective pretence that nothing could have been
further from their minds'. This was *not* a collective pretence. Many indeed
admitted they had wanted an appointment but it does not occur to most lawyers
to apply for judicial posts and all High Court judges are fully aware of the horrific
workload of Court of Appeal (CA) judges depicted in this book. Why on earth
would this be considered 'promotion'? Indeed, what needs explaining is why an
autonomous QC, choosing her cases, organising her yearly calendar to fit in long
holidays and earning millions would opt to take a massive pay cut and then work
long hours in the High Court and Court of Appeal, in the conditions described in
this book. Even more puzzling: why would she want to join the circuit bench for
even lower pay and the shocking conditions described in chapter seventeen? We
saw that it was difficult to recruit to the circuit and High Court benches in the
1970s and 1980s. Lord Mackay, Thatcher's Lord Chancellor, then Labour Lord
Irvine, went to great lengths running recruitment 'road shows' and making
speeches, especially to minority lawyers, and publishing large adverts in the legal
and national press and online, yet by 2006 the Department for Constitutional
Affairs (DCA) still felt the need to commission research into why most lawyers,
especially minorities and women, do not apply. A key finding was that 'a great

---

[1] A friend.

number of respondents…had simply never considered the judiciary as a possible career route'. There was 'a general lack of interest'.[2] The next year, the judiciary commissioned Professor Dame Hazel Genn to find out why highly qualified candidates do not apply to the High Court bench. One female QC said:

> It's a very jolly life *not* being a judge. Getting loads of money, making jokes and doing really interesting work. You do really unusual, fascinating things working with people you like. There is lots of flexibility, long holidays, no bureaucracy. Why would you stop?

Genn found that:

> The majority of practitioners interviewed had no immediate intention of applying, and thought it unlikely that they would apply in the future. … Moreover, of the 21 barristers interviewed for the research, four had been 'tapped on the shoulder' at least once…and had turned down the offer of appointment … men and women gave similar sorts of reasons for not being interested in judicial office …

— Workload and conditions
— Circuit—absence and environment
— Salary—differential and demographic change
— Loss of autonomy
— Prefer to advocate than decide
— Temperament more suited to the Bar than Bench
— Isolation and lack of support.[3]

The 77 judges here were asked when they had first wanted to sit full-time and what it was like being approached or applying. They recounted selection experiences between the 1980s and 2004. All but one senior judge and many veteran district judges (DJs) and circuit judges (CJs) were invited to join the bench, that is, given the metaphorical 'tap on the shoulder' by the Lord Chancellor. The newest group had an enormously different experience, passing though the competitive application process which had become progressively more lengthy, elaborate and challenging, since 1994. One senior judge had applied. All were asked to comment on the selection process, then under scrutiny.[4]

---

[2] *Judicial diversity: findings of a consultation with barristers, solicitors and judges*, DCA archived website.

[3] H Genn, *The attractiveness of senior judicial appointment to highly qualified practitioners* (London, Directorate of Judicial Offices for England and Wales, 2008) 16–17. The main attractions were less pressurised existence, being the decision-maker, 'giving something back to society' and prestigiousness of a High Court appointment, at 15.

[4] Posner said that among the factors influencing judicial behaviour, is 'the judicial career, which affects selection and self-selection into the judiciary and the incentives and constraints that click in once a person is inducted', R Posner, *How Judges Think*, (Cambridge, Mass, Harvard University Press, 2008) 11.

WHEN DID THEY FIRST WANT TO BE A FULL-TIME JUDGE?

District Judges

Five wanted to become full-time before applying part-time. Another five enjoyed sitting part-time. 'I thought this could be a very nice life.'

> My very first case, I thought, 'Right, that's it. This is what I want to do ...' So everything I did after that was designed to get me out of private practice.

> I liked being the engine-driver ... Perhaps I am a bit of a control freak ... As a solicitor, you are forever arguing someone else's cause ... but not having to make decisions that affect things.

Three solicitors found their business partners resented their part-time sittings, or they were difficult to fit around practice.[5]

> My life revolved around the country practice, my clients and the local community ... those partners that I brought into the practice started making my life unpleasant ... 'you're never here!' They didn't seem to appreciate that my high profile and involvements were potentially good for the practice ... I never contemplated being a full-time judge [until then]. Frankly, I was making too much money in private practice. When I became a judge I halved my income ... I've never looked back or regretted it for a moment.

District Judges (Magistrates' Courts)

They had a different recruitment system. It was assumed by them and their recruiters that if accepted part-time, they would progress to a full-time appointment.

Circuit Judges

Their interviews are distinct. The stories they told disclosed that there used to be a very strong assumption, at least in certain chambers, that joining the circuit bench was a 'natural' career path for a barrister not obviously destined for the High Court. In the 1970s and 1980s, the circuit bench was apparently seen as an alternative and interchangeable career path to taking silk, becoming a QC. Barristers became judges when it was their 'turn' in certain chambers, unless they took silk, in the 'Apostolic succession' parodied in the quotation opening the last chapter. Provincial circuit bars and judiciary were (and are) very close knit. Routinely, in court dining rooms, judges indicated to me all of their colleagues

---

[5] According to the JAC research cited in the previous chapter of this book, this is still discouraging solicitors from applying.

round the table who had been recruited from their own chambers. The circuit bench seems to have been seen by most as a less prestigious job than QC and consequently recruitment was difficult. Hazell, 1979, quoted in the previous chapter, was understating the judge shortage but lawyers were aware that, if they chose the judicial ladder, they had to become a judge by 50 to earn the full pension so, for those unlikely to be elevated to QC, the pressure was on to secure a full-time post.

Twelve of the 32 were invited to put their names forward or to apply, including three who 'let it be known' that they were interested. Astonishingly, four were offered it by civil servants as an alternative when they applied to be QCs. 20 applied unprompted. For eight, it was a long-term desire, for one since she was 12. 11 enjoyed sitting part-time (one decided on his first day). Seven mentioned that practice was losing its attractions. 'The Bar had lost all its fun' and 'I thought there was more to life than being head of my chambers'.

> The basic insecurity of being at the Bar ... whether there is going to be any work when you come back from holiday ... Also, I enjoyed ... being ... in charge of the courtroom.

> Unlike the High Court bench, I was able to sleep in my own bed each night...and it had a pension.

Eight had never had any desire to take silk. One applied and then changed his mind, when the life of a rural circuit judge began to look attractive.

> I was beginning to enjoy [being a recorder] ... I was in my forties and up until then I wanted to be some famous QC but then you suddenly realise you are out in the country with your wife and your children and you think 'Well it is not a bad job really. It cuts down on all the hassle'. (1996)

Four barristers, appointed in 1988–95, had wanted to be QCs but found their applications met with attempts by civil servants to persuade them to be a judge. Before this research, I was unaware of this method of recruitment. Again, the third person here was concerned that he did not appear in front of the 'right' judges to support his application to take silk, reminiscent of the last chapter.

> I had ... made two applications for silk. I had a letter ... inviting me for an interview to discuss whether I would like to become a circuit judge. (1989)

> I always wanted to be a silk. I was asked ... would I consider being [a circuit judge] and I said 'not really' ... then you get the dreaded letter saying 'Dear [X], you haven't got silk but would you like to come and discuss your career with us?' ... they say 'Sorry for not getting silk, Old Chap, but how about becoming a judge?' and I said 'No, actually, thanks, I'd rather be a QC still.' [then he was rejected again and received the same letter ... By that time you are not forced into it but they point out to you that you are 49 and a half and if you are going to earn your pension this would be a jolly good time to start. (1990)

> I went along to [the LCD] because I had not got silk ... My problem at the Bar was that I settled most of my cases ... [so] ... You didn't appear in front of High Court judges ...

so really one's chances of silk were severely reduced. I said 'What an earth is going on?' as I had applied [for silk] four or five times. He said 'At the moment you have got no As. You are mostly Bs but one or two have given you a C'. I didn't know what those categories meant ... He said it was up to me. I could apply again or I could apply to become a circuit judge, although there was no guarantee of anything but it was open to me. I didn't realise that A meant that you would be appointed a silk this year, B meant you would be appointed a silk next year and C meant you would be appointed a silk but not next year. (1995)

Those judges were from three different circuits. The interview with this silk from a fourth circuit, who decided he wanted to give up his busy practice and was confident he would be appointed, explains how the circuit bench was viewed by many barristers and why the Lord Chancellor's Department (LCD) was so persuasive.

Being a circuit judge ... wasn't a very plum job and they were very anxious to get whoever they could ... it certainly wasn't very well-regarded [or] ... well-paid ... Two of my colleagues ... were approached and turned it down flat. (1988)

They were offered their jobs as an unpopular consolation prize for not getting silk but for others, they were interchangeable career routes.

I sort of graduated to taking silk ... if someone had offered me the circuit bench on the day I took silk I would have taken [it]. Silk was something that other people were suggesting that, as I had got to a certain stage in my career, I should take. I was very nervous of the idea. So I *drifted* into silk.

This raises the question of why the 10 successful QCs in the 32 CJ sample would want to relinquish lucrative careers, especially as the successful and eligible lawyers in Genn's sample listed reasons not to apply even to the High Court, let alone the lower paid circuit bench. One high-earning QC replied that he was 'bogged down with work', by 2000. By the late 1990s, because of competition, there had been a big shift in the way that the circuit bench was viewed. Obviously, it was no longer the booby prize, nor scorned by silks.

I thought the Bar was going to kill me ... I was travelling; hugely stressful work, mountains ... and though I enjoyed it, I just realised I couldn't do it forever ... Having six foot of paper delivered at nine o'clock at night and having to be in the court the next day—that all went. (Appointed 2001)

[I] wanted a new stimulus ... Doing a lot of frauds, I was spending a lot of time preparing ... skeleton arguments. I missed the day-to-day cut and thrust of being in court. ... time for a change, despite ... the significant drop in income.

The Senior Judges

There was something unrealistic about asking them when they first wanted to be a judge, since 25 of the 26 had been invited. Nine insisted that they had never thought about it. The judge below was very approachable and down-to-earth, modest and self-effacing. He still seemed to be surprised that he held a senior administrative position in the Court of Appeal (and was probably more shocked when, soon after this interview, he was appointed a Law Lord).

> Frankly, I never really applied my mind to it until I was summoned by the Lord Chancellor's Permanent Secretary ... I never really thought that anyone would want me.

One thought it was dangerous to think about it as it might not happen; another said he was happy with his split life as a part-time judge and another, in the CA, reacted:

> Gosh! ... I knew I was joining a set that practised in the county court. It never crossed my mind that I would become a High Court judge. I always thought ... I would have the problem of whether I would apply to be a circuit judge ... Then I thought I would take silk ... [and] things changed quite quickly ... I was asked after four years of being an assistant recorder by the then Vice Chancellor ... it sounds a bit fairytaleish.

Four assumed they would be invited because of their high profile practices. Ten had allowed themselves to want the job, one since school. One was thinking of applying. Another changed his practice to 'mainstream' and *again* he was anxious about not appearing before the right judges.

> [My practice] was in an area that ... had no ... prospect of going onto the Bench. It was specialist and didn't take me into court and get me known to any relevant people.

I asked why a commercial or chancery silk would relinquish a highly paid and famous career.

> I had ... handled some pretty heavy cases prior to becoming a judge and I think there is a danger that if you spend your life as a QC, it is very tempting to go on too long.

> The idea of spending another 20 years at the Bar doing the same thing is more than one could stand ... people would like to put something back into the system that they have been taking out of.

This altruistic idea of repaying 'the system' or 'public service' was mentioned by many senior judges, whose incomes had fallen sometimes from millions to under £175,000. The one who applied 'always thought it would be quite a nice way of ending a career in the law...I marshalled for a judge when I was a student'. Three had taken a positive decision, as silks, that if invited, they would *not* want to be appointed as circuit judges. Two were invited twice and declined. Another was already an eminent CJ when he was invited to see the Lord Chancellor, 'out of the blue'. His reaction below shows his mixed feelings and by the time of the research he still complained bitterly of the workload, the demanding variety, the travelling and being away from home. Indeed, his CJ friends in this sample cited him as an example of why they would not want to be a High Court judge. (They did not know he was in the research sample.)

THE TAP ON THE SHOULDER

The stories below of the old boy network, the casual, short 'interviews' for permanent posts and the desperation to recruit to the bench would be unimaginable to the modern lawyers in the following section. Lord Mackay, the 1980s Lord Chancellor, recently described the system he employed before the mid-1990s. For the High Court, there were regular meetings between senior officials, senior judges and the Chairman of the Bar. He consulted the Heads of Division and Senior Presider before recommending a candidate. As for potential recorders and circuit judges, his officials conducted an annual review, following circuit visits to collect 'assessments' from presiders, senior judges and 'local leaders of the profession'.[6]

The Senior Judges

Twenty-five were invited, including the one above. He was asked to go and see the Lord Chancellor.

> I was so surprised that I didn't even have the presence of mind to ask what it was about…a tense few days. There were three possibilities … One is that he wants to ask you to do a project … The second was a bollocking … and the third was to offer me another job … I discussed it with my wife and I didn't know what I would say… I didn't want to be a High Court judge … I had a very good job in [X]. It was the senior criminal job in the region. It gave me influence … I stayed at home virtually every night. I had four children…The prospect of being away from home either in London … or … on circuit was not attractive … I eventually took the job but it was a very close call.

Two suspected that they were the butt of a practical joke. One called directory inquiries to check the number. The other was used to a mate's tricks.

> I was vain enough to hope I would be invited … I was involved in heavy negotiations with an old friend … called Peter Frisk … He is the biggest practical joker in the world. He has never, ever phoned me saying 'Peter Frisk'. It is always Inspector of Taxes, Germaine Greer, Arthur Scargill … Fortunately, I was on the phone and my clerk came in and said 'The Lord Chancellor wants to talk to you' and gave me the number. Now, if they had put the phone through, I would have said 'Fuck off Frisk! I am not taking your offer' so I was in deep shock … I rushed round to my wife with my knees shaking.

Another was 'gobsmacked' but negotiated a three-year postponement.

> Sound(s) a bit … cheesy but I was asked to go and see the Vice Chancellor in 1993 … I had a standard-form note … saying would I come and talk to the Permanent Secretary … I thought I was only a middling silk … but I … was then shown into the Lord

---

[6] *Judicial Appointments—Balancing Independence, Accountability and Legitimacy*, 2010, a collection of essays published jointly by ILEX, The Bar Council, The Law Society and the JAC.

Chancellor and asked did I want to become a High Court judge … I … had to say to him that I was gobsmacked, completely … I had made no plans for it. I went away and … really thought over the financial side, three children at school and no real provision … so I said 'Not yet' … I talked to my wife and my accountant. I tried to work out the earliest I could do it and I said 'If you come back in about three years I would probably say "Yes"' and, rather flatteringly, they came back almost three years to the day. (1996)

His description demonstrates the civil service habit of talking in euphemisms.

I was summoned by the … Permanent Secretary… It was a strange meeting. He started off by saying had I thought how I would like my career to develop.

I bumped into the … civil servant in charge of … appointments … He came to see me … and I asked what doors might be open and what doors might be closed. He said 'No doors will be closed'.

I had a mysterious conversation. … saying 'If you were asked would you say now, later or not at all?' so I said 'Now' and within three months I had a phone call saying 'Would you see the Lord Chancellor in a week's time?'

This habit of beating about the bush caused confusion about another judge's willingness but circuit gossip prevented him losing the opportunity.

The … chat … wound its way to the question of whether if there were a vacancy … might I conceivably be interested in becoming a High Court judge? [I said yes]. Stage two … was in July … I was asked to go and see the Lord Chancellor … The preliminary stage wasn't altogether that satisfactory, partly because it was so oblique and…it nearly didn't work … because later … I learnt from a judge … that, although I thought I had said … that I *would* be interested in appointment, the message that Sir Thomas Legg had gone away with was that I *wasn't* interested!

One wag wished he had taken advantage of this delicate approach.

The Permanent Secretary … asks you a few questions which includes whether there is anything in your past that might embarrass the Lord Chancellor. One nominee, not alas myself, answered 'It depends how easily the Lord Chancellor is embarrassed!'

The hiatus between the 'sounding out' and the invitation to see the Lord Chancellor caused problems. One talked of an 'agonising' four months. Another found it 'unsettling'.

I was approached by a senior judge who I had done a case in front of and asked if my name was put forward by the judges to the Lord Chancellor what would my reaction be. I was given a very short time to think. It was a very unsettling experience because it immediately put into my head possibilities that I hadn't really been contempla-ting…There were … four or five months where nothing happened and other people were made High Court judges … It was a difficult time because I was unable to throw myself into my work as a QC.

Most accepted readily, one describing her feeling of 'unmitigated ecstasy' and a number of the sense of duty. One deferred for three years and two had 'huge doubts', one because 'I was earning a lot of money and I had very heavy financial commitments' and the other took six weeks 'to think about whether I would enjoy it … and whether … it wasn't nonetheless my public duty to accept'.

Curiously, these last two, despite misgivings, threw themselves into the task of being excellent judges. Appointed in 1988 and 1992, they have dedicated their judicial careers to the service of the law and litigants in their specialist fields. They are renowned for their compassion and humanity, their forward-thinking development of precedent and promotion of reform. They work exceptionally long hours and are passionately dedicated to promoting international judicial co-operation and procedural harmonisation in their fields. They both describe themselves as public servants and most other judges and lawyers would consider that they have *served* the English legal system, despite their initial reluctance to join the bench. For one, his massively diminished income meant a radical change from a very opulent lifestyle and his sudden devotion to public service and law reform seemed to me almost tantamount to a personality change. Having been a playboy barrister, he transformed into a workaholic, zealous, reformer who seemed to carry the weight of the world on his shoulders. If he ever stopped for lunch, it was a working lunch. International law reform conferences, organised by him, seemed to have supplanted his summer holidays.

Court of Appeal and House of Lords/UK Supreme Court

The eight CA judges and two Law Lords (Justices) were asked about their experiences of promotion from the High Court (HC). Four HC judges were promoted to the CA during the research and two have since been promoted. One received a phone call from the Lord Chief Justice after my first day with him, when he had told me how much he loved being an HC judge, travelling on circuit, and by my second day, he had to give his decision. While we chatted, the Lord Chief phoned him and he rushed off, grumbling, so I taped his reaction a few minutes later.

> I had almost made up my mind that if I was asked I would refuse but … it is quite difficult … I know they are short of people to do the criminal … but I have told the Lord Chief … that I have real reservations and I accept with some trepidation … I have thoroughly enjoyed my time as a High Court judge and if you asked me last week, I would have said I wouldn't dream of accepting … I just hope it works out for the system as much as for me … There is no going back.

What put him off?

> The lack of variety … of getting out and about around the country. I commute … I am determined not to … get a flat … on my own in London. That would be soul-destroying, apart from the expense.

Five did not receive the consulting telephone call. Other people knew before them. With the third, his head of division knew of the pending invitation, having been consulted.

I got a letter out of the blue from the Prime Minister asking me whether I would like to be a member of the Court of Appeal ... I said yes ... I thought a change is as good as a rest and ... [the work] is extremely varied, whereas the civil work I did was mostly commercial/maritime.

I got a letter from the Prime Minister...people had dropped hints ... I was excited. I was thrilled ... A bit daunted ... I had always thought that everyone was very clever up here. I found that throughout my life ... when you get there, you find there are some who are absolutely outstanding but a lot who are just like me, competent and conscientious and get on with it.

I had a couple of comments made to me ... The next thing ... the LCJ said, 'Have you had a letter from No 10?' and I said ... 'No' ... I welcomed the invitation. I had stopped going on circuit ... because I was so bogged down in [running a specialist section of the High Court]. I am not a natural manager or administrator. Although I enjoyed it, I don't miss it.

I got a telephone call from [his head of division] ... saying 'John, have you had a letter?' and I said 'No, Brian' ... I was rather surprised. There were a lot of judges who were senior to me ... at least as good.

My clerk ... was a great gossip. He kept saying 'Have you received a letter from the PM recently?' and I kept saying 'Push off. Don't be so stupid'. Then, there was this letter from ... Mr Major saying 'Please can I book you in?' ... I didn't have any hesitation in accepting ... It was a service and you were there to serve.

This judge, who was quoted in the previous section, lobbied to go up to the CA, on his law reform mission.

I wanted the opportunity to play a significant part in the evolution of family law through precedent, so I was very anxious to fill the vacancy ... I was actually talking to the senior family Lord Justice who was putting my case, because they weren't necessarily going to appoint a family specialist ... in order to ensure that the statutory law is interpreted and applied in a way that is relevant to social change and social development it has got to be the judges who ... deliver this evolution, because Parliament isn't going to.

I asked the two Law Lords about being summoned to sit in the CA and the Lords.

It didn't really take me by surprise. I had done eight years on the High Court bench ... I think I would have been quite disappointed not to have been put in the CA.

I asked if appointment as a Law Lord took him by surprise.

That rather did. A lot of people had been saying ... 'You are going to get there' ... I was less and less keen ... I said, 'I would love to be asked, only if I can say no' ... When it was leaked ... by a chum, I said 'You'll expect me to be thrilled to bits but actually I can't tell you how deep a gloom you have sunk me'. The disruption ... of one's life at the Court of Appeal was considerable. All my friends were in the Court. I had lunch every day with them, which I greatly enjoyed, picking up the legal gossip ... I had mastered the routines … It was extremely hard work but I had learnt how to manage … and I had presided for years so I was able to decide which case I wanted to give the leading judgments.

'So there was no turning back?', I asked.

You can't say no … One or two people sounded me out did I want to be considered for this, that and the other and I said absolutely totally and emphatically not, because I loathed administration, which is a huge and growing part of all these … special jobs such as the heads of division. I had no interest in that and was appalled at the prospect.

The second explained 'It was quite a surprise', to be asked to join the CA but 'I have never heard of anyone refusing elevation … It never occurred to me that it was an option'. As for the summons to join the Law Lords:

I had another letter from the Prime Minister and it ended up by saying that 'In the meantime please keep this with the utmost confidentiality' and it had arrived through the post in an envelope with 10 Downing Street on it in letters about an inch high … I was very surprised and great satisfaction, from the very specialised background that I had. It seemed then and … now, amazing that I got to the House of Lords at all and certainly as quickly.

The Circuit Judges

Seventeen, appointed pre-1994, showed that the system used to be an opaque mixture whereby barristers would be sounded out in a euphemistic chat about their 'career', as above, or would 'let it be known' that they were interested, or might be diverted from fruitless applications for silk, or press-ganged, if high-earning silks. The interviews showed that the full-time circuit appointment system was little more formal than the system for recruiting part-timers, depicted in the last chapter.

As we have seen, one silk knew he was pushing at an open door and four were diverted from repeated silk applications, in 1988–95. Two solicitors were invited. One who became the designated civil judge for his region, mainly hearing HC cases, had never been interviewed for any of his judicial posts—assistant recorder, recorder, CJ or specialist CJ. One barrister knew he was destined for the High Court but he asked to be diverted to a circuit appointment for 10 years for family reasons, as he needed to live at home. One gave in to repeated requests, to 'get people off [his] back'. Two high-earning specialist silks had to be heavily persuaded to take up specialist appointments. One had already been offered a judicial post in Hong Kong. Five had long hoped to be judges. The first was keen to move things forward. Again, as we saw in the last chapter, there is the casualness of the 'interviews' and the keenness to snap up barristers into an understaffed bench.

I rang up the LCD man … and said I would like to know how I was getting on … He said 'Providing things go alright I'll contact you in a few years time' … sure enough …

in 1991, there was a letter … This led to a proper interview. It was just him and a retired Lord Justice of Appeal and there wasn't any competition … I think I was just being given the 'once over'. (1992)

I received this letter … I was interviewed … by Tom Legg … He, the note-taker and I sat round a table, discussed my background…and whether I had any outstanding debts to the Inland Revenue … It ended with him saying 'If the Lord Chancellor were minded to recommend you to Her Majesty to the circuit bench, what would your reaction be?' I said 'I would be minded to accept'. He said 'You understand we can't guarantee anything … but against the eventuality perhaps you would like to go and speak to your circuit administrator' … and he said 'Right, when can you start?' (1986)

One silk CJ considered it 'outrageous' that he had entered the full-time judiciary after a 15-minute interview yet, as a school governor, he had spent three days putting an applicant head teacher through tests.

District Judges and District Judges (Magistrates' Courts)

For the longest serving DJs, provided they 'made it known' that they wanted a full-time appointment, it was more or less automatic

I made it clear very shortly after I started … that I'd like to do it full time. I was told that they would not appoint me before I was 40.

Remember that for the DJMCs, most had assumed they would sit full-time.

NEWER JUDGES—THE COMPETITIVE APPLICATION PROCESS

The district and circuit application process became a formal competition, advertised in newspapers and on the Lord Chancellor's website and promoted in recruitment 'road shows' from 1994–95. The annual round has become progressively more competitive, elaborate, tougher and formalised. Again there are complaints about the delays, like those in the last chapter.

a much longer and more detailed form … you don't hear anything for months … [at the assessment centre] I did the box work and a judgment but I felt that was all quite rushed. Then … the interview and you give the judgment and they fire all these legal questions at you … for about an hour. (DJ, 1999)

The forms … are enormous. You have to do a self-assessment … I think the more you put down the better … It is not just 'Well I am so good at the law' … but actually 'I have quite a lot of other experience which is going to be quite useful as well'…having brought up children and having managed all the various toddler groups, teaching at Sunday school…you know what makes people tick … the interview was … pretty gruelling. You come out … feeling exhausted … There are also some politically correct questions just to check that you are not going to do anything outrageous. (DJ, 2000)

> The interview was a nightmare … you had to give your judgment and then the DJ just tore into me…and you are on the back foot … I thought I'd blown it … That was in the October … I heard nothing until February. (DJ, 2000)

This circuit judge, appointed in 2002, described the sequence of applying part-time and then full-time.

> Prolonged, stressful and with a high degree of uncertainty … When it came to recordership, I was on tenter-hooks for a couple of years … The circuit bench I applied three times for…[He was put on a reserve list after the second application but heard nothing] … one person I know … is coming on to the reserve list for the third time and if he doesn't get it I think that will be cruel in the extreme.

Judges very commonly complained about the time taken between the application, the result, and eventual appointment, as did the interviewees in Genn's 2008 paper. A number of this sample were taken aback that other people on their circuit knew before they did.[7] The only senior judge who had applied had sat as a deputy High Court judge.

> An advertisement appeared in the paper … At first I thought it might be simply a smoke screen … in 1999 I applied … I don't think [the form] was nearly as complicated as … now … I wasn't interviewed. I had, of course, been interviewed for my recordership. I had sat for quite a long time [since 1993]. There would have been some track-record … I suppose for my judicial work. I think I was pretty well-known to the senior judiciary anyway because of the nature of my practice. (Appointed 2001)

The delays and uncertainty go beyond lack of professionalism. They are almost cruel, as one of the interviewees said, above. One CJ applied for the HC bench and was told she was suitable in 2004. Despite repeated applications, she had still not been appointed some years later. They not only inculcate frustration and lack of confidence in the applicant, delays after selection stultify lawyers' careers as solicitors or barristers because if they have been told they are successful, they cannot take on any major, new cases and when other people find out, they cease to be offered work, as can be seen from the comments below.

Judges' Comments on the Selection Process

The main research period was 2003–05. In July 2003, the Government announced that it would be creating a Judicial Appointments Commission (JAC), as described in the previous chapter. By 2005, the Constitutional Reform Act had been passed, creating the new Commission, with a further consultation underway about diversifying the judiciary.[8] Thus, most judges could reply from three perspectives: their own and colleagues' experiences; their position as consultees

---

[7]   Similarly, Genn's interviewees complained of the lack of confidentiality.

[8]   DCA, *Increasing Diversity in the Judiciary* and responses (2004, DCA archived website).

or referees for applicants, and from the standpoint of an interested party responding to the reform consultations.

Of the 66 who commented, seven long-standing DJs and CJs said they were relieved that they had not had to go through the annual competition and the demanding assessment process. One CJ described the system as 'horrific'. The comment below was typical.

> The selection process is very difficult and one I am jolly glad I don't have to go through. Six of my chums at the minute have these dreadful letters saying 'You have got the job, you are on the waiting list and you have been deemed to be Class B so watch this space'. Once I heard I was going to be a judge, I couldn't stand on my feet as an advocate … How those people who know they might get a phone call any day in the next two years live on, being advocates, I don't know.

Thirteen criticised the pre-2006 system of collecting 'soundings', from existing judges. One DJ, appointed in the late 1990s, had suffered from a negative comment, like those that scandalised the Commission for Judicial Appointments, below.

> I managed to find out that … I'd had an extremely adverse reference from a DJ who was motivated for personal reasons … [We] didn't particularly get on. He'd never seen me in court. He didn't know me very well but he went to great lengths to write an extremely damaging comment. I was only able to stop it continuing because I was able to establish who it was. I asked the Department why I'd been unsuccessful. They told me of a [comment] that they'd received. I knew who it was from, by … the language … I wrote … and asked if he'd let me sit in with him so I could learn from his experience and I asked if he could sit in with me so he could give me some constructive criticism. He completely avoided me but he didn't give me another bad [comment].

The watchdog Commission for Judicial Appointments, staffed with recruitment experts, attracted wide media coverage when they published, in their 2003 report, some of the inappropriate comments judges had made about applicants, such as:

> She's too primly spinsterish

> She's off-puttingly headmistressy

> Down and out scruffy

A senior CJ spoke from the perspective of one of those asked to express views on lists of applicants.

> They have moved away from an absolutely dreadful procedure which was passing round these pieces of paper for people to tick A, B and Cs … I wonder what information it threw up which was of any value. I felt I could only really fill in the forms where I could only give people As, otherwise if you gave them a B it might be better not to fill in the form at all.

But another senior CJ regretted that the process had been reformed.

> I find it quite difficult to be really helpful because you can't now include anything which is about general reputation ... I quite understand that is objectionable in the sense that people should not be blackballed by tittle-tattle.

One CJ told me a story of how 'soundings' once backfired. I heard this story from others, too.

> There is a famous story on our circuit ... Some High Court judge really liked the look of Smith when he saw him at the Bar and he turned out to be a really good circuit judge. However, he got his name wrong and he told whoever they told in those days 'This man Jones is the man to appoint' ... He didn't know Jones, who was Smith's opponent, and Jones was duly appointed and Smith wasn't appointed at the time. The next time this High Court judge came round, sitting in the same court centre as him was Jones. He said 'Who appointed *him*?' and then he found out *he* had appointed Jones.

Three of the solicitor CJs, such as the two below, were critical of the soundings process as benefiting the Bar, because judges were free to offer comments on a large number of applicants and naturally they came into daily contact with barristers not solicitors. We are *again* back to the same point about 'knowing the right judges'.

> It is very hard for solicitors and for district judges, because in neither case have they got a large pool of people who they can ask to be referees ... you won't have any senior counsel or High Court judges who know anything about your work, which is the reason why so few solicitors get appointed. I think the process is biased.

> Someone turned to my late wife at a dinner. Clearly he ... didn't know her and said 'These chaps who apply—we don't know them really do we? The Bar is like a club' ... [Then John] was instrumental in introducing me...to the Head of Judicial Appointments ... we had a couple of evenings together over a glass of something and so when I went for the interview, I at least knew the person who was going to be heading up that interview. It shouldn't be like that ... I was at a ... meeting last night in London and there were a lot of very high-powered people there. They can open doors that I can't even get near and it is all because ... there are a very small group of people who wield a lot of power. I can count on one hand the amount of High Court judges I know ... In the old days ... they just had no training at all but some ended up on the Bench because they just had common interests, such as they had a good war!

This senior judge was highly critical.

> In every other public appointment process you have proper criteria ... sensible selection procedures ... very sophisticated tests for ... suitability ... the judicial selection procedure has been based very much on soundings ... which has resulted in comments which are no better than 'he is a jolly good chap' or 'safe pair of hands' ... the procedures have been tightened up. You now have proper selection criteria ... against which judges are asked to assess individuals. The problem is [they] haven't had any training ... [This] has invariably meant that judges tend to select those that they know who are in their image, which is why you have perpetually had a succession of white men, able as they undoubtedly are.

The soundings system had five defenders, including one CJ who said 'It is the judges who know who the decent people are'. Two of these, plus another three, including an interviewer, considered that too much emphasis was now placed on the applicant's performance in interview. She considered that people sometimes did not do themselves justice in an interview and welcomed the 2006 development of a Judicial Appointments Commission and further reform.

Eight who had very recently been through the competitive process considered it very fair. One found it 'truly excellent' and another 'as good as it could be'. Three long-standing judges praised it, as did one CA judge who had been on an HC selection panel in 2005. Seven said the system needed speeding up, one calling it 'chaotic' and another 'appalling'. Some recent appointees were taken aback when it seemed that other people knew of their appointment before they did, spreading the news around their circuit and thus freezing their legal practice.

> Everybody at the Bar [here] and all the judges knew … exactly who had been interviewed, who had applied and had not got an interview and by the March/April it was quite untenable for me to practice because all the time people were saying 'You won't be doing the final hearing in this because you'll be a judge by then'. I was thinking 'You know more than I do' because I had not been appointed. All the judges had told everybody and the leader of the circuit had spoken to one of his mates. So when there was a wedding in chambers, a QC then told everybody who had been appointed … I think it is very hard that the [appointers] impose this confidentially and I genuinely stuck to it, I didn't even tell my own chambers, yet the whole world knew. The process was deeply unsatisfying. My husband has been through a similar situation and it has had immeasurable damage on his income and ability to work because they stop giving you cases. (2001; 2004)

Thirteen judges said the previous and existing systems had worked well in producing good judges, regardless of whether they agreed with reform plans. One CJ said, 'I think the world looks at England and says that the judges are of a very high calibre'. Eleven were apprehensive about further reform, mentioning 'political correctness', or opposing quota systems, and/or more lay involvement in the selection process, and/or the fear that quality might be sacrificed to diversity. On the other hand, 18 (in addition to those critics of the existing system, above) welcomed further reform, or considered it inevitable, mentioning the need to enhance diversity and public confidence. One senior judge said he had benefited from the 'tap on the shoulder' 'in the worst sort of way' and another described the old system as 'outrageous', both observing that they probably would not be selected under a new system, if it emphasised diversity. One CA judge did point out though that, despite his strong approval for the post-2006 appointment system, Linda Dobbs was the last HC judge recruited via 'the tap on the shoulder' and the first black one and she had made it clear that she would *not* have applied, so he regretted the loss of opportunity to diversify the judiciary by that mechanism. These judges' views typified the mixed feelings shared by many to whom I spoke casually: that the old system had produced good judges but was democratically indefensible.

> It is not modern or really defensible, ... in the same way as a non-democratically run country, however well-run it is, is indefensible in at least Western minds ... On the other hand ... the present system does seem to produce a very good judiciary ... highly respected ... These are two irresolvable conflicts.

> It does work remarkably well but the need for change is probably now sufficiently made ... [my concern is] that they are trying to diversify the bench in a way that will undermine the merit criteria.

This last point was a very common judicial concern about the duty of the JAC, under section 64 of the Constitutional Reform Act 2005, to encourage diversity. Of course, the sacrifice of 'merit' to 'diversity' is a classic fear when recruitment to any organisation is reformed in the attempt to recruit under-represented groups—in this case solicitors (about nine-tenths of practitioners), women, non-whites, academic lawyers and barristers unknown to 'the right' judges. The classic counter-argument is that organisations that discriminate deprive themselves and their clients (here, the public) of all the talented members of the excluded groups. To illustrate the point from an issue raised later in the book, we shall see that in the biggest Crown Court, two solicitor CJs were universally praised by barrister judges for their talents in relating to juries, because solicitors interface with clients, yet we have seen in these two chapters how difficult it was for solicitors to get onto the circuit bench. Stories of the prejudice against solicitors will resurface later.

The post-2006 application process is still the subject of criticism. Astonishingly, the first competition the JAC organised was re-run, because judges, now deprived of the opportunity to comment in 'soundings', were indignant that their views were not taken account of. Some of those applying in 2009 were critical. I asked a DJMC who had previously applied why she did not apply again for a recordership. She said 'I won't get in cos it's still an old boys network', and referred to the fact that the judiciary had 'made them do a re-run' of the annual competition when they were not consulted 'and their protégées didn't get in'. She said deputies' recruitment is 'all done by exams now and the first hurdle is exam technique'. This affected her, because it would not have allowed her to demonstrate her judging skills. She said 800 took the exam. Her friend, a DJ, showed her the papers. There were many questions requiring answers of only one line. Further into the paper were answers carrying 30 per cent and 40 per cent of the marks available so people with good exam technique flicked through the paper first, realised that, and started with them.[9] By 2009, she said candidates who knew they had been successful in an annual competition were being kept in suspense

---

[9] D Page sought judicial review after he was not shortlisted for a post after sitting a written test. He said it did not test his judicial skills. He thought it was part of the process yet it was used to sift out 60 people for interview from 850 applicants. He thought the JAC did not have the power to use a written test. He claimed that it was not an holistic approach and discriminated against mature, better experienced applicants: F Gibb, 'Written tests are no guide to your ability to be a judge', *The Times*, 29 January 2009.

for two years before they could take up a post. 'How are solicitors expected to run their businesses?'

CONCLUSION

How these 77 lawyers came to be judges needs explaining because most lawyers do not become judges. Their frank stories spell out just how intense and small the pre-2006 old boy circle was for some. Also, there were clear differences in the experiences of older and newer judges and between the different ranks of judge.

DJMCs were administratively and culturally unconnected from the mainstream judiciary and seen as magistrates. Deputies took it for granted that they would progress to the full-time bench. As for county court DJs, they bore the strain of working in the evenings after a day's judging. For some, pressure from their resentful solicitor partners forced a choice.

All but one of the senior judges and many of the veteran DJs and CJs had been 'tapped on the shoulder'. One solicitor had progressed to senior CJ level without an interview at any stage. In certain provincial barristers' chambers, there was indeed the 'Apostolic' succession spoken of in the last chapter. When it was 'your turn', you would either become a QC or a judge. Barristers who had grown up together now found themselves in the same court as judges, with their former colleagues and Bar pupils appearing before them. Most surprisingly, lawyers who applied repeatedly to take silk were offered a circuit judge job as a less desirable consolation prize.[10] Equally laughable was the amateurish nature of this press-ganging, thinly disguised as a selection system, with interviews lasting 15 minutes. Civil servants spoke a euphemistic language and rated lawyers with As, Bs and Cs, gleaned from a formalised version of the soundings system that was somehow meant to make it more respectable but which some of these lawyers clearly did not understand.

Some senior judges were genuinely surprised by the tap on the shoulder. They suddenly had to work out how to live within a limited budget. There were also mixed reactions by existing judges to 'tap on the shoulder' promotions. The CJ promoted to the High Court had been very happy. He was a home-bird, like a lot of CJs.[11] Throughout the research, he was still complaining about the travel and the broad and heavy workload of the Queen's Bench Division (QBD). One HC judge was telling me about how much he loved travelling on circuit when he was summoned to sit in the punishing Court of Appeal (Criminal Division). There is no 'collective pretence' of not wanting to be 'promoted' to the upper courts. By analogy, most university readers and professors do not want to head a law school, whatever the financial incentives. Indeed, there was barely any 'collective' attitude

---

[10] This was so unexpected in their interviews that I laughed and had to ask them to repeat themselves.

[11] As will be seen in ch 16.

among judges on anything relating to recruitment and promotion. Some HC judges, by contrast, said they welcomed promotion and one actively lobbied to get into the CA. As for the Law Lords, it will be seen later that the instant reaction of many was a desire to get back to the camaraderie of the CA, to which Lord Neuberger did indeed return in 2009.

The casualness of the old application process and 'interviews' would be completely unrecognisable to judges who went through the 'prolonged, stressful' highly competitive post-millennium assessment process and the 2009 exams. However, it can be seen that the system is still open to criticism, such as the view of the some DJs applying for recorderships that in the JAC's anxiety to be egalitarian, it does not take account of their developed judging skills. Moreover, the interviews and the events from 2009 demonstrate the tenacity of the old boy network and the consequent anxiety of 'outsiders' like solicitors about getting known by the 'right' judges. The judiciary successfully intervened in the workings of the independent JAC. Despair over this perceived persistence of the old boy network and the unreality of the new exams put off at least one talented DJMC in this sample from re-applying for a recordership in 2010. The delays and uncertainty persist.

6

Training

Nothing more than a public relations gimmick.

A judge quoted in Lord Justice Bridge's 1978 *Report of the Working Party on Judicial Studies and Information.*[1]

THIS CHAPTER[2] examines the 77 judges' experiences of training. These differed radically from the longest standing, who, thanks to the type of sentiment above, were 'thrown in at the deep end', to newer judges who have benefited from the demanding skills-based courses designed for them by those very judges who suffered too little training. While initial and continuing training for the district and circuit bench is well-developed, training and induction for new High Court (HC) judges is in its infancy.

Remarkably, some of the longest serving judges, such as 19 here, and even three appointed in the 1990s, received no training before sitting in judgment.[3] This seems derisory to modern judges. Many were keen to point out that thanks to the establishment of the Judicial Studies Board (JSB) in 1979, the position has gradually reversed. The history was told by Kate Malleson in *The New Judiciary.*[4] Many 1970s judges opposed training, as a threat to independence. It was seen as unnecessary, since all were experienced barristers or solicitors, the implication being that performing advocacy in front of judges sufficed. The most prominent opponent to training was Lord Devlin. *The Judge*[5] contains his 20-page tirade. Notice his confidence that, despite having no experience, he was fully equipped to try and sentence the most serious of crimes (including handing down death sentences).

---

[1] Cited by K Malleson, *The New Judiciary: the effects of expansion and activism* (Aldershot, Dartmouth, 1999).

[2] Details here of current policy and training were checked in September 2010 by the Director of Training, HH Judge John Phillips CBE, to whom I am very grateful.

[3] PB Wice observed that 'American judges ... rarely receive any training or education prior to assuming office': 'Judicial Socialization: The Philadelphia Experience' in JA Cramer (ed), *Courts and Judges* (Beverly Hills, Sage, 1981) 149. L Alpert interviewed Florida judges in 1979, finding self-education and 'sink or swim': 'Learning About Trial Judging: The Socialization of State Trial Judges', in the same book.

[4] Malleson, above n 1.

[5] Baron P Devlin, *The Judge* (Oxford, Oxford University Press, 1979).

> [W]hen in 1948 I was appointed to the High Court ... not since my early days at the Bar had I appeared in a criminal court ... Two days [later] ... I was trying crime at Newcastle Assizes ... for centuries judicial appointments have been made on the basis that experience at the Bar is what gives a man the necessary judicial equipment ... where the independence of the judges may be touched ... it is a good thing to have a protocol. Protocol should, I think, decree that in the acquisition of background information a judge should be left to his own devices.

Judicial training belonged on 'the Continent'. Malleson quoted similar opposition by Lord Hailsham, a Lord Chancellor who, in 1983, expressed his view as 'a degree of indifference verging on contempt'.[6] Such hostility was shared by other common law judiciaries, with some only accepting the need for training far more recently than 1979.

To meet the perceived threat to independence, the JSB was not based at a university as Bridge had recommended. Training should be devised and provided by judges. It still is, with professional assistance. At the commencement of this research, in 2003, the JSB website, adopting the (strangely punctuated) words of the Bridge report, proclaimed the most important objective of judicial training to be 'To convey in a condensed form the lessons, which experienced judges, have acquired from their experience'.[7] The chairman, most of its Executive Board and all directors of training are judges. The secretariat are civil servants. The planning groups are course-director judges, training advisers and staff. All tutors are trained judges, recruited in open competition. Academics and professional lawyers are engaged as speakers.

It has continually added to the range and type of training and enhanced its quality. In April 2011, it evolved into a Judicial College,[8] a facility which European career judiciaries had last century. The 'college' is virtual, because there is no money for a real one. Sentencing exercises were the first training to be offered, in the early 1980s, continuing those initiated by Lord Chief Justice Parker in 1963. The JSB rapidly developed residential courses for assistant recorders hearing criminal cases but civil training for deputy registrars in the county courts was not introduced until 1985. Twenty-three of the research judges were current or past trainers and some were pioneers. Continuing post-appointment training was eventually developed. At the time of the research, district judges (DJs) and circuit judges (CJs) and part-timers were expected to attend residential 'continuation seminars' in crime, family and civil work, every three years,[9] in accordance with the cases they were authorised, or 'ticketed' to hear. Attendance at specialist courses is also required of those ticketed for specialisms like fraud, 'serious sex'

---

[6]   Malleson, above n 1 at 158.

[7]   See the current annual report of the Judicial College.

[8]   Judiciary website. The first step was an annual seminar prospectus, 2010–11 'from which judges may choose those that best match their individual requirements', responding to demand expressed in a review by Professor Dame Hazel Genn. The lack of references here to prior literature reflects the fact that there is not much. There was a *JSB Journal*, until 1999.

[9]   Though from 2010, this is more fluid, as explained below.

crime and public law cases involving children. Training was geared for the lower judiciary but is now, belatedly, being offered to senior judges. All are expected to attend courses on important legislation. Specialist conferences, like that for the Technology and Construction Court, or the President's conference for family judges, will include judges at every level. In addition to JC training, judges attend circuit seminars and conferences which are also open to local lawyers. Some participate in international conferences. Any may visit practitioner or academic seminars. Many senior judges lecture or make speeches at training events, conferences and meetings. This chapter relies on interview material and observation of a one-day conference for newly-appointed recorders and an annual Technology and Construction Court (TCC) Conference.

EXPERIENCES OF INITIAL TRAINING

I asked the 77 to describe their training, before sitting part-time, and whether they would have welcomed more.

1975–82: Being Thrown in at the Deep End

The 22 without initial training told some extraordinary stories:

> We went up to the Royal Courts of Justice and spent a morning in the Lord Chief Justice's Court ... he said 'Welcome good chaps, good to see you, wish you well and now I will just give you the bones of a summing up' ... He said 'That is all you have to do ... Sentencing you don't need to worry about. You will get the feel of it. Goodbye and good luck.' ... I was helped enormously by the Bar... They ... helped me in their submissions ... I was very careful about sentencing so I would look at the current law for examples ... I would also ask other people what the range was. (CJ and solicitor, on his 1975 appointment as one of the first solicitors to be a deputy CJ. A High Court judge told the same story)

> If someone ... in your chambers was, say ... the Recorder of Salford and said 'Well actually, I can't sit next week,' he would say to his clerk ... 'Is there anyone who is up for sitting as my deputy?' ... and that person would ... find himself sitting ... as chairman [of quarter sessions]. A friend did that and his preparation consisted of writing on a bit of paper, which he propped in front of him, 'Keep your mouth shut!' (CJ; appointed deputy 1979)

> I sat in the Old Bailey ... very nerve-wracking ... completely absurd. Looking back, it is frightening how I must have disgraced the office. (UKSC Justice; recorder 1979–80)

> There was a very nice usher who looked after the deputy judges. He had ... once been a classics teacher ... and he said 'This is your notebook and at the end of the week give it back to me'. (UK SC Justice; deputy HC judge 1979–80)

A wonderful clerk here got me on the Friday evening before my first ever sitting and said 'You better just have a look at the register and see how we do it.' That was the most valuable two hours of training that I have ever had. (DJMC; judicial trainer; acting stipendiary magistrate 1982)

None whatsoever. I remember my very first case. The defendant had met one of the jury in the lavatory and had said 'Do your best for me mate!' and I had no idea what to do. (CJ; deputy 1979)

You learnt through reading textbooks. Another district judge and I were the first to introduce training for deputies … in about 1984. (CJ; deputy registrar 1978)

Early JSB Inductions—1980s

Thirty attended JSB inductions in the 1980s, mostly the three-day residential criminal course for assistant recorders. They also sat beside circuit judges for a week or two, as new part-timers still do. Three described the course as 'rudimentary' and one as 'primitive'. Six commented positively: 'fantastic', 'quite excellent', 'rigorous, tough, fairly good and it has got better and better'. Barristers inexperienced in crime were especially enthusiastic.

necessary for someone in my condition. I then had a week sitting-in with a circuit judge. These days I would have to do two. As a civil practitioner, a week wasn't enough. (HC)

quite good … for somebody who had done no crime … While I was nervous as Hell … in my first criminal case … if I hadn't been on that course I probably would have run out of the building. (CA)

I had never been in a criminal court in my life … short, sharp and intense … There were lots of people to take advice from and there was a refresher course within 18 months, then continual training. (HC)

Some experienced criminal lawyers were more cynical.

It was conducted by a High Court judge called [Hasty Ogre], who really was a very unpleasant person who frightened everybody … You have a mix of very high-powered civil advocates. In my group there was [JJ], who is one of the top chaps earning millions a year now, who thought any sexual offence, when we did a sentencing exercise, was a £10 fine but the company director who put his hands in the till and stole £10,000 was put into prison for four years … so those sort of people obviously did need to have a week of thumbing through *Archbold* and reading it from cover to cover and then they would become good criminal lawyers. For the rest of us who were just the ordinary common lawyers, I think it was very limited, apart from frightening us by Ogre shouting at us.

The course contained practical exercises, designed to alert recruits to *some* of the snake-pits in the criminal trial.

We had to prepare a jury summing up ... It involved a very complex case of recklessness ... I was told it was ex tempore but I noticed that everyone else had it all written out ... So I started extemporising ... I was totally at sea and filled with mortification ... total ... ineptitude. Some other very Ritzy judge called Nigel ... took it up and did it brilliantly and very aristocratically and I had made a hopeless case of it. So I thought the chances of ever becoming a judge were remote. (CJ, now a trainer)

When you are that age you think you know it all ... I remember [another trainee] ... we were both reasonably young ... We were both saying, because we had done the mock trial and all sorts of things happened, like people refusing to take the oath, and we had done 10 years at the Bar and nothing like that had ever happened, 'It is so unreal'. Anyway ... the very first case he did, a lady defendant, who was barking mad, suddenly ripped open her blouse and exposed herself to him! (CJ, now a trainer)

The DJ below is prominent in the Judicial College.

I was self-taught ... I was the judge who brought PowerPoint into judicial training because I was appalled to find how amateurish judicial lectures were. At the moment, I'm working on a DVD ... I'm also a 'trained trainer' and syndicate leader.

1990s to Post-millennium

The induction became much more challenging—requiring a lot of preparation and intensive work in residence but was well-received. The first comment below is from a civil DJ, appointed as a deputy in 1997 and as an assistant recorder (criminal) in 2001.

They set you work in these little tutorial groups ... You come away pretty whacked but you have been put through your paces and you are better informed ... It is also a chance to meet other judges in a very nice and informal way and ... pick their brains ... The recorder course was a bit like joining the SAS, as the only thing you didn't do was sleep under canvas. We were working from nine in the morning. With your preparation you wouldn't go to bed until two and by the time you left you could hardly drive but it was brilliant.

Sitting-up to three ... but noticing lights were on all over the hotel. (CJ, QC, 1998 induction)

Almost like doing your finals again (CJ, 1997 induction)

(1) Excellent ... the course materials ... are ... a Godsend ... (2) ... The judges couldn't have done more to help ... [especially my tutor judge] ... and (3) [when you start judging] you are not given some horrendous case. (CJ, 1993 induction)

absolutely brilliant, truly fantastic. I never learnt so much in three days since I was at university or school ... by the end ... together with sitting-in with an experienced circuit judge and prison visits, it equipped me from literally a standing start to ... start the job possibly slowly and maybe a bit pompously. (HC, 1993 induction)

Some found it daunting. The four below are women, trained in the 1990s. Three are CJs and the last was a High Court judge. She found criminal cases so nerve-wracking that she refused to conduct them.

> Terrible. I came back thinking I shouldn't be doing the job, I was simply not up to it. Very worthwhile though.

> Horrible … I was doing training in something I hadn't done for a long time and they really sort of shocked you and scared you … the training was pretty good.

> Turmoil because I appeared to be the only woman, with about 45 large egos and I really wanted to run but fortunately another girl turned up…It was a good course … I was quietly supported by the senior judge … [because] I was not one of the blokes and I knew nothing about crime … It was boozy and competitive. I did a week's sitting-in with [a CJ] and he said 'You are too nice. I am going to send you down to Inner London for a bit of rough' … I didn't feel that I had much empathy with my supervising judges. I was so worried about showing my colossal ignorance … that you don't actually ask a sensible question.

> Truly awful … all in crime and I had to go to Weybridge and it was snowing and it was a horrible hotel and the old lags' course for the existing recorders was going on at the same time … There was nobody I knew from my circuit … terrifying.

Terror was not confined to women.

> The most terrifying three days of my life since I had taken finals. (Solicitor CJ)

> a mock trial, which, though I hated it…unbelievably stressful … basically a trial from Hell … it was productive in the longer term. (QC, CJ)

> as stressful an experience as I have ever had, because it really was necessary to acquire a lot of knowledge and skill literally overnight when one discovered one was going to do a summing-up or judgment the following day … immensely competent administrative lawyers [were] stressed and pale. (CA)

> Frightening … all these people who were going to become Lords of Appeal and we arrived as specialist advocates having circles wrapped round us by these people who were amazingly bright. The mock trial was terrifying. I was told I had to do the whole summing-up. I was up till four. [Lord Chief Justice] Bingham walked into the back of the room. I thought I'd faint. (DJMC, recorder)

Despite their horror, of the 26 who first sat after 1990, 12 made positive comments (seven saying 'excellent' or 'brilliant') and six considered it satisfactory. Curiously, three of this group, all district judges (magistrates' courts) DJMCs, sat part-time, supervised by a full-timer, without any induction. This sounds horrific but it must be borne in mind that they had the benefit of a full-time legal adviser next to them, who was used to advising and running criminal proceedings on behalf of lay justices. One DJMC explained that he did not need induction training, as he was a justices' clerk. This is not surprising. Justices' clerks are the chief legal advisers to lay magistrates, on law, procedure, sentencing powers and practice. They train lay justices. Thirty-four of the 77 said they would have welcomed more initial training. Four civil DJs thought training should be more personalised, according to gaps in prior knowledge and skills. This is a clear aim from 2010–11. Three CJs would have liked more time observing other judges in varied work but now that there is a judge-shadowing scheme, any lawyer may ask to sit with an unlimited number of judges of different types.

Regardless of their date of appointment or opinions, 19 remarked that 'you only learn by doing'. For this reason, new part-timers and even some experienced judges will stop a trial and seek advice from the court's resident or designated judge. This is a part of their job. All judges will readily pop into one another's rooms or ask advice at the lunch table. Since the early 1990s, they have also had access to intranet chat-rooms, buzzing with questions and updates. Most DJs and CJs checked these at least once a day. Several thought their experience as advocates had equipped them for their role as judge.

> I practised at the Bar for 15 years. I saw judges day-in, day-out. I knew which the good ones were … you see…in a very intimate way, how advocates behave. You learn … the tricks of the trade…You do them yourself … You are working in precisely the same environment … you are just adopting a different role.

While deputy DJs and lay magistrates have an established system of appraisal and mentoring by trained, experienced full-timers, the setup for recorders, at the time of the fieldwork, was amateurish, and ripe for abuse. While shadowing residents, I learned that part of their job was reporting on new recorders. Given that the judge did not observe the recorder in court, I asked the pilot judge what evidence the resident relied on: 'Tittle-tattle from the clerks'.

INITIAL KNOWLEDGE OF EVIDENCE AND PROCEDURE

The 77 respondents were asked whether they were initially confident in their knowledge of evidence and procedure and whether, in hindsight, it had been adequate. This was asked in the light of the following background considerations: solicitors' training pre-1979 did not include evidence; civil procedure and evidence have become more straightforward since the mid-1990s but criminal evidence and procedure have become a complex nightmare. These questions provoked some interesting answers, ranging from a new HC judge who considered that you should not be applying if you were not confident, to 30 judges who thought their knowledge had been deficient. Ten were senior judges, including a Court of Appeal (CA) judge who explained:

> No … in the civil world, evidence and procedure nobody cares about. In the criminal, they care very much. Since I didn't have a criminal background, I was at a considerable disadvantage.

Two CJs, both QCs, found that, although they had been confident, with hindsight their knowledge was inadequate, 'I was far too cocky'. Three solicitors said they lacked adequate training. One CJ said that, as a barrister, he had taken advantage of this vulnerability of solicitor judges, to play tricks.

> Our favourite ... were civil district judges who sat as recorders because they have got no grasp of the rules of evidence. So if you are in a criminal case you can just play around with them.

Only 13 of the 77 judges thought applicants should be examined in evidence and procedure, although some thought training should be strengthened. From court observation, I would endorse the comments below. Indeed, proper application of the rules of evidence is sometimes routinely neglected, or misunderstood.

> Certainly a bit more attention to evidence ... For example, I think hearsay rules are operated in quite a sloppy way ... The areas of previous convictions and character are handled in a substandard way. (QC, CJ)

> There ought to be some sort of assessment ... Evidence ... is not particularly well demonstrated by advocates at our level anyway. (DJMC, former justices' clerk)

The majority replied negatively. These answers were typical.

> Controlling a court and applying rules of evidence and procedure really is practical ... You don't have to hear the advocate asking the question and then think about it and say 'Does that offend against a particular rule?' because if you are thinking at that speed, the witness has already answered the question and the damage is done and you have to discharge the jury. (Barrister, CJ)

> Anyone who now comes onto the bench will have been through continual education as a solicitor or as a barrister. (Solicitor, civil DJ)

TRAINING FOR THE FULL-TIME JOB

I asked the district, circuit and High Court judges 'Do you feel you received adequate preparation for your present job, or are there aspects of it for which you would have welcomed more training?' For the CA judges and UK Supreme Court (UKSC) Justices, I asked if they felt they had received adequate preparation as an HC judge.

District and Circuit Judges

None had received training for their *full-time* jobs. Many who missed out on induction training had attended courses later. One DJMC had attended induction after five years' sittings. Most had had continuing education. Thirty-eight of the 51 in this group considered that this had provided adequate preparation. Eleven considered sitting part-time, especially while maintaining their advocacy practices, was sound training. Another group mentioned that they had learned a lot from asking for help from full-timers.

You learn so much more from your peers … and you have had all those years of watching good and bad judges.

As a barrister, having conducted a murder case or rape, when the judge is summing-up … you are actually clocking in your head how you would approach that case. You are teaching yourself.

Of the 13 who considered their preparation deficient, two felt it was wholly inadequate. This included the High Court DJ, who criticised every stage of her training. When she was appointed part-time in 1996, she received only two evenings' training. Two judges would have welcomed more time sitting with experienced judges and the others mentioned that they would have appreciated help in specific subjects, such as IT, costs, housing, or the Civil Procedure Rules. Four said that they felt that there should be training in inter-personal skills and court control and how to handle litigants in person. It will be seen in later chapters just how much these skills are needed.

The Senior Judiciary

Although 23 of the 26 had sat part-time, (or, in one case, as a circuit judge) and most had been trained accordingly, their full-time HC jobs were significantly different so I was interested to discover whether they would have welcomed more training. Judges in the specialist divisions, family and chancery, are appointed from QCs, elite advocates, in those fields so they do not need any *legal* training, as this Family Division judge pointed out.

It was my world. I knew the work backwards … It was simply a question of adapting and adjusting. The roles aren't that different. You are a silk in the front row and your job is to capture the single arbiter … and you have to use all your skills of advocacy to get him on side … so you can move from front row … to bench … without any induction.

The problem of lack of training and preparedness arises in the generalist Queen's Bench Division (QBD). Most HC judges will have had specialist practices but are expected to become a 'Jack of All Trades', conducting serious criminal and civil trials and sitting as part of the Court of Appeal (Criminal Division). Many are expected to adjudicate in the Administrative Court, because there are never enough specialists to cope.[10] One described the problem.

I gave a party in my old chambers to say goodbye and I asked some friends who came from outside the law. One said … 'Well I imagine you go off now for three months' training?' I said 'As a matter of fact you don't'. He said 'When do you start sitting?' I said 'Tomorrow morning at half past ten'. He said 'Well I imagine then that they are giving

---

[10]   In 2010, 44 of 74 QBD judges sat in the Administrative Court. Very few will have practised in administrative law. From 2011 there is at last an induction programme for deputy HCJs in the Administrative Court but the HC judge who was most unprepared came straight from the circuit bench.

you a case of the kind that you used to do at the Bar because you know all about them'. I muttered that they don't and that I was doing an asylum case in the Administrative Court. He said 'How many of those have you done before?' I said 'None'. I know that sounds appalling … to train someone in all the range of what the QBD does in an academic way would take a very long time.

The last point is a good one but it must be remembered that HC judges do not deal with trivia. Their decisions affect people's livelihood, freedom and, in asylum cases, possibly prospects of life or death. I was accompanying the pilot judge when he was asked, with no notice, to handle a pre-trial issue in a case of misfeasance in a public office, a tort of which he had never heard. I was sitting with one of the judges below, from a criminal background, when he was allocated a case where an executive of a multi-national was sued by his ex-employer for breaching his contract by working too soon for a rival. As will be seen, in the High Court chapter, this judge readily acknowledged he was a fish out of water. Fifteen of the 26 senior judges, including those appointed to the specialist divisions, felt they ought to have been given some induction and some felt very strongly. A QBD judge, aware of the lack of training, had taken steps to prepare.

I was well-equipped for my job because I had put myself out … I had been and found people and asked advice … I had sent judgments I had written, as a deputy, to my [circuit] Presider and asked him to mark them like Greek prose. I had got one of the High Court judges to sit in the back of my court and watch me and tell me, so I don't think it is adequate. I think I was adequately served by myself and, yes, I do think there should be more and there should be some sort of mentoring system.

Another felt strongly that HC judges should receive more help and should not be expected to do everything with equal competence.

It is one of these myths about the High Court bench that you can do everything … Being shown the job by your clerk is one thing. What you need is a sponsor judge or a mentor … There is no point putting me in to do an action on a subject I know nothing about. I will do it. I might get it right but it will take me twice as long as somebody who knows what they are doing. What is the point of putting a commercial lawyer in to do a two-week murder?

This issue is addressed in the High Court chapter. Two Chancery judges, like some of the DJs and CJs, felt they should have been offered tuition in handling litigants in person. As will be seen, they need considerable help from judges. Apart from this, one family judge complained of his unpreparedness in dealing with HC emergency applications; two said they would have valued tuition in judgment-writing and the chance to sit with experienced judges, and several pointed out that the criminal cases they had heard as recorders were no preparation for the extremely serious cases they now handled as HC judges.

I remember going to try my first murder. I was infinitely more frightened than the defendant. (UKSC Justice)

I did three months of trying murders before I actually went on the course. (CA)

Three felt (one very strongly) that judges with no knowledge of administrative law should not be expected to sit in the Administrative Court. I asked a judge appointed to the QBD during the research period what his induction had amounted to but, as the reply indicates, HC judges are appointed in small numbers so fully-fledged courses like the recorder induction are impossible.

> I went to see a QBD judge who talked to me about being a judge. He gave me ... a sort of kit, with standard forms ... and things like the code for getting an international line ... Then I saw May LJ who is really the timetable monitor and we ... talked about what work I would like to do ... I find it interesting they have got an induction course ... If it was there, I would have taken it. I was sworn in on 29 April and Mr Justice T ... was sworn in the next day so it would have been a class for the two of us.

CONTINUING EDUCATION

I asked the judges how often they attended continuation seminars and whether they would welcome more such training and/or broader subject matter. All of the DJs and CJs joined residential continuation conferences lasting between two and four days. The number depended on what type of case they were 'ticketed' to hear so those who did a variety of work undertook all three types, civil, family and crime, amounting to one per year, as well as circuit and specialist conferences.[11] Tutor-judges did this over and above their own training. Welsh speakers also joined a two-day annual residential course. Only one of the 51 CJ/DJ group missed out on continuation training. *Again*, this was the HC DJ in the Family Division.

> I don't think we have nearly enough. We have one continuation seminar every three years for public law children work. I was supposed to go this year but because the President decided to have a blitz on public law work, which, incidentally, didn't work, I was unable to go ... Half a dozen of us weren't allowed to go. It means I am not going for a period of four years and I think that is wholly wrong.

Most valued continuation training.

> It's terrific for meeting other DJs ... because it can be quite isolating and you can get a bit lonely.

Nine praised the material that they downloaded from the JSB website. Nineteen suggested that continuation seminars should be shorter and annual. Only three would welcome broader subject matter.

Continuation training is not obligatory for senior judges but 18 had chosen to attend the CJ/DJ residential seminars and 15 mentioned the specialist evening

---

[11] Now, 'there is a minimum annual training requirement for all salaried judges except HCJs of four days per year. The JSB would wish to implement the same system for fee-paid judges but it does not have the resources. For them the training requirement is somewhat less' (JSB Director of Training, September 2010, by email).

seminars at the Royal Courts of Justice. (There were six in 2008–09). Only three said they would welcome more. Like 19 of the others, they suggested annual updates and three QBD judges thought continuation training should be obligatory for senior judges. Many participated in international judicial exchanges and specialist seminars where they lectured and absorbed ideas from other jurisdictions, such as this patents judge.

> JSB evening seminars … [and] once a year a three-day conference for European patent judges and European trademark judges. I go most years to the IP seminar in New York and from time to time … to other miscellaneous conferences or to give lectures.

CURRENT PROVISION

The Judicial College's current strategy and training details are in its annual report and (from 2009) prospectus.[12] It acknowledges the difficulty of evaluating the success of training. The first prospectus, 2010–11, aimed to offer judges a choice of continuation seminars, instead of standardised ones, and to move away from black letter law to the acquisition of judicial skills, though, as can be seen from the stories above, the new recorders' mock trial was ahead of its time as a challenging, skills-based session. Delivery of law updates is shifting to e-learning.[13] CJs and DJs are required to attend one national seminar a year, plus usually one day on circuit. They have piloted a much-trumpeted generic skills seminar on 'The Craft of Judging', including peer review[14] but it is not mandatory. For circuit judges who hear criminal, civil and family cases, their four days per year may be used up on one of those jurisdictions every three years so if they were to attend the judgecraft course, they would have to sacrifice one of those. Training for handling litigants in person is embedded in a variety of training exercises. In 2008, the JSB published 'a single consolidated *Framework of Judicial Abilities and Qualities for the High Court and the Circuit and District Benches* to replace the previous framework which was for the Circuit and District Benches only'. It supplements the selection criteria. The judges' version is meant to be a self-help guide. It emphasises fair treatment in every aspect of judging and explains how this is to be integrated into training.[15]

In 2009, the JSB's senior judiciary committee proposed that new HC judges have five days' training in their first year and two days thereafter and that was agreed. It piloted a three-day serious crime seminar for them in 2010, also open

---

[12] Judiciary website.

[13] Jurisdictionally specific updates, emailed to judges.

[14] According to the 2011–12 prospectus, it includes 'Assessing credibility, making a decision and giving a well-structured oral judgment; dealing appropriately with unexpected and high conflict situations in court; managing a case and giving a well-reasoned oral ruling; dealing with ethical and other problems that confront judges inside and outside court'.

[15] The judges' version is available on the website, with a shorter public version. They were developed after discussions with 500 judges and with practitioners.

to Class 1 CJs ticketed for serious crime, and the 2011–12 prospectus also contains HC seminars in civil cases and family (also open to the CJs who do most HC work). There is at last an HC Director of Training. Deputy DJs have had the benefit of mentoring and appraisal since 2002, as have lay magistrates before them. A mentoring scheme was introduced for recorders in 2009 and another has been developed for HC judges. They are given an information pack. JSB judges have discussed with the Presidents of the Family Division and QBD how to fulfil senior judges' training needs. In July 2010 the JSB explained to me that new HC judges are *offered* a flexible programme of sitting-in and visits, devised with their Head of Division and they may, as before, attend continuation seminars and the Royal Courts of Justice (RCJ) evening seminars, and they have access to e-learning and written material. The RCJ seminars are normally chaired by a CA judge and are attended by CA and HC judges.[16]

CONCLUSION

The traditional hostility to judicial training, seen as an invasion of judicial independence, set back the development of training so that while judicial colleges were developed in the twentieth century for continental career judiciaries, the JSB has only now become a (virtual) judicial college. Some of the longest-serving judges, and even three appointed in the 1990s, received no initial training. Thanks to the establishment of the JSB in 1979, the position has gradually reversed. Range, depth and techniques of training are continually improving and, in line with lay magistrates' training for more than a decade, it is geared to needs and competences. To quell fears that it would erode independence, training is done by judges, like 23 here, some of whom pioneered skills-based training because of their own frightening first experiences. It is no bad thing that training is done by judges. Watching them in tutorials and seminars, they bring their own full-time experiences to teaching. It does not matter that they are not professional educators. Judges who want to be trainers have to apply for the job and they are trained trainers, unlike, for instance, university academics of their generation, who received almost no initial teacher training and who certainly do not enjoy comparable compulsory continuation training.[17] Judges have so embraced the culture of training that it seems that at any court one visits, there will always be judges away on training courses, or away doing the training or planning a training session on circuit. This seems to be an enlightened reverse of the 1979 culture but it does take its toll on a judiciary that is already understaffed because, of course, judges who are training are unavailable for judging.

---

[16] Seminars have been held on, eg, the Mental Capacity Act and the new tribunal system.
[17] New lecturers are required to complete a one-year part-time course. This varies. It is not followed by compulsory CPD and part-timers are normally untrained.

Judges were pioneering skills-based training before it was common in professional training and now that imparting information on black letter law is to be confined to e-letters and e-learning, all training can focus on skills. Continuation training focuses directly on judges' practical needs and they do actually attend the sessions, as they are residential (and anyway, they are generally keen—several wanting more), as opposed to lawyers' continuation training which is merely nominal, generally amounting to a random offering of privately organised black letter law sessions, to which lawyers sign-in before disappearing for the day. The compulsory regime for the district and circuit bench is spelled out in transparent detail in the prospectus on the internet, organised well in advance and intensely geared to match needs and delivered by expert judges.

Though many of the judges here identified gaps in their training needs, most of these gaps have now been plugged. There are some outstanding problems. Though continuation training has just switched from black letter law to offering an annual choice of seminars, geared to needs and competences, there are budget restrictions. Criticisms identified here have not been met entirely. Training in judgecraft is limited, when one would have expected it to be compulsory and a prerequisite. For senior judges, training is not compulsory and this is an enormous gap.[18] Extremely belatedly, a sensible induction and continuation regime is at last available from 2011. QBD judges suffer from the same problem as some circuit judges. They sit in so many jurisdictions that it is very difficult to train them in all of those and they are unlikely to have time to take the judgecraft course. Worse, it is scandalous that training for the Administrative Court is only now being offered to deputies and, as we shall see in the High Court chapter, full-time judges with no knowledge of this complex field are being asked to deal with the full range of this court's work, including asylum cases.

---

[18] Many CA judges now have demanding management roles and have attended specialist courses.

7

Judges' Working Personality

THE JUDGE IN HIS IVORY TOWER

He sits and listens every day
To tales of human depravity,
The depths of man's inhumanity to man
And children subjected to savagery,
Minute by minute
And hour by hour
The diet of the Judge in his ivory tower.

The problem for the Judge is not
That he's out of touch with reality
But that he sees so much of it
Too aware of man's bestiality.

'Tis said a man can only take so much
But this man's diet has to be such
It pervades his every working hour
The diet of the Judge—in his ivory tower.

From the late Mr Justice James Hunt—sent to the author in 2004

THE CHAPTERS IMMEDIATELY following this one, that is, eight to fifteen, are the 'working' chapters, portraying judges' behaviour, their working world and their attitudes towards it. This chapter pulls together some common threads.

WORKING PERSONALITY

The way people approach their work is somewhat dependent on personality.[1] Judges outside the sample would sometimes say 'I expect you're finding we're all very different'. On the contrary, it seemed that judges' courtroom *working* personality was much more consistent than they imagined. Trial judges do not appreciate this because they do not have the opportunity to watch others. They

---

[1] Personality affected magistrates' clerks' approach to running the court: P Darbyshire, *The Magistrates' Clerk* (Winchester, Barry Rose, 1984).

were sometimes curious to know whether their way of doing things was the same as the judge next door.

A working personality refers to distinctive cognitive tendencies in an occupational grouping. It was developed in the sociology of occupations in the mid-twentieth century and most famously applied in legal systems to the field of police work, by Banton[2] in the UK and Skolnick[3] in the US. They showed how occupational environment influenced police perceptions and behaviour. When judges were told that they were much more similar than they thought, each attributed this to training, which, as we have seen, has become progressively more sophisticated. Kritzer likened judging to a craft, learned by a training process and/or apprenticeship[4] and we saw that induction training for criminal cases has for decades focused on skills. It was apparent in observing judges and discussing work that the way they did their job was also influenced by the following factors

— birth family and childhood experiences;
— education;
— experiences in practice, especially watching nice and nasty role models;
— whether or not they were a solicitor, directly serving clients, or a barrister;
— socialisation among their peer group as part-time and new full-time judges;
— status awareness and acute image awareness and the fear of catching 'judgitis';[5]
— current and domestic circumstances;
— experiences in court and behaviour of others towards them in court; and
— working environment.

Judges' similarity in 'working personality' also appeared to be a product of the pre-2006 recruitment system under which Lord Chancellors published desired characteristics and, as we have seen, judges recommended their chosen candidates in the 'soundings' system—possibly in their own image. By similarity, I do not mean universality. It is obvious that *who* judges matters[6] in terms of approach and case outcomes, otherwise there would be no need for appeals or devices to prevent forum-shopping.

---

[2] M Banton, *The Policeman in the Community* (London, Tavistock, 1964).

[3] JH Skolnick, *Justice Without Trial* (New York, Wiley, 1966).

[4] HM Kritzer, 'Towards a Theorization of Craft' (2007) 16 *Social and Legal Studies* 321.

[5] Rumpole, created by John Mortimer, 'comments on the phenomenon of "judgitis [pomposity] which, like piles, is an occupational hazard on the bench"', *Rumpole of the Bailey*, Thames Television, 1978, Museum of Broadcast Communications website. The concept spread through the US judiciary. See L Alpert, 'Learning About Trial Judging: The Socialization of State Trial Judges' in JA Cramer (ed), *Courts and Judges* (Beverly Hills, Sage, 1981) 126.

[6] S Berns said 'Gender matters, race matters, and class matters ... not as potential sources of bias but as a necessary and inevitable part of the story which is unfolding': *To Speak as a Judge* (Dartmouth, Ashgate, 1999) 8.

One High Court (HC) judge was aware that his *working* personality was not the same as his personality. Asked whether his self-image had changed on becoming a judge, he replied:

[I'm] probably a bit kinder and more sympathetic than I used to be. In my capacity as a judge I think I am nicer as a judge than I am as a human.[7]

BIRTH FAMILY BACKGROUND

I did not enquire about birth family background specifically but judges sometimes mentioned it in explaining their behaviour. One circuit judge (CJ) from a council estate said he was harsh on sentencing violence because when he was young, he would travel home on the train from Southend on Saturday nights and see people getting their heads kicked in for no reason: 'Wot you lookin' at me like that for?'[8] It was apparent that most judges were born into families who valued education, which helped them to become high achievers, regardless of class. One child of a refugee family was very sensitive to what she perceived as potential threats to judicial independence: 'I feel privileged to live in a peaceful period but you can't bank on it'. As has been seen in chapter three, childhood images of lawyers prompted some to study law.

CAREER AND SOCIALISATION AS LAWYERS

The judges' career achievements were not representative of lawyers in general. Senior judges and some CJs were ultra-high achievers, with a strong work ethic and a capacity to be focused. This sustained them in the face of long working hours. Other CJs with less demanding jobs and all district judges (DJs) remarked that their hours had diminished on leaving legal practice but most still manifested a strong work ethic.

Fifty-nine of the 77 judges were barristers. I quote at length from a passage entitled 'A cloistered profession' in Hazell's 1979 book, *The Bar on Trial*, to illustrate the hierarchical working world they had entered, years before becoming judges.

The Bar's geographical isolation within the Inns is symptomatic of a wider social and professional isolation … Many … never have lunch outside … their Inn … they have

---

[7] Judge Posner argues that judges are motivated to be and to develop a reputation as a good judge: *How Judges Think* (Cambridge, Mass, Harvard University Press, 2008) 60–61. Here, what constitutes a 'good judge' has been promulgated increasingly vigorously, by the Judicial College, so it should not be surprising that judges are anxious to behave so that they appear 'good' in the courtroom. They have the insight to separate this from their real persona, as the quotation illustrates.

[8] Magistrates' clerks often claimed that magistrates from humble origins were harsher sentencers of their childhood peers who had resorted to crime: Darbyshire, above n 1.

little knowledge of the world outside the Temple … the ranks of the Bar are drawn overwhelmingly from the middle and upper classes … they never shake hands when introduced, because in theory they know each other already … Q.C.s … not only wear different clothes … they sit in a different row…The little courtesies ('May it please your Lordship, 'I am much obliged' …) and the legal pronunciation of Latin … are the equivalent of a sort of school slang—a private language … the Bar has a clearly identifiable uniform … the barrister's fee is an *honorarium*, a gratuity … barristers are still considered too superior to discuss such mercenary matters themselves … it is against professional etiquette …

Officially the Bar is no longer the superior profession, but unofficially there is a widespread feeling that barristers are still the superiors of solicitors, both intellectually and socially … other counsel are referred to as 'my learned friend', solicitors simply as 'my friend' … when a solicitor wants to write a letter to a barrister [he has to do so] through his clerk. When barristers were consulted in 1973 over the design of new court buildings, they asked that whenever reasonably possible counsel should not be asked to share a room with solicitors for luncheon. And when a conference is held, however busy the solicitor and however junior the barrister, it is always the solicitor who comes to see the barrister … Most barristers like the importance conferred on them by their wigs and gowns … The arrogance and complacency of the Bar do more than simply create a bad impression on its clients … The Bar has consistently opposed all measures of law reform which appear to conflict with its own self-interest; and it has opposed many others simply out of conservatism and a resistance to change.[9]

So this described the cloistered London Bar which developed most of the research judges' working personalities as lawyers but not judges. Cliques in the provincial Bar were more close-knit, since it was common to have only one or two sets of chambers in a city.

Because the legal profession has suffered from repeated attacks on its monopolies and restrictive practices since 1985, the Bar's working methods have had to reform and their public image has been manipulated by PR consultants since 1980. Nevertheless, barrister-judges in the Royal Courts of Justice (RCJ) (High Court (HC) and Court of Appeal (CA)) still lunch in their Inns sometimes but are confined to an elite group of contemporaries on the benchers' table. Barristers did not and still generally do not interview clients initially[10] and until fairly recently, they were forbidden to interview witnesses. This is normally done by the solicitor. The long-hours culture, the career achievements of many judges and the need for networking added to the isolating factors of the Bar.

The passage graphically portrays professional pecking order—still a matter of great sensitivity to solicitors and solicitor-judges. We have already seen how handicapped some solicitors felt in applying for judicial posts because they did not know the 'right' judges to support them in 'soundings'. We have seen that

---

[9] R Hazell, *The Bar on Trial* (London, Quartet, 1978) 28–31. Professor Robert Hazell CBE practised at the Bar in 1973–75.

[10] Exceptions were made under the direct access scheme and the rule is now modified following the Legal Services Act 2007.

some were repeatedly re-directed down to the district bench when they were aiming for the circuit bench and how they were bizarrely 'stigmatised' with an 'S' on the trainee list. Solicitor-advocates with higher court audience rights were refused permission to wear wigs until recently. Solicitors and barristers, in trying to protect their monopolies, were locked in what became known as 'Bar wars' over rights of audience in the 1980s and 1990s and this animosity continues, with barristers asserting their superiority as advocates and solicitors resenting barristers' arrogance and the professional hierarchy, with them at the bottom and QCs at the top. (QCs are called 'silks', as they are entitled to wear a silk gown instead of a 'stuff' one.) This was exemplified by the chairman of the Criminal Bar Association at the Bar Conference 2008. He expressed concern over the 'huge rise' in the number of solicitors with higher court advocacy certificates and said some were 'truly appalling'. He said it was 'upsetting' to watch 'the destruction of the system' by 'cheap and inadequate labour'. He repeated the complaint at the European Bar Presidents' conference in 2009. This argument continues.[11] In 2010, the Solicitors Association of Higher Court Advocates objected that the Quality Assurance for Advocates Scheme relied heavily on judicial opinion and they were biased towards barristers.[12] The hierarchy perpetuates another source of conflict. The rank of Queen's Counsel has been the subject of prolonged criticism and a boycott, by solicitors, prior to reform in 2003. In a 2008 Law Society survey, over half the respondents considered that QC status 'should become a broader mark of excellence among lawyers'. Over half felt that the Society should withdraw support if the rank is not opened to a wider range of lawyers.[13] Several judges in this research complained of the arrogance of barristers they had met when practising as solicitor-advocates, or who appeared before them in court. The judicial hierarchy in England and Wales and this research sample strikingly reflects this professional 'hierarchy', as we have seen. This is a product of the pre-2006 'old boy network' selection and of the legal minimum qualifications for judges which were linked to audience rights.

Solicitor-judges considered they had gained insight from their direct contact with clients. Parties appearing before DJs reflected their former clients, from when they practiced as solicitors. Solicitor-judges sometimes had a much wider world experience than barristers. One CJ had travelled the world at a young age, taking witness statements on cargo-ships. She had been in some dangerous

---

[11] In 2010, the Law Society commissioned a report into the training of solicitor higher court advocates after complaints of incompetence by barristers and judges. The review found that solicitors' advocacy training in general was 'not fit for purpose' and must be immediately improved if they wanted to stop being viewed as inferior to barristers: C Baksi, 'Solicitor-advocate training "not fit for purpose"', Law Society *Gazette*, 16 December 2010. The online version is followed by interesting comments.

[12] P Rogerson, '"Mixed practice" warning for publicly funded barristers' Law Society *Gazette*, 2 December 2010.

[13] The survey results were reported in *Queen's Counsel Appointments* on the Law Society website.

situations, clambering into accommodation decks and going into the hold to interview injured foreign seamen. It should be emphasised, though, that there was no evidence that barrister-judges in this research sample considered themselves superior to solicitor-judges. At one Crown Court, barrister-judges praised two solicitor-judges for their ability to communicate with jurors. Nevertheless, the above description of the pre-Dickensian pecking order of lawyers must be borne in mind. Clearly, solicitor-judges carried with them the memory of being part of an 'inferior' profession.

NEGATIVE ROLE MODELS—JUDGES OF YESTERYEAR

A mere mention of this research in a judges' dining room would invoke in judges' minds the stereotype depicted in chapter two. This would trigger tales of the characters of yesteryear. These were invoked to make the point that the stereotype was anachronistic and that such eccentricities would be unacceptable nowadays.[14] In the county court, DJ Hulbert said that as an advocate, he used to adjust behaviour according to which registrar was hearing his case.

> The guy who used to sit in this chair wouldn't be appointed these days. He was mercurial. He'd suddenly lose his temper for no reason … As a judge, you've got a lot of people appearing in front of you, finding their feet, learning the job. Twenty years ago, the judge might have shown them how much he knew and how little the advocate knew but not now.

DJ Homer described idiosyncratic registrars. When he tried to hand in a form, one had said,

> 'Does it say FILING CLERK on my door Laddie? No! It says Mr. Registrar' … You used to get some characters in those days … No respect. One regularly threw the green book at people saying 'That's not what the green book says'. Another one asked you to leave if you went beyond your allotted time, even in mid-flow. He put on his hat and coat at four o'clock and left!

Another used to have his dog in the corner. Another would never take a decision. One was always making empty threats, '"Tell him if he doesn't do it, I'll nail his ears to the wall". Those were the days when a registrar said to someone, "We need a deputy. Do you want to do it?"' I asked Homer why judges were no longer like that. 'Selection, training and our own experiences', he replied. '[Cartman] and I had to *suffer* judges like that.'

District judges (magistrates' courts) (DJMCs) told stories of the criminal courts. Grumpy said that when he had practised at the Bar, Crown Court judges

---

[14]   L Alpert found Florida judges modelled themselves on judges in front of whom they had appeared. Lord Clarke MR cited horror stories told by nineteenth and twentieth century judges of their predecessors, 'Selecting Judges: Merit, Moral Courage, Judgment & Diversity', speech, 30 September 2009.

would pressurise defendants into pleading guilty because they wanted to go home. 'Judges in those days had all been in the war and were merciless'. Now they were 'massively different—very approachable'. Some London DJMCs explained 'If you'd had a good war and had no means of support then they'd make you a stipe'.

Circuit judges[15] told stories of the tetchy and irascible, or odd, or self-important 'characters'. A Midlands recorder remarked 'I'm not trying to curry favour but judges are *so* much easier to appear in front of these days'. In the south, there was a story of a cranky ex-judge who was immediately taken off judging crime when he placed someone on probation who did not consent to being placed on probation, a legal requirement. Midlands judges told of a judge whose sentencing was 'in the stratosphere' and who never read anything on sentencing. Up north, there was a description of a judge who used to have his wife, knitting, next to him on the bench. A resident (managing) judge in London explained he had written a student textbook because his predecessor sat at the head of the dining room table and 'held forth every day. No-one could get a look in'. He got bored and started spending lunchtime in his room, writing. At a second big London Crown Court one judge explained that the resident judge had replaced a 'lazy time-server'. A third such court still had a resident of the old school. 'The resident is a wanker and idle…He's never had a meeting in the time he's been here…The paperwork here is a shambles.' By the time of the research and probably because of these unfortunate appointments, resident judges' demanding managerial jobs were advertised in open competition and attracted some highly qualified CJs.

In the CA, it was explained that there used to be senior judges who would not talk to one another, who sat with their backs to one another on the bench and I watched this for myself as a 1970s student. The Law Lords told of their predecessors they used to appear in front of in the 1980s, who would be 'arguing amongst themselves'.

Judges generally told the story that they were much more approachable and that the hierarchical barriers had broken down. A CA judge said 'Thirty years ago, judges would never have spoken to administrators' and another said:

> I am now in my sixties and when I started, a QC wouldn't speak to a trainee and a judge was someone who was seen as a mini-god … My colleagues … are quite happy to mix with everyone. (CA/UKSC)

In telling such stories, judges were reaffirming their individual and collective image of themselves as reasonable, humane, modern judges who behaved appropriately. It is clear from this research that, as Posner said in 2008, 'most judges, like most serious artists, are trying to do a "good job"'[16] and one obvious comparator was the stereotype of the judge from the bad, old days. Further,

---

[15]   Many stories came from judges outside the research sample.
[16]   Posner, above n 7 at 12 and discussed in more detail at 60 ff.

Posner points out that since no-one is forced to become a judge, applicants self-select, so it is plausible that they do want to be a good judge, and to develop an image as such.

RECRUITMENT CRITERIA

By the mid-twentieth century, lawyers and judges readily complained, in print, of judges who lacked the qualities advocates sought, even naming bad judges.[17] By the time these 77 judges were appointed, Lord Hailsham had listed the qualities he sought, in 1986, in a leaflet entitled *Judicial Appointments*, as 'personality, integrity, professional ability, experience and standing'.[18] Only 14 were appointed full-time in the late 1980s. Most were appointed after 1990, 24 being appointed after 2000. By 1994, Lord Mackay LC had published unusually detailed job descriptions and recruitment criteria for district and circuit judges on the internet and, like his predecessors, he required that full-timers should have sat part-time for two years. They had to be in good health, able to 'sit and concentrate for long periods of time' and conduct themselves professionally and privately in a way that would maintain 'public confidence in the judiciary'. Candidates were required to declare anything that might be a source of embarrassment to themselves or the Lord Chancellor. They were required to have 'legal knowledge and analytical skills, sound judgment, decisiveness, communication skills and authority'. Personal qualities required included 'integrity, fairness, understanding of people and society, sound temperament, courtesy and humanity and commitment'. These requirements were highly publicised by Mackay and his 1997 successor Irvine. The assumption is, then, that these were the criteria applied in selecting these judges.[19]

DESELECTION AND SOCIALISATION—BRINGING THE ROOKIE INTO LINE

The resident judge's job was to report back on recorders, part-timers on the circuit bench, in a fairly unstructured manner. If they allegedly manifested undesirable characteristics or behaviour, the resident might swiftly draw this to their attention. Part-timers are watched from all sides—by court users, lawyers (often colleagues), by the judges they meet in court dining rooms and by the Court of Appeal. Concerns and rumours might be fed back into the recruitment process via 'soundings' with the judiciary, to block a full-time appointment. We

[17] Such as RE Megarry QC, *Lawyer and Litigant in England* (London, Stevens & Son, 1962).

[18] A list condemned by Malleson as 'nebulous' in *The New Judiciary: the effects of expansion and activism* (Aldershot, Dartmouth, 1998) 96.

[19] The criteria applied by the JAC since 2006 remain similar, with the addition of 'an ability to understand and deal fairly', and 'efficiency' (detailed). The *Framework of Judicial Abilities and Qualities* is on the Judiciary website.

saw in chapter four how the gay solicitor deputy DJ kept quiet in the judges' dining room when judges made homophobic remarks.

Part-timers are socialised into adopting the 'working personality' and occupational culture, like all workers. This was observed, first-hand. At one southern court, lawyers had protested to the resident about a recorder's behaviour. He had complained about advocates' clothing and lack of sufficient deference, as he saw it, towards him. The resident asked him in immediately. 'I told him *that* behaviour went out with the Ark.' On one circuit, in two Crown Courts, the judges were laughing about a new circuit judge. (I did not disclose that I had met him in a third Crown Court.) The local Bar had complained about his behaviour in court, where he had been similarly demanding more deference. His pomposity had led to an appeal. Coincidentally, he was based at a fourth Crown Court, where the resident, unprompted, also mentioned this problematic rookie.

> [He] is being a pompous idiot. He has already had the Bar into his room to complain that they are not bowing low enough when he comes into court. Come on! Behaviour like that does bring us into disrepute. And because the barrister wasn't there when he was in another court, he dismissed the case so they had to go to the Court of Appeal to unpick the problems!

The resident had plans for the experienced judges to tackle the problem: 'We'll all take the piss out of him mercilessly'. By the time I reached the Midlands, the story had reached this circuit's dining rooms and the judge was correctly named. Judges were highly amused, on two circuits, about another rookie who had complained that members of the Bar were not bowing low enough. Judges' dining rooms, like Bar robing rooms, are a gossip radio. Recorders and new circuit judges move swiftly round the circuits, transmitting stories. Many judges are email addicts so tales spread instantly. The errant rookie may thus find that any manifestation of judgitis results in the resident reminding him of cultural and behavioural expectations but behaviour like this can generate a life-long reputation among lawyers and judges on all six circuits.[20] With deputy district judges, appropriate judicial behaviour was affirmed by a well-developed formal appraisal and mentoring system, which includes full-time judges observing them in court.[21]

---

[20] Shetreet produced a whole chapter on the Bar as a mechanism for checking judges. He said 'The most important means of control is through informal social and professional pressures, exercised both by individual barristers and by the collective action of the Bar' (at 225), through the Inns of Court, chambers and Bar circuit messes, which is an accurate description of the position today: S Shetreet, *Judges on Trial* (Amsterdam, North Holland, 1976).

[21] Extended to recorders, since the research.

KEEPING JUDGES IN LINE

In 2004, the Judges' Council produced a *Guide to Judicial Conduct*,[22] explaining the practical implications of the requirement for independence, impartiality, propriety, equality of treatment, competence and diligence. These were laid down in the Bangalore Principles of Judicial Conduct, initiated by the United Nations in 2001. All judges here receive equal treatment training and a substantial handbook.[23]

Civil judges commonly remarked that they drafted their judgments with the Court of Appeal in mind. Similarly, Crown Court judges would try to make jury directions 'appeal proof' by asking both sides to comment on a draft. In a manslaughter case, one spelled out his reasons for sentencing and asked counsel to comment, explaining, 'I'm doing this for the benefit of the Court of Appeal', though another Crown Court judge, who constantly contemplated the CA, found it somewhat unpredictable 'You might get Lord Justice Commercial and Mr Justice Motorway Inquiry'. The CA is vigilant in quashing decisions involving bad behaviour as much as mistakes of law. Its language in castigating discourteous or partial judges has become more exasperated and unrestrained in recent years. All judges are aware of this, which may explain why there are so few such appeals. In 2005, one judge, who has since retired, was the subject of three highly-publicised appeals. In one case he demonstrated his preference for the prosecution case by rolling his eyes, throwing down his pen during the defence and treating prosecution witnesses much more politely;[24] in another he told defence counsel she was being silly, in front of the jury, and showed personal animosity towards her and questioned her integrity.[25] In the third, he told defence counsel, in front of the defendant and before hearing from the prosecution, that he had 'never heard of such rubbish' as the defence version of events.[26] Research judges were conscious of these cases, drawing attention to the newspaper reports. *R v Cordingley*[27] was another in which the CA said a Crown Court judge 'should be ashamed' of his rudeness and discourtesy.[28] If judges use inappropriate language or behave badly in a way not connected with the conduct of a case, an aggrieved person can complain to the Office for Judicial Complaints. In 2009–10, two members of the mainstream judiciary were removed.[29]

[22]   Judiciary website.
[23]   ibid.
[24]   *R v Patrick Bryant* [2005] EWCA Crim 2079.
[25]   *R v Lashley* [2005] EWCA Crim 2016.
[26]   *R v Dickens* [2005] EWCA Crim 2017.
[27]   [2007] EWCA Crim 2174; report and comment at [2008] *Crim LR* 299.
[28]   1970s judges could not get away with unlimited bad behaviour, as Shetreet explains, examining appellate and other checks.
[29]   Its annual reports contain no information on the nature of complaints.

'JUDICIAL QUALITIES': COMPONENTS OF THE WORKING PERSONALITY

The judges were asked an open question, 'What personality traits do you consider to be desirable in a judge?' With hindsight, they should have been asked about 'qualities'. Nevertheless, judges had clear ideas and answered as if it had said 'qualities'. Forty listed patience, 30 fairness/objectivity/lack of bias, 28 humanity/ sympathy/understanding, 22 the ability to listen, 22 decisiveness, 20 courtesy, 17 firmness/ability to control proceedings, eight sense of humour, seven humility/ not arrogant/not pompous, five efficiency/organisation, four clear communication.

Asking an open-ended, unprompted question meant that judges did not list as many qualities as they would have done by reference to a list. The answers were more revealing, however. Examples included:

> Calm and good humour … avoid being irascible or too hot-tempered or too quick to interrupt…patience and tolerance … [when you've] been sitting listening to the same litigant in person for the last forty-five minutes making the same incomprehensible point (CA/UKSC)

and from a civil judge:

> robust, able to take control when necessary … don't jump to conclusions … patience, to listen and don't just try and listen to what you want to hear but what they are trying to tell you. You then have to be able to take in large quantities of fact, juggle it round in your head, sort out the wheat from the chaff and make a decision. Right or wrong be strong. Make it clear what you are doing and lay down the law.

A Crown Court judge conducting jury criminal trials emphasised:

> Humanity … the one thing a judge should say to him or herself every morning is that all people are equal, wherever they come from and whichever part of the court they are sitting in.

Judges manifested qualities that they did not list. Very kind judges would not necessarily list kindness, nor funny judges a sense of humour. Below is a discussion of the main characteristics observed in this research, which can be tested by anyone observing a wide variety of judges.

Patience

Within the first week of the first pilot study, I realised I would never have the patience to be a judge. This was the most important quality they listed. Judges' patience sometimes made me impatient. They normally remained calm and polite in the face of repetitive and irrelevant litigants in person; grossly inept advocacy and lack of preparation; impolite advocates who routinely did not take responsibility for their failure to produce or exchange evidence, documentation and skeleton arguments; bombastic, aggressive or argumentative advocates who had to be warned repeatedly about their inappropriate behaviour; warring parents bound up in self-centredness; rudeness and lack of respect by court users; and routinely poor tools such as inadequate computer hardware and software, defective video equipment and poor office backup caused by underpaid, untrained staff. Judges' patience was striking. When asked why they had tolerated a waffly litigant in person, or had not admonished an advocate, or stopped a cross-examination, judges normally had a reasoned explanation, such as giving a litigant in person 'a fair crack of the whip', or not wanting to place an advocate in a bad light in the view of their client. Court staff would sometimes remark on the patience of judges. An HC judge's clerk said that while his judge 'might get out of his pram here in this room', over irritating events, he was faultlessly patient with the litigants in person who populate the Chancery Division.

Courtesy and Kindness; Good Humour; Lack of Judgmentalism

Judges were generally more polite than some advocates were to them and markedly more courteous than many parties. Jurors are usually struck by the courtesy of judges. They took great care to put jurors and witnesses at ease. Judges were normally courteous in the face of court users' neutrality or discourtesy. Not *all* judges were unfalteringly kind. One addressed defendants tersely by their surnames and spoke sternly when a juror's mobile phone rang. I saw only one display of judicial ill-temper. This involved a judge who was not in this sample, who allowed me to sit with him. He shouted at a barrister who arrived late, keeping all court users waiting. He repeated his complaints despite her repeated apology. He later explained that he was disappointed to sit as a criminal judge, which he considered to be a waste of his expertise in commercial law. He served for a very short time and has since retired. Some judges extended their kindness outside the courtroom, routinely befriending staff, even the most junior, and daily enquiring of individuals' welfare, taking an interest in personal problems, health and family. This research indeed was dependant on judges' kindness and courtesy. Senior judges and judges' group representatives spent hours helping to set it up. Judges' kindness, courtesy and good humour was striking.

Most of the judges appeared to be unnaturally unjudgmental over stories that would have outraged some news columnists, especially those writing for the *Sun* and the *Daily Mail*. Lawyers have to develop objectivity, otherwise repugnant criminals and claimants would not find anyone prepared to represent them. Modern-day judges are required to behave in an impeccably objective manner in court, otherwise the appeal courts are swift to castigate them. As will be seen from the jury chapter, judges will not deliver biased summings-up of the evidence, whereas this was common in former times.

Listening Skills

Only 22 mentioned 'listening skills' but another striking quality observed was their ability to listen very attentively and to absorb testimony. While observing each Crown Court judge, there was at least one incident where a question arose as to what someone had said, days earlier in a trial, or the judge would have to correct lawyers' erroneous narrative. Judges were swift and accurate in intervening to paraphrase what had been said, later substantiating this by reference to their notes. They always remembered testimony much more accurately than lawyers. Listening skills had become a natural part of their makeup and were manifest outside the courtroom too. In everyday conversation, judges normally looked the speaker in the eye, listened without interruption, then responded in a way that showed they had listened, not just heard. This ability was so striking that other people's lack of listening skills became noticeable, during the research period.

Ability to Absorb, Analyse and Apply Written Information

All senior judges and some CJs performing High Court work have to pre-read massive bundles of documentation, including reported cases and technical experts' reports, as well as lengthy skeleton arguments. In court, they demonstrated that they had absorbed and remembered this and they often corrected the advocates whose material it was.

Diligence

As will readily be seen in the 'working' chapters, the senior judges, some circuit judges and the family judges had enormous workloads, which required long hours before and after court, pre-reading and writing judgments, plus weekend work.

THE PERSONAL IMPACT OF BECOMING A JUDGE

The judges were not asked what qualities they thought they had but how becoming a judge had impacted on them, allowing them to describe their working personality:

Did becoming a judge alter your

a. self-image?
b. attitudes towards other people?
c. attitudes towards society and the legal system?
d. behaviour, in any way (eg spare time activities)?

Self-image

Thirty-two said their self-image had not changed. Twenty-nine said they had become more confident or were pleased with themselves.

> It gave me more self-confidence because I knew I didn't have to be nice to judges anymore. I can't tell you how dreadful it was going to these dinners and having to be polite to people, knowing they could ruin your career—also being nice to people in the LCD, wondering why I had got drunk at Bar Mess and said to a judge who had just been appointed to the circuit 'This is your reward for twenty years of mediocrity', when everyone had just wished him congratulations. I didn't know why I had said it.

Several women clearly lacked confidence before appointment, such as 'I suppose it was an external endorsement, that you can't be such a hopeless person' and 'Yes because for the first time in my life somebody had decided that I was good enough'. One CA/UKSC judge whose parents had looked down on him and his wife said:

> I was very pleased … My wife and I both had … difficult childhoods and it was quite nice to sort of feel that 'that showed them!' So I felt I had got somewhere that I didn't expect to get.

One male CA/UKSC judge who had difficulty entering the Bar and was very self-effacing said:

> For the first few years I would pinch myself and say 'now you are a judge', like, having moved to the Court of Appeal, I quite often get asked what I do and I say I am a High Court judge and then I remember that I am not.

Eight said appointment had made them more self-conscious.

> I changed. I think because I was aware of my position, I was more careful. I would avoid situations of being aggressive, if you like, to a shop-keeper with whom I might have fallen out or something like that, whereas previously, as a litigation solicitor, I might have been pretty aggressive … I'm always frightened of abusing my position.

One CA/UKSC judge, as previously mentioned, underwent an astonishing change, leaving a decadent lifestyle to become an internationally renowned rights campaigner.

> it changed me radically … I necessarily had to become much more responsible, … serious-minded … committed. The advocate is permitted a degree of personal irresponsibility … I don't think the judge has the same liberty. I have probably become quite dull and boring to lots of people who thought I was quite good fun when I was a silk.

Attitudes Towards Other People: Humanity

Forty-nine thought these had not changed and 20 said they had. Fourteen said it had made them more understanding or compassionate, or less judgmental and/or introduced them to a broader section of society:

> more fair-minded, perhaps less prejudiced or bigoted and less inclined to have entrenched views, because one comes across a whole series of problems, a whole plethora of parts of society ... much wider ... than in my specialist area, [commercial law]. (CA/UKSC)

> You think much longer and more carefully. You are not so much judgmental ... If you leap in and you are over-hasty ... that is bad. (DJ)

> more aware of other people and their needs ... people who were more disadvantaged. (CJ)

Some of the 49 replied that becoming a judge had not altered their attitudes because legal practice had already broadened their experience and taught them not to be judgmental. For instance, a family judge said she was already used to dealing with 'hopeless, vulnerable people' and a Crown Court judge said:

> [Some barristers] develop a sort of professional patois. They sometimes talk about their clients and [their] level of society as 'pond life' and I find that very distressing because I think if you ... cease to have some sort of respect for people that is very damaging. You can be critical but if you despise them that is awful. It is inhumane really ... it is very important that judges should be conscious of the very real difficulties that so many other people have.

This book is peppered with stories of judges' humanity. In 2000 and 2010, two samples of 50 DJs were tested on left/right and authoritarian/libertarian scales. Forty-eight scored within the left-wing, libertarian quartile.[30]

Attitudes Towards Society and the Legal System

Thirty-three said becoming a judge had not changed their attitudes towards society or the legal system, though again some answered that being in practice had already 'opened their eyes'. A judge known for his left-wing views as a barrister said:

> Attitudes towards society haven't changed at all. I like to think I am radical politically with a small 'p' ... If anything, you come up against government in some of its more unattractive forms in this job, particularly if you do ... a lot of asylum work. (HC)

---

[30] DJ G Edwards, 'Judges and other right wing fascists', *Association of HM DJs Law Bulletin*, 22(1), Winter 2010/2011, 22. He warns that the respondents may not be representative.

Eleven said they had become more critical of or 'worried about', or cynical about the legal system, aware of its shortcomings or lack of resources.

> My attitude to the legal system has changed; I am appalled by it. I think it is so much worse than it was and I am so concerned with the lack of ... resources. I see people suffering a lot. (CJ)

Nine said they had become more thoughtful or knowledgeable about 'the way things work'. For instance, an HC judge had not appreciated the number of litigants in person who might appear in front of her, 'a hugely difficult and growing problem'. By definition, paid advocates are unlikely to be aware of the population of unrepresented parties. Nine had become more 'protective of' or 'defensive about' the legal system. Most added that they were more aware of its shortcomings:

> You find yourself becoming defensive ... if people say it is all terrible, the cases take too long, juries are hopeless and similar ... criticism.

Six said they had become more critical or aware of government policy.

> I saw the effect of government policy on housing and deprived people. And that profoundly affected me ... It opened my eyes to a world which I didn't really know existed. (DJ)

Six were more aware of social problems, such as drugs, bankruptcy, and family violence.

> I am definitely more streetwise ... Some of the things I come across are quite appalling. (DJ)

> Yes. By reason of the large volume of family work that I deal with that includes children whose circumstances are largely unfortunate, and a large number of parents whose behaviour is extremely damaging ... a lot of cases with ... horrendous allegations of violence ... I see it as a very major problem on a national basis, with not very many signs that it's either in the public eye or is being addressed in an adequate way. (DJ)

One CA/UKSC judge said being a judge had made him more 'left wing': 'I used to be a Tory'. One circuit judge compared his 'buccaneer attitude' at the Bar with the moral responsibility he now felt:

> Towards society, I feel more protective ... more of a responsibility ... I wouldn't tell [judges] around the lunch table that I feel this way ... because it is a sort of sissy thing to say...but I do feel you have a duty to do what is right, rather than what is right for the client ... I am the voice of the public to some extent ... I am very aware of the fact that what I am doing could have repercussions ... Some would say you become more pompous but I think you become a lot more aware of the importance of what you are doing.

Self-importance

The quotation above captures the social responsibility judges feel. There was a fear of being 'pompous'. Judges very commonly used this word. Twelve used the word 'judgitis' in answering these questions. It was mentioned at most courts.[31] Judges feared that they or any judge might catch it, and let the side down, and this led to the scorn and ridicule of the pompous rookie judges above. Several mentioned that their family would 'take the piss' out of them, to inoculate against self-importance.

> I am not by nature a person who has airs and graces. Lots of judges do suffer from a disease called judgitis. (CJ)

> you can lapse into judgitis … There is a risk that you are so impressed with your ability to reason that you have to share that with everyone … we have enormous powers over citizens. (DJMC)

> there is a propensity to become pompous, but I don't think my family would allow me to, as I get ridiculed at home. (DJ)

> It is very hard not to change, not to become pompous and authoritarian outside of family … I have got children in their twenties who are extremely rude to me and disrespectful and haven't changed their behaviour one bit. But you spend your days laying down the law and sending people to prison and doing awful things. (HC)

DJ Homer chose his codename because he was wearing his Homer Simpson boxer-shorts when he was sworn in, 'as a protection against catching judgitis'. An experienced CJ said he always told an anecdote, in training. He warned new recorders that if they were going to get cross in court, they had better memorise the courtroom layout. He told the story of a judge who flounced crossly out of a busy courtroom, into the broom cupboard. He had to stay there a long time, over lunch.

Behaviour Becoming of a Judge

Sixty had changed behaviour, doubtless cognisant of the requirement that they conduct themselves professionally and privately in a way that would maintain public confidence in the judiciary. Nine said they were careful not to break the law by speeding or drink-driving. Eleven had given up visiting their local pub or *El Vino's*, near the Royal Courts of Justice.[32] On the other hand, one UK Supreme Court (UKSC) Justice said he made a point of visiting his local pub weekly, and talking to strangers on buses, in order to get over his natural shyness. Four said they were more careful about drinking, two having given up 'drinking or dancing

---

[31] In a 2002 Radio 4 programme, experienced judicial trainers, Kay LJ and Judge Dick Pollard explained that judgitis was the occupational hazard of self-importance, caused by the erstwhile gregarious advocate suddenly finding themselves working alone and isolated from colleagues' criticism. If unchecked, a judge might start doing things they hated judges doing when they were at the Bar: *Inside the Judiciary*.

[32] Shetreet, above n 20 at 65, 'Another barrister is said to have been excluded from the bench on the grounds that he was a most frequent visitor to a public house near the Law Courts'.

in front of lawyers'. Two were careful not to dress scruffily in the supermarket and two had given up swearing. Two circuit judges had given up clubbing and casinos but two went clubbing during the research period (to the disgust of wives), as had a CA/UKSC judge, in breach of his intentions. One CJ said she was careful not to attend parties where drugs were taken. One gave up chairing club committees, one gave up acting and 'dressing up' in musicals, moving to a backstage role. Four gave up charity roles such as mediation, free advice, taking children on holiday or acting as trustee. By contrast, others had ramped-up their charity work, two noticing that their judicial status helped enhance fundraising. Four gave up active party politics and five more said they were careful not to comment on politics. Twenty, mainly DJs, mentioned that the job spared more time for family and recreation. One new judge (who had probably watched too much *Judge John Deed*) assumed judges would be monitored:

> I am well aware that various parts of the system are interested in propriety and ethical behaviour of a judge so ... I am probably monitored and observed covertly because I am a judge. My husband says that is the beginnings of paranoia.

JUDGES IN THE OUTSIDE WORLD: THE SOCIAL IMPACT OF BECOMING A JUDGE

The judges were asked whether becoming a judge had had an impact on their relationships with family, friends, and former colleagues and acquaintances, and strangers' reactions. Fifty said there was no impact on their relationships with family. Fourteen said their family laughed or 'took the piss', seven said they were proud or pleased and five experienced some negative reaction. Fifty-nine said there had been no impact on friendships, eight said friends were 'amused' or 'took the piss' and seven mentioned a negative reaction, such as, 'I think I have lost one set of friends…because they feel uncomfortable and I am really surprised by that. I feel embarrassed about [being a judge]'. Another found 'girlfriends' husbands' were intolerant:

> some of the husbands from where we live don't like working wives and particularly women judges ... They try and argue with you sometimes, seeing if they can better you.

The biggest impact was on the relationship with former colleagues, with 54 mentioning a distance from practising lawyers: 'I never went back to the [solicitors'] office'; 'I made a conscious decision not to go back to chambers'; 'It has to change. You can't be seen having a drink with lawyers'.[33]

---

[33] Alpert found that social isolation from attorneys was a key social adjustment: Alpert, above n 5 at 120.

When I left chambers we were all a very friendly bunch and everybody was saying 'you must come back and see us' and you say you will but you don't … You know that you are different animal and you shouldn't … I feel uncomfortable about it.

For most judges, the question on acquaintances' and strangers' reactions did not apply because they would not disclose to a stranger that they were a judge, preferring to pretend they were a lawyer or civil servant. No two responses were the same. One senior judge found his knighthood could get him upgraded to club class on an aircraft but another said his elevation to the judiciary had not persuaded his builders to provide a better service. Civil DJs complained that people did not understand their job and inevitably asked how many people they had sent to prison that week. One woman used it as a 'secret weapon … At dinner parties people ask what does your husband do and I just play along, but sometimes I will just come out with it'.

Isolation

The solitary life of the trial judge, responsible for conducting the hearing and taking crucial decisions, and being in the courtroom limelight, was a stark contrast to the camaraderie, banter and teamwork of the lawyer. While most judges made up for this, chatting and joking to court staff and colleagues outside the courtroom, the life of the peripatetic DJ portrayed in the county court chapter, tannoying-in his cases and only able to speak to other judges over the phone, was indeed a lonely one. There was no question on loneliness in the interview schedule because it is a cliché but judges sometimes mentioned it, like the new solicitor-recorder in chapter four, surprised by loneliness, and these circuit judges.

> There was a withdrawal period, because the camaraderie at the Bar is a remarkable thing and so at the end of the day you could go down into the robing room, take off your wig and say 'Do you know what that silly old fool did out there today' and really let off steam. As a circuit judge … you couldn't. … I was the only judge sitting in the court centre, perhaps for 70 or 80 per cent of the time.

> Suddenly, as a judge, you realise you are answerable to no-one … if I had finished work at half-ten, I could just … drive home and for quite some time after I became a judge, I felt that I had to stay until 4.30 and tell somebody I was going to go home … There are other changes … you are on your own; no-one comes into the room unless they knock and when you go into a room everyone stands up—that sort of stuff.

> What I then discovered was how lonely it is … I think it was six months before I met the resident judge. There was one judge I was introduced to at … one of the sets of chambers and someone said 'of course you two will know each other, you both sit in Citytown' and I said 'No I don't know him' and I think that is quite sad. Chris [former resident] did quite a lot to change things and Fred … has ensured that people do enjoy going to lunch now and you do meet people … quite pleasant, because it is a lonely job.

You miss your mates, even with the people in front of you, you can't say 'come round for a cup of tea' … so it is quite nice when a trial comes to an end, to perhaps be able to say 'come through for tea'. I don't know whether they enjoy it or not but for us it is an opportunity to chat.

FAMILY LIFE

Judges often mentioned family issues or events so information was gleaned in this way and from *Who's Who*.[34] Sixty-two of the 77 judges were married with young children or adult children. Only four had never married. Nine were childless. Five were divorced or separated (four with children) and a further eight had been divorced. Two were currently widowers who had had children and two more had been widowers with children from that marriage, who had since remarried. Only one was overtly gay and living with his partner. This disproportionately high number of ostensibly 'happily marrieds with children' reflects a tacit policy by the Lord Chancellor's Department during and prior to the Mackay years to appoint those in stereotypically 'safe', stable relationships and an overt policy to exclude gays from the judiciary that lasted until the 1980s.

Seven had suffered the death of a child. Three of the male judges spoke at length about the profound effect this had had on them. One showed me a life-size photograph of his son and we discussed this before he could talk about anything else. He described how this had altered his career. He applied to be a local circuit judge, cutting short his career as a high-flying barrister, often away from home. One judge's son died during the research period. A third said the experience helped him in being a judge, 'You know what a strain it is, having a sick child'. Three judges were busy carers, one for her disabled husband and two men shared the care of special needs children. At least five had been brought up by single mothers, three of whom were widows.

Judges' experiences and family ties affected their working lives, world view and capacity to understand people or issues. For instance, when I remarked to one interviewee that jurors found waiting irritating, he said he was used to it himself, having spent hours in Great Ormond Street Hospital with his special needs daughter. One judge presided over a rape trial and out of court appeared to become increasingly disturbed at the evidence of casual sex and binge drinking at a nightclub that had been frequented by his daughters. Another judge said outside court that he sympathised with police officers who had to rummage through restaurant bins for evidence in another rape trial:

When my wife ran a restaurant it was my job to take out the rubbish and clean up the bins on a Sunday night. People just chucked stuff all over the sides and it attracted flies.

---

[34] I asked DJs direct questions on family ties because they are not in *Who's Who*.

One family judge said her husband had walked out on her and her children, 18 months earlier. She wondered if it affected her approach to family cases. One judge bristled defensively at my labelling her care case clientele as being in a cycle of deprivation: 'My Grandad was unemployed all his life. My Dad only escaped 'cos he went into the forces in the War'. Judges with children made frequent references to families, discussing the chore of getting children to revise for GCSEs, or 'A' levels, and proudly showing new graduation photos. Work was juggled around children and grandchildren. Two male judges refused to travel to distant courts because they insisted on dropping their children to school. Two HC judges travelled to circuit early on Monday mornings, not Sunday nights, as they wanted to spend the weekends uninterrupted with husbands and children. Another HC judge listed 'babysitting' his grandchildren as one of his hobbies. Several, mostly male, took half-terms off. One CJ had little sleep during the research. Overnight, one of his grandchildren was rushed into hospital and he and his wife drove over to babysit the siblings. Another, sitting at a court remote from his home, got a call from a school when his 16-year-old was injured. The child had emergency surgery before he could get there. He did not interrupt his trial. In the CA, one presider started work at five every day to free up time to visit his dying family member in hospital. Judges took regular calls and emails from children. One HC judge took repeated lunchtime calls from her teenage son about car insurance. She did not explain to him that she was part-way through a demanding case and was trying to spend the whole of lunchtime sorting out IT shortcomings. As explained, judges with teenage or young adult children claimed that constant 'piss-taking' and disrespect was an antidote to self-importance and some said their families made them do servile tasks. Apart from the bin-cleaner above, one CA/UKSC judge said he was required to clean the family farmhouse floors every Sunday. One judge served behind the bar in her husband's pub and ran the quiz night. 'I've got a karaoke machine, a pink one.' Judges sometimes remarked how their family kept them in touch with outsiders' views of the legal world. Most had spouses and adult children who were not lawyers.

So, family life impinged on work but equally, work impinged on family for some CJs and all senior judges who spent some weekends and evenings writing judgments and pre-reading. Nevertheless, work did not extend to influencing family relationships and identity outside, in ways that the sociology of the police demonstrates that police work affects private lives. Judges were usually keen to separate their identity. Fifty-one would not admit to a stranger that they were a judge, unless forced. Two women lived in the villages where they had grown up. 'No-one at the pub would know I'm a judge when I'm there in my jeans. Some local taxi drivers know I'm a judge but I never told them.' Another CJ ran the real ale club at his village pub for years before his friends discovered he was a judge. One DJ described how she encapsulated her judicial identity:

> You think you are going to become frightfully pompous but I suppose having two teenage children there is no question of that ... I work under my maiden name and as

soon as I go home I am Mrs B. I have this split personality. I find it very easy to switch off from being a judge and become a mother, wife, housewife, whatever ... I think some girlfriends at home, whom I became friends with when I was taking my break [to have children] find it a little difficult. Some say 'Can't you come to lunch today' and I have to say 'Well no I can't' ... They just don't understand.

This generation of judges were in the TV audience laughing at Rowan Atkinson's 'What is a digital watch' judge. In the Royal Courts, an HC judge was keen to dispel the image of privilege: 'We have to come to work on the Tube like anyone else—smelling people's sweaty armpits'. The Law Lords and other senior judges in this research also walked or cycled to work and, like other middle-aged folk, some rode motorcycles. Like their Cabinet counterparts, these judges came from the dope-smoking generation. One HC judge said I should have asked judges if they had smoked cannabis. Plenty of them, he said, would openly admit it. Judges suffered mishaps and were victims of crime like anyone else. One judge was burgled during the research and in the Old Bailey I was introduced at tea-time to 'Judge D-I-Y'. He waved his plastered limbs and laughed, 'I fell off the draining board'. Judges were always aware of and often titillated or irritated by media portrayal of their cases. Several had wives who read the *Daily Mail*, the judges' greatest irritant. 'According to them, we can all go around shooting burglars. *She* reads it. We live in different worlds'. A CA judge turned up to a pre-trial deliberation with a copy of *The Metro*. 'This is what *The Metro* says about the case but according to my wife's *Daily Mail* we should...' provoking laughter from the others.

The time-lagged image of the judiciary is 'huntin'-shootin'-fishin'' but these judges were much more mundane. When asked what they did in their spare time, judges listed 59 activities, from embroidery and beekeeping to fencing and flying, most of which were not solitary and did not involve mixing with judges or lawyers. The most popular was walking (21), followed by gardening (18), music (17), travel (16) and kids/family (15). Only 15 listed football but these were the hard core fans, several of whom held season tickets and attended matches every week. One travelled from the south coast to watch a northern team every fortnight with his father. Other than this hard core, many others, including three women, followed team progress and would join in the continual football conversations in court dining rooms. Next popular were theatre (14), reading (11), golf (9), opera (8), school governor/charity work (7), tennis (7), cricket (6), socialising (5) and cinema (5). Many ran or did keep fit or went to the gym but most did not list these as leisure activities.

Judges were sensitive about their out-of-touch image and one seemed to have internalised it as a self-image, without apparent reason. 'I seldom get the chance to meet ordinary people' he said. This was bizarre. He was born in the Welsh valleys, into a working-class family. He lived in a formerly industrial town. His wife was a teacher. They had four children. He was a school governor. They were heavily involved in their church and charities. He went to local football matches and the gym. He spent his days in the Crown Court steeped in tales of dishonesty and depravity.

JUDGES' CHARACTERISTICS

Trying to describe what judges are like is dangerous but it is one of the aims of this book and hopefully the reader will gain an impression from the following chapters.

Old, White and Male

In accordance with their public image, judges are predominantly white and male, as can be seen from the statistics on the Judiciary website. They are much older than their counterparts in countries such as France with a career judiciary, trained from graduation, and the elderly appearance of male judges is exacerbated by wigs.

Not Party Political But Politically Aware

Whereas it was very common in the early twentieth century for judges to be appointed as a reward for party political services, or to have combined the Bar and a Parliamentary seat,[35] modern judges in England and Wales are scrupulously apolitical, unlike some other judiciaries. Four had been party-politically active, as lawyers. Two London CJs had served as councillors, one Conservative and one Labour. Despite this, they unwittingly shared radical attitudes on the disadvantaged and such issues as poor housing and the lack of legal aid. The Conservative had been active in the Legal Action Group and the other was currently very busy chairing a housing trust. Two northern judges, the only judges in their court, had both stood for Parliament, one for Labour and one as a Conservative but, watching their behaviour in court and interactions with civil servants about court management, one could not detect a hint of difference. Local lawyers said they both had 'a tendency to judgitis' but both were 'very kind'. They said the Conservative had married a social worker, known for her left-wing opinions, and spent much of his spare time in charity fundraising.

I never heard a judge express a *party* political opinion. As many had said in their interviews, they were scrupulous not to do so. Nevertheless, because of the nature of the cases that occupied most judges, as will be seen from some of the quotations later, not a week went by without an out-of-court attack on some

---

[35] JAG Griffith, *The Politics of the Judiciary* (London, Fontana, 1977).

social problem caused by government: the lack of legal aid or social housing, plight of litigants in person, lack of provision for drug users, under-resourced agencies such as the Crown Prosecution Service (CPS) and probation service, the appalling low pay of court workers, poor court resources, bad housing, unfair treatment of asylum seekers, lack of support in family breakdown, lack of attention to deprived children and/or child abuse, public confusion over the benefits system, and social exclusion. Publications such as the district judges' *Bulletin* reflect these concerns. It often carries a column written by a representative of Shelter, the homelessness charity. Some judges felt they had become radicalised by what they witnessed in court. Politicians' failure to appreciate judicial independence angered judges.

Three everyday examples from the field notebooks illustrate this. In the pilot study, I was walking over to Middle Temple with an HC judge for lunch. We bumped into another HC judge, carrying a copy of *Private Eye*. My judge asked what the other was up to. He said he was hearing a cluster of judicial review applications challenging government treatment of asylum seekers. 'It's a disgrace! Do you know they come to London and they have *nothing*? Nowhere to sleep and they can't get benefits. They go knocking on the door of the Home Office but by then it's too late.' In a county court, two London circuit judges were highly critical of their poor court facilities. 'Well', said one, 'if you send missiles to bomb Iraq, you can't afford another usher, can you?' In a Northern Crown Court, a judge was pre-reading evidence in response to a public interest immunity application prior to a manslaughter trial of staff at a care home. 'This'll be the scandal of the future—how we treat old people now. The police are not bothered. The cases are not sexy and lots of victims are dead or old.'

Happy

Almost all 77 were very happy. Two CJs were bitter, disappointed not to be doing more challenging work. One was a commercial lawyer, who found himself hearing general county court cases and another was a civil lawyer who was a designated civil judge (managing judge) who found most of his time allocated to the demands of serious crime in the Crown Court.

Middle class and Well-heeled

Though some judges claimed to be working class—the ones from Welsh mining communities and London and Midlands council estates—of course they were middle class by dint of membership of the legal profession and the middle class tastes that university education (usually) and decades of practice had given them, despite not supplanting the passion for soccer. One of the council estate lads liked port-tasting and another, who called himself 'working class', had a passion for dangerous (and expensive) sports. The ambivalence of their class and cultural background is quaintly illustrated by this taxi-driver-cum-circuit judge's complaint: 'I thought Glyndebourne tickets were expensive till I bought a ticket for the Tyson fight'. Similarly, at least four judges originally from council estates sent their children to independent schools. Almost all the senior judges and a third of the circuit judges had been Queen's Counsel and so had had a large earning capacity and had taken a massive drop in earnings to join the bench. Nevertheless, judges are well-paid and they perceived themselves as well-paid. Judges who campaigned for better pensions were generally criticised as 'greedy'. As discussed before, judges' accents tend to be centred on received southern pronunciation, acquired at the Bar, though I noticed that a recorder with a posh accent was excluded from the conversation in an Essex court dining room.

Funny

The Bar attracts some show-people with a skill for witty banter and/or a delight in practical jokes and they carry these characteristics onto the bench. A popular activity in the corridors of Royal Courts of Justice and the dining rooms of some Crown or combined courts was banter and laughter and a few judges used humour in the courtroom to good effect, to ease tension. Several were natural comedians. Counsel and jurors were smiling in anticipation of entertainment as soon as they walked in. The straightest judge could crack-up everyone, especially jurors, with a one-liner, such as very politely and calmly requesting that an indictment be re-drafted 'in something other than the Star Trek version of the English language'. This is not to say that all judges were a barrel of laughs.

IT Literate

Contrary to the quill-pen image, almost all were IT literate and some were trainers of 'legacy judges', the cute name for those who were not. Most chose not to take laptop notes of evidence. They took longhand notes, leaving their laptops out of court and thus probably giving the court users the impression they were IT illiterate. By the research period, IT proficiency was a requirement for some posts. For example, a CJ could not progress to resident (managing) judge without being fully IT literate.

INTERFACE WITH THE PUBLIC

An increasing number of civil cases involve litigants in person (LIPs), sometimes on both sides. In the criminal courts, DJMCs are trained to 'engage' with young people in the youth court, discussing their offending behaviour, and in the

Crown Court some judges took a pride in engaging directly with defendants. Crown Court judges speak directly to the jury at the beginning and end of a trial, instructing them on the law and summing up the evidence and, in order to put them at their ease and express the state's gratitude, most judges did a lot more than merely communicate the essentials in a clinical fashion. While solicitor-judges are used to talking to ordinary people as clients, this skill has to be learned by some barrister-judges. Judges at all levels often demonstrated more sensitivity to witnesses' and defendants' needs than the advocates and would readily insist that advocates address parties, especially non-native speakers, in plain language. One CJ addressed a rape defendant in Turkish. He invited me to 'Imagine what it's like being in his shoes—an asylum seeker from a Turkish village. Imagine what a culture shock it is to him. He won't have had time to make friends'.

Court users' behaviour that would have provoked castigation in the 1970s was tolerated. If a mobile phone went off, a judge seldom batted an eyelid. Some explained that lawyers had to be in and out of court using their phones all day. One circuit judge said a magistrate's phone had gone off on the bench. Another trumped this story—his own phone had rung. Judges were used to court staff and users exposing bare midriffs or sporting baseball hats. A circuit judge was happy for a homeless applicant with a bad back to lie down in the courtroom. Judges were used to occasional rudeness, especially from the unrepresented. A DJ said an 'ex-army type' had called him 'an upstart', complaining 'I get much better service from the High Court'. Judges are faced with emotional outbursts. Cases have drastic consequences for liberty, livelihood, home repossession, relationships and crime victims. Murder cases attract Greek choruses supporting victim and accused. Judges need to remain unruffled by tears and tantrums, verbal and sometimes physical attacks on other court users, and themselves. Court users do not represent a cross-section of society and many need very careful handling. Many are disadvantaged by poverty, low intelligence, homelessness, ill health, mental illness, learning difficulties, immigrant or asylum status, lack of English, or a combination. The purpose of equal treatment training, mentioned above,[36] is to provide information on religion and belief systems, and a guide to treading sensitively among issues of gender, race, children, disability and sexual orientation. I asked 67 whether they had benefited from such training and how, if at all, it had affected their approach in court. Of the 58 who had been trained, opinion was divided. The training and handbook provoked some strong and some mixed reactions. There were 41 positive comments and 27 negative. This ambivalent reply was typical.

> We learnt quite a lot about the ethnic minorities ... I believe, as do most of the judges here, just to be courteous to everybody. If you are doubtful of somebody's belief or how

---

[36] 45 CJs now act as community liaison judges: see F Gibb, 'Out of Ivory Towers and Into Mosques', *The Times*, 26 June 2007.

somebody might want to be addressed, just ask ... So although I did find the training very interesting, I think the benefit was marginal. (CJ)

Many understood the need to alter judges' understanding and approach, though doubted the efficacy and execution of the training. Indeed, many praised the factual information but considered their training, involving interacting with ethnic minority guests, to be a waste of time. One (married to someone from an ethnic minority) said the training was 'farcical'.

> I didn't feel it was at all useful ... a bit of a PR exercise ... one of the telling moments was when one of my colleagues who is black turned up and was immediately shunted off by the organisers to the ethnic minorities group who were the guests—pathetic! ... it is good that people keep trying ... I was on a JSB course ... an elderly judge made the most outrageous racist remark and he just looked stunned when I said 'You can't say that' ... The problem was about an Asian family and about the impact of the child's ethnicity on how you might determine the residence application and he made an 'all Asians are' type remark and it was derogatory. I wanted to report him but didn't ... everybody in the group was prepared to back me up. (CJ)

> We went to [A] Hotel and though we all lived within three or four miles of it, we all had to stay the night. They invited people from the ethnic minority communities and we had a dinner ... to get to know them and then ... the seminar the next day ... The lady I was twinned up with was ... a professor of law. What the benefit was is very hard to imagine. The fact that she had a different colour skin made not a bit of difference. She was just like me. (CJ)

Of the judges who were in favour, one said he felt he was a typical modern judge—he thought he did not need it because he was politically aware but clearly he did need it. Like many judges, he remarked on a change in judicial behaviour in the recent past:

> The difference from when I started at the Bar [1970s] ... is indeed extraordinary ... I saw an LJ treating a black litigant in person appallingly. You could see the other two LJs trying to hide under the seat as he shouted at him ... 1979 or 1980. He was a decent man but he had a very short temper ... These days somebody would have reported him. (CA/UKSC)

When he started as a judge, he said male judges had a typical 'public school boy' attitude to one female. He said some female HC judges were accepted because they behaved in a 'laddish' manner.

Public Deference and Respect

The judges were asked, 'Since you commenced legal practice, have you noticed a change in attitude towards judges by court users?' One pilot judge said people would walk into court carrying cans, if you let them. By 2000, the front row of his Crown Court public gallery had been taped off because of people throwing missiles. In the Court of Appeal (Civil Division) there are paper signs facing court users—signs of the times—warning against chewing gum, consumption of drinks and sweets, use of mobile phones, recording equipment and iPods. Lack of respect sometimes causes lack of restraint. In the Crown Court, I noticed that lawyers would not normally apologise to the judge for failures of pre-trial preparation on the part of their 'team'. In the CA, much of the grovelling language portrayed by Hazell, in 1979 had gone. Some experienced barristers would address the CA bench as equals, as if they were in a business meeting: 'Well, you've heard my submissions on constructive trusts. I don't think I can take it any further'. Fifty-three reported a change in attitude, with 13 adding that less deference was 'not a bad thing'.[37] They often linked it to the change in judicial behaviour and/or remarked that people were generally less deferential to those in authority:

> Yes ... court users are perhaps a little less fearful of judges than they once were but judges are a little more sympathetic ... and less likely to bully or humiliate the court users. (DJ)

> Less respectful but again less terrified by the judges and there is some advantage to that. I think people are much cheekier than they used to be but again that just reflects society. (DJ)

> Yes but only to the same extent that the public attitude towards teachers or doctors and any other professional office has changed. People are a lot more challenging of people in so-called authority.

Thirty-two reported this observation in neutral terms, such as:

> In common with just about everything else, I think there is a reduction of formality. The number of times the defendant will say 'cheers mate' to me. It is not worth getting cross about. (DJMC)

Civil DJs took informality in their courtrooms for granted. 'Quite often in small claims we will find [unrepresented parties] having a slanging match across the bench' but eight judges commented in negative terms:

> I would never ever have answered back ... or shown the fact that I disagreed with their sentence ... Now [lawyers] will argue with you and tell you that you are wrong. When I was in a Saturday court, one CPS chap, very cocky ..., got so bad he was almost shouting at me and interrupting me. (London DJMC)

CA judges were not more insulated than other ranks and they, too, were happy to be perceived as human.

> People are a lot less frightened and consequently less respectful. It is both a good thing and a bad thing. I don't object to people knowing that I am perfectly ordinary ... In the Family Division, a care case, I took children away from this couple on a Friday afternoon. I went off [to Sainsbury's] ... I was in my scruffy jeans ... wheeling my

---

[37] Of the judges interviewed by Wice in 1980, some cited declining respect: PB Wice, 'Judicial Socialization: The Philadelphia Experience' in Cramer's *Courts and Judges*, above n 5.

trolley round. I came across a member of the Bar who said 'Hello judge, strange to see you here', at which point from right behind me I heard this voice behind me saying 'Look, there is that fucking judge!' and it was the couple. We had this conversation and they were perfectly nice.

Parties' readiness to challenge authority was manifest in complaints about judges. They resorted to complaining once they found out that appealing would be costly. At one court, judges were alarmed that staff had festooned the building with instructions on how to complain about a judge but not about how to complain about court staff. Some disgruntled users did much more than challenge judges in court or complain. Members of the campaigning group Fathers 4 Justice have brought their campaigns to court houses and onto judges' front lawns. Examples are described in the family chapter. Fuelled by the media sensationalism, members of the public would write angry letters about sentencing. I watched a judge open one: 'You are off the planet ... May the Lord save us from weak, pathetic, misguided "judges" like you! The late Lord Goddard would have turned in his grave.'

CONCLUSION

The description of real judges in this chapter needs to be matched against the media and comic stereotype in chapter two. The purpose of the chapters that follow this one (eight to seventeen) is to sharpen that image by providing a lot more detail and setting the judges against the backdrop of their working world. The stereotype judge is old, white, male, pompous, outdated, part of an old boy network of the educationally privileged, who are out-of-touch and class biased, sexist, racist, homophobic and prone to insensitive comments, who is up to hanky-panky or drunk or perverse and gets off lightly for misdemeanours, is soft on sentencing and so on. As we saw, judges were bought up with Rowan Atkinson/Peter Cook lampooning and the 'out of touch' mantra and absorbed it like other members of the public.

Judges told yarns of the 'characters' of yesteryear, especially bad judges who fitted the negative stereotype, reaffirming their image of themselves as the antithesis of the folk-devil. They saw themselves as reasonable, humane and modern. As part-timers, they had been watched by practitioners, by full-timers and the CA. They knew the impression they gave would influence their chances of appointment. Simultaneously, they were adopting the 'working personality' and adapting to the occupational culture. Judges shared a fear of 'judgitis'. Rookies who acted pompously were derided and became the subject of widely-broadcast gossip. Full-timers were kept in line by the CA and superiors. Judges are undeniably older than European judges and more white and male than the population upon which they judge. They were a product of a strictly hierarchical profession, in which barristers were a close-knit coterie and solicitors were made to feel inferior. Solicitor-judges resented the arrogance of barristers but barrister-judges in this research did not consider themselves superior. The judicial hierarchy reflects the legal hierarchy, with solicitors at the bottom. We will return to this.

Judges' working personalities were much more similar than they thought, thanks to training and to the recruitment system that targets specific characteristics and that permitted judges to recommend people in 'soundings'. We have seen here that working personalities were influenced by past and present work and home experiences, socialisation as judges, status and image awareness and the fear of becoming self-important. Contrary to their irascible image, judges listed patience, fairness, humanity and listening ability as the most important qualities, alongside courtesy, firmness, humour and humility. Judges' patience, listening skills and courtesy were striking. Compared with the anachronistic image, their leisure activities were mundane: walking, gardening, music, travel, family and soccer. On appointment, some had changed their behaviour, being careful not to break the law, by speeding or drink-driving; others had given up the local pub, or *El Vino's*, or behaviour such as clubbing, social drinking and activities in social organisations.

Unlike their predecessors a century earlier, they were careful never to comment on politics. Being lawyers, the judges were, by definition, middle class, regardless of any boast of humble origins. The sample contained a very high proportion of happily marrieds with children, reflecting decades of 'safe' recruitment. They experienced parenthood as any other parent does but astonishingly, seven of the 77 had suffered the death of a child. They were involved in the ordinariness of family life. Two thirds said becoming a judge had had no impact on family or friends, whose teasing, especially by contemptuous teenagers, fended off self-importance and pomposity.

In deep contrast to the out-of-touch image, the judges were strikingly concerned about social problems because these were displayed before them every day in court. They were scrupulously party-apolitical but many were outraged by the effects of government policy on the courts and court users, notably the socially excluded. Strong views were expressed on the dispossessed—views traditionally associated with left wing politics. Individually and en masse they opposed government policy from the (unspoken) liberal left. Some said that joining the bench had radicalised them. Judges were *much* less judgmental on human frailty than the news media, unabashed by courtroom stories that would have sent the *Daily Mail* into fits of self-righteousness. Some acknowledged that they had become more compassionate. Surrounded by horror stories and poor judicial working conditions, all but three judges were nevertheless very happy workers.

Contrary to their rude image, judges were much more polite than court users were to them. Some commented that diminishing deference to authority was a good thing. They ignored behaviour that in the 1970s would be perceived as a contempt of court. They had mixed feelings on equal treatment training, acknowledging the need but criticising the execution. Most judges thought attitudes towards other people had not changed, though some said legal practice had enlightened them.

The modern judge, then, only matches the anachronistic stereotype that has stuck in the public mind to a limited extent. They are not privileged and upper-class and are far more in touch with social problems than 'ordinary people' and much more empathetic than the journalists who criticise judges.

8

Criminal Business: District Judges in the Magistrates' Court[1]

Here, it's like *easyJet*. You turn up and take off.

BACKGROUND, SAMPLE AND RESEARCH METHOD

THIS IS THE first chapter examining judges at work. Here, three very different district judges (magistrates' courts) (DJMCs) are portrayed. Like county court district judges, they are at the bottom of the hierarchy but they are the important judges to most court users. These DJMCs, as we have seen, have traditionally been cut off from the mainstream judiciary, because they were seen as a type of professional magistrate and not called 'judge' until 2000. Their courts were not managed by the same body as others until 2005–06. They were not overseen by the Senior Presiding Judge in the circuit system and they were recruited and trained separately.[2] To a significant degree, they were and are culturally distinct.

The English and Welsh legal system is unique in that about 95 per cent of criminal court proceedings take place in magistrates' courts[3] where most cases are heard by lay justices. Some are heard by these professionals, formerly called stipendiary magistrates. They too are Justices of the Peace and have the same powers.[4] They sit alone or, occasionally, with two justices. All magistrates are very powerful because they are judges of fact and law (guilt and innocence) and they do the sentencing so they perform the functions of both judge and jury in the Crown Court. Additionally, many Crown Court defendants are sent there by magistrates. Very importantly, almost all young offenders appearing before a

---

[1] An earlier version of this chapter appeared as 'Cameos from the World of District Judges' (2006) 70 *Journal of Criminal Law* 443–57.

[2] The JSB provided training but now the DJMCs can choose from the diet of general JC courses, like all other levels of judge, and mix with them in training.

[3] 1.64 million defendants in 2008. Business has decreased since 2004, replaced by fixed penalty notices (FPNs): 108,400 in 2008. Source: *Criminal Statistics, England and Wales 2008* (Ministry of Justice, 2010) esp ch 5. Portia said her workload had decreased because of FPNs. In August 2009, she telephoned to say that there was nothing listed in her court, Court 1, that day.

[4] A few are also authorised to hear terrorism and extradition cases.

court[5] are tried in the youth court, within the magistrates' court. This is a significant jurisdiction, as the peak age of convicted indictable offenders is 17.[6] The proportion disposed of by magistrates has increased recently because magistrates have been instructed to accept jurisdiction even in rape cases. Magistrates also have a substantial civil jurisdiction, especially in family cases. Family work is discussed in chapter twelve.

For centuries, criminal business has been shifting down from the higher courts but that trend accelerated in the twentieth century.[7] Magistrates' courts can now deal with causing death by aggravated vehicle taking, all but the most serious assaults, most sex offences, most burglaries, thefts, frauds and forgeries, arson, all drugs offences, perjury, betting and gaming offences and most firearms offences. Prosecutors prefer to bring cases in the magistrates' court because proceedings are much cheaper and the conviction rate is higher. It should be obvious from the statistics that magistrates' courts hear some very serious matters but some more senior judges and the public think they only deal with trivia.[8] Centuries ago, jury trial was much more common. A defendant really could be hanged for stealing a sheep. Despite its factual decline, the more melodramatic jury trial is still portrayed by the media as the *normal* criminal trial. If people are asked to describe a court, they describe the Crown Court.[9] 'The public know little about how the magistracy works ... (and) hugely underestimate the proportion of cases heard in the lower courts.'[10] Textbooks concentrate on jury trial. Parliament and the senior judiciary tend to develop the law on the assumption that jury trial is normal.[11]

Justices have been commissioned to keep the monarch's peace in their locality since 1195. Stipendiary magistrates were introduced into eighteenth-century London because of corruption among lay justices and the lack of police force.[12] Until 1964 they replaced lay justices in London, in everything except very minor crime.[13] Owing to this history, most Inner London cases are tried by DJMCs. In Outer London and the provinces, most are heard by lay justices. Stipendiaries outside London were appointed to meet perceived local need, normally in metropolitan areas with a large caseload but sometimes in rural areas, where they sat with two justices. Only after the Access to Justice Act 1999 were they made into a single stipendiary bench, each having jurisdiction throughout England and

---

[5]   Many are disposed of by way of a reprimand or final warning: 97,900 in 2008.

[6]   Magistrates can impose 24 months' detention and training on 12–17 year olds.

[7]   1990s legislation shifted down even more business: *Criminal Statistics*, ch 5.

[8]   P Darbyshire, 'An Essay on the Importance and Neglect of the Magistracy' [1997] *Crim LR* 627; D McBarnett, *Conviction* (London, Macmillan, 1981): 'the ideology of triviality'.

[9]   H Genn, *Paths to Justice* (Oxford, Hart Publishing, 1999) 230–33.

[10]   A Sanders, *Community Justice* (London, IPPR, 2001) and see R Morgan and N Russell, *The judiciary in the magistrates' courts*, Home Office RDS Occasional Paper 66, 2000, para 5.5.2.

[11]   Darbyshire, above n 8.

[12]   T Skyrme, *The Changing Image of the Magistracy* (London, Macmillan, 1979), quoting Jackson.

[13]   From 1964, lay justices were reintroduced.

Wales. They became known as district judges (magistrates' courts) in 2000. In 2010, there were 143 full-time DJMCs and 151 lawyers sitting part-time, as deputies.[14] DJMCs and lay justices are advised by a legal adviser, a magistrates' clerk, who *may* but need not, be a barrister or solicitor. (No other type of judge has a legal adviser.) The chief legal adviser, normally in charge of a group of courts, is known as a justices' clerk.[15]

There are two very useful research reports analysing how stipendiaries (DJMCs) were used, compared with lay justices. In *The Role and Appointment of Stipendiary Magistrates* (1995),[16] Seago, Walker and Wall found:

1. Few courts had rules for allocating work to stipendiaries.
2. There was a striking difference between their work and that of their deputies, who were kept away from more complex cases, especially in the provinces.
3. Metropolitan stipendiaries heard contested cases almost twice as quickly as provincial stipendiaries.
4. Most of their judicial work was everyday cases but they also heard long, complex or highly publicised trials and they had a heavier caseload than lay justices.
5. Stipendiaries dealt with all types of work more speedily than lay justices.
6. Lawyers considered that speed, efficiency and legal expertise made them preferable in some cases.

In 2000, research by Morgan and Russell was reported in *The judiciary in the magistrates' courts*.[17] They found:

1. All professionals sat in court around four days a week, rarely with lay justices.
2. Work allocation was the same as found by Seago et al.
3. Professionals' hearings involved more questioning and challenging.
4. They showed command over proceedings and would challenge parties responsible for delay. Adjournments were less likely to be applied for or granted.
5. They were more likely to refuse bail and to use immediate custody as a sentence.[18]
6. They relied very little on legal advisers.
7. Court users had more confidence in professionals. They were seen as more

---

[14] Judiciary website.
[15] P Darbyshire, *Darbyshire on the English Legal System*, 10th edn (London, Sweet & Maxwell, 2011) ch 14.
[16] P Seago, C Walker and D Wall, *The Role and Appointment of Stipendiary Magistrates* (University of Leeds, Centre for Criminal Justice Studies, 1995).
[17] R Morgan and N Russell, above n 10.
[18] Supporting departmental research and SS Diamond 'Revising Images of Public Punitiveness: Sentencing by Lay and Professional English Magistrates' (1990) *Law and Social Inquiry* 191–218.

efficient, consistent in decisions, asking appropriate questions and as giving clear reasons.

8.   Lawyers admitted to preparing better.

I sat with the three DJMCs for three or four days each, in a variety of work, in their range of courthouses, in 2004–05 and have continued to sit with at least one, every year since then. They are codenamed here Portia, Guy and Pole.[19] They were chosen because of their geographical spread and range of experience.[20] Portia, newly appointed, sat in a busy Inner London court. Pole, with 13 years' experience, sat in two outer London courts and one in Inner London. Guy, full-time for six years, sat in three provincial courts, one of which was in a high crime city. Three additional interviewees represented the same variety. I arrived at court before the day's business and lunched each day with all judges at those courts so was able to speak casually to eight more DJMCs. I sat in court next to the judges and retired with them. They commented continually.

WORKLOAD

DJMCs are expected to spend 215 days per year on judicial business. One interviewee said he sat for 240. Morgan and Russell found that sittings averaged 196. While Portia and the other novice spent most of their time in court, the senior four were involved in alternative 'judicial business', such as prison adjudication, judicial training and recruitment. Guy spent around four days per week at his three courts and the fifth on other judicial business. One interviewee spent 50 per cent of her time on such jobs as appraising and selecting deputy DJMCs. Like Guy, she sat as a Crown Court recorder for four weeks per year.

THE CONTRASTING WORLDS OF PORTIA, POLE AND GUY

Portia sat in an ethnically diverse, high crime area. Confirming Seago et al, she found her new job significantly different from her part-time sittings.

> It was a big shock…I had always sat in [Countdownshire] … 'Serious' down there was an ABH … Here, 'serious' is a drive-by shooting; it is drug related; it is multiple rapes and quite a lot of this is in the youth court … the pressure of dealing with the heavy sort of crime that you get round here did start to take its toll on me.

She had developed a stress-related illness in her first year. London DJMCs are well-known to work at a fast pace, as the research above confirmed. 'One day I

---

[19]   Portia chose her codename. I chose the others.
[20]   I knew from experience that courts were highly diverse: P Darbyshire, *The Magistrates' Clerk* (Winchester, Barry Rose, 1984) and see 'Legal Pluralism' in RB Flemming et al, *The Craft of Justice* (Philadelphia, University of Pennsylvania Press, 1993).

had 136 "bodies" through my court. In the Crown Court they think they're busy if they have six up for sentencing in a morning.'[21] Like several DJMCs, she felt other levels of the judiciary were ignorant of their work. At her first Lord Chancellor's Breakfast, Portia had asked Charlie Falconer LC to come and watch her court for a day but 'He blanked me'. Young, sleek and chic, her appearance was exceptional in 'the mags', home of the drug addicts, the disaffected and the deprived. It marked her out as the person in charge of the court, as did her authoritative demeanour. The clientele differed from the more benign miscreants of Countdownshire and brought with them the problem of keeping order in court. One afternoon in her first month, she was surprised by the trial of a National Front member for a racially aggravated offence.

> He did his utmost to run rings round me ... I remember feeling really tired ... he kept repeating the racist comments that he was alleged to have made ... Every time I interrupted, he would shout out and point his finger at me and say 'You are just part of the system. You are here to make sure that I get a fair trial' ... I put him downstairs ... It was part of a big learning curve for me.

Another first year challenge typified stories heard at other London courts.

> We have another group here, Commission for Truth and Justice ... a group of black residents ... they latch onto to any case that involves a black person...They don't recognise the authority of the judiciary ... They will bring a McKenzie friend ... The whole group ... will sit in the gallery, a very ... confined space at the back. They will not stand up when you walk in. They will interrupt proceedings and outside ... you can hear drums banging ... just to make the point to the local community that they are here and they don't recognise us ... that was another shock for me, because people don't behave like that down in Countdownshire ... As much as you try and do a great job and be fair and even-handed with them, they will not give you the same courtesy back ... If you start talking about contempt or you start telling them that they have got to stand up when you come in or to take their hats off, you could have a riot on your hands ... You then have the problem of when you finish the case and you leave court ... to get on your bus, they are all at the front of the building.

I mentioned that a barrister colleague said that he found the front steps of the courthouse cordoned off as a murder scene. 'Oh just the one murder?' reacted Portia, 'We've had six here before now'. In 2009, the police had searched outside the building and found 25 hidden knives. Her court was in the middle of junior gangland. Her lists were filled with youth knife crime, child drug-runners and gun-runners and youth gang rapes.[22] One day there were armed police in the

---

[21] See K Mack and S Anleu, '"Getting through the list": Judgecraft and Legitimacy in the Lower Courts' (2007) 16 (3) *Social and Legal Studies* 341–61, on Australian professional magistrates. Half of all matters were completed in two minutes and 20 seconds. The need to satisfy time constraints threatens due process values: M King, *The Framework of Criminal Justice* (London, Croom Helm, 1981).

[22] A Fresco, 'Girls accept gun running and rape as price of joining gangs', *The Times*, 26 October 2009.

building, acting on a tip-off that rival gangs planned a shoot-out. She did not venture out at lunchtimes. She demonstrated the disguise she used for travelling by bus to her flat.

> I do look like a bag lady...the scruffiest coat ... shoes...[like trainers]...a long hood which I pull up ... and ... a scruffy old hat right down over my eyes ... I put my glasses on and take my contact lenses out.

She got off the bus if a public order incident broke out, as occurred during the research period. Despite all this, Portia loved her job.

> It is something I think I am good at ... I had a number of years in the magistrates' court both as prosecution and defence ... I have ... watched decisions [when] I don't think the public have been treated properly ... and now I am in a position where I can treat them properly. I can say 'please' and 'thank you'. I can be hard but I can be fair or firm ... I like the legal points and I have had a number of judicial reviews which I have been successful on. I had this nine-handed robbery trial last week with all the points of law which I really enjoyed getting my teeth into.[23]

I asked what aspects of work she found most satisfying.

> Being able to make a difference and being able to show the public that the court system isn't necessarily against them just because they are a defendant in the dock; that it is seen as an impartial place and that I am not on anybody's side.

Portia sat in the youth and adult courts. Occasionally, she escaped to a country court. She shared her caseload with four DJMCs, and lay justices. The youth court was her passion.

> A lot of the kids here come from hopeless backgrounds—been in care since they were babies. We had kids who were regularly injected with heroin by their mother. Three boys. What a waste. They were bright boys, lovely. The mother's had three more kids since. We're not supposed to put people in detention and training because they might learn how to become criminals but I send people away and they come back better fed and disciplined ... Kids have more allegiance to their gang than their family. They have no respect for the court. They love being tagged. (2009)

I first sat with her in 2004. By 2009, she despaired of parents and had become cynical about the youth justice system. A 15-year-old, accompanied by his aunt, pleaded not guilty to kicking-in his mother's door. They argued. Portia asked if he could go home. Apparently not. The boy said he did not have his father's number. Portia needed proper information. 'I cannot render a 15-year-old homeless.' She asked the Youth Offending Team (YOT) to help. 'I'm not a social worker.' Afterwards she explained to my American students:

[23] A repeating theme is that judges say they want to do a good job, explored in the previous chapter.

It's not my job but morally I cannot leave a 15-year-old sleeping on the street tonight. Parents here abrogate responsibility. When you were kids did your parents call in the police? I wonder if we're using the right system. In this case, in New Zealand there'd be a mediation meeting with specialists. Mother and child should resolve it. Trying him for criminal damage will cost thousands.

Pole had been a magistrates' clerk in a high crime city,[24] then a provincial justices' clerk. After 35 years in magistrates' courts, nothing unnerved him. He was 'ticketed' for the adult crime, youth and family courts. I sat with him in family proceedings so there is less to say here. He recollected his first year as being a strain but, like one of the interviewees, was glad to be rid of the managerial job of justices' clerk. 'The first few months I had never worked so hard. I spent some of my time in a court which had a big backlog of cases which was horrible. It was exhausting and I had a rather long commute but I loved it' but being a DJMC 'beats working for a living'. I asked what he found most satisfying.

> intellectual satisfaction in doing a job well … human satisfaction … that people leave feeling they have been fairly treated.

Several DJMCs sat at his Inner London court. In Outer London, he shared the case load with lay justices. His criminal lists were not as burdensome as Portia's, though one of his courts was a 'robbery hotspot'. The most striking thing about Guy, apart from his kindness and capacity for making everyone laugh, was his love of the job.

> It gets better all the time … Here, the staff treat you with respect. [They are] fantastic. The solicitors have been wonderful and the job is just stimulating … There is nothing negative I can say about it … Every day I say I am the luckiest man in the world to have this job.

He enjoyed the variety. His case lists were not as overcrowded as Portia's but his experience solidified his confidence and he thrived on the speed of proceedings, the *summary* nature of summary proceedings. He liked the absence of pre-reading to prepare for cases, compared with his Crown Court practice at the Bar. 'Here, it's like *easyJet*. You turn up and take off.' He was the most senior DJMC in his court group and devoted energy to ensuring that everyone was treated considerately, staff and court users alike.[25]

---

[24]   I had work-shadowed and interviewed him as a research subject three decades earlier.

[25]   Clerks, in *The Magistrates' Clerk* (Darbyshire, above n 20), kept saying 'this court runs on goodwill'. Guy emphasised the importance of keeping everyone happy. *The Craft of Justice*, like the 1970s American sociologies and like McBarnett, Carlen and King in England, refers to the court community, 'the courthouse is a workplace for people with common occupational backgrounds … norms and common understandings develop [forming] … a local culture … etiquette and courtesies encouraging cooperation', Flemming, above n 20 at 10.

THE YOUTH COURT—OUT OF SIGHT, OUT OF MIND

Since only the gravest of youth crime is sent to the Crown Court,[26] the youth court, hidden from public view and rarely reported on in the media, deals with some very serious cases. Portia was cynical about the appropriateness of the child-friendly forum for near-adults tried for serious offences such as gang violence and rape. 'You might have a 17-year-old. The informality's lost on them.' Portia's colleagues told me that one London DJMC called the youth court 'The Snake Pit' and another, 'The Church of the Fifth Chance'.

First Morning with Portia

Defendants were sometimes accompanied by their solicitor and parent or guardian. Portia made a point of thanking them, as did Pole. The diverse local population[27] contrasted with Guy's white court. There was a white Crown Prosecution Service (CPS) representative and usher, and six members of the YOT, of mixed ethnicity. A mixed-race clerk sat near Portia. Almost all the solicitors were white, like Portia, and most defendants non-white. I include timings to portray just how 'summary' summary justice is, in a DJMC court, despite the seriousness of some charges.

10.15 am Criminal Damage

A tall, 16-year-old black boy was arrested the previous night. His solicitor explained he was 'turned in by Mum'. Portia asked if 'Mum' might wish to drop the charge. Always frustrated with her powers, she commented aside: 'This is just the sort of problem you get in the youth court. You can't keep a 16-year-old in custody with no previous'. She sent him back to the cells to await Mum.[28]

10.20 am Possessing an Imitation Firearm

Portia spoke directly to the defendant, a brown 17-year-old. DJMCs and magistrates are trained to 'engage' with young offenders. In the 1970s, I observed that they did this naturally, before the jargon was invented.

> You're 17 aren't you? I can't believe you did this. Walking around with a gun. I'd have been terrified if I'd seen that. London is full of police in this day and age of terrorism … [She explained the eight-month referral order she was imposing]. This means you're

---

[26] See *CPS v SE Surrey Youth Court* [2005] EWHC 2929 (Admin).

[27] Skin colour is included here to depict its diversity. I did not guess ethnicity from appearance. Terminology is the same as Barack Obama's 'black, white and brown', in speeches on the White House website. See K Sharma, 'Race and the Criminal Process: Breaking the Mould to Ensure Accurate Ethnic Monitoring' (2002) 66 *Journal of Criminal Law* 541.

[28] 'Mum' is used here, copying court vernacular.

going to go before a panel and they'll decide what to do. [Later, she said she found it difficult to explain referral orders 'cos you don't know what the panel will do'].[29]

10.23 am Failure to Stop

A black 16-year-old appeared unaccompanied. He was caught driving a car. Portia asked him why he thought the police stopped him. 'Cos they recognised me.' She emphasised the seriousness. 'You have no insurance. This means if you hit someone the person couldn't get compensation.' She imposed a six-month disqualification and a £50 fine.

10.27 am Threatening Behaviour, Pre-trial Review

There were eight police witnesses. Portia listed it three months ahead. Aside to me: 'You see what delays we have here?'

10.34 am Trial Rescheduling

10.36 am Fixing trial date

A solicitor took 30 seconds to confirm he had received disclosed evidence.

10.39 am Driving with Excess Alcohol

A black 15-year-old appeared with his frazzled-looking white Mum, a widow. Portia asked the boy why he was unrepresented. He thought he did not need a lawyer. She asked Mum why. 'Because he is guilty and just wants to get it over with.' This typified the 'get it over with syndrome' some of us identified in the 1970s, where unrepresented defendants are so anxious to get out of the criminal justice system, that they do not share the court's concern (and legal obligation) to ensure that they are legally guilty of the offence charged.[30] Portia protested to Mum.

> But these excess alcohol cases can be complex and I don't know how a 15-year-old can be confident he can understand the technicalities. I can't. If I just put it back till 11.10, that's only half an hour so it won't delay you that much … *Please*. It'll put my mind at rest. Just tell the caller you want to see The Duty. He'll be outside.

Mum smiled and thanked Portia and they departed to find the duty solicitor.

---

[29] See M Lynch, 'Preliminary Notes on Judges' Work: The Judge as a Constituent of Courtroom "Hearings"' in M Travers and JS Manzo, *Law in Action—Ethnomethodological and Conversation Analytic Approaches to Law* (Aldershot, Ashgate/Dartmouth, 1997) 122. Judges' lectures invoked a communal morality and were a punishment in themselves.

[30] Darbyshire, above n 20 at 176–81.

10.45 am Criminal Damage Boy Again

His solicitor reported that Mum was here, 'miraculously' but could not be persuaded to drop the charge. Petite, black and 16 inches shorter than her boy, Mum said he had smashed her £3,000 TV. His solicitor said they had a volatile relationship. Mum wanted a referral order and to work with the YOT. The boy was due to sign a contract with Crystal Palace FC today so would have a full-time job with good prospects. Portia asked if he could come home tonight. Mum declined. 'He beats me and rips my clothes off … He has a problem with is temper. He takes drugs.' His solicitor interjected that if Mum would not have him back, the YOT would not be able to work with him. Portia spoke gently to the boy. 'Everyone listens to *her* cos she's an adult', he sulked, and asserted that he was not going to sign for Crystal Palace, after all. 'Alright then', accepted Portia, explaining that she was making a referral order and the panel of people 'will listen to you. I've listened to you even though you are only 16. Are you going through a difficult time at the moment?' she asked, repeatedly, 'We all go through that'. She concluded, 'I wish you well. I'm sure you'll look back on this period later in your lives and ask yourselves "How did we get into this state?"' Aside, as they departed, she asked 'Do you know about referral orders? They're useless'. She later explained that, such were the delays, a child had often reoffended before the panel meeting had activated the referral.

10.59 am Trial Date Fixture

11.01 am Excess Alcohol Boy Returned with the Duty Solicitor

Portia asked Mum if there was an alcohol problem. 'No. This was a one-off.' She made a referral order.

11.10 am Possession of Spray Cans with Intent to Damage Property Belonging to London Buses

A fat, white, 16-year-old, was represented by a brown solicitor. He asked for the bail condition, a ban from buses, to be reduced to the top deck only, as his client always sprayed graffiti on top decks. Portia fixed the trial date six weeks hence. There was a racket outside, above the cells. She spoke to the boy.

> Did you hear all that noise outside? That's someone who doesn't want to go into custody. If you commit offences between now and your trial, that'll happen to you. Do you understand?

11.17 am Possession of an Offensive Weapon

A black 17-year-old appeared with Mum and a solicitor. Portia ascertained the issues and listed the case for trial.

11.25 am Robbery

A brown 15-year-old girl appeared with Mum. Charges were under negotiation. Portia sent everyone out. One minute later they returned. Trial date and pre-trial review were fixed.

11.32 am Threatening and Abusive Behaviour and Criminal Damage

A small, brown child appeared, accompanied by a black solicitor and a brown guardian. With a squeaky little voice, 'she' looked about ten but it was a 14-year-old boy. Having been arrested for bad behaviour in his children's home, he had flooded a police cell by stuffing a blanket in the toilet so criminal damage was added to his charges. He pleaded guilty. The YOT team produced an update on a previous referral order. Portia spoke to the boy, 'I think I remember you 'cos I made this referral order. Obviously, it's not worked and I'm going to have to start again'. Later, Portia expressed her concern about net-widening in such cases. She felt the police would not have been called in these circumstances, in the past, when she practised as a lawyer. Through this one domestic incident, the boy faced a list of ostensibly serious charges. Pole agreed.[31] By 2009, Portia was disgusted to find in her list a youth who had been detained overnight after 'swearing at a policeman'.

11.39 am Pre-trial Review

The 13-year-old was absent. The solicitor explained that, after the previous court appearance, 'Mum' had sent him to Africa. Mum explained that she wanted to send him to private school 'because he was stabbing people'. She could not afford the fees here so had taken him abroad. Aside, Portia explained that she had known of other children having been sent to Africa. They had 'come back transformed'. One had escaped the local drug culture and gone to university. She spoke kindly to Mum, asking her to keep in touch with the CPS. She said she understood that the CPS 'can't take a view now' but might be able to in future: a coded request to drop the charge if there were favourable reports.

11.50 am Criminal Damage

A white 17-year-old appeared with the duty solicitor. He pleaded guilty but was bailed for reports, as this offence ended his referral order.

---

[31] In 2006, Rod Morgan, then head of youth justice, criticised net-widening. Teachers were refusing to deal with discipline problems at school and instead calling in the police: news media, 21 August.

11.56 am Robbery with a Weapon

A black 16-year-old was brought from custody. His father had come. He was alleged to have waited outside tube stations at night and followed women, robbing them at knife point. 'I'm going to decline jurisdiction', announced Portia, sending it to the Crown Court. Bailing the child, Portia gave a strong warning to obey the conditions.

At 12.10 am, the morning's list was completed.

We went to eat our packed lunches with the other DJMCs. The afternoons carried on at the same pace or were reserved for trials. The next day, Portia dealt with 23 similar children, many charged with multiple offences, including six robberies, thefts, burglaries, wounding, GBH, two possessions of a bladed article, two assaults on police, one arson, a fine defaulter and two 15-year-olds charged with multiple driving offences, finishing the list by 3.46 pm. Portia asked her clerk to offer to help out other courts. A bench of lay justices were struggling with a long list of traffic offences and two trials. Portia took some of their cases but was too tired to start a trial at 4.00 pm. She grumbled again about lay justices: they should have sent the trial away that morning, as soon as they realised that the police had wrongly been briefed to appear. A child, their family and solicitor had been kept waiting all day, fruitlessly.

Guy's Youth Court

This too was in a high crime area but almost everyone was white. The defendants were strikingly different. Instead of towering over their mothers, most looked puny and underdeveloped. Skinny boys who looked 10 were 14–16. They resembled the unhealthy children I had seen in city juvenile courts in the 1970s, the product of generations of deprivation and malnourishment.[32] The second difference was Guy's court management. He used the novel device of dealing with many children *before* their solicitor arrived. In the first case, he spoke swiftly to the child, 'Your case is being adjourned till 19 May. Make sure you tell your solicitor that'. I wondered if the child would remember the date and have his solicitor's contact details. The second defendant, an unrepresented Persistent Young Offender, was charged with travelling without a valid ticket. Guy took his guilty plea and imposed a conditional discharge, explaining aside, 'Amazingly, he's turned up to face the music. This is trivial'. Guy routinely[33] took the

---

[32] Jamie Oliver drew public attention to modern levels of paediatric malnutrition in his Channel 4 series in 2005–06, *Jamie's School Dinners*. The *International Journal of Pediatric Obesity* was launched in March 2006, focusing on the 'dual burden' of obesity and malnutrition in children.

[33] In *The Craft of Justice*, it was said, 'The idea of craft … recognizes that over time and through repetition practitioners discover that what at first appeared to be separate, distinct

defendant's plea, asked them about previous convictions and imposed a conditional discharge. His practice with adults was the same. 'I don't involve solicitors in plea and sentence.' Since I had never seen a court dealing with offenders in the absence of their lawyers, I queried this. Guy explained that this building was badly designed so it was difficult for the ushers to find solicitors. (One experienced solicitor to whom I spoke called it a cattle-market.) Also, they might be in another courtroom, or down the road at the neighbouring magistrates' court. He empathised with solicitors who took on so many cases, just to make a living, that they had to be in 10 places at once.[34] 'It's OK so long as we touch base at some time in the morning … No harm was done.' He did it every day of the week. He explained that even if a solicitor were there, he might not hear from them, as he preferred to speak directly to the defendant. 'Solicitors trust me.' After all, he had not locked anyone up today. Had he had any doubts about the appropriateness of a plea, he would have advised a child to plead not guilty. If a solicitor complained, he would apologise. 'If the solicitor doesn't like it, you can change your mind … It's all a matter of practicalities.' Solicitors seemed to be used to Guy's practice. When they eventually appeared, Guy politely explained what he had done with their client and, without exception, they thanked him. Guy imposed many conditional discharges, remarking 'These cases are all rubbish. This is not a street crime court'. He asked me to note that he spoke sternly to street crime offenders and was a harsher sentencer, in appropriate cases. 'I've seen the videos. Really awful offences. Lots of violence. Jumping on people's heads in the gutter.' Just such a child appeared in front of him, another day. He spoke sternly, 'You and I have met before. You know if you so much as breathe out of place I'll have you back in here and you'll be inside. Do you understand?'

THE ADULT CRIMINAL COURT

Confirming Seago et al and Morgan et al above, the DJMCs dealt with mixed lists of bail applications, road traffic offences, pre-trial reviews, mode of trial hearings, applications for adjournments, fine defaulters, sentencing (on reports) and guilty pleas to such matters as drugs offences and assaults.[35] Also confirming their research, their working style was characterised by speed, command and readiness to challenge CPS representatives and lawyers (compared with lay justices). Their

---

problems … have enough in common that a single solution is satisfactory for most of them', Flemming, above n 20 at 5.

[34] Posner referred to the insight of judges into the constraints on lawyers wrought by time, money and client pressures, Posner, *How Judges Think* (Cambridge, Mass, Harvard University Press, 2008) 74.

[35] These common offences and the defendants accused of them generally shared some characteristics, which were specific to the local community, as famously portrayed by D Sudnow in 'Normal Crimes: Sociological Features of the Penal Code in a Public Defender Office' (1965) 12 *Social Problems* 255.

legal advisers were generally silent. On a typical October morning, Portia was anxious to keep the cases flowing swiftly and to resist delays. Listing a case for trial, the clerk was heard muttering about January. 'What's wrong with 21 December?' interjected Portia and, to the CPS representative, 'Got two [police officers] on rest days have you? Well, that can be changed can't it?' She cross-examined a CPS representative who sought an adjournment because 'the forensics' were not available. 'You and I both know in a drugs case you get the forensics organised. This never used to happen.' She reluctantly adjourned for seven days, 'Otherwise, it'll be dismissed'.

Nor was Portia an easy touch for the CPS when it came to Anti-Social Behaviour Orders (ASBOs). A vociferous Rastafarian was brought from the cells. He interrupted the CPS from the secure glass dock 'Alright Mr D', Portia reassured, 'We'll hear from you in a moment. I need to hear from the CPS first'. The police had arrested him for possessing a bladed article but sought an ASBO banning him from the centre of a London borough because of his regular drug-dealing there. Portia asked the CPS why they expected her to make an ASBO on untested evidence. Aside, she scowled 'This is the Crown coming in through the back door'. She asked why they had not applied through the local authority.

Defendant, interrupting again: 'Law and justice is meant to go for everyone but it's not applied fairly.'

P: 'Mr D, you've got three previous for possession. This has got to stop, otherwise the police'll keep on stopping you.'

D: 'Yes, Ma'am. It will stop. I've had time to reflect on this.'

[Portia grumbling, aside, about the CPS, refused the ASBO, imposed 28 days' custody, knowing he would go free immediately, and remitted his fines].

D: 'God bless you, Ma'am!'

After he left, she remonstrated with the CPS and later explained, aside, her concerns that the defendant was unrepresented and it was unreasonable to make an ASBO banning him from his home borough. 'Also, you don't know if police records are correct. They make mistakes, don't they?'

Guy and Pole remarked that they gave sentence discounts for guilty pleas, 'because it frees up court time'. Guy said all local DJMCs were fast but he was fastest. He hoped I would not see him being impatient with lawyers but he would not tolerate messing about in trials and he would not involve lawyers in plea and sentence unless he saw fit. Typically, Guy would take the plea, examine the defendant on his previous convictions and just as he was explaining the sentence, the solicitor would walk in.

Hello Mr L, I'm just binding over your client.

I'm grateful, Sir.

He called his court a 'law free zone'[36] and said this caused one lawyer to hide books under a table. He said he never took notes on legal submissions because he knew they would be resolved. He had twice refused to state a case for appeal but had been upheld by the High Court. 'Don't give a 20-page judgment', he warned, as that would provide ample opportunity 'to have a go at you' on appeal. 'Give a one-page judgment'. He regretted that more people were trying to raise legal arguments.

> Legal arguments don't belong here. They belong in the Court of Appeal with proper judges who know the law … It's common sense here. We've got magistrates doing most cases.

His exclusion of the law was not absolute, however. I noticed one day that he carried with him a folder of hard copies of new law reports. Like the secret school swot who pretends not to have revised, Guy *was* up to date on the law.

TRIALS: 'NO MESSING' WITH DISTRICT JUDGES

Because DJMCs have the powers of judge and jury, they were sometimes privy to more information about an offender than a jury would have been. For instance, a clerk might pop in to explain what negotiations were going on, as clerks and ushers did with Crown Court judges. Also, like lay justices, they all had their 'regulars', members of local extended families of repeat offenders.[37] Pole and Guy had travellers' families camping on their patches, 'always shooting people' (Guy).

Summary trial could be *very* summary before a DJMC, compared with a trio of methodical lay justices, regularly taking legal advice and conferring on every decision. Trials were also much swifter than trial on indictment, as we shall see in the Crown Court chapter. Portia started trying a youngster for driving a scooter without due care at 2.30 pm and had dismissed the case by 2.51 pm. 'The evidence of the police officer is less than satisfactory.' Pole heard a 25-minute contested case of parking on a 'red route'. 'Pointless me coming in then, wasn't it?' growled the defendant, after Pole found him guilty, and stomped off out of court. More typical was Portia's trial of a girl for common assault. It started at 10.20 am, after Portia had sentenced children from last week's robbery trial, finishing at 1.22 pm, with a swift, reasoned, extempore judgment, without her retiring. The DJMCs were also used to long trials. Portia had just finished a seven-day robbery with nine defendant children. She felt obliged to conduct it

---

[36] Confirming an argument based on observation of magistrates' courts practice in P Darbyshire, 'Previous Misconduct and Magistrates' Courts—Some Tales from the Real World' [1997] *Crim LR* 105. See also a trial attorney in *The Craft of Justice*, 'The law is a backdrop, but if you use too much law, you're probably gonna lose', Flemming, above n 20 at 3.

[37] Each magistrates' court has its regulars, well known to the bench and legal advisers. See Darbyshire, above n 36.

herself, having accepted jurisdiction, a decision which she proudly reported had been upheld by the High Court in judicial review.

They readily dismissed prosecutions through lack of evidence. Like some stipendiaries I observed in the 1970s, they appeared to be determined to emphasise their independence, so they did not appear to operate a presumption of guilt, associated with magistrates' courts by many previous socio-legal researchers.[38] Guy told me that at the Bar, he knew that 98 per cent of his clients were guilty. Now, he found 50 per cent not guilty, on the evidence. He felt it was better that 100 guilty people go free than that one innocent should be convicted. He was impressed with DJMCs who were ex-prosecutors yet scrupulously fair. Pole said he never inferred that a defendant had previous convictions simply because a lawyer did not mention a clean record, 'because some lawyers are so incompetent'.[39] Guy, who also sat as a Crown Court recorder and was, therefore, used to explaining to jurors their proper role said of DJMCs

> You are the judge and jury. It is an inquisitorial system ... It is ... a hands-on approach.[40] I don't convict unless I am absolutely sure. I remember Lord Justice Auld gave us a question 'how sure must you be before you convict?' I turned round to my colleague and said 'What a stupid question' but she had written 70 per cent and she was a senior magistrate![41]

One of the interviewees described DJMC's technical trial work in terms strikingly like the researchers above.

> We tend to get excess alcohol challenges on the admissibility on the law and on the type of machine ... [and] ... abuse [of process] arguments ... [and] pre-trial review courts in which there may be a stronger and more disciplined control of the case management, merely because that is what I expect and advocates will not mess district judges around.

---

[38] There is a socio-legal literature ranging back to the 1970s, claiming that lay magistrates apply a presumption of guilt. See, eg, M McConville et al, *Standing Accused* (Oxford, Clarendon Press, 1994).

[39] This is an example of the point Posner was making: 'preconceptions play a role in rational thought'. Posner gave the example that judges convict more criminal defendants than juries because of their prior knowledge of prosecutors bringing cases where evidence is clear, Posner, above n 34 at 68. Here, Pole is interpreting evidence in a manner favourable to the defendant because of his prior knowledge of lawyers' incompetence so *prior knowledge and experience* probably account for the fact that professional judges here and in the research above are more challenging than lay justices and do not operate a presumption of guilt.

[40] Doran and Jackson found that Northern Irish judges were more likely to probe key witnesses in depth in non-jury Diplock trials than in jury trials: J Jackson and S Doran, *Judge Without Jury* (Oxford, Clarendon Press, 1995) 160.

[41] I have previously expressed the concern that some lay justices set the quantum of proof far too low and bordering on probability, 'For the New Lord Chancellor—Some Causes for Concern About Magistrates' [1997] *Crim LR* 861. In this research, I found that some DJMCs and CJs share this concern about lay justices, as do some advocates. DJMCs share other judges' acute awareness of the high standard. See research by Zander into the interpretation of 'beyond reasonable doubt' by magistrates and others, M Zander, 'The Criminal Standard of Proof—how sure is sure?' (2000) 150 *New Law Journal* 1517.

I watched Pole hearing a day-long disclosure application in just such a trial, with precedents cited where his decisions had been judicially reviewed by the High Court. He hated this type of case. The defences were often 'crap' and he felt the public would agree with him.[42] He described the badly argued, boring case as 'like paddling through mud in the fog'.

Neatly illustrating the point about not being able to 'mess district judges around', Guy went to the lengths of manipulating the list one day to ensure that he would try a case where a solicitor was raising what he considered to be a spurious point that would confuse lay justices. The solicitor argued that his client would be prejudiced if the assault complainant were permitted to give her evidence from behind screens and this would breach the Human Rights Act. Guy showed me a copy of the submissions, which he declined to read, 'All garbage'. We went in to court.

> I've had the benefit of reading your very helpful skeleton argument and the prosecution's submissions … Let's get to the nitty-gritty. The court has an inherent power to order screens … It's up to the court of trial. Forget all these Acts of Parliament, the Human Rights Act. The magistrates are not going to take against the defendant if the witness is giving evidence from behind screens. A jury might, but not people who are used to taking decisions. We've reached the point where most people in the youth court are giving evidence on video link.

Guy adjourned to speak to the listing office. 'Someone has raised a spurious legal point and they might mess about with a lay bench. Am I free to deal with it?' The trial was two days later. Guy's trouble-shooting paid off. Laughing, he remarked that as soon as the solicitor had realised Guy was judging the case, he had sent an agent. He too objected to the screens but, in the event, the witness gave evidence without, 'which is why I won't rule on it as a preliminary matter. You can imagine, if we'd had a weak prosecutor and Mr G here, it could've taken ages'. Guy explained that, despite his favoured 'inquisitorial' technique, he had left the questioning to the advocates because they were both very good. He had known them for decades. 'You've seen a very typical trial; some adversarial, some inquisitorial.' He said he would sometimes 'lay into' a complainant if he thought their evidence did not add up and 'demolish them' but would not do so to a defendant. Guy reached his guilty verdict and gave extempore reasons, without retiring.

The defendant, it transpired on sentencing, was convicted five years earlier of battery of the same wife. 'It speaks volumes that he was fined only £100', remarked the defence solicitor, hoping this was mitigation. 'It means lay justices probably take a less severe view of domestic violence than district judges', corrected Guy, imposing six months' imprisonment and illustrating another

---

[42] Doran and Jackson, quoting Diamond, above, pointed out that stipendiaries saw themselves as responsible to the community, whereas lay justices viewed themselves as 'the public', as representatives rather than delegates, Doran and Jackson, above n 40 at 223.

research finding above, by Diamond, that district judges are harsher sentencers than lay justices and Morgan and Russell's finding that they are more likely to impose custody. When we left, Guy explained he took a dim view of violence against women. The defendant was a 'nasty man, whose wife was clearly terrified of him'. When the prosecutor deliberately rattled him he had shown how aggressive he could be. 'If he could be like that *here*, what would he be like bevvied up?' Six months inside was a deterrent sentence. 'With his next partner he'll think to himself "Oh. I don't want to go through that again".'

COURT USERS

Each magistrates' court has a regular set of professionals: lawyers, CPS representatives, the YOT and so on, and they all have a common interest in maintaining a good working relationship together and with the bench and legal advisers, for the sake of future harmony in their years as a team. Portia, when first interviewed, had only been at her court for just over a year so had not had time to build this up but Guy had known for decades some of the lawyers appearing before him. He pointed out those solicitors older than him who used to brief him when he practised at the Bar. He was happy to bring an afternoon case forward for one of them to play in the Law Society golf competition and teased the solicitor about his handicap. In the trial above, the prosecuting solicitor

> used to be an old style clerk. She used to be like your Mum when you appeared in front of her. She used to joke 'sit down Mr G, or I'll kick your shins'. I've known her for 27 years. There's no substitute for that.

He regaled me with stories of a number of the local solicitors, as did Pole in his courts. It was useful, said Guy, to know all the local solicitors but DJMCs were moved around so that they did not build up a cosy relationship anywhere. He explained that the senior partners of two rival firms had been involved in fisticuffs.[43]

Prosecutors in front of Portia were consistently poor, to the extent that, in 2009, my accompanying students remarked on them, shocked that a prosecuting barrister looked mystified by the bundle of case files she fumbled through. Cases routinely collapsed because of poor prosecution. Portia remarked on the waste of police time in preparing the case. I was as used to this as Portia, having observed magistrates' courts and unprepared prosecutors since the 1970s.

---

[43] This almost beggars belief but is true. The rivalry is explored in the Crown Court chapter, because, coincidentally, I researched in the city's Crown Court (unbeknown to either set of judges).

RELATIONS WITH THE LAY BENCH

Although he would have been content to see lay justices replaced with DJMCs, Guy worked constantly to maintain a good relationship with all those who populated the court. He ensured he mixed with lay magistrates every day in the city court and, in the suburban court, a lay chairman came to sit at the back of his court to observe. Apparently, this was a regular occurrence. One interviewee, a former justices' clerk and thus used to shepherding a lay bench, also made this a policy.

> I always attempt if possible to get to the court I am sitting at by nine so that I am available to meet the lay benchers, to interact with them just so they see that I am human.

The Royal Commission on Criminal Justice 1993,[44] however, found that some lay benches distrusted the role of professionals. Some justices entertain a long-term conspiracy theory that there is a plot to replace them with professionals, though the statistical trend demonstrates otherwise.[45] Seago, Walker and Wall also alluded to this.

> It is clear from written sources and from our wide-ranging personal contacts during the research that a significant number of lay magistrates fear that a plan exists whereby lay magistrates will be gradually replaced by stipendiary magistrates ... Even more fear the appointment to their bench of a stipendiary magistrate will inevitably lead to a decrease in the level of interesting or rewarding work for the lay bench. (para. 3.4)

In Inner London, there were instances which suggested a mutual hostility, in some respects. The professionals claimed that they could be deeply resented in provincial courts. One DJMC had been told he could not sit at the end of the justices' room and plug in his laptop. Another had found himself referred to as a 'hired hand'. It was said that at one London court, DJMCs and magistrates did not communicate.

Pole appeared to have a friendly relationship with the justices. This was hardly surprising, since he had spent half his career as a magistrates' clerk. Like Portia, however, he had doubts about the competence and impartiality of some of them.[46] One day, a clerk told him that one lay justice had said 'He must be guilty because we sentenced him for all the same offences in the youth court'. The clerk had advised on a retrial. Portia always distrusted lay justices. She expressed concern as to whether the right people were appointed as magistrates. A black Jamaican magistrate had told her off for granting bail to a Trinidadian. 'Don't you know Trinidad is the new Jamaica?' Portia was appalled at this racism and

---

[44]   *Royal Commission on Criminal Justice Report* Cm 2263 (London, HMSO, 1993) ch 8, para 103.

[45]   Explained in Darbyshire, above n 15 at ch 15.

[46]   See ch 12 below.

wondered if she should have reported the magistrate. Every time I sit with Portia, she tells some new story of behaviour unbecoming of a magistrate. As will be seen later, some circuit judges were equally contemptuous of magistrates.

LEGAL ADVISERS

Morgan and Russell raised the question of whether DJMCs needed legal advisers rather than the non-qualified clerks who serve all other judges. Logically, professionals ought not to need one. This study is too small to draw any conclusions but all the legal advisers sitting with these DJMCs were entirely passive. Pre-court, though, they could provide the judges with much more useful information about the listed cases than could a Crown Court clerk with a circuit judge. During hearings, they swiftly fed useful information to the DJMC on sentencing, defendants' records, reports and the defendant's status, all of which helped the DJMCs keep up their speedy throughput. Pole and one interviewee checked their written reasons with their legal advisers before giving judgment after a trial. By 2008–09, there were experiments with professional judges sitting without an advisor.

A NEGLECTED BAND OF JUDGES

Sometimes the DJMCs referred to other judges' and government's lack of understanding of their work. If DJMCs or lay justices feel their sentencing powers are insufficiently robust for the gravity of an offence, they send the offender 'upstairs' to the Crown Court for sentencing. Portia was continually frustrated with circuit judges imposing inappropriate penalties or those within her range of powers, when she had clearly intended a stiffer sentence. 'We know what we're doing.' She had sent a violent offender to the Crown Court. He was given a lenient sentence, 'Now he's up for murder!'

> Crown Court judges don't understand youth court sentencing and they don't want to understand it. We got the resident judge here from the Crown Court because a defendant from here had been tried with an adult, was sent back *here* by the judge, for sentencing and meanwhile remanded for *seven weeks* for handling a *bus pass*! By the time he was sentenced here, he'd done the equivalent of a year's remand! The judge should have sentenced him, sitting as a DJ.

Like all other research judges administering criminal law, the DJMCs found constant and ill-conceived changes to criminal procedure and sentencing to be exasperating and unworkable and they felt ministers and civil servants ignored the problems that beset their courts. One interviewee said, 'There isn't one area that they haven't started to interfere with or change. I am deeply concerned that the criminal law has become a political issue'. Portia was a constant critic of her sentencing powers, especially in the youth court. Her 2004 frustration with referral orders was still acute in 2009. A first offender under 16, pleading guilty, had to be placed on a referral order, even if carrying a knife in the early hours of the morning. She regarded some initiatives as ill-disguised money-saving tactics.

> You see all the hurdles we have to go through? I think the Government ... still think 13-year-olds are committing offences like riding a bike without lights. They haven't got a clue ... I had a chap from the Home Office come down of his own volition [she explained a problem with ASBOs]. He didn't understand at all. He said 'We should have sent a consultation paper out to you. Do you have a grouping?' I said 'Yes we do. We are based in Bow Street and we have been there since the 1600s'.

By 2009, she was equally cynical about the effect of fixed penalty notices (FPNs), readily imposed by police on the streets to keep people out of court and concentrate on violent crime. As a result, she had children appearing in her youth court having 'clocked up' £600 worth of unpaid fines for disorder offences, with no chance of ever paying them.[47] Virtual court hearings were being piloted, with a video link to offenders in the police station. She could not imagine how lay magistrates would hear the 50 cases per day that were scheduled before them and wondered about the effects on due process. 'What'll happen if someone doesn't want the duty solicitor? Will they be put to the back of the list?'[48] Another new cost-saver was a novel use of tagging: 'Offenders can be straight back out on the street'.

DJMCs felt that other judges were ignorant of their lot. Pole, commenting on the 2006 restructuring of the judiciary, felt his new circuit presiding judge would 'know as much about my work as I know about rocket science'. Between my days with Portia, I lunched with a big city Recorder and explained the in-court demonstrations she suffered. 'Oh I'd use my contempt powers', he responded. I reported this back to Portia and her colleagues and it caused hoots of derision. One asked 'Have you *seen* the security here?'

There is an important tailnote here. This chapter appeared as an article in 2006. In it, I urged Lord Chief Justice Phillips to go and watch Portia's court. He did. He also asked her to see him, accompanied by the London's Chief DJMC so that put the top judge in a little more touch with the ones at the bottom. DJMCs have now been absorbed into the circuit system, thanks to the Courts Act 2003 and they are included in the mainstream judicial hierarchy and remembered in

---

[47] The over-use of FPNs and cautions instead of bringing offenders to court, especially in cases of serious violence and burglary, was the subject of a BBC *Panorama* documentary on 15 November 2009. The same criticism was made by the outgoing DPP in BBC Radio's *Law in Action*, on 3 November 2009 and by the current DPP, Keir Starmer QC, in 'Chief prosecutor demands curb on police cautions', *The Times*, 8 November 2009.

[48] In December 2010, the Ministry of Justice announced that virtual courts were worth further development, despite their expense exceeding savings, a decision which the Law Society criticised as 'wholly irresponsible', J Dean, 'Ministry of Justice backs virtual courts scheme', Law Society *Gazette*, online, 23 December 2010.

judicial training regimes and so on. In the meantime Portia said Jack Straw, when he was Minister of Justice, had become a 'regular visitor'.

CONCLUSION

The most important point revealed here is that the public image of judges as 'out of touch' is ludicrous, when contrasted with the junior gangland that constituted Portia's world. The war zone she tiptoed through from her bus, in disguise, outside the building, penetrated the inside of her courtroom and placed her under enormous psychological and physical strain. These judges cannot help but be involved in the community they claimed to serve and they knew it very well indeed, especially its criminal families and teenage gangs. Its most disaffected and frightening elements faced them daily in the courtroom, often across nothing more than a table. Portia did not need to be a parent to understand the problems of reasoning with troublesome teenagers and to recognise what constituted good parenting. Ironically, because they sit daily, professionals are probably more 'in touch' with the community than many lay justices, who are meant to represent it in an abstract and concrete sense.[49] These three each had an adult lifetime's experience of magistrates' courts around the country, which generated strong opinions on the futility of modern responses to youth offending and caused them to worry about 'net-widening', trapping youngsters who would have had their misbehaviour interpreted as naughtiness, not crime, in the 1970s and 1980s. They were scrupulously polite to defendants, who they treated as equal members of the community and they scolded some youngsters, in the role of a type of extra 'community parent', trying to get them to see the error of their ways.

In the context of the legal system, however, these judges were a fairly isolated and distinct group. Historically, they were unconnected with other judges. They were seen as a type of professional magistrate and were called 'stipendiary magistrates' until 2000. They felt that higher judges had little or no understanding of what they did and by 2009–10, Portia and her colleagues were still trying to educate those immediately above them, local Crown Court judges, about what they did, because DJMCs suffered the constant frustration of sending cases up for tougher sentencing, only to find that circuit judges passed sentences they could have passed themselves, or made inappropriate orders, not understanding either DJMCs' powers or their own. This ignorance about them is shared by the senior courts and Parliament. As I pointed out in articles in the 1990s, they develop the criminal law and procedure as if most cases were still decided by judge and jury, yet criminal business has shifted down into the magistrates' courts which hear 95 per cent of it. This makes DJMCs and lay magistrates enormously important to

---

[49] Lay justices used to be required to reside within a 15-mile radius of the jurisdictional area of their bench and most are still local people. Over 80 per cent are over 50 and they sit, on average, 40 sittings (half days) per year. For detail, see Darbyshire, above n 15 at ch 15.

the public at large who, nevertheless, think they deal with 'trivia', just as other judges do. In the reality described here, we have seen that youth gang rapes, stabbings and muggings were hidden away in Portia's and Guy's youth courts, unseen and unreported.

These judges were also isolated in a second manner, from the lay bench. Historically, they were invented to supplant corrupt lay justices in London, then brought in to take over from overloaded lay benches in some provincial cities. When I was researching in lay magistrates' courts, in the 1970s, the 'stipe' at most cities was a revered but elusive figure who I never met and who never rubbed shoulders with lay justices. The DJMCs here who were former justices' clerks had served, shepherded and advised lay justices for decades so they made it their business to mix with them, as did Guy, because of his friendly nature. In the meantime, DJMCs were and are the subject of a lay magistrates' conspiracy theory that there is a plot to replace them with professionals so some DJMCs got a hostile reception and Portia and colleagues reciprocated with disrespect and constant criticism.

DJMCs were isolated in a third way, dotted around the country, often the only professional at a courthouse. They were not even unified as a bench until 2000, because they were all appointed locally by magistrates' courts committees and answerable to them. While Inner London stipes shared courthouses with other stipes and they were trained together and organised, the provincial stipes were unorganised and, as we have seen earlier in the book, most of these DJMCs started to do this job as part-timers without *any* training. This probably explains their idiosyncrasies. In the 1970s, I encountered two London stipes who sat in adjoining courtrooms but interpreted the law differently. Advocates had to adjust their arguments accordingly. Nevertheless, in three decades of court watching, I had never encountered a judge like Guy who routinely dealt with defendants, including children, *before* their solicitor arrived. Yet no lawyer objected to this. They were used to Guy and, indeed, Guy felt he was doing them a favour. As a former practitioner, he understood practising lawyers. Like Portia, he knew exactly what the scene was like offstage, outside their courtroom. All three knew all about clients not appearing, last minute plea deals, duty solicitors and legally aided advocates running between multiple courts because each had played a different part, lawyer or clerk, in the cast of regular characters that populates each magistrates' court. Of course, judges who are appointed from different careers, such as academics, or lawyers practising in other fields lack this prior knowledge. They would pick up some of it while sitting part-time but they would never be able to experience the chaos of lawyers and clients outside the courtroom and they would lack Guy's insight into what it is like to try and represent 10 clients in a morning in different courtrooms.

They knew all about lawyers' games too. This research puts flesh on the bones of previous more large scale and more scientific research on professional judges in magistrates' courts. Unlike lay justices' courts, where there is always a danger that the clerk appears in control, there was absolutely no doubt who was running these judges' courts. They were the central, solitary figure of authority. They announced the orders, did the talking, the praising and the scolding. They controlled the speed of the lists. Previous research found stipes were authoritative and challenging. Guy was *so* challenging that he described proceedings in his court as 'inquisitorial'. Using almost identical language to that previous research, these judges asserted that they would not be 'messed about', in contrast with lay justices who lacked legal knowledge and their experience. They were merciless with weak prosecutors bringing weak cases, dismissing cases within minutes for lack of evidence, in the same way I had watched London stipes doing this in the 1970s. As the previous research had concluded, they were much more challenging than lay justices. Unlike some of them, Portia was not an easy touch for unenforceable or unreasonable ASBOs requested by the Crown. Similarly, defence lawyers relying on spurious points of law that might have worried lay justices for hours were given short shrift. When Guy manipulated the court list to fend off such a claim, the solicitor involved went to the extreme lengths of escaping his wrath by sending in an agent and that did not work either.

Also supporting previous research, and certainly when the main observations in this research took place, the DJMCs had enormous caseloads. They rattled through long lists, sentencing guilty pleas and case managing trials with just minutes spent on each case. Of course this is not a surprise. In the twentieth century stipes were always brought into handle overcrowded case lists because they are far quicker than magistrates. In contrast with three lay people, a single lawyer does not need to confer on guilt or sentence and does not need advice on criminal law, criminal procedure or sentencing. But there was another reason why cases moved swiftly. The DJMC's presence on the bench raised an expectation of speed among the advocates appearing before them. Portia continually sent out the usher to call in the cases to keep her list moving and Guy was so keen to shift the cases through the court that he dispensed with many defendants before their lawyer arrived. DJMCs were pro-active in managing the cases, in the way that their civil counterparts are now expected to be, as we shall see from the county court chapter, where their role has also been described as 'inquisitorial'. As the previous research had shown, professionals resisted the adjournment culture for which magistrates' courts have long been notorious. Portia's experience as a lawyer meant she knew how the police shift system worked and this enabled her to challenge a prosecution request for a long pre-trial adjournment. Summary justice in the magistrates' court is truly summary when dispensed by a professional. Justice is summary for another reason. Guy called this level of court a 'law free zone'. This was not just one of his idiosyncrasies. To a large extent he was right and again this point is not new. It is true that legal arguments are seldom raised in magistrates' courts but that does not mean that the law is not applied. It simply means that most cases are routine and the law involved is so well known there is little room for argument. Where a lawyer does want to raise a defence in, say, a theft case, he will advise the client to opt for trial on indictment in the Crown Court where it can get the unhurried attention of a circuit judge and, if necessary, a 'proper judge', as Guy would have said.[50] Cases raising complex points of law are exceptional in magistrates' courts and this research reaffirms the previous finding that such cases were listed before professionals, like Pole's breathalyser case, one of a long string since the drink drive laws were invented, where clients pay creative lawyers to find legal loopholes in the expensive endeavour to avoid a driving ban. Lawyers who raised 'spurious' points of law, like the human rights argument, created unwelcome work and disturbed the steady, balanced relationship between local solicitors, local prosecutors, the clerk and the bench, which had probably lasted for years.

There is another contrast with lay justices that was not identified in the previous research but seems clear from this chapter. These lawyers were well aware of the reputation of lay magistrates for operating a presumption of guilt, because this is not just a phenomenon identified by researchers like McConville et al in *Standing Accused*. It is a wider reputation among practising lawyers, which partly explains Portia's contempt. Each DJMC was anxious to assert their objectivity and to show that they applied a presumption of innocence and a very high standard of proof.

The DJMCs felt that civil servants and ministers neither knew nor cared about the inefficacy of their sentencing powers. They were just as much the victims of ill-conceived, constant bombardment of soundbite, inoperable 'tough on crime' policy and procedure changes as the judges above them. At least there was a glimmer of hope. The Minister of Justice had at last 'become a regular visitor' in Portia's court and, partly as a result of this work, the Lord Chief Justice had sat with Portia. The DJMCs are gradually being recognised as proper judges.

---

[50] *'The James Report': The Distribution of Criminal Business Between the Crown Court and Magistrates' Courts*, Cmnd 6323, (London, HMSO, 1975); D Riley and J Vennard, *Triable Either Way Cases: Crown Court or Magistrates' Court* (London, HMSO, 1988); C Hedderman and D Moxon, 'Magistrates' Court or Crown Court? Mode of Trial Decisions and Sentencing', Home Office Research Study, no 125, 1992.

9

Criminal Business: Circuit Judges in the Crown Court

The legislation's the usual bugger's muddle.

Sir Monty Everard, *Judge John Deed*, BBC1, 9 January 2007[1]

THIS CHAPTER EXAMINES the work of a variety of circuit judges in the Crown Court, which sits above the magistrates' courts, dealing with the remaining five per cent of criminal business. There are just 77 Crown Court locations, compared with over 330 magistrates' courts.[2] The 680 circuit judges (CJs) and 1,233 recorders[3] (part-timers) conduct most Crown Court trials and hear the most serious county court cases. These were the judges Portia was complaining about in the last chapter. The Crown Court is the stereotypical court, reinforced by news and dramatisations. People rarely visit it and overestimate its business.[4] It is more melodramatic than other courts. In the public imagination it is old, dark, oak-panelled (because filming takes place in disused courts),[5] with a raised, central dock and the judge, bewigged and gowned and elevated, addressed by counsel in fancy dress. This theatre has a captive audience—the jury. As Rock commented in 1993[6] there had been no attempt to analyse its complex social world.[7]

---

[1] In *R (on the application of Noone) v The Governor of HMP Drake Hall* [2010] UKSC 30, Lord Phillips said 'hell' was a fair description of the confusion surrounding transitional provisions for very short-term prisoners on 'custody plus' release. Lord Judge said 'For too many years now the administration of justice has been engulfed by a relentless tidal wave of legislation'.

[2] Though in December 2010 the Coalition Government announced its intention to close 93.

[3] 2010 statistics, Judiciary website.

[4] See previous chapter.

[5] Courts were opened for filming by HM Courts Service Film Unit in 2006.

[6] P Rock, *The Social World of an English Crown Court* (Oxford, Clarendon Press, 1993) 1.

[7] Partly because it was viewed by social scientists as hostile to research, said Rock, ibid ch 1.

SAMPLE AND METHOD

The 32 CJs were the biggest group. Of the 16 core, 13 sat in the Crown Court. I observed 11, having spent days over many years with the pilot CJ. The 16 interviewees sat in the Crown Court. The sample was drawn from the six circuits but underrepresented judges in the South East: only 12 of 32, although it accounts for around 40 per cent of all CJs. They reflected a broad range of experience, including two appointed six months earlier and two about to retire. In 2007–09, I supplemented this by observing three more London Crown Courts and speaking to their residents. I did this because Lord Judge considered that many of the trial problems highlighted in this gloomy chapter must have been resolved by the Criminal Procedure Rules 2005. On the contrary, I found that by 2009–10, the position had significantly worsened in some London courts, with a case backlog and judge shortage to add to judges' frustrations.

The 32 were selected according to a wide spectrum of 'ticketing' (authorisation). Seven had given up criminal business. Of the remaining 25, 10 did only criminal work.[8] The 'ticketing' system was criticised for lack of flexibility by Auld LJ in his 2001 *Review*.[9] These judges were also concerned about the lack of logic and transparency.

Seventeen did some non-routine work. Nine were resident judges, the senior managing judges at each Crown Court centre. They had a pastoral role and managed judicial deployment and were gaining more onerous case and court management duties. Five sat in the Court of Appeal (Criminal Division) (CACD). Two sat part-time at the Old Bailey, four on Mental Health Review Tribunals and two on the Parole Board. Two were magistrates' liaison judges, involving weekend training sessions and court open days. Two were chancellors of a Church of England diocese, presiding over consistory courts. Two were heavily involved in training and four were on committees, such as the Judicial Advisory Groups, advising government on court matters. Two were on committees of the Council of Circuit Judges.

I spent at least four days with each of the 11 core judges, usually non-sequential, in a variety of work. They showed me how they took notes and drafted jury directions. We discussed their cases and paperwork. They involved me in hearings in chambers, court-user meetings and discussions with advocates and court staff. One tutor judge took me to a recorder training seminar, another

---

[8]   The need for CJs to hear criminal cases far outstrips the needs of civil cases. Five heard crime and civil cases, three heard crime and family and seven did all three. Of the 25, eight had 'class one' tickets, which included murder, 12 were ticketed for serious fraud and 17 for serious sex offences.

[9]   'One of the greatest ills of the system is its lack of flexibility in the matching of judges, courts and cases': *Review of the Criminal Courts of England and Wales* (London, The Stationery Office, 2001) (the Auld Report or CCR, or Auld Review) 226. He cited the (Beeching) *Report of the Royal Commission on Assizes and Quarter Sessions*, Cmnd. 4153 (London, HMSO, 1969) para 67.

to a civic function. I lunched with them, usually in the court dining room, in the company of other CJs and recorders, and sometimes district and High Court (HC) judges. This, and time spent shadowing HC and district judges, meant I met over 160 additional circuit judges.

HAPPY JUDGES—WORKLOAD

Their level of job satisfaction was striking.

Beats working for a living. I never have the Monday morning blues.

My wife wants me to retire but I don't want to. I really enjoy the job.

Everything I had hoped for ... I think it's a vocation.

I can't think of a better job.

Very interesting and fulfilling.

The job satisfaction is enormous.

Far better than I could ever have dreamed.

I am amazed somebody is prepared to pay me.

I was told ... I was being appointed to one of the best jobs in England and seventeen and a half years later, I still think so.

Very interesting ... the aspect of public service is ... very rewarding.

Exceeded my expectations ... as if this had been what I had been waiting to do all my life.

Even better than I expected. I had got to the stage in silk where I was utterly exhausted. I was mentally stressed and life was just a hassle ... I [hoped] this would be a relief but it is even better.

Very fulfilling ... an enjoyable job.

The opportunity to concentrate on one ... case or a small number ... free from the additional stresses of ... practice, the daily politics, the payment of fees and wondering when your next brief was going to come ... you could do things at your own pace and to the best of your ability and help to produce the right result.

One of the best judicial jobs in the system, because you have more interest than the district bench and you are not travelling away from home ... as ... the High Court [judges] ... You are also not doing things that you are not comfortable with. I, for example, am not comfortable in civil. Someone I know who was appointed to the High Court from the circuit says that he hates doing civil ... More interesting in many ways and more rewarding than my time at the Bar. What I liked about the Bar was the ... comradeship but we are a pretty happy team here.

Each was used to taking work home, especially the residents, seven of whom were also 'ticketed' for the most challenging trials. Residents, especially city recorders, were also expected to attend civic functions. They had actively sought a variety of challenges throughout their careers. They had normally done more than one of the extra jobs listed above.

> A good friend of mine said 'you can either make a 15-year career out of this job or you can be one of those judges who will do anything to be away by half past 10 … Take any offer that comes your way … I hope all the new judges see it as a new career not as a retirement job, which it used to be seen as when I started.

This quotation is a reminder of the 1980s attitude to judicial service that was exposed in earlier chapters. Most judges sat at more than one court, one at nine venues, requiring hours of travelling. Two stayed away from home. None considered themselves overworked. Almost all found the stress and hours much less than in practice. One, who sat at five venues, handling crime and harrowing family cases, described her job as 'a complete picnic compared with being at the Bar'. Crown Court judges in central London had heavy caseloads and more frustrations.[10] One provincial resident who called himself a 'workaholic' said normal circuit judges outside London were underworked and another said of London judges:

> I feel sorry for them because they are on the same pay rates as me and they work much harder … if one trial collapses, there is another one immediately available … We had the most horrendous day once when Lord Irvine[11] turned up at Bristol and found only three of us.[12]

Despite this, none of the London judges complained of overwork. Judges were asked what they liked about work and what were the most satisfying aspects of the job. Five liked all aspects; four 'public service'; seven 'taking decisions'. Typical answers were 'Playing my part in trying to ensure a just outcome'[13] and 'Making decisions that affect people's lives'. Four mentioned the ability to control their working environment.

---

[10] A 2009 Audit Commission Report noted that while some provincial Crown Courts had spare capacity, some in the South East were working to capacity. London tries to relieve burdens by shifting cases around: NAO, *HM Courts Service—Administration of the Crown Court Report by the Comptroller and Auditor General HC 290 Session 2008–2009*, 6 March 2009.

[11] When Lord Chancellor and head of the judiciary. The story was repeated by other CJs and by HC judges. I would have assumed it to be apocryphal had I not heard it from this judge involved.

[12] Edward Leigh MP, chairing the Parliamentary Public Accounts Committee on 16 March 2009, said 'When I was a young barrister it was common knowledge that Crown Court judges wanted to play golf on Fridays … so they just listed the cases that way … I'm sure it's completely different nowadays' (Parliament website).

[13] Again the point made by Posner that since people *choose* to be judges, most want to do a good job and be well thought of.

> At the Bar you are self-employed … but a lot of barristers … don't want to take holidays just in case someone else steals their practice … suddenly, as a judge, you realise you are answerable to no-one.

Several liked controlling the court or the 'cut and thrust of the courtroom', or 'dealing with people'.

> Keeping everyone happy. In criminal cases nobody wants to be there … so my satisfaction is trying to keep everyone … happy and getting justice done at its best.

> the cut and thrust of being in court, observing human behaviour … making decisions … listening to points of law.

Two enjoyed summing-up to juries and four making the 'right decision' in sentencing.

Two explained why they no longer handled criminal business, though.

> I didn't want to send people to prison because they are just going to be worse when they come out … hopeless.

The second, formerly a commercial QC, was unhappy in hearing simple civil and criminal trials, which he considered a waste of his abilities. He was shifted to a county court and was 'much happier', handling challenging High Court commercial work. A third interviewee, EC (Eats Counsel),[14] the only unhappy Crown Court judge, was also a former commercial QC. He was a designated civil judge but handled mainly criminal cases. He worried that he might become case-hardened.

> Most of that time I spend trying rapes, or child sex abuse, or attempted murder, or occasionally a bit of murder … all very depressing … I really don't think it is a huge legal ideal for anyone to be trying the same kind of stuff in huge quantities … I suspect you become like magistrates with shoplifting. You have heard it all before and you don't believe it.

EC has since retired.

THE WORKING WEEK AND THE WORKING DAY —*TRYING* TO MOVE CASES ALONG

For most, there was no fixed pattern. Court was scheduled to commence at 9.30 am or 10.00 am, with brief hearings such as bail applications. Trials were meant to commence at 10.30 am, with all business finishing at 4.00 pm. The hours in the building depended on whether they were a resident and on preferences. Typically, one non-resident arrived by nine, after dropping children at school. She spent pre-court time writing summings-up but expected to spend an hour working at home, if she were presiding over a long and complex trial. Another stayed till 6.00

---

[14] As described by his colleagues.

pm to avoid taking work home, but spent three hours driving, during each half-year outside his base court. Some would go home if a trial collapsed but not in London. There were always ample cases to shift into judges' lists. One London judge commenced every day at 10.00 am with bail applications, ran trials virtually every day until 4.00 pm then case managed trials of young offenders charged with street crime until 4.30 pm or 5.00 pm. On the other hand, three provincial judges were able to spare many hours chatting to me because their scheduled trials had collapsed. The unpredictability of the nature, length and effectiveness of trials meant their working weeks differed but the variety fuelled their satisfaction.

The normal day with no trial consisted of mixed bail, sentencing and pre-trial management hearings, or plea and case management hearings (PCMHs). The Crown Court pilot was in a big London court, where, every year, 1997–2010, I have watched judges struggling to move business along in an underfunded system. The building is gloomy, overcrowded and decrepit and rain comes in. Electronic facilities often do not work; staff are overworked, underpaid and ill-trained; files are a mess, incomprehensible to the judge unless he reorganises them himself, and post takes eight days to get to him. The probation service cannot keep up with the demand for reports. Barristers are routinely incompetent, ignorant of their own case details and unapologetic. The full description appears in chapter seventeen. Things have worsened. By 2007, after a fraud trial collapsed, the pilot judge listed his normal litany of things that stall or destroy court business: the poverty of resources of agencies and the courts; two courtrooms unused through lack of judges. Every year, including 2010, he said that the London probation service was in 'meltdown'. By October 2009, I watched an entire morning of ineffective business with his colleague, whose trial failed to start because of the prosecutor's illness, while the research judge's trial was postponed, awaiting a witness. In the former's court, there were problems getting information from either advocate in a series of applications. For example, there was a bail application for a 15-year-old. Part-way through, prosecution counsel mentioned, in passing, that the defendant was on bail for another offence. The judge asked, 'Well, why didn't you mention that *before*?' Obviously, counsel had not set eyes on the file until he was in the courtroom.[15] In a probation review, the judge spoke to the unaccompanied defendant, to find out about the case. There was no probation officer. Eventually he appeared. The judge summoned him into his room to politely ask for an explanation. The latest report on the defendant was three months old, which the judge considered useless. A new one was ordered and the procedure re-started from scratch. Another case could not proceed because a defendant had not bothered to turn up to instruct he solicitor. Why would he? In between fruitless attempts at progressing each case, there was a long

---

[15] Reminiscent of prosecutors appearing before Portia in the last chapter.

wait for each defendant to be brought from the cells. Meanwhile, in the provinces, Peter sat in a gleaming, sunny, new court…

FOUR DAYS WITH PETER MATTHEWS—THE JUDGE IN WAITING

Time with this non-resident portrays this unpredictability and the fact that much time may be spent out of court, waiting for prisoners to be delivered and so on, or, on northern circuits, waiting for plea negotiations to take place.[16]

Monday

12.30 pm: In a mixed list, 'PM' was sentencing a dangerous driver. He questioned whether £800–£900 per day on a cocaine habit was a printing error. It was not. Used to London, I was struck by the advocates' strong regional accents and their flipping from prosecuting to defending on a case-by-case basis.

1.10 pm: We retired for lunch, expecting a 'floating' trial at 2.10 pm but waited till 4.10 pm, since lawyers were negotiating. The judge next door, EC, kept popping in, complaining about lack of progress in his burglary. PM remarked that our defendant had not asked for a sentence indication and this was 'very rare nowadays'.[17] We discussed whether plans for judicial criminal case management[18] would stop such delays and last minute plea negotiations.

4.10 pm: The clerk summoned us into court. PM expected the trial had collapsed into a guilty plea. It had not. The prosecution insisted that all 10 counts should be tried as redrafted, unless the accused was prepared to plead guilty to all. Defence

---

[16]   There are not only court cultures but circuit cultures. The reputation for plea bargaining on the northern circuits is born out by the *Judicial and Court Statistics 2009* (Version 1.1, revised October 2010, Ministry of Justice), which disclose that the highest cracked trial rate was in the NE circuit (60.3 per cent, almost double that of London), followed by the NW circuit (52 per cent). RB Flemming et al, *The Craft of Justice* (Philadelphia, University of Pennsylvania Press, 1993) ch 4, and previous research referred to therein, observed that court differences depend not just on law or procedure but judicial preferences. Here, the differences seemed to be driven more by the local practitioners but the judges were recruited from the local Bar and thus part of the culture. By contrast, PW Tague examines London barristers' motivation in *proceeding to trial* to develop their advocacy reputation, in 'Barristers' Selfish Incentives in Counselling Defendants over the Choice of Plea' [2007] *Crim LR* 3. See further below.

[17]   See Sentencing Council guidelines, 'Reduction in Sentence for a Guilty Plea' and *Goodyear (Practice Note)* [2005] EWCA Crim 888, explained in P Darbyshire, 'Transparency in Getting the Accused to Plead Guilty Early' (2006) 65 *Cambridge Law Journal* 48–51.

[18]   Criminal Procedure Rules 2005 and 2010, Part 3 places the courts under a duty to manage cases, explained in P Darbyshire, *Darbyshire on the English Legal System*, 10th edn (London, Sweet & Maxwell, 2011) ch 12.

counsel said he was professionally embarrassed and could no longer act.[19] PM explained to the accused (D) that the trial would go ahead the following day and asked if he understood that this meant he might have to represent himself. PM sent the listing officer frantically hunting for a substitute barrister. She failed. PM instructed her to try the neighbouring city. 'Let's hope they get someone robust with a bit of experience to sort this out' (meaning persuading D to plead guilty).

5.00 pm: We left.

Tuesday

10.00 am: No counsel had been found from three cities. PM worked on a large pile of files. He had done an hour's reading at home the previous night.

10.10 am: In court, PM rescheduled the case two months hence, warning D that this was his last chance. He should find a solicitor within 24 hours. D was in custody so I wondered if this would create difficulties.[20]

10.15 am: We retired. PM explained today's list: adjournments, sentences, a 'mention', two floating trials and an application for a bench warrant.

10.30 am: Into court. Defence counsel in the robbery asked for time to see the editing of the video evidence because he had only just been served with it by the prosecution. PM consented but said the trial would go ahead in 30 minutes. He adjourned another case in which D had appendicitis. He sentenced an unconnected defendant.

11.15 am: We awaited a defendant, late from prison because Category A prisoners could not be mixed with Category C. (I waited with judges for prison vans on three other circuits. The Old Bailey's chief clerk had told me, in 2001, that some days he 'struggled to start any courts before midday'. This problem may have eased slightly since some interim business can be conducted via a live video link from the prison.)

11.45 am: Sentenced another dangerous driver.

12.10 pm: Retired.

12.25 pm: Into court, because the advocates in one of the floating trials wanted to speak to PM in private. He insisted on doing this in court, having asked the

---

[19] Because the defendant had admitted his guilt to him.

[20] Note the litany of problems for prisoners trying to communicate with lawyers, Auld Review, above n 9 at 405–06.

public to leave, as he wanted the discussion to be taped. All judges took this precaution. Phoning the listing officer, PM had instructed 'Tell counsel this could be listed for this afternoon before Judge EC' and he repeated this in court.

12.30 pm: He explained, outside, that this was a coded threat. EC was known for 'eating barristers' and 'making them cry' in court. 'Counsel will be bending over backwards to agree if they're threatened with *him*.'

12.55 pm; In court. PM had asked everyone to discuss what was happening in the two floating trials and a third, scheduled for Monday. In the first, D had changed his plea to guilty. In the second, counsel asked for a discussion in chambers so PM again asked the public to leave. Counsel explained that negotiations had included the criminal responsibility of a child. D had changed his plea to guilty but when the indictment was put again, he objected. PM asked for an assurance of the basis of plea and for the details to be recorded, to reassure D. When the public returned, PM explained what had been discussed in their absence. The other floating trial would go ahead.

1.46 pm: Sandwiches in his room. Another judge wandered in to tell us he was going dog racing that night and the visiting High Court judge had asked to come. 'You'll find them more out-of-touch than us.' The judges discussed their children's graduations.

2.46 pm: We returned to court for the street robbery trial but counsel were still not ready. The jury were sworn in at 3.15 pm. PM apologised for the delay. The prosecution case was excruciating. The witnesses were acquaintances of the young defendant. Their evidence contradicted their statements and they were making it up as they went along. PM asked D to stop pulling faces. This was a designated street crime court and at other such courts, on different circuits, I noticed that judges expressed surprise at the trivial incidents that were prosecuted as robbery. One amounted to an argument between a woman and her boyfriend over a mobile phone. In 2006, HM Crown Prosecution Service (CPS) Inspectorate repeated the criticism that the CPS was responsible for an unacceptably high number of cases being discharged in the Crown Court.

4.15 pm: PM sent the jury away then warned prosecution counsel that if there were a defence submission of 'no case to answer', he would accede to it, because the prosecution evidence was 'riddled with inconsistencies'.

Wednesday

10.00 am: PM refused three bail applications.

10.30 am: Moved courtrooms. The robbery prosecutor had decided to offer no evidence. PM explained this to the jury and thanked them. We retired. I had a long conversation with EC. After lunch, PM and his wife took me on a tour of the local beauty spots.

Thursday

With no notice, PM was sent to a court 66 miles away to try an indecent assault because a 'Class 2' ticketed judge was needed.

12.15 pm: D had allegedly assaulted a 13-year-old at a fairground. In the courtroom, counsel asked for more time because they had new information from another area, where D was facing further charges.[21]

12.25 pm: We waited in the judge's room during plea negotiations. These observations had confirmed the reputation of this circuit: counsel expected to commence plea negotiations automatically, on arrival at court. En route in the car, PM explained that this and other smaller courts had 'their own' procedures. 'It's not been unknown that a judge from here goes into the [barristers'] robing room first thing and says "This is not a *trial* is it?"'. One judge was famous for 'getting rid' of everything so that he could play golf in the afternoon. 'Are you coming to lunch?' PM teased, affecting shock when he assented. A young judge offered us a share of his room, since PM was moaning about being in 'a cupboard'. A third judge came in to seek advice on sentencing. The resident popped in. PM explained that this was a friendly court, whereas such interchanges were impeded at some other buildings because of the layout. It seemed to me that relations were also facilitated by the amount of time spent out of court awaiting plea negotiations.[22]

12.40–1.00 pm: Into court. D pleaded guilty to indecent assault in exchange for prosecutorial concessions.[23] PM sentenced D.

---

[21] D had a record of 18 sex offences and many other offences.

[22] See considerable literature on plea bargaining: J Baldwin and M McConville, *Negotiated Justice* (London, Martin Robertson, 1977); J Baldwin, *Pre-trial Justice* (Oxford, Basil Blackwell, 1985); M McConville, 'Plea Bargaining' in M McConville and G Wilson, *The Handbook of the Criminal Justice Process* (Oxford, Oxford University Press, 2003) 353 and citations therein; A Ashworth and M Redmayne, *The Criminal Process*, (Oxford, Oxford University Press, all editions); A Sanders and R Young, *Criminal Justice* (Oxford, Oxford University Press, all editions); P Darbyshire, 'The Mischief of Plea Bargaining and Sentencing Rewards' [2000] *Crim LR* 895, and references therein.

[23] Dropping charges of a failure to report a change of address and using a false name, in breach of the conditions of the Sex Offenders Register.

1.05 pm: Lunch in the judges' dining room with the circuit and district judges. The resident opened a bottle of wine to share with me. The judges teased about how the research sample had been selected. PM was known to be kind so they insisted the senior judiciary must have steered me away from two local judges, including EC. This sparked stories of eccentric judges of yesteryear, discussed in chapter sixteen. We drove back to PM's home court.

With two other provincial judges on different circuits, even more of the week was spent out of court. One judge's scheduled fraud trial had collapsed and, as he was on leave the following week, he could only be given brief applications or short trials.

MANAGERIAL, PASTORAL AND OTHER OUT-OF-COURT WORK[24]

By contrast, residents of big courts and those with heavy out-of-court commitments needed to get on with paperwork, emails or phone calls every time they left the courtroom. Residents are under government pressure to reduce the number of 'cracked' and ineffective trials and the description of Peter Matthews' schedule demonstrates how wasteful of court time these could be.[25] Residents were constantly aware of their court's statistics, which they compiled and disseminated.[26] They liaised with listing officers and court managers over judicial deployment. The resident's role is to 'offer support and guidance' to other judges. The resident was normally the first resort for legal and practice advice, especially for recorders (part-timers) and new CJs. For example, a recorder asked a resident about a street 'robbery' which amounted to a domestic argument and asked if he should 'lean on the Crown'. Staff saw residents as being in a pastoral role for them too. They popped in wanting to take time out for surgery, or to discuss other welfare issues. Residents had warm relationships with staff. Indeed, judges were generally polite and welcoming, very appreciative, supportive and protective of staff, who they considered to be obliging, underpaid and overworked. Residents signed 'release forms', releasing serious cases normally listed before High Court

---

[24] Drawn from observations and checked against a 2004 Judicial Office document, 'The Responsibilities of Resident Judges and Designated Civil and Family Judges'.

[25] The latest policy designed to bring forward plea negotiations is in Ministry of Justice, *Proposals for the Reform of Legal Aid in England and Wales* CP 12/10, 2010, ch 2 (and see ch 18 below).

> we have already asked the Sentencing Council to consider how sentence discounts might form part of a package of measures to encourage those who acknowledge their guilt to do so at the earliest opportunity. The earlier the guilty plea, the less trauma likely to be suffered by victims and witnesses at the prospect of giving evidence in court; and the lower the costs to the courts and other agencies.

[26] See Lord Chancellor Falconer's June 2003 speech launching the Case Preparation Project (DCA archived website) and the Effective Trial Management Project, announced in 2003 by the Attorney General.

judges, to a 'ticketed' CJ, then referred them to the circuit's presiding judge. They continuously contacted presiders about judicial deployment, such as where and by whom big trials should be heard. They helped organise swearing-in ceremonies and retirement parties (usually involving sketches or pranks, depending on their sense of humour and the court's culture).

Three courts were in the Effective Trial Management Programme pilots, prior to the Criminal Procedure Rules 2005, attempting to manage criminal business more effectively. One acting resident was uncomfortable that judges would be expected to report on the efficacy of counsel in ensuring that scheduled trials were well-prepared and effective. 'We're being asked to act as taxing masters.'[27] At a court users' committee, there were representatives of magistrates' clerks, the listing officer, the Bar and the probation service. They measured the court's performance against targets set by their local Criminal Justice Board. An attempt had been made to persuade local practitioners to adopt a secure email system. The judge hosted a meeting but although 12 barristers came, only two of 90 local solicitors turned up, a problem reflected on another circuit.[28] Residents are the court's contact-point for managers or representatives of court users, such as the CPS, the probation service, and defence lawyers. For example, one resident had complained, like many research judges, about the poor quality of electronic recordings and interviewing of child witnesses in abuse cases. The CPS asked him to join in with their proposal for a new editing system. He declined but was happy to write a letter of support. The management role required residents to spend time away from court, though the loss of judicial days put a strain on the system. One spent Monday at a meeting about the state-of-the-art recording equipment at his court, only to have to tell his fellow judges on the Tuesday that it was being withdrawn, as it was only a pilot. He was away on the Friday at a residents' conference.

One resident complained of too much 'admin' work. When I examined the 18-inch pile of paper on his desk, however, I noticed that none of the decisions required was administrative. They were all judicial. The fact that a decision results from a paper application does not make it administrative. For example, permission to appeal may be applied for on paper.[29] The pile of 'box work' might include applications to extend a trial timetable, or to revoke a community penalty order, or for a witness summons, or to reveal a child's name, or to appeal out of time, or applications from jurors to be excused service. Every resident was bedevilled with constant applications from defendants wanting to change their lawyers, sometimes for the third time. One explained that these 'clogged up the

---

[27]   Criminal Procedure Rules, Rule 3.5.

[28]   Despite the fact that solicitors could earn CPD points just for turning up.

[29]   Case management decisions are judicial. The European Convention on Human Rights requires judicial decisions to be taken by those in a judicial position, independent of the executive. See P Darbyshire, 'A Comment on the Powers of Magistrates' Clerks' [1999] *Crim LR* 377 and see Darbyshire, above n 18 at chs 4 and 12.

system' because every new team had to be given a month to prepare the case. Several reminded me that solicitors in Manchester had been caught bribing remand prisoners with radios in an attempt to poach clients from the competition. At another city with turf wars between two firms, to which Guy had alerted me in the last chapter, a resident showed me a pile of applications, each of which gave the reason 'I have lost faith in my solicitors', which he pointed out was not in the normal vocabulary of defendants and was obviously drafted by the rival firm. One judge showed me an application from the defence to see the social services reports of a child complainant in a sex abuse case. He remarked that this was a fashionable 'cottage industry' among barristers and another judge explained that abuse of process applications had been a similar delaying tactic, 'until the Court of Appeal put a stop to it'.

Some satellite applications and preliminary hearings and all sentencing required pre-reading by all judges. Difficult points of law needed researching, sometimes in frantic lunchtimes, especially if counsel could not be 'trusted' to have researched properly. Some judges were more keen than others to pre-read papers in routine cases. One resident said that, as he might expect to have to deal with over 40 PCMHs in a Friday session, it was impossible to read all the papers. In any event, he was 'quick to pick things up'.

One resident dealt with a number of applications under the Proceeds of Crime Act 2002, as he was the only local judge ticketed to decide them. These involved brief appearances in his chambers, preceded by reading fairly lengthy applications. Consultation papers from various bodies were addressed to each resident and two complained of being 'bombarded'. One resident, a chancellor, worked his way through a pile of consistory court decisions. He emailed queries to other chancellors such as 'Are Mum, Dad and Gran acceptable on a gravestone?' Another dealt with a complaint arising from his conduct of a mental health review tribunal and another spent a whole day, when a trial had collapsed, completing 16 consultation forms on applicants for recorderships, in other words the 'secret soundings', discussed in chapter four. Ten had named him as a referee. Another conferred police commendations and another swore-in new magistrates.

Some residents were also City Recorders.[30] This office is in the gift of a city, requiring participation in civic functions, such as dinners, royal visits, religious and remembrance services. The offices of Recorder of London and Common Serjeant carry substantial obligations, such as livery dinners, the election and presentation of Sheriffs and the Lord Mayor's Show. Several require speech-making.[31]

---

[30] Not to be confused with recorders, part-time judges.
[31] Honorary Recorders are entitled to be addressed as 'My Lord' or 'My Lady', as are all CJs at the Old Bailey: The Consolidated Criminal Practice Direction Part IV.30.

The busier and bigger the court, the harder the resident worked, like two here, Mortimer and Fergus. Both were conducting murder trials, one legally challenging and the other many months long and very difficult to manage. Both commenced work at 8.00–9.00 am, with hearings in unrelated matters at 10.00 am, and the trial restarting at 10.30 am. Breaks and the 4.15–6.00 pm period were filled with boxwork, management decisions, phone calls or emails. They left at 6.00 pm or 6.30 pm and took home their trial notes to research the law and/or write their summing-up for the jury.

A TRIAL: JUDGE MORTIMER DEALING WITH DEATH

Every observed trial was affected by a delayed start, or disruption, or was abortive, or protracted by poor presentation of the evidence or unnecessary evidence and, contrary to some circuit judges' assumptions, business before the HC judges was even more ineffective, as we shall see in the High Court chapter. Trials normally suffered from more than one of these defects. Little wonder then, that trial times have lengthened considerably since the mid-twentieth century and that the executive has been concerned, for decades, to reduce the number of cracked and ineffective trials.[32] This story is of legally complex murder retrial that would normally be handled by an HC judge but, such was the murder rate in his city, was released to Mortimer, the resident, who squeezed in his managerial jobs and other caseload around it. Circuit judges readily admit that they are of mixed ability. Mortimer, like HC judges, was exceptionally intelligent. He needed to be, to understand and apply the House of Lords judgments that had written off the first trial of this defendant. His trials were almost all murder and attempted murder.

Monday

9.00 am: M worked through boxwork and staff and other queries. He preferred email but word-processed letters. He had been offered a personal assistant but declined.

10.00 am: In court, M heard brief applications, including one to vacate a trial date. Defence counsel had obtained a psychologist's report. M repeatedly explained that only a psychiatrist's report would do. Exasperated, he remarked, aside, that some barristers did not understand the difference.

---

[32] See especially *the Royal Commission on Criminal Justice Report* (London, HMSO, Cm 2263, 1993) ch 6 and The Auld Report, above n 9 at ch 10. Policy prompted by the latter and applicable during the research period was set out in the 2002 white paper *Justice for All* (London, The Stationery Office, 2002).

11.00 am: We awaited the 10.30 am trial, the security officers explaining that there was no-one available to accompany the accused. M continued his boxwork. His court clerk was fussing. There were members of the victim's family in the public gallery. 'They'll be wondering why the trial hasn't started.' M called the court manager and asked that Group 4 be 'given a rocket'. Delays were common.

11.20 am: In court. Counsel wondered whether 'some story' should be given to the jury to explain the delay since the offence. M said not. M refused an application for handcuffs, as there was no evidence of violence on this occasion. M made a public complaint about Group 4, though it later transpired that the trial could not have started on time because all counsel requested extension leads for their laptops.

Witnesses were lined-up in court to check that they were not known to any juror. Air conditioning made the room icy cold but, as it was July, three unfortunate jurors had dressed in short sleeves. Twelve of the deceased youth's family faced them, including his two brothers, who resembled him. The prosecutor added an extra prompt: a coffin-like box as a lectern. M said Queen's Counsel for both sides were very competent and well-known locally. Under their silk gowns, they were dressed expensively and flashed bright white tabs, gold watches, cufflinks and fountain pens. M did not feel the need to impress the jury sartorially, accessorised with a scarlet robe, plain watch and a handful of cheap ballpoint pens.

4.10–5.10 pm: M completed a pile of release forms. He recited, '"The steak-knife murder"—she killed her boyfriend in a restaurant—"the single blow murder"'. He examined four applications to transfer from one firm of solicitors. A letter from the losing solicitors complained that they were 'sick and tired' of clients transferring. There were several other applications. I left and he continued working.

Tuesday

Problem: a judge had been off work for a month, with stress. His wife called to say he was not returning and he had a fresh doctor's note. Finding no statute prescribing sick leave requirements for judges, M emailed his circuit presider and the Secretary of the Council of Circuit judges for advice.

10.20 am: We were waiting for anything among the 10.00 am list to be ready, as the trial was due to re-start at 10.30 am. In one minute, M fixed the PCMH date on a murder then gossiped with the clerk.

10.25 am: Applications to vacate trial dates.

10.40 am: Trial counsel wanted a discussion in the absence of the jury. Defence counsel sought to argue provocation, drunkenness and diminished responsibility. The prosecutor had found no new model jury direction following a Law Lords' ruling on a previous appeal but M had obtained one from an HC judge. The jury returned, clad in thick fleeces or body warmers. Agreed prosecution witness-statements were read to them.

11.40 am: The prosecution concluded. M explained to the jury, gently, politely and slowly that they could have the afternoon off while we awaited the defence psychiatrist but could 'rest assured' that he and counsel would be 'working on other cases'. They left and legal discussion resumed. Outside, M explained that the prosecutor did not like dealing with questions of law but the defence counsel did, having argued his point in the original trial up to the House of Lords.[33] I asked M if he was nervous about directing the jury on law, in case he made an error in this sensitive retrial. He was not. He was confident he could rely on counsel to help him. That, he said, was the advantage of knowing counsel in a provincial court. He sent a copy of the new specimen direction to both, remarking 'It's probably all academic for the jury. They'll just look at that little body and they'll look at the defendant [ugly and twice his size] and think he needs convicting for murder'.

M continued his managerial jobs and legal research while we waited for counsel to discuss the jury direction. The presider telephoned. He wanted a case to be sent to a neighbouring city, F, but both counsel wanted it to be heard at city G, fearing adverse publicity. A sensitive private prosecution was listed for a pre-trial hearing the next day. The prosecutor was an estranged son, accusing his relatives of perjury in considering his father's cremation. M logged an inquiry into *Felix*, the judge's intranet at that time, to ask if the DPP's consent to prosecution was required. We went back into court to hear legal submissions on what questions the expert witnesses could be asked and what issues were matters for the jury.

Wednesday

M was word-processing his jury direction. The perjury case was listed for 10.00 am but the unrepresented prosecutor had not appeared so M made phone calls about his autumn schedule.

10.16 am: Into court to fix the timetable for an attempted murder. The perjury prosecutor (P) appeared. M feared he would have to rule that P should be represented. M had written to the CPS to ask if they would take over the prosecution (in the hope that they would stop it) but they declined. M entered

---

[33] He was successful. D's conviction following his first trial was quashed.

into a dialogue, in simple language and sympathetic tone, with P, about whether he should be represented. Speaking gently, he patiently pointed out that the indictment specified perjury yet the committal had been for an offence under the Cremation Act 1902. 'Mr P, doesn't all this show you need legal representation?' P said he had been declined legal aid. 'Mr P, this looks like a very sad family dispute which doesn't belong in the criminal courts.' He explained that the statements contained a lot of irrelevant and inadmissible evidence which would have been filtered out by a lawyer. After more explanation, M said 'The judges are not here and the courts are not here to give legal advice'. M asked for these problems to be resolved before the PCMH and urged P to seek a solicitor's advice. As we left the courtroom, M wondered how this case had 'got past the district judge' in the magistrates' court.

10.47 am: The trial resumed. The prosecutor wanted to bring evidence of the accused's violence in prison. Defence counsel objected. M looked quizzically at the prosecutor and this was enough for him to concede the point. The jury were brought in and the defence case opened. D was examined about his previous convictions for violence and his relationship with his aunt, who was his 'common law wife', his addiction to drinking prison 'hooch', and his post-prison binge of alcohol and amphetamines which preceded the murder. He was cross-examined. A row broke out, with defence counsel angrily objecting to the prosecutor's questions.

12.00 pm: The jury were sent out and defence counsel alleged that prejudicial gestures had been made by a police officer in the public gallery. M and the prosecutor said they had not noticed this. Defence counsel leaped up, 'If counsel is calling me a liar!' M stopped the argument. 'Mr N, Mr Y! If you're going to have a spat, do it out of my earshot!' We rose, as M considered it politic to take a break. M explained that they headed two rival sets of barristers' chambers.

2.15 pm: The defence case resumed. During a tricky part of the prosecutor's cross-examination of the psychiatrist, defence counsel ostentatiously filled his fountain pen from a bottle of ink, which seemed to me to be an effective jury-distraction tactic.[34] M kept asking her to speak up for the jury's sake and asked some questions that would doubtless have been in their minds.

---

[34]   Rock, above n 6 at 55, fn 69 recounts 'John Mortimer recalled that his father had told him about how Marshall Hall had been "preceded into court by a clerk bearing a pile of clean handkerchiefs, a carafe of water and an air cushion. When the prosecution evidence became awkward, he would blow his nose, a sad trumpet, on one of the handkerchiefs. If it became worse, he would knock over a glass of water. If it became really damning, he would slowly inflate the cushion and then the jury had eyes and ears for nothing else. ('Playing to the Jury', *The Times*, 22 April 1992.)'

4.15 pm: Out of court, M's clerk told him she had been asked to clerk another court the following day. M was aghast and called the court manager. The shortage of clerks meant they had to be shared between courts but M clung to one of his privileges as resident.

4.30 pm: M completed another pile of release forms and an application to revoke a community penalty order. We discussed the Street Crime Initiative. He was informed that Fathers 4 Justice planned a day-long demonstration outside the court the following day.

5.50 pm: An administrator brought in a request for police presence in a trial and another brought in a fresh pile of boxwork. After working through this, he assembled all the material he needed to prepare his direction in the murder trial overnight—the Law Lords' judgment, the new specimen direction, notes on counsel's submissions, law reports and law review commentaries on the new ground of argument.

Thursday

9.40 am: The 50 Fathers 4 Justice demonstrators formed a colourful spectacle in front of the building. The aims were to draw public attention to the alleged pro-mother bias of judges and protest to the judges but this was defeated, as all judges had arrived earlier, via their rear entrance, and the demonstrators left before any had finished court. They were not visible from the judges' rooms. M had spent from 10.00 pm to 1.00 am word-processing his summing-up from his handwritten notes and refining his jury directions on the law. I asked whether he had tried using his laptop in court. He had but, like all but three of the 32 CJs, had decided he was not quick enough.

10.30 am: In court, there was a discussion about the psychiatrist's report and it was added to the jury bundle. She gave evidence from 10.40 am. M was frustrated by counsel's questioning but said nothing. Their differences in technique reflected their attitudes to the law.

12.20 pm: The defence closed and M sent out the jury. The prosecutor offered a copy of his closing speech to M and the defence counsel, in case the latter took exception to it. He replied that it contained points of law with which he disagreed but he would be addressing the judge. 'Then why not object *now*?' snapped the prosecutor, anxious not to have a second conviction overturned on appeal. Outside, M sighed about counsel's acrimonious interchanges. He sent them his proposed jury directions. Defence counsel had submitted his proposed address. It sought to correct a line of prosecution questioning that he considered had misled the jury. I wondered why he had not objected at the time of the questioning and asked M whether he felt that defence counsel was employing a deliberate tactic of letting things go wrong at the *trial* in order to fuel an appeal. M agreed that this seemed to be so, adding that at the first trial, this barrister had approved of the judge's direction, but had later attacked it on appeal. I asked M if this sort of behaviour was common. 'Not here; we think of it as a London thing.'[35] At lunch, other circuit judges confirmed this. 'Up here they've got enough work not to create it. Also, it's a bad tactic. You may not win on appeal.'

2.00 pm: Counsel made their closing speeches.

3.40 pm: M took the jury through his written directions and sent them home to await his summing up in the morning.

Out of court, the clerk came in to mention part of tomorrow's business, a preliminary hearing in a murder case where the prostitute victims had been found chopped up in plastic bags. I left M to continue with his boxwork.

THE FRAGILITY OF THE TRIAL AND THE JUDGE AS 'UMPIRE'

In 1990, one Wood Green judge told Paul Rock that:

> Trial by jury has become, as a result of decisions by the Court of Appeal, an inordinately fragile process which may have to be aborted on the most (apparently) trivial pretexts.[36]

Mortimer's trial was fragile. It was scheduled with difficulty. Because the Law Lords had written off the first trial, it was crucial that M directed his jury meticulously and ensured that counsel stayed within the strict legal boundaries of this impossibly complex field. Defence counsel was looking for any weakness. M needed to understand and apply the Law Lords' judgment. A new defence was raised. The alternative defences had different burdens and standards of proof. Two prima donna QCs squabbled. This is why complex murder trials are normally restricted to High Court judges, whom CJs generally consider to have a more finely tuned intellect, like Mortimer.

Criminal trials are fragile for other reasons. They may be shattered by prejudicial testimony, blurted out by an uncontrolled witness, or in calm response to an illegitimate question. A successful pre-trial or mid-trial objection may persuade the judge that the prosecution evidence has not satisfied their burden of proof and the case should be dismissed. Trials may be aborted or

---

[35] See below on trustworthiness of lawyers. M also referred me to D Ormerod's comment on *Kimber* [2001] *Crim LR* 897, on the *per curiam* reference of the Court of Appeal to the *Code of Conduct for the Bar of England and Wales*, that counsel has an overriding duty to the court to act with independence and in the interests of justice. An advocate should not do anything which knowingly encourages or permits the court to proceed on a false basis.

[36] Rock, above n 6 at 27.

delayed by non-appearance of a witness, or loss or corruption of evidence. Their very survival as a contest is unpredictable, as they may be 'carved up' at any time, by plea negotiations. Twelve of 25 Crown Court judges said delays or things going wrong in the case were their worst frustrations.

The judge's pre-trial job is to expedite the scheduling and to ensure, at the PCMH that it is ready to go ahead. During the trial, they still have the job of speeding it along but must also exercise vigilance over its conduct and contents. It is often said that in the Anglo-American common law adversarial trial, the judge merely acts as an unbiased umpire.[37] Undue interference in the advocates' presentation may render the trial unfair, as explained by Lord Denning in *Jones v National Coal Board*.[38]

In a jury trial, the judge must also ensure that information is delivered intelligibly, though they have no means of testing juror comprehension. They have never been entirely passive, though, nor is it accurate to portray the circuit judge as the arbiter of law and the jury as the sole arbiter of fact. If the judge considers the prosecution evidence to be too weak, they can withdraw the case from the jury or acceded to a defence submission of 'no case to answer', at the end of the prosecution case, and PM threatened to do this, in the street crime case, above.[39]

There have been inroads into the judge's passive role and the adversarial model, from the 1990s. The Royal Commission on Criminal Justice 1993 recommended that judges manage complex cases, pre-trial.[40] A 1995 practice direction regularised pre-trial hearings[41] as an opportunity to gather information and make management decisions. Defence statements were required by the Criminal Procedure and Investigations Act 1996, with a judicial power to punish a defaulter by inviting the jury to draw an adverse inference. Judges showed me defence statements and I was surprised to find that none amounted to more than three unhelpful, cryptic sentences. Such was the level of judicial antipathy

---

[37] M Zander, *Cases and Materials on the English Legal System* (Cambridge, Cambridge University Press, any edition) ch 4. It is not up to the judge to initiate grounds of argument or lines of questioning, or to call witnesses. JH Langbein cites the French observer, Cottu, in 1820, describing the English judge as 'almost a stranger to what is going on': *The Origins of the Adversary Criminal Trial* (Oxford, Oxford University Press, 2003) 253.

[38] [1957] 2 QB 55. 'The judge's part in all this is to hearken to the evidence, only himself asking questions of witnesses when it is necessary to clear up any point that has been overlooked or left obscure; to see that the advocates behave themselves seemly and keep to the rules ... to exclude irrelevancies and discourage repetition; to make sure by wise intervention that he follows the points that the advocates are making and can assess their worth...If he goes beyond this, he drops the mantle of a judge and assumes the robe of an advocate: and the change does not become him well.'

[39] Judges also have the power to call witnesses, although from my observations this seems to occur very rarely and this is confirmed by J Jackson, 'Judicial Responsibility in Criminal Proceedings' (1996) 49 *Current Legal Problems* 59 at 70. See also his chapter 19 of McConville and Wilson, above n 22.

[40] Recommendation 245.

[41] Now PCMHs.

towards enforcing this requirement, though, that an experienced circuit judge asked his colleagues, in 2005, whether there was any penalty for not producing one. Other judges were not surprised at his ignorance. They too had never mentioned such a 'defence failure' to a jury, as the defendant would naturally blame his lawyers. Incidentally, I was surprised to find that no judge, given the opportunity, invited the jury to draw an adverse inference against a defendant for exercising the right of silence. There were two reasons. Most occurrences were a 'partial failure', where the defendant answered some questions not others. Secondly, again, judges knew that defendants would claim they were acting on legal advice. Although these powers were described by Sir Philip Otton in 2002[42] as if they were operating as intended, this was far too optimistic, according to these surprising findings above. It is telling that the piece was not written by a practising circuit judge. This epitomises the gap between law in books and law in the real world, which renders empirical research essential. Indeed, Parliament has now extended the required contents of defence statements, in the Criminal Justice Act 2003, Part 5 and in 2006, the Court of Appeal (CA) issued a protocol on disclosure which called for a 'complete change of culture' among judges and lawyers in their attitudes to enforcement of the disclosure rules. Commenting in 2007, though, one of the research judges said that when faced with an inadequate defence statement, he made a declaration of inadequacy 'which is met by blank looks on the faces of *both* counsel'. This contrasts with fraud trials, which have specialist practices and a different culture. One London resident who specialised in them said in 2007 that he demanded full defence statements for years and showed me a 45-page statement.[43] Elsewhere, another London judge said that the biggest recent culture change had been in defence lawyers' willingness to outline the defence and answer questions.

On scheduling, it used to be said that a premium was put on the judge's time and court time. Court users supposedly had to organise themselves to accommodate this. Doubtless this was the case when judges travelled on circuit around assize towns and counted their schedules in days[44] but recent observations in the Crown Court confirmed what I had already learned, that the opposite presumption now prevails. The judge provides a service to be called on as and when it suits the parties and for the period that they and the surrounding circumstances dictate. The Crown Court judge is an umpire who has no more control over the progress of a 'match' than a tennis umpire at Wimbledon has over the rain. If witnesses, the defendant or jurors turn up late, or advocates request more time to

---

[42]   In McConville and Wilson, above n 22.

[43]   Strict trial management and demands for thorough preparation in fraud cases appear to have produced results, according to nine fraud judges. A culture change resulted from the 2005 Rules and a 2005 Protocol on the conduct of fraud and other complex cases: RF Julian, 'Judicial Perspectives in Serious Fraud Cases—The Present Status of and Problems Posed by Case Management Practices, Jury Selection Rules, Juror Expertise, Plea Bargaining and Choice of Mode of Trial' [2008] *Crim LR* 764.

[44]   Prior to the creation of the Crown Court in 1972, by the Courts Act 1971.

prepare, the judge is powerless to move the trial forward.[45] The following instances demonstrate the tension between the judge's legal obligation[46] and practical need to expedite the trial and the legal constraint to stay off the pitch and yet regulate the legality and fairness of the trial's contents.

Last-minute Preparation Delaying the Trial

In the main research period, 2003–05, only one trial started on time. Last-minute preparation is inherent in the Crown Court *partly* because of the UK's (unusual) divided legal profession. The split legal profession is taken for granted by lawyers working within it. They cannot step outside it to view it objectively, yet American and other foreign lawyers, like the law students I take into court, can immediately pinpoint its pitfalls. These are not acknowledged by lawyers and judges here, because they lack experience in other jurisdictions, although the problem is well known to commentators.[47] A communication problem arises in this way: although a solicitor may have taken instructions from the defendant weeks before, defendants are represented by barristers, many of whom receive the brief the night before the trial, because the barrister originally briefed is unavailable. Many defendants do not see their barrister until the morning of trial. If the prison van is late, and then the barrister needs to take instructions, there is a double delay. Defence barristers often asked for time to view evidence. One explained he had only received it at 5.30 pm. Dixon commented:

> I couldn't believe that chap hadn't seen that video before … if that had been my brief, I would have taken that video home … You invent all these systems of ticking the boxes or whatever [the Effective Trial Management (ETM) Programme] but no one actually does the work until the last minute.

---

[45]   Rock made this point in relation to a trial he described. 'The judge was powerless to move the trial along: he could not forbid counsel to consult his client. He had simply to wait.' Rock, above n 6 at 100.

[46]   To protect the accused from undue delay, under Art 6 of the European Convention on Human Rights.

[47]   M Zander and P Henderson's *Crown Court Study* for the *Royal Commission on Criminal Justice* Research Study No 19 (London, HMSO, 1993) found that in 688 contested cases, 31 per cent of defence counsel and 49 per cent of prosecutors had not been briefed until the day before, or trial day. In 59 per cent, prosecution barristers said the brief had been returned by someone else, as did defence counsel in 44 per cent (at 30–32). In 60 per cent, there was no pre-trial meeting between client and barrister before the hearing day. In 70 per cent of last-minute guilty pleas 'cracked trials', the defendant met his barrister on the morning of trial (at 55). Defendants complained of shoddy service after meeting their barrister on the morning of trial: AE Bottoms and JD McClean, *Defendants in the Criminal Process* (London, Routledge & Kegan Paul, 1976) and M McConville et al, *Standing Accused* (Oxford, Clarendon Press, 1994). See discussion in Darbyshire, above n 18.

Barristers blame the courts.[48] Two trials were delayed because of last-minute production of prosecution videos. As we started a 10.30 am trial at 12.12 pm, another resident said he had resigned himself to trials 'never' commencing as scheduled, despite the fact that he insisted on a 'house keeping' meeting, in addition to the PCMH. Judges permitted last-minute preparation because of their legal obligation to ensure a *fair* trial.

By comparison, another resident was keen to emphasise that his court had held pre-trial hearings for decades before they were adopted nationwide. He liked to conduct them himself, or limit them to 'robust' judges, scheduling trials two weeks later and insisting on strict timetables. He was in the interview sample but I decided to observe his court, to see how and whether this worked. He used these hearings as a tool to emphasise to all defendants and advocates present that he would not permit delays. One barrister explained that the defence had only just written to the prosecution to clarify certain matters. 'Why leave it till last week when you knew the PCMH was today?' The judge said these oral hearings worked well because in court you had nowhere to hide. Also, a small local Bar meant people knew they had to co-operate and 'play the game according to the local rules'. It was clear in court that local lawyers were on their toes. Over years of robust insistence, this resident he had cultivated a 'no excuses' attitude, administered firmly but jovially, and had apparently made inroads into the culture of sloppiness that prevailed elsewhere.

Inadequate preparation was also a product of the culture and fee structure of lawyers, who were not rewarded for preparation but for longer trials, in a way that Auld LJ considered perverse, already recognised by the Royal Commission on Criminal Justice in 1993[49] and at last, in 2010–11, the Minister of Justice proposes tackling this, as discussed in chapter eighteen. It was clear in this research that 1990s' reforms had not achieved the efficiently managed trials that the Royal Commission envisaged, which is why the Effective Trial Management Programme (ETMP) was introduced, and why the Criminal Justice Act 2003 and Criminal Procedure Rules 2005/10 tried to strengthen judges' trial management powers. Lords Woolf and Falconer[50] announced that they were designed to bring about 'a culture change', with 'case managing' judges empowered to impose penalties on dilatory lawyers. Similarly, CA guidelines on disclosure in 2006 said 'there must be a complete change in culture'[51] and the *Goodyear* practice

---

[48] G Vos QC, 'Objective opportunities' (2006) 156 *New Law Journal* 433, on the listing of criminal trials without reference to the advocate's availability. This has the knock-on effect of causing cases to be returned, so that the client does not get the advocate of his choice, and the high quality of the service is impaired.

[49] As cited above n 32, 2001 and 1993. See especially Auld LJ at ch 10.

[50] Then Lord Chief Justice and Lord Chancellor.

[51] *Disclosure: a protocol for the control and management of unused material in the Crown Court.*

direction[52] on discounts for guilty pleas referred to 'this different culture'. As research has shown though,[53] merely insisting on a culture change will not bring it about.[54]

The 2005 Rules introduced mechanisms such as a case progression officer at every court and certificates of readiness that advocates are expected to sign, signifying their legal responsibility for ensuring that their 'side' is ready for the trial. Residents were trained as managers. Judges are encouraged to take proactive control. In 2007, to assess whether the Rules had effected a change, I circulated this chapter to most of the sample judges. I visited three additional London Crown Courts and spoke to the judges, after observing case management hearings. By 2006, the national ineffective trial rate had *ostensibly* been reduced to 12.5 per cent from the 2002 baseline of 23.7 per cent (it was 14.6 per cent in London in 2009).[55] One London resident wrote:

> Things are moving forward in terms of more effective trial management … It is a bit like altering course on the Queen Mary and will never be a 'Woolfian' transformation but then it cannot be without the very effective sanction that a costs order against an ineffective party provides in a civil jurisdiction.

This resident has correctly pinpointed the problematic distinction between these Rules and the *Civil* Procedure Rules (Woolf Reforms), which they copied. Whereas most civil cases involve just two parties and an unco-operative party can be punished by striking out his case in whole or part, or a costs penalty, the judge cannot, in fairness, stop a person defending himself from criminal charges, nor is it in the public interest to stop a prosecution of a serious offender (by the underfunded CPS, because the underfunded forensic services have not produced the evidence), because this would be a loss of crime control.[56] Nevertheless, a century of research on occupational culture shows us that workers respond to targets, even if they have to cheat. One judge, not a resident, wrote to me:

---

[52]   Cited above n 17.

[53]   H Quirk, 'The significance of culture in criminal procedure reform: why the revised disclosure scheme cannot work' (2006) 10 *Journal of Evidence and Proof* 42.

[54]   The problem of the remuneration structure remains, unless the Minister's 2010–11 proposals work. Lord Chief Justice Judge said in the 2009 Kalisher lecture 'The arrangements by which advocates are paid for trial work do not proceed on the stark premise that those who work efficiently and well should be better remunerated than those who do not.'

[55]   *Judicial and Court Statistics.*

[56]   It seems obvious that for these reasons, sanctions cannot work in the same way that they do in civil cases. Auld LJ said in his *Review* (para 231) that the search for effective sanctions in other jurisdictions had been in vain. He is cited by a Crown Court judge, RL Denyer QC, 'Non-Compliance with Case Management Orders and Directions' [2008] *Crim LR* 784, who spells out the practical inefficacy of sanctions. For instance, costs against a defendant will not work because they rarely have any money. Prosecution failures will only result in the exclusion of evidence if a fair trial is prejudiced. Indeed, the very contents of the PCMH form 'suggests what common experience tells us, namely that time limits laid down by statute or by rule are not routinely complied with'. The meaninglessness of sanctions was also noted by a judge interviewed in the preceding article by Julian, above n 43.

I know of at least two resident judges who refuse the Bar's request for extra time to negotiate and swear the jury at 10.30 am. They then adjourn for negotiations to take place. If it results in a guilty plea then it is not recorded in the statistics as a cracked or ineffective trial. Manipulating the statistics? Most doctors will agree!

The statistics, then, must be interpreted extremely cautiously.[57] Judges at one London Crown Court told me that while they thought there had been something of a culture change, it was impossible to get defence lawyers to be more co-operative. Two provincial judges, again, note, *not* residents, emailed:

It has made little difference ... 'circumstances' conspire to defeat the best intentions and carefully drafted pre-trial directions. We have a long way to go.

The case management rules have made a slight difference. The defence seem to have taken them on board more than the Crown, however, we are still bedevilled by late disclosure and exhibits not being sent to them, despite a rain forest of letters. This is usually complained of at PCMH, orders are made, then, at trial there are profuse apologies by the Crown, with understaffing, police, etc blamed. This is to be 'remedied' apparently by not sending CPS representatives to cover trials or perhaps even PCMH lists so that they can devote more time to file preparation! Chaos will follow, that is fairly clear.

Other judges emailed that they were horrified at this plan. I watched a London judge adjourning an abortive case management hearing, as no papers had been served. 'Lamentable. I suppose the CPS reviewing officer has been away and the CPS are so understaffed that no-one has looked at this file.' At another London court, I sat with the resident. Although he had reduced his court's ineffective trials, his efforts were undermined by a lack of resources. A judge shortage meant that, in January 2007, he scheduled every trial for September, so some serious offenders would have to be released on bail. In one day he made four public complaints in court.[58] First, he demanded a letter from the borough police commander, to explain the non-attendance of two officers; twice he called for a written explanation from the chief inspector of the local criminal justice unit to explain why they had provided available trial dates only up to July. Fourthly, he complained about the court's failure to produce documentation and the indictment in another case. In some cases, the prosecution had not served papers. In another, the defence made a verbal application to change legal teams, ignoring the correct procedure. In another, the listing officer had confused two defendants and the wrong defendant had been produced from prison. The judge challenged requests for pre-sentence and psychiatric reports. 'In London things don't proceed', he told me 'but here we move things on as much as possible, even if every bit of paperwork isn't ready.' At the third court, the resident showed me how the judges took tight control over the preparation of serious and complex trials but some of them had to be delayed for 18 months because of the lack of HC judges to try them. In others, his requests for HC judges had been denied and he had been left to try them himself.

In another London court, in 2009, things were much worse. One judge claimed that they expected three trials out of 10 to commence each Monday morning. People would not obey judges' orders. Case progression officers were 'lower level clerks, without the education, gumption or training' to progress cases. Only judges could do so and, without their own dockets (allocated cases), they lacked motivation.[59] The new resident, laughing, said his court had the worst statistics for case progression in London. All London Crown Courts were overloaded, with backlogs, since the conversion of the Middlesex Guildhall Court into the UK Supreme Court (UKSC). Worse, the UKSC had cost millions and running costs came from the HM Courts Service budget.

> I've asked how much it cost and no-one will tell me the true cost. They've commissioned a tapestry and we're told the Crown Court now has no budget for tissues for witnesses![60]

The Cast Arrives Late

Proceedings often awaited a prison van. In 2007, several judges said they had routinely complained, publicly, but to no avail. In a four-day child abuse trial, jurors' late arrivals caused delays totalling three hours and 45 minutes. The judge said he did not remonstrate because he did not want to alienate them. In another trial, a witness delayed one day of a trial until noon. Defendants might get shorter shrift. One resident remonstrated with defence counsel for not getting his client

---

[59]   This judge cited German and Spanish judges who have their own dockets. A case is always listed before the same judge, who will manage it pre-trial and conduct the trial.

[60]   As explained, I spent additional time in the Crown Court in 2007–10 because Sir Igor Judge, as he then was, considered that the original draft of this chapter painted too gloomy a portrait. Nevertheless, as Lord Chief Justice, in 2010 he admitted that the he was 'troubled' that Criminal Procedure Rules, which were meant to 'enable the courts and parties to manage cases in an efficient way…are honoured more in the breach than in compliance': *The Lord Chief Justice's Review of the Administration of Justice in the Courts.* In a 2008 speech, he had acknowledged that the inefficacy of sanctions under the rules against a non-compliant defendant were an intractable problem. Unlike a defendant in a civil trial, a criminal defendant could not have his defence struck out: 'The Criminal Justice System in England and Wales— Time for Change?' In the 2010 report he said 'the efficiencies currently demanded of the CPS, Probation and the courts are having a very real impact on the administration of justice. At present, problems such as custody time limits or cancelled sittings are relatively isolated, but there is an undoubted danger they will become increasingly commonplace.' He also said Crown Court work had increased by 10 per cent. By 2010, the pilot judge simply commented 'case management doesn't happen'.

to court on time. Another remarked, though, that he was surprised that things ran as smoothly as they did. We should consider ourselves lucky that most defendants *did* answer their bail, often with their bags packed in readiness to be sent to prison, 'like turkeys voting for Christmas'.

The Equipment Does Not Work

A child abuse trial was meant to commence on Monday. The day was wasted because the live video link from the child witnesses' room to the courtroom was not working and there was no available member of staff trained in its use. The judge was anxious that small children had been kept waiting all day. I saw this repeated in 2007. At another court, delay was caused for lack of a tape-recorder to record a hearing in the judge's room.

Poor Preparation Protracting a Trial

A trial might be prolonged by too much evidence, which should have been truncated or excluded. One judge did nothing to intervene in lengthy and repetitive examinations, of dubious relevance. Elsewhere, in a simple homicide, where a man shot his wife, the jury was shown very slow video footage of the crime scene, the body and entire house *twice* then given still photographs. The post mortem report was read in grisly detail. All this seemed superfluous, as there was no argument on the cause of death. The entire, unedited transcripts of the police interrogations were read out (one was 2.5 hours), with the police witness and counsel taking parts. The trial had started one hour late then been suspended for one hour for the defendant to view the video footage, produced late at the court by the prosecution. The judge was passive. I asked why he did not use his inherent common law power to control the proceedings and question whether all this was necessary. He felt it was not his job to tell the prosecution how to conduct their case. Had he prosecuted, he would have edited the transcript. 'The prosecution have taken to briefing juniors in murder cases, presumably to save money' (whereas the defendant was represented by two QCs).[61] 'As soon as I see Mrs X prosecuting a murder, I know it's good news for the defence'. Another resident was more willing to intervene. He told of one case where he had required a prosecutor to reduce 600 pages of evidence to 10. He said he often told this story to advocates in the hope of persuading them to do likewise but this was unpersuasive, as they were not paid for editing evidence. Bizarrely, prosecuting barristers are paid for the number of pages of evidence, as the Minister of Justice

---

[61] One had been a junior when they received the brief, which explains this abnormal extravagance.

pointed out in 2010, a point explored in chapter eighteen. At a PCMH with a third resident, the advocates had not considered editing a DVD.

> I'm a bit worried about this DVD ... My view is to start with a blank sheet and say 'What do we *need* from this interview?' rather than saying 'We've got this DVD. Let's see what we can cut out.'

Spurious Applications

One judge said, in 2007, that delay in staging and running trials was inevitable 'because villains don't want to be tried'. Many satellite applications before or during a trial are made by the defence to delay, postpone or destroy it. Abuse of process applications used to be made very frequently but other ad hoc, groundless applications wasted time. In the shotgun murder, there was a curious request for a reporting restriction on the name of the deceased's former lover. 'Under what provision?' asked the judge. Another heard spurious applications in a trial and in a second matter that interrupted it. Pre-trial on the second day, he heard a public interest immunity (PII) application, which he remarked was 'totally irrelevant load of rubbish'. In an indecent assault trial, where a man was alleged to have fingered a sleeping woman's bottom, the whole of the first afternoon was occupied with arguments about the reliability of the complainant. On the second day, the defence requested an adjournment to consider the social worker's report on the complainant.

> No, I'm not having that. You can ask questions like that in open court, in cross-examination if you like, so that I and prosecution counsel can comment. If you do intend to, let us know and we might object that you're on a fishing expedition.

One judge remarked that if counsel were unco-operative in running the trial at a speed he judged appropriate, he would happily threaten them with sitting on a Saturday.

Carve Ups

Most of Peter Matthews' time was spent waiting for plea bargains. A resident on the South Eastern circuit confirmed that northern courts were notorious. In his practice as a London QC, he had frequently been called in where a northern solicitor wanted a case to progress to trial. Some northern counsel would take on two trials simultaneously, expecting one to 'carve up'. Several judges resisted requests for pre-trial sentence indications, thinking this encouraged bargaining. Counsel asked Dixon for a sentence indication. 'I don't do numbers. It's up to you to advise your client.' Dixon's predecessor as resident at a big city court had been 'brought in to sort out the close relationship between Bench and Bar, and judges who wanted things carved up so they could go home by eleven'.[62] This Midlands court evidently fulfilled the London barrister's concept of 'northern'. Despite all the boasting about reducing the *ineffective* trial rate over the last decade, to 13 per cent in 2009,[63] the national rate of (last-minute) *cracked* trials in the Crown Court has increased and remains an astonishingly high 42 per cent which collapse on the trial day, because

> on the trial date the defendant offers acceptable pleas or the prosecution offers no evidence. A cracked trial requires no further trial time, but, as a consequence, the time allocated has been wasted and witnesses have been unnecessarily inconvenienced thus reducing confidence in the system.[64]

So 55.4 per cent of trials do not go ahead on the scheduled day, of which about 11 per cent are re-listed. This wastes courtroom facilities and judges' time, lawyers' time and expensive fees, witnesses' time and fees, police time and an astonishing amount of public resources. Commenting on this chapter, a northern judge said:

> As I keep saying, defendants often cannot face the prospect of pleading until they get to the door of the trial court and all the rules in the world will not alter that.

Illness, Jury Nobbling and a Difficult Trial

In complex or multi-defendant trials, the possibilities for delay or derailment are multiplied. This was epitomised in the collapse of the Jubilee Line fraud trial, in 2005.[65] An Old Bailey judge predicted its collapse (to me) three months into the trial. In a multi-handed trial, one judge needed all her energy and adrenalin to take control and ensure progress. Because of jury problems, the trial had had to be restarted with a new jury. Each defendant in turn had taken time off for sickness. She responded by hiring a doctor and required them to satisfy the doctor that they were ill, under threat of having their bail withdrawn. She even lost her voice but sent out the clerk to buy a karaoke machine to make herself heard. Through inventive devices, she had endeavoured to eliminate disruption but she faced a further continual challenge. All the defence advocates were simultaneously trying to find weak spots in the trial. Witness testimony was constantly disrupted by their objecting to one another's lines of questioning. Each was up and down like a Jack-in-a-box, like a fictionalised American trial.

---

[62] In his 2010 Review, Lord Chief Justice Judge said 'I am concerned about the increasing number of defendants who elect for trial by jury and subsequently plead guilty at the first hearing in the Crown Court'.

[63] *Judicial and Court Statistics 2009*, ch 4. An ineffective trial means: 'on the trial date the trial does not go ahead due to action or inaction by one or more of the prosecution, the defence or the Court and a further listing for trial is required'.

[64] ibid, 110.

[65] See Darbyshire, above n 18 at ch 12.

They bickered and challenged her rulings. She addressed them like naughty children. One growled at another's questioning. She twice told him not to interrupt.

Judge, 'Mr V, what did I tell you?'

Barrister, 'Then I object.'

Judge, 'Mr. V, I've heard your objection. Sit down.'

Outside, she expressed exasperation, 'Barristers have such big egos'.

Meltdown—The Victim Writes Off the Trial

Where a witness utters inadmissible evidence, the fairness of the trial is compromised and the jury has to be discharged. Testimony has to be kept under tight control and witnesses are not permitted free narration. In the 1970s, it was common to see a judge or advocate barking repeatedly, 'Just stick to answering the question', but nowadays it seemed some judges were so careful to treat witnesses sympathetically and gently that they were given much more leeway to vent their spleen. Defensive anger is a natural reaction to cross-examination, whose very intent is to provoke. Further, the victim's or witness's appearance in the box may be an opportunity to unleash months of tension and emotion.

In one witness intimidation trial, the alleged victim and his family had been subject to the witness protection scheme for 10 months. They had been rehoused three hours' drive from the court. The trial had been delayed by a day. The complainant had made a fruitless six-hour roundtrip in a police car, then been brought back on this second morning. The trial was then delayed by late appearance of another defendant and defence counsel in an unrelated preliminary matter in the judge's list. The trial, scheduled for 10.15 am (the previous day), started at 10.35 am. Once in the box, in response to defence counsel's question as to whether he was sure of something, the witness entered into a tirade.

> Do you *really* think I'm going to rip my wife and kids out of their home, my kids out of school and give up a job I've spent 10 years working on and be subject to the witness protection scheme—my life turns to crap, for something I'm not *sure* of? [It was much longer than this.]

Without comment, the judge stopped the trial and asked the jury to leave. Defence counsel applied for the jury to be discharged because the witness had disclosed that, after running checks on the defendants, the police had given him one hour to leave his home and, secondly, that he was a protected witness. We retired. The judge said that had he been defence counsel, he would have applied to discharge the jury. As resident judge, he contemplated aborting a trial taking place before another judge in order to steal his jury and restart this trial but declined. He concluded that the witness would have to come back on another occasion. 'But then it's his fault.' I disagreed, arguing that witnesses, not being versed in criminal evidence, do not know what they are permitted to say. Back in court, the judge asked prosecuting counsel whether the witness had been warned not to talk about the defendants' record. He said not. The judge discharged the jury. We argued about the predictability of the witness's utterances. I suggested that allowing a witness any free narration was dangerous and I asked whose responsibility he considered it to be to stop the witness. He thought defence counsel, whereas I considered it the joint responsibility of counsel and the judge.

The Unrepresented Defendant with a Cut-throat Defence—Judge on a Knife Edge

Fergus presided over a much more tortuous trial than Mortimer's. His trial of three Jamaican Yardie-gang defendants for a contract killing was taking several weeks longer than the scheduled 10 weeks because one of the defendants (D) had dismissed his lawyers on the first day, having dismissed previous defence teams, and was representing himself. 'This shows the criminal justice system only works where the defendant is prepared to play the game', remarked Fergus. The defendants were challenging one another's evidence so D had to be permitted to cross-examine defence witnesses and the other defendants, as well as prosecution witnesses. It is notoriously difficult for lay people to represent themselves in a common law trial because they are placed in the false situation of having to tell their story through the medium of asking questions in examination and cross-examination.[66] The judge has to be extraordinarily vigilant that they do not ask illegitimate questions. Whereas the judge can generally rely on trained lawyers not to do this, an unrepresented defendant is dangerous.

Fergus frequently paused the trial, sent out the jury and instructed D as to what he could ask. He called a daily meeting with the prosecuting counsel and D, in which he asked them to help him advise D on how to conduct his defence. The judge and lawyers planned what they would do, as if they had been D's defence team. He then checked with counsel for the other defendants whether they would object to each planned tactic. Fergus clearly overstepped the normal role of judge as umpire but, in securing the defence lawyers' agreement, he cleverly protected himself from accusations of bias. Such meetings protracted the trial considerably and placed Fergus under the enormous strain of running a very vulnerable trial as judge *and* acting as a substitute defence adviser. The only assistance Fergus had in helping the defendant was from a Trinidadian lawyer who had come over to advise D for a few weeks at his own expense and from the fact that D was intelligent enough to make a good job of asking questions. There was a visible strain on Fergus's face. He said that in such long trials, the strain on the judge was cumulative. He seldom smiled. He must have been living on adrenalin during the

---

[66] Explained in P Darbyshire, *The Magistrates' Clerk* (Winchester, Barry Rose, 1984).

trial but, as resident at one of the country's biggest Crown Court centres, his hours before and after trial were filled with other hearings and a mass of boxwork and managerial tasks. One day, he dealt with paperwork from 8.00 am, minor matters in other cases from 9.00 am, the trial from 10.30 am–1.00 pm, a terrorist pre-trial hearing at 2.00 pm, the trial from 2.15–4.15 pm and then was faced with a queue of bail applicants, with no notice, before getting a chance to tackle his managerial tasks, write up his summary of the trial evidence until 7.00 pm, then attend a civic function that evening.

THE JUDGE AND THE PUBLIC

Aside from personality differences, Crown Court judges' demeanour was remarkably similar. They spoke politely to witnesses and juries. They took care to offer water, tissues or a seat to an uncomfortable witness and to suggest breaks. They thanked them, sometimes profusely, and apologised for delay. They took care to explain why delays or collapses had occurred. With one exception, they spoke very politely to defendants. One said he treated everyone as innocent until proven guilty—'It's easier that way'. Another said she always 'tried to build up a rapport with defendants'. Another asked a visiting senior HM Courts Service manager to note how he tried to 'engage with each defendant' in directions hearings. A fourth was very patient and polite to a defendant asking to change lawyers for the third time, despite the exasperation he expressed outside the courtroom. Only one judge spoke brusquely to defendants, 'Sit down…stand up', without a 'please' and without addressing them by name. All remained courteous to advocates, regardless of various degrees of ineptitude or shortcomings in professionalism. They showed remarkable patience, even where lawyers had caused inconvenience to the whole court by failing to prepare, or appearing late. The worst a judge would administer was a mild reproof.

LAWYERS

I observed judges' interactions with advocates and they commented in asides. I asked them how much contact they had with lawyers out of court and whether they had any general views on the lawyers appearing before them. Of the 27 answering this question, 11 commented positively, seven considered the standard variable and nine complained of poor standards.[67] Of those who commented positively, most had been barristers in local chambers. Five of these were residents who spoke of their close relationship with the local circuit Bar. Ten of the 11 sat outside London. They often remarked that the local Bar could be

---

[67] In the 2009 Kalisher lecture, the Lord Chief Justice listed the six competency frameworks for advocates.

'trusted'. One provincial resident said that there were only four or five local 'slippery customers'. Barristers could normally leave their papers in court without risking the opposition looking at them. A number of judges considered provincial barristers to be more trustworthy than their London counterparts. One said 'I think there is more of a professional rapport between lawyers in the provinces than lawyers in London'. Another said:

> There is a difference in attitude. In the big cities you will get the very hard-hitting advocates who will take every point going and they are undoubtedly representing extremely hard criminals.

One London judge confirmed this.

> When the numbers were small you did have a fair idea about everybody ... I am afraid there are inevitably some people who are more easily persuaded to go over a line.[68]

One provincial judge pointed out that it was normal there to prosecute and defend in turn and in all courts outside London this was indeed the case. Noticeably, they did not tend to affect received southern pronunciation as many London barristers do. Their local accents and dialects were probably good for building up a rapport with witnesses and jury. One spoke like a mate to a 15-year-old witness, 'Some of yer kisses were snogs, weren't they, Kerry?' Provincial residents were keen to maintain a good working relationship with the local Bar. They saw the same advocates regularly, they had formal contact out of court in court users' meetings and they often maintained close social contact with former colleagues.

> There is the three-monthly court user meeting, my bi-monthly trial group meeting ... dinners for new judges ... four or five semi-formal occasions during the year.

They saw it as their job to keep a close eye on local advocates and expected to write recommendations on many of them in their applications for recorderships. One resident said he did not get 'het up' when prosecuting advocates were ill-prepared because he appreciated how 'stretched' they all were.[69] Two other residents said how uncomfortable they were when one London judge came to sit occasionally because he disturbed this relationship.[70] He was 'hated' by the local Bar because of his habit of telling them off. The two residents were left to field

---

[68]   There seemed to be a widespread view that advocates were not as trustworthy now as in the past, especially in London. Lord Chief Justice Judge said in the 2009 Kalisher lecture, 'I was called to the Bar in 1963. I left it in 1988. It was a privilege to have been a barrister. In 25 years in practice in what is a very competitive profession only one dirty trick was played on me by another advocate.'

[69]   Empathising with practitioners, like Guy in the previous chapter.

[70]   While court communities and relationships, mentioned in the previous chapter, were readily maintained in provincial Crown Courts with a local Bar, the Crown Courts in London had a much less stable company of actors, as there are so many more judges and lawyers moving around. This not only disrupted the lawyers' ability to learn whether to 'waltz or rumba', in the metaphor of *The Craft of Justice*, above n 16, it clearly disrupted the development of trust and

barristers' complaints but neither could work out a tactful way of discouraging their unpopular colleague's visits.

Of the judges who made negative comments on lawyers, three, on three circuits, mentioned the poor standard of advocacy of solicitor-advocates. One of these was a solicitor-judge.[71] Judges who did a variety of work, including civil and family, often mentioned that the standard of criminal lawyers was comparatively low. One of these was shocked when she was first appointed and angry at the lack of help she received from London barristers, until an experienced judge told her it was her job to prepare the law and she should think herself lucky if advocates had even read the papers. Her high profile solicitor's practice had been in civil law and she had a perfectionist habit of meticulous preparation so she was disappointed with criminal advocates' lack of preparedness. A Commercial Court High Court judge thought criminal cases should be tightly managed, like his cases. He demanded skeletons on legal points. There were a lot of weak advocates in crime. 'They half-make points.'

SENTENCING

Being consistent with practice and not being overturned by the CA were the chief concerns of CJs in the Crown Courts. They routinely popped into one another's rooms to ask for a second opinion and it was one of the most popular dining room topics. Most relied on DA Thomas's *Sentencing Referencer*. One called it 'the best book in the world'. Circuit sentencing exercises and Judicial Studies Board (JSB) training were the more formal mechanisms for trying to achieve consistency. A JSB session for novice recorders demonstrated how difficult it was to achieve this. The trainees had prepared sentences for hypothetical cases. These were displayed by a tutor CJ on *PowerPoint*, demonstrating that their sentences varied from six months to four years in one case and four months to four years in another. Some judges in the audience mentioned how difficult it was to pass sentence in the abstract. The same remarks were made by others several times in the course of the research. One said, 'Of course we do all this dining-table sentencing but it may all be different when you see the defendant in front of you'. Ten judges considered sentencing to be the most frustrating aspect of their job. They complained of the lack of sentencing options for drug addicts, the mentally ill and young offenders. They thought it inappropriate and fruitless to send many such offenders to prison. Three explained that this was the reason they had given up trying criminal cases. Judges were, however, enthusiastic about drug treatment

---

goodwill. At the time of writing, 2011, there are almost nine times as many CJs in London and the South East as on the Welsh circuit (Judiciary website).

[71] This point has been referred to in ch 7, as the problem of solicitors' advocacy standards in the higher courts has been the subject of controversy and consideration.

and testing orders (DTTOs) which resulted in a successful outcome.[72] Two rated these as the most satisfying elements of their job. One said he had 'wanted to hug' a successful defendant on a DTTO and court staff told me of one resident who took off his wig, walked across the courtroom and shook the defendant's hand. I asked judges whether they found any cases difficult to decide or manage and five responded that sentencing for causing death by dangerous driving was their most difficult task. Two used almost identical words to paint the scenario:

> There you have the family of the victim and they are baying for blood and you have this tragic figure in the dock whose life you are about to smash by sending him inside and leaving his family without him.

Many expressed disquiet that they were obliged to announce the earliest parole date for prisoners, on sentencing them, as this often outraged victims' families in the courtroom and set judges up as news objects of loathing and derision, as described in chapter two.

CONCLUSION

This is the central chapter of the book, numerically and symbolically, because, when we visualise a judge, these are the judges that come to mind and that fill the newspapers. Like the DJMCs, the CJs were very happy, despite the fact that some had to travel a lot. It must be borne in mind, though, that the sample under-represented judges on the South Eastern Circuit. London judges and residents in charge of big courts generally worked harder than their country counterparts and suffered more frustrations.

Now that every judicial job had to be applied for, resident judges were in transition from being a group of time-servers, waiting for a pension, recruited when it was difficult to fill the bench. New ones had fended off competition with CVs demonstrating a variety of out-of-court responsibilities, IT competence and a preparedness to actually manage their courts and judges, and to garner statistics. It was these residents, at the top courts, like Mortimer and Fergus, who were among the most intelligent of circuit judges, handling serious crime normally reserved for HC judges and interlacing their management jobs and other courtroom business into the breaks in these exhausting and harrowing trials. One of these was appointed to the High Court after the research. One of the reasons for doing this research was to find out what judges did outside the courtroom. Some provincial judges went home. Residents of big courts worked 10-hour days and took work home.

In contrast with the speed of case progress in the last chapter, this chapter tells a depressing story of cases failing to progress. It could be renamed 'an analysis of

---

[72] They were all aware of the statistical analysis of DTTO's success rate, which was one third during the research period.

what goes wrong in the Crown Court'. In London, judges always struggled to make progress and no trial anywhere started on time and progressed smoothly. This chapter demonstrates the value of empirical research, especially observational research. According to statistics, case progression has improved but we saw that judges, like doctors and other workers, manipulate statistics. We will find circuit judges doing so in the family chapter too.

It used to be said that the judge's time was at a premium and everything else and all court users were geared to that central organising feature. Here, judges were at the mercy of everyone else. Peter Matthews and 'Northern' colleagues spent much of their time out of court waiting to see if plea bargains would be struck. Others, especially in London, failed to make progress because of court users. Much of this, such as prosecution failure to disclose evidence in a timely manner, or lack of probation reports, or failure of court equipment, boiled down to a lack of resources. The expensive judge in the expensive courtroom and the time of all the other court users was wasted. This can only get worse, with cutbacks in public spending announced in 2010, and this point will be revisited in chapter eighteen. The observations also demonstrate the poor preparation of some prosecutions. They expose the defence lawyers' culture of last-minute preparation, exacerbated by the common problem of late briefs, caused by the UK's unusual, divided legal profession. In London, except for the fraud trials court, lawyers failed to take responsibility for their lack of preparedness. By 2009–10, the Criminal Procedure Rules 2005, trumpeted as changing this culture, had made not a jot of difference. In a criminal case, there was always someone else or a lack of resources, onto whom or which the blame could be passed. In 2010, Lord Judge himself acknowledged that sanctions were not working. On the other hand, there were mixed reports from the courts I did not revisit as to the success of the Rules and the resident at the London fraud trials court and one of the provincial residents had worked for years to insist on a culture of trial readiness.

Again, the value of empirical research is demonstrated by the observations on plea bargaining, which I had previously written about only from an academic standpoint. Late briefs tempted barristers to plea bargain. The observations found evidence that the 'Northern' circuits' reputation for endemic plea negotiation was real: neither historic nor a rumour. It was the normal way of proceeding. Many judges appeared to spend much of the day out of court, as it was taken for granted by them and the barristers that negotiations between prosecution and defence would start as soon as the prisoner eventually got to court and met his barrister, very often for the first time. The judges were part of this local culture and facilitated it, without getting involved in negotiations. Southern judges knew all about it. As barristers, they had been hired in certain cases to insist on going to trial. Indeed, I was told that Dixon's predecessor as resident at a busy Crown Court in a high crime city had been appointed with a brief to stop plea bargaining. (He later became an HC judge.) In 2010, Lord Judge acknowledged that there were too many late guilty pleas wasting public money.

The value of observational research is also shown in the context of the the right of silence and the disclosure rules. Practising and academic lawyers were heavily critical when the law was changed in 1994 then 1996 to permit a trial judge to invite a jury to draw adverse inferences where a defendant exercises his right of silence or fails to produce a statement of his defence. Later, a Court of Appeal judge, Sir Phillip Otton, described these laws as if they were operating as intended. This research is too small to make generalisation but I found that the defence statements judges showed me amounted to a couple of unhelpful lines. This caused no reaction from them. In all cases where a judge could have invited an adverse inference from silence, he contemplated it then declined to do so, fearing that he would trip in the minefield of the highly complex jury instruction he would have to devise, and be thrown straight before the Court of Appeal. In changing the law, Parliament and these Bills' sponsors had overlooked the fact that judges were also lawyers and so probably valued the presumption of innocence as much as critical practitioners.

There was a big difference between bench and Bar relationships in London and the provinces. It was seen in chapters four and five that provincial judges were recruited to sit, with their chambers contemporaries, in the courts in which they had appeared. Lawyers and judges knew one another very well, working together as court habitués, like those different groups in the magistrates' courts. These circuit judges and barristers joined together in circuit sentencing exercises and training seminars and socialised together in chambers parties and circuit dinners. Crucially, the judges trusted local lawyers, whereas the London Bar is so big that judges cannot know all advocates and found some untrustworthy. The same phenomenon recurs in the county court chapter. An outsider judge from London failed to understand this relationship of mutual tolerance and respect. It was seen here how incompetent or lazy lawyers wasted public money and placed a strain on judges, by poor preparation. The barrister who could not tell a psychiatrist from a psychologist had wasted public money on a psychologist's report when every second year law undergraduate should know that fitness to plead is a psychiatric issue. There are accounts of incompetent lawyering elsewhere in this book, notably from Queen's Counsel appearing in another Crown Court in the High Court chapter.

In this chapter, it was seen that the unrepresented prosecutor was making elementary mistakes and had to be reminded that the judges were not there to provide legal advice. Fergus went to extremes, however, to help an unrepresented defendant. This trial, lasting months, put Fergus under a visible physical strain. In later chapters, we shall see how unrepresented parties slow case progress and place the judge under considerable strain, as well as disturbing the adversarial ideal of judge as umpire.

One tiny point here is that most of these judges *appeared* in court to be non IT users, consistent with the out-of-touch image, because they took trial notes of evidence in longhand and kept their laptops outside, which they used for preparing the summing-up and jury instructions, for writing letters and doing emails.

This chapter draws attention to a massive waste of public money, of which judges are all too aware. Some could be resolved through simple expedients, like warning a witness in advance of trial to stick to answering the advocates' questions and telling them what not to say. The Crown Court system is shot through with false economies, like the rest of the English legal system. If underfunded agencies cannot provide the people and the evidence to progress criminal cases, then the underfunded HMT Courts Service wastes an expensive courtroom and the time and cost of all the other actors, including the judge. Things can only get worse, especially in London. Since 2005, there has been a twenty per cent increase in defendants disposed of by the Crown Court.

10

Judges and Juries

I enjoy creating a balanced résumé and telling the story to the jury in a way that brings it to life yet helps them with their decisions.

MOST JURIES IN England and Wales sit in the Crown Court.[1] This chapter draws on the circuit judge (CJ) interviews and on observations of CJs and High Court (HC)judges interacting with jurors. I had a double interest in the judge-jury relationship because I had published a summary of jury research and a series of recommendations for reforming jury composition and the handling of jurors, for the Auld Review.[2] I drew 32 conclusions in 2001. Some are not discussed here. For instance, jurors have a great deal of difficulty understanding the burden of proof, they are influenced by evidence that they are told to ignore and it is questionable whether a juror is effective at judging truthfulness of a witness from demeanour. Examples of the 2001 findings discussed in this chapter are as follows.

— The most popular [psychological] theory on how jurors individually consider the trial and verdict is the cognitive story model. The juror reorganises information into a narrative story.
— Juries are much better at remembering evidence than individual jurors but real juries sometimes argue in the jury room over the contents of the evidence.
— If English judges are to continue to sum up the evidence, they should be told not to recite their notes but to draw attention to the main points, to areas of conflict and to how the law applies to the issues of evidence.
— Juries have a great deal of difficulty in understanding and applying judicial instructions. The model instructions should be subjected to rewriting by

---

[1] Civil jury trials in the county court and HC are infrequent. There were none taking place during any of my county court visits, nor during the weeks I spent in the RCJ. Juries occasionally sit in inquests, which are outside the scope of this research. I observed the CJs and HC Queen's Bench judges interacting with juries.

[2] P Darbyshire, A Maughan and A Stewart, 'What Can the English Legal System Learn from Jury Research Published up to 2001?', downloadable from the author's webpage on the Kingston University website. The Criminal Courts Review is entitled *Review of the Criminal Courts of England and Wales* (London, The Stationery Office, 2001) (the Auld Review or CCR). It has its own website.

     English and Welsh psycholinguists, possibly in accordance with guidelines developed in the US.
— Juries should be given written as well as verbal instructions on the law after the trial. These should be drafted by the judge and agreed by counsel and explained verbally by the judge. Where possible, juries should be given a pre-trial summary of the issues, as they were in the Harold Shipman murder trial, in October 1999, and pre-trial instructions, which could be agreed by counsel and the judge.
— Real jurors in England and Wales experience a great inhibition against asking questions, sometimes to the detriment of their deliberation. Encouraging jurors to ask questions, take notes occasionally and discuss the evidence at an interim stage may all help to keep them awake and alert and to make sense of the trial, to help them remember the evidence more accurately, to understand the case and make their deliberation more focused.
— Real jurors' accounts from England and Wales show jurors suffer a lot of discomforts, in addition to boredom and inconvenience, which may affect their performance. Heat and cold, boredom and their passive role may reduce their arousal levels and ability to concentrate on the evidence. Court managers should regularly check courtroom temperatures and it may be wise to give jurors frequent breaks and encourage them to be more active, as described above.
— Small discomforts all irritate jurors. All court personnel should be taught to be polite to jurors and respect the fact that jurors are making a personal sacrifice for the public good.

Most of our recommendations were adopted by Auld LJ in his Review but the practical ones that do not involve a change in the law have apparently not been fully discussed. Certainly many have not been implemented and they had apparently not filtered down to trial judges. The CJs in this sample, plus all the senior judges who conducted or had conducted jury trials were asked about their training for handling juries, what they though of some of the suggestions above, how they composed summings up and whether they gave written directions, what they thought about juries and so on.

JUDGES' TRAINING

Sixteen of the 25 Crown Court judges considered that they had received adequate training for handling a jury, especially the nerve-wracking mock jury trial. Those who had practised regularly in jury trials said that this had provided a good grounding. The 12 High Court Queen's Bench Division (QBD) judges handled the most serious jury trials, which are shared with 'ticketed' CJs like Mortimer and Fergus described above. Before appointment, HC judges had sat as recorders and thus been through the same training as the CJs. Three CJs said no amount of training could prepare you for every eventuality.

Only doing the job prepares you for one juror being sick over another. It happened to me in my first week … For instance, having a complaint by two women jurors that the male juror that was sitting between them was masturbating; you cannot train people to deal with that.

Eight veterans had had no or 'inadequate' training. Several CJs at a big city court told me that two solicitors among them were reckoned to be 'the best' in handling juries. One of these explained[3] that solicitors had the advantage over barristers, thanks to their experience in explaining matters to their lay clients. 'I look at my jury and think about handling The Thickie, like explaining something to one of my thick clients.'

QUESTIONS, NOTE-TAKING AND CLARIFYING MATTERS FOR THE JURY

In 2001, we reported that jurors who had published stories of their jury service in England and Wales frequently mentioned a strong inhibition against asking questions.[4] This confirmed Zander and Henderson's *Crown Court Study*. Forty-four per cent of jurors had wanted to ask questions but under a fifth had done so.[5] Matthews, Hancock and Briggs[6] made the same point. Sixty-seven per cent of their sample had wanted to ask questions. Many felt uncomfortable about holding up the trial. Some felt they were actively discouraged. Some felt it would be embarrassing.[7] In the present research, no judge suggested to a jury that they might ask questions. Judges neither encouraged nor discouraged it. In some American jurisdictions, it is recognised that jurors experience this inhibition so they are actively encouraged. Although English and Welsh jurors are told that they may ask questions, in 2001 we recommended that it may be helpful to alert judges to this inhibition and to encourage them to ask the jury at certain points in the trial whether they need to ask questions. Matthews et al recommended that 15 minutes per day be set aside for this.

We reported that in some parts of the US, jurors are prohibited from note-taking because it is thought this inhibits concentration on the witnesses.[8] In an article on my own jury service, I reported that, despite being an experienced

---

[3] These judges were outside the research sample but this illustrates how I was able to glean information from many extra judges in lunchtime conversations and other out-of-court interaction. It was routine for the research sample judges to introduce me to others who they considered would be of interest.

[4] Darbyshire, Maughan and Stewart, above n 2 at 48.

[5] *Crown Court Study* for the *Royal Commission on Criminal Justice* Research Study No 19 (London, HMSO, 1993) 213.

[6] R Matthews, L Hancock and D Briggs, 'Jurors' perceptions, understanding, confidence and satisfaction in the jury system: a study in six courts', Home Office Online Report 05/04.

[7] ibid 40.

[8] Darbyshire, Maughan and Stewart, above n 2 at 47.

note-taker, I had given up taking notes, for the same reason.[9] Matthews et al reported that a small number of jurors found difficulties with note-taking. No judge in this research was observed to mention the subject of note-taking to a jury but there were two extremes. In Fergus's long murder trial, almost all of the jurors took notes. One had accumulated 30 notebooks. In Mortimer's one-week murder trial, no juror took notes. Writing equipment was not visible. Mortimer explained that it was available but he hoped jurors would not take notes, as he wanted them to watch the witnesses. Some judges shared this view. Elsewhere, I noticed another jury where no-one was taking notes. There was no chance that they could have remembered all the evidence or the judge's verbal direction, during their deliberations. There were clear inconsistencies in judicial approach, reflecting the complete absence of general policy or even discussion of this issue in England and Wales.

Judges were good at interrupting witness examination to ask for clarification of technical evidence. Interruptions were kept to the barest minimum, as all the judges were extremely passive. For example, one judge in a rape trial asked for an explanation of 'high vaginal swab'. Judges were also good at keeping the issue simple. Another quietly interrupted a prosecutor's opening speech in an indecent assault trial, as follows.

> Mrs F, your case is that he put his hand up her skirt. The jury don't need a lecture on indecent assault.

In the trial of a Sri Lankan, a judge stopped the prosecutor using the phrase 'My Learned Friend'. 'Well, I was hoping the interpreter would translate!' sneered counsel. 'It doesn't *translate*', retorted the judge, exasperated. 'They don't say "My Learned Friend" in his village', at which the jury erupted into giggles.

Judges did not watch juries for signals that they were in difficulties. All the judges took longhand notes of evidence in their standard-issue, court notebooks. Even when they were not writing, they did not look at the jury, other than to address them. All avoided eye-contact with the jury during testimony. When I asked some judges about this, they denied it was deliberate policy, explaining that they were simply busy noting the evidence. Thus, they did not notice jurors giving visible clues that they could not understand or hear the evidence. Jurors frequently pulled faces, or tried to indicate that they could not hear a witness, or asked questions of one another. For instance, in a trial where an interview transcript was read out, the jurors were at first rifling through their bundles to see if the document was in there, because no-one had told them whether it was. This distracted them from listening to the transcript contents for many minutes. In the same trial, the jury looked bemused at technical evidence on handwriting and blood alcohol levels. The judge did not explain matters but reassured them,

---

[9]   P Darbyshire, 'Notes of a Lawyer Juror' (1990) 140 *New Law Journal* 1264.

'Ladies and gentlemen, don't worry, I'll be reducing it to five clearly understand-able lines.' Elsewhere, a defendant in a murder trial spoke with a thick Jamaican accent which was almost impenetrable. I assumed that the judge understood him because he continually took notes without asking for clarification. So did some jurors but some turned to one another with quizzical looks and asked one another what the defendant had said. The judge did not notice, because he kept his head down, writing.

PRE-TRIAL SUMMARIES, WRITTEN DIRECTIONS, SUMMING-UP AND ACCESS TO THE TRANSCRIPT

In 2001, we had recommended that, where possible, juries should be given a simple pre-trial summary of the issues, because of the illogicality of receiving all trial information (evidence) before being told what to do with it. If a group of people is expected to take a decision, it is abnormal to provide them with all of the information first, and then to tell them afterwards what decisions are expected of them, especially when the delivery of the information takes days or weeks. As the paper was written for Auld LJ, he adopted that recommendation in his *Review*. Sixteen of the 27 circuit judges commenting on this were either opposed, or considered that it would only be of limited use in, say, complex trials. Almost all gave the same reason, 'Issues shift during the course of the trial'. Several considered it ought to be done in the prosecutor's opening speech. Of those in favour, however, some had already done it.

> I see no problem in giving sort of mini-directions before the trial starts or before the speeches—'Members of the jury, you will be invited to consider this' … I may say to the jury 'The only issue that I anticipate that you may have to decide is whether he had these drugs with him and he intended to supply them to someone else.'

Written defence statements were discussed in the previous chapter. If the Criminal Justice Act 2003 is working as intended, resulting in fuller defence statements, then surely the provision of a pre-trial summary of the issues would be more feasible now, as we recommended and Lord Chief Justice Phillips repeated in 2007, in a speech, 'Trusting the Jury'.[10]

> Sir Robin Auld in his report recommended some more radical changes to the nature of jury trial. Issues should be identified before trial, with better use being made of the defence statement. At the start of the trial the judge should give the jury a summary of the case and the questions that they will have to decide, supported by a written aide memoire, agreed with counsel before-hand. The jury should be told the nature of the charges, a short narrative of the agreed facts and a summary of the facts in issue and a list of the likely questions for their decision.

---

[10]   Judiciary website.

The 2010 Bench Book, *Directing the Jury*, which was supposed to be a response to his concerns, is silent on this precise point, as is a 2009 training guide written by His Honour Judge Inigo Bing, a Crown Court judge.[11]

We had recommended that judges be encouraged to give written directions to jurors. We did not ascertain how many judges did this. In the present research, it transpired that the practice was much more common than the 2001 paper anticipated.[12] Twenty-three of the 27 circuit judges questioned on this point said they had given written directions. (Two were newly appointed and had not yet had the chance.) Most supplied copies of examples and it was clear that the instructions usually took the form of a sequence of questions, or sequences following alternative routes, rather like a flow-chart. Judges did not give written directions in routine cases where the issues were simple but they generally gave them in murder, reckless arson, rape, joint enterprises and dangerous driving. Judges showed me how they prepared written directions in murder cases. Nevertheless, written directions were the exception. Frequency varied from one resident who had given written directions twice in his career to another resident who said 'I do it all the time' and certainly in every murder case. Both conducted many murder trials. One judge said that he was becoming increasingly willing to give written directions. Two judges outside the research sample said, in 2007, that they gave written directions in *every* case. One had been influenced by a 2006 article on the subject.[13] Continuing his endorsement of the Auld *Review*, Lord Phillips went on:

> At the end of the evidence the judge should no longer direct the jury on the law, nor sum up the evidence in detail. He should remind the jury of the issues and of the evidence relevant to them and, of course, of the defence. He should put to the jury a series of written factual questions, the answers to which would lead to a verdict of guilty or not guilty. These proposals were made seven years ago. They have not been taken up. The time may come when they receive further consideration.

In the Judicial Communications Office response to Cheryl Thomas's research report and recommendation that jury directions should be simplified, they said 'The Judicial Studies Board now recommends that written directions be given to juries in all but the most simple of cases'.[14] All judges in the present research

---

[11]   Not a public document. I am very grateful to have been given a copy.

[12]   Zander and Henderson, above n5, found that written directions were given in only two per cent of cases.

[13]   HH Judge N Madge, 'Summing up—a Judge's Perspective' [2006] *Crim LR* 817. He tried written directions in all cases and reported the results: quicker verdicts, fewer questions and more convictions.

[14]   Her paper is *Are Juries Fair?* Ministry of Justice Research Series 1/10 (2010). In our 2001 paper, we had recommended that specimen jury directions be simplified with expert help, as in some states in the US, and we expressed concern that current specimens responded to the Court of Appeal's requirements and had not been 'road tested' on real people. In Thomas's report she concluded 'While over half of the jurors perceived the judge's directions as easy to understand, only a minority (31%) actually understood the directions fully in the legal terms used by the

asked advocates to approve written directions before offering them to the jury. By doing so, they protected themselves from disapproval by the Court of Appeal and the consequent quashing of a conviction. One novice told me of an instance where the advocates had disagreed with her proposals and she had redrafted the directions and then checked them with the resident judge.[15]

Judges demonstrated how they prepared the summing-up of the evidence day-by-day as the trial progressed, from their longhand notes. Some explained that it was time consuming to sum-up in a relevant and concise manner. Merely reciting everything in one's notes was regarded as a bad technique of judges of yesteryear.

> Someone said ... the ideal is to have no more than one hour [for every] week of evidence ... most summing-ups are too long because people haven't taken the time to make them shorter.

> You have got to be able to analyse and organise material. If you are going to help a jury ... it is no good just reading through your notebook. I saw this 20 years ago ... horrendous.

> I often work at home in the evening ... as the trial is progressing. It is only at the end that the issues ... and the pattern become clear and you can pick out what is important, so you are left with a massive workload at the end.

> I was summing-up for most of the weekend on this big contract killing. All of that work is now down the drain as I had to abort the trial. The most boring part is reading through the evidence and highlighting the parts of interest ... You can't just read it from your notebook because it has to be tailored to what the issues are in the end, and that is very time consuming.

> I really enjoy ... say, at the end of a case that lasts a fortnight ... to sum it up in less than an hour and a half, to have distilled it into a series of issues and to present it to a jury in a digested and balanced way which I hope helps them ... I enjoy creating a balanced résumé and telling the story to the jury in a way that brings it to life yet helps them with their decisions.

In 2001, we recommended that in summing-up, judges 'should be told not to recite their notes but to draw attention to the main points, to areas of conflict and

---

judge'. The 2010 Crown Court Bench Book *Directing the Jury* (Judiciary website) tries to change the judicial approach and to stop some judges slavishly following the specimens. It explains the law's requirements, then presents examples. These have still not been tested on non-lawyers (they were drafted by judges again) but simplifying some instructions seems an impossible task when the law is so complex. For example, the section on a defendant's failure to mention facts he later relies on (exercising the right of silence) amounts to 9.5 pages, including a two-page suggested direction. There is another large section on how to instruct the jury on a defendant's failure to account for evidence. The 2010 Bench Book may result in directions being more varied but it in no way guarantees that they will be more comprehensible to juries. See also D Perry, 'direction' *Counsel*, March 2011, p 36.

[15] As we saw in the last chapter, this is typical of the advice recorders and novice judges seek from residents.

to how the law applies to the issues of evidence'.[16] The research judges clearly endeavoured to do this and judges' interviews acknowledged the time and care that must be taken in preparing a summing-up that is sufficiently brief and focused to help the jury. In the last quotation, the judge was unwittingly confirming what we found to be the psychologists' consensus that jurors operate an internal 'cognitive story model' in which they try to make sense of the evidence by constructing a feasible story, in their minds.[17]

Zander and Henderson, in 1993 and Jackson, in 1996[18] referred to judges summing-up for the prosecutor or the defence[19] but the judges I observed would have been horrified at this suggestion. They tended to see it as an archaic practice. Typically, in 2006, one judge explained this to a group of curious American law students, who asked him if he tried to get the jury to acquit or convict.

> If you try and tell a London jury what to do they may well rebel … Nowadays judges don't try and sway a jury. There used to be some judges who were masters at telling the jury the verdict they wanted them to bring in.

I would be astonished to witness this nowadays. While judges may, in law, express an opinion, modern circuit judges seem to strive to be neutral, out of a sense of real neutrality and fairness, a distaste for the role of fact-arbiter and a realistic fear of being appealed. Although I did not question judges on this, I would expect that many would not even realise it was *legal* for them to comment on the evidence.

On being asked whether they considered that juries should be given access to a trial transcript, 19 of 25 Crown Court judges thought this a bad idea. They felt jurors would become 'bogged down' in a 'mountain' of paper. Many had experience of reading *Livenote* instantaneous trial transcripts and pointed to the fact that these could generate about 70 pages of transcribed text per trial day, which was difficult enough for a judge to cope with, let alone a jury. They warned that concentrating on a fragment of the dialogue could give a biased impression of the evidence. They felt that judges were there to take notes and juries could ask them to clarify testimony if necessary. The job of the juror was, as they saw it, to note the demeanour of witnesses. This answer was typical.

> juries are there to sit and watch and listen. Judges miss such a great deal when they are … trying to make a note. The great value of the jury is they hardly ever miss a trick … I am not happy when I see jurors writing too much down … if they were given a

---

[16]   Darbyshire, Maughan and Stewart, above n 2 at 60. The 2010 Crown Court Bench Book makes the same point, noted above.

[17]   Darbyshire, Maughan and Stewart, above n 2 at 22.

[18]   J Jackson, 'Judicial Responsibility in Criminal Proceedings' (1996) 49 *Current Legal Problems* 59.

[19]   D Wolchover, 'Should Judges Sum up on the Facts?' [1989] *Crim LR* 781 said 'judicial habits vary'.

transcript ... they would be tempted to answer those little questions that sometimes have to remain unanswered ... combing through it in almost an attempt to review the entire case.

Several judges said the jurors' job was to watch the witnesses and this is confirmed by Rock, 'Judges would invite jurors to consider how witnesses had acquitted themselves ... this was evidence about evidence'.[20] Of the six judges who were prepared to allow jurors access to a transcript, one gave the following reason.

I think otherwise they are very often saying 'a witness said this or the other' when what they really have in their mind are counsel's questions and I think that to be a good defence advocate you are getting a view of the events across to the jury by way of your questions which actually isn't reflected in the evidence at all.

HELPING THE JURY, JURY WELFARE AND EXCUSALS

In our 2001 paper, we recommended reforms that would help jurors to do their job. I asked the 25 Crown Court judges here an open-ended question as to whether they had any other recommendations. No two answers were the same. Eight recommended practical aids to decision-making. Three of these suggested simplifying the law and the JSB specimen directions, and five suggested schedules, plans, diagrams and agreed chronologies. Five had regard to jurors' general welfare. One said 'A judge should really look after his or her jury' and another said he would 'move mountains to reduce the length of trials'. One very new judge said:

I am astonished to learn that they have nothing provided for them by the state. I think they should be given complimentary tea and coffee in pleasant surroundings; be looked after properly.

Whilst doing jury service, I had had the same experience as some of the jurors in Mortimer's trial. I reported for jury service in flimsy clothing, as it was a hot summer's day. The air conditioning made the courtroom icy cold. As a consequence, I found it difficult to concentrate. In our paper we said:

A group of us visiting a London Crown Court in October 2000 found the air conditioning to be unnecessarily cold. Since cold depresses arousal levels, this must make it difficult for jurors to concentrate. The judge, clerk and barristers were probably not affected, as they were all gowned and bewigged ... court managers should keep a close check on room temperatures.

Nothing came of this recommendation. Matthews, Hancock and Briggs found that several jurors complained of the air conditioning being too cold and fewer

---

[20] P Rock, *The Social World of an English Crown Court* (Oxford, Clarendon Press, 1993) 53.

complained of being too hot.[21] In four Crown Court centres I noted that the air conditioning made the temperature cold but the judges seemed indifferent to or oblivious of the discomfort that this caused to jurors. In Fergus's December murder trial, the coldness of the courtroom led to farcical results. Two women were wearing thick coats, another had an extra coat over her, back to front, and others wore fleeces. One juror had an obvious cold, with constant nose-blowing and a red nose. The one next to her also had a cold and cough. The trial was delayed on my first morning, as one juror complained of flu-like symptoms and asked for time off to see the doctor. Fergus asked a nurse to see her and then requested a verbal report as to whether the juror was fit to serve.

Judge: 'Is she swinging the lead?'

Nurse: 'I have to believe what my patient tells me. She's feeling sorry for herself but she doesn't have a temperature.'

After discussions with the usher about the juror and a reassurance from the nurse that the juror would not infect others, Fergus decided that she should serve. The trial would proceed. He asked the clerk to arrange a doctor's appointment for her that evening. I asked Fergus why the courtroom was so cold. He replied that he kept it 'as cold as I can get away with' to enhance the jurors' attentiveness. Fergus seemed unaware of the point made above, that cold reduces arousal levels. Medical research was published in 2005 that confirmed the 'old wives' tale' that cold ambient temperatures induce colds and flu.[22]

If a person summoned for jury service wishes to be excused, they must first request deferral from the Jury Central Summoning Bureau.[23] They will not normally be excused but may be permitted to defer service. If they are refused, they may apply to a judge.[24] Judges have a statutory power to excuse people 'for good reason', under sections 9 and 9A of the Juries Act 1974. Letters to a Crown Court seeking excusal are directed to the resident judge and this research found that such letters are quite common, arising every week. On some occasions, jurors will appeal in person to the trial judge. Those judges with whom I discussed excusals expressed extreme differences of view. Some would excuse almost any applicant, explaining that they considered it undesirable for juries to contain reluctant participants. Others were very strict. For example, at a very big court, Fergus told me that once the Bureau had commenced operating, he had received about three applications a day. He granted three or four per year. He gave examples:

---

[21]   Matthews, Hancock and Briggs, above n 6 at 57.

[22]   Research by Cardiff University's Common Cold Centre, widely publicised in 2005. See website.

[23]   Explained when the person is summoned and on the Directgov website.

[24]   A point which we did not take account of in our paper for Auld LJ.

'I have lost faith in the justice system' ... 'I am an IT contractor on a crucial contract.' One was from a 'captain of industry' who said he 'really couldn't serve' and sent a barrister along to say so. I asked whether he hadn't got a holiday booked and why he couldn't serve for a fortnight at some future date.

Another resident at a small Crown Court received two letters a week. He gave an example: one person had said he despised all criminals and was very prejudiced so the judge excused him. During the research, another person explained that he had not appeared for jury service because of language problems and the judge accepted this and took no further action. One judge refused to excuse a television producer in the difficult football hooligan trial described in the previous chapter. She explained, 'He said he was working on a current series. I asked him if his absence would result in a blank screen and he conceded it wouldn't'. In order to try and regularise the operation of excusals and deferrals, guidance has been published on HMT Courts Service website.[25]

JUDGES' VIEWS ABOUT JURIES AND BEHAVIOUR TOWARDS THEM

Since most CJs were former barristers who had made their living from jury trials, I expected them to be strongly in favour.[26] Conversations with the core sample Crown Court judges, interviews with the remainder and dining room conversations with dozens of judges at the research courts and two other big London Crown Courts confirmed this assumption. They supported the jury system for another reason—if the jury were to be abolished, they would have to decide on the verdict themselves. Many could not imagine a criminal trial conducted by a judge alone and were incredulous that laws permitting it could ever work. For instance, one asked, 'What'll happen in the courtroom when a judge retires to bring in his verdict?' This is like the issue about the divided legal profession, discussed in the last chapter. It demonstrates not so much the ethnocentrism of English and Welsh lawyers but an ignorance of comparative legal systems. The research judges were ignorant of the fact that in our common law daughter jurisdictions, such as Canada and the US, New Zealand and some Australian States, the defendant may opt out of jury trial in favour of a 'bench trial' by judge alone.[27] Worse, in response to such questions, I had to remind them that procedure would be just the same as with a district judge (magistrates' court) (DJMC) conducting trial. This showed that judge-only trials conducted by DJMCs never entered their consciousness and they had almost certainly never

[25] For further details and discussion, see P Darbyshire, *Darbyshire on the English Legal System*, 10th edn (London, Sweet & Maxwell, 2011) ch 12.

[26] RF Julian, 'Judicial Perspectives on the Conduct of Serious Fraud Trials' [2007] *Crim LR* 751, found that nine serious fraud judges were strong jury supporters and considered that juries could understand evidence even in complex frauds. There was no support for judge-alone trials.

[27] See discussion in the Auld report at 177–81. In some jurisdictions, the majority of defendants opt for bench trials.

witnessed one in practice. This is a testament to CJs' astonishing ignorance about their magistrates' court counterparts of which Portia and colleagues complained in the magistrates' courts chapter. Hidden away in her closed youth court, Portia would be conducting judge-alone trials of violent youth-gangs which were much more serious than many Crown Court jury trials. There is also a big overlap between the adult magistrates' court work undertaken by DJMCs (long trials) and the Crown Court trials because of the extensive category of offences of medium seriousness, 'triable-either-way', such as all thefts and so on, explained in the magistrates' courts chapter, yet this was an area of work of which these Crown Court judges seemed completely unaware.

In 2007, I found that a group of 10 judges who routinely presided over fraud trials (outside the research sample) were strongly opposed to the Government's repeated legislative attempts to permit judge-alone trials in serious and complex frauds.[28] Typically, one judge said:

> I think the jury system is absolutely great and by and large works amazingly well … whatever the weaknesses are … I think it is such an important part of civic duty.

Nevertheless, the interviewed judges did have concerns about some jury decisions. They mentioned cases where they would have convicted, on the evidence, but the jury had acquitted. They tended to see this as an injustice but accepted it as inevitable. One judge outside the sample remarked that he had never experienced a perverse conviction but his last four trials had each resulted in a perverse acquittal. Another, in the main sample, remarked that he and his fellow judges at his large city court were strong supporters of the jury system because they would not like to be the sole arbiter. He said juries 'often' acquitted in circumstances where he would have convicted. He cited a recent case of an office 'groper' who, from a position of trust, took advantage of a junior employee. He cited a second case, earlier that year, 'a nasty case of rape' of two prostitutes. The jury convicted only of actual bodily harm, despite serious injuries to the prostitutes. He gave the man three years' imprisonment. Had the jury convicted, he would have imposed life imprisonment. 'Now the bloke is out, and a serious danger to women. He'll kill someone.' Two judges, also jury supporters, expressed the concern that juries were 'racist',[29] one of these recounting that he was 'furious' at an acquittal for racially aggravated offences where the complainants were from a Turkish kebab shop. At one high crime city, a group of judges outside the research sample told me about their court's high acquittal rate,[30] joking that 'the bells ring on the town hall clock if one of our juries convicts … they have to

---

[28] Having failed to gain support for the implementation of the Criminal Justice Act 2003, s 43, the Government sponsored the Fraud (Trials Without a Jury) Bill 2006–07, defeated in the House of Lords.

[29] Thomas, above n 14, found no evidence of this.

[30] 'There are no courts with a higher jury acquittal than conviction rate.' Thomas, above n 14 at v.

go back to their estates'. One of them was presiding over a 'jury nobbling' trial and they said jury interference was quite common in their court. They told me that had the jury convicted in the fraud trial of a popular local figure, the jurors would have been 'nutted'. I found that it was taken for granted in the Crown Court, by advocates as well as judges, that there will be a proportion of unpredictable acquittals, where it appeared to the judge that there was sufficient evidence to convict. This was accepted, however, as the application of 'jury equity' (though the judges did not use this phrase).[31]

As mentioned in the last chapter, judges were very polite to juries, welcoming them into court, thanking them profusely and apologising for delays. Advocates and judges are aware that they can 'play to the gallery' in the jury box.[32] Four of the 25 Crown Court judges were natural comedians and two bore a remarkable resemblance to TV comedians. All their juries were attentive and smiling broadly even when they were addressed on minor housekeeping matters. Their juries rapidly learned to expect facetious remarks, smiling attentively while they watched for the next joke, and then giggling in response.

> Now off you go into your cosy little jury room again … I can't come into the jury room and listen to you discussing the facts and you have to go out … while I'm discussing the law. [Later, when a police witness recited the caution from memory] They always get it right on *The Bill* don't they?

These observations are supported by the findings of Matthews, Hancock and Briggs.[33] They found the role of the judge to be a key component in influencing jurors' confidence in the court system, in a survey of 361 jurors. The media had played the greatest role in shaping people's attitudes to the criminal court system but

> In contrast to those decontextualised studies which claim that judges are 'out of touch' with the views of the general public or that do not do a good job, (*sic*) our research found an overwhelming degree of support for the work judges carry out in managing and summarising cases. It was clear that the vast majority of respondents were extremely impressed with the way judges performed … were praised particularly for their perceived professionalism, the consideration they showed, particularly to jurors, their ability to summarise and clarify information and their impartiality … While it was evident that judges were drawn from privileged social groups … they gained considerable acclamation as a result of their competence and commitment … in some

---

[31] Their right to bring in perverse acquittals is deep rooted in pro-jury rhetoric: P Darbyshire, 'The Lamp that Shows That Freedom Lives—is it worth the candle?' [1991] *Crim LR* 640. The furore following Auld LJ's 2001 recommendation (at 176) that they should provide grounds for a prosecution appeal demonstrated that any attempt to limit such a right is pointless.

[32] See Rock, above n 20 at 55 on 'stagecraft'.

[33] Matthews, Hancock and Briggs, above n 6 at 30–31.

cases the perceptions they had of judges before engaging in jury service were transformed … Jurors took particular offence at the denigration of judges and the ways in which they are sometimes represented in the mass media.

Zander and Henderson found that over 85 per cent of 8,000 jurors surveyed rated judges as doing their job very well, in respect of controlling proceedings fairly and explaining things to the jury.

CONCLUSION

In researching in the Crown Court, sitting next to the judge, I had a perfect, elevated, close-hand view of the jury and I was sometimes sitting nearer than the judge so I often had eye-contact with jurors. I sometimes had to avert my gaze when a whole jury was staring at me, wondering who the judge's unexplained companion was. Having read almost all of the English language literature on juries and jury psychology for my teaching and research, I was naturally watching the jury as well as the judge, and examining judge-juror reactions.

The longest serving judges complained that their training for handling a jury was inadequate. Indeed, in the training chapter, we learned that one of these veterans considered the training so useless that he was one of the pioneers of the mock jury trial that continues to terrify all new recorder recruits. This highly effective invention was ahead of its time in skills training and clearly the newer judges had benefited, though we saw here and in that chapter that no amount of training would prepare a judge for all surprises that a group of strangers could bring into a courtroom.

In making recommendations based on findings from existing jury research in 2001, my assistants and I were concerned to suggest improvements to jury trial to help the jury do their job. Observations here showed that during the course of testimony, judges were sensitive to jurors' needs to have things explained in plain English and were swift to interrupt counsel or witnesses to seek plain English translations. I did not identify any lapses. It was not surprising to find that there were differences in judges' attitudes to jurors' note-taking, given that no thought has been given to the issue in this jurisdiction, yet we had recommended that note-taking be encouraged as an aid to keeping jurors less passive and more alert.

Judges showed me the results of their evenings and weekends carefully crafting their summings-up so as to select the most pertinent evidence, going beyond our recommendations in the 2001 paper. The days were gone when the judge would bore the jury for hours or days, drearily reciting the evidence. They knew it took hard work and concentration at the end of a trial to produce a short and pertinent summing-up, gearing the factual evidence to the legal issues. There was no evidence whatsoever that today's judges used the summing-up as a tool to support the prosecution or defence. I would expect them to have been horrified at the suggestion. They appeared to be scrupulously neutral, doubtless in fear of provoking an appeal but also because they seemed to have developed a repugnance to the idea that they should bring in a verdict themselves and take responsibility for it.

This is reflected in their incredulity at the suggestion that they should conduct trials all by themselves. Their distaste for judge-alone trials is shared by journalists, parliamentarians and probably the public at large, as was seen in the aftermath of Auld's suggestions in the *Criminal Courts Review*[34] but it also reflects lawyers' general ignorance of procedure in other common law jurisdictions and a shocking disregard for the role of the DJMCs, an unseen group of judges, outsiders (as we have seen) to the mainstream bench. These people never entered the consciousness of the CJ, confirming the DJs' complaints, noted in chapter eight.

As for jury directions, some had developed these into an art form, with complex use of highlighted longhand notes, a word processor and an understanding of diagrams. It was heartening to see that almost all judges gave written directions, with some using flow-charts to guide the jury decision-making process, though it took a 2006 article by a judge in the *Criminal Law Review*[35] to persuade one of the judges here to produce written directions in every trial. Apparently, the same recommendation made by us, five years earlier, had not filtered through to practising judges. At last, however, the Judicial College apparently recommends that written directions be given in all but the simplest of cases. It is good to see the gradual demise of the pretence that juries can absorb and memorise the evidentiary summing-up and complex written directions and apply them to days of remembered testimony while deliberating in the jury room.

Judges were unreceptive to our 2001 suggestions of a pre-trial summary of the issues and access to the trial transcript. Judges often dismissed the former on the grounds that the issues change during the trial but Lord Chief Justice Phillips clearly considered the suggestion feasible and judges probably dismissed it simply because such a device had never occurred to them. I would repeat the recommendation here because in other contexts it would seem unthinkable to present information to a group of decision-makers and tell them afterwards what they were expected to do it. In this context, I also speak from my experiences as a juror.

Nevertheless, when judges were asked what they would do to help jurors to do their job, they had clearly given some thought to this over the years and some of the suggestions, such as more written and diagrammatic aids to decision-making, reflected the move in recent years to provide far more printed or electronic information than jurors would have been given in the 1970s or 1980s and this

---

[34] A clause in the Criminal Justice Bill 2003 permitting defendants to opt for judge-alone trial, as they can elsewhere, was defeated. Another clause permitting bench trials in complex and serious frauds was enacted but never implemented.

[35] HH Judge N Madge, above n 13.

parallels the very belated acknowledgement that written directions might help jurors in their deliberations.

Unlike any judge except one in the sample of 77, I had served on two juries and written about my experiences so unlike them, I knew what it was like to be one of the only passive and silent actors in the courtroom, an unpaid conscript: like the defendant, penned into a box like his dock but with much less room, being squeezed in with 11 strangers all day. I knew from this and from the research cited above that jurors experience a great inhibition from asking questions. From conversations with judges in this research and from the interviews, it was apparent that judges were unaware of this. It is worth drawing attention to this in judicial training and reiterating the suggestion made by previous researchers that judges ought to set aside a few minutes at the end of the day to allow jurors to ask questions. While jurors often ask questions that have an inadmissible or irrelevant answer, it is not difficult to devise ways of dealing with this and would go some way to acknowledging jurors as intelligent, human decision-makers rather than passive sponges, as we called them in our paper for Auld LJ. As two Lord Chief Justices, Lord Phillips and Lord Judge have suggested, the jury should be trusted more.

Judges were big fans of the jury system. Previous research had found that unlike the public at large, jurors were big fans of judges, too.

11

Civil Business in the County Court

A judge gives judgment for two audiences, the loser and the Court of Appeal.

We are operating on the margins of effectiveness, and with further cuts looming we run the risk of bringing about a real collapse in the service.

Judge Paul Collins, Resident Judge of the Central
London Civil Justice Centre, 2007.[1]

T HIS CHAPTER IS about the civil, non-family work of district and circuit judges (DJs and CJs) in the county courts. It is a story of a dwindling caseload, even more dwindling resources, and of judges facing litigants in person. The Courts and Legal Services Act 1990 aimed to shift civil business down into the county court, reserving the High Court (HC) for complex and unusual cases. It achieved this quite radically in the HC Queen's Bench Division (QBD). In 2009, around 18,600 proceedings were issued, compared with 120,000 in 1995. Coincidentally, county court business also declined, from over 3,311,000 cases in 1990 to just over 1,879,000 cases.[2] This research reflected this trend. I spent two weeks in Central London Civil Justice Centre, the 'flagship' county court. One week, there were no trials for the 10 CJs, the only two being heard by recorders (part-timers). The settlement rate was so high that judges were competing for trials. In other London courts, CJs resented the fact that meaty multitrack trials were sent to Central London. This did not mean that all civil judges were underworked. Most CJs had more than enough family cases or crime. DJs had endless boxwork. Indeed, at three courts, judges felt they needed help. DJ Joel was doing the work of two judges, after a colleague retired. DJs Elizabeth Bennett and Stuart wanted another DJ half-time and CJ Vincent Jones showed me an empty courtroom where a retired judge had not been replaced. In 2009, Genn called civil judges 'heroic', because of pressure of work, little support, strained resources, little security, increased unrepresented civil litigants (LIPs) and habitual litigants.[3]

DJs are the most important civil judges. In 2010, there were 448 and 640 deputies. After the downshift of most civil business onto their shoulders, the

---

[1] BBC News website, 'County courts system in chaos', 13 February 2007. See ch 17.
[2] *Judicial and Court Statistics 2009* and previous editions.
[3] *Judging Civil Justice*, below n 4 at ch 4.

district bench expanded. They deal with the bulk of civil cases, mainly unseen by the public, and very often adjudicate between unrepresented parties.[4] Thanks to the 'Woolf Reforms', resulting in the Civil Procedure Rules 1998 (CPR), they manage almost all county court cases and most High Court cases outside London.[5] This is important, as most claims do not progress to trial. They also dispose of most claims, since 70 per cent are small claims. DJs and CJs share the remaining fast track and multitrack cases, around 20 per cent of county court business.[6] High Court cases have similarly shifted down onto the shoulders of CJs, who hear most such cases outside London.

Therefore, for most people caught up in debt, divorce, or a property, business or consumer dispute, their case will be decided by one of the DJs, yet they have *no* public image. As we have seen, most judges do not admit to strangers what they do. A DJ appearing on *Who Wants to be a Millionaire* was disguised as a 'lawyer working in government service'. DJs' hearings are mainly conducted in their chambers and have only been opened to the public since 1999[7] but outsiders rarely visit. They would have to discover what a county court is, learn that they may visit, then pluck up the courage to persuade an astonished usher to let them through the security-coded door into a small office, where they would squeeze in with the parties. DJs' invisibility was fostered by their old title 'registrar', until the Courts and Legal Services Act 1990 renamed them. They used to administer the courts and were generally recruited to sit part-time, from among local solicitors.[8] They have been neglected by most writers and researchers. Baldwin pointed out, in his pioneering study of small claims, that researchers have been much more fixated with the criminal process[9] and Genn made the same point, 'Criminal justice may be easier to comprehend, it is more dramatic, and politically it is more sexy'.[10] County court civil business is also neglected by the media and the public. Because the archetype court is the Crown Court, DJs tire of people asking 'How many people have you sent to prison this week?'

Most county court research days were spent with the 12 DJs because only three of the 32 circuit judges were hearing civil cases during observation. The drop in civil work caused frustration for some. Judge EC, from the Crown Court chapter,

---

[4] Professor Dame Hazel Genn cited a QC saying DJs grapple with issues that would be worthy of three days of argument in the High Court Chancery Division: H Genn, *Judging Civil Justice* (Cambridge, Cambridge University Press, 2009) 176.

[5] Inspired by Lord Woolf's *Access to Justice* (HMSO, London, 1996), 'The Woolf Report'.

[6] *Judicial and Court Statistics.*

[7] Access to Justice Act 1999, necessitated by the European Convention on Human Rights, Art 6.

[8] In 1939, they had jurisdiction in disputes up to £10 and heard one third of county court contested cases: RM Jackson, *The Machinery of Justice* (Cambridge, Cambridge University Press, 1940).

[9] J Baldwin, *Small Claims in the County Courts in England and Wales* (Oxford, Clarendon Press, 1997) 13.

[10] H Genn 'Understanding Civil Justice' (1997) 50 *Current Legal Problems* 155, 159.

was saddled with serious criminal cases, despite being the Designated Civil Judge and thus manager of local civil business.

> The problem, these days, is that you do not get to *try* anything. It all settles. I used to go down to the QBD, for six weeks a year ... either doing nothing or you were being given real rubbish to do.

THE JUDGES AND THEIR WORK

I work-shadowed six DJs on six circuits but gathered eight 'bonus' observed judges, plus one recorder. I interviewed 12 and spoke to many more. Their courts varied from Central London to tiny, rural Welsh courts, where the judge sat alone, tannoying-in the cases himself, since he lacked even an usher. The DJs spanned the widest possible range of ages and experience. Their work consisted of case management 'boxwork', small claims, fast track and some multitrack trials. They heard mortgage and public sector property repossessions, debt, defective goods and services, personal injury, road traffic accidents and so on. Most also heard family cases, which will be examined in the family chapter. Three were ticketed for bankruptcy and one for Court of Protection work. All research DJs dealt with a mixture, though at two very large courts outside the sample, I encountered two sets who specialised.

All three CJs had practised as solicitors, making them unusual. One, William Highbury, was a designated civil judge (DCJ), managing civil business and judicial deployment in two trial centres and 13 county courts. The other veteran, Vincent Jones, split his time between civil and family. Circuit judges also sit in the Crown Court, as we have seen, and both had extensive criminal Crown Court experience and were ticketed for High Court work. Shakespeare was relatively new and spent half her year in the Crown Court. Highbury managed his region's Technology and Construction Court (TCC) (High Court) business.[11] He was ticketed for chancery and mercantile[12] HC trials. He and two colleagues shared all that specialist work in their region. (Cases were allocated in rotation, to prevent 'forum shopping'.) Highbury sat at the High Court in London but found that his local HC cases were more challenging. HC judges only visited his court for three-week periods so, paradoxically, were given shorter trials. Of the remaining 29 CJs, 18 did some civil work but only three spent 50 per cent or more of their time on it, two being ticketed for the TCC and the Commercial Court and one for the Admiralty Court. Eleven did no civil work, as, nationwide, the criminal

---

[11] I tried to work out what types of case were allocated to the TCC. Highbury said his court was 'generous' in classifying cases as TCC, as they would be managed tightly and heard more quickly. I concluded that the court should really be named 'the technical and construction court'.

[12] Outside London, the Commercial Court is known as the Mercantile Court, in order to preserve the unique international identity of London's Commercial Court.

caseload is much more demanding. As usual, the ticketing system was a mystery to the judges, several being authorised for chancery High Court work, about which they professed to be 'clueless'.

Each DJ performed judicial business for 215 days per year and worked from around 9.15 am to 4.30 pm except at two busy courts, where they left at 5.30 pm or 6.00 pm, occasionally taking work home, such as pre-reading, or writing reserved judgments. One DJ who had experienced the introduction of the CPR 1998 spoke of the impact on DJs at his busy trial centre.

> The workload is vastly greater … it does threaten to become intolerable … The jurisdiction has increased enormously … there is boxwork that builds up and it is high-pressure decision-making … When I started … I could go home at four … Now, if I'm not careful, I could find myself in the position I was in as a practitioner—going in at seven and working into every evening.

Each DJ was fully occupied. One remarked after an unremitting housing list, 'It's like doing a seven-hour meeting without a break'. There were no slack periods, as there might be for a CJ, spare minutes being filled with boxwork. Workloads were not evenly balanced from court to court. Nevertheless, all were agreed that the only workload impact on their private life was to restore it, compared with the pressures of private practice as a solicitor.

> I had a load more spare time. I joined a gym … started playing bridge … spent a lot more time with the kids. I do stuff around the house; see more of my wife. It's like a holiday.

They were relieved of the worry of running a business. On holiday as solicitors, they would phone the practice daily then return to the office to find work piled up. 'Now we come back off holiday to a normal Monday workload.' Two judges who 'liked to be kept busy' spent some personal time writing for judicial publications and working on judicial IT projects. Three were active in judicial training and appraisal but the other DJs had very few out-of-court jobs and virtually no managerial tasks. Two of the six core DJs sat only in one location. Others moved around. One travelled to four rural courts each week, requiring early rising and lots of driving.

CJ Highbury worked from 9.00 am to 6.30 pm. He needed the two hours after court, plus Friday afternoons, for management and boxwork. As well as being a DCJ, he helped to manage local court buildings. He had transformed his court into a 'civil justice centre', proud of his chosen design. He demonstrated plans for new courts, saying he 'played hell' if he were denied sufficient input. Because of his High Court work, he took home pre-trial papers and judgment writing. During the research week, all his trials collapsed but this was the first lull in six months. The others had similar hours. Shakespeare, the novice, was anxious to learn about all aspects of civil work and thus willing to take on novel cases and do legal research at home. None considered that their work affected their private lives.

Like their magistrates' court counterparts, DJMCs, and Crown Court judges, the DJs were happy. Those at the first court said 'We think it's the best job in the world and you'll find that wherever you go'. At the second court, they endorsed this. 'I still pinch myself when I wake up', said Homer. When asked what they liked about their work, three liked 'all of it' and each typically replied that they liked 'resolving disputes', especially where even the loser thanked them, or 'making a difference to people's lives', or 'helping the underprivileged'. I asked the last one, DJ Tierce, what he meant.

> Example: if I'm asked to approve a settlement for a child who's been injured…and it's not infrequent that a child is poorly represented … I can say, 'Right, well I don't think this is fair. Go away and rethink it then come back'. I had one … where a poor little girl who was a mental patient injured her foot very, very badly and they had approved a settlement of £7,000. I sent them away and it came back at £22,000. That gave me an enormous sense of satisfaction—I was able to do for her something to put right a wrong.

DJs appreciated the variety in their work.

> Making decisions which impact on people's lives … which you think are fair and right. Also, you become a bit of a Jack-of-all-trades so you know about everything from double glazing to psychiatric problems.

Of the six CJs who handled a substantial amount of civil business, all were happy and three spoke in hyperbolic terms, 'I think it is the best job in the Principality'. Another said:

> I like resolving the issues that other people can't resolve and the more I do in a day the better I feel.

They enjoyed the variety of issues and being the sole decision-maker, in contrast with a criminal trial judge, who leaves the verdict to the jury.

> In civil law, you make the decisions. That may sound as though I am a megalomaniac.

> I do like taking decisions. I like to be independent.

Typically, the DJ's week included one or two days of family work, a day of small claims, a day of housing possessions, and a day or half-day for a fast track trial. Two ran fast track trials for one week every two months. They sat in open court, gowned up. Otherwise, they all worked generally in their offices (chambers), ungowned. The lists were overloaded in the expectation that many trials would collapse into a short hearing or a non-appearance of one or both parties. Case management hearings were by telephone conference, normally at 10.00 am. Gaps between appearances were filled with boxwork, containing a mix of civil case management and family applications. I asked one whether he found judging a lonely job. 'No, it's just like my work as a solicitor. I sit here at my desk doing paperwork all day, interrupted by clients coming in'.

One DCJ[13] at a busy trial centre explained that, although he liked to keep all his judges and recorders busy, civil CJs had no control over their work because of the settlement rate. Civil listing was tricky. Seventy-five per cent of trials settled on the day but if they did not, then the parties whose trials could not be heard were eligible for compensation. This unpredictability was illustrated by the days spent with Shakespeare and Highbury. Most of the time was spent chatting.

FOUR DAYS WITH JUDGE SHAKESPEARE

Monday

9.30 am: Preoccupied with a computer problem, a typical waste of judicial time. She had had software installed on her laptop when last sitting in the Crown Court and now the civil templates would not work. She was exceptionally computer literate and was trying to solve the problem from written instructions but was unsuccessful and arranged for technical help on the earliest available date *10 days* hence, a wait that would be considered intolerable in academia.[14]

10.32 am: In court, delivering judgment in a four-day commercial property trial heard the previous week. She had written part of the judgment on Friday but had spent Sunday morning and two hours before court preparing it but had not word-processed the entirety so apologised for reading. Commenting on the witness testimony, she unwittingly mimicked the witnesses.

12.50 pm: She left counsel calculating interest on the damages. Aside, she explained that she had quoted the defendant's evidence in detail to illustrate why she did not believe him, in case he considered appealing. 'He was making it up as he went along.' The trial had been difficult because defence counsel 'wasn't up to the job'. Worse, counsel had not agreed on *anything*. This was a product of the defence counsel's inexperience. When we returned to the courtroom, counsel were arguing over the interest. She suggested that if they needed more time, she would deal with costs after lunch. This had the desired effect. They rapidly agreed. At lunchtime, the DCJ managing this court queried why she had not written the judgment in advance. She replied that she had not been prepared to devote more of the weekend to it than Sunday morning.

---

[13]   Outside the sample.
[14]   I normally receive technical support, in person, in under two minutes, whether at my desk or in a lecture theatre.

1.15 pm: A clerk asked if she would like to deal with a half-day housing review, or a couple of directions hearings. She chose the review. We lunched in the court dining room. Typically, we were the only females in a group of 13 CJs and recorders.

2.00–2.25 pm: Reading the skeleton arguments and trying to mark the relevant sections of the documents, a task that could not be done in 25 minutes. She glanced at a 'crib' on the Housing Act. She grumbled that the case had not been listed for a day.

2.30 pm: In court, she asked the applicant what section of the Housing Act was involved and what document was being appealed against. 'I just want to know what decision I'm being asked to take.' Defence counsel, catching my eye, smirked at her frankness.[15] The applicant had been refused housing on medical evidence and she lay prostrate along the chairs at the back.

3.35 pm: Retired to write her judgment.

4.07–4.25 pm: Delivered judgment. Left at 4.45 pm.

Tuesday

No matters in court so S read the papers for a meeting. She had asked for boxwork but none was brought.

Wednesday

10.00 am: S heard a brief housing possession application and spent the rest of the day doing boxwork. She knew she was slower than a DJ, because she kept looking things up, but tried 'to make up for it by working long hours'. In the afternoon she attended a judicial meeting.

Thursday

She came in at 7.45 am, to read the papers for a complex property matter. At 10.40 am, when the parties had not appeared, she called the listing office, only to be told that the case had settled. She did not resent the hours wasted in pre-reading, as her research was educative. She was given a commercial rent

---

[15] I found little evidence of advocates playing 'lawyer-games' with new judges, unlike L Alpert's Florida judges, 'Learning About Trial Judging: The Socialization of State Trial Judges' in JA Cramer (ed), *Courts and Judges* (Beverly Hills, Sage, 1981).

dispute. Only one party had turned up so this took one hour. We went out to lunch, 'I get a chance to see young faces, compared with the old males I work with'.

There were no effective CJ trials that week.[16] One judge was writing up a long technical judgment. Another had returned from holiday, to find nothing to do. He asked one of the DJs to show him how to handle housing possession hearings so that he could share their list. Work had been slow in the previous three months.

Circuit judges have often been likened to a Jack-of-all-trades because, as well as their criminal work, they are expected to adjudicate on any area of civil law, with the exception of specialist jurisdictions such as patents and TCC. (This epithet applies equally to most DJs, High Court QBD and most appeal judges.) All civil judges relished the challenge of novel areas of law. They were not afraid to ask the advocates to explain the law to them. Experienced judges could find themselves in uncharted water. 'I hope they're going to explain pollution to me', remarked Vincent, nearing retirement, as we walked into court, 'I've never done a pollution case before'. Judicial ignorance should not generally matter, since the advocates are meant to bring all the legal arguments to the court. A problem arises where the litigant is unrepresented or the advocate is inexperienced, poorly trained or supervised, or lazy.

BOXWORK AND CASE MANAGEMENT HEARINGS

Most DJ time was taken up with considering applications and correspondence in paper case files, then dictating or word-processing pre-trial case management orders. These are all judicial decisions. It is the DJ's job to allocate defended cases to the appropriate track: small claims (under £5,000), fast track (under £25,000, lasting a day or less) or multitrack (longer or more complex). All fast track and multitrack cases are managed, as are some small claims, dependent on local practice. DJs fix the pre-trial and trial timetable, moving the case along 'expeditiously and fairly', in accordance with the overriding objective of the CPR. The DJ has wide powers to group the issues, dispose of issues or the whole case summarily, monitor pre-action disclosure and make orders on what witness evidence will be admitted.[17] Two of the research courts were experimenting with software to enable DJs to read and handle case files electronically but both were beset with problems and were abandoned. One DJ demonstrated that it took nine minutes to open an electronic file, when he could have read the paper file, made an order and disposed of the case in five minutes. At the second court, the DJ was

---

[16] Ironically, the DCJ had given trials to the three recorders, less experienced part-timers, as he felt they they had to be kept occupied.

[17] Detailed in P Darbyshire, *Darbyshire on the English Legal System*, 10th edn (London, Sweet & Maxwell, 2011) ch 10.

unable to demonstrate the software as it was not working and no technical help was forthcoming during the research period. Belatedly, in 2004, some courts introduced facilities for email document filing but this only went a minuscule part of the way to fulfilling Lord Woolf's 1996 desire for universal electronic case handling.[18]

DJs talked me through their boxwork. A pile would be two feet high but they worked very swiftly, provided the files were well-organised and it was clear what was required. All too often, this support was missing. Since there were hundreds more files awaiting attention, it was left to the judge to determine the end of the working day. CJ's case management decisions were similar, but preceded more complex trials. For instance, Highbury and colleagues managed all their mercantile and TCC cases through to trial. CJ's box work contained appeals from DJs and, if they were DCJs, case allocation decisions.

In multitrack trials, or if pre-trial issues needed discussing, the DJ would arrange a case management conference, normally by phone. In one court group, all local DJs required attendance at case management conferences. Statistics showed that this caused most cases to settle and saved time on trials. Solicitors unfamiliar with this local practice could be taken by surprise. A solicitor called from across the country, expecting a telephone conference, only to be told that she should have attended. DJs on other circuits knew of this practice but some considered it unfair, because of the confusion and the unreasonableness of requiring that all parties attend, in those cases which failed to settle. A practice direction has since banned this local requirement. Conferences in substantial cases, including High Court cases, were conducted by CJs.

As required by the CPR, all judges took a robust line, speeding cases along, reducing the issues and preventing parties 'keeping their cards close to their chests', perceived by Woolf to be one of the evils of the unreformed adversarial process. Judges have a duty under the CPR to ensure that litigation is conducted fairly and prevent powerful parties manipulating the pre-trial process for their own benefit. The pilot DJ imposed a costs penalty on a defendant multi-national corporation who disgusted her by failing to respond to requests from an injured worker's solicitor to disclose information about her workplace and thus not acting in the spirit of Woolf, or according to the letter of the pre-action protocol. Telephone disputes were often about expert witnesses, with the DJ expecting the solicitors to agree on a joint expert, as required by the CPR, and the solicitors taking an adversarial stance, trying to justify employing separate experts. One April, a DJ remonstrated with solicitors for not agreeing a single joint expert by January; 'Timetable's going haywire'. He reminded them of the costs they were wasting and the importance of agreement and speed. I watched part of a seven-day £150,000 building dispute before a recorder. The DJs asked him who had managed the case, perceiving case management to have been a failure, since

---

[18] Expressed in *Access to Justice*, above n 5.

the claimant had refused to agree on a joint expert and the recorder reckoned the claimant's expert was inflating the case. They all suspected that there might have been a generous offer to settle by the defendant, in which case the claimants would get their come-uppance for their obstructiveness.[19]

TRIALS

This book gives no insight into judicial decision-making in trials. There is little to report. In 10 weeks observing county courts, so few trials were effective that no meaningful generalisations can be made.[20] With DJs, I observed five small claims. With three civil CJs, one had no effective trials and I observed just two short trials with one judge, plus part of a hearing on quantum of damages. When I planned to watch QBD High Court judges, all their civil trials settled too.

Small claims were examined comprehensively by Baldwin. At one court, I watched DJs Homer and Cartman dealing with a day's claims. The list was deliberately overbooked, in the expectation that some cases would collapse.[21] Occasionally, this tactic backfired. The judges said that if they could not get through the list, they sent home the litigants in person and heard the cases of those who were paying for a solicitor. Before work, they shared out some of the files, then left the remainder to the usher to distribute. At lunchtime, they tossed a coin to see who would hear the remainder. The usher said she could barely believe this practice at first. It occurred to me that there could be no better way to prevent 'forum shopping', though. Cartman explained that his colleague, Homer, was 'a bit of a reader'. Homer had read all the files the previous afternoon, whereas 'I take the view that I'm not going to read something that's not going to go ahead'. Baldwin found that most DJs did not pre-read the files and he criticised this policy as it might have 'a number of unfortunate consequences'.[22] DJs in this research were divided into pre-readers and non-readers. At one court, DJ Hulbert had taken a file home to read the previous evening. When the hearing collapsed because the parties did not appear, his neighbouring DJ, a non-reader, came in to tease him. 'I told you so!'

Small claims courts were developed independently of the courts in 1971 and, since being absorbed into the mainstream in 1973, the judges have been given statutory power to conduct the proceedings as they see fit, within the boundaries

[19]   A CPR Part 36 offer. The defendant calls the claimant's bluff by offering a sum that he considers to be appropriate in damages. If the claimant refuses the offer, wins the case at trial and the judge awards the same or less, then the claimant has to pay both parties' costs from date of the offer. This can total more than the damages. Thus the winning claimant can end up out of pocket. The judge knows nothing of the offer, or the bluff would not work.
[20]   Genn remarked in 2009 on the dearth of UK research into styles of judging and influences on decision-making, above n 4 at 131.
[21]   Baldwin, above n 9 at 51 observed that DJs found it notoriously difficult to schedule small claims, not knowing which parties and witnesses, if any, would turn up.
[22]   ibid 55.

of fairness. Flexibility is needed because the hearing may be more informal than full county court procedure and the process must be simple enough for the parties to represent themselves. Most are unrepresented and the DJ needs to take an interventionist and somewhat inquisitorial role to help them. Baldwin found considerable variation in the way proceedings were conducted. He also found that some DJs did not explain their intended procedure to the parties. The judges in this research did take the trouble to explain. They had personal standard explanations of such matters as burden of proof, addressing the evidence to the judge, avoiding a 'tennis match' and avoiding interruption. Three of the small claims observed resulted from road traffic accidents where the DJ had to decide between competing plausible accounts. Three said these were the most difficult cases they had to decide. Judges used their own experiences as reference points. In one case, where I preferred a woman driver's account, the judge explained why he preferred the male lorry driver's account. The small claim below (Hens) falls under both elements of the next heading.

LITIGANTS IN PERSON AND MCKENZIE FRIENDS

I had not appreciated the prevalence of unrepresented civil litigants (LIPs) and I doubt that academics, lawyers and government understand how much they impact on court facilities, staff and judicial resources.[23] All civil judges, including those in the Court of Appeal, are regularly faced with LIPs. Much staff and volunteer time is spent in explaining procedure and helping them complete forms. In court, LIPs are at an inherent disadvantage in our adversarial system, which requires each party to bring their arguments and information to the court, and requires the adduction of evidence through presentation of witness statements, and by examination and cross-examination of witnesses. Very few lay people can cope[24] so the judge has to 'discover' the LIP's argument and evidence and turn their stories into questions.[25] Parties do not always understand that they have to *prove* their case, with evidence.[26] They think that all they need to do is tell their story. The judge has to depart from normal procedure and the 'neutral

---

[23] The most detailed and comprehensive writing is by Richard Moorhead. See especially R Moorhead and M Sefton, *Litigants in Person: Unrepresented Litigants in First Instance Proceedings* (Department of Constitutional Affairs Research Series 2/05, 2005), also R Moorhead, 'The Passive Arbiter: Litigants in Person and the Challenge to Neutrality' (2007) 16 (3) *Social and Legal Studies* 405–24. They found that only 15 per cent of total county court defendants were represented.

[24] In P Darbyshire, *The Magistrates' Clerk* (Chichester, Barry Rose, 1984), I found that the court's statutory duty to help an unrepresented defendant was undertaken by the clerk. They varied in empathy skills, training and the legal knowledge needed to help an LIP to adduce the defence case. See 172–76.

[25] Moorhead, above n 23, cited one judge who considered it inappropriate to cross-examine witnesses.

[26] Baldwin, above n 9 at 10.

umpire' role. This slows proceedings significantly, like an unrepresented defendant in a criminal trial, as we saw with Fergus in the Crown Court chapter. The Civil Justice Review Body 1988 supported an interventionist judiciary in small claims, because they recognised the inappropriateness of the 'neutral umpire' model.[27] In foreign jurisdictions, it is widely accepted that freedom for the judge to enter into the arena and help the unrepresented is fundamental to small claims.[28]

Public funding for representation (legal aid) will not be granted for most small claims but the impact of LIPs on judges stretches far beyond small claims. People represent themselves in housing cases, case management hearings and fast track or multitrack trials. In both of Vincent Jones's multitrack trials, one on pollution and one on personal injury, one party was unrepresented. Highbury had a string of LIPs appearing before him on pre-trial matters. With circuit and High Court judges, I encountered LIPs in the Technology and Construction Court and the Commercial Court and indeed discovered that they dominate the High Court Chancery Division.

In 1997, Applebey[29] remarked on an 'explosion' of LIPs but, by 2003, numbers had risen dramatically.[30] There are several reasons: the withdrawal of much legal aid; the increase in the small claims limit to £5,000; the cost of UK lawyers and the fact that some litigants choose to represent themselves,[31] because the CPR are written in plain English and available on the internet.[32] From 2011 there will be an increase in LIPs in family and many other cases, because of the further reduction in legal aid. The prevalence of High Court LIPs caused the Judges' Council to establish a working party, chaired by Lord Justice Otton. They found that LIPs were occupying disproportionate resources. They could be 'seriously disadvantaged', compared with represented parties. Some had no case; others could not cope. They lacked objectivity and advocacy skills.[33] Otton's report

---

[27]   This resulted in the Courts and Legal Services Act 1990, s 6 and consequent delegated legislation, providing for judicial flexibility in the manner of taking and questioning evidence in small claims.

[28]   Baldwin, above n 9 at ch 3.

[29]   G Applebey, 'The Growth of Litigants in Person in English Civil Proceedings' (1997) 16 *Civil Justice Quarterly* 127. See also J Plotnikoff and R Woolfson, 'A Study of the Services Provided under the Otton Project to Litigants in Person at the Citizens' Advice Bureau at the Royal Courts of Justice', Research Report 7/98 (London, LCD, 1998).

[30]   Moorhead and Sefton said that there was little evidence of an explosion but Moorhead, above n 23, said that in family cases one third to one half of parties were unrepresented, depending on the type of case and a significant minority of these had vulnerability problems.

[31]   In the High Court chapter, there is an example of a multi-millionaire who chose to represent himself.

[32]   Though they are much-amended and accompanied by a battery of practice directions.

[33]   Moorhead, above n 23, noted that participation by LIPs fell far short of what would be expected by a represented litigant. They were less likely to defend, file documents, make applications or attend hearings. They struggled to identify legal issues or the purpose of litigation. They sometimes confused law with social or moral justice. They sought to adduce legally irrelevant evidence and argue each 'twist and turn' of their dispute. Judges were faced

recommended strengthening the resources of the Citizens' Advice Bureau in the Royal Courts of Justice (RCJ) (High Court and Court of Appeal (CA)) and encouraging staff to recommend that LIPs should seek their legal advice. High Court judges were given a pool of judicial assistants on whom they could call for help in researching the law, where one or both parties were unrepresented. Lord Woolf considered that courts should be more pro-active in helping LIPs, with information and advice provided via people, leaflets, kiosks and IT. Judges should be interventionist, treat them with respect and not give priority to lawyers. Much of this has been achieved. The CPR are simplified, courts have developed user guides, simplified forms and multi-lingual leaflets. Legal advice and other support is provided in the RCJ but remains patchy elsewhere.

The Citizens' Advice Bureau in the RCJ was described by Mummery LJ as 'a kind of legal casualty department'.[34] It employs solicitors and over 250 volunteer legal advisers. It helps 11,000 people and deals with 14,000 inquiries per year, which gives an idea of the scale of support needed. He remarked on how much CA judges appreciated the help. This was supplemented, since 2001, by the Personal Support Unit (PSU). Its volunteers help LIPs with advice on court procedure, and accompany them in court to provide emotional support. The PSU remarked in their 2003 report that LIPs could behave in an unrestrained manner, were often obsessional and usually stressed. Their behaviour sometimes caused stress in court staff and judges.

Judges have to be very patient and sensitive, in handling LIPs, and they must take care to ensure that their fair trial rights are upheld. The law provides LIPs with some rights to help in court.

1. A 'litigation friend' may represent a child or mental patient.[35]
2. A 'McKenzie Friend' may accompany the LIP but has no right to speak, although the judge may permit this.
3. A lay representative may represent an LIP in a small claim.[36] The court has a general discretion to hear anyone.
4. A lawyer with rights of audience may represent someone without charging (*pro bono*).

There is a growing industry of people acting as paid lay representatives and the courts are often prepared to hear them. There are competing values and uneven results here, Moorhead observed.[37] On the one hand, the judges sympathise with

---

with bundles of confusing and irrelevant paperwork. There was some evidence of poorer outcomes. Non-representation significantly prejudiced some LIPs.

[34] 'Litigation crisis? This way to the casualty department', *The Times*, 18 May 2004, 5.

[35] CPR, Part 21.

[36] Under the Courts and Legal Services Act 1990, s 27. The LIP must be present.

[37] R Moorhead, 'Access or aggravation? Litigants in person, McKenzie friends and lay representation' (2003) 22 *Civil Justice Quarterly* 133–55.

LIPs who cannot obtain legal aid.[38] On the other hand, they have to protect the legal profession's audience rights. Some judgments have observed how useful a lay representative can be but incompetent ones are a nuisance.[39]

The LIP's first face-to-face contact is at the front desk, seeking advice, the correct forms and help in completing them. While litigants at the RCJ are well served, they are not always helped at county courts, as judges were swift to point out.[40] I visited a county court (outside this research) and observed a typical incident. A red-faced man was holding up the queue, becoming increasingly angry and frustrated as he demanded help in completing forms, but the counter staff repeatedly asked him to read the notes. A DJ there explained that (very low paid) staff were placed on the counter after just three weeks' employment.

None of the research judges had received any training on how to handle LIPs. Their Equal Treatment Bench Book now, belatedly, contains a section on 'judge-craft', written by a DJ.[41] and the CA has provided guidance in case law and judicial publications.[42] The lack of training means that the treatment an LIP receives depends on the judge's self-developed skills and on their experience, attitude to the party, interpersonal skills, capacity for sympathy, and appreciation of the party's level of understanding.[43] All judges observed in this research, from DJs to the CA, were sympathetic and patient. They were aware that LIPs were under stress and were adept at putting them at their ease. An LIP arrived late, and flustered, in front of Judge Highbury. 'Not to worry, Mr P', he reassured him, 'You take your time'. Like Vincent Jones, his smile and politeness never lapsed. Like other judges, he was concerned to warn LIPs how to avoid saddling themselves with extra costs.

Judge: 'Looking at the justice of this Mr P, you do owe HSBC some money. How much do you say you owe? £2,500?'

Mr. P: 'Well, it's getting on that way.'

Judge: 'If they are saying you owe them £3,000 and you say you owe them £2,500, the sooner you file the defence the better, and get this sorted out.'

---

[38] In defence of volunteer McKenzie frends, 'welcomed with open arms' by magistrates, see J Kennedy, 'McKenzie Friends Re-United' (2011) 160 *New Law Journal* 416.

[39] Moorhead, above n 37, described the case of *Paragon Finance plc v Noueiri* [2001] EWCA Civ 1402. The McKenzie friend submitted futile appeals and told the LIP he would win £250,000 and that he wanted 20 per cent. The CA held that he was practising advocacy as an unqualified person.

[40] Moorhead and Sefton, above n 23, found that the help received from courts and other providers was patchy and courts were not confident signposters to alternative help. Court staff were unsure of what help could be given, because of the way that the 'no advice' rule was managed.

[41] See ch 6 above. LIP training is now spread through seminars in general.

[42] Mr Justice N Wall, 'Litigants in Person— a Personal View' (2003) 15 (2) *Association of District Judges Law Bulletin*, 6.

[43] Moorhead and Sefton, above n 23, found that judges responded to the inappropriateness of the neutral umpire role with varying degrees of intervention.

He dictated his interim order, spelling it out point-by-point in plain English, for the benefit of the LIP. Judges automatically looked after the LIP's financial interests as well as guiding them through procedure. One London DJ said 'Lots of people here are non-English litigants in person and you've got to look after their interests'. In addition to their obligation of fairness under the overriding objective of the CPR, some judges will instinctively help an unrepresented person faced with a more powerful, represented party, such as a creditor, to the annoyance of the latter. In 2003, the Civil Court Users Association complained to the Association of District Judges that 'There is a general belief amongst creditors that judges unfairly favour Litigants in Person'[44] and this supports the views of commercial litigants interviewed by Baldwin.[45] Judges' sympathy was further fuelled by their disgust at the shrinkage in legal aid since the Access to Justice Act 1999. The pilot High Court judge was upset about injustice caused by the withdrawal of legal aid from personal injury cases. DJs deprecated the lack of local legal aid solicitors. On the first research day, three drew my attention to this. DJ Rooney said:

> Virtually no-one is prepared to do aided family work now. Another good firm has pulled out.[46] Huh—'access to justice'! People who've been beaten up walk up and down the High Street looking for someone to take them on and they can't find anyone.

Vincent Jones and Bede complained that their court's advice centre had 'dwindled to one person'. Much court time was wasted by cutbacks in advice. Vincent had a shelf full of *Legal Action* bulletins, the news journal of the concerned legal aid solicitor. His wife was a Citizens' Advice Bureau adviser. Judges' concern was expressed by the editor of the Association of DJs *Law Bulletin*.

> Those on the rent and mortgage lists ... if they are lucky are able to see a worker from Shelter ... there is only one solicitor in my area with a housing franchise ... respondents in injunction applications attend alone ... the respondents in committal applications who are told to come to court on their own ... husbands and wives [who] cannot afford solicitor and counsel[47]

In 2006, the President of the Association admitted that one of the main 'bees in his bonnet' were the mounting difficulties in obtaining help for people living in rural communities.[48]

In one case management conference, a care home was acting against 15 unrepresented residents. A local authority representative at the hearing explained that their average age was 81 and some had legal guardians. The authority had

---

[44] ADJ *Law Bulletin*, Vol 15 No 2, 23.

[45] Baldwin, above n 9 at 100.

[46] Family legal aid practices fell from 4,500 in 2000 to 2,800 in 2006, falling to 1,300 *providers* in 2010: F Gibb, 'Vulnerable youngsters put at risk by plans to slash legal aid', *The Times*, 26 October 2009 and News (2010) 160 *New Law Journal* 1127.

[47] Nigel Law, winter 2005–06 issue.

[48] Profiled in the ADJ's *Law Bulletin*, Vol 17, No 2, summer 2006.

had great difficulty seeking solicitors and legal aid for them. DJ Tierce decided to order a litigation friend. He stayed proceedings and ordered the authority to report on each defendant's ability to manage their own affairs. The claimants were a charity on the verge of collapse and their solicitor was perturbed at the delay.

Where judges were not alert to the dangers faced by LIPs, the latter could find themselves in deep water. One LIP was suing her vet for wrongful removal of her dog's leg. The DJ laughed at the anthropomorphism in the heads of damages: negligence, personal injury (to the dog), blood on the car upholstery and shock at seeing the dog, and the dog's pain and suffering. Nevertheless, the costly consequences to the claimant were very serious. The vets, represented by a barrister, were prepared to use any procedure open to them to scupper the case so the amount of court time (and costs) expended thus far was alarming. Although the LIP had doubtless expected this to be an inexpensive small claim, it had been allocated to the multitrack, where costs are unpredictable. The claimant had appealed this point to a circuit judge and a judicial review was pending in the High Court. There had already been a two-hour case management conference. One of Woolf's aims was to keep costs proportionate to the sum claimed but the DJ did not raise this point. The LIP, a law student, protested that the costs incurred by the defendants were disproportionate. In light of the overriding objective of the CPR and the emphasis on proportionality, I was shocked that no judge involved had come to the LIP's rescue.

Judges were generally very good at explaining procedure to lay people.[49] Most DJs were solicitors so had decades of experience in this. Where they were anxious about a potential injustice, judges would urge the LIP to seek legal help. DJ Homer was conducting a case management conference where the claim was £4,000 but the unrepresented defendant was counterclaiming £30,000 so the claimant solicitors had submitted a costs estimate of £8,000. Homer explained the nature of the civil case tracks, the order he would be making and disclosure, in simple terms.

> It's not like *Perry Mason*. We don't have trial by ambush. You might see the documents they provide and think 'Well, this is a load of rubbish' and they might see your documents and think 'Ah, well we didn't realise all this' and be prepared to discuss a settlement … I don't know. I haven't looked at the merits of your case and I can't see into the future.

He explained costs, again urging the defendant to seek legal advice. DJs sometimes appeared to be tempted to offer advice but had to remind themselves of the

---

[49] Moorhead, above n 23, said that judges ensured procedural correctness but quoted judges who admitted that they could not be confident that all points of law supporting an LIP's case had been explored and it was not their job to do so. Instead, they saw their role as making time for advice-seeking.

requirement for impartiality.[50] An LIP appeared at a case management conference in front of DJ Hulbert. He was the defendant in a personal injury action. At the instigation of his estranged wife, his children were suing him for injuries sustained 12 years earlier in a car accident he had caused. The claimants' solicitors did not appear, having only just received a chaotic file, but they had not bothered to inform the court. Hulbert initiated a long conversation with the litigant, explaining how to discover who his insurers were at the date of the accident. He stopped himself short and said that he could not give partial advice. I asked Hulbert if he felt tempted to intervene. He said he did when someone had been 'badly done by', like this.[51]

An LIP might lose sympathy if they had inexplicably failed to comply with procedure in a way that the judge felt was within their capacity. An LIP appeared before DJ Joel, defending against the application to repossess his pub. The claimant owners were represented by a barrister. They claimed possession, rent arrears, arrears of business costs and the £6,000 deposit. The LIP had not bothered to submit a defence, or defence statement, or counterclaim, but announced to the judge that he 'ought to make a counterclaim', as the claimants had seized his stock and catering equipment. 'But you can't just submit a counterclaim in the face of the court', tutted Joel. He insisted on dealing with the matter immediately, as an adjournment had already been granted, following a letter from the LIP's solicitor. The judge answered questions from the defendant's father and explained that the defendant could take separate proceedings in conversion for his losses. After presentation of the claimant's evidence, the defendant repeated his claim for his stock and equipment. The defendant's father interjected with another question and the judge called an end to his advice session.

> I'm here to adjudicate, not to advise. If you want to advise your son, you may do so and appear as his friend. It's called a McKenzie Friend but if you think there's a question you'd like your son to ask, you should speak to him.

The father interjected again, explaining that his son was out of work with no benefits. Father and son clearly felt an injustice had been done, when Joel made an order for £6,000 plus £1,500 costs. The son retorted 'I can't pay. I'm going bankrupt soon' and remarked loudly and sarcastically that the pub's barrister's costs were 'Not bad for two days' work'.[52] After they left, Joel remarked, 'You feel sorry for some people but Quaffers Pub won't get anything. He's going bankrupt.'

---

[50] In the Crown Court chapter, we saw that Mortimer had to stop short and remind a prosecutor in person that the courts and judges were not there to give legal advice.

[51] The Association of HMDJs is piloting a scheme supported by the Judicial Communications Office to publish a guide to small claims, written by a DJ, in local papers throughout the country. They hope this will also enhance public perception: S Gold, 'Putting the public straight', AHMDJ *Law Bulletin*, Vol 22, No 1, winter 2010/11.

[52] Moorhead and Sefton, above n23, found that half of the LIPs interviewed were left with a sense of unfairness, often wrought by judges excluding legally irrelevant evidence. They

Typically, the LIP here was accompanied by a friend or relative who expected to speak to the judge and participate in the hearing, as if they were one of the parties. It seemed that such an expectation was partly raised by the fact that DJs' hearings were conducted casually, like roundtable discussions, in their offices, with the DJ at a desk.

UNHAPPY HENS

Similar expectations were raised in a disappointed hen party. It illustrates how lay people cannot distinguish between a party to litigation, a witness and a McKenzie friend and have to be repeatedly constrained by the judge, endeavouring to keep to a fair, ordered procedure, when all parties want a row. It also illustrates that the strain on the judge is doubled where both parties are unrepresented. In this case, the DJs were alarmed that a deputy DJ had listed this small claim hearing for two hours, despite the fact that 19 lay and two police witnesses were listed. DJ Elizabeth Bennet offloaded the trial to a colleague, DJ Stuart. He commenced at 2.00 pm, ascertaining who the 12 people were in court. Both sides were unrepresented. The claimant was the unpaid publican and the defendant bride was counter-claiming false imprisonment. Her defence was that the entertainment was inappropriate and the drinks were not free. The nervous, young defendant was accompanied by an older woman and asked if she could sit in 'as a McKenzie friend'. Stuart replied 'Not really, because she's also a witness but you'll probably find you're OK, because I'll explain the proceedings to you.' He addressed them all in simple language, checking that they all had the relevant documents. He summarised for the defendant what she had said in her defence, outlining in simple language what he thought her story was and allowing her to correct him. He then explained the procedure to all parties. He questioned the claimant and noted his answers in longhand, pointing out discrepancies between his statement and testimony. The claimant then challenged the defendant.

> Claimant: Have you got any witnesses, other than in your group?
>
> DJ: Just a minute Mr. X, you can't ask questions. You're giving evidence.

DJ Stuart reminded the claimant publican that he was the one bringing the claim so should give evidence of what happened. When the claimant was examining the second and subsequent witnesses, he was increasingly challenging and aggressive. He looked physically strong. He listened to the answers and then asked questions of the claimant instead of the witness, and was corrected by the judge. Then all the women from the hen party started to chime in. The claimant started making

---

contemplate why this strict insistence on 'neutrality', excluding everything that is legally irrelevant, causes feelings of substantive injustice and he suggests an alternative judicial approach, emphasising the communication of legal principles so that LIPs can understand them, and a greater willingness to understand disputes in the way the LIP sees them.

a statement, challenging the witnesses' evidence, instead of asking questions. Smiling, the DJ interjected, explaining that he was aware of what he needed to decide and this was not helping. 'Let's try to conduct the procedure as decorously as we can.' (There was no chance of *anyone* understanding the word 'decorously'). By 3.50 pm, the witness testimony was complete, the defence witnesses having been whittled down to eight, and DJ Stuart explained that the parties could both give closing speeches. 'The issue for me to decide is whether the girls were asked to leave or went voluntarily.' (It occurred to me that some of the 'girls' over 40 might not like this label.) DJ Stuart asked them to leave the room while he wrote his judgment, then called them back in at 4.20 pm. (There was no usher.) The judgment took 12 minutes to deliver. He mentioned the volatility of the claimant then the claimant interrupted with a lengthy speech, insisting that he was not volatile, raising his voice. 'I thought this was not about *me*! I was just trying to run a business'. DJ Stuart dismissed the claim and asked the claimant to speak on the counterclaim. The claimant looked aghast and angry, 'I don't believe this! What more can I say?' trying to catch my eye. DJ Stuart explained that all the witnesses were entitled to expenses of £50 each and loss of earnings. As the DJ asked them in turn to state their expenses, the claimant interrupted, 'Do I have to sit through this?' and stomped out. As the women left, one turned to DJ Stuart and thanked him, 'Can I just say thank you. That was nicely done. I really wasn't looking forward to this.'

English, adversarial procedure expects each party to research the law to support their case. Judges have a problem where an LIP has failed to do this. This is why the senior judiciary are supported by their judicial assistants but lower court judges have no such support. DJs explained that they found these cases especially hard.

> When you have two litigants in person, particularly where there are issues of law which neither have worked out, you have to make sure you get the law right and that they understand. The difficulty is in small claims as they normally have very entrenched views and no matter what your decision, somebody is going to go out dissatisfied. Occasionally they both go out dissatisfied

Circuit Judges Highbury and PM were managing a construction case in the Technology and Construction Court (TCC) where both the claimant property owner and the defendant builder were unrepresented. They moaned that it was very technical but there were no specialist reports. No Scott schedule had been prepared. They added '*And* they're *both thick*'. Both dreaded trying the case. They kept handing it to one another in case management then PM trumped Highbury by retiring. Highbury explained that, despite the fact that the claim was for a substantial amount, £60,000, he planned to conduct it like a small claim. He would get both parties to 'sit down and tell their side of the story'. He said he would not send them away to seek legal advice, since they probably could not afford it. 'Another judge might have got them to write a proper pleading, whereas I think it's hopeless, as they're not very intelligent.'

All the judges were extremely patient in explaining procedure, and tolerant when LIPs went wrong, in, for instance, asking inappropriate questions of witnesses, or repeating themselves. Where an LIP appeared opposite a lawyer, judges expected professionals to demonstrate similar tolerance. Judge Vincent Jones found himself in two sequential trials, each with an LIP facing a lawyer. In the first trial, for pollution, the judge had to stop the LIP asking one of the witnesses what the law was and then counsel for the Environment Agency objected to his asking a witness to speculate. The defendant was clearly aggrieved at the action being taken against him. He was hoping the agency would have acted against his business tenant, as it was he, the defendant, who had reported the tenant to the water authority for pollution. The judge allowed the LIP a significant amount of repetition before he responded to the advocate's objections and politely stopped this line of questioning. By lunchtime, Vincent had concluded that there was no defence. There had already been a successful prosecution for pollution in the magistrates' court. The LIP repeatedly tried to argue that the lay magistrates had used the wrong legal test of criminal responsibility and the judge repeatedly and patiently explained that he could not act as an appellate court from the magistrates, nor could he 'go behind' their line of reasoning but it took until 3.20 pm before the LIP conceded defeat.

During the next two days, Vincent heard an unrepresented claimant suing his employer for work-related injuries. The LIP was fairly competent in presenting his case and when he made statements, Vincent carefully translated these into appropriate questions for examination or cross-examination. Throughout, he maintained a smiling demeanour towards the LIP. The obstructive defence barrister disrupted the trial. Vincent was annoyed at his failure to produce originals of documents. He produced photocopies and tried to argue with Vincent that this was sufficient. Vincent, provoked by his rudeness, remarked that counsel should have the sense to 'know his judge' and apologise.[53] He halted the trial and waited for 1.5 hours while the originals were couriered over and then insisted in sitting into the evening to make up for lost time, as he was scheduled to commence a two-day family trial the next day. Once this barrister had vexed Vincent, the relationship was irretrievable. He tried to address the judge while sitting down and was reprimanded. The trial inevitably spilled over into the next day. At one point, counsel objected to the irrelevance of the LIP's questions and Vincent finally lost patience with the unhelpful advocate.

> Well, the questioning is bound to be wide-ranging where the skeleton arguments and the evidence say different things. I'm *trying* to conduct a fair hearing Mr X! This is a

---

[53] This London court suffered from the same lack of 'community' as the London Crown Courts, with judges complaining about being unable to trust lawyers because there were so many of them. This stranger barrister did not know his judge and had not mastered courtroom craft, as depicted in RB Flemming et al, *The Craft of Justice* (Philadelphia, University of Pennsylvania Press, 1993), cited in ch 8.

litigant in person. Judges in the county court need to offer latitude and tolerance to litigants in person and *you* need to learn the same!

By this time, counsel had learned to apologise. He thanked Vincent and sat down contritely.[54]

VEXATIOUS LITIGANTS

For some LIPs, litigation becomes an obsession, a full-time pursuit. When LIPs become obsessive, attempting to persecute one or more parties or making multiple hopeless applications, they may be classed as 'vexatious litigants' and banned from suing people. An examination of the facts in the case law was confirmed by this research: both indicating that the civil courts are astonishingly tolerant. Often an LIP makes the lives of counter staff and judges a misery before being classified as vexatious.[55] DJs Elizabeth Bennet and Stuart discussed a problematic LIP who appeared in their list. He regularly brought claims two days inside the limitation period. They suspected these were fraudulent. Unfortunately, he regularly obtained judgment in default, as Elizabeth explained.

> because the claim sits on someone's desk at the insurance company and then they apply to strike out the judgment and a DJ says 'The court has no evidence'; then he always appeals to a circuit judge. He's built up a knowledge of procedure. The court office has late-opening till seven, once a month, and he's had loads of the office's time. I drew up a table of all this, including costs ordered against him, all unpaid. I've done it in my own time. My husband asked why I bothered.

DJ Stuart came in later and dropped a bombshell. The defendants in this latest case had settled, paying out £1,400. 'But there's no evidence!' DJ Stuart told us how alarmed he had been when he saw the LIP coming in with 'petite counsel' for the insurance company. She had intimated that she might ask for the case to be struck out but her instructing solicitors told her to settle and pay him off. The judges were horrified. 'This'll mess up our statistics, won't it?' They could not now report him as a vexatious litigant. The report would go to waste and the fraudster would be encouraged. Elsewhere, DJs Homer and Cartman told me of one of their vexatious litigants. He kept suing Royal Mail for non-delivery of his registered letters to all the various courts in which he was suing. Vincent Jones

---

[54] He seemed ignorant of 'a long tradition at the bar that where a litigant is in person, the lawyers in the case will endeavour, insofar as it is consistent with their duty to their clients, to assist LIPs in the presentation of their case': Wall, above n 42.

[55] In *Bhamjee v Forsdick and others* [2003] EWCA Civ 1113 and *R (Mahajan) v Central London County Court and Another* [2004] Civ 946, the CA set out guidelines. In *HM Attorney General v Chitolie* [2004] EWHC 1943 (Admin), C was found to be a vexatious litigant after involvement in 18 actions. In October 2004, a new Rule (3.11) set out the courts' powers to make a civil restraint order. For some, vexatious litigation is a disease, known in Europe as De Clerambault's syndrome. They try to sue their lawyers, the judges and the courts. In 1997–2003, the Lord Chancellor's Department spent £3 million defending itself from such actions.

showed me a massive bundle of files relating to one litigant he described as 'volatile'. The council had evicted him and taken his possessions into storage. He claimed that they were worth £30,000. On his last visit to the court information desk he had smashed doors and windows, so Vincent had persuaded HM Courts Service to take out an injunction forbidding him to come to the court except for a hearing.

DEALING WITH DEBT

County courts are not filled with the middle classes and business folk.[56] A 2003–04 survey of over 5,000 adults showed that socially excluded groups were especially vulnerable to civil justice problems, which were experienced by 80 per cent of people in temporary accommodation, two thirds of lone parents and half the unemployed. Issues frequently occurred in clusters, such as personal injury leading to loss of home or income.[57] Typically, DJs Tierce and Rooney heard 16 local authority housing possession actions per hour, one morning a week, then heard private landlords' applications in the afternoon. Most tenants did not put in an appearance to fend off eviction and many who did were unrepresented. The DJs were unhappy about this hasty treatment, in view of the gravity to the defendant. 'These are people's *homes!*' I was reminded, around the country.[58] Through housing cases, personal bankruptcy and their family work, where they were frequently splitting the debt not assets, judges were brought into contact with society's poorest and most disadvantaged and disorganised people, who suffered disproportionately from drug addiction and depression.[59] Unwittingly, DJs share many of their 'clientele' with DJMCs in the magistrates' courts, who punish their crimes and hear their family problems. DJ Hulbert remarked, as we examined the debts of a depressed chef who earned £5,500 per annum, 'I think many of them have borderline personality disorders and they medicate themselves on drink and drugs'. Coincidentally, there had been a news item that morning about people with multiple debts, like the very people appearing in front of Hulbert. Judges were often upset at social injustices. In all six circuits,

[56] Two thirds of county court claims are produced by the Northampton Claim Production Centre, acting for bulk claimants such as banks and credit card issuers: *Judicial and Court Statistics.*

[57] P Pleasance and others (2004), *Causes of Action: civil law and social justice* for the Legal Services Research Centre, confirming H Genn, *Paths to Justice: what people do and think about going to law* (Oxford, Hart Publishing, 1999).

[58] This concerned attitude was universal. No judge said the cases were 'pretty boring stuff', like the DJ quoted by D Cowan and E Hitchings, '"Pretty Boring Stuff": District Judges and Housing Possession Proceedings' (2007) 16 (3) *Social and Legal Studies* 363–82. DJs did not underestimate the gravity and consequences of the proceedings, as can be seen from the remainder of the quotation in the body of the article.

[59] And see Genn's account of a judge being harangued by an LIP who clearly had special needs. The judge retired to chambers to telephone social services, above n 4 at 178.

defendants on the possession lists suffered from slow receipt of housing benefit and were confused by the fact that they had to apply for it from the local authority, not central government like the rest of their benefits.[60] They suffered delays in receipt of family tax credits, including one woman who caused some ironic mirth by disclosing that she worked for that very section of HM Revenue and Customs. One lunchtime, two judges discussed whether claims-farmers touting for business in personal injury cases 'offered a way out of social exclusion'. DJ Rooney had accompanied the bailiffs to witness the consequences of homelessness. As a 1970s law student who had read Griffith's *Politics of the Judiciary*, I never dreamed I would one day accompany judges agonising about social exclusion and legal advice deserts but then this generation of judges were brought up on Griffith too.[61] All of this demonstrates the absurdity of judges' 'out-of-touch' image.

One such judge was DJ Jurd. A housing association applied for an injunction requiring a tenant to remove a giant caravan from his garden. The unrepresented defendant argued that he put it there to accommodate some of his six children. He wanted an adjournment so that he could obtain advice but asked if he could 'counterclaim', because he felt the association were in breach of contract, having failed to rehouse him. Jurd repeatedly explained that he could not give legal advice any more than he could advise the housing association. The defendant replied that he could not get advice quickly enough: there was a three-day waiting list for the local Citizens' Advice Bureau. Jurd explained that he would grant the adjournment but the defendant was still in breach of his tenancy agreement and he would be told to remove the caravan. 'Well I'll have to put my kids on the street then', raged the defendant. 'I'll have to go to prison for my kids [repeatedly]. There's nothing I wouldn't do for my kids…There's no fairness here.' He threatened to bring his children to the next court appearance. Afterwards, the DJ explained that he had considerable sympathy for the defendant. The housing association should have rehoused the family. He felt so strongly about this injustice that he had considered listing the case before a circuit judge so it would attract publicity.

People could lose their credit rating as swiftly as they could lose their homes. At 11.22 am one day, an usher slipped a bankruptcy applicant in between small claims, before the 11.30 am slot. The man appeared unrepresented.

DJ Cartman: 'Have you taken advice?'

Applicant: 'Yes, I went to the CAB.'

---

[60]   Cowan and Hitchings, above n 58, said lack of housing benefit was a major cause of rent arrears.

[61]   J Gallagher reported a 'highly positive' view of the county courts from Shelter's case workers and solicitors providing advice and representation in possession cases. They were routinely welcomed by district judges. 'Keeping the Roof', ADJ *Law Bulletin* (Winter 2005–06) Vol 17, No1, 11.

DJ: 'Did anyone explain the alternatives?'

Applicant: 'Yes but I can't pay my debts. I haven't got enough coming in.'

The DJ accepted this and explained that the bankruptcy would take immediate effect. The man asked for further explanation and the DJ explained the summary administration and the role of the official receiver.

DJ: 'Do you still want me to make the order?'

Applicant: 'Please, Sir, yes.'

A petitioner for bankruptcy appeared, unrepresented, before DJ Hulbert. He was the 20-year-old chef. Having read the papers, the judge wondered, aside, whether the young man had received advice. He spoke very gently and sympathetically to him as he explained that he suffered from depression and had moved in with his father, as he could not cope on his own. He owed money to utilities companies. He owed £30,000 on his mortgage on a property now worth £10,000 and he was paying £30 per week for counselling. The judge asked if he had received advice about administration orders but he insisted on being made bankrupt, to 'wipe the slate clean'.

Judges were not sympathetic with serial bankrupts, however. DJ Jurd spoke harshly to a young lady in jeans.

DJ: 'How have you got yourself into this mess again? Seven credit cards and no income?'

Applicant: 'I was robbing Peter to pay Paul.'

The judge later explained his abruptness. 'She knows the system and she's done it before. She's clocked up forty thousand pounds of debt and never worked.' DJ Tierce, who dealt with hundreds of housing possession actions per month, considered that only one defendant in 10 was undeserving of sympathy. He berated one of these. Looking over his glasses, he scolded an immigrant squatter, challenging him in an inquisitorial manner. '*Why* are you in these premises? Is there any reason why you should not take your place in the housing queue?' His colleague DJ Rooney said he often gave people on the housing list a lecture.

> because they don't understand the importance of the order for repossession. I ask them 'What's the most important thing in your life?' They say 'My child' and I say 'Think again—the roof over your head'. They'll be out on the street and they won't be rehoused—not in this authority.[62]

As will be seen in the family chapter, DJs readily lectured warring parents, too.

---

[62] Cowan and Hitchings observed judgmental attitudes in some DJs: 'At one end, all occupiers were worthy because this was *social* housing and deviant behaviour was therefore forgivable; at the other extreme, the contract was sovereign and its breach unforgivable. Generally, the construction of the worthy occupier was in tune with neo-liberal concerns broadly coalescing around governing understandings of responsibility', above n 58 at 374. A DJ might give a feckless tenant a telling off.

JUDGMENTS AND APPEALS

All civil judges said it was preferable to give an extempore (immediate) judgment. Reserved judgments *always* took a disproportionate amount of time, as Highbury explained:

> I try and give extempore judgments … but obviously in a heavy case you can't do it and those cases take an enormous amount of time … If you say at twelve o'clock 'I'll give a judgment at half past three' and you go into your room, you get it together and it is done. If you reserve it, it takes an eternal amount of time to do.

Civil circuit judges were placed in the uncomfortable position of hearing appeals from DJs' decisions, judges sitting in their own court. Given the necessity for working harmony, the procedure was unsatisfactory. Vincent Jones said it was 'embarrassing, especially when it's part of my job to look after everyone here'.

Civil judges felt the CA sitting on their shoulders, as they drafted a judgment. Judge Duke called me into his chambers to show me how he constructed a judgment, where he thought both parties were lying but one was lying more than the other. He said that a judge gives judgment for two audiences, the loser and the CA. (I heard that said frequently by circuit and HC judges.) He said that a civil judge directs himself to have regard to the law and the evidence, in the same way that a judge directs a jury. I asked Shakespeare, experienced in civil and criminal (jury) trials how she decided who was telling the truth. She said she looked at the documents and weighed the evidence systematically.

> Well, I don't think 'I don't like the colour of this man's skin' or 'He's got a lisp that irritates me' or 'I wouldn't want to go out with him'. Judges are trained to disregard all that and concentrate on the evidence. Some jurors probably go on looks and dress.

She said her judgments were seldom appealed because they were detailed. 'I think it sells the decision to them.' It was hard to know what litigants expected in the way of judgment because 'when I was in practice, all my cases settled'.

LAWYERS AND CIVIL JUDGES

DJs understood cash-flow logistics of solicitors' firms and the consequences of shrinking legal aid. They taxed solicitors' bills swiftly so as not to delay payments. As former solicitors, they understood solicitors' day-to-day work. 'Those guys appearing in front of me this morning—I can understand what their clients are like'. Nevertheless, poor quality legal work prevented them exercising their legal obligation to take swift case management decisions. They encountered incorrectly completed forms in *every* pile of boxwork, such as unsigned claim forms, letters which should have been forms and cases sent to the wrong court. Forms were routinely completed by illiterates. Phrases like 'tripping over refuge bags' and other gems caused giggles or groans.[63] Jurd said he might correct errors.

---

[63]   There is a list of such howlers in every issue of the DJ's *Bulletin*.

People don't know what they're doing. Newly qualified solicitors haven't a clue how civil procedure works. In road traffic cases, they'll say 'I haven't a clue what I'm doing' and sue the wrong person, such as the insurance company.

Joel had given up correcting errors. 'Why should I make work for myself?' The pilot judge had created a proforma top sheet with a tick list to denote errors. In most instances, though, the forms had to be returned to the solicitors' firm. This caused delay to the client and to case progress, extra work for the court staff and a bill for the taxpayer, as well as wasting judicial time. The judges said errors occurred because solicitors employed paralegals or low grade staff to do the basic case work. The problem is widespread. In 2006, a DJ complained in the *New Law Journal* of the frustration of the CPR's aims to take case management decisions promptly by the shoddy completion of allocation questionnaires by solicitors. He listed routine errors, demonstrating a lack of understanding of the CPR and wholesale disregard of the parties' obligations under the CPR, causing delay and extra cost.[64] The care taken in file preparation was very variable. The judges' work was much easier if the files were in order. The pilot DJ opened one claimant's file, prepared by a solicitor who was a deputy DJ. It was in a ring-binder, in a logical order, with a list of agreed evidence, statements and so on. 'It's such a pleasure when something's properly prepared.' In one case, a claimant had sent in a draft order on disc. All she needed to do was amend it. By contrast, the next fat bundle was 'a dog's dinner—all back to front' and she struggled to put it in order before working on it.

When asked if they had any comments on the lawyers appearing before them, judges considered the standard of advocacy to be as bad as the paperwork. Nine of the 12 DJs replied negatively. These represent five of the six court circuits.

You'd be surprised how many lawyers ... don't seem to have a clue what they're doing.

There are a lot of people who ... don't know what they are doing. They are not solicitors or barristers ... It is annoying and frustrating not just for us but for the people they are representing.

Competence has gone down ... solicitors can no longer afford to put solicitors ... in front of judges. More often than not we get legal executives or non-partners.

We tend to get a lot of new lawyers, or trainees. I'm not always convinced that the training ... suits them for [court] work ... We, almost as default, take on part of their training role ... My approach ... would always be, 'Next time Mr So-and-So, would you bear in mind this or that ... '

I don't think the training of young solicitors is as good as it used to be. They ... disregard the law ... don't address the issues properly.

---

[64] District Judge TJ John, 'The district judge as scrutineer' (2006) 156 *New Law Journal* 569.

Another said 90 per cent of solicitors did not understand the CPR. Judges said the office staff were 'fed up' with lawyers telephoning for legal advice. These comments are supported by an editorial in the 2006 DJ's *Law Bulletin*, complaining of falling standards:

> I would never have been allowed to send to counsel my file [in place of a brief] ... or to ignore directions of a Judge ... or to know so little of the facts that within a three-minute review prior to the hearing the Judge knows more than the advocates do.[65]

Baldwin observed that lawyers were untrained in small claims procedure.[66] This is now clearly part of a much wider problem.

In court, circuit judges William Highbury and Vincent Jones demonstrated why it was counterproductive to argue with a judge. The story of Vincent, the LIP and the argumentative barrister is told above. One day, Highbury heard a contested application to activate an 'unless' order. The party in breach had delivered bank statements but they were useless as all the entries had been blanked out.

> Barrister for respondent: 'We want to move on from here. Where are we now?'

> Highbury: 'Where you are now is *struck out!*'

As the barrister whinged that the original solicitors, now sacked, had possession of the cheque book stubs, Highbury reposted 'You know perfectly well that you could have had a witness summons to get them to come and produce them'. The barrister then foolishly tried arguing that the DJ had not meant to make an 'unless' order, according to her notes.

> Highbury: 'Judges don't make *notes*, Mr X. Everything's tape-recorded! It's as clear as it could be that your client should have produced the bank statements disclosing all entries!'

> Barrister: 'Well maybe the tape should be heard then.'

> Highbury: 'And you could have *applied for a transcription!*'

As the barrister repeatedly insisted that he could apply to vary the order, the judge repeatedly explained that he could not. 'It has to be done under the Rules and supported by evidence.' Despite the defence barrister's incompetence, Highbury gave judgment in the defendant's favour, saying the overriding objective of the CPR (justice and fairness) would not be furthered by striking out her defence, but he listed the litany of legal errors. It was not a surprise that Vincent Jones' assessment of the lawyers who appeared in his court was similar to that of the district judges.

---

[65]   N Law, Editorial, *Law Bulletin* Vol 17, No 2, summer 2006.
[66]   Baldwin, above n 9 at ch 3.

They are not very good ... As this court is not very far from the Temple, it is used as a training court by many young barristers. Barristers who become very good at their specialism then stop appearing at county courts ... outside London the quality is generally much better.

His view was supported by his colleague, Bede.

[As barristers] we did a mixture of common law, crime, civil and family. We were in court morning, noon and night and we acquired advocacy skills ... Nowadays the young Bar are much more specialised, go less to court ... With the diminution of public funding, less of them are able to learn their trade ... less preparation and less focus upon important questions like 'what jurisdiction does a judge have?'

Circuit judge Duke was similarly concerned.

When I took this job it was a total culture shock. I had been a silk for 10 years ... then suddenly to find people who had not even read the papers and did not know what they were talking about. They didn't even know what statute they were quoting from ... I had someone come here the other day who had not even brought the document on which they were seeking an *ex parte* injunction, which is a penal order for which you could go to jail and I had to chuck it out.

Duke, Vincent and Bede sat in London and Bede expressed a distrust of the London Bar in strikingly similar terms to Crown Court judges, on the loss of trust.

There are inevitably some people who are more easily persuaded to go over a line ... I am talking about ethics and morality ... client pressure, money pressure ... as the number has grown, I think there is much less trust within the Bar ... one used to have discussions ... with the opposition on a gentleman basis.

JUDGES' VIEWS OF THE WOOLF REFORMS/ALTERNATIVE DISPUTE RESOLUTION

The Woolf reforms, notably the introduction of pro-active case management in the CPR 1998, have been generally evaluated as a success in enhancing access to justice. Litigation has continued to decrease and settlements are achieved more speedily but the cost has not been reduced in the way that Woolf hoped.[67] I asked those judges who heard civil cases what they thought of the Woolf reforms. I had noticed that, when I first sat with DJs, in 1996, they were enthusiasts and claimed to be pre-empting reform. 'We act according to a strict timetable now, in view of Woolf.' Seven years later, 11 of the 12 research DJs rated them as a success, four responding in strong terms: 'brilliant' (twice), 'amazing' and 'incredibly successful'.

---

[67] See Darbyshire, above n 17 at ch 10. The Ministry of Justice consulted on plans to curb costs as a result of Lord Justice Jackson's *Review of Civil Litigation Costs: Final Report* (The Stationery Office, online, 2009), Judiciary website. See MoJ CP6/2011.

Absolutely brilliant ... they have transformed civil justice ... It has brought an end to the endless sniping ... extraordinarily tedious and a waste of money.

An amazing change ... There was some worry that judges were going to become very draconian and try and dictate things ... I think there is a good working relationship and that is to the advantage to the people who litigate.

The 21 CJs were significantly less enthusiastic, with only 10 commenting positively, although two considered them 'extremely good'. Of the 33 district and circuit judges, 16 expressed concern about increased costs, with some CJs voicing strong views that this was a denial of access to justice.

The costs seem to be out of all proportion ... judges often say to each other that we could not afford to go to court ... a lot of decent people can't go to law.

Another complained of a personal injury case where the damages recovered were £30,000 but the costs £16,000.[68] Four judges wanted to see strict curbing of costs by extending the fixed-costs regime in small claims to larger claims.[69] Four of the 33 were concerned that litigants were now under undue pressure to settle and four considered that the rules, intended to be an exemplar of simplicity, were too complex.

Although some commercial litigants have embraced arbitration as an alternative dispute forum since the eighteenth century, 'alternative dispute resolution' (ADR) as a generic concept was imported from the US as recently as the early 1990s. Lawyers were very slow to refer their clients to ADR and it was left to the enthusiastic senior judiciary to promote it, in their speeches and in the case law of the Court of Appeal. The CPR, rule 1, requires case managing judges to check that the parties have considered ADR and that lawyers have explained it to their clients.[70] I was surprised to find that DJs barely mentioned ADR. I never witnessed one of them raising the subject during case management. I did not ask them about this but the first DJ I shadowed said he almost never referred people to mediation because he felt it was not appropriate for the type of cases DJs heard, small claims and small fast track cases.

The client wants his hearing. He's paid for it. A court order is enforceable. Why send him off to look for an alternative? Where's he going to get it? What's it going to cost?

While it is understandable that ADR is not promoted as an alternative to the small claims procedure, itself developed as a cheap, informal alternative to regular county court procedure, it makes far less sense that there was no mention of ADR in managing fast track and multitrack cases. There are indeed many small claims that would be better dealt with by ADR. I witnessed a pre-trial hearing

---

[68] There were many cases in this research, including HC and CA cases, with astonishingly disproportionate costs.

[69] One solution contemplated by Jackson and in the 2011 consultation. Lord Woolf recommended this in 1996 but it was not adopted in the CPR 1998.

[70] See Darbyshire, above n 17 at ch 11.

before one DJ, where the claimant appeared alone, in a dispute over a £26 mobile phone bill. The explanation may partly lie in DJs' lack of understanding of ADR and knowledge of its availability. In 2003, the editor of the DJ's *Law Bulletin* confessed:

> I am in favour of ADR but do not really know how to approach it in my Court ... There must be many colleagues who share my feelings of inadequacy yet the District Bench is in the best position to promote ADR due to its role in case management.[71]

Other writers in the same edition wondered how to change the county court culture in favour of ADR. Given that Woolf had been emphasising ADR since his interim *Access to Justice* report in 1995 and given that DJs, as managing judges, have a *duty* to promote ADR, this was surely a serious gap in the operation of the Woolf reforms, some 20 years after ADR entered the UK legal lexicon.

On the other hand, the DJs, as former solicitors, were very familiar with negotiation, the type of ADR of first resort, so they expected the parties to negotiate before litigating. In 1996, one DJ would not permit parties to enter his courtroom unless they assured him they had already discussed the case. Baldwin found that in one in six defended small claims, the parties had reached a settlement before the court hearing and some were negotiated in the court building.[72] As noted already, lists were overbooked, expecting this would happen. While legal representatives expect to negotiate, LIPs may not. According to Baldwin, some small claims litigants assumed it would be improper to initiate contact with the other side[73] and LIPs, if left to their own devices, would rarely negotiate. Being then faced with the judicial expectation of negotiation, the meeting outside the courtroom provided a crucial first opportunity.[74]

CONCLUSION

The powerhouse of civil litigation is neglected by researchers and not understood by the public. Since 1990, litigation has dwindled. There has been a downshift of business into the county court, especially onto the shoulders of district judges. This parallels the trend in criminal cases. DJs do work formerly done by circuit judges. CJs hear most HC cases outside London. Travelling HC judges do not spend long enough in one place to try lengthy provincial cases. DJs are the most important judges to most people involved in a civil case because they determine most cases (all small claims and many fast track) and manage most cases pre-trial

---

[71]   Vol 14, No 3, spring 2003. M Trent, President of the Association of HMDJs called for all DJs to be trained in mediation, News (2010) 160 *New Law Journal* 470. On disparity of ADR and lack of judicial training, see T Allen and K Mackie, 'Higher resolution' (2010) 160 *New Law Journal* 1143.
[72]   Baldwin, above n 9 at 65.
[73]   ibid 34.
[74]   ibid 65.

(and most never get to trial). Like DJMCs, they remain invisible to the public and they only became known as 'judges' in recent history. At least other judges were aware of them, because they shared courts and dining rooms, but this made the appeal system uncomfortable, with CJs determining appeals from their workaday colleagues.

While CJs' work was sporadic and the high settlement rate left some with free time, they were not generally underemployed. DJs were fully employed, spending most of their time alone, with unlimited boxwork (judicial case management). CJs normally loved their work. DJs too were happy, because their 9–5 weekday hours contrasted with their workload as solicitors and they were free of business responsibilities. Judges enjoyed doing justice, as they saw it, in individual cases, having an impact on people's lives and they appreciated their independence in decision-making. Nevertheless, they drafted their judgments for two audiences: the parties and the appellate court. County court judges have often been called 'Jacks of all trades'. The novice, Shakespeare, was happy to give up evenings and weekends in self-education on unfamiliar laws. Some experienced DJs had learned that so many cases settled, though, that they could take the risk of not pre-reading the papers. The settlement rate is indeed so high that no meaningful conclusions can be drawn in this book about civil trials.

County court judges are not generally occupied in resolving the problems of the rich but the homeless, the debtor, the bankrupt, the unemployed, the poor, the vulnerable (children, the elderly and the mentally infirm) the immigrant, the drug addict and so on: people who often present with multiple civil and family problems, sometimes the same chaotic clientele of the magistrates' courts. Judges face litigants from the same social groups as their former clients so they have a very clear understanding of their needs. These real judges are far from the out-of-touch folk-devil, portrayed in chapter two. Like the legal aid solicitors most of them formerly were, they see the widest spectrum of civil problems, brought by parties who are disproportionately representative of the dispossessed, the underclasses, the 'marginalised'. The judicial stereotype is not just wildly unrealistic but unfair. We are back to the point made in chapter two that 'judges cannot win'. The public think they are out of touch and privileged yet professional commercial litigators accuse them of siding with the underdog.

One striking finding was the dominance of judges' time by litigants in person. Until I spent so much time in all levels of court, I had no appreciation of the proportion of time spent on civil cases where one or both parties are unrepresented. The presence of an LIP in court significantly affects the judicial role. In the adversarial system, the judge is kept strictly in the role of non-interfering, unbiased umpire and if he steps outside that role he raises grounds for appeal. The parties are meant to bring to the court everything the judge needs to take a decision, in terms of law, evidence and witness testimony. They raise their arguments and he decides who has the strongest case. The passive umpire is entirely dependent on the parties to bring all this to the court in a timely manner and to argue their case. Exacerbating this dependence on lawyers, the common law trial, civil and criminal, functions by the adduction of testimony via examination and cross-examination. This is a skill developed through training and practice as a lawyer. Ordinary people come to court expecting to tell a story. The passive judicial role does not work where parties are unrepresented. Seventy per cent of claims are small claims. Procedure presumes that parties will represent themselves. The Courts and Legal Services Act 1990 and the Civil Procedure Rules recognise this so the DJ is allowed leeway in helping people to argue their cases. This is feasible because most small claims do not require legal argument. They depend on known law frequently applied: debt, faulty goods, car accidents and so on but the parties are invariably dependant on the judge to extract their story. The law lays procedure open to idiosyncratic interpretation, however. When I unwittingly followed John Baldwin round the county courts after his small claims research, in 1996–97, district judges asked anxiously whether they did things the same as the judge in the next room. This procedural flexibility means its quality is dependent on the judges' skills, in extracting the party's story and turning it into a series of questions. The problem is, LIPs are not confined to small claims. In fast track and multitrack trials, people represent themselves where thousands of pounds of compensation or their pension depend on the outcome. These cases are likely to invoke complex law or technical or complex evidence. They also last longer. They place a strain on the judge. PM and Highbury, specialist judges, with years of experience in practice and as judges hearing High Court cases, were struggling to manage the construction case where both parties were unintelligent and failed to comply with pre-trial procedure. As we saw with Fergus in the murder case, where a judge *helps* an unrepresented party, he treads a thin line. In this context, the Civil Procedure Rules place judges under the duty of 'ensuring that the parties are on an equal footing'[75] and the judges' instinct, developed from compassion and years of practice, is to help and advise the unrepresented, especially when so many are vulnerable, but they *must* stop short of giving advice.

The prevalence of LIPs is not just important because of the strain it puts on judges and the derogation from the common law adversarial model but because of the degree to which it protracts trials and the consequent expense. Judges have warned that the proposed cuts in legal aid in 2011 will slow cases considerably as parties represent themselves.[76] Years ago, judges were left to initiate their own solution to the problem of the mismatch between the adversarial expectation and the prevalence of LIPs in the higher courts: the judicial assistants. It was left to the European Court of Human Rights, though, to point out to the UK that leaving

---

[75] Overriding Objective, CPR Rule 1.1(2)(a).

[76] News release, 'Proposals for the reform of legal aid', 24 February 2011, Judiciary website and A Hirsch, 'Legal aid will cost more in the long run, say judges', *The Guardian*, 24 February 2011.

people unrepresented in complex litigation, defending against a multi-national is not just impractical, it is unfair.[77]

The judges here understood how solicitors' practices work. Thanks to decades in practice, like Portia and Guy in the magistrates' courts, they empathised with the struggle of legal aid lawyers to run a business at a profit. Nevertheless, judges' work suffered from poor advocacy and sloppy form-filling by inadequately trained or illiterate employees. Mistakes were so prevalent in boxwork that there was doubtless a considerable cost in judge time and court administration and mailing. I concluded during observations that it might be cost-effective to set up an independent research project and remedial training on form-filling.

While the judges' comments on the Woolf reforms were predictable and in line with the 2009 commentaries on their tenth anniversary, it was surprising to see almost no reference in any case to the desirability of alternative dispute resolution. Highbury told me of two £3 million pound mediations I had just missed but there was no routine encouragement of ADR. On the other hand, there is a compelling logic in not offering ADR as an alternative to a small claim. Small claims were originally introduced as a speedy, cheap, informal *alternative* to the county court. What is more worrying, however, was the lack of attempt in some cases to keep costs proportionate, in line with the aims of Lord Woolf and the overriding objective of the CPR. While the dog's leg case gave the judge and me a laugh, the consequences were serious for the unsuspecting and impecunious law student and none of the judges before whom it had appeared, DJs, the CJ or the HC judge, had put a stop to its escalation completely out of proportion to the ill-advised small claim the student had thought she was bringing. In 2011, Jackson LJ told D Regan that our costs regime was the 'laughing stock of the world'.[78] We will return to examples of disproportionality in the High Court and Court of Appeal.

---

[77] *Steel and Morris v UK* (6841/01) [2005] 41 EHRR 22.
[78] D Regan, 'What next?' (2011) 161 *New Law Journal* 305.

12

Family Judges: The Patience of Job and the Judgment of Solomon

It doesn't matter what findings of fact I make. Fuck! The problem is to get her to co-operate with contact!

Circuit judge

Being a family judge is so different from any other type of judging.

Baroness Hale, Society of Legal Scholars Conference, September 2007

THIS CHAPTER EXAMINES the work of the range of family judges: district and circuit judges (DJs and CJs) in the county court, a High Court (HC) judge in London and on circuit, an HC district judge in the Principal Registry of the Family Division, a district judge (magistrates' courts) (DJMC) in Inner London and a Lord Justice of Appeal working on family business. It is a story of an extremely confusing court system and procedures overloaded with lawyers and experts, with judges struggling to deal with an ever-increasing caseload and failing to stop massive delays in determining the futures of children.

Family cases are heard at the High Court (Family Division), county courts and magistrates' family proceedings courts, as follows.

1. *Undefended divorces (including judicial separation)* are normally granted by the county court following paper applications. Complex or publicly important cases are heard by the HC.
2. *Financial orders*, dividing the capital of spouses or civil partners, can be granted by the county court or HC. Maintenance orders can be made and enforced in all courts. Contested child maintenance is handled by the Child Maintenance and Enforcement Commission but magistrates' courts enforce most spousal and child maintenance orders.
3. All three courts have jurisdiction over *domestic violence.*
4. All have concurrent jurisdiction over *children*, under the Children Act 1989.[1]

---

[1] Except wardship: HC only.

The detail is complex, with county courts exercising five types of jurisdiction[2] and most provincial HC cases being heard by nominated ('ticketed') CJs. A family breakdown may require appearances in different courts. This has been confusing users for decades. A unified family court has been debated since the 1960s but has come to nothing.[3]

THE JUDGES AND THE MYSTERIES OF FAMILY TICKETING

I spent 57 days observing 21 family judges, in 14 courts, in six circuits, in their full range of work. Observations lasted four days, sequential or spanning 2003–07. The 12 county court DJs scrutinised and granted uncontested divorce and financial provision applications and issued private law family proceedings. Two were ticketed under section 8 of the Children Act to determine 'private law' contested applications for residence of and contact with children. Eight were Nominated Care DJs, with jurisdiction in 'public law' matters, managing contested care cases (excluding final hearings) and unopposed care and supervision orders. One was ticketed for adoptions. DJs' family hearings were generally separated from non-family but most of their time was spent on mixed boxwork. The one DJMC, Pole, spent 10 weeks per year making orders for emergency protection, adoption, interim care, non-molestation and hearing contested private law and care proceedings. Care cases over five days or with many experts were transferred from his court to the county court. The HC district judge, Caroline, at the Principal Registry of the Family Division, had full private and public law jurisdiction, like a circuit judge with all possible 'tickets',[4] spending half her time on care and the other half on money (up to £10 million) and private residence and contact (including conciliation hearings) and adoptions. She could issue orders stopping people moving assets abroad.

I observed five CJs in complex contested care and contact cases, including a designated (managing) family judge. I spent two days in the Royal Courts of Justice (RCJ) and two on circuit with Stanford J, a Family Division Liaison Judge.

---

[2] Allocation and Transfer of Proceedings Order 2008 SI 2836 (L 18).

[3] See Finer Committee 1974 and Judge J Graham-Hall, discussed by SH Bailey and others, *Smith, Bailey and Gunn on the Modern English Legal System* (London, Sweet and Maxwell, 2002) 113–14 (not later editions). In introducing the Children Bill 1989, Lord Mackay said he hoped it was the precursor of a unified court. See also The Nuffield Foundation's 2002 report, *Family Matters*, below; J Westcott, 'The Family Court Revisited' [2002] *Family Law* 275 and Wall J in (2001) *The Magistrate*, 281. Responding to the DCA consultation paper, *A single civil court?* the Government said it was a long-term objective. See also DCA press release 324/05 and 'A Single Family Court' [2005] *Family Law* 935. In a 2008 speech, 'The Family Courts of the Future', Ryder J said 'We are on the cusp of…a unified family court' but this claim is far-fetched and lacks insight into the confusion exposed here. The Family Justice Review 2011 revived the recommendation.

[4] HCDJs are officers of the Supreme Court within the meaning of the Senior Courts Act 1981, s 88. County court DJs are not. When managing civil HC cases, they act as registrars of the HCt.

HC judges typically hear financial disputes over £10 million and those with a complicating feature such as an international element, a complex trust or point of law. They tend to be allocated child cases involving injuries over which the experts disagree, or the death of a sibling, or an international element, such as abduction. I spent four days with a Lord Justice of Appeal engaged in family court administration and family appeals. I interviewed the judges above plus 11 more involved in family cases—one DJMC, eight CJs, one HC judge and another Lord Justice of Appeal (32 in total).

Ticketing was controversial at the time of the research.[5] County court DJs resented the fact that they were not authorised to determine contested care but magistrates and DJMCs were: 'The President doesn't *like* district judges. She said if we want to do care, we should become circuit judges.'[6] A CJ said this impeded access to justice in remote courts, staffed only by DJs. Magistrates were considered biased and incompetent.[7] Some CJs were outraged by a 2003 letter from President Butler-Sloss, warning that unless they spent 50 days per year on family work they would have their 'tickets' withdrawn. Given the caseload, they could see no logic. Years later, some had retained their 'tickets' by sleight of hand. One explained that if he had a family 'mention' (brief matter) listed first, his day of criminal business would count statistically as family.[8] One new CJ found herself inexplicably allocated to full-time crime in the Crown Court:

> What I cannot get my head round is, having been a family silk, I haven't got a family ticket … I went to see the administrator and said 'Are you going to put me into family work?' I was one of the few recorders that had a public law ticket and the answer was 'No no no!' … I didn't know anything about crime.

One rank of judge mystified the others: the 19 HC district judges in the Principal Registry of the Family Division. Caroline, the one depicted here, resented their isolation and lack of contact with HC judges and the President, across the road.

THE NATURE OF FAMILY JUDGING—AN OUTSIDER LOOKING IN

To an outsider,[9] family judging appears distinct, in judicial role, work and professional culture. These are my observations, not taken from any prior literature. First, where a family unit is broken, emotions are almost always charged. Secondly, in children's cases, third parties and state agents (often in

---

[5] Potter P promised to simplify ticketing: 'Comment' [2008] *Family Law* 4. His intention was that there should simply be public law and private law 'tickets' and, following a 2007 review, this was done.

[6] From 2005, some DJs were nominated to hear contested care through to final hearing.

[7] See ch 16.

[8] See CJs manipulating statistics to satisfy targets in the Crown Court chapter.

[9] I have not studied or practised family law. Natasha Slabas assisted with footnoting.

multiples: grandparents/local authori*ties*/children's guardians/Cafcass)[10] may generate multiple arguments in a case which has multiple elements of dispute (fact finding/decisions on different children), which may be one of a series of judicial decisions (divorce/asset distribution/child residence and access/ maintenance) which may be recurring and/or prolonged. Thirdly, arguments of law very seldom arise. Indeed, I never heard mention of the law in all my time in the family courts, including the Court of Appeal (CA). Fourthly, the judicial role appears to be distinct. The judge will not grant a divorce, in some cases, unless they are satisfied that a fair settlement has been reached between the parties, whereas in ordinary civil cases this is not a condition. In child cases, (except for fact-finding), the judge is not applying a standard of proof between two or more competing versions of events, as in civil and criminal cases. Their paramount duty is to uphold the interests (welfare) of the very *subjects* of the dispute, the children, and to remind adults that children are parties not objects. Indeed, they are the primary parties.[11] In an otherwise adversarial legal system,[12] the judge's job is to dissipate the natural adversarialism that has arisen between estranged parties.[13] To this end, the judge cannot be passive. Some describe their role as inquisitorial.[14] It is frequently interventionist. Some manipulate the proceedings (witnesses, evidence and argument) to achieve their chosen outcome, which may not have been advocated by any party. Because of their role as peace-makers and because some alternate as formal mediators or conciliators, they readily slip into the *informal* role of negotiator, mediator, conciliator, counsellor or, indeed, scold.[15] Fifthly, family lawyers and judges are culturally different from

---

[10]   Children and Family Court Advisory and Support Service.

[11]   Children Act 1989, s 1 and preceding statutes; also an obligation under the UN Convention on the Rights of the Child 1989, Art 3 (1).

[12]   In 2010–11, the Ministry of Justice is undertaking a joint Family Justice Review. It is required to examine 'The extent to which the adversarial nature of the court system is able to promote solutions and good quality family relationships in private law family cases and what alternative arrangements would be more effective in fostering lasting and positive solutions'. The interim report was published in March 2011.

[13]   It seemed to me that the parties' mutual hostility generated adversarialism, contrary to the view of Matt O'Conner, founder of Fathers 4 Justice who reportedly said 'the trouble with the courts is that it is all so adversarial, with both parties having to discredit each other', D Ross, 'Unmasked', *The Independent*, 4 July 2006. Part II of the Family Law Act 1996, if implemented, would have introduced no-fault divorce. Many argue that fault-based divorce introduces blame: N Shepherd, 'The Divorce Blame Game', Association of HM District Judges's *Law Bulletin* Vol 20 no 2, summer 2009, 24. Research in 2009 by Mishcon de Reya found 20 per cent of parents wanted to make separation 'as unpleasant as possible' for their ex-spouse. Fifty per cent of parents sought a day in court, despite knowing it made matters worse for the children: Bennett, below n 33.

[14]   B Cantwell thought family law was becoming adversarial: 'What is Contact For?' [2005] *Family Law* 299. The Family Justice Review is examining 'the options for increasing more inquisitorial elements into the family justice system for both public and private law cases'.

[15]   A Bainham observed that English family law was predicated upon a fault-based system, unlike that of the US, 'Men And Women Behaving Badly: Is Fault Dead in English Family Law?' (2001) *OJLS* Vol 21(2), 226. J Dewar observed that family proceedings are incoherent and

others.[16] The work is mysterious to other lawyers and judges. One Queen's Bench Division (QBD) judge I met teased family judges as 'tree huggers', or 'child minders'. Wilson J said to an audience of non-family lawyers, 'most of you will admit that your private perception of the Family Division is, in every sense, as the Third Division, the Leyton Orient of the High Court'.[17] There is a specialist core of lawyers and professionals who are repeat players in the same courts. On the circuits, long-term relationships between them and with the bench may be close and fluid and affect their actions in individual cases. Solidarity is enhanced in child cases by their shared legal obligation to further the best interests of the child. They must exercise dispassionate, collaborative patience and remain focused, in the face of adults propelled by emotion and self-interest.[18] Sixthly, the distinctiveness of this non-legal culture in courts of law is practically encouraged and abstractly symbolised by the fact that no-one is gowned and it takes place in private. In children's cases, it seemed that the whole business was simply too serious to be conducted by characters in pantomime dress, strutting egos and scoring points. Judges' levels of job satisfaction were high.

> Many of the decisions that I make for children I believe are making huge differences to their lives. I have a chance to play an important role ... in what happens to people and what happens in society and that gives me a good feeling. (CJ)

Most agreed that they found 'the responsibility daunting or emotionally disturbing'.

> I wouldn't like to do family work exclusively because I think it would do me head in! ... I look forward to crime as light relief. (CJ)

THE ROUTINE: COUNTY COURT BOXWORK

DJs spend most of their time dealing with boxwork: paper-based judicial decisions, a mixture of family and non-family cases. DJ Rooney processed a pile of divorce petitions: 'Look, I'm granting all these divorces at the stroke of a pen. I feel as if I'm in the Post Office—stamps, driving licences, divorces!' Boxwork contained agreed financial orders between divorcees. Judges checked that the settlement was fair. If not, or if one party was unrepresented, they might ask whether parties had taken legal advice, or summon them in. Judges were

---

variable due to the relationship between the law and the state: 'The Normal Chaos of Family Law' (1998) 61 (4) *MLR* 468.

[16] C Piper argued that family lawyers are much more devoted to non-law aspects, 'How Do You Define A Family Lawyer?' (1999) *Legal Studies* Vol 19 (1) 96, 97 and 98.

[17] Mr Justice Wilson, The Atkin Lecture 2002, 'The Misnomer of Family Law', The Reform Club, 17 October 2002.

[18] M Henaghan, 'The Normal Order of Family Law' (2008) *OJLS* Vol 28(1), 171.

frustrated by errors, made by solicitors' firms,[19] court staff or the parties. In DJ Tierce's morning boxwork, the court had sent out the wrong forms in three divorce petitions; in other cases his orders had not been complied with or were wrongly drafted and all the other forms were incomplete. All files had to be returned to the office or solicitors' firms for correction.

'Parents Behaving Badly'

Procedure in child residence and contact applications varied. Cafcass officers met parents pre-court but their role in hearings differed. One town required officers to speak first, taking some lawyers by surprise. DJ Joel prepared for a contested contact application from another circuit. The file included the mother's statement. He groaned, 'We don't order statements here, it inflames the situation'. The place of alternative dispute resolution (ADR) differed. Mediation, which is now to be promoted by the Family Procedure Rules 2010, from 2011, proposed changes to legal aid, and the Family Justice Review 2011, grew independently of the courts pre-1990. Local practices developed. Judges may act as mediators; elsewhere this is left to professionals. DJ Rooney referred contested cases to mediation, conducted by himself or colleagues, with the court welfare officer present. There was no consistency in using mediation.[20] Stanford J had been called in during the vacation and 'effectively ended up as a mediator', with the husband's McKenzie Friend grumbling that she was 'using a procedure not known to man'. She felt 'It was ridiculous that it got before a High Court judge before anyone mediated'. Nevertheless, even under the Children and Adoption Act 2006, which widens the judge's range of powers in contact disputes, no party may be compelled into mediation.[21]

Conciliation[22] was controversial. Designated family judge, Harriet Vane, disapproved of 'children brought into court … seeing parents in dispute' but Caroline, in the Principal Registry, defended it, explaining that she worked with the Cafcass officer to explore the possibility of settlement. Children over nine, and sometimes younger siblings, were not in the courtroom but saw the Cafcass officer, who reported back. Parents sat in the front row, with lawyers. She engaged in a 15-minute conversation with each. She cited research on the procedure's success

---

[19]   Discussed in ch 11.

[20]   Mediation would have been universal, had the Family Law Act 1996, Part II been implemented. M Trent, President of the Association of HMDJs called for all DJs to be trained in mediation, News (2010) 160 *New Law Journal* 470.

[21]   In force from 2008: S Blain, 'A new era for contact?' (2008) 158 *New Law Journal* 1585.

[22]   In-court conciliation was found to be useful only in certain contact cases: L Trinder et al, *Making contact happen or making contact work? The process and outcomes of in-court conciliation*, DCA Research Series 3/2006.

rate.[23] 'The nettle on post-separation contact is being grasped all over the world. Judges are visiting one another's systems to find out how others do it.'[24]

DJs Cartman and Homer called their family day Parents Behaving Badly Day. Judges emphasised that courts only became involved in the pathological 10 per cent of cases.[25] Homer would not interfere with a 'carefully crafted agreement where both parties were represented. That's what Parliament wanted in the Children Act'. Where parents could not agree, or one disobeyed a court order, there were endless hearings.[26] Where both parties paid for representation, there was a strong incentive to settle. By 2004, family cases absorbed 80 per cent of the civil legal aid budget and in 2005 the Government announced that strict control would be exercised over multiple and repeat applications in private law family cases, to deter unreasonable conduct.[27] DJ Joad explained that a lot of people passing through the courts were inadequate or inarticulate and had difficulty seeing reason. This did not stop him trying. Like all DJs, he saw this as a legitimate part of his role.[28] Where parents were self-interested and vindictive, judges reminded them that their children's interests were paramount, often in strong terms. Homer asked why a sibling contact order had been flouted. The father said he could not afford to travel. He was about to be made bankrupt. The

---

[23]   She did not name this but see L Trinder and others, above n 22, and L Trinder and J Kellett, *The longer-term outcomes of in-court conciliation*, Ministry of Justice Research Series 15/07, 2007. See also E Walsh, 'Judges Talking to Children' [2008] *Family Law* 809. See a July 2007 address by Baroness Hale drawing attention to the UN obligation on courts to ascertain 'the wishes and feelings' of the child: E Walsh, 'Newsline Extra: Baroness Hale: The Voice of the Child' [2007] *Family Law* 1041(4). Also R Hunter, 'Close encounters of a judicial kind: 'hearing' children's 'voices' in family law proceedings' [2007] *Child and Family Law Quarterly* 283 and other articles in the same volume. See now Family Justice Review 2011.

[24]   Australia promoted shared parenting in Part IV of the Australian Family Law Act 1975. The symbolism in shared residence promotes settlement, argued C Piper: 'Shared Parenting- a 70% solution?' [2002] *Child and Family Law Quarterly* Vol 14 No 4, 367.

[25]   B Clark, 'Cafcass, the Courts and the Children and Adoption Act 2006', Association of HMDJ's *Law Bulletin* Vol 20, no 2, summer 2009, 27.

[26]   In a July 2010 speech, Lord Judge said private law applications had increased by 19 per cent in 2008–09. The courts could no longer 'afford the luxury' of allowing parties to dictate the length of the case. In October 2010, the Revised Private Law Programme Practice Direction came into force, aiming to achieve early intervention. Some judges have considered policing contact disputes but this would counteract the principle that parents should resolve issues privately. A statutory presumption of contact might impact on attitudes of resident parents and aid the judge's role but this could be resolved through a public education programme. Research has shown cases take far too long because of the complexities in each individual hearing: J Hunt and A MacLeod, *Outcomes of applications to court of contact orders after parental separation on divorce* Oxford Centre for Family Law and Policy, Ministry of Justice (2008). The revised Private Law Programme above will not reduce delays, because of the Cafcass backlog. In 2010, private law battles were in a 14-month queue because of a 60 per cent increase in care cases.

[27]   But the cost of family legal aid continued to rise. It costs one quarter of the £2 billion total: E Walsh, 'Newsline: Legal Aid and Graduated Fees' [2008] *Family Law* 710.

[28]   Three interventions were proposed by L Trinder et al, *A Profile of Applicants and Respondents in Contact Cases in Essex*, DCA Research Series 1/2005.

mother had asked a friend to bring the children but the friend only visited once a year. Homer retorted:

> Not good enough! It's no good just saying 'There's a problem'. Why has nobody tried to sort it out? I can't *believe* you have the bare-faced cheek to come before me today and tell me you can't do anything to comply with this order!

One morning, Joel's Cafcass officer was off ill. This was a setback. Cafcass always effected some settlements.[29] In the first case, both parents had declined mediation. Both were represented but he spoke to them directly.

> I'll put this back for half an hour to see if you can reach an agreement. I want you to think 'What's best for the children?' not 'What's best for me?' … Now, if you can't reach an agreement, the matter will have to be referred to the Cafcass officer. She will interview the children, whatever their young age … Do you want to put the children through that?[30] … I don't want to see this matter coming before the court again and again.

They did not agree and requested a report. They both enjoyed legal aid. In another rural court, he sent out two unrepresented couples. With Cafcass help, the first agreed to mediate. Joel smiled broadly when the second settled: 'In the nicest possible way, I hope we don't see you again. You've got to have a relationship for the rest of your lives, over the children, even though your own relationship has broken down.'

Like Joel and Homer, Joad made it plain that he expected reasonable parents to agree, again portraying court intervention as pathological. In one case, the mother objected to the father's new girlfriend being in immediate contact with the children, despite inconvenience to the father, 'I suspect what you *don't* want here surely is a *hearing*, do you? How about if I adjourn this and you see how you get on?' In the next case, he asked, 'You don't want a *fight* in this case do you?' At the Principal Registry, Caroline took a firm line with an unreasonable mother.[31] She waited while parties negotiated for an hour and then went into court. The father was a waiter so was unable to see his children Friday to Sunday but the mother insisted they go to Arabic lessons after school on Monday to Wednesday. Caroline made the order, spelling out the mechanics of contact. She pointedly asked the barristers to remind their clients that these arrangements were for the benefit of the children, not their parents. The young mother slammed out of court. Twice, solicitors asked DJs to 'talk some sense' into their clients.

---

[29]   Many parents complained that Cafcass officers did not spend sufficient time with families: C Smart et al, *Residence and Contact Disputes in Court, Volume 2*, DCA Research Series 4/2005 but see much worse backlog by 2010–11, above.

[30]   Children's short-term stress is seemingly ignored over the long-term aim of preservation of contact with both parents, according to A MacDonald, 'The caustic dichotomy—political vision and resourcing in the care system' [2009] *Child and Family Law Quarterly* 300.

[31]   The state is obliged to respect the right to family life, which may contradict some interference by courts: MacDonald, above n 30.

The consequence of withdrawing legal aid is that more people represent themselves. As seen in the last chapter, this slows and disrupts procedure considerably[32] and places a much greater strain on the judge and a financial burden on represented parties. In 2007, DJMC Pole was scheduled to hear a hotly contested contact dispute in the magistrates' court but the hearing proved abortive directly as a result of the unrepresented mother's ignorance of procedure. The father applied for contact which had ceased in 2006. The mother, a 'part-time Open University law student', alleged rape. After 15 minutes, the mother unexpectedly applied for an adjournment. The father was paying for counsel and a solicitor. They 'strongly resisted' the adjournment but Pole granted it. The mother seemed to expect that part of the case would be heard, because she brought two witnesses. The witnesses and father had wasted time and the father had wasted money. Court, judicial and staff time was wasted. In granting the application, Pole publicly observed 'a represented party might have realised the importance of this but it's not a perfect world'.

In some cases the parent with residence has refused contact for years, in the face of court orders. Until 2008, there was little the court could do.[33] They could attach a penal notice which, if activated, would send the mother to prison. These would rarely be activated. The children would suffer and the parents' relationship would be destroyed. In 15 years, Vincent Jones only sent two mothers to prison. The Children and Adoptions Act 2006 now permits courts to direct activities such as anger management classes and to make contact enforcement orders requiring unpaid work.[34] The courts' reluctance to act prompted the establishment of the activists calling themselves Fathers 4 Justice. DJs in this research spoke of 'parental alienation syndrome'. One parent convinces themselves (and the child) that the child does not want to see the other.[35] Joel heard a typical case. The mother had been arrested for possessing crack. The father was in prison for dealing. Both were represented. The child was on the Child Protection Register. Joel grilled the mother's solicitor as to why the father had had no contact, despite attending all court hearings. The mother had repeatedly failed to appear. 'This

---

[32]   Endorsed by President Potter in the *Times*, below n 53. Writing in the 2008 Association of DJs *Law Bulletin* (19 (2)), Wall LJ said judges would increasingly find themselves facing two LIPs. See now, the Judges' Council's strong opposition to the 2010 proposals to further cut family legal aid: February 2011.

[33]   See the Honourable Mr Justice Munby, 'The Family Justice System' [2004] *Family Law* 547 and case law and papers cited therein on intractable contact disputes. Judges may transfer residence: R Morgan, 'Facing the Consequences' (2010) 160 *New Law Journal* 857. See further R Bennett, 'Third of children lose touch after divorce', *The Times*, 16 November, 2009, reporting research by Mishcon de Reya.

[34]   See Blain, above n 21.

[35]   See T Hobbs JP, 'Parental Alienation Syndrome and UK family Courts' [2002] *Family Law* 82. Under Australian law the term 'parental alienation syndrome' is used where 'selfish' mothers are the primary controllers of contact: H Rhoades, 'The "no contact mother": reconstructions of motherhood in the era of the "new father"' [2002] *International Journal of Law, Policy and the Family* 74, paras 2 and 3.

has been going on for two years.' The mother claimed the father was violent.[36] Joel was sceptical. She wanted him assessed and contact to be supervised.[37] The father wanted residence. Joel sent them out to draft an order permitting assessment of the father's motives and requiring supervised contact. He congratulated the mother before they left 'Miss B, I'm glad to see you've got yourself legal advice and you have attended these proceedings'.

Judge Vincent heard an application for a penal notice on a contact order with a four-year-old, born when the unmarried couple had split.[38] The mother had flouted the order throughout, generating many hearings, and had not appeared. Next door, Judge Antony Bede had to make a finding of fact on a rape allegation made against a father by a mother, to justify years of disobedience of a contact order. He gave Vincent a running commentary. The judges urged observation of Bede's approach, the antithesis of Vincent's calm courtroom.[39] Bede was extremely interventionist, in trying to secure agreements. He sent out the parties to negotiate for the first afternoon and most of the second day. Meanwhile, he demanded court files relating to another child of the mother, by a different father. Both sides' counsel had failed to disclose these. They revealed that the mother had made a false allegation of arson against the *other* father, resulting in a trial and acquittal in the Crown Court. Bede concluded she was a liar and, on medical evidence, that this father was incapable of rape.

> I've spent the whole morning discussing sexual positions. I don't believe a 29 stone bloke who's damaged his cruciate ligament is capable of raping his girlfriend. Anyway, he's a mummy's boy who should be wearing an apron and she's got a brown belt in karate. I think she's a loony. I wish I had a psychiatric report on her.

By the second afternoon, Bede was animatedly dictating a contact order in minute detail, interrupting himself to negotiate with the parents about mobile phones and transport. Despite mutual hostility, both parents could not suppress smiles, thanks to Bede's enthusiastic and down-to-earth negotiating style, his casual language and optimism.

In a number of cases, violence had been found proven by criminal and civil non-family courts. In Joel's contact list, a father did not appear because he had assaulted someone and been hit with a hammer. In the next case a father had assaulted the mother, had been the subject of criminal and civil proceedings and

[36] C Sturge and D Glaser, 'Contact And Domestic Violence—The Experts' Court Report' [2000] *Family Law* 615. Fathers were often excluded from contact where violence was present.

[37] H Reece described women's rights campaigners as using domestic violence to disallow contact: 'UK women's groups' child contact campaign: "so long as it is safe"' [2006] *Child and Family Law Quarterly* 538.

[38] Unmarried fathers did not have automatic parental responsibility rights. A dramatic change was brought about by mandatory joint birth registration in the Welfare Reform Act 2009, s 56. J Wallbank believes this will have a detrimental impact upon mothers exposed to violence: '"Bodies in the Shadows": joint birth registration, parental responsibility and social class' [2009] *Child and Family Law Quarterly* 267.

[39] Another example of observing a bonus judge, outside the core sample of 40.

had just been released from prison. In Joad's list were two cases where fathers were in prison, one for an armed robbery and another for assault. During the research, campaigning by Fathers 4 Justice against judges was at its height. They claimed that judges were biased against fathers in disputes over children.[40] They occupied a courtroom at the Principal Registry and staged a demonstration outside a city court in the sample. In 2007, the Judicial Communications Office criticised their 'judge-buster' campaign, publishing judges' home addresses. Their arguments fuelled some angry behaviour. An aggressive approach or vendetta against a judge could be counterproductive. Frank, a CJ, chatted with Joad about a father who had organised demonstrations outside the court and Frank's home. He had uploaded information about his case on a website, which Frank had had closed. He had recorded interviews with his children with 'provocative' questions then submitted the tapes to the court, commenting 'I told you so'. The judges considered this self-defeating. Frank barred him from contact.[41]

Joel had a case where a mother opposed any form of contact. The father had been arrested. She was represented but absent. He was represented and angry. The solicitors were hostile. As Joel predicted, the submission of a 46-page statement from the mother, with none from the father, proved provocative. The father was talking as well as his solicitor. Joel gave up trying to stop him but asked 'Is that your opinion or your client's opinion?' Joel ordered a Cafcass report and listed the case before a circuit judge. The father interrupted, sobbing, '*Excuse* me! None of you 'as met my kids. I brought my kids up. Why don't yer listen ter *me*? I 'aven't made a statement. You judges, yer not interested in wot fathers've got ter say. [Shouting, standing up] The law needs *changin*!' Joel was rescued by a scheduled telephone hearing. When they returned, Joel explained calmly that there would be a full hearing. The father stood up to leave, shouting. 'These're my babies. I brought em up! [From the doorway] Yer all for the mothers. Yer not interested in fathers'. Joel persuaded him to sit down while he finished the order.

In the Principal Registry, the judges had recently watched Bob Geldof's television programme making the same arguments. It annoyed them.

> I wish Geldof would come and watch these courts. 'Just ignore the man at the back with the bag over his head.' Geldof doesn't appreciate fathers can be so *violent*. I've just had a case where a man raped his daughter and threatened to murder his wife.

---

[40]   J Hunt and A MacLeod found no evidence of bias against non-resident parents: *Outcomes of applications to court for contact orders after parental separation or divorce* (2008) Ministry of Justice website.

[41]   D Ross observed of the founder of Fathers 4 Justice, 'Matt is bright enough, but I don't think he can see that too much anger can be self-defeating, particularly where little children are involved', above n 13.

Caroline did not sympathise with the campaign for a legal presumption in favour of joint residence.[42] 'Where are all these houses coming from? Lots of people in this court are very poor. Is a London borough meant to provide two homes?'

Many in the family courts are angry and where litigants appear in person (LIPs), there is no protective buffer of an advocate between them and the bench (and this raises questions of security, below). Most are fathers. Stanford J gave a judgment in a case where she had cut off contact for a father whose behaviour had been so difficult that he had 'driven the mother to the edge of a nervous breakdown'. During the hearing, he 'argued with everything and after two weeks started arguing all his points over again'. She eventually left the courtroom. 'Even giving judgment was a challenge.' Most of Kind LJ's days in the Court of Appeal commenced with a LIP renewing an application for appeal.

Anger can degenerate into violence. DJs are vulnerable when hearings are in their 'chambers' that is, their offices, with parties round a desk and table. Tierce considered this unsatisfactory: parties in a family dispute would not want to face one another. He arranged his furniture like a courtroom, with parties facing him over two large desks. DJs' rooms had secure escape holes and coded door locks. Sometimes judges had to escape through neighbouring chambers. A barrister told of a recent escape. A father had stormed out of a DJ's chambers and stood outside while the lawyers exited via the surrounding DJs' rooms, apologising as they clambered through startled sets of judges and parties. With Joel, a mother involved in a care case before a CJ started roaring through the courthouse at a social worker. Joel contemplated his contempt powers, 'But my judicial role conflicts with my desires as a human being. My instinct is to go out there, ask if there's anything I can do and sit her down with a cup of tea ... If she behaves like this...how will she keep her temper with her children?' That afternoon, she was screaming at the advocates, who locked themselves in their room. Court staff flurried around and locked us in Joel's room, 'What about the kitchen? Get the knives!'[43]

Splitting the Debts

DJs remonstrated about money in the same way as they did with warring parents, emphasising their expectation that the parties should resolve differences, not the court. Homer said most parents before him were in the lower socio-economic

---

[42] Fathers' groups campaign for a presumption in favour of 50–50 shared contact but this was rejected by the 2004 consultation paper, *Parental Separation: Children's Needs and Parental Responsibilities*. C Smart conducted studies on the effectiveness of shared parenting and found that unsuccessful cases were mainly due to 'fairness' conceptually based on parents' rights and not for children's benefit, 'Equal Shares: Rights for Fathers or Recognition for Children?' (2004) Vol 24 *Critical Social Policy* 484.

[43] See further F Gibb, 'Lawyers call for protection from threats and attacks', *The Times*, 23 February 2004.

groups. The judge's task was often to split the debts. Elizabeth Bennet contemplated a debt schedule of £23,000, set against £70,000 property equity.

> Not enough to buy a house round here. I talk to the parties quite frankly. I tell them what the costs in the eventual hearing will be and today has cost a thousand, to concentrate their minds.

They appeared before Elizabeth in the morning but returned at 2.00 pm with no settlement. Their offers were drafted in adversarial language. The husband's barrister contested everything.[44] The husband had already spent £6,000 on legal fees. From 2.05 pm to 2.50 pm, he looked sulkily out of the window. Elizabeth spelled out her provisional view and urged it upon them. 'Today is *crucial*. If this goes to a final hearing, *more* assets will be dissipated.' Before Homer, a couple were arguing about £2,500. The solicitors explained, in their clients' absence, that they had tried their best to persuade them to agree. Homer co-operated. 'Well, tell them the judge'll go ballistic if they're still arguing about two and a half thousand. You can paint me as an ogre if you want.' In the Principal Registry, one DJ said she had shouted at people 'You're mad', when they had wasted £20,000 on legal fees, arguing over dwindling assets. The Court of Appeal took a similar view of a protracted dispute over a valuable family home, relished by *The Metro* and other newspapers, 'It's a *tragedy* that this case cannot be resolved by mediation' said Kind LJ, presiding, 'A clean break was clearly necessary here. Counsel suggested that the Court of Appeal should do it but that is *not* the function of this court!' What the newspapers did not know was that the parties had spent over £350,000 on legal fees, excluding the appeal.[45] Joad considered it was part of the judge's job to protect the state's interests too. He said if a wife were settling for a low sum, he might ask 'What if your new relationship breaks down?' If she replied 'I'll claim social security', he would ask 'Why live at the state's expense? It's your husband's responsibility'.

---

[44]   These barristers were openly hostile. Judges and lawyers launched a campaign to support 'collaborative law', in 2007, copied from the US. If parties fail to negotiate, lawyers must resign: F Gibb, 'Family judges campaign to take the bitterness and costs out of divorce' *The Times*, 4 October 2007. *Resolution*, solicitors' code of practice states 'Members … are required to: conduct matters in a constructive and non-confrontational way, avoid use of inflammatory language … [and] retain professional objectivity and respect for everyone involved'. See L Jones, 'A change in attitude' (2008) 158 *New Law Journal* 1477.

[45]   See D Burrows, 'A scandal in our midst' (2009) 159 *New Law Journal* 217, citing Munby J, in *KSO v MJO and ors* [2008] EWHC 3031 (Fam) on 'ruinous expense'.

THREE CIRCUIT JUDGES—TALES OF DELAY, PROFESSIONAL DILATORINESS, CONFUSION AND OVERLOAD

Three CJs, Judges Jodie, Soar and Harriet Vane suffered from intense workloads.[46] Delays were astonishing.[47] Soar wrongly assumed that a shortage of judges was confined to her circuit.

Four Days with Judge Harriet Vane

Harriet spent 75 per cent of her time on family and 25 on civil. She was a designated (managing) family judge.

> I am ... in charge of family policy and administration [locally] ... I liaise very closely with administration and listings ... and the district judges. I do ancillary relief appeals and most appeals from district judges. I go round family proceedings courts helping with training ... I liaise with Cafcass ... and the local authority solicitors ... Any applications to vacate [proceedings] come in front of me.[48]

She commenced boxwork around 8.30 am and spent every minute out of court on managerial calls, emails or meetings. She wrote judgments and read massive care document bundles in the evenings and weekends, as did the CJs and HC judge below. She denied that this was counter-productive in disguising the need for more judges. She tolerated the workload out of concern for the number of children waiting in the lists. She felt her workload was light compared with the Bar. 'I wish I'd had this workload when my kids were young.'

May 2004, Monday

Harriet's court was two CJs short. In her first contact case, proceedings had commenced in 2001 and had remained part-heard, because of the difficulty of reconvening. Two hearings had been cancelled. Listings reminded her on Friday that the judgment was due, so she had spent Sunday writing, struggling to make sense of her notes. There had been a finding of fact that the father had not abused the daughter. The mother was unconvinced and prevented contact. Harriet considered she was alienating the girl against the father, and a toddler sibling would be denied paternal contact.

---

[46] Things are worse by 2010–11. In his 2010 *Review of the Administration of Justice in the Courts 2008–09*, Lord Judge LCJ said increased family work placed great strains on family judges.

[47] See criticism of 'shocking' delays in the Family Justice Review 2011.

[48] Responsibilities are set out in a paper obtainable from the Judicial Office.

10.20 am: The grandmother was present. Harriet mentioned in judgment that the grandparents and the mother drove the child to the contact appointments, to which they were all hostile. She ordered a psychologist's report to determine whether resuming contact would harm the child, given the mother's allegations. The parties argued about who would pay.

11.05 am: Rushed back to read additional papers that she had just received for a 'five-day' contested care hearing.

11.15 am: Into court for a 'three-day' final care hearing. The parties had been told on Friday that unless it was settled it would have to be re-listed. They were expecting a 15-minute directions hearing. The mother had not appeared, despite having been telephoned and a taxi arranged for her. There were six lawyers, the father, the guardian and three other people. The case had shrunk to 'one day'. She rescheduled it two weeks hence. It raised disclosure. Harriet had found the father of one child to be a 'Schedule 1' offender: he burned a child with a cigarette lighter. Harriet sought to prevent this information falling into the hands of the children of the new partner of the father of a second child, because if they found out, it could cause vigilantism in the close-knit neighbourhood.

12.40 pm: Out. She asked the clerk to tell the parties in the 'five-day' case to find dates into which it could overrun.

12.53 pm: In court, she made her order in the first case.

At lunch, Harriet introduced all the judges who had been Bar colleagues in her local chambers. They discussed jury-nobbling, Bar yarns, new judges and football.

2.25 pm: Listing asked her to do an interim order. Harriet asked them to give it to a DJ.

2.30 pm: Having freed up the afternoon for the 'five-day' case, the lawyers asked for it to be stood down. One barrister had just received the new papers. The afternoon's court time was wasted.

2.35 pm: Marched to the listing office, muttering 'shambles'. They found the three extra days that this case would now need, beyond this week. She felt complaining to the lawyers would be pointless. None wanted to start the case without reading these new papers, despite the fact that Harriet considered it unnecessary. She knew them: 'a very good team'. She summoned one barrister in for a chat and asked her to help out at a training conference.

Tuesday

9.30 am: Harriet gave up trying to get her new laptop to function (again, no in-house IT support) and met the DJs over coffee. She got 'gowned up' for an adoption. Adopters always requested this, for photos. Harriet gave the little boy a congratulations card. As they departed after five minutes' chat, he asked 'Is that it then?' (CJs often listed adoptions as the most rewarding part of their job. One said he cried throughout one adoption 'It makes you wonder how many mantelpieces we're on').

11.10 am: Into court: 'So much for getting started early'. There was an interim application.

11.20 am: The parties in the five-day contested care case asked to commence at noon.

12.15 pm: They were ready. Today's delay was caused by the local authority solicitor arranging Harriet's document bundle. Harriet groaned. There was a solicitor and barrister for each parent, the guardian, and the local authority. Eight lawyers and parties had been waiting throughout Monday morning and today.

2.10 pm: Listings came in to discuss scheduling. Harriet corrected a judgment.

2.40 pm: The hearing recommenced. As the social worker gave evidence, the mother shook her head and tried to catch Harriet's eye.

4.30 pm: Harriet took the papers home.

Wednesday

9.55 am: Listings crisis: next week's judge was overrunning on crime. A case would have to be rescheduled and the father was very active in Fathers 4 Justice. 'Can it be shifted to a DJ?' There were no free DJ days until September. They contemplated importing a civil recorder.

10.40 am: The clerk reported parties were ready in the first matter, a directions hearing. 'Well, I'm not.' Harriet flicked through the papers.

10.46 am: It resembled Monday's case. The mother refused contact, alleging paternal abuse. Investigating police declined to take criminal proceedings. A psychologist refused to report without a judicial finding of fact. The mother was accompanied by her parents. The father sat with his face in his hands. The maternal grandmother applied to be joined in proceedings but Harriet explained that she could not give leave for the grandfather to be joined without a formal application. Harriet listed it for further directions and a four-day perpetrator hearing. There would be another hearing for the grandfather's application. The gaggle of lawyers asked for a Cafcass officer to be appointed as guardian. Harriet queried this.

11.15 am: Outside, Harriet explained her reluctance: 'These kids have already got lots of professionals involved in their lives'.[49]

11.30 am: The care case resumed. A psychologist gave evidence on the mother's condition. The mother was smiling and shaking her head. There were four barristers, one pupil, four solicitors' representatives, two social workers and the guardian.

12.20 pm: Out again: the psychologist needed time to read a report.

12.45 pm: The social worker was back in the witness box. Her bundle was incomplete so Harriet left them to sort it out.

12.50 pm: Harriet summoned the guardian into her room about a different case. She had applied for permission to see a girl at school. Harriet declined during GCSE time. The mother had attacked other professionals in the case by running them over with her car. The children were seeing their father in secret for 15 minutes a week.

12.56 pm: Draft directions in the first case were ready: into court to approve them.

2.15 pm: Continuing problems with the bundle. Listings came. An application needed a judge with a High Court 'ticket'. There had only been one family judge available for three weeks now.

2.28 pm: The care case recommenced until 4.30 pm.

Thursday

9.50 am: Coffee with the DJs. Harriet expected to hand down a judgment in an appeal from one of them.

10.40 am: The clerk told us an expert in the care case had arrived but needed half an hour to read the papers. Harriet wondered why this had not been done before.

---

[49] Greater co-operation was encouraged between Cafcass and other professionals by L Trinder et al, *'Making Contact Happen or Making Contact Work? The Process and Outcomes of In-Court Conciliation'* DCA Research Series 3/06, 99.

11.10 am: They needed another half-hour. Harriet made calls about the training conference and went to see listings about next week's potential mayhem.

11.50 am: The care case resumed. The father's counsel related an agreement between two experts who had just seen new reports this morning so the other counsel wanted half an hour to discuss this. Harriet asked them to return at 12.30 pm 'to explain how you plan to progress this case'. Out of court, she said she thought one expert had 'got at' another. There were four experts. Harriet had previously expressed concern about the proliferation of experts in child cases but thought they might prove useful here if they could persuade the parents to agree on care. The information they were discussing was not new so she wondered why experts had not met before.

12.37 pm: Despite some measure of agreement, two experts still wanted their evidence heard. The psychologist gave evidence that the mother had a 'histrionic narcissistic personality' and the father had 'a lot of borderline personality disorders'. The father could not withstand pressure from the mother, so his contact must take place without the mother.

4.30 pm: Adjourned until the following week.

Friday

Harriet had a double-booked 'short appointment' lists, as no other CJ was available.

Commentary

Procedure

The vulnerability of children and ephemeral nature of childhood means that their cases are the most urgent in the courts but they progressed scandalously slowly. The backlog in Harriet's court was cumulative. There was a shortage of judges. Court and professional time, all paid for by the taxpayer, was wasted by unprepared lawyers and experts in the care case. Harriet could have accommodated the one-day case she postponed. In 2006, the Government published a *Review of the Child Care Proceedings System in England and Wales*, with the aim of ensuring that resources were used in the most timely and effective way (county court care cases taking an average of 51 weeks). A Public Law Outline and Practice Direction, requiring pre-court preparation by local authorities, guardians and lawyers, was introduced in April 2008[50] but is not succeeding in

---

[50] Speech by Sir Mark Potter, 1 April 2008.

achieving this aim any more than its predecessor Protocol,[51] or the Children Act 1989[52] because of the lack of court and local authority funding.[53]

Substance

The unproven maternal allegations in two of Harriet's cases, like the mother's false allegations in Bede's case, had the effect of stopping paternal contact for *years*, because they triggered a panoply of procedures and hearings, and the involvement of multiple lawyers and professionals. Such allegations are easy to make and are common. Contact stops immediately because judges cannot take any risk to children and some allegations are true.[54] The allegations in Harriet's cases had been dismissed but the delay in the first case, plus the mother's disobedience, plus her and her parents' alienating effect on the child, meant that Harriet was forced to contemplate depriving both children of contact with their father, against whom the accusation was unproven.[55]

Judge Jodie

> I love the job. It's all the peripheral crap that does my head in.

Jodie's time was divided 1:3 between crime and family, at six courts, on a weekly basis. It was inefficient. 'I could do the job a lot better if I had a [secure] room where I could leave work out.' She carted multiple lever arch files containing intimate family details, her laptop and judicial paraphernalia, sometimes with the parties in tow. On Tuesday (below), she learned that that she was scheduled to sit in the Crown Court on Friday. All parties in her care case would have to travel to a criminal court in a neighbouring city to receive judgment. Communication was

---

[51] The Protocol for Judicial Case Management in Public Law Children Act Cases, implemented in November 2003 to cut delay in care cases.

[52] Also emphasising judicial case management with a view to cutting delay in care cases.

[53] See analyses by C White, 'Child law update' (2007) 157 *New Law Journal* 1424 and P Cooper, 'The right protocol' (2008) 158 *New Law Journal* 1057. J Masson's expert evaluation is somewhat pessimistic: 'Improving Care Proceedings: Can the PLO Resolve the Problem of Delay? Part 1' [2008] *Family Law* 1019. All courts are now affected by a budget shortfall: F Gibb, 'Courts face closure as judges are told of £90 million shortfall in collection of fees', *The Times*, 4 September 2008 and F Gibb, 'Reforms threaten family courts' (interview with Sir Mark Potter), *The Times*, 23 October 2008. Further, in 2010, the £9 billion Ministry of Justice budget was cut by £2 billion. At the same time, in 2008–09, public law applications increased by 31 per cent: Judge LCJ, July 2010 speech referred to above.

[54] Contrast *Re L (Contact: Domestic Violence)* [2000] 2 FLR 334. Domestic violence could not be proven so other children in the family could not be displaced and were exposed to potential further violence.

[55] See G Vallance-Webb, 'In Practice: Child Contact: Vengeful Mothers, Good Fathers and Vice Versa' [2008] *Family Law* 678, discussing cases such as *Re C (A Child)* [2008] EWCA Civ 551, where Ward LJ spoke of the 'drip, drip, drip of venom' from vengeful mothers who systematically turn children against their fathers and *Re M (Intractable Contact Dispute: Interim Care Order)* [2003] EWHC 1024 (Fam).

challenging. I arrived unannounced on 5 January, having failed to track her down for five days before Christmas. She did not receive a message. She could not read emails as she did not have internet access. Locating the court demanded orienteering skills. She sat at F County Court, sitting at a building labelled *G and H County Court and Magistrates' Court*, at town J but it was accessed via K station and when I got there, the usher asked me which county court I wanted, as L County Court also sat there. Finding the court doubtless added to the stress of parents who were about to have their four children removed forever. That week, two sets of lawyers apologised for the absence of parents in other cases because they were on state benefits and could not afford, or work out how, to get there on public transport. Navigational problems caused by courts sitting in annexes like this add to the confusion caused by family jurisdiction being shared by three courts. A new family justice centre had been promised there in 1989. Jodie was in her 'chambers', a six by eight foot magistrates' retiring room with unpainted breeze block walls, no window and no internet. This was a bone of contention with the magistrates' courts committee who 'owned' the building.[56] The advocates' room had been locked since lawyers using laptops had been accused of 'abstracting the magistrates' electricity'. This exacerbated the judges' contempt for magistrates.

Jodie and her circuit colleague, Deed, like Bede, described their role as 'inquisitorial'. They were always in a dialogue with the lawyers. If a civil case were badly argued, said Jodie, the aggrieved party could sue their lawyers but in a family case she was seeking 'the truth and the best solution'. (In commenting on a draft of this chapter, Judge Vincent Jones agreed that some judges, like Bede, were 'inquisitorial' in approach but added 'Most judges still respect the adversarial system though they will intervene in a child's interests if they think there is otherwise a serious risk of a proper line of enquiry not being pursued'.) In the Court of Appeal, Kind LJ's non-family colleague accepted that family judges will be considerably more interventionist than other trial judges. 'The criticism that the judge asked leading questions is a *wholly inappropriate* criticism. The judge is not in the position of counsel.'[57]

To maintain consistency, Jodie felt that a sole judge should be responsible for each case's progress.[58] She was extremely interventionist, trying to move cases forward to what she considered to be the best outcome, but was sometimes frustrated. She gave examples of her achievements. Notice that in the first case, the outcome she sought had not been argued for by any party.

A couple of weeks ago a baby had very severe head injuries … The local authority, the guardian and both parents, astonishingly … all said that the court can't decide who has done this and therefore the case has to proceed on the basis that it could be either

---

[56] MCCs allocated the budget until replaced by courts boards, in 2005.
[57] CA judgment citation not provided, to maintain anonymity.
[58] Now supported by the Family Justice Review Interim Report 2011.

parent and therefore this child is not going home to either. I felt quite clearly on the papers that it was probably the dad who had done it and it required the mother's advocate to do his job properly with the evidence. The evidence came out very much as I expected ... and at the end ... everybody accepted that I could make a finding that the father had done it...the child will go home to Mum, ... who did not harm him. He would otherwise have been adopted. So there are cases where a judge's intervention makes a positive difference ... Then the adoption case ... where we have managed to keep five children in a family together, albeit at vast expense to the local authority, but those children are thriving.

Jodie and Deed said they had much more night and weekend homework in family cases than crime.

Monday

On Sunday, she had read the files for the five-day care case, only to be told that the father was no longer contesting. She had managed the case except for the pre-trial review. This information had not been relayed. She wished she had conducted the pre-trial review. 'I'd have been saying "You don't need seven witnesses to prove *that* do you?"'. The start was adjourned until Tuesday as the social worker was unavailable. She worked through boxwork.

Tuesday

The first case was a directions hearing and the second a case management conference. Overnight, she had read the files for the first. It was a 'no hope' care case. The father had been convicted of burglary and assault and had repeatedly raped a five-year-old. The 25-year-old mother had been convicted of child neglect. Their other three children had been adopted. The baby had had surgery for a severe congenital disability. While we waited for the parties, Jodie found another 'no hope' baby case in her boxwork and expressed disgust at the local authority's inaction, after birth. The mother was inadequate. She had gone to see her GP 'legless', claiming that she 'couldn't cope'. Still the local authority had not reacted. It was listed for August. 'No, not good enough! You get fed up with saying "No, this case can't wait" because it's clearly another baby who's not going back to its parents and needs to be placed as soon as possible.' She relisted it for February.

The local authority solicitor in the 'no hope' hearing kept everyone waiting until 11.00 am. She had locked herself out of her home and was waiting for a locksmith. 'I might have known it'd be Drippy Daphne.' Jodie was ferocious. She demanded to know why the local authority had only just started looking for adoptive parents and why the final hearing was not scheduled until April. Daphne whined that they were awaiting an adoption panel meeting. 'I'm sorry! I cannot acquiesce in this little boy's case being kept waiting another two months.

Can't an emergency panel be convened?' Retiring, Jodie exploded about the Drip's lack of a sense of urgency over children's welfare, remembering years of frustration with her, while practising as a local barrister. She explained that adoption panels were 'a relic of the days when the local authorities decided on whether unmarried mothers were genuinely prepared to give up their babies and checked that they had no infectious diseases … All they do now is rubber stamp things and get in my way'. By 11.30 am, the Drip reported that a panel could be convened in eight days.

11.15 am: The usher came in to report that the conference Jodie was expecting, about another baby, had been relisted for February. 'No it bloody well *has not*! I listed it myself. Look! That's my handwriting!' She re-listed it for two days' time. Listing asked if she could hear a two-day contact case. 'No! I hate private garbage from Foldingham. They're always trivial arguments that don't need to come before a circuit judge.' They added it to her list.

12.35–12.52 pm: The care case commenced. The files exposed the inadequacies of both parents, the 30 allegations of abuse by the father against an older family and the description of the oldest child, 10, who had copied bullying from his father. His violence and destructiveness was occupying five care workers in secure accommodation. There was no issue about him or two readily-adoptable siblings. The debate was about the eight-year-old, bullied by the 10-year-old. He had a good relationship with his foster carer. Jodie hoped she could be persuaded to adopt. She could not. Aside, Jodie explained the financial incentive to foster, via an agency, rather than adopt (£200 per week for the fosterer) but her interest was in keeping the child in this settled relationship, regardless of the expense to the local authority. Through three days, the parents sat silently muffled in Parkas, their eyes downcast, completely disengaged from the proceedings.

3.40–5.55 pm: Jodie agreed to sit late so the psychologist could give uninterrupted evidence. To Jodie's disappointment, she insisted that research showed that adoption was preferable. Jodie (aside) commented that the witness was insufficiently independent of the local authority.

Wednesday

12.00–12.55 pm and 2.15–6.00 pm: Jodie sat late to accommodate another professional. Despite pressing by Jodie, she was not prepared to agree that the boy would be better off in long-term foster care. Another care directions hearing was abortive. The carer had gone to the wrong court and the child's file was at a third court.

Wednesday night: Jodie horrified the advocates by requiring written submissions to be prepared overnight, as she was obliged to give judgment on Thursday. A courtroom could not be found for Friday. She drafted judgment overnight.

Thursday

All cases culminated at once.

1. Despite an irate call to the senior listings officer, she had been unable to escape criminal work on Friday in the Crown Court. The guardian, well known to Jodie at the Bar, gave evidence intermittently throughout the day, agreeing with Jodie that the boy should remain with the foster carer, so Jodie got her way, despite the other expert opinion opposing this.
2. The aborted case management conference was fitted in at 12.15 to 1.00 pm. Jodie relisted the September final hearing for March, double-booking it precariously with another case.
3. At noon, she called in the parties in the 'private garbage', giving her provisional view, from the papers, that the child should see its father. They returned at 1.25 pm with a draft consent order, having resolved their differences during the days she had kept them waiting in the courthouse.

Commentary

Jodie's natural impatience here paid off. She was explosively intolerant of listing delays and this spurred the passive listing office and the 'Drip' local authority solicitor to speed children's cases forward by months so she was acting in the spirit of family procedure and the aims of the President of the Family Division and speed was obviously in the (paramount) interests of each vulnerable child. She was extremely interventionist and effectively decided what ultimate outcome was in a child's interests and achieved that result, even if the weight of expert evidence was against her and if none of the parties had argued for it. Notice her contempt for the private parental dispute over children. By keeping them waiting in the court building all week and not permitting them any courtroom time before her, she forced them to negotiate an agreement with the help of their lawyers. In this way, her approach was a more extreme version of the district judges above depicting a judge-imposed solution as pathological.

Judge Soar's Shuttle Service

Soar split her time between family and crime in three courts and unlike Jodie, did not manage her own cases, reckoning that her peripatetic work-style made this impracticable. She remarked on the local shortage of family judges and court-rooms and the national increase in family work, especially care proceedings. I met her in February, when three-day hearings were being timetabled for September. Against this background, it was tragi-comic that Soar spent her week waiting for a mother to be tracked down for a care case which ultimately proved abortive. This was caused by the inefficiency of social services and the tripartite family jurisdiction which apparently befuddles social workers as much as parties. The mother 'Angela' had severe learning difficulties and was incapable of looking after herself, let alone a child, evidenced by photos of their squalid home. At 11.50 am on Monday, Angela had been given £20 by a social worker and wrongly put in a taxi to the magistrates' court. Soar's court was part of the county court sitting at a combined court in a building unhappily labelled *Crown Court*. Soar spent much of Monday and Tuesday discussing with the professionals how Angela might be found and brought to court. Each day, Angela met an 'appointee', a social worker from whom she collected a cash allowance. By Tuesday, Soar suggested that someone should alert the appointee and that Angela could be escorted to court. She adjourned until Wednesday afternoon. At 2.20 pm on Wednesday, Soar was informed that Angela had been tracked down and had been waiting in the canteen since 11.00 am (no-one had thought to inform Soar) but her social worker had a fear of heights so could not enter Soar's third floor courtroom. Soar requested a ground floor courtroom. A jury trial was shifted out. She waited there until 3.05 pm when the social worker arrived, looking ill and traumatised. It was too late to commence a contested care case. Angela's solicitor would have to take instructions for two hours. The case was adjourned for six weeks. Soar ordered public funding for four lawyers who had been waiting for three days, with two social workers and the guardian. Judge Jodie was unlikely to have taken Soar's sanguine approach.

Much of the remainder of the four days was spent waiting. This was not all wasted time for Soar. Most other matters were directions hearings in care proceedings so the lawyers and professionals were in the courthouse negotiating and drafting orders placed before Soar for approval. She had pre-read the papers. Each hearing was scheduled for half an hour. Soar said she 'trusted' the lawyers, who were 'all very experienced', to cover all the issues. She would only question something in a draft order if it 'jumped out of the page'. Soar operated a week-long shuttle service with these cases, calling each into court in turn, for a few minutes, or asking the clerk to report on negotiations. Each occupied four to six lawyers, plus a guardian and social workers. On Monday, Soar made a one-minute injunction for a bandaged father against his violent son. On Tuesday, she spent just 15 minutes in court, approving two sets of draft orders in directions hearings. On Wednesday, all parties in a brief directions case were kept waiting until 11.20 am for a mother, who, on a previous occasion, had fled the courtroom and taken a drug overdose in the toilets. On this occasion, she had been with the witness service since 9.00 am, though no-one informed the court. Thursday was busier, with most of the time from 11.45 am spent in a one-day final care hearing, punctuated by an emergency application and two sets of directions for approval. In the hearing, the parents were disengaged, like those in

Jodie's court. The mother sat near the back of the court, tearful. The father sat at the very back. He could not see the softly spoken social worker, let alone hear her.

Commentary

Again we see the confusion wrought by the lack of a dedicated family court, with even the social worker sending the mother to the wrong court. Effectively four days of judge time and court time were wasted, as was the time of the social workers and the lawyers. Then on two occasions mothers were waiting in the court building but the judge was not informed. With a case backlog of months, this was time that could be ill-afforded. The fourth day was wasted because the social worker arrived late and had a fear of heights. All the while, multiples of lawyers were being paid out of the legal aid fund to wait around. Judge Jodie would probably not have tolerated this. She might have been on the phone to the head of social services by the second day. Social services inefficiency was probably caused by their own case overload but both the family courts and social services have become much more overloaded since the research because of the increase in care applications since the Baby P case. With cutbacks in public funding from 2010–11 both will become more overloaded and inefficiency may increase.

Circuit Judges, Lawyers and Other Professionals

These judges mentioned their close working relationship with advocates and others. They sat in three circuits outside London, where they had practised. The trust this generated (or contempt for the Drip, in Jodie's case) affected their work. Harriet described the lawyers in the care case. The local authority barrister was her former pupil; counsel for the father was a good friend from her chambers, as was counsel for the guardian. Counsel for the mother was a former solicitor who had briefed her. They were a 'good team'. You could trust them. 'The advantage of knowing everybody is that if they are asking for something daft you know they are doing it under instructions.'

Soar indicated all lawyers appearing before her who were members of her former chambers. She asked one barrister into chambers for a chat about her children. Jodie pointed out that relationships might not be the same in future. Many new judges were appointed outside their circuits and while 'We're blessed with good lawyers in care cases' she feared this would not last: 'The current level of remuneration for the family Bar…is so dismal that anybody in their right mind will not want to practise'.

IN THE HIGH COURT—DEALING WITH DEATH

The striking thing about Stanford J's work was that there was far too much of it. When I met her in 2004 in the Royal Courts of Justice she was squeezing an international contact case 'with masses of witnesses', into two days scheduled for judgment-writing, because, mistakenly, it had not been listed. At night she was writing a reserved judgment that would become a precedent and knew she would also have to write her judgment in the present case forthwith since it would be impractical and onerous to reserve more than one judgment. Her overload was relentless. She had sacrificed a week of her Christmas break and all Whit to judgment writing, including her 50th birthday. She travelled home every weekend but routinely spent it working. She started workdays before eight and worked virtually every night, declining many Bar and social invitations. Family Division judges complained of a serious shortage of judges and although numbers increased during the research period, this made little impact. 'It really is *much* worse than five years ago.' Unlike the CJs, she was busier than in her career at the Bar and, unusually among the 77 judges interviewed, would not enthusiastically recommend the job. Like the CJs, she attributed the workload to the number of care cases, complicated by the use of experts.[59] Insisting on more time for judgment-writing would deny an endangered child access to justice. She had no time to keep up with relevant news. In 2005, on circuit, I watched her hearing a shaken baby case. She was unaware that the Court of Appeal (Criminal Division) was that day reopening a cluster of convictions in such cases. She had not seen the two-page spread in *The Times* the previous day. 'I don't have time to read a newspaper.'

Although she too was dependent on the honesty and integrity of lawyers, she lacked the interdependent, beneficial relationship enjoyed by the CJs. Her workload was warped by lawyers' unrealistic estimates. She was writing a judgment on an 'eight-day' case that took five weeks. Then another overran. 'I'll get a bollocking from the listing office and I can already see I'll be saddled with writing this judgment at the weekend.' Watching her a year later, a 'three-day' case followed her around the circuit for 10 days. There was no room for slippage caused by lawyers' dilatoriness. Pre-reading was essential. She cross-examined lawyers as to why she had not received material. On circuit, she read bundles from 6.00 pm but received the skeleton arguments very late. They were badly drafted and did not direct her to the important issues. One Monday, in London, she conducted two case management conferences before continuing a long case involving a dead baby but had received no papers in either conference, one of which required 16 decisions. Her clerk had wasted Friday chasing the papers. Stanford assembled all the lawyers in court and expressed exasperation. One set

---

[59] Research by J Brophy concluded that there had been no significant increase in the use of experts in care cases in the previous 10 years: *Research review: child care proceedings under the Children Act 1989*, DCA Research Report 5/2006. The judges' memories go back much longer. There was a massive growth in the use of multiple experts in criminal, family and civil cases from the 1980s, leading to concern by Lord Woolf in *Access to Justice* (London, HMSO, 1996) and over the lack of regulation in criminal cases by Auld LJ in the *Review of the Criminal Courts of England and Wales* (London, TSO, 2001).

meekly explained they had sent notes of an advocates' conference to the court on Friday lunchtime. 'I want the profession to understand how difficult it is for us to be dealing with too many cases with no papers.' She spent 10 hours a week fielding phone calls from the circuit of which she was Liaison (managing) Judge, and was hampered by a shortage of courtroom staff to keep her cases running smoothly and by IT problems. She shared an associate (court clerk) with two other courtrooms. This caused delays in sending messages back to 'listings' and obliged her to type her own orders. She bought her own laptops because those provided were not robust enough. She spent hours on circuit troubleshooting IT hardware and software problems.[60]

In court, her demeanour was authoritative, as was her voice production and enunciation, compared with the CJs. She was very interventionist, cutting examinations to the quick, to move cases on. She was a more incisive examiner than counsel. She dived in speedily to clarify points. She apologised to one counsel for 'hijacking' her examination. She dismissed opening statements and the repetition of anything in the document bundle. She said her cases were very emotional. It was a big responsibility, if a child had died, determining what had happened, because the welfare of the other children depended on the judge. 'Lots' of her cases were difficult to decide or manage.

> For instance the ones that are on the cusp of medical science, where one half says that there's been a non-accidental injury of the most serious kind and if there has then the child's at real risk for the future. The other side says that it's an organic cause. The law has left us in a position where, if you find that it's not proved on the balance of probabilities, we behave as if it was not there at all so the child's unprotected.

Unlike the district and circuit judges, additional stress-factors were that she made rulings which became precedents and she sat in the Court of Appeal.

Typifying the judgments of Solomon expected of her and some CJs, the shaken baby case involved evidence of serious injures. Both parents conceded on the evidence that the injury was non-accidental, yet neither could offer an explanation and, in tearful solidarity, neither was prepared to believe that the other had inflicted the injuries. They appeared to be articulate, competent and devoted parents, desperate to be out of the traumatising environment of the court system and free of the stigmatic label. The local authority apparently had doubts about causation, since the child was left with them, and the social worker was convinced of their innocence and effectively a hostile witness for her authority's application to renew the supervision order.

Stanford often found herself dealing with death. In one case, a two-year-old twin had suffered serious injuries, consistent with suffocation. A sibling had died at eight months from injuries. There had been a police investigation but insufficient evidence of causation to prosecute. Although Stanford had ordered 'parallel planning', a search for adopters, social services had disagreed and so her order

---

[60] See ch 17.

had not been executed. Stanford's demeanour towards witnesses was unfaltering empathy and neutrality. By this device she hoped to induce honesty. The mother trusted Stanford so she opened up in a way that she had not done to other professionals, despite speaking from a High Court witness box. Stanford gently reassured 'I won't mind if you're a pool of tears'. The mother conceded she 'could have' killed her other child. 'You could have heard a pin drop', remarked Stanford, as we left the courtroom.

PATHOS AND INSIGHT INTO THE REAL WORLD

By this chapter of the book, the message must now be clear that judges' 'out of touch' image is derisory. Family judges penetrate the financial, sexual and emotional affairs of thousands of people and examine the narrative and photo-graphic detail of injuries and squalor and human misery and cruelty to children that most of us could not stomach. Chic Elizabeth Bennet was born into privilege but as she read her boxwork through her Gucci glasses, she drew attention to the level of debt of the households she was divorcing. Many county courts in this research were in poor areas. Shuttered, graffitied streets are a shock to middle class eyes. The visitor can kick litter past the pawn shops and porn shops all the way from a scruffy station.

As we have seen, civil and family courts are filled with the most vulnerable, when their disorganised lives are in total disarray. Some stories are so pathetic they beat *Cathy Come Home*.[61] In Elizabeth's list was a case where the matrimonial home had been repossessed. Four children were not having contact with their father, as he was living with their 16-year-old sister, whose partner was a Schedule 1 offender. Their mother was living in bed-and-breakfast accommodation. The children were having psychiatric treatment as they were grieving for their father. He applied to meet them on Sundays on the pier for three hours' contact.

Pole renewed a secure accommodation order on an innocuous teenager on the autism spectrum, with Tourette's syndrome and OCD,[62] whose parents volunteered him into care because they could not cope. Pole remarked on how difficult it was depriving someone of their liberty when they had done nothing wrong.

That drug abuse drives crime and the criminal process is very well known. Its prevalence in family and civil cases is not.[63] Homer regularly made children's residence orders for grandparents whose daughters were heroin addicts and

---

[61] A classic 1966 British television play, written by Jeremy Sanford and directed by Ken Loach. It prompted questions in Parliament on homelessness and the development of the charity, Shelter.

[62] Obsessive compulsive disorder.

[63] The revised Private Law Programme, above n 26, recognises the growing impact of domestic violence, drug and alcohol misuse.

incapable of looking after their children.[64] A tearful grandmother was embarrassed. 'Don't worry', he reassured her. 'You're not alone. I've just made four in a row this morning.' Applications about family violence revealed a high incidence of drugs and alcohol. Most care orders made by the DJMCs involved addicted mothers.

Tales of hidden violence popped up unexpectedly. One DJ said he had received a divorce application in his boxwork where the wife claimed she was content to settle for none of the matrimonial property. He summoned her in. Tearfully, she explained that her husband, ex-SAS, had threatened to kill her cat unless she agreed to his terms. DJs Elizabeth and Hulbert expressed concern over the level of untreated mental illness manifested in their courts. In one of Elizabeth's cases, a mother had taken her child to jump off the pier.

All care cases are heart-rending. Judges are asked to rip dozens of children from their blood parents forever. Judges are not permitted to handle an unremitting diet of care. They absorb voluminous documentation: psychiatric and social assessments; litanies of cycles of abuse *of* the parents and *by* the parents.[65] They develop techniques for forgetting closed cases. Hulbert's worry was 'the level of child abuse' that was 'hidden' in the county court. If only the public knew, they would be outraged:

> The extent of child abuse in this country is depressing. It's something Middle Britain is totally unaware of. Care proceedings are unseen so it's not on the political agenda. The abuse is often inflicted by parents who've been in care themselves.[66]

CONCLUSION

The research here covered all types of family judge and court except for lay magistrates. In the absence of a family court, parties to a family breakdown are often required to appear in different types of court, in different towns. Given that family courts often annex courtrooms in unrelated buildings, it was unsurprising that parties who were meant to appear in front of some of these judges were unable to locate the court or afford to travel. Some social workers were, apparently, as confused as their clients. This wasted judicial and court time and the legal aid fees paid to waiting lawyers and professionals. The distribution of work between family courts and judges is so confusing that the judges I asked to read an earlier draft corrected one another's amendments. Equally confusing, and unjustified as far as they were concerned, was the distribution of work between

---

[64]   And see R Bennett, 'The cost of keeping grandchildren in the family can be life below the poverty line', *The Times*, 26 October 2009: research by *Grandparents Plus* estimated 200,000 grandparent carers.

[65]   And see Brophy, above n 59.

[66]   Each issue of the HM District Judges's *Law Bulletin* contains educative material on social problems, such as articles on homelessness by Shelter and material on Shari'a family law.

circuit judges and the three types of district judge. The expert family QC, with no experience of crime, was mystified when she was appointed to the Crown Court amid a shortage of family circuit judges, as were those judges who had had their family 'tickets' removed, except of course, for those who had kept their tickets by stealth. More confusingly, procedure differed from court to court, with different judicial preferences, different Cafcass and ADR regimes and different but strongly held judicial beliefs on the efficacy and legitimacy of various types of ADR.

The function of the family judge is very different from that in ordinary civil cases. A family breakdown may trigger multiple issues that need resolution, in different groups of hearings with shorthand labels that are familiar to the coterie of professional insiders but incomprehensible to an outsider. Family issues may generate years of hearings where parties are intransigent. Not only are the problems multi-layered but so are the parties, with grandparents and local authorities often being involved, sometimes in multiples. In children's cases, the children are represented parties, with guardians and their own legally aided lawyers, as well as being the objects of the civil dispute.

Family courts are generally another law-free zone. Observing an experienced Queen's Counsel judge animatedly negotiating about train timetables and mobile phones, the outsider is left to wonder if this is the most efficient use of resources. Governments have been trying to devise ways of getting warring couples to mediate since the mid-1990s. This is back on the agenda in the 2011 Family Justice Review. Judges are in general so enamoured of ADR that most will, formally or informally, readily slip into the role of mediator or conciliator. Importantly, many judges would not consider themselves to be taking part in an adversarial system. In money disputes and most private law disputes over children, there is a gross mismatch between the parties' expectations and what the judge is prepared to deliver. The parties often come to court with an adversarial attitude, fired up with loathing, fuelled over months of waiting. They are expecting a day in court to publicly expose the depth of their suffering and the evils of their ex-partner. They perceive their dispute to be the property of the court and the responsibility of the court to resolve. Judges do not see it that way. They see these as private disputes and they know that those appearing before them are the pathological 10 per cent of couples who cannot resolve their disputes in private: unreasonable people who have to be persuaded to see reason. Adversarialism has no place in their courtroom, and they repeatedly send out couples to negotiate in private, urging them to return with a draft agreed order when they have resolved their own *personal*, as the judge sees it, squabble. As we have seen, a judge may even be prepared to conspire with lawyers, to threaten unreasonable and unreasoning couples. When parents were behaving like spoiled children in court and throwing tantrums, the judges dispassionately, steadfastly and repeatedly reminded them that the real children's interests were paramount. Judge Jodie hated this 'private garbage' and would not have it clogging up her courtroom when there was a queue of seriously abused children awaiting her care orders. Judges spilt the debts of divorcing couples and pleaded with antagonistic couples not to waste their dwindling assets by protracting their disputes.

Squabbles over children rapidly became very serious, where there was evidence of or an allegation of violence or abuse. An allegation against a competing parent was easily made and could trigger procedures lasting years, depriving the alleged abuser of contact with all the children involved for much of their childhood. Judges had to take any allegation seriously, however, because some were true. Where a parent disobeyed a judge's order and refused access to the children, there were repeated court appearances, spanning years, and the judge was almost powerless to sanction the intransigent. Violence and threats to judges, lawyers, and others were not unusual.

Judges needed the patience of Job to deal with people rendered irrational through emotion yet Jodie's impatience with the local authority and the listings office paid off, in speeding the resolution of care cases. Similarly, Stanford, aware of the queue of similar at-risk children behind her current case, cut lawyers' arguments and examination to the quick, to truncate hearings. Judges could be extremely interventionist. Jodie was content to resolve children's futures in a way that she considered best suited their needs, regardless of the arguments of all the other parties. All family judges were fully occupied. Harriet was struggling with the caseload of two judges. Jodie sat into the evenings. Stanford, the High Court judge, never seemed to stop. No judge would slacken, for the sake of the children who awaited their attention.

In Harriet's multi-layered cases, her time was consistently wasted by the many lawyers and experts not being ready. In a case outside this sample, one circuit judge addressed the 16 lawyers and multiple experts in his courtroom and remarked that he could not have afforded to be a party to the proceedings. An outsider in Harriet's family court, where cases had been going on for years and still failed to proceed, while the many children involved grew towards adulthood, was left to wonder whether there was not a more rational way for adults to resolve the welfare of children. To the insiders, though, the familiar group of family lawyers, judges and experts, this bizarre set up was routine.

There are themes that repeat earlier ones: the shortage of judges; the IT problems; the LIP unwittingly wasting everyone's time and money through ignorance of procedure; the sloppily completed forms having to be mailed back to solicitors; the duplication of barristers accompanied by solicitors in Harriet's court (and always in Stanford's court), because of the split legal profession. Again, we see in Harriet's, Jodie's and Soar's courts a familiar group of lawyers they could 'trust', yet Stanford in London had to reprimand a group of anonymous lawyers for making her job difficult. Again, we see that the litany of problems coming before the court are caused by drug or alcohol abuse and the question is raised whether public resources could not be better directed towards rehabilitation and anger management. The overwhelming repeating theme here is, however, that these judges are exceptionally 'in touch' with the intimate details of ordinary people's lives.

13

High Court Business

S ENIOR JUDGES[1] are exceptionally intelligent and have a capacity for extremely hard work. Other judges characterised them thus and none envied them. This chapter endeavours to paint a landscape of High Court (HC) work, in London and on circuit. It is a story of a broad range of very demanding work, executed by conscientious but uncomplaining judges, in impoverished circumstances. The quotation above is offered as a contrasting relic of less pressured travels on assize, when judges considered it reasonable to demand a better bed.

The High Court has three Divisions. The 18 Family Division judges are specialists, as are the 18 in the Chancery Division, which hears cases relating to property, trusts, patents, etc. The 72 in the Queen's Bench Division (QBD) handle all other civil work and conduct serious criminal trials in the Crown Court. The QBD contains the Commercial and Admiralty Courts. HC judges serve in the Technology and Construction Court (TCC) and chambers of the new Upper Tribunal, and in the Employment Appeal Tribunal (EAT).[2] The QBD reviews cases from the lower courts and contains the Administrative Court, which reviews public bodies' actions and hears certain appeals. HC judges also sit in the Court of Appeal (CA). Almost all HC cases are civil, except a few criminal appeals and reviews. The aim of the Courts and Legal Services Act 1990 was to reserve the

---

[1] Judges from the HC, CA, UKSC.
[2] A superior court of record, like the HC.

High Court for complex or substantial or public interest cases, shifting the rest to the county court.

THE JUDGES AND THEIR WORK

I work-shadowed and interviewed eight HC judges, including two women: one chancery, one family and six QBD, including one from the Commercial Court. I shadowed a ninth in the pilot study and collected two more when core judges' trials collapsed. I interviewed a further eight, including one woman. I selected the sample to provide as broad an insight into their work as possible. Additionally, because of the time these judges spent in the Court of Appeal (Criminal Division) (CACD) and the time spent shadowing appeal judges and travelling on circuit, I spoke with and observed many more HC judges. I joined five judges for two days each on circuit, staying in three sets of lodgings and dining at a fourth. The rest of the time was spent in the Royal Courts of Justice (RCJ) or annexes, or the EAT. I spent around four working days with each judge, plus breakfast and evenings in lodgings. I usually sat next to them in court. They showed me skeleton arguments and trial bundles and talked me through out-of-court work, such as judgment-writing and determining paper applications. The four days were spread out, sometimes by over one year.[3]

Four of the 16 sample judges were QBD presiding judges, one was a Family Division Liaison Judge and one had a similar role in Chancery. These six had a supervisory and pastoral role on circuit. I accompanied one to a court users' meeting and watched each interacting with circuit judges and administrators. Three judges: chancery, commercial and administrative, spent the whole year in the RCJ. Another commercial judge spent all but six weeks there. The remaining 12 generally spent half the working year on circuit. For the QBD judges, this involved serious crime and occasional civil business. In London, one QBD judge sat in six-week blocks in the EAT and all sat for three-week blocks in the CACD and in civil work. Seven sat in the Administrative Court. One spent four weeks per year on the Parole Board, one chaired a committee of the Judicial Studies Board (JSB) and two sat on judicial committees. Family work has been described in the family chapter. I describe HC judges' appellate work in the next chapter.

The High Court and Court of Appeal only function thanks to the recruitment of high-achieving lawyers who have developed workaholic habits. Most expected to work long hours during term times, including some weekends.[4] Workloads were heaviest in family and for circuit presiders and commercial judges. Only one judge was unmarried. All found that, quite apart from living on circuit, their

---

[3]   HC Masters manage most RCJ cases. They are not included here as their case management powers are almost identical to those of DJs. They have HC powers but do not try issues without consent of the parties.

[4]   Term dates are on the Judiciary website.

work impinged on family life, albeit less so than at the Bar. There were always fat skeleton arguments and bundles to be read. Like circuit judges, no-one was happy to reserve a judgment because it took longer to write. Judges were discouraged from reserving more than one. Although reading time was permitted on one day per week in the CACD and for big commercial cases, it was not permitted in the Administrative Court and not normally in other lists. Reading days were routinely lost to other work. The family judge Stanford, was *always* sent into court. On a 'reading' Wednesday in the EAT, Mrs Justice David had to write a judgment for a clinical dispute she had heard the previous week, approve transcripts of CACD judgments, and read skeletons and bundles for Thursday and Friday. Weekly, she also provided reasoned determinations on eight written applications for permission to appeal to the EAT. Some took 10 minutes. Others took considerably longer, if there were a 40-page tribunal decision and a long-winded argument from a litigant in person (LIP). Awaiting the evening attention of all QBD judges was a constant pile of paper applications for leave to appeal to the CACD. Around a quarter of applications are granted but some prisoners occupy 'time' with fruitless applications. There is no word limit. The judge must read through rambling, or illiterate, handwritten texts, appended with items such as birthday cards, illustrating the prisoner's loss as a father. Time off for judgment writing had to be requested. Judges were reluctant to ask.

> If you do a long, complicated trial, you really need two or three days to write the judgment … you have to … say 'Please can I be kept out so I can write this judgment' … Obviously, I know I am a resource … You don't suddenly want to start saying *that* in the first three months of your appointment.

Not all work was equally pressured. The CACD was described as 'relentless' so judges normally served in three-week blocks. The EAT was described as 'relentless', because although the lay 'wingers' and judge took a collegiate decision, the judge had to write it, with legal reasoning. The Administrative Court was described as 'intolerable', 'a pig' and 'a sweat shop' and family as 'sometimes intolerable'. Commercial judges spent much of *each* vacation writing judgments and had the extra burden of handling their own case management.

> a very significant additional strain … very long hours on Thursday evenings to prepare … five or six hours … There is a strong case for increasing the number of judges.

Because QBD timetables were fixed in six-week or three-week blocks, problems arose where hearings spilled over. One presider was dismayed when prosecutors in the CACD submitted extra evidence on a Wednesday, when he was scheduled to be on circuit by Friday.

A significant minority of QBD judges complained of 'inefficiency' caused by its generalist nature. They were expected to be all-rounders, yet the Bar from which they were recruited was increasingly specialised. They were slower at doing unfamiliar work. The pilot-study judge was sent to the EAT, as a new judge. He protested that he knew nothing of employment law. The bizarre response was 'Well, you did personal injury at the Bar didn't you?' One cited a friend, newly appointed from the commercial Bar, who described having to hear criminal appeals as 'like paddling through treacle'. Whaley was rendered miserable by the Administrative Court, because of unfamiliarity with public law. His struggle to write reasoned decisions required night shifts. He delivered tapes to the RCJ at 2.00 am and his clerk came in to type up his orders at 6.00 am. He would have preferred to have been given a greater share of criminal appeal applications. Obversely, both commercial judges considered these applications a waste of their expertise. One presider described her routine on circuit and in the RCJ.

> I get up six, six thirty, and start working straight away in my pyjamas then … scrub myself up and have breakfast … then work again until … court. I always try to have lunch with the [circuit] judges. [After court], I will have a cup of tea and begin again and do as much as I can after supper, although I am very tired by then so the bulk of it has been done. I would expect to lose part of every weekend. I might lose the whole of Sunday … In London, I would get to my desk here by seven something and … work…until seven or eight. I go up to Gray's Inn very infrequently.

One ex-presider said his workload had been measured by HM Courts Service and found to average 55 hours per week. I witnessed his successor's hours in lodgings, but for the period when I failed to stay awake:

> I start at about 7:30 am … Then off to court, then back here … I normally stop at about 1:30 am.

Seven of the newest judges were critical of the workload and what some perceived as a 'macho' attitude.

> There is a macho tradition in the QBD … you do it, you don't complain and you don't say 'I haven't got time to do this. Give it to someone else'.

> There is a genuine commitment to doing the work—not upsetting the punters but there is another force at work too—a type of machismo: 'We can do any type of case and as many as you want'.

This judge was promoted from the provincial circuit bench where, as we have seen, the cultural tendency is maximising happiness and minimising strain. Another former circuit judge used the word 'macho' in describing the unfamiliar culture. Some judges perceived this as a danger to the public and to the development of the law, and a handicap to diversifying the judiciary.

> That is done at the expense of personal life … and therefore has implications for diversifying the judiciary. I don't see how anyone can do this job if they have young children … the Court of Appeal … is a truly staggering workload. The problem with it is whether we reduce our standards to meet it.

> The reading load in the CACD is also, I think, too great. The remarkable thing … is that there are no major mistakes made.

It's assumed that everybody will give 120 per cent ... if you do have a very difficult case, or something that you really want just a morning or a day to reflect on, or to write a judgment on, you have to be quite assertive and I think that is wrong ... The Administrative Court is extremely hard-pressed so it is easier to get judgment-writing time in the QBD or in the Employment Appeal Tribunal. You could say that at trial level that is not our job. Our job is to get decisions out and the Court of Appeal will make it fancy but it is a terribly expensive thing to send people to the Court of Appeal. I think sometimes, giving you a little more time would have increased the quality of the product inordinately.

Several judges mentioned that the Administrative Court manager encouraged them to produce multiple rulings quickly, on permission applications, with the words 'Don't get it right, get it *writ!*' reminding them that an aggrieved party could appeal. Judges expressed concern over potential injustice. Experienced judges were more sanguine and confident to ask for reading time or to call a halt to the piling-on of work and most reckoned work to be more predictable and less stressful than at the Bar.

It just goes with the job. There are very few two-day weekends. In fact there have been none during term time.

I am 66 now and most of my friends are retired. They all say 'Why are you working fulltime and with that sort of workload?' ... It is no good complaining as it comes with the territory ... I don't find it as stressful ... as when I was at the Bar. If I need to take time to write a judgment, I will take it and ... I will end up eating into my holiday but at least I can do that and the holiday is a good one. We normally find that a significant chunk of vacation is spent working.

It is not like it was at the Bar ... I find it far easier to get weekends off.

I watched a veteran judge returning four sentencing appeals to the CACD office, when he and a colleague were asked to hear 12 in a day. He worked long hours and went home up north at weekends. I asked if he took work home. 'No, that would be the last bloody straw!' Most spent time travelling. A judge from the west commuted to London weekly. When sitting in Newcastle, he would drive from home on Sunday afternoons. Northern judges commuted weekly to the RCJ or circuit courts. One would not sit anywhere south of Leicester. He resented the fact that the RCJ was treated as the home base of all senior judges, requiring him to pay for his travel to London. He rented a London flat which reduced his net income to that of a circuit judge. Others bought flats. The circuit judge interviews demonstrated how they valued living at home and were put off HC jobs by the travelling and disruption to family life. A former circuit judge said he and his wife 'thought long and hard' before he accepted the HC job.[5]

---

[5]   See ch 5. The grumbles about travelling on circuit away from family and about having to handle cases outside their specialism were identified by Professor Dame Hazel Genn as some of the 'downsides' of HC life that discouraged some high-achieving lawyers from applying for senior judicial appointments: *The attractiveness of senior judicial appointment to highly qualified*

Although senior judges have generous holidays, the RCJ still has some courts sitting. All judges sat in the emergency court, on a rota basis, contactable by telephone through the night and at weekends and bank holidays. By their terms of appointment, new judges had to sit for six weeks of their summer vacation. After that, they were expected to give up two weeks of vacation but were entitled to time off in lieu. One chancery and both Commercial Court judges spent some of the summer abroad at international judicial conferences and one spent time in newly independent democracies, advising on the formation of their legal systems. Another participated in the Anglo-American judicial exchange each September. On the other hand, for those who were not presiders, nor slogging through big commercial cases, nor engaged in other judicial business, the generous holidays made up for hectic terms.

> At Christmas we get ... three weeks ... Easter ... is 10 days. Whitsun ... we have been able to go away for a week.

Seven of the 16 found that the job had lived up to their expectations and all except one family judge would recommend the job to a friend. Three were taken by surprise by the workload but six found it more enjoyable than they expected, though their enthusiasm never matched that of the circuit and district benches. The quotations below are typical.

> Very hard work ... I am surprised at the levels of support ... that makes the job harder ... I wasn't given a computer for quite a while ... On the other hand, the work itself is very stimulating.

> Much more work than I expected ... The Bar was immensely hard work but I don't think you really appreciate ... how hard it can be on the bench ... I wasn't aware of all the tasks beyond the strict judging, [such as] presiding ... You expect a judge to be deciding and not managing and administering and looking after other people.

> It is a fantastic job ... hugely rewarding and you get to do some really interesting cases. There are some bizarre aspects: the way that the RCJ is run; the way you don't even have a room [at first] ... the way you have to beg to get anything ... the traditions; the way you select which circuit you are going to go out on; the trappings of the job and the five sets of robes.[6]

Two enjoyed the variety, four enjoyed all of it and six enjoyed decision-making or writing judgments. One liked meeting foreign judges and helping to develop foreign legal systems. Two mentioned running a trial. The three women (two below) enjoyed dealing with people, as did some of the men.

> As presider, I find it very satisfying when personalities are accommodated ... My whole approach is ... most people have strengths—find them and allow them to play to them.

---

practitioners—*Report to the Judicial Executive Board* (London, Directorate of Judicial Offices for England and Wales, 2008, Judiciary website).

  [6] Civil robes have been reduced since his interview.

I love being a trial judge ... controlling the courtroom ... You want people to feel confidence in you ... and ... that they have had a fair hearing.

I asked the 16 what frustrated them, what cases they found difficult to decide or manage, and whether they found the responsibility daunting or emotionally disturbing. Seven found poor or confrontational advocates or LIPs frustrating, or that this made cases difficult to decide or manage. Five mentioned 'hanging around' on circuit, waiting for prisoners or witnesses; three mentioned doing things under pressure so that the job might not be done properly, and four named HM Courts Service, IT or the civil service. The challenge of developing the law was a pleasure. Chancery judges found cases with complex facts the most difficult (and complex facts were what rendered the commercial cases that I observed difficult). Three QBD judges considered managing multi-handed criminal trials their most difficult job.

I am doing a case that has threatened to take 12 months ... it had 14 defendants and 34 barristers.

Three who lacked a public law background found the Administrative Court the most difficult and an experienced public lawyer explained why.

I find a lot of cases difficult to decide ... the arguments seem to me to be fairly balanced ... the responsibility daunts ... having to make a first instance decision with nobody to talk to about it ... if you make it one way you will have a minister exploding; if you make it another way, you will have all sorts of public interest groups saying you are chickening out ... I am talking about cases which are quite capable of producing a split view even in the House of Lords.

A far greater proportion (10 of 16) than the lower judiciary found cases could be daunting or emotionally disturbing but explained their coping mechanisms, 'you just detach'.

I used to be terrified of these high profile cases ... when you are surrounded by press the whole time ... not emotionally disturbing. You get completely case-hardened to murders and horror.

My wife said that even though I don't talk about work much, she could tell when I was doing yet another cerebral palsy baby case.

In the emergency applications court, I refused an application by a woman who had a ... long-standing row with the DSS ... She stormed out of court and wrote to me saying that she was going to kill herself and all would be revealed at the coroner's inquest as to how badly she had been treated by the DSS and now by me. She did kill herself two years later ... I found that emotionally disturbing.

A defendant committed suicide in the course of my summing up ... anybody who has tried some really serious criminal cases would find them ... disturbing. I can remember one murder trial where a member of the navy selected young men under his command ... for homosexual activities, and murdered them, triple murders. I can remember other murderers who were terrifying people. You just learn to handle it.

It is like walking a tightrope. If you look down you would fall off so you have not got to think about that otherwise you would go mad.

I just think very carefully about what I am doing ... a judge who doesn't find the responsibility daunting perhaps ought to think about whether they are in an appropriate job.

PRESIDERS

Circuit presiders never have an idle moment.[7] Travelling half the year, they respond to circuit queries daily, by phone or email. Each circuit has two QBD presiders, with a third in the South East. The junior's job, described below, is for new judges. After two years they become senior presiders for two years.

Judicial supervisory management ... pastoral...you get judges with career issues ... Trying to ... get the best out of your judicial team ... You recommend people for doing types of work ... [and allocate Crown Court cases] and advise the senior judiciary on who should be appointed to do particular types of cases, such as serious sex cases... murders and attempted murders.

The Chancery Division has two judges supervising the six circuits.

[It] requires me to be aware of what is going on in terms of problems with staff ... local judges ... adequacy of resources. I may be ... representing the judges vis-à-vis the Court Service, or representing the Court Service vis-à-vis the judges ... or I may be helping to bid for more resources...or discussing with the ... Head of the Chancery Division ... how procedure should be developed.

This judge, Jennings, took me to a circuit court users' meeting, attended by local chancery-ticketed circuit and district judges, court staff and lawyers. Its agenda was typical. The listing officer reported that late case collapses had been reduced. Jennings hoped his new protocol requiring pre-trial reviews would help but a circuit judge complained that he had only been in court half the summer and was wasted 'on gardening leave'. Jennings raised the problem of trial bundles reaching

---

[7] In his 2008–09 *Review of the Administration of Justice in the Courts* (2010), the Lord Chief Justice said there were 26 HC judges with 'substantial leadership roles': 14 Presiders; eight Family Division Liaison Judges; two Chancery Supervising Judges; two Administrative Court Liaison Judges; one in charge of HC lists; two in charge of the Commercial Court and TCC. Three are Presidents of the EAT, the Administrative Appeals Chamber and the Competition Appeal Tribunal. All Chancery judges sit as Chairmen of the Competition Appeal Tribunal and are assigned to the Upper Tier Tax and Chancery Chamber. One is its President. One is the Chairman of the Special Immigration Appeals Commission (SIAC) and one is President of the Asylum and Immigration Chamber. Ten have outside responsibilities: one on the Judicial Appointments Commission; one responsible for judicial diversity and one in charge of parliamentary relations. Two assist in dealing with judicial discipline. One is in charge of judicial welfare. From 2010, the JAC requires that applicants for the senior judiciary demonstrate leadership and management skills.

him on time, as the paperwork followed him too slowly around circuit. There was a court service presentation on 'Customer Facing Email Accounts'.

One QBD presider was attempting to dissipate rivalries between barristers' chambers, which he considered to be damaging their service to the public. He was trying to initiate a Criminal Law Association, to distract lawyers' energies into professionalism. Over the years I saw him, he was dogged with a problem about a new court building. Its architect had no experience in court design and it had proven unusable for criminal business. A typical interchange with a circuit judge occurred one lunchtime in the Crown Court. The resident popped in to seek moral support about his vilification in the local press. He had allowed a convicted man to go on a pre-booked holiday to Turkey, while remanded, resulting in headlines like 'Turkish Delight—Anne Widdecombe disgusted'. It became worse when *The News of the World* picked it up, portraying the judge 'alongside a Turkish beach and a cocky defendant'.

JENNINGS ON CIRCUIT

Jennings of the Chancery Division made a site visit to a moorland farm, where a claimant alleged the narrowing of a drive, a right of way. We huddled with the solicitors, under golf umbrellas. Jennings showed me an aerial photograph. Lorries had been driven in until the 1960s but the drive had been narrowed by automatic gates, walls and flower beds. The bucolic-kitsch scene was embellished by an ornamental pond, over which a team of cricketing gnomes grinned at a solitary Muscovy duck. I wondered why the simple case was listed for four High Court days. Jennings explained: in his time on circuit, he and a local chancery 'ticketed' circuit judge would normally have three trials listed, in the expectation that one would settle. Jennings' trial had settled so he used the time for the site visit. This case was listed for chancery, because it was a property case and problems had arisen with inexpert judges.[8] Jennings reported that the hearing took three days. He had decided for the claimants and the result was 'very expensive' for the defendants. Afterwards, he learned that the claimants had attempted mediation and made some 'quite generous offers' to settle. In lodgings, with two veteran HC judges, they explained how quarter sessions worked in the 1960s. That evening, we went to a concert. Royals were among the guests but Her Majesty's judges and I sat with the plebs, after nodding a greeting to the High Sheriff, who was roped off with the Glitterati.

Next, Jennings started a two-day hearing in which the claimants sought an order for sale of a jointly owned property, another clear-cut case, where Jennings

---

[8] At the time of writing (2011), certain chancery (equity) cases over £30,000 must go to the HC. The Ministry of Justice launched a consultation in March, proposing to increase the statutory county court equity jurisdiction to £350,000: *Solving disputes in the county courts: creating a simpler, quicker and more proportionate system—A consultation on reforming civil justice in England and Wales* CP6/2011.

considered the defendant to be stubborn or badly advised. The claimant's counsel started by seeking to call a surveyor, 'to ask him supplementary questions'—a big mistake.[9] Jennings declined. Counsel explained that the witness was already en route to a neighbouring town, mistakenly thinking the trial was there. 'Well you'd better call him on his mobile and tell him not to bother, then', instructed Jennings. 'I appreciate this matter is important to the parties but extra costs should not be accrued.' When counsel started asking his first witness his date of birth and occupation, Jennings interrupted to ask when he was going to stop asking non-controversial questions. The barrister, with a nervous, fixed grin, cringed. After one more question and an objection from defence counsel, he stopped. Defence counsel fared no better, Jennings querying the relevance and appropriateness of his questions. 'I can see that feelings have been running high here but this line of questioning is not going to help me decide'. Jennings excluded the second witness. The hearing proceeded in this way. After lunch with the circuit judges, Jennings, now repeatedly challenging the relevance of the claimant's cross-examination, interjected at 2.48 pm, 'Perhaps I should make myself clear … We can finish this case *today*'. This did not work so at 2.55 pm he tried again.

> Mr B, is this relevant? The issue is: this property is jointly owned. Neither party is in a position to buy the other out so there has to be a sale unless Mr F can satisfy the court that there is a good reason why not.

At 3.30 pm, Jennings gave an extempore judgment, ordering a sale. He gave the parties five minutes to agree on a sale date, then sent them off to type and lodge an agreed order. Like the cricketing gnomes case, the property was worth over £200,000 but both cases fell readily within the skill-set of a county court judge. Their inclusion in Jennings' list was a product of the circuit system—Jennings' *short* stays in each city. Jennings' function was symbolic and practical. He represented Her Majesty's HC judges bringing centralised civil justice from London to three circuits. His practical function was to apply the exacting standards of a senior judge to local advocates. By constraining disorganised and unfocused lawyers, he was 'keeping local barristers on their toes', as HC judges argue is their function, below.

THE SPAN OF QBD WORK

General QBD Work: Civil Trials

Outsiders doubtless visualise the bulk of QBD work as general tort or contract trials but this is not how judges spend most of their time. There is little general work left and, as the frustrated EC said in the Crown Court chapter, 'it all

---

[9]   Under the CPR 1998, an expert's statement normally substitutes for examination-in-chief.

settles'.[10] I was defeated in all attempts to observe non-specialist trials. Judges offered theories. One said a provincial listing officer called him 'The Cracker' because of his persuasive capacity to settle. She would stand at the back of the court and enthusiastically give him the thumbs-up sign.

Dealing with Death in the Crown Court

Just as Stanford J specialised in cases involving the death of a child, the nastiest of murders are reserved for 'red' (HC) judges.[11] Whaley J was conducting a retrial. A body had been found in a drug dealer's car boot; there were bloodstains all over the defendants' flat; they had swapped sofa cushions for those in their cellar and there was a Tesco receipt for cleaning materials. The defence was 'We didn't do it'. The sheriff was visiting today. We flanked Whaley. He did not introduce us. I wondered what the defendants made of these unexplained characters in the second act of the panto, especially the sheriff in her velvet and lace suit and hat.[12] Each side was represented by a QC and junior, after a full rehearsal at the original trial, yet the trial was more of a shambles than those described in the Crown Court chapter. By 11.40 am, Whaley interrupted dreary blood-staining evidence to ask that photographs be copied for the jury. They could not be copied in the building. The prosecutor procrastinated for 15 minutes so Whaley suggested we wait outside. He was in despair.

> He's doing it all the wrong way round! Why didn't he tell them what was on the Tesco list, *then* refer to their copies in the bundle, *then* show them the original?

After 20 minutes, counsel had still not agreed how to present the blood-staining evidence to the jury so we left. By 12.50 pm, counsel were debating how to present the Tesco receipt. At 1.10 pm, Whaley broke the trial for lunch and hoped aloud that the evidence problems could be resolved by 2.30 pm. Whaley's clerk drove us back to lodgings in his private car, because the lodgings' Mondeo was too small. Lady Whaley joined us. Whaley said this posh treatment was for our benefit and he would 'normally have lunch in the Crown Court dining room with the lads' (circuit judges). 'It'll be a jam butty tomorrow, with the boss', chimed in the clerk. By 2.40 pm, the prosecution were still not ready, counsel explaining that the Crown Prosecution Service (CPS) did not have a colour photocopier in this city. Their nearest was in a neighbouring city, so the defence solicitors had taken the photos for copying.[13] Outside, Whaley expressed disgust.

---

[10]   5,694 claims and originating summonses were issued in the RCJ in 2009 but there were only 196 concluded trials: *Judicial and Court Statistics 2009* (London, Ministry of Justice, revised October 2010).

[11]   And the rest are distributed to 'ticketed' CJs.

[12]   Another icy courtroom, in June. The sheriff complained and was given the usual explanation, 'Temperatures are controlled from Bristol'.

[13]   I wondered why the police had not taken digital photos, or digitised those they had taken.

What must the public think? The jurors? 'We disregard the inconvenience to them of an eight-week trial, yet get them in here and they're left hanging around!' The sheriff, bored and cold, escaped after lunch. We returned at 3.20 pm. The photographs had been copied but the jury still had to number them themselves. Whaley stopped the hearing at 4.15 pm. Almost the entire day had been wasted. Whaley remarked, aside, that the blood evidence could have been dealt with in one hour. These two silks were 'not so brilliant'. One resented the fact that he had been appointed 15 years after the other, after seven rejections. He had become 'paranoid' and had started canvassing people, 'He even approached me in the gents' loos, at a function!' In lodgings, Whaley had a meeting with the local Bar. Lady Whaley joined us for dinner. Whaley continued working until the early hours on a reserved judgment and his summing-up. He got up very early to work on criminal appeal applications.

The trial recommenced at 10.35 am. The forensic scientist was still trapped in the witness box.[14] We broke for lunch at 1.20 pm. At 2.30 pm, prosecuting counsel came to see Whaley in his room about timetabling the trial. This new QC wanted Monday off, to take his wife to a Buckingham Palace garden party. After he left, Whaley and I realised we had been unable to share his enthusiasm, both having declined Her Majesty's invitation. Whaley regaled me with the story of his 20-minute private audience with her, on his appointment to the High Court, accurately mimicking her voice. In the trial, I struggled to stay awake in the cold. Whaley was anxious, as the courtroom was needed soon for another drug dealer's trial. £1 million had been offered to free him. Several million-pound drug dealers were on trial at this courthouse, yet Whaley earned about £150,000, significantly less than the incompetent QC.

I spent two days on a different circuit with David J. Her work progressed no faster. She travelled up on Monday mornings. Today her train was late. The delay allowed her more time to read the papers for her manslaughter trial. She arrived at 11.35 am, read the pre-sentence reports on cases listed for sentencing and we entered court at 12.15 pm. The clerk had prepared her red summer robes with grey silk cuffs and David showed me the white gloves and black cap (ready for passing the death sentence)[15] that she carried into court. She quickly renewed a drug treatment and testing order on a 19-year-old. In the second case, the pre-sentence report was not ready. Defence counsel explained that he was notified on Friday that the case was being brought forward from the end of the month but no-one remembered the pre-sentence report. No other case was ready.

The jury were sworn in at 2.00 pm. The trial commenced but stopped at 2.55 pm, because defence counsel had mistakenly thought the witnesses had been summoned to appear on Tuesday, though, according to the prosecution, they were ready and waiting in the building. We waited until 3.45 pm for a prosecutor

---

[14]   I secreted reading matter under the bench to fend off boredom.
[15]   Hanging was suspended in the UK in 1965 and abolished in 1969.

in a case that should have been heard that morning but was not because the defendant had mistakenly gone to the magistrates' court. David accepted his apology but explained that she could not sentence him without more information. 'Nothing was ready *all day!*' she reported to her clerk, at 3.55 pm. We were driven to lodgings. After tea, I talked to her clerk and the lodgings manager. She wrote her jury summing-up and worked on a reserved judgment. The trial progressed smoothly on the second day, except for a break while documents were copied for the jury. David wondered why we needed so many witnesses whose evidence could have been given in statements, as we tried to concentrate on the third loss adjuster. Luckily, we rattled through the witnesses quicker than expected so the day's hearing finished at 3.50 pm. The only excitement occurred in the afternoon, when one juror exclaimed 'That's my nephew!' as a witness entered the box. I wondered why no-one had checked the list of witnesses' names with the jury before the trial started.

Conclusions cannot be drawn from two cases. Nevertheless, circuit judges had told me criminal business before HC judges would be better run because the advocates would be QCs. They were wrong. These judges performed a symbolic and educative function, like Jennings. A 'red' judge on the bench emphasises the gravity of homicide. Whaley, like Jennings, took *exactly* the same approach that we saw Stanford applying as a Family Division judge: with their experience as top class advocates and their highly-developed intellect, HC judges require high standards. By expressing dissatisfaction, without losing patience, Whaley was trying to keep these lawyers focused and hoping to subtly indicate how he would have preferred the trial to have been run, by laying evidence before the jury in a manner that optimised jury decision-making. Whaley, an ex-circuit judge here, was no longer part of the small and tight-knit local judicial/Bar group that had in some way supported the conferment of the elite rank of 'silk' on this strikingly poor advocate.

The Administrative Court

This court is now so busy[16] that its cases have displaced general QBD work[17] Even judges like Rathlin and Whaley, with no experience and 'no feeling for public law'

---

[16] Judges developed administrative case law from around 1963. The application procedure for judicial review was simplified in 1981, encouraging applications. The Access to Justice Act 1999 expanded public funding. The Human Rights Act 1998 expanded the grounds of challenge.

[17] In his 2008–09 *Review* (2010) Lord Chief Justice Judge said 'There remain real concerns about the pressures on the Administrative Court and the judges who sit there'. Over 12,000 applications and appeals were lodged in 2008. Some of its cases are being moved to the Upper Tribunal and to provincial centres.

(Rathlin) are drafted in. Many have not studied the subject.[18] Ossian J *had* practised here at the Bar so his expertise was exploited and he spent most of the year in the Administrative Court. He enjoyed judicial review. His week, with four days in court and one doing paper applications, allowed no time for pre-reading or judgment writing. 'We get papers ... whenever we come out of court, for the following day, and you simply have to read them in the evening.'

I watched Ossian spend a day deciding 12 paper applications for permission to apply. He was able to read and understand these detailed files rapidly, touch-type each reasoned decision, and explain everything to me. Whaley would have been struggling through this pile in the middle of the night. The list was a mixture, requiring scrutiny of the different statutory powers of each public body concerned: immigration, asylum, parole, planning, housing, and magistrates' sentencing. Ossian drafted reasons carefully. Judicial reviews challenging the legality of government action can be highly political. He referred one application, challenging the legality of the Iraq war, to be decided by the head of the Administrative Court. I wondered what happened when Ossian spotted a ground of challenge on which he was not addressed. He was reluctant to invite written submissions: 'dangerous—there isn't the time'. He had once invited written submissions on his powers in interpreting a European Directive. Neither party could help him so he decided the case on another ground, and it was appealed to the House of Lords. He was so used to his decisions being appealed[19] that he was amazed when he met a Family Division judge who had never had a decision successfully appealed. (Obviously, he did not realise it was a law-free zone.) As the applications had been dull and hard work, we took Ossian's five sets of robes out of the cupboard and giggled at their ostentatiousness.

I watched Peter J in his 'worst ever day in the Admin Court'. There appeared to have been a breakdown in communication between the lawyers, the listing office and himself, as to the timing of his list and what decisions he was required to take. Although he had not practised in administrative law, Peter was 'not phased' by the challenge of learning new areas of the law. In Case One, a group of professionals sought to challenge a regulatory body, 'hopelessly out of time'. 'I don't begin to understand it', admitted Peter. Case Two involved a company asking for documents 'on a fishing expedition'. In Case Three, a social worker challenged a decision by her ex-employers. In court, Peter asked for time estimates, 'realistic ones, not ones dreamed up by the office'. Lawyers in the first,

[18] Solicitors expressed anxiety over judicial inconsistency in granting judicial review applications and the criteria judges applied, in V Bondy and M Sunkin, 'Accessing Judicial Review' [2008] *Public Law* 647: 'A consistent concern was that claimants felt unsure as to whether judges sufficiently understood the claims being made'. There was a wide variation in grant rates between eight judges.
[19] As we have seen, judges were encouraged to 'get it writ' not 'get it right'. Bondy and Sunkin refer to pressure on judges to clear unarguable cases out of the lists.

listed for 30 minutes, estimated they would take two hours. The 'fishing expedition' wanted half an hour, so Peter heard them first, at 10.40 am. The applicants complained that the opposition were making them out to be crooks. 'Oh litigation is such good, clean fun, isn't it?' quipped Peter. It was 12.25 pm by the time judgment had been given. Counsel in Case One explained that the substantive application was listed for three weeks hence. This was merely an interim application. Peter was furious, having prepared for three hours the previous night. Worse, he was only given one skeleton argument that morning. 'Mr X, have the admin law Bar got no intention of complying with the practice direction?' He struck the case out. An argument started. The lawyers blamed one another, resisting the threat of costs and protesting 'injustice'. The public body claimed to have 'bent over backwards to help the court', because of defects in the applicants' papers. The applicants pleaded that their solicitors were acting for free 'for altruistic reasons', as the applicants had no money. The third case commenced at 12.49 pm. Peter asked the parties to have just the necessary papers ready at 1.50 pm. They were ready by 2.05 pm. The applicant showed Peter a draft injunction. 'Oh wouldn't it have been *wonderful* to have had this last night, Mr Y? … It's OK. I'm not saying it's your fault.' After struggling through confusion for the afternoon, Peter gave an extempore judgment at 4.30 pm, ordering 'logically produced bundles' for the substantive hearing. 'This hearing has been hampered by lurching from one set of bundles to another.' Later, he said the Administrative Court was his least favourite. Twelve weeks per year usually yielded only two interesting cases. It was a waste of his talent 'if I have any'. He was often 'served up with a Horlicks'. Counsel were much worse than in ordinary cases. 'My heart sinks.' Unlike Whaley, veteran Rathlin was not rendered miserable by the Administrative Court. He had only taken one public law case whilst at the Bar. Counsel would give him mini-lectures on the law on homelessness and immigration, 'You tell *me*, Mr Jones [laughing]. I need all the help I can get!'

The Commercial and Admiralty Courts—London's Hidden Assets

Judges pleaded the importance and neglect of their own jurisdiction.[20] Commercial Court judges were anxious to demonstrate the poverty of their facilities, relative to the court's value to the UK economy. 'Look, if you're the chairman of Shell, this is your waiting room', indicating a plastic chair next to the lift shaft in St Dunstan's House, the cramped office block then used for most admiralty and commercial cases. In 80 per cent of cases, one litigant is foreign and in 50 per cent, all parties are.[21] All the cases I observed with Trollope J fell into the latter category. One involved a sovereign state suing another for over $80 million. There

---

[20]   For instance, the significance of the Welsh courts and Welsh language and the shortage of family judges.

[21]   *Report of the Commercial Court and Admiralty Court*, annually, Judiciary website.

were three claims ranging from $62 million to $100 million, another about the Australia to Japan Cable, another where international loan sharks had bought up sovereign debt of an African country and another involving the misappropriation of fuel-oil off the Emirates. Disputes come to London partly because England is the mother of all common law jurisdictions. This, and the longevity and stability of English common law means that contracting parties routinely agree that English law should be used to resolve any dispute.[22] It also results from the historic importance of the City as an international centre of commerce, banking, insurance, shipping and aviation. One party may fight to establish jurisdiction in London.[23] London's pre-eminence also rests on the incorruptibility of British judges. The 14 Commercial Court judges are businesslike and understand the importance of speedy dispute resolution. Trollope was cognisant of his judgments' impact on the stock market.

Their brilliance was not matched by the court's facilities. Decades ago, the Government decided civil courts should be self-funding.[24] By 2007, there were only two video-conferencing suites in the RCJ. Some cases were heard in tacky rented offices. Fifteen years after email was routine, I watched Trollope explain to a group of incredulous City solicitors (doubtless each earning five times as much as him) that his email could not receive attachments over two megabytes. He would have been better served by a free Hotmail account. An electronic case management system was belatedly developed from 2007. Trollope said one solicitors' firm spent more on IT annually than did the entire civil court system. At last the court is being housed in a new building.[25] In the meantime, judges are wary of losing business to forums more *conveniens*, such as Singapore, Scotland or Ireland.[26] Commercial Court judges loved the job, despite exasperating conditions.

> Hopefully we contribute to certainty in international trade by our judgments, which are referred to throughout the world … it is satisfying if you can achieve an overall market settlement.

Trollope kept proactive control. One inter-state case was part of a series. He conducted monthly case management hearings. Among the papers, I spotted a note from another judge, congratulating him for narrowing the issues, despite the lawyers' combative attitude. 'There were lots of rows', explained Trollope. In the list of issues, masses had been literally crossed out. The trial bundle contained the 're-re-re-amended points of claim'. The remaining issue was quantum,

[22] English and US law were the 'law of choice' for most global transactions: T Burke in a College of Law podcast, cited at (2010) 160 *New Law Journal* 743.

[23] The commercial list was started in 1895. The court was given statutory status in 1970.

[24] P Darbyshire, *Darbyshire on the English Legal System*, 10th edn (London, Sweet & Maxwell, 2011) ch 6.

[25] But it is being built by a private developer and leased by HMT Courts Service.

[26] F Gibb, 'A court for the world to solve its business disputes', *The Times*, 5 September 2006.

occupying expert witnesses on accountancy, valuation and foreign law. He had started trying the case a year earlier but, such was its factual, technical complexity, both sides sought postponement, 'so they could get on top of it'.

Before opening any of his cases, Trollope started preparing his judgment. He demanded an outline, a litigation history, a factual scenario or statement of differences, a list of *dramatis personae* and a 'Scott' schedule of damages. Lawyers emailed these to his clerk, for him to cut and paste into his judgment. He then sent them a statement of law and allowed them to correct it. 'You have to keep on top of the judgment in a long and complex case like this because you don't want to leave writing to the end.' Livenote software produced the transcript on his laptop. He highlighted the parts he needed. He 'tried to keep the number of experts down' and often had them simultaneously sworn in and questioned.[27] 'You've got to make them understand they are helping the judge.' He enjoyed having his judgments upheld in the House of Lords, if he had been overturned by the Court of Appeal. 'The trouble with the Court of Appeal is that you might get one commercial lawyer and two with no experience.'[28]

I sat with Trollope a year later in a South American oil-drilling case. In the meantime, applying the law of Ohio, he had decided a $110 million dispute arising out of the bombing of the Twin Towers. In the South American case, the task was to determine contractual liability through six sets of contracts and subcontracts and a further six side-contracts and agreements. The contracts and facts were impenetrably technical. This was an $80 million side-issue of the main issue. Trollope 'grasped the scale of the case' when a witness explained they were losing $3 million per day by delaying construction of an oil platform. He wondered if he should 'slice off' some issues for determination by maritime arbitrators. Alternatively, in factually technical cases like this, commercial judges felt they should decide the preliminary points of law, then 'pack the case off to the Technology and Construction Court' but parties resisted this. It was unpopular because not all TCC judges were HC judges.[29] This oil case was not going well. The lawyers had not provided the agreed factual matrix he had requested and he kept asking one QC to stop speaking too quickly for the foreign witnesses, explaining outside, 'I feel very strongly ... Can you imagine being cross-examined at this speed in Portuguese? We should be providing a *service*.' To compound his embarrassment, there was nowhere but the floor for all the ring-bound documentation in this pokey, dark courtroom in the RCJ, which was unsuitable for computer equipment.

---

[27] This practice is fairly common in Australia and New Zealand and is known as 'hot-tubbing'. It was recommended to be 'piloted' by Jackson LJ in his 2010 costs review, para 3.23. There was no reference to the fact that the system is already in use in England, at least in Trollope's court.

[28] CJs expressed similar frustrations.

[29] Five HC judges were added in 2005.

The Employment Appeal Tribunal

The EAT was a model of the egalitarianism it is tasked to promote. The CJs and HC judges and Registrar squashed around one long lunch table, beside the non-lawyers: trade unionists and multi-coloured captains of industry. Young David J was teased about negative media coverage. I sat near newly-appointed Kevin, a thick-set, shaven-headed man who travelled from Wales to sit in two-day shifts. He had seen the job advertised by the Department of Trade and Industry (DTI). He was a Welsh speaker so could sit in Cardiff too. I was surprised to learn that he had not sat on an employment tribunal.[30] In hearings, David was flanked by Kevin and a black entrepreneur. On the second day, she sat with a white trade unionist and an expensively dressed brown senior manager with a smooth American accent. All the applicants were black and their lawyers were brown or white.[31]

Tribunals generally comprise a lawyer and two expert laypeople. The EAT, however, is only empowered to rule on errors of law so I asked David what contribution these 'wingers' made. She said they were very useful because of their vast experience in industry. Whereas the law prescribes legally correct procedures for hiring and firing, they experienced its practical operation. On the second day, in deliberations, the American, whose day job was developing new Tesco stores, gave us a mini-lecture on how the company before us *ought* to have been restructured, modelled on good practice, from his experiences of restructuring a family firm. Employees should have been matched to new jobs only if they had the appropriate skills. David laughed, remembering my query.

> This is the perfect illustration for Penny of how we [judges] benefit from hearing how things work in the real world. The Court of Appeal have no idea. They are all commercial judges or patents or something.[32]

All had pre-read case papers. On the first day, David led pre-hearing discussions and asked the questions, during the hearing, just as lay magistrates now leave questioning to the chair. On the second day, the wingers were much more experienced. They were very knowledgeable about the case and assertive in pre-hearing discussion, expressing strong views. They had discussed it before joining her. In the hearing, they each questioned the advocate, entering a dialogue, like CA judges. The three explained they were nervous in determining this appeal. The CA had recently restricted them to finding perversity in the tribunal's decision, yet in cases like this 'you can see the tribunal just got it wrong—there's inconsistency in the evidence'.

---

[30]   The lower-layer tribunal from which appeals go to the EAT.
[31]   In ch 8, I explained why I used Obama's terminology to denote skin colour.
[32]   The same point as made by Trollope, above.

Room 101 and the Judge on the Clapham Omnibus

I thought the name of the RCJ emergency applications court was a parody until I learned that it used to sit in Room 101. David had been on duty over Christmas. 'Christmas eve was a nightmare. Christmas day was quiet': deportees seeking injunctions, bail, immigration and homelessness applications and commercial applications for freezing orders.[33]

> You get teams of commercial lawyers with ring-binders and a draft order thrust at you, then nutters or poor folks from Hackney. There was a well-dressed nutter applying to commit the Lord Chancellor and Lord Chief Justice. I thought he was OK for a minute.

Mostly, on weekend or evening duty, judges need not wait in the RCJ so when the news media report that 'a High Court injunction was granted last night' (for instance to stop the Blairs' ex-nanny publishing stories of life in the Blair-Booth household), they are referring to a virtual court, a single judge on the telephone. One judge had been called on his mobile while on the Clapham bus at 11.00 pm. He got off, to hear the application for an injunction. Overnight applications must now be made by a lawyer, since the night when Mrs X phoned one HC judge 40 times.

I spent two days in Room 101. I was meant to be observing Whaley in a QBD trial but, typically, 16 QBD trials had settled that Monday morning. At 10.35 am, I found Pitt J[34] was hearing a team of commercial lawyers applying for freezing and search orders. Counsel had spent the weekend with the senior partner of her briefing solicitors preparing the massive, well-ordered bundles, 'diamond-studded, My Lord'. Next were applications from student barristers, working for free. From 11.30 am, Pitt was left waiting for the next party's lawyers to prepare. His room was so far away that that if the parties wanted time to themselves in court, he sat on the windowsill outside. The usher popped in with a large box. 'That's your two o'clock Sir.' I left him to read. The following day commenced at 10.00 am with an application for an injunction to prevent an industrial dispute, attracting four journalists. Pitt delivered a fluent extempore judgment at 12.40–1.07 pm. He had not received the union's papers until 9.45 am. The afternoon was filled with applications from LIPs. The first at 2.10 pm was a lady claiming 'A thousand million pounds, because the Queen said I should have it'. Pitt patiently explained that an order striking-out her claim was not a judgment in her favour. She handed up a picture postcard. 'Yes, I can see this explains your feelings.' He dismissed her claim.

> Your Lordship, how can you come to that conclusion just like that?

---

[33] Freezing assets of another party.
[34] Pitt J was not in the sample but, happily, I already knew him, from appearing with him at a foreign conference. This was another example of a 'bonus' judge. I met him again, in the Court of Appeal chapter.

Well, I just have.

I did not receive these documents.

I've made my order Miss Thornton. Thank you.

The 2.40 pm case was another appeal from a Master's dismissal of an appeal from an order striking out a claim. Pitt explained that there was a procedure the LIP could have used, as a tenant claiming that he had enhanced a property. The applicant started listing all the home improvements he had made. 'You're going over the facts now Mr Ahmed. I've read all the papers, thank you.' The LIP did not stop. 'I've heard all I want to hear. Thank you, Mr Ahmed.' The opposing solicitor applied for a civil restraint order. 'We have many judgments against him.' The next LIP had had his car clamped. Its contents had been stolen; it had been driven and it had collected parking tickets. The case had been before a DJ, a CJ and an HC judge. The man was articulate but the injustice had taken over his life. Pitt stopped his explanation. 'I fear you're going to find against me', turning red, 'I think you're bound by the decision in *Vine*.' Pitt read the law report the litigant proffered and allowed the claim to be reinstated. He enquired in a friendly manner where the LIP had learned the law. He had enrolled on a law degree. Pitt advised, smiling, 'It looks as if you got cross about this. It's a good idea to get a lawyer because they don't get cross.'

Later, Pitt explained that the emergency applications list had moved to a proper courtroom after an HC judge was punched. I asked how he coped with such a legally wide range of applications with little or no notice. 'You're flying by the seat of your pants.' He had only received the papers for Monday's commercial case that morning, despite the fact that there was a lot to read and the freezing and search orders requested were draconian. Some people came back repeatedly, even if classed as vexatious litigants, though they had to apply on paper. 'You usually try to make orders to maintain the status quo.' He had only been fooled once. He had had to overturn his own order once he had heard from the other side. He said you were dependent on people being honest. You needed to be able to trust solicitors and barristers. He wondered what it was like to live in a country where you could not trust lawyers.

MORE LIPS

Litigants in person (LIPs) populate the High Court and Court of Appeal. Many have meritorious claims or defences which they struggle to bring without legal aid. Some are obsessive. One chancery judge's clerk said 'there are people who *live* in the Royal Courts of Justice'. As soon as the building opens, in they trundle, through the Great Hall, armed with ring-binders, bottles of water and multiple carrier-bags. He said judges sometimes struggled to save this type of LIP from being bankrupted by obsessive litigation. Judges would plead with them to stop ruining their health and squandering their assets. One LIP had spent £20,000 on a six-month dispute. The judge reminded him that this left him just £17,000 equity in the property in dispute, 'You're ruining your life!' His clerk praised the judge, 'This guy gets out of his pram sometimes, in his room, but he's very, very patient with litigants in person'.

In the Administrative Court, Ossian enjoyed the unusual gift of a reading day, to prepare for an LIP challenging a grant of planning permission. The LIP had requested a five-day hearing. The listing office granted two. His 20 ring-binders were delivered late. Ossian said 'the problem is getting him to stick the salient points'. He had been aggressive. He insisted on representing himself, despite being a multi-millionaire.

In court, Ossian warned him to confine his arguments to a day. The LIP, in a very thick Greek accent, retorted that there must be a fair trial. Ossian smiled and asked if he would like to sit down, attempting to put him at ease. The LIP had applied to cross-examine all the planning authority's witnesses but Ossian released them, rapidly dismissing an application to join-in another applicant. Ossian endeavoured to clarify the grounds, continually steering him off a stream of pedantic, irrelevant challenges. Luckily, the planning authority was represented by 'one of the best planning silks'. A chorus of supporters sat at the back of the courtroom. Next to them was a messy-haired boy on work experience, looking catatonic. I wondered if this would put him off studying law. I slept next to Ossian for most of the morning and Work Experience Boy was fast asleep, head on hands. A press reporter read a novel. At 12.31 pm an elderly supporter made an early start on her packed lunch. As the litigant played to his audience, counsel used devices to fight off sleep—pretending to take notes or admiring the elaborate gothic light fittings and wood-carving high above. The authority's silk stared at us, face contorted in consternation or alarm, failing to understand the LIP, but Ossian would not have his eye caught. At 12.50 pm, the elderly lady bedded-down into a post-lunch snooze but was woken at 12.55 pm when Ossian interjected, smiling 'Mr X, you must be in need of a break, having done *so well*'.

After lunch, as the LIP waxed melodramatic, Ossian politely reminded him that this was not a theatre. He insisted he needed five days but Ossian firmly reassured him that he was 'doing very well'. As we approached 3.30 pm and Work Experience Boy was horizontal, Ossian attempted to truncate the separate arguments of bias against five councillors, punctuated by political speeches.

I've taken this point, Mr X.

Well, I've got many more examples, My Lord!

Well, judges sometimes say 'Give me your best point', [smiling].

My Lord, I can't choose! [Laughter from the 'audience'].

At 3.40 pm, 16 schoolchildren entered. At 4.30 pm, Ossian smiled, 'I think you're drawing to a natural conclusion now, Mr X'. Ossian reported, later, that the LIP had tried to continue his argument on the second day. The authority's silk took the whole morning and some of the afternoon. 'I discouraged the young lad [counsel] for the developers from saying anything.' Ossian acknowledged that most of the transcript would report the LIP's speech as 'inaudible'.

One Friday afternoon, an LIP was squeezed into Trollope's busy case management list. Unusually, commercial judges insist on managing their own cases. He was insolvent and suing one of the world's biggest underwriters over insurance contracts placed by a Khazac insurance company. Another commercial judge had urged alternative dispute resolution (ADR). The claimant said he could not afford it. 'Most regrettable', remarked Trollope to the LIP and his McKenzie Friend, groaning, aside, that the witness statements 'should have been exchanged years ago'. McKenzie Man (MM) claimed to have practised as a commercial solicitor for 25 years yet Trollope said he had to instruct him on how to take a witness statement. MM interrupted Trollope as he was ordering that Khazak law could not be relied on. Trollope patiently explained that the LIP would need to *argue* Khazac law and bring an expert to prove it. MM repeated the point. Trollope re-explained and the argument went round in another circle. There was a repetitive interchange about estoppel, MM announcing he was going to argue it, without citing any authorities. He mentioned three witnesses were 'experts in their own right', ignoring Trollope's warning that they could not give expert evidence unless acceptable to the court. Trollope refused MM the right to appear at trial and strongly encouraged the LIP to seek counsel's help. Outside, Trollope explained that he could have requested a Friend of the Court but it would be a waste of public money as there was no basis in this claim. The Bar Pro Bono Unit had declined free help. This had lasted all afternoon, Trollope repeatedly explaining basic points of procedure to this faux-solicitor, who was bent on using a procedure of his own devising. In Trollope's chambers, we re-enacted the bizarre interchanges, giggling.

One morning outside Jennings' room, I bumped into a departing barrister. He had appeared as an LIP in a series of cases relating to shares in a family company. 'This case has followed me around' for years, with hearings in two cities and London. I asked what it was about. 'Hate and money', replied Jennings. LIPs made such frequent appearances in the Chancery Division that a notice below Jennings' bench read:

Please address the judge as My Lord and please keep your voice up.

Both chancery judges said that the only omission from their training had been in how to handle LIPs. In one case, an LIP sought permission to appeal out-of-time against the Pension Ombudsman's decision affirming his ineligibility for a pension. In all interchanges, Jennings smiled warmly, though he was not naturally smiley. The nervous LIP had two supporters from the Personal Support Unit in the RCJ. Jennings had requested an Advocate to the Court.[35] The pension fund was represented so, after hearing the application and checking with the LIP that he had correctly interpreted his arguments, Jennings checked with counsel that they had not overlooked anything that could have been argued by the LIP. In his judgment, refusing permission, Jennings took care to sympathise. The fund sought £4,000 in costs but Jennings ordered the LIP to pay £400, in £20 instalments. He concluded, 'Mr V, that's it. I'm *very* sorry'.

One day in the EAT, every applicant was alleging direct and indirect (race) discrimination and victimisation. One was bringing a case against a city council for refusing her a job, having brought a case each time the council rejected her 16 applications. David considered it curious that the applicant, a law graduate, had listed these: 'evidence of her own vexatious litigation!' Another applicant was more extreme. David and her wingers laughed that my mere presence might provoke him into alleging bias. David thought there had been an increase in LIPs claiming discrimination.[36] Their sense of grievance was exacerbated when the EAT ruled that their applications disclosed no error of law. They were normally unaided in preparing because legal aid is not available but most were represented in the hearing by lawyers offering free services under the Employment Lawyers Advice Scheme. David had been a member and was greatly relieved by their help. In most instances, LIPs' claims disclosed few arguable points of law. David dreaded cases where the lawyer opened by explaining 'I am going to argue two grounds and Miss X is going to address you on grounds 3 to 97'.

The stories are indicators of all the points made on LIPs in the county court chapter. LIPs place an onus on the judge to shift from neutral umpire to pro-active helper, for which they are untrained. HC judges seldom request help from an Advocate to the Court. Most striking, here, is the disproportionate amount of resources painstakingly devoted to them—staff and court time, judge time, free legal help and emotional support, and corporate and public bodies' resources in opposing them. The law affords multiple bites of the cherry. Some are hopeless repeat-players, paranoid, or have lost all sense of proportion, yet the case law and this research shows that judges are remarkably tolerant and the LIP needs to become an outstanding nuisance before they will classify him as a vexatious litigant. Obviously, many LIPS have meritorious cases but all but one here had a hopeless case.

---

[35] Any judge can do this where there is a danger that an important and difficult point of law might be decided without the court hearing relevant argument.

[36] In 2005–06, these constituted one quarter of the EAT's cases: F Gibb, 'Sex, race and religion—the growth industry', *The Times*, 9 January 2007.

LAWYERS

Commercial judges appreciated being served by the best advocates. Family Division judges felt lawyers were generally well-prepared but almost all other HC judges considered lawyers 'a mixed bunch', such as this Chancery judge.

> They range from completely incompetent, almost incompetent and really have very little idea...to experienced QCs who it is a pleasure to have conducting a case. They may not be experienced chancery counsel because the demarcation lines have been hugely eroded. When I started in the Bar, if a case was in the Chancery Division ... almost certainly the counsel instructed would be from chancery chambers, who would have at least some idea of what he/she was doing.

Two QBD veterans felt judges were much more tolerant nowadays.

> Perhaps we are not fierce enough...our user-friendly attitude...doesn't keep them up to the mark.

> The young are much less cowed by judges...and I think that is rather splendid. I don't think they are frightened of us the way I used to be frightened.

This reflects the experiences of DJs and CJs, though no HC judge complained of 'untrustworthy' lawyers. The Administrative Court had the most mixed-ability lawyers, as well as mixed-ability judges. Inexpert judges suffered from amateurish advocacy, partly because many inexperienced barristers represent people without charging and partly because many cases are emergencies. Ossian explained the dependence of the judge on the lawyer.

> At the top end are the best barristers ... at the bottom end the worst ... some immigration cases, frankly, where the quality of advocacy is hopeless ... The norm is good. We do depend quite heavily ... on high quality advocacy. We don't have a lot of time to conduct our own research into cases or to rethink the arguments.

ON CIRCUIT AND IN LODGINGS

HC judges sit for 189 days per year. Duties such as Parole Board count as sitting days but judgment writing does not. The four-term legal year commences in October. Judges' sittings are divided into six half-terms of six weeks. Most Chancery judges stay in the RCJ. Family judges only go on circuit to hear specific cases, except for Liaison Judges, like Stanford. QBD presiders tend their circuits. Some judges are allocated to big circuit trials. Non-presiders choose unfilled 'slots' on each term's timetable on a rota basis, alternating with London duties. Most go out for three six-week periods.

Auld LJ examined the circuit system in his *Review*.[37] At any one time around 40 per cent of QBD judges would be on circuit. He considered whether the system should become more flexible, because of various problems, such as delays in listing long murder cases and the waste of judges as a resource, if a circuit trial collapsed. He recommended that the long vacation, August and September, be reduced to August and the regime of sitting in six-week blocks should end, permitting flexibility, deploying judges to try particular cases. It was clear from this research that more flexibility has been injected, as Ossian spent most of his year in the Administrative Court and others did in the Commercial Court and so on. I spoke to the judge managing QBD judges' rotas at that time. He tried to be flexible. People could sit full-time in London, by choosing appropriate 'slots'. Some trials were advertised so judges could select them. Some judges resented 'hanging around' on circuit or dealing with trivia if a long trial collapsed. The managing judge said this should not happen. The circuit's presiders were meant to offer a redundant judge back to him for reallocation. There was plenty of alternative work at big trial centres. At Manchester, there could be about 50 trials queuing and at Liverpool, over 80 murders. A judge would only be left with trivia if a trial collapsed on a Tuesday and he had to wait until the following Monday to commence a new one. The inflexibility of HC judges' timetables still causes problems. In 2007, a resident CJ had problems in securing HC judges to hear serious and complex frauds. This caused trial delays and their eventual allocation to CJs.

Jennings was scheduled to sit his chancery circuit courts for one, two or three-week periods. His important scheduled case had collapsed so, as we saw, he was left with trivia. It seemed Jennings' presence on circuit was a public relations and supervisory exercise, allowing him to develop a working relationship with 'his' circuit and district judges. Both QBD judges in lodgings with Jennings were redundant that week. Their big criminal trials had collapsed. One described himself as 'resting', hearing routine Crown Court cases, and the other stayed in lodgings, writing up a judgment.

I asked the 26 senior judges for their opinions on the circuit system and on judges' lodgings. All were in favour. They felt some cases were so serious that they needed the attention of an HC judge. It would be inappropriate to ask all parties to travel to London. Only one suggested having judges attached to a specific circuit or court group, other than presiders. Most argued the benefit of the present system was to break up the bench and Bar 'cosiness' of a circuit.

> The High Court judge comes from London. He sits regularly in the Court of Criminal Appeal. It is very easy for a court … to get its own in-house idiosyncrasies.

> It brings a different approach, a different set of backgrounds and helps to maintain standards … there is a danger that you have local practices developing.

---

[37] The Right Honourable Lord Justice Auld, *Report of the Review of the Criminal Courts of England and Wales* (London, the Stationery Office, 2001) ch 6.

High Court judges going out from London and seeing the circuit judges, working with them … so you don't get little fiefdoms building up.

fresh light on the same problems … keeps everybody on their toes … good for the local Bar … good for local judges … good to have the variety of ideas.

In certain … cities…there is maybe three or four sets of barristers … who get most of the work. The people who rise to the top … will be made circuit judges … the whole situation becomes a little comfortable and deals are done. Trials are cracked when they shouldn't be. Corners are cut and procedures aren't as rigorously enforced when they should be[38] … I go … somewhere and they haven't got a clue who I am. All they know is that I am some stuck-up character from London who has more guns on board than they do. I enjoy it but I don't enjoy the lodgings thing … It is a break from this place. You work less hard. You see parts of England that you have never seen. You meet people and it is an invigorating experience generally.

The High Court should be recognised as a national and not local cadre of judges who are visible in all parts of the country … There should be a level of seniority of judges specifically perceived as being there to try the gravest cases … they meet and are met by the local Bar, solicitors, magistrates, locals, judges, dignitaries and non-dignitaries … the burden of proving a good case is on the shoulders of those who would wish to get rid of a … continuous practice since the time of His Great Majesty King Henry II.

The deployment of QBD judges had its critics. Three of the eight CA judges wanted a greater move towards a docketing system (listing cases for particular judges and they usually manage them pre-trial). One HC judge wanted 'an overhaul'. Another called it

very badly managed … a very silly waste of public money and…judicial time. There is a lot of sense in presiding judges going out … and obviously big cases where it is important to have a High Court judge to try them … They always over-estimate the time and so you are sitting there afterwards. Well, I just go out walking.

There was niggling criticism of the cost of lodgings, such as a 2003 *Daily Mirror* article, 'Judge Bread—Free lodgings for High Court cost the taxpayer £5m a year'. An answer to Andrew Dismore MP disclosed that some lodgings provided very expensive accommodation for the small number of nights they were used per year.[39] Costs had been cut by the time of the research. Butlers and chauffeurs were dispensed with, provocative as much for their symbolism of anachronistic class privilege as for their expense. No judge rued their passing. One criticism is repeatedly made: given the sporadic or rare use of lodgings, it would be

---

[38]   Neatly illustrated by ch 9.

[39]   At Caernerfon 10 nights' accommodation had cost £235,232. Some efficiency savings have been achieved since then but in 2005–06, the cost was still over £5 million. Accommodation at permanent lodgings cost £3–8,000 per judge per week. The economics of lodgings' management was scrutinised by the Lord Chancellor's Department in 1995 and again in 2000. I was privileged to be given a spreadsheet of a full, detailed breakdown of the cost of each set of lodgings, audited on 10 January 2007.

economical to use hotel accommodation. Most judges objected but Auld LJ said HC judges 'manage well enough' in hotels, in Scotland, Northern Ireland and the Commonwealth. Some under-used lodgings have since been closed. Judges are accommodated in Wolsey Lodges, which 'offer superior bed and breakfast accommodation' (website).

Judges spend up to six weeks in lodgings about three times a year. They may spend most of their waking time there working. They hold meetings and entertain the local sheriffs, judges and others. Judges are permitted to bring partners and children but are mostly unaccompanied. Each is aided by a clerk. Each needs a bedroom and a study so some judges pointed out that, in comparison with well-used lodgings, secure hotel accommodation would not be cheaper. Most regarded lodgings as a necessary, albeit inadequate 'home from home', where they could relax after stressful trials, with colleagues, and feel their persons, papers, electronic sources and conversations were secure.

> We carry quite a lot of clobber … paper has to be left lying around and much of it is highly sensitive … To have to get in the lift in the hotel with one side [of a case] … and there is the other side peeking through the door saying 'God, he is going up in the lift with the judge?'

> I can't imagine having gone out and done high profile murder cases and stayed in a hotel. I simply can't imagine it.

> If I had been told that I had to spend six weeks out of town, three times a year…in the Forte Crest, I wouldn't have taken the job … I wouldn't want the chambermaid reading drafts of my judgments … You wouldn't want unsavoury characters knowing where you were…everyone is entitled to a little bit of time off during the day and if you are doing the Soham murder, you really wouldn't want the paparazzi coming and photographing you while you are having dinner would you?

> There is this amazing feeling … that it is bad and wasteful … and the notion is that they are dressing up for dinner and all that. We have never dressed for dinner … if I was a colonel … I would be given a house … car and … a driver.

The three below had a reputation as radicals. They considered lodgings uncomfortable and found the formal expectations of circuit life to be tiresome and distasteful but they too defended the accommodation.

> I would much rather stay there than a hotel…lodgings are ghastly, large buildings … provisions are always so primitive that it sparkles … I tell you after six weeks, even if you are there with your best friend, you are completely mad and miserable. There is something about the quality of the paint, lighting and furniture that is seriously dispiriting after a few weeks.

> The general lodgings are a dingy suburban villa with chintz curtains and fading carpets. I would not be prepared to go out on circuit if I stayed in a hotel … What you get in lodgings is privacy. You are able to kick your shoes off and talk unguardedly and freely

with other judges about the case, knowing there is no journalist overhearing and writing down what you say and you see your remarks in the paper the next day. They are okay.

It is seen by the Government as a mark of privilege ... understandably associated with the kind of social trappings that are inflicted upon High Court judges ... a butler, a chef and big chauffeur-driven car is silly. It existed here until last month ... I have no difficultly in driving myself to court ... I think lodgings are very valuable. I have meetings perhaps three times a week. I have barristers ... the local authority ... magistrates, trying to improve the way the system operates ... It is entirely private ... I don't find lodgings easy ... Every lodgings ... have been wonderful. The people have been kind and generous ... It still isn't a great place to live, frankly ... but ... it is the best one they could devise ... I think the real agenda is not saving money ... It is the socio-political aspect of what appears to be a privileged existence and I think that is rather a pity.

The pilot-study judge and five others said that if lodgings were replaced with hotel accommodation, they would leave the bench. Others pointed out that it was difficult enough to attract lawyers to the High Court Bench. One had stayed in Wolsey Lodges but found it 'very wearing'. He felt obliged to socialise with his hosts, as did another.

I don't want any other customers to be there because it is terribly inhibiting...[and] good manners prevents you from completely ignoring your hosts and hostesses.

One judge had had an off-putting experience in an hotel.

In a small area people rapidly found out who you were. An old ... couple cottoned on to the fact that I was a High Court judge and the wife became a kind of groupie, leaping out from behind doors. My clerk was wonderful. He managed to act as a buffer.

Two lodgings I visited were in cities and two were in the country. All were depressing, as if furbished from a frumpy store in 1960, on a low budget. I sat with Stanford in the sitting room window, as it was the only light chink in the gloomy panelling. We were framed by chocolate brown velvet tasselled curtains and pelmets. The high-backed wing chairs belonged in a home for the elderly. Non-descript pictures hung randomly. Stanford made no complaint about her surroundings, as she enjoyed the company of two QBD mates and she was far too busy working to notice anything much beyond her desk.

Arriving at purpose-built city lodgings, I laughed that it was like a nursing home but less cheery. All it needed was a stair lift, and more departmental savings could be made if it were rented out for geriatric respite care. David J said its nickname was 'The Crematorium'. No judge grumbled at such surroundings. They listed far greater priorities for tax payers' money, such as staff pay, court IT systems and the general social exclusion of the people appearing before them. Lodgings provided a happy opportunity to interact with their contemporaries and they all had their own 'space'. Good company and food made up for the gloom.

Being confined for six weeks with some judges could be trying. Lady Hale's story of being asked to retire with the ladies after dinner in lodgings seems to be universally known. It has transformed into judicial folklore as a scary allegory against judgitis, pomp and farcical sexism. She told it in *Women in the Law*.[40] I had assumed that the events had occurred years earlier but two CJs reported that they had been guests at lodgings in about 2001, when the senior HC judge shocked them as much as Lady Hale by asking her to retire, while they were expected to stay for port and manly conversation. Others said the same judge caused Fisher J to resign from the High Court when he refused to dine with him unless he dressed formally. Baroness Hale explained to me that she was 'a good girl' in lodgings and always retired when asked to do so. There was only one occasion when she refused. She thought it was rude behaviour to ask a guest, the circuit leader, to retire. She said she got a telling off. Men would say to her 'Brenda, don't you realise we need time on our own?'

The pilot-study judge told PJ how jolly one colleague had been at breakfast, wearing his red (Treasury) devil jumper and insisting on egg with marmite soldiers. He always dressed for dinner. PJ said this would not appeal to her. All she wanted to do in lodgings was 'curl up in front of Coronation Street with a cheese sandwich'. In one of the lodgings, I was invited to a 12-person dinner to entertain the sheriff. I was the over-dressed one. Everyone knew Lady Hale's story. One judge's wife announced over starters that the men had better not even think about asking us to retire.

I talked to lodgings staff. Thanks to cutbacks, they were all multi-tasking. In one, the cook answered the door in his chef's outfit. In the second, the manager doubled up as a waitress. As I apologised for getting her up at 5.30 am, to let me out of the security gates, she said she could use the early start to do the ironing. At the third, the manager told me he had qualifications in catering and hospitality. He could justify all his expenditure. His lodgings were heavily used, 37 judges having stayed there in the previous year. With the lodgings' limo system abolished, saving £155,000 the previous year, cars were now supplied by the Government car fleet. The judge, clerk and I were driven to and from court in a people-carrier with dark windows. We joked about being like aged rock chicks, lacking 'the telly and the drinks cabinet'. At the fourth lodgings, a Sierra supplanted the limo. Anyone drove it. The judge welcomed the abolition of limos.

> It really annoyed me when I was in practice, hunting around this court building for some scallywag client, when a summons would come over the tannoy at 11.30 am for the judicial chauffeur, because the judge was ready to go back to lodgings.

The old practice of driving back to lodgings for lunch was, he thought, an 'absurd' relic of circuit life. An HC judge should be content to eat in the court

---

[40] E Cruickshank, *Women in the Law* (London, The Law Society, 2003), repeated in national newspapers.

dining room with the circuit and district judges. At a country lodgings, the excellent cook was a farmer, hired when necessary. The manager, Karen, drove me to the station. She was recruited through her husband who was the grounds man next door. She had been asked to do the lodgings cleaning 'to tide them over'. She stayed on because she loved the job. Driving was added to her job spec. She bought the food. She sometimes worked 60 hours per week in the 36 weeks that the lodgings were used. She helped out at other lodgings when they were busy but she much preferred it to her previous bank job because she had all the school holidays off.

Judges routinely praised staff's kindness. In turn, Karen was defensive of 'her' judges. 'They're all lovely. I've never met an offhand one.' It irritated her when outsiders complained they were 'pampered'. She would point out how they were up and working before she awoke. 'I say they'd be waited-on in a hotel, anyway, wouldn't they? Here, they have peace and quiet and security.' She felt sorry for them in serious trials when 'they have to see and hear awful things'. One had been trying a quadruple child-murder. 'He would come in grey-faced, saying "Karen, I don't want any dinner tonight".'

Staff and judges' clerks had their own social network—real, not Facebook—and both sides looked forward to visits. Clerks, like judges, were great gossips. One said lodgings were their 'information superhighway'. They considered their travelling expenses an essential supplement to their meagre pay so when some HC judges were promoted to the CA, they lost their clerk to new HC judge.

The pilot-study judge was an enthusiast for circuit life. He had made some 'super friends' among sheriffs, whose one-year job[41] is to welcome Her Majesty's judges to the area. One doctor-sheriff had made 'curries to die for'. He had stayed in a sheriff's stately home. A presider could have a 'hectic social life' but he drew the line at two nights a week. It was 'fun' to attend dinners and church services. The highlight was Newcastle's black-tie 'dagger dinner', where judges were presented with a 1620 groat, 'dagger money' to pay for a dagger to ward off brigands as they crossed the Pennines. He told me of processions and services and dinners in Leicester, Liverpool and York, the like of which I had assumed had disappeared with assizes, in 1972. These were defended from extinction by locals and funded by local authorities.

Whaley J was cynical. He thought dinners served a good business purpose to foster links with locals such as the chief constable but he was as embarrassed at having the sheriff sit with him in court as she was to be there. 'I *sometimes* have the guts to introduce them.' He groaned at having sheriffs accompany him from extinct counties. 'Sometimes it's worse—they turn up with their chaplains!' His reluctant sheriff was anxious about having to clean her house thoroughly and

---

[41] Funded by themselves at a cost of up to £50,000. The High Sherrif is the oldest secular office in the UK, dating back to Saxon times. Henry II gave them the job of ensuring the safety and comfort of judges. They used to issue writs, get the assize court, juries and prisoners ready, then execute the sentences: The High Sherrifs' Association of England and Wales website.

cook a dinner for the Lord Chief Justice. She had bought her outfit secondhand and it did not fit. Relatives had nominated her before she got cold feet. The Shrievalty was 'a load of La-La Land if you ask me. I expect you're taking notes on the uselessness of sheriffs'. Lady Whaley, though, found it useful that someone had the job of introducing them to the locals. She had been nervous about accompanying Whaley up North. She worried about what to wear till the sheriff took her shopping.

CONCLUSION

Senior judges were reckoned by the district and circuit bench to be a breed apart, exceptionally intelligent and hard working, confined to the unusually complex, technical and demanding civil cases and on top of this, QBD judges tried the most harrowing and/or complex criminal cases. The High Court and Court of Appeal only function thanks to the recruitment of dedicated lawyers who have developed workaholic habits and for whom a whole weekend or a weekday evening off is a novelty. New judges thought the 'macho' attitude in the QBD—we can do any case and as many as you want—was inefficient, given that they were recruited from an increasingly specialist Bar. They all enjoyed the challenge of having to apply new areas of the law but the Administrative Court was a challenge too far. They considered the pressure of speed was unfair to the litigants. Given that so many had no public law background, it was predictable that researchers recently found its decisions to be inconsistent. The barristers were *much* worse than the judges.

So-called 'reading days' were routinely lost. A never-ending pile of paper applications awaited QBD judges. The dreaded Administrative Court was only eclipsed by the demands of the CACD. Family Division and Commercial Court judges pleaded for reinforcements. Staying with judges in lodgings, I could not keep up, and went to bed at bed-time. Many judges spent about half their working terms travelling. Presiding and liaison judges did even more travelling and added administration and management to their caseload. Northern judges spent the other half a year commuting to London and complained that the cost of travel and renting property in London reduced their remuneration to circuit level. New judges, used to successful chambers and law firms, were shocked to have to wait for office space and a laptop. Although the judges loved their job, none was as ecstatic as the average circuit or district judge. HC judges were far more likely to agree that some of their work was daunting or emotionally disturbing. We saw that they valued wigs as a disguise in high-profile cases where they are surrounded by a media circus or 'where they bury the witnesses'. HC judges deal with death—death of a child in the Family Division; terrorism and the grisliest of gang murders in the Crown Court.

Paradoxically, Jennings ended up with very simple, short cases on circuit. Longer chancery and TCC cases were heard by CJs. The value of the properties took these cases into the High Court allocation but the issues were so very clear cut they could have been determined by a DJ. Nevertheless these HC judges' function was symbolic and practical. They defended the circuit system as bringing the exacting standards of centralised justice to the circuits since 1176.[42] The judges were clear about the shortcomings of local lawyers' advocacy standards but it is impossible to say whether they had any educative impact.

The sheer scale of the multinational cases in the Commercial Court was unmatched elsewhere. Trollope knew he was making international law. The fact that he did this in tacky annexes, without proper IT facilities or an adequate email account, is a testament to the unimportance of the courts, as far as governments are concerned. Lodgings were shabby. Judges did not complain because they knew that there was much more desperate need for spending on court staff and the court system. They were happy that the butlers and limos were gone but they clung to this relic of the circuit system as a home-from-home, somewhere safe and secure and relaxing to return to after yet another day dealing with death. Replacing lodgings with hotel accommodation would have been the last straw.

Apart from mixed ability barristers and shocking tools for the trade, another repeating theme here is LIPs. The judges here were remarkably sympathetic, patient and encouraging, despite their lack of training and lack of interface contact with clients when they practised as lawyers. They pleaded with obsessives to stop bankrupting themselves. Judges were tolerant of litigants without a hope or a case and they received disproportionate court resources and attention. Their increase is not wholly attributable to cutbacks in legal aid, as can be seen by the millionaires appearing before Ossian and Trollope. Their impact on judges is completely unseen and unimportant to governments.

---

[42]   'In 1176 the itinerant justices were organised into six circuits ... investigating crimes and unexplained death, misconduct and negligence by officials...and private disputes', JH Baker, *An Introduction to English Legal History*, 4th edn (London, Butterworths, 2002) 16.

14

The Court of Appeal

3.40 pm, in Rathlin LJ's[1] room, after an appeal turning on statutory interpretation.

> Rathlin, to the two High Court judges: 'Sit down, you two, and don't say anything. I want to hear what Doctor Darbyshire has to say'.
>
> PD: 'You can't ask *me*. That's cheating [High Court judges laugh]'.
>
> Rathlin: 'But you're the nearest thing we're going to get to an academic *now*. You wanted to watch our deliberations'.
>
> PD: 'But not to *participate. I'm* not part of this tribunal [laughing]'.
>
> Rathlin: 'Would it surprise you we've decided to allow this appeal?'
>
> PD: 'No but will you stop asking my opinion? Anyway, I've already given it.'
>
> Rathlin: 'You told me where to find the answers.'
>
> PD: 'And I told you if there was a doubt about interpretation then you should give the benefit of that doubt to the accused.'

THIS CHAPTER EXAMINES the work of the Court of Appeal (CA), including the contribution of High Court (HC) judges in criminal cases. Remarkably, I was permitted unprecedented observation of deliberations.[2] My key findings were that if HC work requires graft, quick-thinking, genius and stamina, then CA work requires these in abundance. Appeals are determined at

---

[1] In this chapter, there are many judges outside the research sample, such as Samson.

[2] Unprecedented in England and Wales. In ch 1, I cited Paterson, commenting on the impenetrability of deliberations to researchers. At 84, he said: 'Denied first-hand access to judicial interaction, dependant on discrepant and ambiguous second hand accounts, scholars in their third-hand efforts reconstruct reality in disparate ways'. I cited Judge Posner, who said we had difficulty in understanding judicial behaviour because they deliberate in secret: *How Judges Think* (Cambridge, Mass, Harvard University Press) 2. Chief Justice Edwards (DC Circuit Court of Appeals) in the article cited at n 54 below, said that academics' analyses were handicapped by the lack of ability to observe deliberations, and thus they underestimated the importance of collegiality. Nevertheless, he was opposed to observers and judicial assistants (JAs) being allowed in. (JAs are allowed in in England and Wales). Edwards mentioned (at 1687) that Latour had observed the deliberations of the Conseil D'Etat over a period of years: B Latour, *La fabrique du droit: Une ethnographie du Conseil d'État* (Paris, La Découverte, 2002).

astonishing speed, given their significance as precedents.[3] Skeleton arguments have transformed judgment formation. On elevation to the CA, judges relinquish the fun element of HC work—travelling on circuit and the cut and thrust of the trial. They seldom escape the Royal Courts of Justice (RCJ) or see a witness under examination but they relish the intellectual challenge and counteract the workload with humour and camaraderie. In a valedictory comment in 2006, Brooke LJ referred to it as 'the friendliest … most hard-working court of the land'.[4]

JUDICIAL WORK

The 37 Lords and Ladies Justices of Appeal (LJs) share appeals with the Lord Chief Justice (LCJ), Master of the Rolls and five Heads of Division, HC judges and a few retired judges. A civil bench may consist of one or more judges,[5] and full appeals are normally heard by three LJs or two and an HC judge. Judges normally gave separate judgments, though there has been a trend to a single or collective judgment. A Court of Appeal (Criminal Division) (CACD) bench consists of at least three for substantive appeals. One LJ normally sits with two HC (QBD) judges, or one HC and one circuit judge (CJ). Sentencing appeals are routinely heard by a pair of HC judges and guideline precedents are set by benches of five.[6] HC[7] and circuit judges[8] enrich the CACD's deliberations with their experience of Crown Court trials. Statute requires a single judgment, with very rare exceptions.[9] In 1996, Pattenden agreed that CACD work was dominated by heavy appeals, from prisoners. It had become much easier to obtain leave, increasing the workload.[10] In 2006, the backlog was reduced[11] but Lord Chief

---

[3]   As it hears thousands of cases per year and the UKSC hears 60, most precedents emanate from the CA.

[4]   *The Court of Appeal Civil Division Review of the Legal Year 2005–06* at 8.

[5]   Senior Courts Act 1981 (1981 Act), as amended by the Access to Justice Act 1999, s 59. Family or Chancery HC judges sit occasionally. QBD judges are too busy.

[6]   For instance, *R v Goodyear (Practice Note)* [2005] EWCA Crim 888 set out important guidelines on plea indications. A five-judge decision is of no higher precedent value. See R Pattenden, *English Criminal Appeals 1844–1994* (Oxford, Clarendon Press, 1996) 38–39. Composition is prescribed by the Senior Courts Act 1981. There is no upper limit.

[7]   See Pattenden, above n 6 at 36.

[8]   A very small number of senior circuit judges are ticketed to sit in the CACD.

[9]   1981 Act, s 59. The presider may permit separate judgments where the question is one of law and he considers it convenient. Pattenden noted that this occurred only twice in the Court's first 40 years (Pattenden, above n 6 at 123).

[10]   Pattenden, above n 6 at 54–56. Since 1997, the total number of appeals entered has declined fairly steadily and slightly: *Judicial and Court Statistics 2009*, version 1.1, revised October 2010, Ministry of Justice. This tells us nothing about the type of appeals or judicial workload, however, because appeals lodged in the HC (also heard by CA and HC judges) have increased from 5,000 to 15,000 since 1996 and the administrative work of the judges has increased. Work is reviewed in depth, with more statistics, in the Court's Annual Reviews.

Justice Phillips remarked that the cases were more complex, caused by 'labyrinthine' legislation.[12] Civil appeals have declined since 1995, almost flat-lining since 2002.[13]

Both divisions describe themselves as courts of review.[14] Given that most appeals finish in the CA, its role in interpreting and developing the law is far broader than that of the UK Supreme Court (UKSC). In the Civil Division, presiders may call on judicial research assistants.[15] Statistical and legal information can be gleaned from the annual *Judicial and Court Statistics*, annual reviews[16] and in depth from analyses by Pattenden[17] and Drewry, Blom-Cooper and Blake.[18]

MANAGEMENT JOBS

CA judges have a role in managing courts, caseload, judges and procedure, because they head the England and Wales hierarchy.[19] Most outsiders are unaware of this.[20] Thanks to the Woolf[21] and Bowman Reports[22] management was intensifying even before Lord Phillips acquired over 60 civil servants in 2006 to help him as the first LCJ to run the judiciary.[23] Senior managers spend up to half their time on management. There are 12 secondary management jobs, such as

---

[11] CACD Review, to September 2006, Criminal Appeal Office. The LCJ's remark is quoted from there.

[12] Sympathising with trial judges struggling to interpret the Criminal Justice Act 2003 in the context of other legislation, Rose LJ repeatedly called it 'labyrinthine': *R v Ford* [2005] EWCA Crim 1358, para 11; *R. v Lang and others* [2005] EWCA Crim 2864, paras 16 and 153.

[13] *Judicial and Court Statistics*.

[14] *R v McIlkenny and others* [1991] 2 All ER 417, the Birmingham Six's successful appeal, and CPR, r 52.11, which, taken together with *Assicurazioni Guerdi SpA v Arab Insurance Group (BSC)* [2002] EWCA Civ 1642, *Jaffray v Society of Lloyds* [2002] EWCA Civ 1101 and other cases means all appeals in the CA Civil Division are reviews, according to G Drewry, L Blom-Cooper and C Blake, *The Court of Appeal (Civil Division)* (Oxford, Hart Publishing, 2007) 22–23.

[15] They are not normally attached to individual judges.

[16] By the Lord Chief Justice and the Master of the Rolls, on the Judiciary website and HM Courts Service website, respectively.

[17] See Pattenden, above n 6.

[18] Drewry et al, above n 14.

[19] When judges move to the UKSC they shed management jobs and have a less frenetic life.

[20] The HC judges were unaware, as lawyers, of the HC management jobs, let alone CA jobs.

[21] The Rt Hon The Lord Woolf, Master of the Rolls, *Access to Justice: Final Report* (London, HMSO, 1996).

[22] Sir Jeffrey Bowman, *Review of the Court of Appeal (Civil Division)*, 1997. Summary on the DCA archived website.

[23] Implementing the enhanced separation of powers and wrought by the Constitutional Reform Act 2005. Lord Phillips, new Lord Chief Justice at that time said:

It was plain that the functions that were to be transferred to me would have to be shared among my senior colleagues … if I was to have time to continue to sit as a judge … I formed a Judicial Executive Board consisting of the Master of the Rolls, the President of the Queen's Bench Division, the President of the Family Division, the Chancellor, the Vice-President of the Queen's Bench Division, who performs the crucial and challenging function of organising

chairman of the Judicial College, head of IT and judges in charge of specialist lists.[24] They liaise with other judges, ministers and civil servants; chair courts boards and rule committees and court user groups; visit circuit administrators and judges; spend hours with IT providers; train judges and manage sections of the Judicial College; organise national and international conferences and host foreign judges and delegations. The bonus is escape from the Royal Courts of Justice (RCJ).

Managers did not appear resentful. The current generation appear to throw themselves into management enthusiastically.[25] They expand out-of-court jobs by producing annual reports, devising conferences, fostering international links and travelling on circuit (and indeed sitting—Sir Igor Judge[26] sat in the Crown Court in 2006). They enthusiastically demonstrated software they were keen to promote.[27] Nevertheless, three cited their interface with the executive as the most frustrating element of their job: 'chairing a difficult committee' and

> the enormous amount of effort and time it takes me to get anything like a [departmental] decision ... the culture ... of civil servants is so different ... We were brought up as barristers to think everything was dealt with. People come with a crisp point ... or series of points. It sometimes takes a bit of time to unravel; you give the answer and everyone goes away happy.

> The necessary, perhaps the excellent caution of senior officials and junior ministers to contemplate any sort of family law reform that promises to be contentious, innovative, daring.

> the deployment of the High Court Queen's Bench Judiciary, and the Senior Presiding Judge, who acts as my Chief of Staff.

(Speech and video, 'Constitutional Reform—One Year On', 22 March 2007, JSB annual lecture, Judiciary website). According to Lord Judge's *Review of the Administration of Justice*, February 2010, it meets weekly. A full list of responsibilities is on the Judiciary website. The team also includes the VP of the Family Division, the VPs of the CA Criminal and Civil, the Deputy Heads of Civil and Family Justice, the Deputy Senior Presiding Judge (SPJ) and the Senior President of Tribunals. There are Nominated Judges for Complaints and Discipline. Lord Phillips' speech also describes the relationship of the Executive Board with the Judges' Council, also detailed on the Judiciary website.

[24] Judiciary website.

[25] In the 2007 speech, cited above, Lord Phillips said:

rather to my surprise, I enjoy the administration, and I believe that this is true of most... Judging is necessarily a solitary task, and can be lonely. It contrasts with the teamwork involved in the administrative duties ... Judges at all levels are working much more closely with members of the Court Service than has ever been the case in the past.

[26] Then SPJ and Head of Criminal Justice.

[27] Drewry et al, above n 14 at 65 observed how seriously CA judges now take their management jobs and 'things have moved on' since J Plotnikoff and R Woolfson, in 2002, found 'little judicial appetite' for management: *Judges' Case Management Perspectives: The Views of Opinion Formers and Case Managers*, LCD Research Report No 3/2002, summarised on the DCA archived website. Lord Phillips, 2007, explained: 'None of us had gone on the Bench because of a love of administrative duties...This led us to enrol in ... a short course on management and leadership'.

THE RESEARCH SAMPLE AND BONUS JUDGES

I work-shadowed four LJs and interviewed them and four more[28] but because the core four and the HC sample judges sat in various constitutions, I observed 20 CA judges, some repeatedly, and consulted four more about this research.[29] Five HC judges were elevated to the CA in the research period. I observed one as an LJ. I watched three of the HC sample sitting in the CA, plus a further 13 HC judges. I spent 26 non-sequential days in the CA, in 2003–05, and watched deliberations in all but one constitution. I have been casually observing the court since 1971.

All LJs are generalists, though around 15 do only civil work.[30] None sits only in crime.[31] The CACD supervising LJ said he tried to construct balanced constitutions. Ideally, each should contain a crime specialist. A new HC judge had to be accompanied by an experienced colleague. There was little flexibility. Seven constitutions can sit contemporaneously, using the six RCJ courtrooms with cell-access. Supervising LJs tried to fix civil benches of three to contain two specialists. The eight research judges came from non-criminal backgrounds: family, admiralty, administrative, chancery and construction law. Two were senior managers and had two days per week set aside. Four had secondary management jobs but no time allotted.

WORKLOAD AND INTELLECTUAL STIMULATION

Conversations with LJs in the 1980s alerted me to their workload.[32] There can be no lapses in concentration, given that most precedent emanates from the CA. Because the workload is known to be an 'ordeal',[33] judges normally only sit on criminal appeals for three weeks, although some stalwarts do them 'back-to-back'. Rathlin, a civil lawyer, was offered a CA post during the research period on condition that he would do 'double crime', an indication of the demand. Ebony LJ sat for four three-week blocks per year in the CACD, in four constitutions. Each included four reading days. A routine day consisted of a dozen or more

---

[28]   This chapter also includes interview-clips from two UKSC Justices.

[29]   Including Lord Judge, who gave me intense help and Sedley LJ, one of my research consultants.

[30]   Including the President of the Family Division and the Chancellor of the Chancery Division.

[31]   Though till 2006, Rose LJ sat exclusively in the CACD and QBD Divisional Court.

[32]   In those days the workload was civil, resulting in a 'backlog of major proportions', R Matineau, *Appellate Justice in England and the United States: A Comparative Analysis* (Buffalo, Hein, 1990) xiii. Now civil appeals have declined but the Court is driven by its criminal workload.

[33]   Pattenden, above n 6 at 56. In 1980, Lord Roskill likened the CA job to slavery: D Pannick, *Judges* (Oxford, Oxford University Press, 1987) 5. In *R v Fortean* [2009] EWCA Crim 798 the Court condemned meritless applications, saying it was 'coping' with 6,000 applications a year.

sentencing appeals, or eight sentencing appeals and renewed applications for leave to appeal in the morning and a substantive appeal on a point of law or mixed fact and law in the afternoon. One said 'Nothing beats the 16 sentencing appeals I had one day'. Judges often caught me laughing at the farcical contrast between the speed of creating precedents, and the leisurely, nit-picking, academic analysis to which they would be subjected for years to come. One HC judge said:

> The reading load … is … too great. The remarkable thing about the CACD is that there are no major mistakes … the judgments … are sometimes analysed semantically, as though they are statute, and the reality is that [they] are off-the-cuff thoughts of a very clever and a very learned Lord Justice. Generally speaking, he has had the papers a day or two before … it is only the enormous ability of these people that keeps the train on track.[34]

HC judge Ossian complained of the 'moral pressure' to get judgments written, despite the fact that writing-time is not scheduled, even in complex appeals, as can be seen with Brewer LJ and Whaley J, below. A UKSC Justice described having been a new boy.

> The criminal stints … were extremely exhausting, gruelling and relentless. But to start with in the civil sphere you were always 'number three' and the presiding judges were undertaking the bulk of the work so you might only write a judgment every three or four weeks.

Judges all worked long hours but organised their schedules differently. Lee LJ worked in the RCJ until nine on three weekdays, staying in a London flat and commuting home on Wednesdays. He came into the RCJ on Sundays, to avoid working at home. Others had established family homes close by. One of these worked at home as much as possible, including weekends. Two did a long daily commute and a northerner commuted weekly. They worked on the train. Lee's clerk gave me an account of a December week in the CACD. He arrived around 8.15 am:

Monday morning, reading papers for cases on Monday afternoon and Tuesday, repeatedly interrupted by phone calls on his management job. 1.40 pm, his two accompanying HC judges came to discuss the afternoon's cases. In court until 4.55 pm. Worked until 9.10 pm.

---

[34] UKSC Justice Lady Hale was not so confident about mistakes. She acknowledged that one argument in favour of retention of a top UK court

> lies in the manifest deficiencies of the Court of Appeal (at least in its civil division where I sat). We worked under considerable pressure of time … The quality of our decisions was very heavily dependent on the quality of the arguments before us, and this is very variable … Above all, the Court sits in approximately 11 constitutions each week. Inevitably, members do not always know what the others are doing … There is a real risk of outright inconsistency: B Hale, 'A Supreme Court for the United Kingdom?' (2004) 24 *Legal Studies* (1 & 2) 36, 39.

Tuesday 9.00 am admin meeting. Met his HC judges at 10.10 am to deliberate. Sat until 4.30 pm. Went to party briefly at 5.00 pm. Worked until after 9.00 pm.

Wednesday Handed-down a judgment then worked in chambers all day. 'Poked his nose' into two parties. Caught the 6.45 pm train home.

Thursday Handed-down a judgment at 9.45 am. At 10.15 am his HC judges arrived. Court all day. Civil CA party at 5.00 pm. Worked until 9.00 pm.

Friday 'A long day' in court. Took his two HC judges out to lunch, 1.00–2.00 pm, as one of them was retired.

Sunday All day in the RCJ, writing a judgment.

Some lost 'reading days' to admin meetings. All said the workload impacted on family life but this had been the case since they had joined the Bar. The judge above said he liked hard work but a senior manager, who looked tired and whose clerk complained he was overworked said:

> It seems to get worse ... from year to year ... that may be because ... I am getting older and ... my stamina and resilience are inevitably reducing.

Much of his vacation was spent organising international conferences and hosting foreign judicial visitors. Others called the work 'relentless'. Another, who had avoided being recruited onto senior management, considered his workload demanding but acceptable. A new boy, Bland LJ, who only heard civil appeals, found the workload of a novice less demanding than chancery HC work.

> From time to time it has been jolly hard work ... but half the time it is significantly less than I expected. We have three reading days a fortnight ... I don't think I had a day without sitting in the Chancery Division ... the idea of having three days a fortnight is just ludicrous to me ... I do give up part of my vacation to write judgments.

Why do judges put up with this? As corny as it sounds, many said this was pay-back time, repaying the society that had given them such a good living, as lawyers. As Posner has remarked:

> The hypothesis that judges are motivated by a desire to be good workers is supported by the superficially puzzling existence of a judicial work ethic ... most federal judges work pretty hard, often well past the age at which they could retire ... most ... derive considerable intrinsic satisfaction ... and want to be able to regard themselves and to be regarded by others as good judges.[35]

What stimulated them, most in their seventh decade, was the intellectual exercise. Every interviewee named judgment writing as the most satisfying aspect of their work.

---

[35] Posner, above n 2 at 61–62.

Very interesting ... demanding intellectually ... hard work, which I like.

I like the intellectual challenge ... and the variety ... I have been lucky really because some of the work in the commercial courts and the CA is quite academic ... I also like the oral argument.

I like law as a discipline and a subject ... You enjoy the responsibility.

I see my primary role as the evolution of family law, given that the evolutionary process through statutory reform is impeded by the weakness of government ... They are extremely loathe to embark on family law reforms because they are regarded as negative...in terms of electioneering and public image, and of course family law requires constant evolution if it is not to fall behind social change so the Court of Appeal is very important ... My second is to develop the significance of international family law and the influence of the UK ... [and then my role within this jurisdiction] by getting the various disciplines to really share the problem and look for common solutions.

Posner has called judges 'occasional legislators'[36] but the quotation below shows that in some fields of law, neglected by Parliament and seldom coming before the UKSC, CA judges are *regular* legislators.

It is a fascinating job ... I like intellectual problems ... By the time it comes to the Court of Appeal, the thing has been distilled and refined. The first instance judge has to make all the findings and he may have had to decide 10 points ... there may be an appeal on one or two ... we put the microscope on those points ... We have the luxury ... of being able to concentrate on those points and with the benefit of usually three of us. So I love it.

Intellectual satisfaction of grappling with a problem

I like making decisions about deep questions which may have, I hope, beneficial effects in important areas of people's lives ... I am very interested in ... constitutional law ... cases which engage the differences between [the three organs of government] and the tension between them.

Four of the eight found family cases or those involving children the most difficult or emotionally disturbing. One was gratified not to have been a family judge.

... cases where I find it very difficult not to cry ... my wife says it right—they normally involve parents and children. I am quite an easy crier ... In the Court of Appeal it is much easier because you don't have witnesses ... I would have been in a permanent state of waterworks if I had been a family judge.

One family judge described some of the disturbing trials he had conducted. He found the CA 'much easier, because you can share it'.

---

[36] Posner, above n 2 at 5 and the chapter entitled 'The judge as occasional legislator'.

BEING 'MESSED ABOUT' BY LAWYERS

Pre-trial reading of skeleton arguments and document bundles has transformed HC and appellate work since the 1980s.[37] Drewry et al cited Lord Evershed describing the very different procedure in 1950, 'the Court knew nothing of a case until it was opened by the appellant's counsel' and 'it is well within the memory of the writers that counsel for each party commonly read to the court at dictation speed the main points they wished to make'.[38] It was within the memory of judges too. 'Years ago, the Court of Appeal would have had 20 minutes leisurely conversation before going into court', remarked Kind, wistfully, having taken home the papers only to discover that three vital documents were missing. His clerk had frantically borrowed copies from another judge, leaving just five minutes' vital deliberation time, pre-court.

Until the 1990s, CA judges resisted copying their US brethren[39] to supplant oral advocacy with written arguments and although judges now take pre-reading for granted and they have been encouraged to limit oral argument since 1994–95, they would be highly unlikely to limit it to the 20 or 30 minutes permitted before the European Court of Justice or the 60 minutes before the US Supreme Court. UK appellate judges love the forensic verbal polo of the oral hearing, smiling as they take turns to question a good advocate, refining the advocate's argument and their thought processes. Bland, gleeful in these interchanges, said 'I know I talk too much in court'. Ebony said 'I like the oral argument. I wouldn't like to spend

---

[37] Cemented by Practice Direction in the CA in 1989, discussed by Martineau, *Appellate Justice in England and the United States* (Hein, Buffalo, 1990), copying Commercial Court practice, on the urging of the Civil Justice Review 1988 (*Report of the Review Body on Civil Justice*, CM 394, London, HMSO) ch 4, then reinforced by the Heilbron-Hodge Report: *Civil Justice on Trial—the Case for Change* (London, The General Council of the Bar and The Law Society, 1993). Practice directions requiring exchange of skeleton arguments emerged the next year. The directions permitted the court to limit oral submissions, discovery, examination of witnesses and reading aloud. See P Darbyshire, *Darbyshire on the English Legal System*, 10th edn (London, Sweet & Maxwell, 2011) ch 9.

[38] Drewry et al, above n 14 at 40 and 38. And in my memory, of course. Taylor LCJ said in 1993 that when he started at the Bar, 'one started by reading out loud to the court of three, the whole of the trial judge's judgment and such parts of the transcript of evidence as were material', lecture cited in ch 2.

[39] They were aware of American practice. They experimented with written material from 1962, when the CA had 12 judges. See D Karlen, 'Appeals in England and the United States' (1962) 78 *LQR* 371. A more concerted effort was made from 1982, provoking resistance. The state of the CA in 1987, with its overwhelming backlog, is portrayed by Martineau, above n 37. Per judge, they heard one third of the appeals of their US counterparts. Lower courts determined their workload. Parties dictated the length of oral argument. He demolished the English defences of orality, highlighting the appalling standard of advocacy and preparedness, the lack of research and other staff, the time-wasting, the pointless duplication in judgments and so on. See whole book, esp from 123, on his observations.

my life only reading American-style briefs and hardly ever going into court'.[40] Sedley LJ has defended orality. If the advocate wants to keep the court's attention,

> they must steer the court to those documents which matter … And it's surprising how often the dialectic of courtroom discussion changes one's mind—usually by direct persuasion, occasionally by the process noted by the Italian lawyer Piero Calamandrei, when the joyous victor fails to appreciate that it's the other side's lawyer he should be embracing.[41]

Scheduling works on the interdependent assumptions that paperwork will be delivered to the opposition and judges in good time and that judges' schedules will permit pre-reading. One striking finding of this research at every level of court and in each jurisdiction, criminal, civil and family, was that in a substantial proportion of cases, the scheme did not work as intended by rules and practice directions. CA judges, like HC judges, lost reading days to other work. Documentation was frequently delivered late, lawyers not appreciating how long it would take to filter through the building. A crucial family appeal was heard in the glare of publicity and a BBC documentary. The BBC team argued that new evidence should be admitted but gave the judges no time to read it, as it was delivered on the morning of the hearing. One judge was preoccupied in trying to draft a press release, to correct the BBC's version of events. In an administrative law case, one judge was told en route to court that a supplementary skeleton had been submitted. The barrister did not apologise, merely acknowledging it should have been delivered two weeks earlier. In an appeal from the Technology and Construction Court (TCC), lengthy, amended skeletons were delivered 10 minutes before the hearing. In an employment appeal, a clerk wasted time looking for missing pages and no judge had received the bundle of authorities. 'Oh well, less for us to read then', laughed one, as they walked to court. The clerk grumbled that this barrister's chambers were 'a shambles'. In court, the barrister did not apologise, explaining he had emailed his chambers to ask them to send the authorities but they did not receive the email. The judges did not complain, merely observing that an earlier judge had remarked on the shambolic state of the papers.

In the CACD, Ossian was tired and had lost his reading day to writing the planning litigant in person (LIP) judgment. At lunchtime in a crowded list, he received a new skeleton in a big fraud starting the following day. The fax, in 10-point font, was barely readable. Late delivery was caused by the appellant dismissing his previous legal team. The following day, the presider chastised.

> Presider   'I was reading this between five and six this morning! It's hopeless if you don't get the skeleton to us before the reading day or, at least, before the weekend.'

> Counsel   'My Lord, I can only apologise. I have no excuses.'

---

[40]   Martineau (above n 37) remarked on this hostility to 'American style briefs', articulated for the best part of a century.

[41]   S Sedley, 'Second Time Around' (2007) 29 *London Review of Books* 14–15.

Presider	'When the Criminal Appeal Office contacted your chambers, they were told you were on holiday and couldn't be contacted and nobody knew about this. That's not good enough.'
Counsel	'[squirming] I can only repeat my apology, My Lord.'
Presider	'We haven't got a skeleton from the Crown and they haven't had time to prepare one, I expect.'

Crown counsel had started working on a skeleton the previous night and could get 'something' prepared by two. The judge asked for a time estimate, warning that they might not be able to hear the case today. Counsel left. The judges disposed of a long list of sentencing appeals. After lunch, Ossian and the other HC judge, Lucinda J, started worrying about how long this appeal would take. She suggested he could defer judgment. 'Oh no!' he said, horrified. By 3.00 pm, though, they had heard arguments and dismissed the appeal. The presider thanked Crown counsel for preparing a skeleton so swiftly 'and enabling us to deliver our judgment *today*'.

Lawyers caused another problem—wasting judicial time by withdrawing arguments after judges had pre-read them. One said that last-minute settlement of civil appeals was the most frustrating aspect of his job. In the pilot study, three complained in the CACD that they had been reading from daybreak and then adjusted their day's case list to accommodate a 'big European point', only to be told the appellant was withdrawing that ground. 'It's not on is it?' grumbled the presider, as they left the courtroom, 'Messing us about'. In most cases, lawyers did deliver in time for pre-reading but *every* CA and HC judge was affected by failures. This defeats the object of procedural rules and makes judges read into the night. If no documentation is delivered, the judges may not grasp all the issues. Court time is wasted in oral explanation. Because scheduling is tight, the timing of other cases is affected. If judges cannot grasp a case by the end of a hearing, they reserve judgment. They dread this.

Judges showed remarkable tolerance. Occasionally, the CA loses patience and issues a reminder of the rules. They amended a Civil Practice Direction (PD 52) in 2004 and explained the changes in *Scribes West Ltd v Relsa Anstalt (No 1)*.[42] Brooke LJ complained bitterly of a 'proliferation of bundles' and 'widespread ignorance of provisions which were designed to assist the court'. He warned of cost sanctions and reminded advocates that if they failed to file papers a week ahead they could be summoned before the presider to seek permission to proceed. This followed other complaints of lawyers failing to inform the court when a case was settled[43] and failures to comply with practice directions on the citation of authorities that 'verged on the scandalous'.[44]

---

[42] [2004] EWCA Civ 835.
[43] *Yell v Garton* [2004] EWCA Civ 87.
[44] *Bank of Scotland v Henry Butcher (a Firm)* [2003] EWCA Civ 67, para 77, per Munby LJ.

As all interviewees said, the quality of advocacy was very variable, as advocates of all levels of experience, from six circuits, bring their appeals. In the CACD, barristers are generally unaccompanied by solicitors. On a morning of sentencing appeals, a barrister said it was Northern Circuit practice to remind trial judges of their sentencing powers. 'I think you can take it there's some judicial knowledge of practice on the Northern Circuit', smiled Deer LJ, a northerner, accompanied by the Northern Circuit Presider. Another lawyer invoked the *Leicester Mercury* in his argument. 'It has a good circulation in Leicester.' 'But not in the Court of Appeal, Mr X', quipped Deer. Later, the court heard accents from South London, Devon and Northern Ireland.

Ossian and a retired judge, Lucinda, believed there were lawyers who touted for criminal appeal business in prisons. They would concoct lots of 'plausible and impressive' grounds, said Lucinda.

> Then in court you hear prosecution counsel who was there [at the trial] … and it's all rubbish … Often the defendant is dismissing a defence team who you *know* are excellent and will have done their best.

Ossian thought there were lawyers who went looking for judicial review work in prisons too.

Judges would sometimes discuss the lawyers who were to appear before them. 'He's the shittiest barrister'; 'He got X off'; 'He's *awful*'. Most advocates had dropped the grovelling language, traditional in the 1970s. If the bench anticipated a groveller, this provoked derision and mimicry. 'He's such a *smoothie*—"The last few minutes have been such a *pleasure*, your Lordships".' In their pre-hearing discussion above, the Old Hand warned Ebony about a barrister. 'He's awful. He's been complained about to the Bar Council.' 'What? For being awful?' laughed Ebony LJ. In court, the advocate was hamming it up, with gesticulation and flourishes. Ebony was trying to speed him up.

> With the *deepest* of respect … I would be insulting my Lords if I were to take the matter further … I will be brief, following the great examples set before me.

He waffled until Ebony LJ asked what his points were. One lunchtime, a colleague came in to laugh with Whaley J about a long-winded cross-examiner, appearing before him. 'He's a cross between Hugh Grant and the bloke off *Blackadder*', mimicking Hugh Laurie, head cocked sideways.

In big civil appeals, judges engaged in practical, enthusiastic dialogue, smiling and debating with lawyers who were their intellectual equals and with whom they might be familiar. Although the Bar has expanded from just over 1,900 in 1960 to 15,000 now, the elite of the London Bar ply their trade in the Royal Courts of Justice. I watched a QC who was the opposite of the groveller. His behaviour would not have been tolerated in the 1970s. He was angry and impatient. The opposition were applying to admit evidence they had just sent in to the judges that morning, in an adjourned appeal. 'We can't have an appeal that is allowed to ramble on and on and we might look at *these* documents and *these* documents!'

he demanded. All three judges entered into separate dialogues with him, smiling and patient. He contradicted Ebony, 'That's not fair!' Outside the courtroom at lunchtime, Cairns LJ smiled to me 'You're seeing the Court of Appeal at its best—or its worst'. 'Is he the son of Lord Lakely?' I asked, recognising the former Law Lord's name. 'Yes, and similarly bombastic', replied Ebony 'but the art of good advocacy is to concede points to the other side. You need to get the judges on your side if you want to win'. Back in court, the more cross and red-faced Lakely QC became, the more serenely patient and smiley they were. 'We really can't proceed like this! It's not fair!' Cairns tried to placate him, intimating that by the time they had finished hearing all of this argument, they may as well have heard the appeal. They did not chide him. They wore expressions like the embarrassed parents of a child throwing a public tantrum.

LITIGANTS IN PERSON—LAST CHANCE

By the CA stage, litigants have become desperate. Some parents have lost their reason along with their children (and irrational, aggressive behaviour may have lost them contact with the children at first instance).[45] CA judges know they are the last hope. They are on the receiving end of volleys of tension, wound up over years. The LIP wants them to re-take the judgment, which they cannot. By emphasising objectivity, they aim to dissipate enough tension to allow them to communicate their reasoning.[46] Experienced judges know that the only way to get through LIPs' circumstantial 'deafness',[47] wrought by anxiety, is to explain themselves repeatedly, slowly and calmly, fully explaining their reasoning, in plain English.

Kind LJ heard two LIP cases in four days. One was represented by a McKenzie Friend who was determined to argue the same point repeatedly, that the father had been denied residence because of membership of Fathers 4 Justice, 'a gross violation of his human rights'. Kind explained that both parents and the children had human rights and where those conflicted, children's rights took precedence. McKenzie Man remained standing, and arguing, as Kind gave judgment. A chorus of four supporting old folk at the back of the court tut-tutted. In another case, Kind spoke gently to a quiet, articulate mother in a hopeless application, on the brink of losing her child forever. He had been taken into care when she became depressed and was about to be adopted. Her fluent submissions were written on notepaper. Kind acknowledged:

---

[45]   See examples of attacks on judges in ch 17.
[46]   Drewry et al, above n 14 at 134, remark of LIPs: 'They exhibit an unremitting commitment to the rightness, even self-righteousness of their cause'.
[47]   In *Magistrates' Justice* (London: Martin Robertson, 1979), P Carlen explained how defendants would agree that they had understood the bench's explanation when they had not been able to listen properly, as nervousness had impeded concentration.

> Your circumstances are tragic. You were raped in 2003, your mental health suffered and you didn't receive sufficient help from the local authority ... Nevertheless [refusing leave] my job is not to ask what judgment would I have made but whether the judgment is manifestly unfair.

Sobbing, she said she was losing her child through no fault of her own.

As can be seen from the annual reviews of the Court of Appeal (Civil Division), the resources occupied by hopeless applications and vexatious litigants became an increasing cause of judicial concern from 2000. In 2002–03 the Master of the Rolls said that almost 40 per cent of applicants for permission were LIPs, of whom 90 per cent were unsuccessful.[48] The rules were changed in 2006 to permit a judge considering a paper application for permission to appeal to mark it as 'totally without merit', in which case it is not renewable orally. The 2005–06 CA *Review of the Legal Year* reported that this measure had 'reduced the scale of the problem'.[49]

DELIBERATION AND JUDGMENT FORMATION IN THE COURT OF APPEAL (CIVIL DIVISION)

Where a trial judgment was given by an HC judge, the LJ will give the appeal judgment. Conviction appeals are virtually always listed for the presiding LJ. In complex appeals, they might delegate part of the writing, as can be seen in Brewer and Whaley's case, below. Otherwise, in each list, the Criminal Appeals Office proposes who will give judgment.[50] Prior to a day's hearing, judges will meet to discuss the cases at around 10.10 am, having read the appeal office summary and the papers. Remarkably, they normally manage to express provisional views on each case by 10.30 am when they enter court. As Posner[51] said, 'judges deliberate in secret, though it would be more accurate to say that the fact that they do not deliberate ... very much is the real secret'.[52] During the research, judges demonstrated how office case summaries formed the basis of a judgment.[53] HC Peter said that, on becoming a judge, he had shared my surprise that judges could pre-deliberate a whole day's work in 15 minutes. Like all judges, he showed me what he had done in preparation. Leaving the pre-read material in his room, he carried a slim ring-binder of essential information and had written a few notes

---

[48]   Examined in Drewry et al, above n 14 at ch 9.

[49]   Drewry et al (above n 14) think parties seeking permission to appeal should be obliged to be legally represented.

[50]   Subject to renegotiation between the judges or alteration by the presider.

[51]   In 2011, he is a Judge of the US Court of Appeals in Chicago, appointed 1981 and chief judge in 1993–2000. He is senior lecturer at the University of Chicago and a prolific writer. See University website.

[52]   Posner, above n 2 at 2.

[53]   Pattenden, above n 6 at 45, describes these and explains that they used to be confidential until 1992. See Practice Direction [1992] 1 WLR 398 and (No 2) [2000] WLR 1177.

on each case and, on the previous day, had handwritten his draft judgments. Others word-processed notes and judgments. One retired judge arrived with notes on scraps of paper but his extempore judgments were just as fluent. Attentive pre-reading prepared judges to be vigilant over lawyers who tried to draw too flattering a portrait of the appellant. In one case, counsel argued that his client should be given credit for not fleeing the scene of a road accident. Peter swiftly corrected him: the appellant *had* fled and been identified by his abandoned motorcycle. In another case, a judge laughed with his colleagues, outside the courtroom, after counsel's compelling speech 'made me forget what a nasty piece of work the appellant was until I read out my own [pre-written] judgment'.

Watching pre- and post-hearing deliberations, I was interested to see whether patterns emerged, or whether the HC judges tended to defer to their seniors, the LJs. I found neither. The approach depended on the presider.[54] Rathlin LJ shared the practice of a very experienced LJ, Matheson. These two *always* sought the views of the two HC juniors before expressing any opinion. Rathlin explained he had copied his Parole Board training. In other constitutions, the HC judge who had drafted the judgment gave his opinion first, then the other HC judge, then the LJ. When an LJ had prepared the judgment, he might give his opinion first, unlike Rathlin. As for the issue of dominance over the deliberation, I observed four constitutions with eminent LJs from civil backgrounds who remained conversationally passive, listening to retired HC judges with extensive criminal trial experience. They were engaging not just their wide and deep knowledge of the law and procedure but of day-to-day tactics by lawyers or defendants in criminal trials, as well as their prior experience of appellate judging. One veteran cynically referred to 'that old trick', when an appellant had made allegations against a juror on the last day of a trial. The LJ asked what his elder thought of calling witnesses to court to give live evidence. 'Well', *I* wouldn't call them.' Most deliberation pre-trial, and in the corridor behind the courtroom during breaks, took the form of the latter answering the former's questions, with the third HC judge, a new (civil) appointee, participating very little. In another case, the retired HC judge was an ex-circuit judge and thus doubly valuable to a new LJ.

> This is where the old circuit judge bursts out of me. We would never send one of these down for so long in Crimespot. There are so many of them. [And in the next case] You have just got to grit your teeth and let them go when they've done all their sentence on remand, however much you find it difficult.

Elsewhere, Ebony commenced deliberations at 10.20 am with a retired old hand and an HC judge but the dialogue was between the first two. In the first case, the

---

[54]   Harry T Edwards, 'The Effects of Collegiality on Decision Making' (2003) 151 *University of Pennsylvania Law Review* 1639 explained that in the Court of Appeals for the DC Circuit, the judges speak in reverse order of seniority (at 1665), like the UKSC. In the USSC, Justices speak in order of seniority. In tribunal training in the UK, chairs are trained to consult their 'wingers' first.

old hand had prepared the judgment. He gave his opinion and the others agreed. Ebony had prepared the judgment in the second, a renewed application for leave to appeal, on the grounds that the trial judge had failed to explain that the burden of negating self-defence was on the prosecution. Ebony summarised the prosecution's position.

> Ebony: 'Once they've got the knives with the bouncer's DNA on it, it's difficult to see how they could run self-defence. Could self-defence ever be a runner?'
>
> [The passive HC judge agreed but the old hand was not happy.]
>
> Old Hand: 'It was fundamentally flawed and the jury asked a question on self-defence.'
>
> Ebony: 'Well, if you're unhappy Phillip, I'll go along with that.'
>
> Old hand: 'I think it's a case for a retrial.'
>
> Ebony: 'They're bloody well guilty but I suppose that's got nothing to do with it!'

Ebony explained that if one judge in the CACD felt that an application for permission to appeal should be granted then it would be, regardless of the views of the other two.

LJs frequently told me how valuable circuit judges were because of their trial experience. I had cynically presumed they were deployed as a cost-saving measure. It appeared that they were performing the very function the 1993 Royal Commission on Criminal Justice[55] envisioned. A number of CJs are respected specialists. One constitution was hesitant in an appeal against a sentence imposed by a CJ who was a renowned sentencing writer. They decided they had better wait to be addressed by counsel.

In about nine out of 10 cases, the judges had made their decision pre-court and they stuck to it. Where they agreed to reduce a sentence, a judge would often suggest 'Shall we make him an offer?' The presider would stop appellant counsel opening and make the offer. Normally, the advocate assented. In about one in 10 cases, including substantive appeals on points of law or mixed fact and law, oral argument would persuade judges to change their minds. Extempore modification after a two-minute deliberation took skill. A more complex change of mind in a case raising a substantial point would require a frantic lunch rewrite but anything requiring reasoned rethinking, perhaps based on further deliberation, would have to be reserved. Like the trial judges in earlier chapters, they strived to deliver extempore judgments.

A change might occur even where the judges unanimously proposed dismissal, especially where a new argument was raised. One afternoon, HC judges David J and Pitt J came to Lee LJ's room at 1.45 pm to prepare for the afternoon's hearing. After five minutes' discussion, the judges had written-off a murder appeal as 'hopeless' and started discussing the next day's list. By 1.58 pm, they

---

[55]   CM 2263 (London, HMSO) 178.

had discussed all their cases for the following day. In their swift discussion of the substantive appeal, most of the points raised were by the presider, giving his opinion initially. In the courtroom, by 2.09 pm, the presider plunged straight into a dialogue with the two QCs. Pre-reading and pre-deliberation enabled the in-court argument to be truncated to staccato exchanges. The presider inter-rupted the appellant's opening, 'You don't have to work very hard on that'. Citing the relevant precedent and statute, the judge articulated the first ground. By 2.25 pm, he invited submissions on the second. 'If [N] had been the case, then you would have been arguing [V].' Counsel laughed, fawning, 'I couldn't have put it better myself, My Lord.' The presider started a new dialogue with the second appellant's QC but he did not want to add to his written argument. By 2.44 pm, the presider asked for submissions from the Crown. The judges retired at 3.55 pm. Pre-court, the presider had observed to the others that the appellant's advocate had made a regrettable concession on a point of law in the trial, without the point having been argued, but the judges had now been 'helped' on the point by the oral advocacy of the responding QC, who had found a precedent on similar civil point. Back in court at 4.00 pm, the judges invited brief written submissions on this new point. The last-minute rescue of the appellant's case by the *Crown* in this way meant that the presider could not give the extempore judgment he had planned but would be forced to reserve. By 4.05 pm, they were proceeding through the remaining list, with David and Pitt giving judgment in turns on renewed applications for leave to appeal.

Most judgments are delivered extempore, orally, prepared in advance by the judge whose job it is to give judgment, after solitary pre-reading by each judge. Judgment may have been written verbatim. This is normal in sentencing cases. The other two do not know exactly what the judgment will say. They will have seen the outline prepared by the appeals office and will have 'an idea' of what their colleague's reasons will be. Judgments are almost universally single. HC judge Ossian explained that it was important that the CACD were unanimous, on the face of it. 'Internally you can be two-to-one but that's not revealed to the outside world' because the liberty of the subject is at stake. Munday was concerned with the trend towards composite judgments, discussed below. In the CACD, these sometimes replace the traditional judgment of a single judge. They are used in long and complex cases but a detailed composite was exemplified by *R v McIlkenny and others*,[56] the Birmingham Six appeal. Lloyd LJ introduced it as the judgment of the court. They read it out in turn, symbolically. It contained an important principle on the constitutional primacy of the jury. The CACD was unusually composed of three Lords Justices, because of the appeal's international notoriety.

---

[56] (1991) 93 Cr App R 287.

CRUCIAL STATUTORY INTERPRETATION

I caught up with Rathlin LJ and his two HC judges at 11.00 am, hearing a criminal procedure appeal, provoked by peculiar behaviour of a trial judge. The judgment, delivered by Rathlin's companion, became a precedent and has been analysed by academics in publications such as the *Criminal Law Review*. By lunchtime, this case was history. We entered Rathlin's room to discuss the afternoon's appeal on an important point of law that they felt was destined for the Law Lords. It turned on interpretation of a new Act. We laughed when I said academics would be analysing the precedent for months though they had half an afternoon for it. They received the skeletons two days earlier but barely had time to read them. They were struggling with the statute. Rathlin asked how I would interpret it. I declined to answer. After the others left, Rathlin said his opinion wavered, and he was 'not helped by the fact that the other two disagree'. With a hint of panic, he asked what I would do. 'Look it up in the annotated statutes on *Lexis* and *Westlaw*; phone an academic.' All judges had access to *Westlaw* and *Lexis* but neither he nor his clerk could remember how to access them. 'Can't you get a judicial assistant?' I asked. 'No, they're only for civil cases. There's no budget. Counsel should be doing all this but they are both juniors and not brilliant.' Had he looked up the point in the *Criminal Law Review*? No, but *Smith and Hogan* said the point was unresolved. Rathlin expected to have to reserve judgment but felt he should not reserve it for long, because the appellant was in prison and so many other cases depended on it. He opened the afternoon hearing: 'We've read the papers. This is not an invitation to hurtle through it. We need all the help we can get'. The HC judges did not take notes, knowing Rathlin would write the judgment. At 3.32 pm, he announced that they would reserve for a week. We returned to his room. There ensued the dialogue that opened this chapter. One judge left and Rathlin discussed the following day's cases with the other, as they would be sitting with a fourth judge in a new trio. He left. Rathlin would write this criminal judgment at the weekend. His reading Monday would be lost to a judicial working-party so he also had to pre-read next week's cases.

QUASHING A MISCARRIAGE OF JUSTICE

The old courtrooms in the RCJ have massive, elevated public galleries which are normally closed. One morning, this upper gallery was filled, as was every ground floor space, with journalists, publicists, expert witnesses, politicians, interest groups, the public and the usual supporters of the accused. Worldwide television crews obstructed the pavement. Only I knew that the judges had decided to quash the conviction, two days before the accused was freed from his iron-barred dock.

At 9.45 am, we had joined Matheson LJ and PJ. They had had the previous day plus the weekend to read the skeletons and big box of documents. Matheson asked 'Who's going to go first?' My judge was adamant, 'I can't get away from the fact that this jury has been misled. I don't care why, but they asked two sensible questions and were misinformed, therefore the conviction is unsafe.' PJ's conclusion was more technical, supported by forensic knowledge, gleaned from being the trial judge in a similar case. Matheson agreed. He knew about the expert whose evidence was challenged. A colleague had alerted him to another successful appeal, discrediting him. They discussed the reliability of expert witnesses, a constant concern of judges, given the lack of systematic accreditation.[57] PJ recounted a trial in which a doctor had called himself a consultant and she had asked why. 'Because people consult me.' They laughed. Matheson thought that the prosecution at trial seemed to expect the accused to seek exculpatory evidence. He asked if they should order a retrial. 'There must be a retrial', said my judge. 'The public will expect it.' He looked forward to hearing the appellant QC. A CA mate had told him 'She's got a mind like a Ferrari.' 'There was no need for her skeleton to be so aggressive', remarked Matheson 'though that's fine coming from me. I'd have been far more aggressive'. Although they had made up their minds, Matheson said they should ask Ferrari-brain to outline her case 'for the sake of the public'. In court, my judge was frustrated, anxious to put her skeleton words into her mouth. '*This* is your point, isn't it?' and fed her a consequent argument 10 minutes later. At lunch, the judges hoped their interventions had encouraged the appellant. 'Mr X's heart [responding for the Crown] must be in his boots by now.' After lunch, they invited Crown counsel to 'give the headlines' of his case but he started arguing it. Matheson grew impatient with his cross-examination of an expert 'You've run up to the wicket for about 10 minutes. Can he now have a question he can answer?' At 4.15 pm, Matheson stopped the hearing with, for the third time, 'I'm at a loss as to why this expert is being cross-examined in such depth. We are not here to take the jury's decision again!' The following day, they quashed the conviction, without a retrial. The ghost-faced, young appellant never recovered from years of wrongful imprisonment and died two years later.

A MANAGED APPEAL—COMPLEX FACTS AND LAW

Whaley J and Pitt J joined Brewer LJ for a complex seven-year-old appeal about a botched prosecution by entrapment. I caught up on the fourth day. The prosecution had sprung a last-minute public interest immunity (PII) application on them, then copious documentation had arrived last night, despite seven years of preparation and a string of case management hearings. 'I thought it was a bloody cheek, didn't you?' asked Brewer. While we waited in the corridor behind the courtrooms, David and her clerk passed, then Kind LJ's clerk, my hook on the RCJ gossip grapevine, then Mortimer. Brewer had started writing his judgment at

---

[57] Discussed by Auld LJ, in the *Criminal Courts Review 2001*. For an update, see Darbyshire, above n 37 at ch 12.

4.00 this morning before visiting his sick son in hospital. The advocates had been on night-shift. A junior barrister had written up a chronology and a QC had been 'explaining to himself' a newly-discovered document. In court, the judges were so blinkered by law reports and Pickfords boxes of ring-binders, that they could not see one another. The stenographer had a permanent frown. She could not hear Brewer's questions, or the lawyers' replies. No-one noticed.

At lunchtime, Brewer asked if I had understood. Aside from the law, it was impenetrable to an outsider, without maps, a chronology and character list. 'It is to us too!' they laughed. They said only one QC understood the case. Brewer expressed frustration in extracting fully-argued grounds of appeal.

> The problem here is that the Court of Appeal is not a court of inquiry and the prosecution have thrown in the towel, though the appellants say 'Hang on a minute'. They want a full airing of everything that went wrong.

Brewer directed Whaley to ask the afternoon questions. (I had noticed other presiders divided up this task.) This case was taking longer than scheduled, because of these last-minute submissions. After two reading days, they had heard the application on Monday afternoon and Tuesday then started the full hearing on Wednesday. They anxiously needed to finish in time for Whaley to drive 3.5 hours that night, to a Friday commitment on his circuit. That weekend, he would write his part of the judgment. On Tuesday he was scheduled to start a murder trial on circuit but dreaded driving back to London on Sunday night to hear this appeal overflowing on Monday, then driving back to his circuit on Monday night. 'I shouldn't have taken the job, I should have stayed teaching.' This story illustrates the points about night-shifts and about tight scheduling being thrown into chaos, at a cost to judges' private lives and probably their health and the quality of judgments.

No time had been allocated for judgment writing. 'Can't you ask?' 'No', said Whaley. 'Why don't you refuse to work at this rate?'

> First, there's a genuine commitment to doing the work. Upsetting the court clerk is one thing. Upsetting the punters is another matter. The second force is a type of machismo.

Luckily, Whaley had less to write than Pitt. How was judgment divided up? 'The presider decides.' Single judgments may be hidden composites. As the advocates had prepared material such as a chronology, I asked if these could not be pasted into the judgment, to save time, just as Trollope J constructed his Commercial Court judgments. It had not occurred to them. Whaley said he would feel guilty if he did that. Brewer laughed, pointing out that advocates who were still preparing the case *during* the hearing could hardly be relied upon to provide useful electronic material to paste into a judgment. As we have seen, this did not stop Trollope. He expected lawyers to prepare material overnight. The crucial distinction here was doubtless the fees extracted by Trollope's commercial lawyers.

THE TREND TOWARDS SINGLE CIVIL JUDGMENTS

Although the Civil Division does not work at the speed of the CACD, Phillips MR said that what had been a four-day case 20 years earlier was now heard in a day.[58] As stated above, pre-reading has radically transformed deliberation and judgment formation. Munday drew attention to the rise of the composite.[59] Judges used to give separate civil judgments. The 1990s trend for composites resembled 'civilian procedure', said Munday, which 'goes entirely against the English legal grain'.[60] In common law jurisdictions where judges formulate principles, the separate, concurring judgment arguably enriches the reasoning process. Diplock LJ once called this practice 'the beauty of the common law; it is a maze and not a motorway'.[61] Munday examined judgments from 1999–2001, revealing 10–14 per cent were composites. He concluded they were used when the CA wished to produce a single, authoritative statement. He highlighted a culture shift to written judgments, stimulated by technology enabling circulation of drafts. He contemplated whether judges had 'borrowed' from other systems, or wanted to make their judgments user-friendly. He thought they had engaged in cascade learning.[62] His argument is based on a meticulous analysis of the law reports but it is speculative. He did not speak to judges.

I was able to do so and to observe judgment formation firsthand. Because of this, I would draw attention to another statistic in Munday's tables: in 2000, 40 per cent of appeals resulted in just one judgment with assents—meaning 60 per cent by then resulted in a single judgment.[63] My conclusions are different from Munday's. Both collective *and* single judgments are generated by the same causes. There is often no practical difference between a composite and one delivered in a single name, where the judge has taken account of the others' views. I found that the *normal* civil presumption was that one judge would write the judgment, or in long and complex cases, it would be a composite. Writing tasks were allocated pre-hearing but the plan could change according to workloads. There was sometimes last-minute horse-trading over who could spare the time to write, or who fancied taking on the intellectual exercise. Chance dictated whether the others had the time or motivation to transform a single judgment into a hidden

---

[58]   S Hawthorne, 'The Master of all he surveys', *Counsel*, April 2002, 8.

[59]   R Munday, '"All for One and One for All" the rise to prominence of the composite judgment within the civil division of the Court of Appeal' (2002) 61(2) *Cambridge Law Journal* 321–50 (2002a) and 'Judicial Configurations—permutations of the court and properties of judgment' (2002) 61(3) *Cambridge Law Journal* 612–56 (2002b).

[60]   Munday (2002a), ibid 322.

[61]   Cited by Munday (2002b), above n 59 at 641, from *Morris v C.W. Martin & Sons* [1966] 1 QB 716, 730.

[62]   Munday (2002a), above n 59 at 330.

[63]   Later, he showed that over 50 per cent of the cases he sampled from 2003 were composites or single: R Munday, 'Reasoning without dissent. Dissent without reason.' (2004) 168 *Justice of the Peace Reports* 968–75 and 991–1000.

composite by injecting their ideas, or whether the writer was consciously aware of adopting their reasoning, or bothered to mention that it was a joint effort.

The pilot HC veteran, appointed in 1990, disagreed with Munday's theories on causes, such as cascade learning, later re-affirmed by senior managing judges. Composites and single judgments with assents were indeed a direct result of requiring skeleton arguments. This is confirmed by Martineau.[64] I noticed that judges could formulate an opinion on the skeletons, do their own research, draft judgments, deliberate/negotiate, refine their reasoning and even swap drafts or modify a single draft *before* the hearing. In the old days, said the veteran, they would have had no papers.

> We would form a view during arguments and then deliver our extempore judgments. We wouldn't have had a chance to discuss the case. I wouldn't know what the man next to me was going to say until he said it!

It was apparent in both civil and criminal appeals that skeletons and the criminal case summaries prepared by the appeals office have been the drivers of this change. This means most judgments are reached before the hearing.[65] Munday and Drewry et al observed that we are moving over to a culture of written judgments.[66] This is a facilitator but is not as crucial as skeleton arguments, as can be seen from CACD practice where most judgments are not reserved. One judge explained that there is a way in which skeletons cause judgments to be reserved. They may contain multiple strands of argument. Some judges feel obliged to address each point. Munday is right to draw attention to the shift in practice, given the historic English hostility to composites.[67] He said it occurred without discussion. A rare judicial acknowledgment can be found in Lord Phillips' 2002 review.

> It is now more common ... to deliver a single judgment to which all members have contributed ... Profusion of precedent is the bain [*sic*] of judges and practitioners alike. A single judgment reduces the material that has to be read, avoids the opportunity for differences of interpretation and provides greater clarity. Providing certainty, and giving clear guidance, are among the Court's most important functions.

Practically, single judgments have become a labour-saving device. Jurispruden-tially, judges claim they are sparing us the pain of extracting the ratio decidendi

---

[64] Martineau, above n 37.

[65] Munday refers to written skeleton arguments (2002b, above n 59 at 616) but wrongly attributes their introduction to the Civil Procedure Rules 1998, whereas they were introduced from the late 1980s, as explained above.

[66] Over 57 per cent were reserved in the year ending September 2008. *Court of Appeal Civil Division Review(s) of the Year* are on HM Courts Service website. The latest ones do not analyse judgments.

[67] Munday contemplated the advantages and drawbacks of multiple concurring judgments. See 2002b, above n 59 at 645. M Kirby, 'Judicial Dissent—Common Law and Civil Traditions' (2007) 123 *LQR* 379–400, seems to be unaware of the English trend towards single judgments. I return to this issue in the next chapter.

from multiple judgments. Judges explained that Phillips' predecessor, Lord Woolf was similarly keen on single judgments, to prevent later analysts finding tiny distinctions between multiples. Phillips' successors, Clarke and Neuberger, shared this view and the latter is now urging a similar change on the UKSC.[68] Munday considered this reasoning problematic because it 'flaunts the lawmaking function of the Court of Appeal' and because 'it will always appear' that one judge has done all the work.[69] CA judges are happy to acknowledge this is not just an *appearance.* Drewry et al 'deprecated' it because it creates 'the impression of dominance by the specialist'.[70] I make no remark on the jurisprudential desirability of single judgments but conclude that judges now give them because they *can.* Skeletons prompted the change. Some critics are concerned. Judges are content.[71] Judges now explain why they are insisting on a separate second or third judgment. Munday examines some of these.[72] They include cases where the Court is reversing the decision of an expert trial judge, dissents, deference to counsel's arguments and cases where they differ on reasoning.[73]

GIVING CIVIL JUDGMENTS—HOW IT WORKS

The administrative head of civil appeals devises the constitutions. There is a supervising LJ for each type of specialist appeal, who decides who will judge important cases. If a judge gives permission to appeal from, say, the EAT, they will require it to come before a judge with EAT experience. The presider decides who will give judgment, explained Ebony. 'Tomorrow's case is commercial so I'll do it. Blue could do immigration. Amber could do employment.' Below, though, when Kind LJ was presiding, he let the experts divide the judging amongst themselves. Kind was gratified when another family judge had joined the CA. He preferred to sit with family judges in a family appeal, because the second judge could give a short, succinct judgment with just the main points. Alternatively, it was useful 'because they can look at it as a trial judge', injecting practical experience. Family Division judges sat in the CA in four-week shifts. Unfortunately, they often wanted a change from family cases.

---

[68] See next chapter.

[69] Munday (2002b), above n 59 at 644–45.

[70] Drewry et al, above n 14 at 129.

[71] Munday observed the trend would 'generate a working practice whereby one member of the court is conventionally assigned the task of writing the judgment and the others see whether they can go along with it': (2002b), above n 59 at 645. In my observations, by 2005, he was right.

[72] Munday, above n 63.

[73] ibid 9–14. eg, *Howell & Ors v Lees Millais & Ors* [2007] EWCA Civ 720. The CA were severely critical of an HC judge. The MR delivered a very full judgment, Judge LJ adding 'a short judgment of my own simply to add emphasis to my entire agreement with his judgment'.

Example 1 New Boy

In a case about negligent cricket, no expertise was required. Judges met at 11.20 am. The presider had given Bland LJ, the new boy, the job of judgment writing. Bland was nervous. 'We didn't do cricket at my school.' He had had to learn about it. He had written out his judgment and hoped to deliver it verbatim. The others, who had played school cricket, teased. All had 'prepared' by watching TV cricket on Saturday. The presider said they should hand down judgment at 2.00 pm but was concerned that this could be difficult if, after hearing arguments, Bland needed to change it. This made Bland even more nervous, now fretting about sounding incoherent. At lunchtime, they discussed the case. Oral argument had changed their views a little. The presider asked Bland if he wanted to hear arguments from the respondents. He did. 'But what happens if we go on till 4.30 pm? Are we together tomorrow?' Smiling, the other two replied that they were not and that *un*fortunately, Bland would have to reserve judgment. Bland's face fell.

Example 2 Presider as Makeweight

Kind, presiding, explained, 'I'm sitting with two chancery judges who are very bright and it's an area of law completely beyond my ken so I'm expecting they'll have decided it'. He admitted he was teasing. As an experienced CA judge, he had dealt with all types of law but he 'would not get excited about the finer points as specialists would'. We joined Bland and Bright LJJ behind the courtroom. 'Well, you two, have you decided it?' They explored the 'Property Law (Muddled Provisions) Act 1989', as they called it. Kind asked some intelligent questions, demonstrating that he *had* read the arguments. The case was scheduled for 1.5 days but he was hoping it would be over in half a day. He had a speaking engagement the following day, up north. They assured Kind that it would take half a day. 'Are you just going to concur then?' I asked. 'That's right. My job is to keep things moving—make sure this is dealt with in half a day.' The chancery judges discussed the case for four minutes alone and for two minutes with Kind. 'Should we quash or remit?' asked Kind. 'Quash not remit', they chorused. In court, Kind was silent, the other two asking questions. At 12.35 pm, the three huddled. Kind announced 'We don't want to hear any more about section 53, Mr X'. Counsel was partway through responding. Kind asked his clerk who was going to give judgment. 'Bright. It's reserved.' 'Well, I'll have plenty of time to get that train this afternoon, then', he sighed, relieved.

They deliberated from 1.50–2.00 pm. One asked Bright to make sure that, in his judgment, he alluded to a particular point. At the end of the morning, Bland had opened up a new line of questioning, on an intellectual frolic. He tried it on his colleagues. 'Well, *everyone* would say that', countered Kind, discouraging Bland's exciting jurisprudential escapade. Kind felt his job was 'to apply common sense and restraint'. He sided with Bright. Bland jokingly threatened to write a dissent. At lunch, Kind showed me an envelope of unrelated paperwork he had been doing on the bench whilst 'presiding'. I asked if he had been paying attention.

> A bit. You get a pretty good idea of how an appeal should be resolved, even in a case where you'd feel inadequate to describe why. You can conclude without being able to make a judgment of the calibre expected of this court. I won't have read the papers in as much depth as the other two.

The chancery judges could have decided the case without him so I asked why he was there. He said the danger of a two-judge court was that the two were so steeped in expertise that they might find a reason to disagree. He told me of a case where he had sat with a family expert and they disagreed. The case was adjourned for three months and reheard by a three-judge court, causing delay and expense to the parties. Two-judge benches were only safe if the case was straightforward and one was an expert and the other a non-expert.[74] In a three-judge court it was rare for an expert to be outvoted but it had happened to him. There was no assumption that a non-specialist should defer to a specialist, especially in family law, because the outcome of most cases did not turn on the law. The CA's job was to review whether the trial judge had exercised his discretion correctly, which needed no expertise.

Example 3 Judge Overruled on 'Hopeless' Application Then Saddled with Judgment

Judges expressed frustration when they found themselves hearing a groundless appeal for which they would not have granted permission. I joined Kind presiding over a 'hopeless' family property appeal. The trial judge had refused leave to appeal. When one party re-applied in person, Kind considered there were no grounds but a non-family judge with him disagreed so permission was granted. In the meantime, mediation had failed. He and two non-experts, Bland LJ and Chatworth LJ, had heard the arguments yesterday. 'We're vehement in rejecting the appeal at every stage.' The case attracted wide publicity. They met in the corridor, ready to deliver judgment. Bland showed us an item in *The Metro* he had found on the Tube. As always, the judges were titillated by news gossip about their cases. 'Good picture,' mused Kind. 'The appeal got further with the press than with us, then.' In the courtroom were 14 journalists and law reporters. In giving judgment, Kind remarked 'It's a *tragedy* this case was not resolved on

---

[74] Contradicting Munday's optimism, 'Obviously, a bench of two rather than three judges is likely to facilitate their agreement': (2002a), above n 59 at 338.

mediation'.[75] Chatworth delivered a brief judgment commenting that one criticism of the trial judge was 'wholly inappropriate'. Bland agreed and added a few brief comments. Kind explained later that he had had no idea in advance what the other judges were going to say, in their brief additions. 'Chatworth probably wrote his judgment while I was speaking.'

Example 4 New Skeletons Pointless—We Decided Your Case Yesterday Lunchtime

Ebony met Blue and Amber just before a 10.30 am hearing of an application for permission to appeal and an application to admit fresh evidence, on appeal from the Technology and Construction Court. Blue explained that they had decided the case yesterday lunchtime. Blue had written the lead judgment. In court, the presider, Amber, attacked the appellant's weak case head-on. Extracting points from the skeleton, he protested, smiling politely, 'Every litigant would like to reopen their case with fresh evidence, if they could'. Each judge entered a dialogue with counsel. After an hour, they rose to discuss what questions they should put to the defendant and waited behind the courtroom. Meanwhile, in court, a clerk came in at 11.45 am to announce that we were waiting for the shorthand writer, so I knew that judgment was imminent. Eventually, the shorthand writer lumbered in with a dripping umbrella, moaning about the rain. As she put on her lipstick, the clerk told her about his football training at Southend at the weekend. With the shorthand writer satisfactorily adorned with lipstick, the judges were called back from the corridor at 11.55 am. Amber thanked the defendants for their arguments, but said the court did not want to hear from them and Blue delivered the lead judgment. Ebony LJ said 'I agree' and Amber delivered a brief, off-the-cuff judgment.

Ebony had shown me the papers. The costs were shockingly disproportionate. (Indeed, watching the CA was an eye-opener on wildly disproportionate costs.) The appellant claimed to have accrued £48,000 in costs since trial, with the defendants spending £35,000. The argument was about a grossly inflated insurance claim of £140,000 loss of business due to negligent building work on a property purchased in 2000 for £36,000. The TCC judgment was cynical and subtly witty about the inflated claim. Ebony remarked before the hearing that he felt responsible for this case, as he had granted permission. 'When you know how much it costs, you'd never do it yourself, would you?' he laughed, on the folly of litigation. At 10.10 am, his clerk had delivered supplementary skeletons and additional priority reading. I wondered what Ebony was supposed to do with it, since he still had to get robed and walk the labyrinthine RCJ to get into court by 10.30 am. These papers were stamped as received by the Civil Appeals Office the

---

[75] Mentioned in ch 12. It had cost the husband £350,000 on legal fees even before the appeal.

previous day. Ebony said he would ignore them anyway as they had decided the case the previous lunchtime.

Example 5 Who's Got Time to Write the Judgment?

Ebony LJ heard a reinsurance appeal with Cairns LJ (presiding) and Grynn LJ. While we waited in the corridor, Grynn expressed surprise to Ebony that Cairns had not asked one of them to give the judgment. Ebony was surprised too. 'He'll write an immaculate judgment but it won't be today or tomorrow.' Blue LJ came past, moaning that he had collected four reserved judgments and now Cairns had asked him to do the judgment in a case next week. 'I tried to get out of it. They're appealing on every point of fact and law.' This must have been a disappointment for Blue. Christmas was coming and he had told me in his interview 'I work incredibly hard to avoid reserved judgments [by working at weekends and evenings] … I am optimistic that I will have no reserved judgments left at the end of this term.' Blue too was surprised that Cairns had said he would do today's judgment. 'In a macho way he said he'd do the judgment in this case next week too [laughing]'. 'He could have got Tony Silverdale to do it. He's young.'

Example 6 Landmark Composite Destined for the Law Lords

Ebony gave me the skeletons, as always, admitting he had not 'got on top of the case'. We walked to the presider, Samson LJ's room and they talked about EasyJet flights. 'This is bloody difficult don't you think?' Samson asked. 'It's a good job we've got John Bland to tell us what the law is.' New Boy Bland came in. 'This is difficult, don't you think?' 'Well', replied Bland, 'Their only argument is [X] isn't it?' 'Let's see what we've read.' They had all read the skeleton and the judgment below. Bland thought the latest clear statement of English law was a New Zealand authority. Samson suggested they ask for 'an early day' this afternoon to read. He grumbled mildly that the skeletons contained many authorities but no 'essential reading' list. They discussed how long they could spare for the case—about a week. 'We've got a reading day on Friday, haven't we?' suggested Ebony. Samson dropped the bombshell that he might not have time to write a judgment and might farm it out to one of them. The case was all over the newspapers. The decision would set an important precedent for media contracts. It would go to the Law Lords. When the rock stars involved had appeared at the trial, the RCJ had been mobbed with TV crews and fans. Discussion contained lots of laughs and media gossip. Bland said 'According to my wife's *Telegraph*, [the claimants] are not suing for [X].' The others teased him for reading the *Telegraph* whilst not wanting to be seen buying it. Ebony had asked his wife what she thought. Although they had not 'got on top of the case', they had each formed a provisional opinion. Samson first sought Bland's opinion, the junior judge and also the expert on the subject. Bland surprised them by raising the issue of estoppel, as he had in Kind's case, above. 'What do you mean?' asked the others, who were not chancery lawyers. Bland dropped this line then said 'I agree with the appellant's skeleton. It's as simple as that'. Samson agreed. Bland thought some of the claimants had suffered a breach of privacy. 'Privacy's not like virginity.' They laughed. 'I wonder if we can get *that* into our judgments', mused Samson. In court, they were a very friendly and good-humoured tribunal. They each relished engaging counsel in a dialogue. As we left at lunchtime, Bland and Ebony remarked that the respondent would have his work cut out. By 4.00 pm, counsel had only reached point 49 on his 77-point skeleton. We went to tea at 4.15 pm in Samson's room. He changed into his characteristic ancient sweater. Neither it nor Bland's gown, in tatters, would have been acceptable donations to an Oxfam shop. They batted ideas around in an unsystematic way on various points underpinning the grounds of appeal. Their mood was jolly and very friendly. No-one took precedence in the discussion. When Samson handed down the 260-paragraph judgment, five months later, he started, 'This is the judgment of the court, to which all members have contributed'. Samson emailed me this explanation:

> Considerable discussion took place in relation to the draft judgment after the hearing, resulting in parts of this being fundamentally re-written. Disagreement or dissent often crystallises when a judge produces his first draft and circulates this to his colleagues.

Example 7 Leave Judging to the Expert—Retired Judge as Makeweight

Young Silverdale LJ and a retired judge were hearing an immigration appeal presided over by Samson. Samson had told Silverdale to give judgment because of his expertise. Immigration and asylum appeals were prolific. Importantly, the court had to decide between conflicting precedents by the Lord Chief Justice and the Master of the Rolls. The retired judge only received the papers that morning. Samson and Silverdale received theirs in ample time but had only discussed the case for five minutes outside the courtroom. Silverdale asked for a shorthand writer at 3.00 pm to take the extempore judgment he planned. Samson scrolled material on his laptop, leaving most of the questioning to Silverdale. The retired judge asked no questions and slept during parts of the hearing but not as much as I did. Samson slept momentarily. The room was icy cold. As we left at 1.00 pm, Silverdale was 'backtracking' on giving judgment at 3.00 pm. Samson contemplated whether the case should be sent up to the Law Lords. Later, alone, Silverdale wondered whether he should give as careful a judgment as possible or refer it up to the Lords. He was finding it very interesting. Silverdale said that Samson was good at delegating,[76] even though he was sharp and decisive on any

---

[76] Samson had one of the busiest senior management jobs so he delegated out of necessity.

area of the law. Silverdale, who knew he was more liberal on immigration than the others, was still in two minds about the outcome but they had expressed concern about the 'floodgate' of immigration appeals they might open. At 2.56 pm, they agreed to reserve. There was no post-hearing deliberation, Silverdale having swiftly established that Samson and he were in agreement. When I expressed surprise at the lack of discussion, Silverdale explained that it had been clear to them on the papers that the Immigration and Asylum Tribunal's decision should be upheld, then it started to seem less clear when they heard oral argument, then it now seemed clear again. Silverdale would devise the reasoning, as the career expert. Samson was far too busy. The retired judge was entirely passive. Silverdale would show them his judgment for approval.

COLLEGIALITY

I referred above to the camaraderie of the CA. A senior LJ said relations had not always been universally cordial. Years earlier, there had been clashes of personality, with some judges not speaking to others. I had detected this, decades earlier, by watching body language in court. One judge sat with his back towards the presider.[77] I wondered whether camaraderie encouraged them to deliver single and composite judgments. The veteran above confirmed this. Naturally, he said, in an atmosphere of mutual respect for one another's qualities and abilities, judges were less likely to insist on delivering alternative judgments.[78] In the highly-developed US literature on judicial decision-making, there are numerous articles on the effects of collegiality.[79] The most convincing,[80] written by a former chief appellate judge, Harry Edwards, who promoted collegiality,[81] accords strikingly with my CA observations and the veteran's remark. Edwards did not mean judges had to be friends but

> judges have a common interest ... in getting the law right ... we are willing to listen, persuade, and be persuaded, all in an atmosphere of civility and respect ... collegiality plays an important part in mitigating the role of ... personal ideology by allowing judges of differing perspectives and philosophies to communicate with, listen to, and ultimately influence one another in constructive ... ways ... In an uncollegial environment, divergent views ... often end up as dissenting opinions.[82]

---

[77] The rudeness of one abrasive character, who left the CA in 1998, was still legendary among the clerks.

[78] Posner, 'Most judges do not like to dissent...Not only is it a bother and frays collegiality, and usually has no effect on the law, but it also tends to magnify the significance of the majority opinion', above n 2 at 32.

[79] Referenced in the copious footnotes of Edwards' article, above n 54.

[80] Edwards, above n 54.

[81] Chief Judge of the DC Circuit from 1994–2001.

[82] Edwards, above n 54 at 1645.

He said that while some commentators worried that strong collegiality would render judges reluctant to challenge colleagues, research on group decision-making demonstrated the opposite, confirming his experience of his collegial court and its non-collegial former incarnation. Redolent of the CA, he had been shocked to join his court in 1980, to find it still 'a collectivity of fighting cats' (Frankfurter).[83] Collegiality made for better decisions.

> The freedom to disagree ... fostered by collegiality, enables judges accurately and honestly ... to identify what is common ground ... all the while remaining open to revising their views ... judges will help one another to make dissenting opinions as effective as possible. Dissents become more precise, focused, and useful to the development of the law.[84]

He thought collegiality had helped foster a useful composite, from judges with diverse opinions, in *US v Microsoft Corp*.[85] He defended composites in terms almost identical to Lord Phillips:

> What the parties and the public need is that answer, not a public colloquy among judges. A multiplicity of opinions ... can contribute to confusion about what the law is.[86]

The present Court of Appeal's and Edwards' emphasis on collegiality is strongly supported by Posner, 'Appellate judging is a cooperative exercise. It does not work well when the judges' relations with one another become tinged with animosity'.[87] Commenting on an earlier draft of this chapter, another CA veteran, outside this research said:

> Of course there are sometimes tensions when judges have strongly held differences about the outcome of a particular appeal. Some judges are easier to disagree with than others: the difficult ones are those (not many) who have poor negotiating skills and defend their position like a dog in a manger. But some differences are serious—for example where dismissing an asylum appeal may be sending someone to their death—and one should expect a certain amount of judicial passion about them.

---

[83] In a 1962 letter, written by Frankfurter: JB Morris, *Calmly to Poise the Scales of Justice: A History of the Courts of the District of Columbia Circuit* (Carolina Academic Press, 2001), cited by Edwards.

[84] Edwards, above n 54 at 1651.

[85] 253 F 3d 34 (DC Cir 2001).

[86] Edwards, above n 54 at 1651. He distinguished his Court's function from that of the USSC.

[87] Posner, above n 2 at 33 and see the chapter, 'Nine theories of judicial behaviour'.

'I DIDN'T HAVE TIME TO WRITE A SHORT JUDGMENT'

Judges and critics are concerned about the length of judgments.[88] One veteran, who did not type, complained that word-processing had enabled judges to cut and paste from precedents. Secondly, judges often remarked, 'I didn't have time to write a short judgment'. Thirdly, as the case law mushrooms, there are more precedents the judge feels obliged to cite. Fourthly, possibly, the longer the argument and the more grounds, then the more points the judge must address, if only to dismiss them.[89] For example, far-fetched human rights arguments have bedevilled every level of judge since 2000.[90] Fifthly and most important, I found that CA judges were loaded with so much pre-reading, that they would expect to be given a list of essential reading, as did Samson in Example 6 above. In *Gulf International Ltd v Groupe Chimique Tunisien*[91] the Court expressed 'strong disapproval' at

> the volume of papers…There were 15 lever arch files…well over 100 authorities and 3 files of documents (to which almost no reference was made) in addition to the core bundle. Midgulf's first "skeleton argument" ran to 132 pages … [with] … a supplementary … 30 pages, in which it repeated many of its previous arguments … the case is a grotesque example of a tendency to burden the court with documents of grossly disproportionate quantity and length. It is a practice which must stop … it makes the work of the court infinitely harder. Hours had to be spent reading … and they were largely wasted hours. It will no doubt also have added greatly and unnecessarily to the costs … All that the court needed … was to have the documents and a summary of each party's argument, which could have been provided in far less than 10 pages. The ordinary principles of contract law in this area are so well known there was no need for reference to authorities, let alone well over 100 authorities.[92]

Both divisions have expressed similar sentiments repeatedly in cases[93] and practice directions. Sedley LJ, like many judges, blames it on the photocopier but argues that at least he and his colleagues are spared from its worst excesses by the requirement for oral advocacy.

> The nemesis of all courts in modern times … has been the use of the photocopier … to tip the whole file on to the photocopier and leave it to the court to find its way through hundreds or thousands of pages. In other countries, where appellate decisions are taken

---

[88] eg, Drewry et al, above n 14. See also L Blom-Cooper, 'Style of Judgments' in L Blom-Cooper, B Dickson and G Drewry, *The Judicial House of Lords, 1876–2009* (Oxford, Oxford University Press, 2009).

[89] In *R v Erskine; R v Williams* [2009] EWCA Crim 1425, Lord Judge cited Viscount Falkland in 1641: if it was not necessary to refer to a previous decision, it was necessary not to refer to it.

[90] When the Human Rights Act 1998 came into force.

[91] *Times* law report, 3 March 2010.

[92] [2010] EWCA Civ 66, paras 71–73.

[93] See *R (C) v SS for Justice* [2009] 2 WLR 1039. Buxton LJ complained of 122 authorities and a 61-page skeleton, cited by Blom-Cooper in 2009. See also, *Tombstone Limited v Raja* [2008] EWCA Civ 1444.

after only perfunctory oral argument, the burden of donkey-work this places on the judges is huge.[94]

CONCLUSION

I learned about the Court's workload by talking to appeal judges in the 1980s. That sparked the curiosity that ultimately led to this research. No CA judge used the word 'macho' to describe the workaholic attitude to long hours, like the new HC judges. Ossian talked of the 'moral pressure' to get through the work and get judgments written. The Court of Appeal hears thousands of appeals a year yet only a handful reach the UKSC from the four jurisdictions—58 in its first year. This is the crucial court that lays down precedent. Added to this pressure in the Criminal Division is the knowledge that the guilt or innocence and freedom of other defendants rest on the cases before them. There were over 30 prisoners convicted of rape waiting for the decision in Rathlin's case, yet in the CACD no-one is allocated writing time and judicial assistance is unavailable.

The contrast between the hasty judgment formation in serious criminal appeals and their later leisurely analysis by academics was laughable, to both the judge and the academic observer. Rathlin's bench had two hours in an afternoon to hear his landmark appeal, turning on technical statutory interpretation and then he wrote the judgment by himself, over the weekend. More than one HC judge considered it remarkable that more mistakes were not made. Judges long past retirement age tolerated this exhausting strain because they thought it was 'payback time'. They had made a good living at the Bar. They all loved the intellectual challenge of deciding points of law and, like the district judges, they hoped their decisions would have a beneficial effect on people's lives.

Apart from the caseload, most CA judges have management jobs but only the senior executives had time allocated to this. They appeared to relish management. This allowed them to escape the confines of the Royal Courts of Justice, though the civil service mentality frustrated these people who had been self-employed barristers in efficient chambers with very simple administrative infrastructures.

Pre-trial reading and the exchange of skeleton arguments and document bundles have transformed CA decision-making since the 1980s, when judges went into court to hear the whole story. CA judges would not willingly dispense with oral argument altogether, though. They felt that debate stimulated their intellectual appreciation of the issues. They loved the cut and thrust of the courtroom. Anyone can visit the Royal Courts of Justice and watch these good humoured dialogues. The system only works, though, when judges have been given the time to pre-read documentation that has been delivered on time. Like the HC judges, they routinely lost reading days to other work and *every* HC and

---

[94] Sedley, above n 41.

CA judge suffered from the late delivery of documents. It was very common to receive them minutes before the judges were due to walk into court. If these were redundant supplementary arguments, the judges just laughed it off but late delivery could seriously affect the judges' work. They had to read overnight, or they wasted time in the hearing trying to grasp the issues, or, worse, they had to reserve judgment writing in order to understand the issues and all judges dreaded reserving judgment. The lawyers seemingly had no idea how tight the judges' schedules were so that last-minute nasty surprises, like those in Brewer's big appeal threatened to disrupt Whaley's scheduled work on circuit and cause him to drive back and forth for hours at night between his circuit and the RCJ. Repeated judgments and practice directions asking lawyers to obey the rules have had no effect, as was clear from the behaviour of the sets of inconsiderate lawyers who made Stanford so anxious and miserable in the HC Family Division, reported in the family chapter. Lawyers were a very mixed-ability bunch in the CA. There were some rude, unapologetic people. As with the public at large, the respect formerly accorded to judges was gone and, as was seen in the Crown Court chapter, there was a failure by many barristers to apologise or take responsibility for not providing what the court required. Yet again, we can see very starkly how the judge in the English legal system is so heavily dependent on the lawyers—not only in terms of efficiency but also in addressing the issues, in intellectually grasping the decisions to be taken and in bringing to the court all and only the necessary legal authorities. Rathlin was left stranded in his job of interpreting a new statute defining rape, because not only did his HC judges drift off to other jobs but the advocates were weak so Rathlin was left in a lunchtime panic.

We can see again that LIPs take up the time of the Court of Appeal (Civil Division) as they do in all the other civil courts. By this stage, they are desperate. Again judges accorded them remarkable amounts of time and patience, probably too much of this Court's precious time.

Posner said that the judges deliberate very little. This was certainly the case in run of the mill criminal appeals: renewed applications for leave to appeal and sentencing appeals. Judgments were written in advance, verbatim, by the judge to whom the appeals office had allocated judgment,[95] with the help of the office summary. Judgment in a substantive appeal or one from an HC judge's trial would be written by the LJ. Three judges could pre-deliberate a whole day's list in about 15–20 minutes, having their say but not knowing exactly what their colleague would say in judgment. Judges reckoned they only changed their minds on hearing oral argument in about 10 per cent of cases.

I used to think that circuit judges' presence in the Court of Appeal was a means of doing justice on the cheap but for the LJs in the research sample, all from civil

---

[95] This point astonished Irish HC and Supreme Court Justices, when I was asked to speak at their annual conference.

backgrounds, trial judges brought unparalleled experience of the criminal practice and sentencing. Two appeal judges always asked the opinions of their juniors
first, to ensure that there was no deference effect. Tribunal chairs and senior ranks
of the armed forces are trained to do this too and it would be worth reminding
LJs that this is good practice. There was no set pattern.

The famous miscarriage of justice case described here demonstrates the
importance of the CA and the pressure of conducting an appeal in the international spotlight. Although the judges were unanimous and adamant, pre-hearing,
that the appellant had been wrongfully convicted, I was the only person in the
crowded courtroom who knew that. The judges strategically staged a 1.5 day
hearing, which was redundant to their decision, in order to expose to the
interested public the weakness of the Crown's case and especially the experts'
evidence. As a result of this exposure, the expert witnesses were all disciplined
afterwards by their professional bodies. Note how the presider was so keen to air
this story that he was repeatedly prompting the appellant's counsel to emphasise
the full horrors of the appellant's case.

In the CACD, a single judgment could be a hidden composite. This was
inevitable in long and complex appeals cases like Brewer's because no-one had
been allocated writing time and Brewer had to write from 5.00 am. Like other
presiders, Brewer also shared out the task of asking questions in the courtroom.
However hard pressed these judges were, they could not rely on the device
Trollope used in the Commercial Court—asking counsel to prepare agreed
material to cut and paste into his judgment. Indeed, the expensive lawyers here
were so incompetent that after seven years' preparation, they jeopardised the
judges' schedules by bringing complex, last-minute applications, backed by
highly complex material.

As for civil appeals, Munday is to be commended for drawing attention to the
rise of composite and single judgments but the judges said his hypotheses as to
why this occurred were wrong. The real reason was the significant change in
practice away from orality. Skeleton arguments and document bundles now allow
judgments to be drafted and circulated in advance of the hearing. The striking,
warm collegiality of the CA encourages debate and the exchange of ideas in
judgment formation, before, during and after an appeal hearing. As Posner said,
it does not mean they have to be friends but that they are free to disagree in an
atmosphere of civility and respect. It has become the *normal* presumption that a
single judge will write most civil judgments, with that task shared out in a
complex case to form a composite to which all three have contributed. As can be
seen from the case examples, the matter of who would be tasked with writing a
judgment might depend on expertise but more likely who had the time to write
it. Plans could change. Practically, single or composite judgments are a labour-
saving device but successive Masters of the Rolls have defended them jurispru-
dentially on the ground that they make life easier for the public and the end-user
because a single judgment is easier to understand. Unfortunately, however,

judgments have lengthened, because there are simply far more previous precedents to cite, because judges can cut and paste them instead of summarising the
principles, because judges are swamped with authorities by sloppy lawyers and
because they just 'do not have the time to write short judgments'. As Lord Chief
Justice Phillips said in his last annual review,

> Whether you talk to Circuit Judge, High Court Judge or presider from the Court of
> Appeal the reaction is the same—a spell in the 'Crim Div' is hard labour.[96]

---

[96] *The Court of Appeal Criminal Division Review of the Legal Year 2007/2008* (Judiciary of
England and Wales, 2009).

15

Brenda and the Law Lords Transform into the Supremes

We're a common law court. Of course we 'make' law as we go along.

US Justice Sandra Day O'Connor[1]

A judge should be anonymous.

UKSC Justice, 2009

'That's the most fun part of the job!'

UKSC Justice, 2009, talking about oral argument

THIS CHAPTER EXAMINES the work of the UK Supreme Court (UKSC) Justices now and in their previous incarnation, as Law Lords. I was privileged to sit with them in 2005 and in 2009–10.

PUBLIC NON-IMAGE

The Law Lords[2], now Justices from October 2009, have been the subject of far more research and scrutiny than other judges and their role has for decades been the subject of debate by lawyers, academics, politicians and judges, yet the public have little understanding of who they are and what they do.[3] TV channels seldom use the live feed of the top court's proceedings. Well-informed citizens would not be able to name one, in the way that Americans can name members of the US Supreme Court (USSC) and describe their political reputations.[4] The Human

---

[1] Cited below.
[2] 12 full-time Lords of Appeal in Ordinary, other Lords of Appeal and top judges who sat occasionally.
[3] Lord Bingham said 'people have very little idea', referring to news of a Law Lords' case, mistakenly depicting a group of CJs in ceremonial garb, though the top judges sit in lounge suits: F Gibb, interview, *The Times*, 20 November 2007. Two TV documentaries in January and February 2011 were unprecedented so a handful of viewers may now be a little better informed.
[4] L Blom-Cooper and G Drewry, *Final Appeal* (Oxford, Clarendon Press, 1972) 154, said they did not produce biographies or attract biographers like USSC Justices.

Rights Act 1998 and the 2003 announcement of a UKSC[5] caused short-lived clamour for candidates to be publicly examined,[6] but this came to nothing. By 2005, the latest appointment went so unnoticed that a *Google* search for Lord Brown of Eaton-under-Heywood retrieved only the Eaton-under-Heywood Swingers. While the 2009 nomination of Sonia Sotomayor was analysed in UK news, the Law Lords' transformation into the first UKSC Justices went unnoticed.[7] They like it this way. In December 2009, one Justice said 'a judge should be anonymous'. Three had just travelled, two in white-tie, with Baroness Hale in an evening-dress, by tube, to Grays Inn Grand Night. They eschew the limos ferrying top judges elsewhere.[8] He said Sandra Day O'Connor might have been called one of the world's most powerful women but 'Brenda wouldn't want that'. This is symptomatic of their image of themselves as apolitical. They are unknown to the public as they were in 1978, when Stevens said, 'Except to the cognoscenti, Reid, Wilberforce and Diplock were unknown, and Kilbrandon, Salmon and Simon were scarcely household words'.[9]

The plans to create a Supreme Court drew attention to how little simple information was readily obtainable on how the UK's top court worked and how inaccessible it was to the public.[10] Yet paradoxically, it has immense power. It is not a constitutional court that can strike down primary legislation,[11] like some other countries' top courts, but Justices can effectively re-write, quash or suspend legislation that conflicts with EU law, strike down Scottish Acts and reinterpret or declare UK statutes to be incompatible with the European Convention on Human Rights.[12] Furthermore, they effectively act as a legislature of five to nine people because their job is to decide points of law of general public importance. Indeed, judges in England, the mother of the common law world, *made* and refined the world's common law.[13] They defined the essentials of a contract and created the law of tort. Also, unlike some of England's daughter jurisdictions, much of our law remains uncodified and has thus been left to judicial creativity. Even murder is a common law crime. Moreover, the UK is one of only three

[5] Followed by a consultation, *Constitutional Reform: A Supreme Court for the United Kingdom* (archived DCA website).

[6] Copying US Senate confirmation hearings of USSC Justices, discussed below.

[7] By summer 2009, there was one item on the BBC News website but nothing about the Justices.

[8] A fourth Justice was fresh from Hong Kong where he had protested that he did not need the chauffered car provided.

[9] R Stevens, *Law and Politics, The House of Lords as a Judicial Body 1800–1976* (London, Weidenfeld and Nicolson, 1979) 598.

[10] The UKSC is very welcoming for visitors, including school groups. Its website is an improvement on the Law Lords' site. By far the most valuable innovation are its press releases summarising judgments.

[11] Thanks to the doctrine of Parliamentary sovereignty.

[12] As with anti-terror legislation, in *A (FC) and others (FC) v SS for the Home Dept* [2004] UKHL 56 ('the Belmarsh case').

[13] R Posner, *How Judges Think* (Cambridge, Mass, Harvard University Press, 2008) calls appellate judges 'occasional legislators' but the UKSC are frequent legislators.

countries in the developed world with an 'unwritten' constitution and this has allowed these judges great power in defining it and their role within it. For example, they have been ingenious in escaping parliamentary shackles[14] and one day in 1966, they gave themselves the power to overrule their own precedents, further liberating their creativity.[15]

BACKGROUND

The UKSC was created by the Constitutional Reform Act 2005 and, like its predecessor, the appellate committee of the House of Lords,[16] acts as the final appeal court in civil cases from England and Wales, Northern Ireland and Scotland[17] and hears criminal appeals from the first three.[18] The Court comprises 12 Justices, including, by convention,[19] one Irish and two Scottish, supplemented by 'acting judges' who hold or have held high judicial office, such as retired Lords of Appeal below the age of 75, the Lord Chief Justice and so on.[20] New Justices are selected under the criteria of the Constitutional Reform Act 2005. For the first time, candidates are required to apply.[21]

Written appeal applications are determined by a private panel of three Justices.[22] Curiously, the Act and UKSC Rules are silent on criteria, although they are identical to those applied by the Law Lords.

> 3.3.3 Permission to appeal is granted for applications that, in the opinion of the Appeal Panel, raise an arguable point of law of general public importance which ought to be considered by the Supreme Court at that time.[23]

---

[14]   *Anisminic v Foreign Compensation Commission* [1969] 2 AC 147 (1968).

[15]   In a Practice Statement. The Constitutional Reform Act 2005 is silent on this.

[16]   For over 600 years but regulated by statute since the Appellate Jurisdiction Act 1876.

[17]   Used here were the old HL Briefing paper, *The Judicial Work of the House of Lords* and the Parliament library note, *The Appellate Jurisdiction of the House of Lords*. UKSC basics are in its first *Annual Report and Accounts 2009–2010*, July 2010, and on its website.

[18]   Though a number of the devolution cases in 2009–10 involved criminal law. The Court hears about 65–96 appeals per year.

[19]   The Constitutional Reform Act 2005, s 27(8) stipulates 'between them the judges will have knowledge of, and experience of practice in, the law of each part of the United Kingdom'.

[20]   Constitutional Reform Act 2005, ss 25 and 38. Lord Chief Justice Judge sat in 2009 and, later, Lord Neuberger MR. Under s 44, they can appoint 'specially qualified advisers', like a 'Brandeis Brief' in the US.

[21]   Submitting a CV, a letter of application and three judgments they consider demonstrate their abilities. The selection panel is chaired by the President, accompanied by the Deputy and representatives of the three jurisdictions' appointing commissions. R Cornes drew attention to the power this gives to the President, 'Shaping the Supreme Court—the power of the presidency', *The Times*, 1 October 2009.

[22]   If not rejected by the Registrar. Interveners may apply.

[23]   Practice Direction 3.

Most criminal appeals must be certified by the court below as raising a point of law of general public importance.[24]

The building is opposite the Palace of Westminster, where, as Law Lords, they sat in a committee room. Panels are normally five but sometimes three, seven or nine. By convention, the newest Justice speaks first in deliberations,[25] the obverse of USSC practice.[26] Law Lords' judgments used to be called speeches or opinions and were handed down in the Lords' chamber. Freed from Parliamentary procedure, Justices now deliver 'judgments' and refer to their fellows as 'Lord Phillips' instead of 'my noble and learned friend Lord Phillips of Worth Matravers'. Parliament broke the Court's historic link with Parliament in order to enhance the appearance of judicial independence. Law Lords Bingham and Steyn started campaigning for a UKSC around 2001.[27]

The Justices also serve in the Judicial Committee of the Privy Council, now cutely known as 'JCPC', since its move from Downing Street. Most appeals are from Commonwealth jurisdictions and UK overseas territories. Its devolution-review jurisdiction was transferred to the UKSC in 2009.[28] JCPC work occupied almost as many sitting days as Law Lords work[29] but is rapidly diminishing.[30] Some countries have established their own supreme courts[31] and it has lost its appellate work over doctors and dentists. Also, procedure changed in 2009, replacing oral leave hearings with paper applications. Hearings are shorter than in the UKSC. Advocates must justify hearings lasting more than one day, rather than the two days normally permitted for UKSC hearings. When Hong Kong was

[24] Administration of Justice Act 1960, s 1. Scottish appeals do not require leave but two advocates must certify the reasonableness of the appeal.

[25] Not a rule but it may have been copied from the JCPC, where it is prescribed by standing order.

[26] Justice Ginsburg, 'Workways of the US Supreme Court', lecture, February 2001, New Zealand Centre for Public Law.

[27] Lord Bingham of Cornhill, 'A New Supreme Court for the United Kingdom', 2002, The Constitution Unit, UCL; 'The Evolving Constitution', speech, Law Society, London, 4 October 2001; Lord Johan Steyn, 'The Case for a Supreme Court' (2002) 118 *LQR* 392. Their predecessor Lord Browne-Wilkinson wanted a UKSC: F Gibb, 'The law lord who took the rap over Pinochet', *The Times*, 19 October 1999. For the post-2001 story, see A Le Sueur, 'From Appellate Committee to Supreme Court: A Narrative', and others in L Blom-Cooper, B Dickson and G Drewry, *The Judicial House of Lords 1876–2009* (Oxford, Oxford University Press, 2009). The inevitability of severance from Parliament was apparent from 1998, in *McGonnell v UK* (28488/95) (2000) 30 EHRR 20, discussed in R Cornes' paper on the UCL CU website, 'Reforming the Lords: the Role of the Law Lords', 1999.

[28] Information is on its website and in the *Judicial and Court Statistics*. Obscure work includes vets' disciplinary appeals and some ecclesiastical and admiralty work. It went to the Bahamas for work purposes in 2006–07.

[29] 106 days and 117 days respectively in 2005: *Judicial Statistics (Revised) 2005*, August 2006.

[30] It heard 105 cases in 2006 but only 47 in 2009.

[31] New Zealand in 2003 and others in 2005, with the creation of the Caribbean Court of Justice.

handed over to China, the agreement required that two judges sat in the Hong Kong Court of Final Appeal and this occupies each for one month per year.[32]

PREVIOUS WRITING

Because the UKSC is essentially the same court, the relevance of research on the Law Lords is undiminished. Apart from the battery of commentaries that their decisions attract, the judges' practices and opinions on their work have been scrutinised in depth, though most books about them say they are under-researched.[33] Sets of Law Lords have granted interviews, since the 1960s. Their working methods are well documented. Their work is easy to examine, since almost all of it is *judging*. They are aloof from the management jobs of the Court of Appeal (CA). Partly because of their involvement in controversial cases and formerly public inquiries,[34] they are more likely to be profiled in books[35] and newspapers than other judges.[36] All are intellectuals so throughout their history many have lectured and published. Out-of-court speeches are on the Internet and reproduced as journal articles.[37] Some have courted publicity, either for the sake of promoting a cause, such as Lords Bingham, Steyn,[38] Walker,[39] and Baroness Hale[40] on the Supreme Court,[41] and Lord Steyn on human rights[42] or, uniquely, in

[32] There are normally about six current or former Lords of Appeal/Justices eligible to sit.

[33] B Dickson, 'The Lords of Appeal and their Work 1967–96' in P Carmichael and B Dickson (eds), *The House of Lords: its Parliamentary and Judicial Roles* (Oxford, Hart Publishing, 1999) 127 said that they were 'surprisingly under-studied', yet the battery of academic analyses continues in 2011. See below.

[34] Serving Justices will not now sit on inquiries, though retired ones may do so.

[35] Such as M Andenaes and D Fairgrieve's collection, *Tom Bingham and the Transformation of the Law* (Oxford, Oxford University Press, 2009) and A Lentin, *The Last Political Law Lord: Lord Sumner (1859–1934)* (Newcastle, Cambridge Scholars, 2008).

[36] For instance, C Blackhurst, 'An ideal judge' (on Lord Nolan), *The Independent*, 4 November 1995; P Webster, 'I will do what I like to find the truth, says law lord', *The Times*, 22 July 2003, on his inquiry into the death of Dr David Kelly. Lord Hoffmann attracted adverse publicity over the *Pinochet* case, provoking articles on the selection process, in 1999. There were many profiles of Steyn, Bingham and Hale.

[37] For instance, David Hope, 'A phoenix from the ashes? Accommodating a new supreme court' (2005) 121 *LQR* 252–72, speech at Strathclyde University. Lord Bingham was a prolific speech maker and writer: *The Business of Judging* (Oxford, Oxford University Press, 2000).

[38] See above, n 27.

[39] Walker, 'Sentence First, Verdict Afterwards—Constitutional Change in the United Kingdom Justice System', speech at the Supreme Court of NSW Annual Conference, 2004, reproduced at (2005) 7 *The Judicial Review* 133.

[40] Hale, 'A Supreme Court for the UK?' (2004) 24 *Legal Studies* 36–44.

[41] A former Law Lord spoke and wrote the most: Lord Cooke of Thorndon, in Parliament, in speeches such as the one cited here and in articles such as 'The Law Lords: An Endangered Heritage' (2003) 119 *LQR* 49.

[42] Steyn, 'Guantanamo Bay: The legal black hole', 27th FA Mann Lecture, 25 November 2003; J Rozenberg, 'Lord Steyn attacks fellow law lord over Guantanamo Bay detainees',

promoting himself, when Senior Law Lord Tom Bingham stood for the Chancellorship of Oxford University,[43] or just because they like to be transparent, such as Baroness Hale, when she placed a blog of her first week as a Law Lord on the Internet.[44] All of this, plus the books below, have given interested academics (but not the public) a clear idea of what the UK's top judges are like and how they work.

L Blom-Cooper and G Drewry, Final Appeal, 1972[45]

'An informed evaluation of the role of the Law Lords', it is a mixture of legal and comparative analysis, statistics and constitutional debate. They analysed performance in 500 cases. There are statistics on cases throughout and biographical information. They examined the pros and cons of having two levels of appeal court, which pinpointed the functions of a supreme court as going beyond review (error correction) to supervision (developing precedents). The pointless debate about whether the Law Lords should make new law was in its heyday, not least among the Law Lords. Some recommendations are highly pertinent here: the Law Lords should normally deliver a single opinion; advocates should submit skeleton arguments[46] and Law Lords should have American-style law clerks.

R Stevens, *Law and Politics, The House of Lords as a Judicial Body 1800–1976*, 1979[47]

Stevens' aim was to examine the social and political attitudes of the Law Lords and to assess their judicial role as part of British society and government. He examined arguments over whether judges made or declared the law. There are meticulously researched chapters on the period's politics, jurisprudence, politicians and judges, the development of substantive law and the shifting approach of the appellate process. He observed that 'the Court' could not be characterised as performing differently over time, in the way that the USSC could, because the Law Lords sat in small panels of five or so, not *en banc* (as a complete bench).[48]

Telegraph, 26 November 2004. Campaigning continued after he had ceased to be a Law Lord: *Panorama* interview, 10 October 2005; Channel 4 News interview, 6 December 2005.

[43] F Gibb, 'Call me Tom, says Lord Bingham in race for Oxford', *The Times*, 21 February 2003; interview with MA Sieghart, *The Times*, 13 March 2003; T Halpin, 'Dirty tricks alleged in fight for Oxford post', *The Times*, 25 February 2003; R Johnson, 'A land unfit for heroes', *The Spectator*, 22 February 2003. He set up a website.

[44] 'Diary of a Lady Law Lord', Association of Women Barristers newsletter, 2 April 2004. She very frequently gives lectures and has been interviewed on the UKSC Blog.

[45] See above n 4.

[46] They did not use this term. It had yet to be coined.

[47] See above n 9.

[48] They cannot sit *en banc* as they are an uneven number (12).

A Paterson, *The Law Lords*, 1982[49]

This is a socio-legal masterpiece. Paterson's aim was to explain how the Law Lords made decisions and to outline developments in their role in the previous 30 years. In hard cases, 'how do the Law Lords demarcate their province from that of the legislature when it comes to "developing" the common law?'[50] Paterson felt that in discussing these topics, jurists had raised empirical questions so he used social research methods—highly innovative and bravely executed. The book still provides a unique insight. It is one of the richest pieces of socio-legal research on any judiciary, because of his copious use of frank and non-anonymous interview material from the most famous, active and outspoken group of Law Lords ever. Demonstrating my point about the Law Lords' approachability, Paterson acknowledged help from no fewer than *20* Law Lords in 1970–80. His data were gathered from 14 in-depth interviews, 14 further judges, 33 advocates and key civil servants. He quoted the interviewees at length, and their plentiful writings and judgments. He observed interactions between the Law Lords and advocates. He summarised his findings as follows.

> Decisions ... are not the product of five individuals sitting in their own rooms painstakingly writing out their opinions. The printed speeches are but the end product of a complex series of exchanges between Bar and Bench and between the Law Lords themselves.[51]

Contrary to claims then current, academics apparently had little influence. Their primary reference group was their fellows. He examined judgment formation and their opinions on multiple and composite judgments. As his work examined the *role* of the Law Lords, according to their and others' expectation, Paterson was writing at an exciting time. He explored the genesis of the 1966 Practice Statement, the restrictions they put on their use of this new power and the hard cases in which they applied it or chose not to. This was a period of intense debate over whether their job was to provide certainty in the law or change it in accordance with their perceptions of social expectations. By comparing what they said and did, in 1966–80, Paterson demonstrated that these two were consistent, contradicting critics such as JAG Griffith.[52]

D Robertson, *Judicial Discretion in the House of Lords*, 1998[53]

This very important book is routinely ignored. It is about how judges make law. Robertson's statistical analysis is rigorous and the narrative on case law is

---

[49]   A Paterson, *The Law Lords* (London, Macmillan, 1982).
[50]   ibid 2.
[51]   ibid 7–8.
[52]   JAG Griffiths, *The Politics of the Judiciary*, 5th edn (London, Fontana, 1997).
[53]   D Robertson, *Judicial Discretion in the House of Lords* (Oxford, Oxford University Press, 1998).

especially valuable, from a non-lawyer. An American political scientist, he made unprecedented use of multivariate analysis. He demonstrated that case results were strongly correlated with which Law Lords determined an appeal, regardless of the arguments presented. Complex interactions took place between pairs or triples of Law Lords, sharply affecting the probability of the stronger or weaker litigant winning.[54] He examined judicial methods in statutory interpretation and common law, much more thoroughly than anyone else, to show how little constraint there was on discretion, regardless of judges' claims to be bound by existing rules. While Blom-Cooper and Drewry had told us 'it really does matter which judges are detailed to hear particular cases',[55] Robertson demonstrated just how much it matters. He said Americans readily performed jurimetrical analysis 'because no-one doubts the importance of particular judicial attitudes to results. In the UK, however, the prevailing belief is still one of neutral technical judging'.[56] As we shall see, the belief is now reversed. All current Justices would agree that who judges matters. In support of his thesis, he commented that the very fact that the Law Lords sat as a large bench in rare cases showed that they recognised the partiality of their normal decisions. 'It should be noted that decisions of sub-panels are virtually never used in other supreme courts.'[57]

A warning comment is needed against Robertson's initial propositions. Citing Stevens, he said that the common law 'is now presented as a complex body of rules, a "maze" as described by Lord Diplock, but a largely fixed body which can generate answers by the basic legal methodology of analogy to precedents'.[58] That is *not* what Stevens said in 1978. Nor was everyone deluding themselves that it was so in 1978 or 1998. On the contrary, Stevens cited Lord Radcliffe in 1964: '[T]here was never a more sterile controversy than upon the question whether a judge makes law. Of course he does. How can he help it?'[59] Stevens pointed out that the Practice Statement was issued against this background debate, and although it was only used six times during that period, its psychological impact was great, adding legitimacy to the creativity of the Law Lords in the 1960s and 1970s.[60] Stevens quoted Lord Reid's delightful metaphor:

> There was a time when it was thought almost indecent to suggest that judges make law—they only declare it. Those with a taste for fairytales seem to have thought that in

---

[54] Ch 2.

[55] Blom-Cooper and Drewry, above n 4 at ch VIII, 152.

[56] Robertson, above n 53 at 35.

[57] ibid 14.

[58] ibid 11.

[59] Stevens, above n 9 at 615, citing CJ Radcliffe, 'Law and Order', 61 *Law Society's Gazette*, 821. Though Radcliffe's insistence ended most UK debate in the 1960s, there now seems to be (tactical) reluctance to admit to law-making in the US. Posner only dared portray judges as '*occasional* legislators' in 2008, above n 13. He cited John Roberts who, in his confirmation hearing as Chief Justice, claimed that USSC Justices were mere umpires, at 78. Sonia Sotomayor insisted that a judge's job was to apply not make the law, in her 2009 confirmation hearing: R Smith, 'Judging the Judges' (2009) 159 *New Law Journal* 1154.

[60] Stevens, above n 9 at 617–19.

some Aladdin's cave there is hidden the Common Law in all its splendour and that on a judge's appointment there descends on him knowledge of the magic words Open Sesame. Bad decisions are given when the judge has muddled the password and the wrong door opens. But we do not believe in fairytales anymore.[61]

Robertson, then, started off with an exaggerated and generalised 'white' proposition (Law Lords claim not to make law) in order to disprove it and show it to be black (they do). The true picture of what judges claim to be doing is in subtle shades of grey, as carefully depicted by Lord Bingham, writing one year earlier.

[Appellate judges] know from experience … that the cases they have to decide involve points which are not the subject of previous decisions, or are the subject of conflicting decisions, or raise questions of statutory interpretation which apparently involve genuine lacunae or ambiguities. They know … that decisions involve issues of policy.[62]

Lord Bingham cited Lord Cooke in 1990, 'The inevitable duty of the Courts is to make law and that is what all of us do every day'.[63] As USSC Justice Sandra Day O'Connor said 'We're a common law court. Of course we 'make' law as we go along'.[64]

To be fair to Robertson, what he objected to is that in their *judgments*, the Law Lords downplayed the level of discretion that they enjoyed by insisting in locating their reasoning in known law. Even when presented with a moral dilemma where there was no precedent and which Robertson suggested was non-justiciable, such as the issue of what to do with a person in a persistent vegetative state,[65] they claimed to be applying rules. '[J]udicial pronouncements in England have always tended towards a pretence of a belief in slot machine jurisprudence'. It was not easy to characterise individuals, nor was it useful to look for broad class-based ideological affinities.

In many cases, and the Law Lords admit this easily enough, they work 'bottom up', from a basic instinct that the plaintiff or the defendant ought to win … Their own sense of being constrained … [by] acceptable legal argument is quite strong. Two ideas were common to the interviews. One is that they all claim to be familiar with the sense of having to give up the attempt to decide a case the way they want to, because the arguments cannot be made to work. The other is that they have, in a phrase that cropped up over and over again, a sense of 'cheating', not playing the game. [Many of them used the word to describe Lord Denning or one of their current colleagues.] Or they used it to describe an inner sense of obligation—'one tries not to cheat' … The Law Lords come to their decisions very freely, with little peer group influence or pressure, largely according to individual conceptions they hold about their role, and

---

[61] Stevens, above n 9 at 621, quoting James S Reid, 'The Judge as Lawmaker' (1972) 12 *Journal of the Society of Public Teachers of Law* 22.

[62] Bingham, *The Business of Judging*, above n 3 at ch 2.

[63] ibid 34, citing Lord Cooke's speech.

[64] J Toobin, *The Nine: Inside the Secret World of the Supreme Court* (New York, Doubleday, 2007) 97.

[65] *Airdale NHS Trust v Bland* [1993] 1 All ER 821.

with an eye either to an immediate sense of justice in the particular case, or to concerns they have about the likely impact in a wider world of the instant decision.[66]

Incidentally, Robertson found the Law Lords to be utterly transparent. He was 'surprised and delighted' that *all* the Law Lords were willing to grant him interviews.[67]

P Carmichael and B Dickson (eds), *The House of Lords: its Parliamentary and Judicial Roles,* 1999[68]

Dickson examined statistical information on the Law Lords' length of service, age on appointment, education and case throughput, the success rate of petitions and number of sitting days. Drewry and Blom-Cooper revisited 'The Appellate Function', finding the nature of appeals had changed since their book. Public law had displaced revenue appeals. There are four commentaries on their performance in aspects of the law.

M Barrett, *The Law Lords: An Account of the Workings of Britain's Highest Judicial Body and the Men Who Preside Over It,* 2001[69]

Barrett said the Law Lords were 'very much unknown to the British public. This book aims to change that'[70] but sadly, by 2007, I was the fourth person to borrow it on interloan. It contains chapters on history, the Lord Chancellor, the JCPC, a statistical analysis of biographical information on all Lords of Appeal in Ordinary and potted biographies, with the novelty of photographs. There are seven pages on working methods. Barrett too interviewed 'various Lords of Appeal past and present'.

A Le Sueur (ed), *Building the UK's New Supreme Court,* 2004[71] and a special issue of *Legal Studies,* 2004[72]

These 30 pieces, and many journal articles were prompted by the 2003 announcement of the UKSC. Some are very informative and thought provoking on the

---

[66] Robertson, above n 53 at 17–18.
[67] ibid Preface, viii.
[68] See above n 33.
[69] M Barrett, *The Law Lords: An Account of the Workings of Britain's Highest Judicial Body and the Men Who Preside Over It* (Basingstoke, Macmillan, 2001).
[70] ibid 2.
[71] A Le Sueur (ed), *Building the UK's New Supreme Court* (Oxford, Oxford University Press, 2004).
[72] *Constitutional innovation: the creation of a Supreme Court for the United Kingdom; domestic, comparative and international reflections, a special issue of Legal Studies* (2004) 24 *Legal Studies* 1 and 2.

constitution, function and working methods of the top court, comparing it with similar courts abroad. They are well worth re-reading now, as the UKSC continues to discuss and develop its practice.[73] As Le Sueur acknowledged, debates about the judicial functions of the Law Lords and Judicial Committee of the Privy Council (PC) have not suffered from insularity.

L Blom-Cooper, B Dickson and G Drewry, *The Judicial House of Lords 1876–2009*, 2009[74]

The 40 items in this tome are diverse, with 15 analyses of performance in specific areas of law, institutional history, analyses of judicial approach and outsiders' perspectives. This is not a complete picture. For a deeper analysis of the Bingham court's approach, and Bingham's impact on other top courts' reasoning, and the use of comparative law, see some of the 51 items in M Andenas and D Fairgrieve, *Tom Bingham and the Transformation of the Law*, 2009.[75] Academic analysis continues in 2011, in another collection of 12 items, mainly on the performance of the Law Lords: see J Lee, *From House of Lords to Supreme Court—Jurists, Judges and the Process of Judging*.[76]

These, and a plethora of speeches by Justices and CA judges, and the articles written by and about the top judges for the last 60 years show they have been the subject of penetrating examination which remains highly pertinent. As there is a UKSC Blog, there is also now a running commentary.[77]

THIS RESEARCH

I too found the judges ultra-transparent and approachable. In 2005, while lunching with three at a small table on Parliament's terrace café, four more squeezed in to join the conversation. Recently, one academic made use of material gained from a freedom of information request to the UKSC but I had already obtained the same information in minutes, by phoning the chief executive and registrar. I spent four days with two Law Lords in 2005 and interviewed them, returning in 2009.[78] I observed and/or spoke to 11, including two panels of five and three deliberating privately in an appeal committee. A different five took

---

[73]   See especially the items by John Bell and Brenda Hale and everything written by both Le Sueur and Cornes.

[74]   See above n 27.

[75]   M Andenas and D Fairgrieve, *Tom Bingham and the Transformation of the Law* (Oxford, Oxford University Press, 2009).

[76]   J Lee, *From House of Lords to Supreme Court—Jurists, Judges and the Process of Judging* (Oxford, Hart Publishing, 2011).

[77]   The amount of commentary has already become overwhelming.

[78]   In the UKSC, I avoided Bingham and Hale, as there is a mass of biographical information, plus their opinions, in the public domain. See above for Bingham. See Lady Hale's

me to the Privy Council. I watched one chairing a Parliamentary select committee. I had previously met four, discussing their work at length with two. I was invited by two Law Lords to the UK-Canadian judicial conference. In 2008, I attended a series of private seminars on the UKSC[79] and in 2010, the closed first anniversary seminar. In 2009, I visited the UKSC four times, observed the two research judges at work, in and out of court, and spoke to the registrar, chief executive, and other Justices. I returned in 2010. This chapter contains quotations from the two interviewees and companion judges, plus comments from two other Justices on a draft, plus published quotations from other Justices, such as a 2009 interview with Lord Hope.

HORSES FOR COURSES—HOW PANELS ARE SELECTED

Lord Cooke said that it mattered more in London than in foreign Supreme Courts *which* judges were selected and graphically illustrated this with the life-or-death penalty outcomes of differently constituted Privy Councils.[80] Blom-Cooper and Drewry wrote in 1972 'No outsider knows how the five judges are selected, but there have been instances where the five selected seemed to an outside commentator to be the least suitable' and there had been occasions when the selection had appeared to present a particular bias.[81] They recommended that the Law Lords should sit *en banc*, like the USSC. Ten years later, thanks to Paterson, we did know how benches were devised.[82] Nowadays, the chief executive and registrar are happy to discuss how the panels are selected but it was clear in 2005 and 2008 that the Law Lords did not fully understand the selection criteria. 'We just say when we're available.' A very experienced Law Lord confessed in 2008 that it was 'a mystery' when seven and five-member panels were convened.

academic writing, her blog (above), and newspaper articles. She was profiled in E Cruickshank, *Women in the Law* (London, The Law Society, 2003) and C McGlynn *The Woman Lawyer—Making the difference* (London, Butterworths, 1998). In 1996, the *Daily Mail* launched a campaign against her as a law commissioner, as a 'twice married' and 'hardline' 'feminist', bent on 'subverting family values'. See *The Guardian* profile by C Dyer, 9 January 2004, at 14. She was a well-known academic, Brenda Hoggett.

[79] Organised by Professors Le Sueur and Malleson of Queen Mary, University of London, attended by future and aspiring Justices, lawyers and academics. Practice and procedure were discussed.

[80] In a 2001 speech.

[81] Blom-Cooper and Drewry, above n 4 at 153, referring to RB Stevens' comment (27 *MLR* 121) on *Hedley Byrne* [1964] AC 465, a case which expanded negligence. The chancery-dominated bench originally convened might have reached a different conclusion.

[82] Dickson used a freedom of information request (B Dickson, 'The Processing of Appeals in the House of Lords' (2007) 123 *LQR* 571) but I found no reluctance from Brendan on selecting Law Lords or from Jenny Rowe, UKSC Chief Executive, or the Justices, to explain the procedure.

Appeal Panels

Paterson reported that selection of the trios determining leave applications was done by the Principal Clerk to the Judicial Office and because of constraints on listing, he often had very little choice. No effort was made to tailor a specialist panel. Nor was there any co-ordination between their composition and the five who heard the appeal. In 2005, the clerk, Brendan, a non-lawyer, confirmed that he chose these trios unaided and 'It's up to them when they meet'. By 2011, the panels of three Justices are selected by the registrar.[83] She said they *may* be specialist but she emphasised that although she drafts the panel rotas they are approved by the President or Deputy.

Full Hearings

Paterson reported that there was often little room for manoeuvre and *this is still the case* in the UKSC. The principal clerk liaised with his JCPC counterpart. The UKSC registrar performs both jobs. She and the chief executive draft the constitutions, for approval by the President. As before, one or both Scottish judges sit on a Scottish appeal (and one gives the lead judgment). New Justices do not sit on appeals they have heard in the Court of Appeal. Lord Mance does not sit on appeals from his wife. Occasionally, individuals are unavailable, such as those[84] who sit in Hong Kong and those who are absent whilst delivering lectures or conducting job interviews.[85] For logistical simplicity, some panels stay together to hear JCPC cases. Blom-Cooper and Drewry reported that chancery judges did not sit in criminal appeals. This was not true by the late 1970s, as some (in)famous decisions demonstrated. Nor is it true now.

Paterson commented that a case might start out with a single specialist judge, then be decided by a Court of Appeal with one or two specialists, then thrown into the Law Lords lottery, where although an attempt might have been made to tailor the bench, it was highly likely to be decided by five mostly non-specialists. There were no *fixed* specialist panels,[86] so the advocate's job was much harder than before the lowest court. From Paterson's 1970s interviews until the 2004 commentaries,[87] lawyers complained that they did not know until quite close to

---

[83] Louise de Mambro, to whom I am indebted, as well as Jenny Rowe, for these explanations.

[84] And, till the convention was abolished, those occupied in inquiries. The Saville inquiry was announced in 1998. Lord Saville was preoccupied with it until late 2009, when he recommenced sitting.

[85] Interviews for Family President and a Justice were conducted in the UKSC building in 2009–10.

[86] On this topic, see the highly informative item by Bell, in the 2004 *Legal Studies* collection, above n 72.

[87] Paterson, above n 49 at 61 and Gordon, in Le Sueur, above n 71.

the hearing which judges would be sitting, though this is now on the website. Richard Gordon QC[88] advocated set panels in constitutionally important cases, because of the danger 'of unspecialised Law Lords deciding cases that require an understanding of the dynamics as well as the literal meaning of the relevant case law'. Responding in 2008, one of the research Law Lords said:

> I think that Gordon's comments about 'unspecialised' Law Lords are misconceived, especially in the context of human rights. The notion that an 'unspecialised' Law Lord is bound to come up with a literal interpretation is absurd.

This view is supported by the fact that the top court has heard so many human rights cases by 2010 (100 of 475 decisions in 2000–07)[89] that all the Justices are specialists. Indeed, the court *makes* human rights law for the UK.[90]

Brendan Keith, principal clerk in 2005, told me he devised the benches for the following term, subject to approval by the two senior Law Lords. 'I know my judges—horses for courses. Lord Nicholls likes this and doesn't like that and so on.' There was by then no shortage of criminal lawyers, one judge pointed out. Two had practised in crime and four were former chief justices (one English, two Scottish and one Northern Irish). They were useful for JCPC work, as it heard so much crime. In 2009–10, the chief executive and a Justice told me that when panels of five were selected, the criterion was to choose the specialists (as Brendan did), then add the others in at random.

Where seven or nine heard constitutional blockbusters, Brendan said Lord Bingham preferred that the most senior would sit, so there could be no accusations of packing the bench. Nevertheless, that very lunchtime, the junior Law Lords asked Lord Nicholls what work was scheduled for the following term. He mentioned there would be a torture case and the judges had been chosen.[91] One judge was sorry that he would be too junior but Lord Nicholls said he was wrong in assuming the seven would necessarily be the most senior. In his 2005 interview, one Law Lord (now Justice) recognised that *who* judges matters and thought the Law Lords should change practice:

> It is … frustrating … to be left out of a case in which one has a particular interest … I think that there is quite a strong argument for us as the final court to hear fewer cases with more of us hearing them. I think there is too great a risk with cases being decided … [by] the particular five chaps you have and by the time you get to this level this shouldn't be the case. I think we hear too many appeals. The Court of Appeal are for the

---

[88]   Commenting in Le Sueur's book, above n 71.

[89]   V Zeno-Zencovich, 'The Bingham Court' in Andenas and Fairgrieve, above n 35 at 824–25. B Dickson, 'Year end' (2010) 160 *New Law Journal* 65, said 24 per cent were human rights cases in 2009.

[90]   Zeno-Zencovich says the court is in constant dialogue with Strasbourg and *no other top European court uses so much Strasbourg jurisprudence* as ratio decidendi. Andenas and Fairgrieve recount how a Bingham judgment persuaded the ECtHR to overrule itself: above n 35 at 835 and, of course, the UKSC has tried to do the same thing, in *Horncastle* [2009] UKSC 14.

[91]   *A v SS for the Home Dept* [2005] UKHL 71.

most part extremely able and unless there are compelling reasons because you are reshaping the whole area of law or eliminating errors ... I don't think we should be touching the case and when we touch it I think we should touch it in a very full way ... It is a very expensive business having a second appeal ... I question whether ... we should really move more towards a system with a conventional supreme court.

Then, there seemed to be no chance of any such significant change of practice. The notion of sitting *en banc* was written off without reasons in the 2003 consultation paper. Robert Stevens sarcastically quoted its smug conservatism.

Obviously the new Supreme Court could not sit in banc (as the US Supreme Court does—'The reason for this is to prevent the possibility that the composition of the panel will affect the outcome of the case'—something that could not be relevant for apolitical English judges) ... The mythology goes deep![92]

The advantage of bigger panels is in eliminating the lottery effect demonstrated by Robertson but it cuts down the number of appeals that can be heard, though some considered this would be an advantage. At the time of writing, 2011, rather oddly, the Justices are have not published clear public criteria as to how the routine appeal panels of five are devised, though they have published on their website the criteria for sitting in bigger panels of seven or nine. This was in response to outsiders asking Lord Phillips to do this in the closed seminar on the first anniversary of the court.[93] The readiness to sit as seven or nine continues a trend they started as Law Lords but this trend has escalated. It must be noted, however, that *most* panels are of five. The same judge who lobbied to be on the 2005 torture case told me that he had been disappointed to be excluded from a seven-panel for an interesting case on pre-nuptial agreements in 2010. He lobbied the President, who agreed to increase the panel to nine: 'the President is infinitely malleable on size and constitution of panels'. All Justices to whom I spoke in 2009–10 favoured more frequent use of big panels. Of the 58 decisions by the UKSC in 2010, 10 used seven judges and five used nine.[94]

Unsurprisingly, there is still rumbling unease that Supreme Court composition matters and that Justices ought to sit *en banc* or at least be more transparent in panel selection criteria.[95] One Justice's 2009 words reflect the sentiments of his colleagues.

I've been advocating bigger panels for some time. The final courts in the US and Canada sit en banc. Quite often in the past we've split 3/2 ... If we split 5/4 we don't lay

---

[92]   R Stevens, 'Reform in haste and repent at leisure: Iolanthe, the Lord High Executioner and *Brave New World*' (2004) 24 *Legal Studies* 1–35, 33, quoting the consultation paper at 51.

[93]   In September 2010. The criteria for bigger panels are potential departure from precedent, conflicting precedents, constitutional or public importance and important human rights points. The registrar emphasised (in response to my telephone query) that constitutions must be approved by Lord Phillips or Lord Hope.

[94]   B Dickson, 'A marque of quality' (2011) 161 *New Law Journal* 153.

[95]   For a useful analysis, see R Buxton, 'Sitting en banc in the new Supreme Court' (2009) 125 *LQR* 288.

ourselves open to the same criticism, because a different constitution wouldn't reach a different conclusion. So we do sit in bigger panels more often now. When we give leave, we indicate this.[96]

At a 2010 conference,[97] Baroness Hale said she had heard that their habit of sitting in sevens and nines more frequently now was 'because of our desire to assert ourselves' but like the Justice above, she explained 'the trigger was really the embarrassment if we split three-two'. The more Justices, the more authoritative their decision. Nevertheless:

> If we sat en banc, there'd be a risk that it'd look as if we were divided on philosophical lines. If we sat all the time it might seem that ABC always agreed and XYZ all agreed. If you have a randomly shuffled pack, as now, people can't take such an interest in who is appointed.

In 2010, another Justice agreed that it would be unwise to sit in panels of nine too often 'because it's impossible to overturn the decision. It sort of entrenches it'.

PRIVY COUNCIL—RELIC OF EMPIRE

When I asked one Justice, in 2009, how there was sufficient judicial time to schedule bigger panels, he explained that (apart from the reduction in JCPC work) they had started to sit as a group of three in the JCPC, because 'many civil appeals raise no real issue of law, do not have much money at stake, and would not be thought worth a second appeal in England'. By 2010, however, protests from the Caribbean persuaded the Justices to start sitting in fives again. Trivial appeals cannot be eliminated because in some instances, they do not need leave from the JCPC itself. In 2008, another judge remarked that some two-day criminal appeals from the Caribbean 'would be knocked off in a morning by the Court of Appeal'. Justices find the waste of their time in the JCPC frustrating but know that a leave requirement would necessitate amending domestic law in all relevant Commonwealth jurisdictions, following negotiations by the Foreign and Commonwealth Office.[98] As I observed the JCPC in 2010, they were hearing a case that arose out of a spat between two businessmen who used to be friends. They had already spent in costs three times the amount in issue in the case, having had a 13-day hearing in their native High Court, then an appeal, before

---

[96] In a November 2010 speech, Lord Clarke also said he favoured large panels in cases of 'real public importance' and that in the longer term there is a case for having a smaller court, which takes fewer cases but on which all the Justices sit.

[97] At the University of Notre Dame, London Law Centre, 'Happiness pursued: a celebration of ten years of the Human Rights Act—an exploratory encounter', 20 October 2010.

[98] Someone in the closed seminars drew attention to a 2007 case on 'a defunct statutory regime that affected two people'. Some have criticised occasional time-wasting Scottish appeals (which the UKSC cannot refuse).

coming over to London. One Justice said he thought that if appeals from Jamaica and Trinidad disappeared then 'some other solution' would be found to handle appeals from the remaining handful of tiny states still sending appeals 'because it's such an absurd waste of [the Justices] time—the worst case was an appeal over a truck crash!'

THE WAY THEY WORK: THE APPEAL COMMITTEE

As Blake and Drewry observed, in 2004, the Court of Appeal employs a self-denying ordinance and rarely grants leave to appeal, leaving this to the top judges. This was a significant change since they remarked in 1972 on the contrast with the US and Canadian Supreme Courts which controlled their own 'dockets'. The best modern examinations of this sifting process[99] are by Dickson[100] and Le Sueur.[101] The main significance of case selection, Le Sueur said, was that it enabled a court to define its constitutional role and powers. A top court in a common law country ought to be concerned not just with error correction but with clarifying and developing the law and exercising judicial management over the whole legal system. In selecting cases, it set its agenda. Nevertheless, as Blom-Cooper and Drewry pointed out in 1972, the Law Lords did not receive enough appeals in some areas of law to enable them to develop a coherent body of jurisprudence and this was most marked at that time in criminal law and in the law of obligations, with 'disastrous' consequences.[102]

Since 1998 almost all applications are determined in writing. Since 2000, each is accompanied by a three to four-page judicial assistant's memorandum,[103] setting out the main points and drawing attention to relevant passages in the judgments appealed, which are included in judges' files. This is a far cry from Blom-Cooper and Drewry's portrait of the 1960s Law Lords, tortured by 'a large number of garrulous petitioners ... appearing in person'.[104] Le Sueur said that in criminal appeals, the issues have been focused by certifying a question for appeal yet in civil cases, the judges tend to select *cases* for appeal rather than *issues*. In the USSC, it was common to grant leave on one point but not others and lawyers were aided by past models of acceptable appeal questions. In the 2008 seminars, several lawyers called for similar transparency, with explicit reasons for refusal

---

[99] In 2007, 52 of 207 applications proceeded to a full hearing (*Judicial and Court Statistics 2008*, Cm. 7697) and there were 62 in 2009, in the HL/UKSC. As Le Sueur shows, the USSC hears about one per cent of applications and the Canadian Supreme Court hears about 14 per cent.

[100] Dickson, above n 82.

[101] Le Sueur, above n 71 at ch 12.

[102] Blom-Cooper and Drewry, above n 4 at 399–400.

[103] Blom-Cooper and Drewry were 30 years ahead of their time in recommending law clerks.

[104] Blom-Cooper and Drewry, above n 4 at 398.

posted on the website, but this has not been done. In 2010, a Justice said they might change procedure to provide reasons 'if we keep getting nagged' but it would add to their workload and lay them open to criticism and challenges by those who were refused leave. 'Also, it's sometimes difficult to explain that a case may raise points of general public importance but the application before us is an unsuitable vehicle for considering the point, because of the facts'.[105] Pointing to the increase in applications, and (wrongly) assuming the Law Lords to be under growing pressure, Le Sueur suggested copying the Canadian Supreme Court, using mature staff lawyers to help sift applications, the advantage being that they 'are more mature and more ready to refuse leave [than law clerks]'.[106] This comment is in danger of wrongly portraying the role of US law clerks and UK judicial assistants, who merely prepare summaries. Justice Ginsburg has described the US petition conference process intimately, down to the coffee cake and beef jerky.[107]

> Every petition, no matter how humble, is summarised and explained in a law clerk's preliminary memorandum. But it is surely not true that the justices simply scan the memoranda, then vote as the law clerks tell them to ... Yes, the justices speed read the law clerks' memoranda, but with the judgment one gains from experience with law and life, and with the Court as a collegial body. When in doubt, a justice will personally check the petition and the response ... and do [appropriate] homework.

Similarly, UK judicial assistants do not filter applications. It is inconceivable that they would, so UK and US procedure are similar but the scale is different.[108] Le Sueur seems to be suggesting that lawyers be appointed to perform the same filtering role as the registrar in the Employment Appeal Tribunal (EAT). There is, however, no evidence that time spent considering petitions is excessive, or that Justices are overworked. *The total of full hearings and JCPC work combined has remained constant.*[109] There are some changes in the UKSC, aimed at transparency. Where an application is filed electronically, it can be made visible to the public. Also, Justices changed their practice, in 2009, so that they may all examine petitions. Any may express an opinion, though permission will be determined by the designated three.

Gordon was concerned that the Law Lords missed cases that were important, and took on inappropriate cases. He suggested more detailed and/or specialist consideration at the application stage.[110] Baroness Hale, before she joined them,

---

[105] Still complained of in 2010: H Tomlinson and O Gayner, 'Hilary Term 2010' (2010) 160 *New Law Journal* 698.

[106] Le Sueur, above n 71 at ch 12, 290. Norwegian Supreme Court permission decisions appear in their law reports.

[107] Ginsburg, above n 26.

[108] 8,500 USSC petitions per year are sifted to about 85 argued cases. *Chief Justice's Year-End Reports.*

[109] As can be seen from the flat lines on the graph in the annual *Judicial and Court Statistics.*

[110] In Le Sueur, above n 71 at 326.

commented on their selection criteria: 'As the senior Law Lord put it before he joined them, the House of Lords "dines a la carte". The real criterion is whether it is something important that they fancy doing. If it is, they may take the case even if there is no real prospect of success'.[111] In 2008, a Law Lord (now a Justice) emailed:

> We do set our own agenda in selecting cases, but only from a very limited menu—those where someone petitions for leave (and in crime where the court below has certified a point of law of GPI [general public importance]). That is a very random and self-selected group, often missing some of the biggest issues of the day because no-one wants to appeal.

Another Justice emailed:

> The expression 'general public importance' might be seen as a formula that pretends to give a reason for our decisions but really, because it is so wide and vague (especially in the mysterious 'at this time') avoids doing so. But we could all give examples ... We are more likely to give leave on a case involving a social security payment of (say) £100 a week, because it affects tens of thousands of people, rather than involving a commercial contract worth £10 million if the latter is 'just a one-off point of construction'. But some commercial points are of general public importance, for instance whether an arbitration clause in a contract applies when the validity of the contract itself is attacked. Lord [X] is quite keen on selecting suitable patent appeals in order to try to harmonise the interpretation of the European Patent Convention. On some topics (for instance big money divorces; the date of knowledge for limitation purposes; when a cause of action arises for pure economic loss caused by professional negligence; artificial tax avoidance; one supply or two for VAT purposes?) I think we are sometimes inclined to feel that we have already dealt with the problem as well as we can, and that a further appeal would not necessarily clarify the law any more.

At 10.00 am one Monday, a Law Lord took me to an appeal committee. Lord Hoffmann joined us, still wearing his Lycra cycling shorts and cerise top. By 10.15 am they had decided all five petitions. They thought I would be surprised but I had learned how the Court of Appeal could pre-deliberate 10 cases in 15 minutes.[112] They had pre-read the applications, the assistant's memo, and the judgments in the court below. On each decision, they completed a tick-box form. Their options were/are to grant or refuse leave, or ask for objections from the other side, or ask for an oral hearing. (Brendan told me this was granted only about six times per year and speeches were limited to 15 minutes.) The junior judge gave his opinion first, each time.

10.04 Case 1: unanimous in granting leave to appeal so no discussion.

---

[111]   Hale, above n 40 at 37.
[112]   Dickson, above n 82, guessed a petition was discussed for 30 minutes. The reality is three.

Case 2, on contract: one felt leave should not be given. Another wanted more guidance. Another commented that one CA judge had given a practical judgment while another's was technical. Leave refused.

10.07 Case 3, on mobile phones: refused leave. 'John Dyson dealt with it perfectly satisfactorily in the Court of Appeal', said one. The senior judge filled in the form, reciting as he wrote '*Not* a European point … No reasonable doubt'.

10.09 Case 4: one said there were two points of law of public importance but it was a puzzle as to whether the Court of Appeal should have decided the case the other way. Another was confused about what the points were. One suggested that they could ask for objections from the respondent. 'It's up to you.' 'Well I'm not going to hold out.' The other filled in the form: 'OK. I'll tick this box. No question of European law'.

Case 5: the first judge said 'I would refuse leave. The law's draconian and it's meant to be'. The others agreed without discussion.

In 2004, Gordon suggested that specialist panels should determine applications. This research found that this is now the case, to some extent. He said they should decide whether a specialist neutral 'friend of the court' should be briefed. Of course they now do this and the UKSC Justices added that they welcome even multiple interveners (as did the Law Lords)[113] and limit them to 15 minutes or a written intervention. 'It would be *insane* to shut them out—very helpful', said one Justice.[114] Gordon argued that cases should be managed by a single judge from an early stage, as is done in the Strasbourg court. Responding in 2008, a senior Law Lord disagreed, 'The sort of case management required in lower courts should simply not be needed'.[115] While this is clearly so, I suggest below that the timing and content of oral hearings does need to be prescribed.

THE WAY THEY WORK: FULL HEARINGS

Every commentator points to judges' keenness to preserve oral hearings, contrary to other top courts, such as the USSC, which allows 30 minutes of advocacy,[116]

---

[113] They allowed 17 interveners in *A v SS for the Home Dept (No 2)* [2006] 2 AC 221: B Dickson, 'A Hard Act to Follow: The Bingham Court, 2000–8' in Blom-Cooper et al, above n 27.

[114] For instance, five interveners in the Jewish schools case, [2009] UKSC 15. Of the 17 cases decided by the UKSC in 2009, interventions were allowed in five: see website. Also Dickson, above n 89.

[115] With certain exceptions: he cited *Kirin-Amgen Inc v Transkaryotic Therapies Inc (No 2)* [2004] UKHL 46 and Privy Council cases such as *Christian v The Queen* [2006] UKPC 47.

[116] USSC Rules, effective 1 October 2007, Rule 28. 3, prescribing 'Additional time is rarely accorded'.

and the European Court of Justice, which might permit 10 minutes, or nothing.[117] The Law Lords have demanded a written outline since before the 1690s,[118]
but Blom-Cooper and Drewry observed in 1972 that 'The Case is merely
regarded as a useful preliminary statement … Indeed it sometimes appears that
their Lordships have not even read it'. Procedure was 'geared wholly to oral
argument' and 'counsel spend a great deal of time in reading authorities (some of
them at inordinate length)'.[119] They suggested copying South African courts with
the pre-hearing submission of 'heads of argument', a full précis of propositions
and authorities, with a general prohibition on raising new arguments orally. The
printed case now contains a skeleton argument, meant to be limited to 20 pages
but which sometimes splurges to 60 and this research found that nowadays they
do read it.[120]

Paterson concluded that the Law Lords relied far more on the oral interchange
than written material. Judges repeatedly told him that the oral approach lent
flexibility to the arguments. More surprisingly, by 2004, Gordon reported that
'the preponderance of legal argument takes place in court. There are rarely any
time limits for the delivery of submissions and, if any are imposed, they are not
usually insisted upon' and 'the statements of case are frequently not referred to'.
He worried about a system where fundamental rights and constitutional issues
were 'determined on so slender a thread as the superior skill of the barrister
presenting the legal argument'.[121] Paterson revisited this point in empirical
research published in 2011. Interviewing 22 current or former Justices or Law
Lords, he found they all said they had changed their minds during oral argument.
Gordon did not suggest abolishing oral argument, because the sort of forensic
examination inflicted by the Law Lords tested the integrity of argument. He
suggested time limits, encouraging court and advocate to focus on the true
questions, plus directions as to which points should be argued.

Paterson said the average appeal took three to four days by the 1970s. The
average is now two.[122] Hearings test the stamina of the strongest advocate. Barrett
remarked that the presence of 'the most brilliant judges in the United Kingdom
endows the hearings with a natural aura of authority'.[123] Sitting behind elite
counsel, I have often watched their silk gowns tremble, as all five brains challenge
them in turn. Gordon likened an appearance to a scene from Hitchcock's *The*

---

[117]   Rules of Procedure of the Court of Justice, 1–1-2007, Art 44(a).
[118]   Meaning seventeenth century—this is *not* a misprint, as so many Justices and commentators thought it was: Stevens, above n 9 at 12. Each appellant was obliged to produce enough
copies for each peer.
[119]   Blom-Cooper and Drewry, above n 4 at 404.
[120]   Supported by A Paterson, 'Does Advocacy Matter in the Lords?' in Lee's 2011 book, cited
above n 76 at 262. He also found what I observed, that some judges also discuss the case in
advance with their judicial assistants.
[121]   Richard Gordon Q.C., in Le Sueur, above n 71 at 316–17.
[122]   *Judicial and Court Statistics 2008*, repeated in the UKSC's first annual report, in July 2010.
[123]   Barrett, above n 69 at 122.

Birds[124] though Gibb remarked that Lord Browne-Wilkinson, in the 1990s, 'put a stop…to the tradition of rudeness, the savaging of counsel'[125] and in 2011, Paterson said Lord Bingham 'finally established the conversational style'. He drew an entertaining portrait of the aggressive behaviour of some predecessors, notably Lords Brandon and Templeman ('Sid Vicious').[126]

Although there are no time restrictions on individuals, there are on cases, based on advocates' estimates. In 2005, some judges grumbled that estimates for the Hunting Act challenge[127] had proven inadequate and they had to ask Treasury Counsel to translate some oral arguments into writing. In another case, they complained that the advocates had underestimated timings, to secure a listing. They blamed the appellants' counsel but when I questioned counsel, they, in turn, blamed Crown counsel, who were clearly the darlings of the Law Lords.[128] One judge said that disproportionate scheduling was the most frustrating aspect of his job.

> The great hunting case … [was] a two-day case, which frankly should have been at least three. It is frustrating to cramp hearings, to give that case a two-day hearing … the same length … as the case on Monday which should never have been more than a one-day case. It is ridiculous. One was a short sharp point and the other a huge constitutional reform … Cases should last as long as we want to explore them and not how long they want to address us.

Another Justice pointed out, though, that they did not all complain that time estimates were too short and there was a strong contrary view. The Justices are aware of the limits on orality in foreign courts but have no desire to change, like Lord Cooke, who had also sat in Hong Kong, New Zealand and a number Pacific islands.

> I confess a strong preference for the practice in the Lords … Adequate opportunity for oral persuasion is a precious asset … Skilfully used and with the stimulus for both counsel and bench of judicial interrogation and disclosure of how for the time being the Judge's mind is working, it can change preliminary impressions derived from reading the papers.[129]

Paterson observed that interchanges between the 1970s Law Lords were aimed at their colleagues[130] though he did not repeat this in 2011 and there was nothing in

---

[124] Richard Gordon QC, above n 121, at 319.

[125] F Gibb, 'The law lord who took the rap over Pinochet', *The Times*, 19 October 1999, Law, 3.

[126] Paterson, in Lee, above n 76 at 256–59.

[127] *Jackson v Attorney General* [2005] UKHL 56.

[128] Paterson, in Lee, above n 76 at 265, remarked on the advantage the 'leading performers' have, because of the trust placed in them by the judges, and he cited a judge who said this gave them an unfair advantage.

[129] Lord Cooke of Thorndon, 'Final Appeal Courts: Some Comparisons', lecture delivered at the New Zealand Centre for Public Law, Victoria University of Wellington, December 2001.

[130] Paterson, above n 49 at 89.

my observations, in 2005–10 to suggest that this was still the case. Judges' enthusiasm for oral advocacy is undiminished, though. Lunching with three, I asked if they had made up their minds on the case they were about to hear, having read the papers. 'Oh *no!*' said one. 'What, then, would be the purpose of counsel?' 'No I definitely haven't made my mind up', said another, 'They are all arguable, interesting points'. The third agreed but by 2005 they were already considering how to draft procedural rules for the UKSC so this prompted examination of the oral tradition, in their interviews.

> There is quite a debate going on among us as to whether we should stick with the existing system ... so long as Lord Bingham is around there will continue to be a strong feeling that our justice system works round oral argument and that it should not be restricted but I think probably there will come a time when ... there will be much tougher time limits. There is a pretty big duplication about the huge detail that one now gets in our printed cases ... plus lengthy oral argument, which is pretty much, 'You say you have read my printed case but I don't really trust you so I am going to say it all again' and I think it is probably is a bit wasteful.

By December 2009, they were still as keen. One remarked, 'that's the most *fun* part of the job!' Nevertheless, some of the oral presentations in the UKSC are neither 'argument' nor necessary. In two autumn 2009 cases, counsel opened by tediously reciting the contested legislation in detail. In the first case, on Article 6, Lord Hope, presiding, occasionally tried to move the appellant on. Accompanied by English and elite American law students, I was embarrassed by the advocate's recitations and lack of flexible, responsive advocacy. The Americans, used to the USSC, remarked on the pointlessness of recitation and repetition and one of the Justices' assistants speaking to the students was even more critical. He added that the Jewish schools case had opened with a two-hour recitation of the legislation. 'A four-day case could have been heard in a day.' He said that Temple Bar Scholars (ex USSC clerks, visiting) had commented that there was far too much extraneous material. The next week, in a tax case, Lord Hope was again repeatedly trying to speed up the appellant advocate but the QC seemed to be stuck on a train-track, from which he could not deviate. He had not finished by the end of the first day of a two-day case.

Lord Hope: 'You must finish by 11.30 tomorrow'.

Appellant: 'I'll try my best'.

Lord Hope: 'That's not a *request*'.

Afterwards, another Justice and I wondered why these Queen's Counsel were so inept. The Justice, who himself conducted advocacy training, responded that you could tell a difference with younger advocates who had been trained. There is an obvious need, I suggest, for tighter, more detailed case management. If a hearing is scheduled for two days but time limits are not placed on advocates, the respondent's case may be unfairly truncated, as in this tax case, or even derailed, as in the Hunting Act case. I suggest that the Justices should place time limits on each stage: appeal, response and appellant's reply, and instruct the advocates on the points on which they wish to be addressed and also ban recitation. In conversation, in 2010, a judicial assistant argued for the same thing, pointing out that there is still too much recitation of the Printed Case. A Justice agreed with him, 'We're *very* patient!' At the 2008 closed seminars on the UKSC, some lawyers and some judges also suggested case management, with any hearing over one day having to be justified and with time limits on submissions, issues simplified at an early stage and the appeal panel identifying the issues on which the full hearing should be addressed.

The 1970s Law Lords interviewed by Paterson considered that they were more courteous and the senior Law Lords better at politely controlling prolixity than some of their predecessors. They found silent presidents such as Radcliffe and Wilberforce disarming for advocates. Advocates saw presiders as having a dominating influence over their colleagues, since they controlled the pace and direction of argument, but this was denied by Paterson's 1970s Law Lords. One of my interviewees agreed with my observation that they were much less vocal than their predecessors 20 years earlier. He remarked on how 'hugely different' his judicial style was now from the dialogues he had indulged in as a presiding judge in the Court of Appeal, where he could shape the argument by interventions.

> Basically you let counsel get on with it and I think you interrupt startlingly little. I sometimes think we ought to try and give shape to the argument. The difficulty here is that not everybody wants it to take the *same* shape and you can't therefore, even as a presider, be too prescriptive as to how the hearing is conducted. Certainly Bingham and Nicholls, Nicholls particularly, hardly interrupts at all and lets the case take whatever shape counsel want to give it. I used to come here between 1979 and 1984 a great deal … and in that generation … the real chatterers were Diplock, Templeman, Bridge, who were all very anxious to argue … and you sat back whilst they had a slanging match between themselves.[131] But it isn't that way now. I know that Tom Bingham thinks that if you just let counsel develop his case, rather than adopting a pre-ordained approach, you are likely to get insights into the arguments and fresh perceptions.

His Lordship's portrait of the 1979–84 Law Lords reflects Toobin's 2007 description of the USSC Justices, 'As usual…the lawyer was largely a spectator as the justices talked to one another'.[132]

There are still inefficiencies in the UK top court that surprise outsiders. Commenting on a draft of this chapter, an Australian Justice emailed:

> One thing I was surprised at was the failure of the Lords to get the transcript of the hearing of the argument. We get it by 11.00 am the following day. That means I make no notes of the argument but am able to follow closely when required or fall into a daze when not. I always read the transcript before writing my judgment and double check it

---

[131] In 2011, Paterson said Brandon and Templeman 'would constantly snipe at one another … if either were rebuffed they would sulk'.
[132] Toobin, above n 64 at 195.

to make sure that I have dealt with all necessary arguments. I think the failure to provide a running transcript must detract from the quality of the work done.

Also, the UKSC also still suffers from some of the defects that were highlighted as bedevilling the unreformed Court of Appeal, by Martineau, in 1990,[133] discussed in the CA chapter: case length controlled by advocates; too little pre-deliberation, poor advocacy and sparse secretarial help.[134]

LAWYERS

In his interviews with 61 lawyers, eight of whom became Law Lords[135] Paterson found that their aim was to persuade the Law Lords, by any legitimate means, to decide in favour of their clients, regardless of their own private views on the state of the law and its desirable or legitimate development.[136] He felt the conventional, adversarial model of judge as neutral umpire was inadequate. 'The battle is not so much between the hired champions as between them and the Law Lords sequentially.'[137] Advocates valued the skill of tailoring their arguments to individual traits of the Law Lords, though they were frustrated at not knowing who the panel was, well in advance. By 2011, he concluded that since all benches are now 'hot benches', where Justices have pre-read the cases, and oral hearings are shorter, there is limited potential to tailor an argument.[138] In his 1982 work, Paterson felt advocates' considerable influence had been ignored in writing on judicial creativity. Just as a judge might adopt an advocate's argument and even wording, he might sell it to his colleagues. One lawyer said 'What one is seeking to serve up to them is how they should write their judgment.'[139] At the 2007 Society of Legal Scholars conference, Baroness Hale reminded her audience that they should not underestimate the quality and influence of lawyers' arguments.[140] Paterson's argument could equally well be applied to the Court of Appeal, whose judges keep up a dialogue with the advocates. The difference now, however, is that

---

[133]   J Martineau, *Appellate Justice in England and the United States* (Buffalo, Hein, 1990).

[134]   A CA judge commented: 'The poverty of secretarial and PA support … is a scandal … There cannot be another supreme court in the common law world which is so pathetically resourced'.

[135]   Ackner, Donaldson, Elwyn-Jones, Slynn, Russell, Bridge, Templeman and Scarman.

[136]   Paterson, 1982, above n 49 at 49.

[137]   ibid 51.

[138]   Paterson, in Lee n 76, at 262.

[139]   Paterson, 1982, above n 49 at 64.

[140]   All researchers remarked that arguments were not tape-recorded, as those of the USSC and the ECJ. Paterson (82–83), concluding that judgments were a product of the oral interaction between lawyers and judges and between judges, was critical of this 'serious handicap to any study of judicial decision-making in the House of Lords … The lack of proper transcripts helps perpetuate the notion … that the real work … are the speeches produced at the end of the day. This … is intellectually dangerous and academically unsound'. UKSC proceedings are recorded–sound and moving image.

they have read the skeletons so these form the basis of all judgments in a manner invisible to the outsider. Paterson's entire piece in 2011 discussed whether advocacy matters and his interviews with lawyers and top judges suggested that it does in some cases but not in others.

Gordon, declining suggestions that lawyers be limited to specialist panels, favoured appointing an additional specialist *amicus* (friend of the court) in most cases, because of the advantage in guiding the (non-specialist) court through 'the morass of case law for the purpose of detecting trends and patterns in the law'.[141] This point is now satisfied by encouraging interveners. This continues a trend started by Lord Bingham, signalling the Court's appreciation of the wider implications of its judgments.[142]

JUDICIAL ASSISTANTS

There is a pervasive myth that USSC clerks take decisions and write judgments and I have heard the same insisted upon about UK judicial assistants (JAs). Paterson found Law Lords disagreed as to whether it was legitimate for judges to base opinions on arguments and material which they had researched, which advocates had not had the opportunity to address, though this was no longer the case now.[143] The Law Lords shared four JAs but there are now eight, some supporting one Justice and some two.[144] They are highly intelligent lawyers taking early-career breaks, appointed for 10 months. They do not draft judgments, as do law clerks in the US (though these are stylised[145] and no more 'belong' to the clerks than the Commercial Court judgments belong to counsel whose texts were pasted in by Trollope in the High Court chapter, above). UK JAs write neutral memoranda on petitions to appeal and the press releases/ summaries of judgments (checked by the Justices) and they help research speeches and lectures. Judges differ in their demands. One, who shared a JA with Lord Steyn, considered the latter to be so demanding that he felt he should rarely use her. It is well known that Lord Hoffmann did not use assistants. In 2007, the JAs sent me a joint statement:

> The level of interaction between the Assistants and the Law Lords varies between Law Lords and between cases (for example, some Law Lords make less use of Assistants ... and the amount of use can depend on the adequacy of submissions by counsel) ... The

[141] Gordon, in Le Sueur, above n 71 at 323.

[142] A point made by B Dickson, 'A Hard Act to Follow: the Bingham Court 2000–8' in Blom-Cooper, Dickson and Drewry, above n 27. He provides details at 264.

[143] This was controversial. Lord Denning had recently tried it and been castigated: Paterson, above n 49 at ch 3. See now his 2011 piece, above n 76 at 260–61.

[144] The chief executive, Jenny Rowe, consulted the Justices on their requirements.

[145] Toobin, above n 64 at 156.

Assistants' role is not political nor do they formally express views on the merits of petitions or cases.

In 2009, one assistant said he was called in where a Justice wanted to bolster his reasoning; another said he was asked to research a point insufficiently covered by counsel. Two Justices were making heavy use of their JA, a tax solicitor, in the tax case. He was called in to discuss it with them. 'We discuss the issues. I like bouncing ideas off him. He's very bright.'[146]

THE WAY THEY WORK—JUDGMENT FORMATION

Paterson said the 1970s Law Lords would start discussing a case every time there was a break in the hearing. Pairs or groups might discuss it over lunch, then the whole panel before they reconvened. This went much further than the 'internal engagement' called for by Arden LJ to reduce prolixity.[147] One commented in 2008:

> My experience is quite contrary to Paterson's finding that there was 'continuous discussion' ... Unlike the Court of Appeal, there is no meeting beforehand to canvas preliminary views (and assign the donkey work judgment), and there is often very little collective chat during the case itself, though sometimes one or two may make comments on the way to and from the committee room. We don't all have lunch together ... there are the odd two-by-two chats and occasionally things are so clear that we discuss what to ask counsel to address us on. Otherwise we wait until 'clear the bar'.

The Justices can meet beforehand now, briefly. They have conference rooms, instead of having to whisper in the Parliament library or a corridor. 'We can now exchange a few words in private about the nature of the case and how we propose to handle the hearing' explains Lord Hope[148] but, crucially, unlike the CA, 'we prefer not to commit ourselves to any material extent to a view before the hearing'. Afterwards, they immediately deliberate, with the judges speaking in monologues in reverse order of seniority, unless the presider truncates discussion by starting with, for instance, 'Well, there's not much in this'.[149] Paterson, in 1982, said if no majority view emerged, there would be a further discussion. If they were all agreed for substantially the same reasons, they would decide who would write the lead judgment (in the UKSC, the first judgment), dependent on expertise and workloads, but this would not prevent anyone writing a separate

---

[146] Confirmed by Paterson, above n 76.
[147] Arden LJ, 'A Matter of Style? The Form of Judgments in Common Law Jurisdictions: A Comparison' 28 June 2008, Judiciary website.
[148] J-Y Gilg, 'Supreme Craftsmanship', interview with Lord Hope, *Solicitors Journal*, 8 December 2009.
[149] Information from a UKSC Justice. Paterson's Law Lords set a high value on continuous discussion. It was unusual for a surprise to be sprung because views had emerged in interim discussions: at 90.

opinion. 'The main idea is that there should be somebody responsible for producing a first draft which can then be built upon by others.'[150] One is given the task of describing the facts.[151]

Opinions are circulated over the following weeks. Paterson said sometimes a judge would delay, to see what opinion colleagues would write. Lord Hope said there is often considerable movement of drafts because you may want to expand when you have seen someone else's judgment. Another explained to me:

> At the end of each oral hearing we ... have an immediate debate and we decide that either someone will write a judgment with which it is likely everyone else will concur. That is one extreme. The other is that the [presider] will say 'obviously we are all going to want to write on this' and all manner of intermediate positions. We reach a sort of provisional consensus. The one thing that is clear is that practice requires that there should be one speech which covers all the relevant veins and all the relevant issues, whereas others can chip in on particular issues if they want and ideally the leading judgment should be one in the majority ... [but is regrettably sometimes a dissent]. But there is a pattern of different possibilities ranging from where we all agree, and all think it would be best just to dispose of it in just one judgment, to all manner of differences of opinion and uncertainties, and people saying they don't really know where they stand and they will reconsider it after they have seen someone else's draft ... Sometimes we go round the room and realise we cannot reach a consensus and that's unsatisfactory. It's an unhappy feeling. We stay for 10 seconds then say, 'Well that's it then'.

Lord Hope said that *after* the initial meeting, the presider normally decides who will write the lead judgment but in this research, more than one Justice expressed frustration

> not knowing, when you embark on an appeal ... who is going to write the judgment. That is ... quite an important practical difference from the Court of Appeal ... Sometimes thinking you would quite fancy writing the leading judgment ... and find that you don't get invited to do it. And there are occasional frustrations because of the limited secretarial help ... Sometimes you ... would like to get your draft judgment out quite quickly, in the hope of possibly persuading your other colleagues and then you find that it doesn't get there instantly.

(Groups of three Law Lords shared one secretary. In the UKSC, the ratio varies). Another Justice was still frustrated by the duplication of work in judgment preparation, caused by insufficient conferring and pre-allocation of work (called for by Arden LJ, below). In 2007 he wrote,

> I think we all feel that the new SC is going to be a great opportunity for change. I would like to think that most of us who expect to end up there hope that we will take the

---

[151] Paterson, above n 49 at 92–93. Paterson's 1970s description was strikingly similar to the modern one below and to Lord Hope's 2009 description. Barrett commented, in 2001, that in the post-hearing discussion, the judges did not attempt to sway one another's votes but Paterson found the opposite, in the 1970s. Also, they might have been persuaded by one another's opinions while discussing the case in the breaks.

opportunity to be more collegiate, and waste less time in duplicating work. The new rules have deliberately been drafted in an open-textured way to allow for this.

But by December 2009 he was disappointed, 'We're still a long way off, having marketed ourselves [the UKSC] as user-friendly to the legal profession and the lower courts'. He complained of the preparation of multiple judgments, repeating facts and issues 'the Presider should immediately say who'll write the lead judgment because, if not, you leave everyone for a week and they'll write their own judgments'. He indicated a four-inch pile of nine judgments in the Jewish schools case.[152]

SINGLE JUDGMENTS AND CLARITY

'You write a separate dissenting judgment if your outrage exceeds your natural indolence', said one Law Lord, quoting another judge, to make his colleagues laugh.[153]

The previous chapter discusses arguments about single, composite and individual judgments. These were reignited in anticipation of the UKSC.[154] Justices readily offer their opinions. The one quoted above was fresh from Hong Kong, 'where the culture of the court is much more to settle on a single judgment...[Here] we made some good resolutions. We're just not carrying them out'. In 2008, some CA and HL judges expressed strong opinions that, as the top court's only job is precedent, it ought to produce clear judgments, rather than multiple, conflicting *rationes* that leave the law uncertain.[155]

In 1972, Blom-Cooper and Drewry recommended single 'opinions of the court', written on a rota basis.[156] Where one judge is assigned to write a single opinion, he takes on board the majority's views. Once the draft has been circulated, differences tend to be settled orally, said Barrett.[157] In their Privy Council job, these same judges give a single opinion. After 1833[158] when lawyers and judges were appointed, this rule made less sense but was thought to lend

---

[152] Lacking the collegiality discussed in the CA chapter and discussed by Edwards, therein.
[153] In the closed QMUL seminars.
[154] See Arden LJ's speech, above n 147, and J Lee, ' A defence of concurring speeches' [2009] *Public Law* 305.
[155] Apart from crime (below), plus *Boys v Chaplin*, another example is the mess caused by *Pettit v Pettit* [1970] AC 777 then *Gissing v Gissing* [1971] AC 886, that 'continued to haunt the law of constructive trusts for almost 40 years': Carnwath LJ in 'The Devil we know or a new start?' *Counsel*, June 2008, p.6.
[156] Blom-Cooper and Drewry, above n 4 at 402. Chapter V of the same book is entitled 'judicial individualism' but mainly discusses dissents.
[157] He observed that with a continuing rise in the number of appeals there was a real incentive to produce a single opinion. However, Barrett's assumption, like Le Sueur's, is mistaken. There is no rise.
[158] Judicial Committee Act: Barrett, above n 69 at 170–71. It dates from a 1620s practice of giving a single opinion.

authority and certainty and since, technically, this was advice to the sovereign, it was thought inappropriate to provide conflicting advice, but 'Enforced unanimity was perceived to result in a certain blandness … Dissenting opinions were increasingly viewed as a means by which the law could be improved'[159] and permitted from 1966.[160] In the Law Lord job, in the 1970s, Paterson found most thought multiple opinions were to be avoided, especially in criminal appeals. (This is astonishing, in the light of their irresponsible 1970s criminal law judgments, such as *Hyam* and *Majewski*).[161] Junior Law Lords were not expected to defer and abandon their opinions, though. Composites were rare. Half said they would withdraw a dissent after opinions had been circulated, considering it served no purpose. If a dissent were published, the judge was effectively appealing to future judges, a law reform body or Parliament. All said they were individualists with a right to free expression. Most said it was not the senior Law Lord's job to act as mediator. Very occasionally, the presider reconvened a panel to try to produce agreement or reduce a multiplicity of divergent opinions such as those in *Boys v Chaplin*, where, clearly, no such effort was made[162] but this was generally seen as too difficult, logistically. Judges such as Reid dismissed the suggestion that they could produce single judgments when sitting as Law Lords. They did not have the time[163] to 'start a sort of committee meeting over a joint judgment … we would never get through our work'.[164] This is bizarre. If CA composites are nowadays justified because judges do not have time to produce multiples, how is it that past Law Lords justified multiples because they 'did not have the time' to make a composite? Paterson concluded the 1970s ethos was 'laissez-faire'.[165] Consequently, bargaining between judges was much less common than it was between US Justices, required to produce a court opinion. Robertson noted that Lord Diplock, senior Law Lord until the mid-1980s, preferred a single majority judgment but Robertson could see a drawback.

> In a real sense, the Lords seldom argue, because they do not address each other's points … This tendency to bland assertion rather than the often quite brutal attacks on other judges' reasoning found in American or Australian opinions has probably become

---

[159]   ibid 171.

[160]   In Lord Cooke's 2001 speech, he explained the second dissent in a death penalty case, where Lord Steyn declined to recognise a rule that there should be only one dissent.

[161]   *Hyam v DPP* [1974] UKHL 2 and *DPP v Majewski* [1976] UKHL 2, where divergent lines of reasoning left the law on murder and the defence of intoxiction in an uncertain state for years. Insolvency lawyers find the indecision in *HIH* [2008] 1 WLR 852 exasperating. See Neuberger, 'Top Dogs: Britain's New Supreme Court', BBC Radio 4, 8 September 2009.

[162]   [1971] AC 356 (this case tortured private international lawyers for decades).

[163]   Paterson, above n 49, 108.

[164]   Ibid, 98.

[165]   Paterson, above n 49 at 96–108. Radcliffe and Reid considered it 'nonsense' to discourage dissents. Radcliffe said that when he became a Law Lord in 1949, dissents were frowned on because it was felt that the exposure of differences weakened their authority but no-one supported that view by the time he retired in 1964. Reid thought there was a danger that later courts treated the language of single judgments as if it were statutory: Lee, above n 76 at 324.

worse [because] … the Lords have moved to the expectation that there will only usually be one major speech … Whatever value this may have for legal certainty … it has reduced the extent of genuine argument and discussion of issues in a way that not only academic lawyers but many leading counsel find distinctly unhelpful … it can also cause problems for their Lordships themselves, who sometimes find that they are deemed to support interpretative positions that they later have to withdraw.[166]

Law Lords told me in 2005 that Lord Bingham was anxious not to be as inflexible as Diplock so most decisions attracted multiple opinions and

Rejecting suggestions that the [UKSC] should strive towards issuing single judgments of the court … Lord Hope says, 'We don't want to follow the example of the European Court of Justice in Luxembourg, where a rather anodyne, anonymous document is produced which doesn't actually contain very much in the way of creative thought. This style of judgment doesn't help to advance common law'.[167]

On the other hand, I found a number of judges, from a district judge to UKSC Justices, wishing that they would produce a single or single majority judgment. Lee and others quoted a Baroness Hale judgment.

On the first two issues, Lord Hoffmann's view is shared by a majority. The least said by the rest of us who take the same view, therefore, the better. There should be no doubt, and no room for argument, about what has been decided and why … Indeed, there would be much to be said for our adopting the practice of other supreme courts in having a single majority opinion to which all have contributed and all can subscribe without further qualification or explanation. There would be less grist to the advocates' and academics' mills, but future litigants might thank us for that.[168]

Carnwath LJ's exasperation over multiple judgments, in *Doherty*, is well known. I have seen him repeat it face-to-face to the top judges at every opportunity.

Was it necessary for the opinions of the House to have come to us in the form of six substantive speeches, which we have had to subject to laborious comparative analysis to arrive at a conclusion?[169]

Lord Neuberger MR, former Law Lord, has joined in, saying, like Brenda Hale, that the problems of an ECJ-type judgment would be avoided if they copied the USSC single majority judgment with individual additions, as desired.

Dissenting [and] concurring judgments can be given … independence and accountability are maintained … the public and Parliament can clearly see the signposts to future possible developments … The majority's judgment sets out the ratio. It obviates

---

[166] Robertson, above n 53 at 77–78. The book covers 1986–95.
[167] Gilg, above n 148.
[168] In *OBG v Allan* [2007] UKHL 21 cited by Lee, above n 76.
[169] *Doherty v Birmingham City Council* [2006] EWCA Civ 1739. See *Counsel* in June 2008, 'Devil we know or new start?' at 6. See also the mess in *SS for the Home Dept v AF* [2008] EWCA Civ 1148 and Clarke MR's and Sedley LJ's comments, referred to by Lee, above n 76 at 306–07, not to mention another plea by Waller LJ in *Grundy v British Airways plc* [2007] EWCA Civ 1020, cited by Carnwath, above n 155.

the need to search through five or more ... it provides a clear picture of why the law is as the court has declared it to be.[170]

Arden LJ called for decisions to be rendered more accessible by roadmaps, press summaries, better headnotes and being shorter. She urged less prolixity, brought about by more internal engagement, before and after the hearing and 'regular consideration of a single majority judgment'.

> Whenever there is a concurring or dissenting judgment, the author ... should (a) make it clear with what reasoning or propositions ... the author agrees or disagrees and (b) avoid...repeating the facts or citations ... in the main judgment ... [A]n early decision that one person is going to write the lead judgment ... and an understanding that the other members of the court will not generally circulate their own judgments until they have seen the lead judgment.[171]

In *R v Forbes*[172] the Law Lords produced a single statement of the law in a criminal appeal and announced their intention of doing so again[173] but only did so in five per cent of their decisions[174] and there is no consistency in when composites will be used, according to Dickson. When I asked two judges (separately) to explain the lack of composites compared with the CA's keenness, they referred to the strong collegiality of the CA. Another told me of a case where the presider had decided that there should be a judgment of the court, then asked a non-expert to write it, so the expert felt compelled to add a separate judgment. Another wrote to me, comparing the CA. 'I would like to instil a bit more collegiality into the House of Lords/new Supreme Court'. At the SLS 2007 conference, Baroness Hale said that the CA had a high workload. There was collegiality and a common approach. Importantly, three judges sat in the same constitution for three weeks. It was decided in advance who would give the lead judgment. In the top court there was no systematic prior discussion, nor was it decided who would give judgment. This very different process was 'a recipe for having five judgments'. In her 2010 anniversary seminar address, cited below, she called for 'a more collegiate approach to judgment writing, which is common elsewhere in world where plurality judgments are the norm'. At the October 2010 conference referred to above, she said, 'We have no tradition of joint or plurality

---

[170] Hale, 'Insolvency, Internationalism and Supreme Court Judgments' speech, 11 November 2009. She repeated this call in her talk at the 2010 UKSC anniversary seminar, now on the website.

[171] Arden LJ, above n 147 at 10.

[172] [2001] 1 AC 473, discussed by Le Sueur, above n 71.

[173] R Munday, '"All for One and One for All" the rise to prominence of the composite judgment within the civil division of the Court of Appeal' 61(2) *Cambridge Law Journal* 321–50, 342. Lord Rodger pointed out that it was delivered by Lord Bingham, who was one of the counsel for the appellants in *Heaton's Transport*, where it was done deliberately to defuse a highly-charged political standoff, where the docks were paralysed by a strike: 'The Form and Language of Judicial Opinions' (2002) 118 *LQR* 226–47, 233.

[174] Lee, above n 76. See also B Dickson, in Blom-Cooper, Dickson and Drewry, above, n 27 at 262.

judgments but this stops the Bar picking them apart'. Nevertheless, regardless of her keenness to promote plurality judgments, even she acknowledged it was not always possible. 'In *Radmacher*, this morning, nine Justices sat. Nine wrote judgments. The President thought it looked bad so tried writing a judgment all would sign up to. He'd never get *me* to sign up to it!'[175]

In outside speeches, Justices refer to foreign decision-making structures, sometimes making their antipathy better informed.[176] Lord Cooke expressed surprise that US Justice Ginsburg claimed the 40 per cent unanimity rate of the USSC to be 'high'. He pointed to the 75 per cent unanimity rate of the Law Lords.[177] This level of unanimity makes it all the more frustrating for the proponents of single judgments that in 2000–08, only five per cent were single majority. Other Law Lords' practices used to make the problem of extrapolating coherent reasoning worse, as Le Sueur said:

> Speeches are delivered in order of seniority … not in any logical order … no attempt is made … to present … a synthesis … High level legal skills are often required … to work out the majority view.[178]

More confusing, as Baroness Hale pointed out, the judgment setting out the facts, did not necessarily come first[179] though in the UKSC, this is now indicated. Formerly, opinions were merely uploaded onto the Law Lords' website, with no summary or head note.

Are Matters Improving in the UKSC?

Repeated discussion has prompted enough Justices to recognise these problems to bring about changes in practice, though they do not go far enough to satisfy the critics, including the Justices themselves. Changes include the following.

— More composite 'judgments of the court', or single, or single majority judgments—31 of the first 57.[180]
— A clear, comprehensive press summary, cross-referring to elements of the judgments. These really are brilliant, as anyone can see from the website, and mean the judgments really can be understood by the taxpayers who fund

---

[175] [2010] UKSC 42.

[176] Note Lord Rodger's horror of the use of footnotes and confrontational tone in USSC judgments, compared with the courtesy of the Law Lords' footnote-free opinions, above n 173.

[177] It was 90 per cent in 1952–68, according to Blom-Cooper and Drewry, above n 4 at 178.

[178] A Le Sueur, 'Developing mechanisms for judicial accountability in the UK' (2004) 24 *Legal Studies* 73, 90.

[179] Plenary session, SLS conference, 2007.

[180] Brenda Hale, *Judgment Writing in the Supreme Court*, address to the First Anniversary Seminar, 30 September 2010, UKSC website. Lady Hale calls jointly authored opinions 'plurality judgments' and gives examples of judgments she wrote with Lord Neuberger.

them, whereas the Law Lords' judgments used to plunge law students and even the CA into despair.

— The printing of the lead judgment first, then majority then minority judgments, with clear labelling, including an indication of which contains the facts.
— Some pre-hearing planning.
— An acknowledgment by many Justices, separately, that, even where there are multiple judgments, they should, in any event, make the ratio decidendi clear, even if they back it up with different reasoning routes.

This still does not satisfy the disgruntled Justice quoted above. No wonder he indicated the Jewish schools case. Readers are spared from misery with this five to four, 91-page decision, by its brilliant summary. There is little attempt to follow Arden's suggestion of curbing prolixity and, clearly, as the Justice complained, there was too little internal engagement. The facts are set out in Lord Hope's minority judgment. Why not get the parties to present a brief summary of the facts, to be pasted in front of the judgments, copying Trollope in the Commercial Court?

WHAT IS IT LIKE BEING IN THE TOP COURT?

Newcomers remark on the shock of leaving the camaraderie of the Court of Appeal, into relative isolation. The judge leaves CA and HC buddies, and the solicitous personal clerk, in the bustling Royal Courts of Justice, severing connections with other levels of the judiciary brought by any management job. In the mid-1990s, a new Law Lord told me he hankered after the CA and often went back. Two later appointees suffered the same shock.

When I found out about [my appointment] ... I said 'You'll expect me to be thrilled to bits but actually I can't tell you how deep a gloom you have sunk me in'. ... All my friends were there. I had lunch with them in the Inns every day ... picking up the legal gossip ... I had mastered the routines of the Court of Appeal. It was extremely hard work but I had learnt how to manage ... I had presided for years so I was able to decide in which case I wanted to give the leading judgments and because of my public law experience I was getting most of the public law cases.

I absolutely hated this place when I first arrived. I found it just so weird and I almost got to the point where I was going to ask to go back to the Court of Appeal ... Partly it is this building.[181] I still pretty much hate it—all these flunkies with white ties and that ... like being in a really posh hotel. The waiters all treat you with deference. You don't know really what they think about you. I do find it a very unnatural place and I don't like the notion that our highest court of appeal is a sort of bolt-on to the upper house of the legislature so I am in principle in favour of the Supreme Court and although my

---

[181] The Palace of Westminster.

colleagues are, without exception, delightful and considerate and all that, it is a very different atmosphere from the Court of Appeal [where] you are just so bloody busy that you all have to pull together because otherwise you won't survive.

He appreciated that the Celts were further adrift,

leading a sort of bachelor existence in London, cut off from their chums ... They are *much* more isolated.

Another drew attention to the 'monk-like' existence of the Celts. A Scot told me he rented a flat in the Inns of Court ('I couldn't afford to buy one'), for which he received no compensation. Unlike MPs, they have never received a second home allowance. He spent 10 hours per week travelling. He arrived home at 11.00 pm each Thursday and set off for London on Sunday at 5.00 pm. 'Put *that* in your book!' but added 'It is an enormous privilege to be a Law Lord, and I have no regrets whatever about the commitments that I have to make to play my full part in the work of our team'. The other adjustment for the new boy was the slide down the pecking order.

moving from being a very hands-on presider ... where I was going to be writing the judgment ... entirely free to shape the arguments to your needs, to being a junior winger here.

Unsurprisingly, after the CA, one English judge did not feel overstretched.

We have extremely generous vacations ... about 14 weeks ... I give two ... to my [statutory regulator] job and...you generally have a judgment or two which have to be attended to ... I don't work now as long hours as I did in the Court of Appeal ... I get away with doing six hours a weekend. I am not sure ... that would be true of the ... more senior members of the court who write more than their fair share of the leading speeches.

But commenting on this, another Justice wrote:

I too felt a release of pressure on leaving my equivalent position (with much admin on top of it) in Edinburgh. But ... constant effort is needed to keep up. I certainly do not get away with only six hours at the weekend. I usually work 15 to 20 ... writing judgments and reading up for the next week ... I have less time off at weekends than I did when I was in Edinburgh ... The time commitment is greater but the pressure is less—a good balance: time to think when not under pressure is what this job requires.

One judge spent about half his summer preparing invited lectures, organising a judicial exchange and helping draft the new UKSC Rules. He described his term-time week.

Monday to Thursday we almost always sit. Fridays hardly ever. Some of my colleagues and I come in on Fridays and work and sometimes we take bundles home ... I arrive here at about 7.30 am ... We sit at 11.00 am on Mondays and 10:30 am on other days ... the working week is divided between reading papers in advance of hearings and attending hearings, discussing hearings, which involves deciding who is going to write, thinking, writing and considering petitions for leave to appeal.

Among intellectual giants, they had had to expand their legal self-education.

> I think I felt very wary about coming here and I think I have always felt that my colleagues are a great deal cleverer ... I used to think I was pretty much on top as a Court of Appeal judge. I think here I have to run very hard to keep up.

> at every stage [of judicial promotion] I knew I was going to be doing a lot of work in areas that I was not familiar with and that I was going to have to make a conscious effort to get up to speed ... the whole of public law which could hardly be a vaster subject, which I knew virtually nothing when I first became a judge ... so it has been a big learning experience and that has added to its great interest ... I think probably at least two thirds of our cases are public law ... a tidal wave of human rights ... and this creates all sorts of new problems about the relationship between judges and other branches of government which are of great interest and importance.

The UK Supreme Court is still under that tidal wave.[182]

The Law Lords' rooms and corridors were festooned with monitors showing Parliamentary business. Being in the Palace of Westminster reinforced the political nature of their job. The first acknowledged some benefit, despite his loathing.

> There is something to be learned by judges rubbing shoulders with legislators and being exposed to some of the pressures of politics ... there is a danger of judges being too isolated from political reality and if we are going off to an ivory tower it is going to be ... even more important, that we educate ourselves and keep in touch with the issues of public life in the wider sense. One of the few bits of self-education I consciously did when I was coming to the House of Lords was ... [taking] ... the *Economist* which I read cover-to-cover every week.

> There is some value in being in this building ... it was helpful to have ... a real appreciation, on a day-to-day basis, of the legislative process; of the concerns of the nation.

In their 2003 response to the SC consultation, the Law Lords were divided but, of those in post by 2008, just two were opposed to the move out of the Palace of Westminster.

FOUR DAYS WITH THE LAW LORDS IN 2005

Monday

9.00 am: Lord Bingham popped in, seeking legal advice on conveyancing from my judge.

---

[182]   In 2009, of 62 decisions, 18 were private law and 24 per cent were human rights: Dickson, above n 89.

10.05–10.20 am: Watched appeal committee whip through petitions, as above.

11.00 am: Full hearing on a trivial point of statutory interpretation.

1.00 pm: Lunch with three in the self-service terrace café. They no longer ate in a dining room, as in Paterson's day but 'in the most subsidised canteen in the UK', joked one. Another emphasised, 'We don't all meet at the gentleman's club nowadays, you know'. He doubted if any Law Lord belonged to a club. I knew this was a mistake. The others swiftly corrected him. 'I dine at my club when my wife's not cooking' and 'Even *Brenda's* in a club'. This legitimised club membership. If Baroness Hale did it, it was obviously OK. She was a constant reference point in Law Lords' conversations (and among the senior judiciary and counsel) as an icon of the 'cool', the humane and the modern judge. In his interview, one said, admiringly '*Brenda!* She is *Queen* amongst us'.[183] In the lift, we met Lord Ackner, a retired Law Lord and active parliamentarian, bent over his walking frame. Casual encounters with their eminent predecessors are now lost to the UKSC Justices.

1.45 pm: The senior law reporter brought in a draft judgment for checking then took me to the committee room. She asked if I was going to write an 'exposé'.

3.15 pm: 'Clear the bar'. We left the room while they had their preliminary discussion. A white-tie doorkeeper praised their hard work, 'I don't know how they do it. Reading at the weekend for their Monday cases. Reading in the evenings for the other cases, as well as writing judgments'. Later, the judge told me they had been unanimous and he would be writing the judgment.

Tuesday

9.30 am: I re-joined him after nine had spent one hour discussing *Jackson*, the Hunting Act case. They were pleased that they all had time to express an opinion. He showed me the printed case: two volumes, with nine volumes of appended material—the statutes, extracts from *Hansard*, Asquith's biography, academic articles from HWR Wade, Wade and Bradley, Bennion. He showed me the 'team' he had assembled for September's Canadian judicial exchange. I went to quiz Brendan about 'horses for courses'.

1.00 pm: In the public café, Charles Kennedy MP, then leader of the Liberal Democrats, was in front of us in the cash register queue. We stared. 'Was that

---

[183] Brenda thought this was a joke, reversing *Private Eye's* name of Brenda for the Queen but it was not.

really *him?*' asked one. 'Yes' replied the other. 'He's smaller than I thought.' I smiled at this irony: two of the UK's most senior judges, touchingly oblivious of their importance as two-fifths of a law-making organ in the mother of common law systems, awestuck by this Parliamentary starlet, a sole voter in a legislature of 1,393.

They called another to join us. Then Lord Nicholls joined our tiny table, fresh from fixing the constitutions for next term's cases 'heavy on human rights'. They asked who I thought the new Law Lord might be, wondering if I had picked up gossip in the Court of Appeal. They said they had all been consulted, at a meeting in the Lord Chancellor's room.

4.15 pm: I was aware of witnessing vanishing history as another Law Lord took me to watch him chairing a Parliamentary sub-committee.[184] A minister flounced in for questioning, proclaiming that she had to rush off to see the Lord Chief Justice. The judge considered her presence pointless. 'I want to get rid of her', aside. He was a novice here. 'I was on a steep learning curve when I took on this job.'

Wednesday

9.00 am: The judge was showing me the papers for a Privy Council hearing. Lord Hoffmann knocked on the door, again in cycling Lycra, this time with a bright green top.

9.30 am: To the conference room to meet a mixed group of foreign students.[185] They had stellar CVs. The judge recognised an Australian name. 'Is your father who I think he is?' He wanted me to see him hosting this, as he considered it an important part of his job. Next day, he entertained a party of Dutch visitors at Lincoln's Inn. Downstairs, I waited with five judges for the ancient Daimler to take us round the corner to the Privy Council. They teased me that it might break down yet again. They had had to 'leg it' to Downing Street through two lanes of traffic. 'The Daimlers on circuit used to break down' remembered one. En route, one asked if anyone knew anything about the latest nominee for the USSC. No-one did. 'Gonzales wasn't right-wing enough for Bush!' he quipped. They all laughed about the distant spectacle of the highly politicised selection system of their American brethren, as if it were unthinkable in the UK. Two judges hoped the new appointment system here would not make a difference.

---

[184] All Parliamentary jobs ceased with the Constitutional Reform Act 2005. Praising the value of Law Lords' select committee work and other contributions to legislation, see Lord Hope, D Hope 'Voices from the Past—The Law Lords' Contribution to the Legislative Process' (2007) 123 *LQR* 547–70.

[185] On the Pegasus Programme, organised by the Inns of Court.

Inside Soane's architectural gem[186] at No 1 Downing Street, the judges sat at a table, the advocates looking down on them. The Jamaican appeal was about the felony-murder rule, a foray into old English criminal law. The appellant's first citation was the 1975 edition of Smith and Hogan's *Criminal Law*. The trial transcripts depicted the patois of the accused. This conjured an image of the convict on death row, in his island cell, waiting years for this appeal. I wondered if he knew that his fate was being determined right now, yards away from Tony Blair's Cabinet room. The proceedings seemed a surreal relic of empire but I knew he stood a much better chance of survival in the hands of these liberal white men than in the hypothetical Supreme Court that the Caribbean had been failing to establish for decades.[187] These five judges were not all English though. They were English, Irish, Scottish and two were South African. The respondent's authorities included American precedents. The Scot quizzed him in depth. The hearing was over by 11.55 am. I walked to the Palace of Westminster.

There was a Transport and General Workers' Union (TGWU) demonstration, with a band, in front of the building, blocking the pavement. The Law Lords' rooms faced this scene. Entering one's room, I noticed it was filled with this racket and traffic noise, through the open window. It did not distract him from dictating a judgment. Nor did the big, flat-screen TV above, relaying Parliamentary proceedings, buzzing whenever the speaker changed. Symbolising the 'inseparation' of powers in the Palace of Westminster, politics was blaring in through the judge's window and his screen. We lunched with the Pegasus students. That afternoon, Committee Room One was filled with 20 supporters of the appellants in a case on a common law crime. The room was eight yards by twelve, with the Pugin flock wallpaper that had caused Lord Chancellor Irvine so much trouble,[188] and a hideous painting of the Burial of Harold. The tall windows did not let in enough light. Two senior Law Lords questioned the appellant's counsel. He was a typical silver-tongued silk, practised in the art of jury seduction in the Old Bailey, who the judges dismissed as the worst of advocates. He started badly. As soon as he dipped into the facts, Lord Bingham said they had read them. One judge looked very cross and he promised he would not take too much time the following day. Another explained he had a low opinion of counsel in this case, except for the opposition, Treasury counsel, well known to them and much praised.

[186]   See M Binney, 'Soane's Privy Council merits more than a judicial review', *The Times*, 30 July 2007. See further P Dean, *Sir John Soane and London* (Farnham, Lund Humphries, 2006).

[187]   Jamaican appeals still come to the JCPC.

[188]   Attacked in 1998 for spending £59,000 on wallpaper to refurbish the Lord Chancellor's apartments, BBC News, 4 March. See Pugin wallpaper video-tour on the Parliament website.

Thursday

9.00 am: I met a judicial assistant. After graduating from Cambridge and Harvard, she was doing this job for 10 months before her PhD. She took me to witness the curious procedure of the Law Lords' handing down of judgments.

9.45 am: They were alone in the House of Lords chamber. The mace came in. They knelt while a bishop read prayers. Lord Bingham stepped aside, onto the Woolsack, representing the members of the House, because, technically, the House had to 'receive' their opinions. The public were allowed in. The QCs stood at the Bar. The Law Lords spoke briefly. I returned to the committee room hearing. The cross judge glowered at appellant counsel. By contrast, Baroness Hale smiled when questioning and made jocular interjections.

1.00 am: As I exited the rear door with the judges, one carefully hurried me ahead so I could not hear the others' discussion. After lunch, he needed time to contemplate the arguments. He wanted to sound coherent in expressing a preliminary opinion. A junior Law Lord explained that this Treasury counsel was briefed as an *amicus* in any case where there was a difficult point of criminal law. He did not find him easy to understand.

2.00 pm: I could see why he was popular. He was very good at answering questions.

2.45 pm: Afterwards, another judge said he was frustrated that they had only heard two days' argument. There was no flexibility in the timetable. Appellant counsel told me he thought the case should have been scheduled as longer but Treasury counsel, beloved of the Law Lords, had insisted on two days, sneering, '*We* know. We're before them all the time.' Counsel praised Baroness Hale's warmth and humour. She had added to her fan club.

4.00 pm: The hearing over, the judges were deprived of their traditional immediate discussion, as one of them hurried off to an academic engagement. The others worried about how they would reschedule deliberations, as it was the last week of the legal year.

Law Lords were keen to pass opinions on the proposed Supreme Court. Two gave me copies of their speeches, now articles. The interviewees complained. One criticised the cost, raided from the general courts budget, and 'the absolutely deplorable and unbelievably inept way that [the constitutional change] is handled by the government'.

It is … in a suitable location if the existing building could be blown up and there was an international architectural competition for an entirely new twenty-first century build-ing … it is mock baronial with Art Deco touches,[189] the personal gift of the eighth Duke of Devonshire to the Middlesex County Council, built in 1908 … It is again an odd reflection that a country like South Africa can expend a huge sum on its new constitutional court, that the UK can't or won't.

The other said the building was

undistinguished Victorian gothic. We will have to keep the Middlesex Regimental War Memorial. We want a vibrant image of a modern looking Supreme Court. It's an iconic site and a barn of a building. I've seen the Supreme Courts of Ottawa and Jerusalem. Why not us? Instead we have a hand-me-down Crown Court designed to intimidate the felons of yesteryear![190]

SUPREME COURT—DECEMBER 2009

By December 2009, however, one Justice's only regret was 'losing the brand' of the Law Lords. Another, who had opposed the move, admitted 'We're all seduced by the comfort and convenience here. Much easier. The lifts work quickly. We don't have to look for a space to eat lunch'. One told me he still went to Parliament for Friday fish and chips, because he missed the experience. The Law Lords' former cleaning ladies popped in with Christmas cards. They missed them. 'There's Baronesses in your rooms now.'

Conference rooms make it easier to meet before a case, then deliberate afterwards, without the need to clear the courtroom. They are proud that the court attracts the public. 'We're playing to packed houses. Have you played with the toys in the basement yet?' By 12.30 pm, I counted 40 visitors watching a Scottish case, including schoolchildren. Tickets had been issued for seats in the Jewish schools case, with an overflow of 50 bodies, watching on screens. This is remarkable, considering that the building has no label and that by 2010 the website still promised tour and visit details would appear 'soon'. One Justice thought it 'a disgrace' that my students could not hear from the back of the Court One. 'It wouldn't happen in the US.' While the white space and iconography in Court Two emphasise uniqueness and modernity, in Court One, Lord Brown implored counsel to 'speak up in this cavernous room', where six massive carved angels presided from the spectacular vaulted ceiling. Like the stained glass, art

---

[189] It was/is neo-gothic with Art Nouveau and Arts and Crafts elements.

[190] SAVE Britain's Heritage said it was completed in 1913. They considered it 'the finest secular gothic revival building in the country'. In 2004, English Heritage said the main courtroom interiors were 'unsurpassed by any other courtroom of the period in terms of the quality and completeness of their fittings'. See now M Binney, 'A stern judgment on their Lordships' refurbishers', *The Times*, 15 January 2010.

work and Westminster war memorial, these grand, irrelevant relics confuse the symbolism.[191]

AN INTERNATIONAL COURT

Spending time with them, it struck me that the top court is characteristically un-*English*. In 2005, there were three South Africans, as well as the usual two from Scotland and one from Northern Ireland. In their conversations and out-of-court activities, there were daily reminders that they were players on an international stage in the development of the common law, human rights and judicial independence. International pre-eminence of the Law Lords was emphasised by Canadian Chief Justice Beverley McLachlin and South African Justice Kate O'Regan, on the day the UKSC opened.[192]

> The judges of the House of Lords over the centuries have represented for us the gold standard in judicial reasoning and writing … they came to epitomise the ideal of judicial independence.

And:

> An ever-lengthening line of public law decisions, admired and cited around the Commonwealth, establishes principles of public law based on fairness, reasonableness and more recently, proportionality. Underlying this jurisprudence is the deep constitutional principle that courts, as a separate arm of government, must protect the rights of citizens against abuse.

The Court's role in developing international common law and human rights is evidenced in dozens of sources, not least the 51 essays in *Tom Bingham and the Transformation of the Law*.[193] Australian former Justice Kirby said 'Decisions have no binding force whatsoever … the greatest tribute to the House of Lords can be found in the fact that … they continue to be cited in so many fields'.[194] Andenas and Fairgrieve, referring to judgments on liberty and anti-terror, said 'Lord Bingham persuades through his reasoning … his judgments are comparative law sources, as persuasive authority, all over the world'.[195] Zeno-Zencovich details the Court's internationalism.[196] Of 475 decisions in 2000–07, 250 centred on interpretation of, or made use of, transnational or international law, including 100 human rights and 50 Community law cases, plus a number citing American,

---

[191] For further details, see website. The building has attracted much more media coverage than the creation of the new institution, reflecting UK citizens' lack of awareness of their constitution (or even the concept of one).

[192] 'Views from Canada and South Africa: we owe a great debt to the work of the judges', *Timesonline*, 1 October 2009.

[193] Andenas and Fairgrieve, above n 75.

[194] Kirby, in ibid 719–20.

[195] M Andenas and D Fairgrieve, 'Lord Bingham and Comparative Law' in ibid 831 and 839.

[196] V Zeno-Zencovich, 'The Bingham Court' in ibid 823.

Canadian and Commonwealth authorities. Listing 24 cases using comparative material, he said 'A comparativist finds in the House of Lords reports a *bonanza* for his classes and case-books'.[197] Andenas and Fairgrieve claimed that Bingham was a pioneer in developing comparative law.[198] They cited his willingness to use European human rights law to develop the common law. Dickson mentioned Bingham's use of foreign judgments, including those of non common law courts.[199] They and judges in other top courts self-educate by visiting other legal systems. They cite one another's precedents.[200] There is a far more intense international interchange of senior judges, in ideas, visits, exchanges, conferences and publications than outsiders appreciate.

THE COURT'S SELF-IMAGE AS 'APOLITICAL'

As the twentieth century progressed, judges distanced themselves from the party labels attaching to their predecessors in the first half of the century.[201] By 2005, it seemed to me that the Law Lords took pains to keep themselves distant. The episode in the car typified their horror at, and derision of, the visible party-political posturing of their counterparts in the USSC, and its nominees,[202] as can be seen from Lord Cooke's speech.

> In the United States formal obeisance is given to the doctrine of the separation of powers ... In reality ... there is no modern democracy where the links between politics and the judiciary are so strong ... Yet I do not even know what are the politics of most of my judicial colleagues ... the Labour Lord Chancellor, Lord Irvine of Lairg, is in many ways more conservative than his Tory predecessor, Lord Mackay of Clashfern, but still has made or played a dominant part in the appointments as Senior Law Lord and Lord Chief Justice respectively of Lord Bingham of Cornhill and Lord Woolf, both of them in varying degrees are probably more liberal than the Lord Chancellor himself in their judicial approach.

---

[197]   ibid 827.

[198]   The trend to cite foreign judgments started in the 1960s. New Zealand Law Lord, Lord Cooke remarked, 'I have sat on...panels...where there has been either no member of English origin or only one', 2001 speech.

[199]   B Dickson, in Blom-Cooper, Dickson and Drewry, above n 27.

[200]   Exceptions are some insular USSC Justices. In 2005, a House of Representatives resolution criticised USSC use of foreign sources in *Roper v Simmons* 543 US 551 (2005), on the juvenile death penalty: Toobin, above n 64 at 198. Some called for Justice Kennedy's impeachment. Ginsburg and O'Connor received *death threats* for stating they consulted foreign precedents in forming their judgments (249). Posner, above n 13 at 347, details law review debate over the legitimacy of the USSC's citing foreign judgments.

[201]   Explored in Griffiths, above n 52. See also K Malleson, 'Appointments to the House of Lords: Who Goes Upstairs' in Blom-Cooper, Dickson and Drewry, above n 27. In the same book, Lord Bingham 'regrets' the absence of public administration experience of all modern top judges: 'The Law Lords: Who Has Served' at 125.

[202]   For discussion of way in which party political public examination warps USSC nominees' professed beliefs, see Kirby and Kavanagh, below n 215.

In 2007, Lord Bingham said 'We see our job as a purely judicial one, to try to get the law right and apply it properly to the facts. I don't think we spend very much time worrying if our decisions are going to be popular or not'.[203] So the top judges saw themselves as rigidly aloof from *party* politics, as did all levels of the judiciary in this research. What is more striking, however, is that some see themselves as apolitical in a broader sense. Their human rights decisions shape the unwritten UK constitution in a profound way that would require difficult constitutional amendments in most countries. Many decisions, like that in the Belmarsh case, provoke the wrath of ministers and Parliamentary rows. This is especially acute at the time of writing, 2011, over the plan to give people the opportunity to apply for removal from the Sex Offenders' Register, following a UKSC decision,[204] yet some top judges think that they are, individually and collectively, somehow objective, and that any new appointee would be such a clone that there could be no interest in public examination of a candidate. Some tend to deny that they have a broad political role in the same way that some Law Lords last century denied that they had a law-making role.

This 'neutral' position was taken for granted in the 2003 consultation paper on the proposed UKSC. Acknowledging the growth of judicial review, the Government emphasised 'It is essential that our systems do all that they can to minimize the danger that judges' decisions could be perceived to be politically motivated'.[205] Academics like Stevens were and are highly cynical. He likened this reasoning to *Alice in Wonderland* in that 'if we say often enough that our judges are apolitical they will be.'[206] The paper emphasised the supremacy of Parliament, yet the European Convention on Human Rights and the European Communities Act had required the Law Lords to apply a fundamental law and act as a type of constitutional court.[207]

Since the growth of judicial review, from 1981, and especially since the Human Rights Act 1998, it was argued by some that the Law Lords had become a constitutional court. The creation of the UKSC turned this into a concern that the judges might arrogate more power, propounded in 2009 by Lord Neuberger and immediately dismissed by Lord Bingham and the first UKSC President, Lord Phillips.[208] Neuberger did make the undeniable point though that:

---

[203] In the 2007 Gibb interview, above n 3.

[204] M Fricker, 'Fury as paedophiles get the right to dodge sex offenders' register for life', *The Mirror*, 17 February 2011.

[205] Department of Constitutional Affairs, *Constitutional Reform: a Supreme Court for the United Kingdom* (2003, on the archived DCA website) 11.

[206] Stevens, above 92 at 31.

[207] See also D Woodhouse, 'The constitutional and political implications of a United Kingdom Supreme Court', also in the 2004 special edition of *Legal Studies*, above n 72.

[208] In 'Top Dogs: Britain's New Supreme Court', BBC Radio 4, 8 September 2009. Lord Neuberger, then a Law Lord, said that with a separate identity, the UKSC 'could start to become more powerful … arrogating to themselves greater power' and 'lead to a real risk of confrontation between the judiciary and the executive'.

> In a way more powerful under the human rights Convention is our ability to interpret legislation which does not appear to comply with the ... Convention so as to comply ... To an extent ... that means we can re-write legislation.[209]

Consequently, some argued that the Court's appointment process should be much more open. John Patten, a former Conservative Home Office Minister, argued in favour of public confirmation hearings, as in the Senate Judiciary Committee when a USSC Justice is appointed.[210] Others reiterated this, especially after the UKSC announcement.[211]

Dawn Oliver examined these arguments but emphasised the problems.[212] She questioned what criteria would apply. A Parliamentary Committee would be less qualified than an appointments commission to determine a candidate's suitability. A hearing was likely to be concerned with a judge's beliefs and politics, which ought not to be relevant in the UK. It could lead to a reduction in security of tenure. Our system assumed judges were open-minded and would not let their prejudices influence them. This had generally worked. In the 2003 paper, the Government dismissed confirmation hearings. Gordon Brown's Government expressed a distaste for copying the US but not before outraging constitutional experts and judges by suggesting it.[213]

> To adopt such an approach in this country could lead to the strong perception that judicial appointments were being politicised, and such a perception could have an impact on confidence in the independence of the judiciary.[214]

For the time being, governments and most interested parties appear to accept judges' insistence that they are apolitical, and there is little sympathy with Patten's suggestion, even from Lord Neuberger MR, who, in a speech later on in 2009, acknowledged that it was difficult to see how the UKSC could have a *Marbury v Madison* moment and give itself a general power to rule on the constitutionality of legislation. He too rejected confirmation hearings as 'a real risk of politicisation of the senior judiciary'.[215]

---

[209] They did so in *Ghaidan v Godin-Mendoza* [2001] UKHL 30, giving a homosexual partner the same rights as a spouse. They said there was no limit to the words that could be read in or out of a legislative measure, provided it did not go against the grain of the measure. The HC and CA have the same powers.

[210] *The Times*, 16 March 1999.

[211] Cornes, *The Times*, 1 October 2009, above n 21. See Gibb, same edition, and Pannick, one week later.

[212] D Oliver, *Constitutional Reform in the UK* (Oxford, Oxford University Press, 2003) ch 18.

[213] In a 2007 Ministry of Justice consultation paper, *The Governance of Britain*. The suggestion was dismissed by Lord Chief Justice Phillips, speech, 'Judicial Independence', 12 September 2007.

[214] White paper, *The Governance of Britain: Judicial Appointments*, Cm. 7210, 2007, para 4.36.

[215] Neuberger, 'The Supreme Court: is the House of Lords "losing part of itself"', speech, 3 December 2009, para 31. The topic of transparency over judges' beliefs and backgrounds in judicial selection was was re-examined from different angles by Michael Kirby, former Justice of

CONCLUSION

The Law Lords and now UKSC Justices have been subject to far more research than any other judges. Their practices, role and appointment have been the subject of debate by academics, practising lawyers and politicians. Comments on their working practices have intensified since 2003, when the UKSC was announced. By now, there is so much academic and journalistic material on them, plus judicial speeches, that it is difficult to keep on top of it. Ironically, however, the public have, generally speaking, no understanding of what they do and would not be able to name one Justice, though a handful of people may have become better informed by two 2011 documentaries. The Justices like being anonymous. They think they are apolitical. This is true in a party political sense but certainly not in the wider political sense and, since many of their cases concern human rights, they are sucked into fierce political controversy whether they like it or not. They have immense power. They make the common law. They reinterpret statutes conflicting with the human rights convention, or declare them incompatible. They can quash UK Acts which flout EU law. Their power is enhanced by the fact that the UK has an unwritten constitution.

Their working methods are extremely well known to academics, thanks to research and the speeches and writings of the judges. For instance, we know that selection of normal panels is on a 'horses for courses' basis, subject to constraints of availability and serving Scottish and Irish needs. They are ultra-transparent and responsive to demands for more transparency. They have placed on their website the criteria for selecting larger panels. All Justices now take the point that composition matters and may sway the outcome so they all say they want to sit in bigger benches sometimes. There is still room on the website for more informa-tion, though, such as full reasons as to why some applications are rejected. This, and some other really important issues, such as bench size, bench selection, format of hearings (length, orality) and judgment formation, are not constrained by the Rules or Practice Directions so the Court's transformation to the UKSC led to soul-searching among the Justices about these important issues of practice. This is still going on. Heeding the academics and the blogging practitioners, and the newly appointed judges, the Justices have been changing their practices. Completing this chapter, I am writing about a moving target, as the Court continues to change its practices to accommodate critics' suggestions.

The English Justices are far less vocal in hearings than they were in the CA. The UKSC still suffers from defects identified in the CA in 1990: too little pre-deliberation, too much time control by advocates and poor advocacy. Like the CA, they are keen to preserve oral hearings but much time is still wasted on the recitation of legislation or other contents of the Printed Cases. Any observer can

the High Court of Australia, in 'A Darwininan Reflection on Judicial Values and Appointments to Final National Courts' and A Kavanagh, 'From Appellate Committee to UK Supreme Court:Independence, Activism and Transparency', both writing in Lee, above n 76.

see this. Even students and the Justices' own judicial assistants remark that there is room for improvement. One would expect tip-top advocacy in the top court but advocates are of mixed ability, as we have seen they are in all other courts. Parties, not cases, should be time-limited. Recitation should be banned. The Court should list the topics on which it wishes to be addressed.

Contrary to the pervasive myth that judicial assistants have a hand in judgment writing, they do not, but Justices do find them extremely useful to bounce ideas off and it is still true that advocates have a big part to play in the basis of judgment and that oral advocacy can change a judge's mind. From reading the accounts of Paterson and others, it is clear that preparation, collaboration and judgment formation have changed according to who leads the court. While Lord Reid was laissez-faire on separate judgments and judges commonly had not read the printed case beforehand, Lord Diplock was so strict on pre-reading that he seemed to have pre-judged cases to the extent that he dismissed some arguments entirely. He preferred the single judgment, especially his own. Under Lord Bingham, the Court swung back to laissez-faire on the number of judgments but by then every judge had read the printed case. Hearing time was halved. Now, things are changing again. Outsiders, like their friends in the CA, press for more single or composite judgments but there has always been the perpetual argument that while the public and the CA may find these more user-friendly, the law is better served by the application of multiple strands of brilliant reasoning.

In the CA chapter, it was apparent that there was a really strong collegiality and that that had undoubtedly helped to foster the trend towards single and composite judgments, but so had pre-deliberation. In this chapter, it seemed that the new Justices sorely missed the collegiality and, indeed, camaraderie, of the CA so much that they even hankered after returning. Lord Neuberger did return. It was also clear that some Justices now feel frustrated over the lack of pre-deliberation, judgment planning and post-deliberation that they took for granted in the CA. Indeed, since I did not find a Justice who did not share this view, I remain slightly mystified as to why they have not changed their ways more by now. Having said that, Baroness Hale has explained how she and Lord Neuberger put their strong opinions into practice and collaborated on judgment writing, and the statistics demonstrate that there is a trend towards single and composite judgments. Doubtless Baroness Hale will keep pressing for plurality opinions.

The new judges felt like fishes out of water in the Parliament building. By 2008, all but two of the Justices wanted to move to the new UKSC and once they had arrived, in 2009, they all appreciated its fabulous facilities.

The Court is strikingly international. Not only does it serve three jurisdictions but much of its workload involves international law, especially EU law and human rights. It is an extremely important hub in the international traffic of ideas. Other courts follow its precedents and it has even persuaded the European Court of Human Rights to change its reasoning. Despite all this, its judges cling to their ordinariness and remain touchingly and astonishingly unaware of their own importance. On reading a previous draft in 2008, one Law Lord emailed:

Part of your chapter gives the impression, no doubt justified, that the junior Law Lords moan a lot but do not do anything about changing things. I think we all feel that the new SC is going to be a great opportunity for change. I would like to think that most of us who expect to end up there hope that we will take the opportunity to be more collegiate, and waste less time in duplicating work. The new rules have deliberately been drafted in an open-textured way to allow for this.

It is clear that this fluidity has enabled the Justices to change their practices in some very significant respects, in response to their own preferences, established after discussion, and to innumerable suggestions for 'improvement' made since 2003. The development of UKSC practice and procedure is still a work in progress.

16

Judges on Judges

Here, the High Court judges now join us for lunch and we have visits from higher still. And sometimes when we go on lectures or JSB seminars we meet with higher judges. But until about 1997, I felt very isolated … It was a problem … I never met circuit judges and *never* met High Court judges or above … there is a barrier there but it is not as bad as it used to be … when we first came to this building from our separate places, there was iciness in the dining room … One circuit judge said … 'We don't mind you coming into the dining room but it's your deputies!' … That was 1996 … in Liverpool and Manchester they have separate dining rooms!

County court DJ

Apparently, immigration adjudicators want to be called judges now—who'd want to do a job like *that?*

DJMC

T HIS BOOK GIVES a much clearer picture than any judge has of what their fellow judges do. This chapter examines the relationships between judges and their perceptions of different ranks and whether they sought promotion. It also examines the aftermath of dining room discrimination referred to above which caused some managing judges to resort to desperate remedies.

THE HIERARCHY

There is no 'career judiciary', unlike some European jurisdictions. A judge cannot expect promotion on passing exams. In the 1980s, it was still rare for a district judge (DJ) to become a circuit judge (CJ) or for a CJ to move up to the High Court (HC). Veterans in the research sample explained that judging used to be seen as a lawyers' retirement job.[1] It is still unusual for a judge to be promoted, with the exception of Court of Appeal (CA) judges who are recruited from the High Court, a handful of whom will become UK Supreme Court (UKSC) Justices. Most DJs are ex-solicitors. Most CJs are ex-barristers. Most HC judges

---

[1] S Shetreet quoted Denning, Scarman and Ensor: *Judges on Trial* (Amsterdam, North Holland, 1976) 78.

are recruited direct from the elite 10 per cent QC rank of the Bar. Most judges in this research only or mainly interacted with those of their own level. Some normally encountered no other judge. I asked the 77 interviewees how they perceived the differences between ranks and I observed how judges interacted with others.

District and Circuit Judges

Four of the 13 DJs routinely met only DJs at work. One worked alone, travelling around tiny rural courts, telephoning a retired colleague most days. When I took him out, court staff thanked me for rescuing him from his solitary cabbage soup diet. Five DJs ate with CJs some lunchtimes. Three saw CJs and HC judges.

It was not apparent until I interviewed them that most county court DJs harboured resentment against CJs, nine answering negatively when I asked a neutral question on how they perceived the differences between themselves and CJs. Five thought the pay difference 'unjustified'; four said 'we do more work'; four said CJs 'go home early';[2] one called them 'stuffy', another 'starchy'; one said DJs were more 'hands-on'; another said DJs were generally solicitors and thus 'practical', whereas CJs were 'cliquey' barristers. Status consciousness was seldom evident in observations of DJs, in their everyday dialogue with me throughout the working day, or in their interactions with others, but their interviews betrayed an irritation they had developed as practising solicitors about the superiority complex of some barristers, a phenomenon that was referred to earlier in this book. One young DJ answered:

> It starts when you are a solicitor … Barristers always think they are better … or at least that is the impression … There are some CJs that continue with that. Also … we are fighting each other for the work we do … There is certain resentment from DJs that CJs attempt to choose the work *they* want to do.

Annoyance about pay differential and work-type were a product of the fact that DJs now do the county court work that used to be done by CJs in the 1980s, so DJs thought they should be better paid. Few acknowledged what this research and court statistics demonstrate: that much High Court business has, in turn, shifted down to CJs.

Many DJs complained that the public and/or HM Courts Service and/or senior judges did not perceive them as judges. This status sensitivity is historic. They used to be called 'registrars', with a jurisdiction far more limited than now. In 1996 a senior Lord Chancellor's Department civil servant referred to them as

---

[2] As we have seen, Lord Irvine visited Bristol Crown Court and found there had been an exodus by Friday afternoon. See case law from the 1950s on judges leaving it to court officials to take a jury verdict on a Friday afternoon: Shetreet, above n 1 at 217.

'bean counters'.[3] Furthermore, these are the only judges, other than 'tribunal judges' not listed in *Who's Who*. Only since the Constitutional Reform Act 2005 have they been appointed by the Queen. In many post-1970s court buildings, DJs have separate dining rooms. This parallels the solicitor–barrister hierarchy. When barristers were consulted in 1973 on new court buildings, they specified that they must have dining rooms separate from solicitors.[4]

> Historically, there would have been social differences ... circuit judges were the Bar and district judges were solicitors. They were slightly different sorts of animal with whom you are not to have too much contact lest you be accused of touting. (Veteran CJ)

The 'dining room saga' is examined below. Four DJs and one district judge (magistrates' courts) (DJMC) mentioned 'separate dining rooms' in answering the question about perceived differences.

If county court DJs were *somewhat* separated from other ranks, then most DJMCs were wholly separated. One solicitor DJMC had never met a senior judge. Five of the six never encountered other ranks in their day-to-day work and two only encountered lay justices. They perceived big differences between themselves and the circuit bench. One said the difference was 'substantial' in pay and 'tremendous' in status. Three drew attention to their different work. 'We couldn't do one another's jobs.' Most perceived a social difference: 'They're Oxbridge, I'm council house!' A barrister DJMC, who sat part-time as a Crown Court recorder, referred to circuit judges' 'snootiness' and the separate Crown Court dining rooms. DJMCs felt excluded from judicial status and hierarchy to the extent of being invisible. Even a new appointee was sensitive.

> When the title was changed from stipendiary magistrate to district judge [in 1999] ... a lot of the circuit would say 'they are not like proper judges; they are just like magistrates'. To a lot of them, perhaps, we don't even exist. When I went on the inaugural meeting of the Association for Women Judges it was quite clear that a lot of them didn't know that we existed.

Their concern over invisibility was borne out by the interviews with the rest of the judiciary who, with one exception, automatically assumed the interview question on 'district judges' referred to county court DJs. There is an historic reason for separateness. Because most magistrates are laypeople, the professional (stipendiary) magistrates, as DJMCs used to be called, had never been perceived as judges. Magistrates' courts were administered by a separate government department until the 1980s and were managed locally until the creation of HM Courts Service and local courts boards in 2005.[5] Most magistrates' court cases are

---

[3] G Lingard, 'The other Gordon, yesterday's man?', Association of HM DJ's *Law Bulletin*, Vol 21 No 2, summer 2010.

[4] R Hazell, *The Bar on Trial* (London, Quartet, 1978), citing the Bar Council *Annual Statement 1973–4*. This was not just about snobbery but about the rule that prohibits barristers touting for business.

[5] Courts Act 2003.

heard by lay justices so it is not surprising that most lawyers and judges do not associate the term 'judge' with any adjudicator in a magistrates' court.

The handful of High Court DJs[6] were even more invisible, with several DJMCs and county court DJs asking me to explain their rank and jurisdiction and one DJ confidently providing an erroneous comparison of their powers. DJMCs asked why these judges outranked them in the parade into the Lord Chancellor's Breakfast in the Palace of Westminster.[7] Two HC DJs told me they had been sure to attend it 'gowned up' so that other judges would notice their distinct rank, and that they outranked county court DJs.

Despite frosty remarks about circuit judges by district judges, only two of the 32 CJs interviewed referred to DJs negatively, the others denying any social or status difference, but many, like this solicitor CJ, who had been a barrister, showed an awareness of DJs' sensitivity. At work, she groaned more than once about the behaviour of barristers appearing before her, 'Barristers have such big egos'.

> I socialise with district judges. Also, at the Association for Women Judges, I get a lot of opportunity to meet district judges ... [they] tend to be drawn from a slightly more diverse economic background. Obviously, there are a lot more former solicitors ... In many ways they are much more exposed than we are because they sit much closer to the punters and people say they have a much less stressful life but actually I am not convinced of that ... They are paid less than we are and some people say they do less work ... They seem to me to be very insecure in their position ... [they] seem to think that all circuit judges look down on them and it is true that some do.

The reflections of two more solicitor CJs who had been DJs were revealing, both on the subject of solicitor-judges and on another handicap to smooth relations referred to earlier in this book—the uncomfortable fact that appeals from DJs go to the CJs in the same courthouse:[8]

> The [work] differences are becoming much smaller ... there is a difference between the solicitor-judge and the barrister-judge. There are still very few solicitor-judges, about 60 or 70 out of about 800 and we are not grouped together, whereas the barrister-judges tend to know one another very well ... when I was first appointed there was resentment to solicitor-judges. I do feel occasionally that I am the odd one out. In Central London [Civil Justice Centre], I am usually the only one out of about a dozen [circuit judges]. I don't really think there is a social difference between district judge and circuit judge but there is *this* problem: if you are hearing appeals from district judges it is very difficult to be friendly with them on a social level.

---

[6] Who sit at the Principal Registry of the Family Division, in Holborn. 18 are listed, as at 2011.

[7] The ceremony at the opening of the legal year.

[8] Access to Justice Act 1999.

The second circuit judge sat in a provincial city and town. He too had been a DJ and told astonishing stories of having been excluded, as a solicitor-advocate, and *still* being excluded.

> We didn't belong to the Bar 'club' ... One of the reasons I wanted to be a judge was because I felt we need more people with a broader range of approach ... An example is the shooting brigade and 'Are you going to Lord So-and-So's party?' Particularly in the provinces it is expected of you, when you become a judge ... So it is quite nice to be someone who doesn't do that sort of thing and who doesn't come from that background. [On DJ/CJ differences] Even though we often share ... similar jurisdictions ... [DJs] don't always exercise all the opportunities they have ... I don't think there is a social difference ... There are some circuit judges who would regard me as a bit of an upstart ... when I was first a recorder there were those of the old school who made it clear that I wasn't part of the club ... There is also the story about when, unlike all the other lawyers who had finished a big case and were taken out to dinner [by the judge], I wasn't, because I was a solicitor-advocate. I had done a 17-day care case ... We were all up there staying and I had known nothing about this dinner and one of the QCs ... said, as we were leaving court ... 'Shall we share a cab to the dinner tonight?' I said 'What dinner?' She was so appalled that she didn't go to the dinner either ... Now, it may be because people haven't got used to the fact that I am now in [this city] that when the new Senior presider came ... I wasn't invited. People forget me because I am not part of the club ... I think there is a different social strata that some of them perceive ... not a barrister-solicitor thing. It is just that they come from a different background, even though they may have come from comprehensive education ... and been brilliant and made good.

Defending CJs, a barrister CJ said the attitude of DJs was 'all about money and jealousy' and another CJ defended the pay difference, making a fair comment, 'They claim they do work which is circuit judge level but they forget the fact that circuit judges do work that High Court judges used to'. Nevertheless, 12 of 32 CJs insisted there was no social or status difference, typically:

> I don't think there is a huge difference any more ... In the past ... a lot of them were solicitors ... it irritates me intensely when certain circuit judges ... have the idea that they are in some way better ... We are different. I don't think very many do have that view these days.

One new CJ, a QC, thought there was no social difference but 'there is snobbery right through the judiciary'.

Judges and Lay Magistrates

Sometimes judges and magistrates shared work harmoniously but some district and circuit judges were contemptuous of lay justices. The hostility was mutual. London DJMCs said provincial magistrates resented them deeply. One told me he was not allowed to sit at the end of the magistrates' room and plug in his laptop. Another said he'd been referred to as a 'hired hand'. I was told that at one London court, the senior judge would not allow the DJMCs to speak to lay magistrates and the magistrates thought there was a plot to replace them with DJMCs. At one court, the DJMCs grumbled about a lay justice who insisted on lunching with the judges. He sidled up to them and broke into their conversation. 'He won't leave until he's spoken to. He's always acting as if he's a DJ, telling you what the law is, arguing with the DJs about sentences they've imposed', hissed a DJMC, aside. She was 'sure' he sat more than the maximum 80 days.[9] In family cases, lay magistrates were considered biased and incompetent. County court DJs laughed scornfully at a care case sent up after an inexplicable year-long delay. Elsewhere, a family CJ asserted 'We do things better here. Some magistrates are biased towards authority—the police and social workers.' Judge Jodie clucked about 'magistrates deliberating with the door open'. DJMC Pole, who used to train and organise magistrates, as a justices' clerk, said that when he sat with magistrates it was

> hopeless trying to get them to agree reasons. I take the case home to draft reasons then ask if they disagree with me. Listening to their deliberations, I sometimes wonder if they've forgotten all they were taught on decision-making.

Senior Judges and the Lower Ranks

DJs did not extend any resentment to HC judges, whom they held in admiration. I asked the 19 DJs and DJMCs how they perceived the difference between the circuit bench and those above. One said there was a 'bigger void'. A DJMC said:

> Chasm! There are lots of awful circuit judges who can't walk and chew gum at the same time but you don't get that at High Court level. It is a different world. They get paid 160 grand a year and they are worth every penny. They work them to death. I might as well be a bus driver or butcher … I have got as much in common with a carpenter as I have with a High Court judge.

He was impressed with the approachability of his circuit's new presider. The presider had invited him to lodgings but it was not convenient so he responded 'Well, I'll come to *you* then. I'll adjourn my murder case early'. The DJ was flabbergasted. 'This wouldn't have happened five years ago *and* he turned up in a Corporation car with no motorcycle outriders.' Another DJMC had never met a senior judge until the week before I met her, when she attended the Lord Chancellor's Breakfast. 'I met three High Court judges there. They were charming. At that level, they have nothing to prove, have they?' I took her to a book launch at Middle Temple, where we spoke a number of CA judges. She was slightly awe-struck and told her colleagues the story the next day. Five DJs referred to HC judges' 'intellect' or 'calibre'. 'They are seriously octane people, to be respected'.

---

[9] The recommended maximum of half-day sittings by magistrates.

Similarly, nine CJs referred to senior judges' 'immense intellect and abilities' and six mentioned their work: 'tremendous work burden and responsibility'. Many CJs recognised that not all had the brains to handle senior work:

> You have to have ... a much more acute intellect. You are under greater pressure; you are assisted because you will get the highest quality of advocacy [a mistaken impression, as we have seen] but nevertheless you will get more difficult problems, more knife-edge problems ... [such as] judicial review...immigration, asylum seekers and the Human Rights Act ... They have got to get important answers where there is not a lot of precedent ... acute judgments ... under pressure of time. There are certainly members of the circuit bench who have that ability but I think they are few ... That group of people are going to go on to man the Court of Appeal and eventually the ... Supreme Court. Of course the cream rises to the top but nevertheless you want good quality cream from which to make your appointments.

There was a general view among the lower judiciary that the state got its money's worth out of senior judges. As a Crown Court resident judge sorted the cases that had landed on his desk, he allocated the murder and rape of an 83-year-old, 'You think you're in the last throes of man's inhumanity to man—terrible injuries to the woman. This is one for a starred judge at least. That's what High Court judges are for'.

Five said senior judges were much more approachable now than judges of 'the old school': 'much less "them and us"'. Two responded identically, 'They come to lunch in the dining room now. That wouldn't have happened five years ago'. A newly appointed barrister-judge said:

> I don't ... sense any division, or have any sense of the High Court judges feeling superior or acting superior to us. It is a very different atmosphere from that when I started [as a barrister, 1976] when everyone knew their place.

Another said:

> It ... surprised me ... The High Court judges ... are very open and accessible and make time available to see us. They join us for lunch every day, or invite us to the lodgings, so there is really quite good contact ... There is no stand-offishness. For the most part, the difference is intellect. One can think of one or two who fall short of the ideal.

The first above regretted that he only encountered HC judges when they visited his Crown Court for four–six weeks per year. Some CJs at big courts met HC judges every day in the dining room, but others at small county courts rarely met them. One of these said 'it would do them good to come here and see litigants in person'. Again, this was another seriously mistaken impression, the notion that senior judges were not equally preoccupied by litigants in person. A number of CJs had shared chambers, as barristers, with friends who were now HC judges so they met them regularly, socially.

By far the biggest group of senior judges is the Queen's Bench Division (QBD). They met county court DJs and CJs travelling around the circuits for half the legal year. HC presiders, liaison and supervising judges from all three divisions see them in management meetings and get to know many of the judges on their circuit. Nevertheless, senior judges were likely to have more frequent contact with CJs than DJs. Some CJs said they were invited to lodgings to dine with HC judges four to six times a year, though only one DJ mentioned such an invitation. Two of the 16 HC judges said they made it their business to meet and lunch with DJs on circuit. Moving further up, nine of the 10 CA/HL judges said they met DJs and CJs occasionally on training courses, or they met them weekly now or in the past, in their management capacity. One said, as a manager, he could visit a different county court every Friday if he chose to do so. Because most of the 26 senior judges did not meet DJs regularly, I was surprised to find that 24 had an opinion on the CJ/DJ differences. They had clearly sensed the atmosphere while on circuit. Ten alluded to DJs' status sensitivities and were aware of the DJ/CJ tension. Typically, one said DJs were

> slightly chippy about their positions … when I was a recorder doing civil work, I was asked to do an appeal … from a district judge and I think I allowed the appeal. I then was told that I shouldn't have agreed to do this … because I was a part-timer … I just sense that they feel they are at the bottom of a pile and I think that is unfortunate.

Another said:

> Some circuit judges feel slightly superior to district judges but then you discover one of the district judges was a senior partner in a large City firm and you know he is more able than any of the circuit judges in the town. So I think in some ways it is historic from when the district judges were registrars and weren't called judges.

A CA managing judge who met a lot of DJs was well aware that able DJs were sometimes deployed to do circuit bench work:

> This is quite a sensitive area … DJs are quite self-conscious about their inferior status … In theory there is no limit to the jurisdiction … there is all sorts of different practices, all over the country … that is understandable because if you have got the really good district judge it may seem … a waste of resources not to use that DJ [for high value multitrack trials] particularly if your circuit judges are all really needed to do crime … It is uneasy.

HC judges were generally too polite to distinguish themselves from CJs on the basis of intellect, as the CJs did. Most denied a social difference and asserted that there was merely a difference in the type of work they did, and that the gap between High Court and circuit judges was 'diminishing', because a lot of HC cases were heard by CJs 'analogous to … my GP practice where things that I used to go to the doctor for, I then went to the nurse for and I now go to somebody called a health care professional', and because an increasing number of CJs were being promoted to the High Court.

It was often said, outside the interviews, by all types of judge, that the circuit bench included a broad ability range:

> It is a very broad church … as, indeed, is the whole of the judiciary. There are some that you think would be able to become High Court judges … there are others like me who ought to be circuit judges but have been lucky enough to get where I am. (HC judge)

As has been seen in the Court of Appeal chapter, appeal judges put a high value on having circuit judges in the CACD.

Some circuit and some HC judges drew attention to the difference in lifestyle between the generally static circuit judge and the itinerant High Court judge. One CJ said the latter's out-of-court workload and travelling lifestyle was 'unenviable'. An HC judge who had been a circuit judge looked back wistfully, 'You get to sleep in your own bed at night'. Conversely, some HC judges could not have tolerated the CJs' work pattern:

> They do a different job, in many respects … more difficult. They get ghastly long fraud and drug cases which we don't get … I didn't want to be a circuit judge because I didn't want the lack of variety … I would hate to sit in the same place every day…trying the same sorts of cases. That would bore me silly … There are many of them who could do the High Court judge's job … as has been shown by the modern practice of promoting circuit judges far more often than they were before … that is a wholly beneficial change.

Another said 'the circuit bench are much more saint-like … they just have to go on and on doing the same thing all the time and I think the joy of *our* job is that we do have variety'. The CA/HL judges said the same. As was clear earlier in the book, although senior circuit judges and senior judges worked very hard, some said they had chosen to take on more and more challenges and that was clear from their achievements as lawyers too. Senior judges thrived on the intellectual challenge of the law, whereas DJs and some CJs were happy because the job freed them from business pressure as solicitors, or case pressure, as barristers, and spared time for more outside life.

PROMOTION

Judges broadly understand what is required of the rank above and they are aware that an increasing number have broken through. The whole hierarchy *could* now become more fluid since the Constitutional Reform Act 2005 created a new, supposedly merits-based appointments system. The hiatus between circuit and High Court *could* be broken because all senior posts have to be applied for. It will not be broken, however, if few CJs apply. The same applies to the barrier between the district and circuit benches.

Do District Judges Want to be Circuit Judges?

Since many DJs described their job as 'the best in the world', it was not a surprise that, despite their relative youth, only one of the 13 wanted to join the circuit bench (and has since done so). Ten did not want to conduct criminal trials.

The reason why I love this job so much is the quality of life is great and I'm quite comfortable with the fact that I have a circuit judge between me and the Court of Appeal ... I'm not interested in doing crime at all.

I considered applying to be a circuit judge but am not interested in crime, so ruled it out. Then came the opportunity to be a circuit judge (civil or family only) and I seriously considered it because I felt I'm up to it in terms of delivering judgments and would welcome getting longer cases rather than lots of small ones. But I backed off because I decided that for me (with my personality and interests) I'm at the right level, close to people, dealing with their problems in a wide variety of situations ... I'm happiest where I am. I came into this with an inferiority complex ... I lived in awe of the city solicitors ... but since joining the judiciary, I've found that I have the edge ... there's nothing I haven't dealt with ... except serious crime or immigration.

I don't need more money. I like being in control and enjoying what I am doing. I like having free time ... to spend with my family and friends.

Similarly, four of the six DJMCs were not interested in promotion. Two had considered it half-heartedly. This one was very frank:

It is most unlikely that I would apply to be a circuit judge ... The QCs are all going for it now; the competition is really hotting up ... A top QC could do a circuit judge's job ... with their eyes shut ... I would never like to be seen as being hopeless at what I do. Of course I think I am brilliant at *this* because I am competing against lay magistrates ... I could do it if I worked hard but ... I think it would start affecting my home life.

There is a curious tail-note. Researchers should guard against affecting their subjects but, by asking DJs this question, this research prompted one DJ (not the one above) and one DJMC to apply to sit as recorders, as a first step to the circuit bench, despite the fact that one insisted she would feel 'like a fish out of water' in the Crown Court.

Do Circuit Judges Want to be High Court Judges?

Twenty-one of the 32 were unenthusiastic, listing their intellectual limitations, the travelling, hard-working, family-unfriendly lifestyle and having to live in London.[10]

The demands ... both intellectual and ... sheer hard work would be just what I don't want. It would be going backwards because I am so relieved not to be under those sorts of pressures. High Court judges are dealing mainly with civil work, which was never my favourite ... categorically no. (Newly appointed)

---

[10]   Compare the similarity of responses to Genn's question to lawyers: Professor Dame Hazel Genn, *The attractiveness of senior judicial appointment to highly qualified practitioners—Report to the Judicial Executive Board* (London, Directorate of Judicial Offices for England and Wales, 2008, Judiciary website).

I don't know anyone who can go on the High Court bench if they have a family, particularly young family. I just don't think it is user-friendly. (Male CJ who said having a child had put him off).

I am doing the job I wanted to do and I don't think I want to go back to the life of living out of a suitcase ... I don't think I am ... of a sufficiently high calibre. (QC)

Firstly, what a miserable life but (a) I don't think they would want me anyway, but ... you would have to spend half the year in London ... acquiring some accommodation in London, which would be costly ... I do a high amount of High Court civil at the moment and I have sat in the QBD as a Deputy ... (b) it is extremely hard work and I think the job involves even more work than I'd want. And what do you get in exchange? You get a bit of status, you get a knighthood and that is about it ... your life would be extremely unpleasant. (QC)

What I am doing at the moment is ... very satisfying ... I am my own boss ... I am able to be at home, apart from when I go to London, which I do out of choice. I am invited there and to the Court of Appeal, which I enjoy ... the moving about would put me off and also the work you would be doing. Crime is what I enjoy ... Here, I do murders, rape and serious crime so...why throw it all to be stuck in Newcastle, or, *worse*, London ... The financial implications of moving to London ... are enormous. The increase in salary is about £30,000 ... but you take tax ... and London accommodation out of that, it is nothing ... the only reason why people do it is the knighthood.

I wanted to be a High Court judge badly, because I thought I was up to the mark. Now I realise that I don't ... I would lose a great deal, I would lose being in touch with human beings in a much more profound way.

Probably to be honest most circuit judges would say they wouldn't want to become a High Court judge because it is very hard and onerous but secretly I think the vanity of every individual would say they would love to have a knighthood and an extra £30,000 a year and the extra status ... *I* wouldn't apply because I would have to live away from home. Six months a year you are in London, Newcastle or living in lodgings with someone else's dog or wife.

Those above were men. Two women said they would consider applying once their children had grown up.

Probably not when the children are still at home and young because one of the reasons why I took this job was to avoid all of that travelling around the country that I used to do when I was a barrister. I quite like the idea of sleeping in my own bed at night and if you are a High Court judge it means relocating to London or Newcastle.

Nine of the 32 CJs said they would have welcomed an HC appointment. One was appointed during the time of the research, one was applying, three were too old to be considered and four were new.

The reluctance of most DJs and CJs to apply for promotion reflects their contentment with their job. It does not mean that the new trend towards more judicial upward mobility will not accelerate. It must be remembered, though, that most university lecturers do not apply to be head of department. Most barristers do not apply for QC status, and so on. The responses above reflect that generality. Given that circuit and HC judges can still be recruited from among practising lawyers under the post-2006 system, my guess would be that the majority will be so recruited in future. The 2005 Act will not generate a career judiciary.

Do High Court Judges Want to Sit in the Court of Appeal?

High Court judges had no such reticence, 11 of the 16 admitting that they would contemplate the CA, whatever their reservations. Given that 14 had been high-achieving, workaholic barristers, this is hardly a surprise. Indeed, four were promoted at the time of the research, including the one who professed reluctance but then received an invitation to join the CA at the time of the interview, quoted in chapter 5. Another two have since been promoted. Two judges were too new to have contemplated the CA. Three were adamant that they would reject it.

> I got a second class degree and I think I have a good second class mind ... if you have a first class mind it would be tremendously exciting either to be an academic or be in the Court of Appeal. If you don't, you have to run very fast to keep up ... and I am fully stretched in the job I do at the moment and I enjoy it. I was also appointed fairly old. I have no desire to blight my declining years by having to work even harder than I am at the moment.

One was ambivalent. As a Family Division judge, the CA represented a chance to get her teeth into more legal issues but the lifestyle was different:

> There's the ladder thing ... part of you feels that you'll have failed if you don't climb ... it would represent the opportunity to do more law, and not being on your own doing trials ... there's also the fact that there's huge amounts of work there. ['You'd also be in London all the time.'] That would be a downside and a positive. ['What's positive?'] All this term, I've just been all over the place. You get seriously disorientated after a while. All your papers are in an in-tray with a rubber band on. You don't know where anything is. You can do it up to a point but it's just been silly. The downside is that you don't get to meet all those nice people in lodgings and you don't get to get out and be your own boss for a bit.

Do Court of Appeal Judges Want to be Supreme Court Justices?

Six of the eight said they would like to, though some thought their chances were very slim. The two others ruled out the possibility. Three have gone up. Two viewed life in the top court with some suspicion, because they valued the collegiality of the Court of Appeal:

> It cuts you off from the main stream of the rough and tumble, running the courts ... It is an academic question as I don't feel it would ever arise.

I think I probably would … it is rather a different way of life. It is a very nice way of life in this Court. It is collegiate, there are 35 members so it is very relaxed. People get on very well together, whereas their House is rather smaller. I am not quite sure how that would work.

This very point was raised by the two Justices and by two Law Lords to whom I spoke in the 1990s. One hankered after the Court of Appeal and used any excuse to return and, as was seen in the previous chapter, the two Justices in the main sample were 'tapped on the shoulder' to be Law Lords and immediately wanted to escape back to their comfort-zone, with friends in the CA.

JUDGES AS SOCIAL ANIMALS AND JUDGES' TRADE UNIONS

Most of the civil DJs sat at more than one court and would chat to other DJs about work or personal lives in one another's rooms and/or over lunch. This judge went home for lunch and to do housework sometimes (taking me with him) but otherwise, the courts he sat at provided a typical variety:

The courts vary. I know of courts where the district judges are not welcome at the circuit judges' dining room, where they have separate dining rooms … courts where the judges meet every day as a matter of habit over a sandwich in one of their rooms … courts where they go out every day. Here we are a fairly gregarious lot … constantly talking to each other about the way things … can be improved.

The district bench was the most collegial at a national level, because their organisation[11] was the most active and inclusive. Each DJ attended its AGM, a training and business day, organised by the Judicial Studies Board (JSB), followed by a dinner, and each attended two or three meetings/training sessions annually within their circuit. Most were not active organisers but universally praised it. Some added that circuit judges envied it. They attended other training sessions and some were trainers, travelling the country. One lunched with DJs, CJs and HC judges most days of the week and met judges at a regional or national level 15 times a year. Unsurprisingly, 11 of the 13 DJs thought they had ample opportunities to meet other DJs. By contrast, all DJMCs, in their isolated state, said they would like more opportunities to meet other judges. Below is a typical London DJMC.

We are very lucky … in and out of each other's rooms … [we meet] people at training sessions [and … quarterly meetings for Greater London … and … area meetings … We have social events … an annual dinner. Round the country they have their own groups and they all come together three or four times a year. We made it clear to the [Ministry of Justice] and the JSB that there is a need … for those who are isolated in singleton posts, to come together. We had a weekend where everybody came … fantastic.

---

[11]   The Association of Her Majesty's District Judges.

Another DJMC saw a need to meet at least Crown Court judges.

> I have suggested that we need to meet at least once a year with the Crown Court judges
> … we can send cases to the Crown Court that we think are too serious to be dealt with
> here … We never get any feedback.[12]

Circuit judges who had practised at the Bar were generally gregarious workmates.
Not only were they in and out of one another's rooms with queries on law and
sentencing and social chat but they could usually lunch together in the dining
room. Two who could not do so complained about it. Most had judge-friends
they had made at the Bar and this was a typical northern judge, though it shows
why the solicitor circuit judge above felt left out of the 'Bar club':

> Training occasions … circuit dinner … in York every year which is good fun …
> Christmas and summer mess so other judges from the Bar are there … Friday night
> chambers functions … the court [cathedral] service where judges are invited for lunch.
> When the High Court judges are up here they have dinner for the high sheriff and they
> will invite some of the circuit judges … JSB trainings are great socialising occasions …
> The North Eastern Circuit really do know each other pretty well.

There are far more circuit judges in the South East than other circuits, indeed 307
of the 680 in post in 2011, compared with 36 in Wales, and they do not know one
another as well. This London solicitor-judge had far fewer opportunities to meet
his fellows than when he was a DJ:

> There are a few social functions … an annual dinner for the Circuit Judges' Association.
> Sometimes … a dinner for London circuit judges, particularly if we are saying goodbye
> to someone … there should be far more business meetings … district judges have about
> four business meetings every year and the circuit judges only have about one.

Nevertheless, 27 of the 32 CJs did not want any more opportunities to meet other
judges. Most CJs spoke positively about the Council of Circuit Judges but did not
attend meetings. They were aware of criticisms and some wished it were a
stronger trade union, though others criticised it for being too much like a
union.[13]

Most CJs and DJs also belonged to a nationwide virtual bench, Felix, as it was
then called, reading interchanges on common problems, legal or procedural, or
joining in, and I noticed, in 1995, that this formed an important social network
for a circuit judge who led a solitary life, at a tiny Crown Court, staying in a hotel.
Felix was a striking penetration into his lonely bubble. Felix may have contributed to the homogenisation of judges referred to earlier in this book and to some
harmonisation of practice and interpretation of the law. Other intranet groups
facilitated networking. Most DJs and CJs logged on every day. Typically, one CJ
said he liked some of the good quality chat, though 98 per cent was of no use to
him. Felix and its replacement probably generated some national camaraderie

[12] See ch 8.
[13] Details on Judiciary website.

and solidarity, since it allowed for a national whinge-fest among a minority of judges about pensions, about ministers who criticised judges, and about media attacks and so on.

HC judges interacted at work with judges in their own corridor in the Royal Courts of Justice and I mentally labelled one 'the corridor of fun'.

> This corridor is very special … There are QBD tea parties which are rather mixed and rather sad … But the main interaction is on this corridor. We had a retirement for [Andy] yesterday and all the graduates of this corridor came back. We generally have a sandwich lunch twice a term and people just take their sandwiches into each other's rooms … I am told that is not typical. My clerk … said I should get on this corridor because it is fun. When [John Doe] was here they sometimes played corridor bowls and stuff like that.

Most lunched at their Inn of Court two or three days a week, when in London. Commercial Court judges met every two weeks, Administrative judges met for seminars and Chancery judges had tea on Tuesdays. Travellers got to know their fellows in lodgings very well. In London, they received regular evening invitations to academic events and chambers parties and, on circuit, lodgings life required socialising with the sheriff and/or other judges about twice a week, though they juggled this around hard work. Unlike the DJs and CJs, they did not have as many training opportunities, as their attendance at JSB seminars was relatively novel. Like the CJs, most retained judge-friends from the Bar. The social pattern for CA judges was the same, though of course they worked together too, in a new threesome every three weeks, and it should be remembered that this applied to HC judges, during their CACD stints.

The Judges' Council is a statutory body established in 1873 to represent senior judges.[14] It was re-launched in 2002, representing all levels of judge, including magistrates and tribunal judges. After reconstitution, it helps the Lord Chief Justice in his duties under the Constitutional Reform Act 2005.[15] Its membership is limited, including only four HC and one regular CA judge. Most of the 26 senior judges said they did not know what it did, including some of those who were or had been members. Only six commented positively. The other 20, including Council members, criticised it or did not know enough to comment. This was the most positive comment.

> It was set up after extensive consultation … designed to get a spread of representation right across the judiciary … It is still pretty top heavy—it has got to be because it is the

[14] It became moribund in the 1980s and was revived in 1988 when Lord Lane LCJ ferociously opposed Lord Chancellor Mackay's plans to alter rights of audience.

[15] The Judiciary website gives details: independence, code of conduct, welfare, employment conditions, budget, law and policy reform, IT, liaising with the Judicial College and Judicial Appointments Commission. The Council is also represented on the European Network of Councils of Circuit Judges, whose main concern seems to be to be threats to independence, according to the account of DJ Walker in the summer 2006 edition of the Association of DJs *Law Bulletin*. They have their own website.

formal body to represent the judges' views in the public arena ... It is a useful body but there is still a lack of understanding and knowledge of its work.

But a CA judge was highly critical of the Council and the other management groups he sat on.

Any organisation which has more than 10 people and certainly more than 30 is completely ineffective. I go to three meetings a term ... the High Court judges' meeting which has about 100 members, the CA which was about 30 and the Judges' Council which was about 30 and they are all a complete waste of time because, first of all you just can't have a sensible discussion and there is also so much to get through. The LCJ in two of the cases and the MR in the case of the CA basically tell you what is going on and everybody nods. The idea that they come away mandated in a sense is perfectly right because whatever they say virtually without exception just gets voted through, with one or two self-regarding judges asking questions, one or two intelligent judges making points and all the points ... disappear under the water and the ship moves one. Frankly ... other than perhaps giving a rather absurd feeling of community ... they are useless.

In response to such concerns, the Council was remodelled in 2011. Its representatives include magistrates and Justices of the UKSC and it holds day-long meetings.

THE POLITICS OF DINING ROOMS

Some Crown, county and combined courts have judges' dining rooms but not the Royal Courts of Justice, which is where HC and CA judges bring their own sandwiches or eat at their Inns. The Law Lords ate in the Parliament café and as UKSC Justices they now have their own dining room. Separate dining rooms for DJs and CJs in modern courts caused enormous lasting irritation to DJs and ongoing embarrassment to managing CJs. A very senior DJ explained his own court's position in the opening quotation above. Indeed, the resident CJ at his combined court (by now a HC judge) was so sensitive about his court's history that he made sure that all ranks sat mixed up around a large table and he went round serving coffee, like a waiter. A family CJ on the same circuit was annoyed by the inconvenience and artificiality of separate dining rooms:

In Z, the circuit and district judges have lunch in different rooms and in many ways the ... district judges are people I am working more closely with than some of the circuit judges. It seems to me completely bizarre ... We ring each other and chat.

A resident judge of a court with separate dining rooms explained that when he arrived in 1993, he considered this problematic and set about devising a means of mixing DJs and CJs. He started a system of one DJ and one CJ going to one another's dining rooms every day but people did not like it. Then he invited all the DJs to join the CJs but they did not want to lose their room to administrators. New, 'aggressive' DJs complained, so the resident invented a system where they all had drinks together, then went to their separate dining rooms, but this broke down because people stopped coming for drinks. He was aware that the Lord Chief Justice and the Senior Presiding Judge disapproved of the separate dining rooms:

I am still struggling … I don't feel they [DJs] really responded by not coming through. So there is that slight sort of tension but when we do have our monthly lunch it goes well but I don't think there is any pressure from them to have it more frequently so it is a difficult and touchy area.

There were divisive patterns at courts with just one dining room. At four, where the resident sat at the head of the table, the DJs sat at the opposite end, with CJs between. One CJ remarked on this—it happened at one court where he occasionally sat, which was exceptionally friendly and welcoming, 'not because of some expectation but because the district judges have their own gossip'. At a big city combined court, I went with the designated family judge to have coffee with the DJs. I asked her why I never saw them in the dining room.

They are invited but they tend on the whole not to. The district judges that do come … tend to be the ones who were at the Bar or sit doing crime. The other district judges will only come if the Lord Mayor is here or … for the Christmas lunch.

At one big city county court, the managing designated civil judge (DCJ), himself a solicitor, was unhappy that DJs sat at the other end of the table and talked about their own cases some of the time.[16] The DJs ate in the dining room two or three times a week and otherwise ate their lunch in the library, which made the DCJ sad. He had initiated the dining room, when he redesigned the court building. He resisted sitting at the head of the table. The kitchen staff laid the table, setting out the cold food that judges had pre-ordered. I accompanied him as he sneaked into the room early, to swap the places around, to ensure that the DJs were mixed with the CJs.

There is still to an extent a sense of 'them and us' and I am against that and I do all I can to alter that. The lunch arrangements are a particular example of that here. I would prefer it if we all had lunch together every day … Circuit judges enjoy talking about things that affect circuit judges and equally district judges enjoy talking about things which affect district judges so I can see arguments why we might lunch separately but you can still talk about things which affect you in the same environment. One of the problems is, [the district judges] are less formal … they keep a less set time and they are going out and doing some shopping and that sort of thing.

Elsewhere, a resident described all the dining room arrangements he had experienced on other circuits, and the politics surrounding them. He regretted that the dining room at his court could not accommodate a round table. 'With a long table, people coming in late might be excluded.'

The Employment Appeal Tribunal (EAT) put its anti-discrimination mission into a symbolic statement in its dining room. On a hot summer's day, people lunched in their shirt sleeves, wherever they could find a space, round the single

---

[16]   In most courts, we all talked together. I expect any novelty stranger might have the same disruptive attraction.

big table, and an observer could not tell a circuit judge from a High Court judge, from a lay member.

WOMEN

At 30 of the courts with dining rooms, I was the only woman. At 10 others, the only other female was the research subject. At five, there were two female judges. Only at the Principal Registry of the Family Division were there more than two women. This should not be a surprise, because family law, for this generation, is women's work. At a number of courts, there were female judges in the building but they did not come to lunch, preferring to work at their desks, or rattle through domestic chores. One woman had done this, as a barrister, but deliberately changed her habits to be sociable:

> I normally go to the dining room most days. As a busy housewife and a mother I used to do so much in the lunchtime to make the rest of the world go round but I don't feel I can do that. I am nosey. I like to know what is going on.

As the absent women were not in the research sample, it is impossible to know whether they excluded themselves because they preferred to work or do domestic chores, or whether they felt alienated by the lack of female companionship, or whether the football discussions, Bar gossip and schoolboy banter did not appeal. Two female CJs who did not enjoy the dining room atmosphere, but did lunch there, organised tiny support groups with other women judges.

> [I meet one] ... district judge and one circuit judge. The two of them in many ways, because they are both mothers and have been married, actually have a closer empathy with one another but I actually organised this. ... We all get quite a lot out of it.

> One of the things I have done to help me: the other woman who started this trip with me. She was appointed a circuit judge two years before I was. When I was appointed, I was in floods of tears. She said she was always on the other end of the phone ... we meet every two or three months ... pour out our woes and we support each other. She is not a personal friend. It sounds daft. I have never been to her house. She has never been to mine. I know very little about her personal circumstances. She is just my judicial support network and she says I am hers and we have an empathy because of our similar situations of being usually the only woman around ... I have appreciated and valued that friendship and I have tried to follow it. I have now got a youngster who has just been appointed a recorder and she was sitting for the first time and I said to her come and stay with me and so she stayed with me for the time that she was sitting and I in turn have listened to all the ups and downs of everything that has happened to her during the day.

Most women judges I encountered in this research were keen supporters and attenders of the UK Association of Women Judges.

CONCLUSION

In judicial training, judges have badges with their first and last name, not title. The expectation is that they will address one another by first names.[17] Lower ranks can find themselves flummoxed, as they were raised in a strictly hierarchical legal profession with a Bar used to genuflecting and fawning to judges and using practice rules, wigs and symbolism to assert its seniority over solicitors. First names and egalitarianism were heavily promoted by Lord Chief Justice 'call me Tom' Bingham, in the 1990s and his successors, especially Lord Phillips and the current incumbent, Igor Judge, 'call me Igor'. This friendly, kind character made it his job to travel the circuits as Senior Presiding Judge and to meet and memorise the names of as many judges as he could. But in 1999, the pilot DJ found herself training all ranks, including Law Lords, whom she was expected to address by first names. She found this disarming—hardly a surprise, given DJs' status sensitivity and their treatment by other ranks until the late 1990s. So the image that the judiciary tried to promote to the outside world and the egalitarianism senior judges try to foster, symbolised by these badges, did not quite succeed.

There is no career judiciary and the divided and divisive legal profession undoubtedly fosters this state of affairs. The pre-Dickensian legal hierarchy is still reflected in the judiciary as it was in the 1970s. It was not until I wrote this chapter, examining interviews and field notes, that I appreciated how distant DJs felt from CJs, though there was no direct evidence that any CJ looked down on them. County court DJs resented the fact that they handled cases heard by CJs in the 1980s, yet they were not as well paid. They thought CJs worked shorter hours and perceived themselves as more 'in touch' with ordinary people, as former solicitors. Their interviews and those with solicitor CJs manifested a strong irritation they had acquired, in practice, about the superiority complex of barristers. Some DJs and DJMCs thought higher ranks did not consider them proper judges and they were not called 'judges' until recently. The relationship was rendered more difficult by the fact that CJs heard appeals from DJs in the same courthouse. As if this were not enough, some courthouses had separate dining rooms. This resentment ran deep. Even DJs who had not visited those courts knew about them. When a new CJ remarked that the judiciary was shot through with snobbery, I have no doubt he was referring to the solicitor-DJ and barrister-CJ spilt but not the senior judiciary. CJs who managed courts agonised about this and had devised various ways of getting DJs to mix but DJs generally kept to themselves and gained mutual support at a national level in their very active and much praised Association. Most DJMCs and the HCDJs were and felt much more isolated and other ranks really were unaware of their existence.

---

[17]   Initiated for security reasons. At training conferences, I was the only person given a badge bearing a title.

In sharp contrast, barrister-CJs outside London generally participated in many circuit events. As seen earlier in the book, they and their court colleagues were recruited from local chambers and preserved their social ties. The South East Circuit has far more CJs, though, over 40 per cent, and London CJs did not always know one another as well. Most CJs were not active in the Council of Circuit Judges, doubtless because many were well-served socially by their circuit connections, though this, of course, meant solicitor CJs felt left out of this close old-boy network. It was acknowledged by all ranks that the circuit bench spanned the greatest range of intellect. Some considered that they did not have the intelligence or stamina to become HC judges.

Lower ranks admired senior judges and DJs were in awe of them, considering there to be a much greater gap between them and CJs than between DJs and CJs. Most CJs did not envy their immense workload and itinerant lifestyle. Many referred to the approachability of modern HC judges compared with predecessors. Most senior judges had interacted with lower ranks on circuit but they had much more contact with CJs. Senior judges were surprisingly aware of DJs' sensitivities, though. The HC judges did not distinguish themselves from CJs on the basis of intellect and most denied a social difference. Indeed, CA judges placed a high value on circuit judges sitting in the CACD.

As an academic, used to a diverse environment, I noticed there were strikingly few women in the courts I visited and at lunchtimes, most were absent from the dining room, though it is impossible to know whether that was because they felt uncomfortable. Most women judges were keen members of the UK Association of Women Judges. In this respect, they are at the stage women academics were in the 1970s and early 1980s.

In the Royal Courts of Justice, most senior judges interacted with others, especially HC judges in the 'corridor of fun'. Some specialists had regular meetings. Most senior judges lunched with others in their Inn around two days a week. They received many invitations to academic and Bar social or legal functions, alongside the UKSC Justices. On circuit, HC judges got to know their lodgings fellows very well, over several weeks, and were expected to participate in formal social functions with local judges and/or the sheriff and others. The Judges Council, originally established for senior judges, was re-launched in 2002 to represent all judges. It is meant to feed the views of judges to the Lord Chief Justice who speaks on their behalf but most senior judges did not know what it did and/or were critical of it so it seemed an irrelevance to them.

The Constitutional Reform Act 2005 *may* result in more CJs being promoted to the High Court but will probably not result in a career judiciary. It seemed to me that the district judge's description of a chasm between the senior judiciary and the rest is right. The senior judiciary occupy a different world, centred around the Royal Courts of Justice, working really hard and making law. The CA and HC judges are indistinguishable elements of the same social and working group because they come from the same top chambers and work together in the CA. Those who go on to become UKSC Justices continue to interact with former colleagues in the very same out-of-court activities. The homogeneity of the senior judiciary is demonstrated by the fact that most HC judges *did* want to be promoted, unlike the DJs and CJs. Six of the 16 here were promoted. Most CA judges would have accepted elevation to the top court but were apprehensive about leaving the collegiality of the CA.

17

Tools of the Trade[1]

Well, if you send missiles to bomb Iraq, you can't afford another usher, can you?

Circuit judge

Staff … half clueless and the other half know what they are doing. We muddle along.

Circuit judge

Inadequate information technology; stressed administrative staff; too few books for the judiciary; rushed listing; and judges required to wander down to waiting rooms to collect their next case.

Professor Dame Hazel Genn[2]

The efficiencies currently demanded of the CPS, Probation and the courts are having a very real impact on the administration of justice. At present, problems such as custody time limits or cancelled sittings are relatively isolated, but there is an undoubted danger they will become increasingly commonplace … the courts have been pared back to the point where there are insufficient staff, an inadequately maintained estate, and not enough sitting days to dispense justice in the manner which society expects.

Lord Chief Justice Judge[3]

---

[1] Extending the metaphor used by Lord Denning on lawyers' 'tools of trade' in Denning, *The Discipline of Law* (London, Butterworths, 1979) ch 1.

[2] H Genn, *Judging Civil Justice* (Cambridge, Cambridge University Press, 2009) 51. See Judge Paul Collins, quoted in ch 11 of this book. Staff were poorly paid. His salary had been cut from £125,000 to £80,000 in 1992–2007: 13 February 2007, BBC news.

[3] *The Lord Chief Justice's Review of the Administration of Justice in the Courts*, February 2010 (Judiciary website). His predecessor, Lord Phillips, said in a 2007 speech, 'The vulnerability of our resources … was causing us serious concern', in 'Judicial Independence'. Funding for courts was an international requirement for judicial independence. The Cabinet had forgotten the assurance behind the Constitutional Reform Act 2005 of close communication with the judges: Lord Phillips learned of the plan to create a Ministry of Justice from the newspapers. Judges have long criticised the policy that the civil courts should be self-funding. See P Darbyshire, *Darbyshire on the English Legal System*, 10th edn (London, Sweet & Maxwell, 2011) ch 6 and Genn, above n 2 at 46.

INTRODUCTION

T HE THREE PILOT studies, with a Crown Court judge, a district judge
(DJ) and a High Court (HC) judge, taught me that I would not have the
patience to be a judge. Sitting with a circuit judge (CJ) in a London
Crown Court, we were in and out of court, waiting for people, documents and
jurors, before anything could proceed. 'Mondays are the worst and August is
terrible. August starts in July.' Documentation was incomplete in *most* case files,
because of the Crown Prosecution Service (CPS) or the court office. Files were in
no logical order. Post took eight days to get through, even when marked 'urgent'.
His clerk for the day had no 'gumption'. She had not been trained, 'Drives me
bloody wild!' There was a very high staff turnover, as they were badly paid. 'They
get them off the Labour.' His Monday paedophile trial was delayed until Tuesday
afternoon because the video-link to the child witnesses' room was not working
and there was no-one in the court building who knew how to repair it. The
children were kept waiting though the wasted Monday.[4] Prosecuting counsel were
disturbingly ignorant of the basic rules of admissibility of evidence and incapable
of sifting out the irrelevant. There was no co-ordination in listing. A defendant in
his list was scheduled to appear on something else, before a different judge on a
different day. 'All you need is a computer that would ring a bell when the same
name comes up!'

The chief probation officer apologised in court that there was no pre-sentence
report for a rapist, because of staff shortages. The circuit Presiding Judge had sent
a memo asking judges not to request pre-sentence reports unless necessary. The
judge explained 'Sometimes London has run out of money for them. The
London probation service is in meltdown'. (He said it again in 2010.) In the trial,
late jurors accumulated 3.75 hours of delay in four days with the result that a trial
that should have taken two days, in fact took over a week. The courtroom had a
clerk only some of the time. Sometimes there was no usher. The air conditioning
kept it chilly. It had veneered walls with tiny frosted windows so appeared
permanently dull, especially in winter. HM Courts Service had installed low
wattage bulbs. Counsel complained the light levels were below the statutory
minimum.

In the corridors, we tripped around buckets catching raindrops. This was the
deluxe end of the building. At the other end—the 'temporary' end of the
building—judges dodged defendants destined for the cells, en route to their own
tiny breeze block rooms, daintily referred to as 'chambers'. The Bar had complained about the tannoy system, 'the common enemy of us all', as another judge
called it. A silk said he was 'so old' he could remember the building's demolition
being promised 'in 18 months' time', in the 1970s. Judges recounted recent

---

[4] Research by the NSPCC showed child witnesses in abuse cases waited for over a year:
NSPCC, *Measuring Up? Evaluating implementation of Government commitments to young
witnesses in criminal proceedings* (2009).

problems: shootings in the street, the lack of security, not to mention a drug dealership among the dock officers. I visited the judge at least once a year in 2002–10 but things became worse. By 2008, he had abandoned the judges' dining room since five judges succumbed to food poisoning. He decided to retire in 2010. By contrast, two southern judges outside London had no intention of retiring. One said he would not be prepared to do the same job in London because of the 'poor quality of life'.

Over in the county court, the pilot-study DJ complained of no secretarial help. She had to write her own letters 'unlike a circuit judge'. (She did not realise that they also had none.) She at last had her own Dictaphone but typed up her orders. Some older judges protested, 'we're not secretaries'. She sent tapes to Gateshead. Some had gone missing. Her court received 8–10,000 pieces of post and faxes per week and had insufficient staff. It affected trial management. Another DJ explained that instead of asking for orders to be complied with within eight weeks, he asked for 10 weeks because orders took a week to get to the post room. He put a two-week time limit on orders that ought to have been complied with within three days.

While this research confirmed that things were not quite so bad outside London, the significance of this gloomy picture is that over 40 per cent of district and circuit judges sit in London and the South East. The courts and the agencies that serve them are run on a shoestring because spending money on this unseen world will not get votes. Under Labour, we saw headlines such as 'Courts face closure as judges are told of £90m shortfall in collection of fees'.[5] Under the Coalition, things are becoming much worse. In December 2010, the Ministry announced the closure of 49 county courts and 93 magistrates' courts. Judges, like court staff, users and government agencies have to suffer in this low-budget production but there is a big issue of principle too: while governments have perpetuated a policy that the civil courts should be self-funding, judges have strenuously opposed this, arguing they are a public service. This chapter examines judges' habitat and the 'tools' of their trade, in terms of buildings, facilities, IT, staff, working and service conditions and the input of other agencies and lawyers.

BUILDINGS

By 2008, the maintenance backlog had risen from £38 million in 2000 to £200 million.[6] Courthouses in this research were variable[7] but, aside from those who suffered accommodation bordering on the squalid, judges did not complain. As

---

[5] F Gibb, *The Times*, 4 September 2008, 20.

[6] Gibb, ibid, discussed rat-infested, crumbling buildings.

[7] Data were held regionally, hampering national assessment: NAO, *HM Courts Service-Administration of the Crown Court Report by the Comptroller and Auditor General HC 290 Session 2008–2009*, 2009.

with pay, staffing and IT, they accepted that one could not expect more in public service and certainly not the standards they were used to as lawyers.[8] They did protest on behalf of court staff and court users, especially families with children.

The Law Lords' habitat, the Palace of Westminster, was lavishly furnished by Pugin but some were uncomfortable at the constant reminders that they were judges living in the legislature. They love their new home across Parliament Square, since it offers every facility for them, court users and the visiting public but everyone else is paying the price for its £77 million outlay plus running costs. In the Royal Courts of Justice (RCJ), housing the Court of Appeal (CA) and the High Court (HC), the first surprise was the lack of retiring rooms. When judges exit the imposing, mahogany-lined courtrooms in this Victorian Gothic cathedral to the law (each uniquely designed and accessorised with wrought iron balustrades and/or tapestries and vaulted ceilings), they stand in the back corridor to deliberate. The modern family courtrooms were windowless, gloomy and depressing, with tacky veneered walls. Commercial Court judges were sent out to conduct court in cramped offices, until now. While RCJ facilities were sumptuous, by Victorian standards, judges mentioned petty economies. Light bulbs were not replaced until 10 had failed. While the appeal judges had no complaints about their spacious rooms and antique desks, new judges had to wait a year for a room. One lived in the basement near the boilers. Another was finally settled in a converted broom cupboard. Another's room had flooded. Another had to move when her ceiling collapsed. There is no dining or meeting room. Judges eat sandwiches at their desks, or cross the road to the Inns of Court: cheap, congenial, quality, fast-food outlets. They do not mind.

Most county, Crown and combined courts provided modern, adequate facilities but there were exceptions. At one old Crown Court a judge indicated a wet porch: the judges' entrance. A sprinkler system had been installed because the judges 'got fed up' with stepping over the sleeping drug-users, and the heroin needles. 'The Lord Chief came here on a visit last year. I noticed the security officers cleared them out. They don't do that for us.' Judges in a Victorian county court pointed out that there were no waiting rooms. Families with crying, bored children and buggies huddled for hours at the bottom of the stairs, in the entrance. Elsewhere, a county court was hidden in a cheap office block above a betting shop, fronted by a bright blue night club. Its grand predecessor, a Greek Revival building, embellished with massive Doric columns, now serves as a wine bar.[9] I drove past a new county court several times, before spotting it in an office,

---

[8] Philadelphia judges made the same point: PB Wice, 'Judicial Socialization: the Philadelphia Experience' in JA Cramer, *Courts and Judges* (Beverly Hills, Sage, 1981).

[9] Architecture aficionados can depress themselves with *Silence in Court: The Future of the UK's Historic Law Courts*, by SAVE Britain's Heritage, 2004. Bow Street Magistrates' Court and its neighbouring police station, world famous for the Bow Street Runners, have since been closed. Buildings are closed because of rationalisation, or because their interiors cannot satisfy modern users' needs. Pitifully, those with the most stunning (listed) interiors are used as theme parks, or film sets, or are left to rot.

strapped to a church. As we have seen, the lack of a unified family court, with courts overflowing into annexes or neighbouring courthouses, caused confusion to stressed families and their social workers.

Until 2004, there was no blueprint for court design and no common use of architects, therefore even new buildings caused problems. Unsuitable design affected judges, who complained of lack of consultation. At three new courts, their rooms were one or two floors from the courtrooms, causing a 10-minute delay every time the judge left and re-entered. At another, the juror nearest the judge could barely see witnesses. In a 1970s court, defendants' and victims' families, could 'eyeball' and intimidate jurors from the public gallery. Judges and jurors shared a corridor. In the Midlands, I was told of a dedicated fraud trial centre that had never been used. Judges refused to sit there because pillars restricted the courtroom view. It was sold for a shopping centre.

Where judges managed to influence court layout they were contented. A designated civil judge proudly showed me his refurbished Civil Justice Centre, explaining he was 'possessive' about his design. He was a member of the civil estates committee and said he 'played hell' if he was not consulted on buildings in his locality. But his circuit presider, Whaley, was concerned over a useless new court. A converted office block, it had opened in 2004 but judges refused to use it because of defective design. Defendants could not hear proceedings from the dock. The public gallery faced the jury box (again) and the benches were too close together. There was no natural light and no advocates' robing room. Whaley wanted separate waiting areas for family and criminal courts in the building, 'otherwise your nice day out for your child's adoption would be marred by sitting with the skinheads'. Yet again, it was conjured by an architect with no experience of court design. Years later it was still unused. In the Royal Courts, an HC judge explained that the courtrooms, particularly the new ones, were badly designed. 'They never bothered to ask the people who worked there how you should design the courtroom—for example, the Thomas Moore Building.'

It frequently happens that old, dignified court buildings, even those with a world-renowned past, like Bow Street Magistrates' Court, are left to rot, if not sold to the hospitality industry. Whaley had sat as the first HC judge for 11 years in one important old building on his circuit. He found a beautiful, old ceiling repaired with polystyrene tiles. The roof was leaking and a frieze was damaged. Court furniture, made by local craftsmen, was damaged. Economising by neglecting repairs inflated damage and cost all round the circuits. One London resident said that a refusal to repair his Crown Court roof for £50,000, five years earlier, necessitated work costing £2.4 million in 2008.[10]

---

[10] He repeated this in his annual report. In 2010 Lord Judge criticised 'the continued under-investment which has resulted in the maintenance backlog remaining'.

In their interviews, 43 of 77 judges said they were content with their facilities. Like this district judge (magistrates' court) (DJMC), they recognised shortcomings but they knew there was no money.

> My base court is a converted music hall. The facilities are not brilliant but the staff are delightful ... The other courts I go to, I don't have a room ... it means taking the laptop and there is nowhere I can sit on my own if I need to do writing or make any telephone calls in private so life isn't brilliant but I have no real complaints.

Of the 17 who gave mixed replies, most were HC judges. While they mostly admired the RCJ architecture, they missed a communal area. On circuit, there were no office facilities for their clerks, who perched in a corner of their room. They encountered mixed court buildings, like this presider. The quotation gives a vivid picture of the state of court buildings in 2011.

> There is no coordinated approach to the provision of justice buildings so that you have, for example, here, a fairly modern Crown Court centre built in 1989 with four very acceptable courts. This courtroom is very big; the other three are very small, *too* small but when it was built it was accepted that it was too small for requirements so we use two old courts in the old Guildhall. We have a wholly inadequate modern civil justice centre, built in an office block, which is a complete shambles, and in a third building we have the magistrates' courts. So there is no justice centre as such, then on top of that we have the various buildings which are used for tribunals then some tribunals ... in hotel rooms, when in fact they could probably use for free or cheaper price an empty courtroom. There is no co-ordination at all.[11] What we are trying to do on circuit now is to co-ordinate these things. The RCJ is a wonderful building but it is a difficult building to be at work in the twenty-first century. The old courtrooms are wonderful but they really aren't geared for modern life; nor are our rooms.

Though judges could see the need to provide modern facilities for court users, they deprecated court closures when historic buildings were sold off or where closures further inconvenienced court users. Lodgings were shabby but judges did not complain, or miss the butlers and limos, knowing the low-paid staff were all multi-tasking now.

Dining

District and circuit judges in old county courts also had no communal or dining facilities so ate packed lunches in their offices. Newer Crown and combined courts had dining rooms, where judges paid for their food from what seemed to be a universal set menu. Its interpretation and quality varied but iceberg lettuce featured heavily and food lacked the quality and imagination of university refectories. The exception was the Central Criminal Court, the Old Bailey, where

---

[11] Lord Judge said 'work is being undertaken to look at where court and tribunal functions can share the same accommodation'.

judges are guests of the City of London and lunch formally, amid the City silver, gowned up. They are expected to entertain the City's guests, famous personalities.[12]

Temperatures

The reverse logic of HM Courts Service seemed to apply to heating, as well as repairs. On the western circuit, air-conditioned courtrooms were like cold stores. Temperatures were centrally controlled in Bristol. At another seven courts, air conditioning induced jurors and shorthand writers to muffle up in coats and body warmers. Judges at one county court explained that, as an economy drive, HM Courts Service had set all the heaters on date-timers so staff bought electric radiators for the whole building: 'Cost a fortune'.

Security

Provision was random. Security has to be taken seriously. In the 1980s, I taught an ex police officer who had been kneecapped in Bow Street Magistrates' Court. As Pannick pointed out, in 1981, a man was found guilty of murdering a judge who had sentenced him. Judges have had missiles thrown at them.[13] This was so routine that carafes and glasses have long since been replaced by plastic. At one county court, judges indicated a dent in a wall, from a carafe thrown at a DJ. Sometimes the front rows of Crown Court public galleries are taped off to stop people throwing missiles.

While many buildings have security screening at the front, this does not apply to other entrances. In the Royal Courts of Justice, an appeal judge listed all the non-secure entry points, reminding me that Dame Joyanne Bracewell had been faced by a woman toting a revolver.[14] We saw that emergency applications were moved from the real room 101 after an HC judge was punched. Lady Hale told of a litigant in person (LIP) who tried to perform a citizen's arrest on her, in the Court of Appeal.

> She advanced towards the bench as we were finishing giving judgment in another case. I was the junior judge so had to wait for my presider's permission (quickly given) before making a dignified exit![15]

---

[12] The Recorder and Common Sergeant have accommodation and are expected to attend City dinners. I was told that Lord Bingham could not bring himself to eat with his gown on.

[13] D Pannick, *Judges* (Oxford, Oxford University Press, 1987) 6 and 138–39.

[14] In the Court of Appeal. See her obituaries in the press in January 2007. See also E Wilson, 'Terror as Mad Woman Aims Gun at Judges; eighty cops fail to find her in court', *The Mirror*, 14 February 1997, 11.

[15] Interviewed by F Gibb, *The Times*, 11 November 2003.

Family judges have had fathers' groups demonstrating on their front lawns and suffered kidnap threats. Family cases can provoke very violent reactions, as we saw in Joel's court. In one county court, they put a red dot on any file where the parties were likely to 'cut up rough' or where custody was likely to be imposed so the case could be shifted into a more secure courtroom. One judge pointed out there was little data security. There was no shredder. Confidential documents on families lay around the building. Civil DJs are constantly aware of risk, with emotionally charged antagonists in their chambers.[16]

> The litigant can come up and stand right behind you to see what you are writing. Because we are not in robes, people can get quite overwrought and if you are just sitting round a table, they feel they can really let rip with their feelings and it can get quite out of control.

At one county court, a litigant had thrown battery acid over his wife. Another county court had been fire-bombed through the letterbox, just before I arrived.

In the Old Bailey, which tries the biggest concentration of gangland killers, I walked into the front entrance, barred to the public and full of security devices and police but no-one stopped me or asked for ID. Normally, I was expected to join the judge via the Lord Mayor's entrance at the rear but sometimes I was not checked. There were no security doors. I could have walked in and shot a row of judges. I noted another Crown Court where I could have smuggled in a gun. Recording is banned in courts but I was only stopped once throughout the years of the research when a security guard spotted my recorder under X-ray. On the other 90 occasions, it remained undetected.

District judges (magistrates' courts) were similarly aware of risks, 'Here ... you would be a fool to go out at lunchtime, as it is a very rough area'. As luck would have it, the battery acid was thrown in a combined court so police were present. Researching magistrates' courts in the 1970s, I noted that police were routinely available in family proceedings but their presence was deemed inappropriate so they were withdrawn before 1980. Police are seldom available in any court nowadays, except at places like Preston, where police outriders guard Eastern European drugs-mafia defendants with prices on their heads. At some courts, guards are present but judges are aware that they are nominal and would not be able to cope with violence or collective action. At one ultra-high crime Crown Court,[17] the Chief Constable had withdrawn officers and re-instated them only when the judges protested.

---

[16] Discussed in ch 11.
[17] Mortimer's court in the Crown Court chapter.

STAFF

Only 36 of the 77 judges considered they had adequate staff and administrative support.[18] Many drew attention to poor pay and high turnover.[19] This is well-documented in courts' annual reports, including that of the Court of Appeal. A CA judge's clerk said that she could only afford to do the job because her forces' pension subsidised her and I heard the same story from other senior judges' clerks. Judges were consistently polite to staff and usually had a warm working relationship, expressing disgust at their low pay and being supportive when they went on strike.

Most circuit and district judges have no secretarial help. A London county court suffered a high staff turnover, as people could earn more money in the City. All staff, even section managers, were very young, evidenced by names like Tara, Carrie, Kiri and Kylie. Judges found matters were referred to them that should have been decided or rejected by office staff but they lacked confidence or were too inexperienced. Judges suffered from incompetent or ill-trained[20] staff but none complained. A file came before Judge X, labelled 'Not to be listed before Judge X'. As we saw in the county court and family chapters, in every pile of court files there were errors. At a western court, a 'good girl' was being moved out of the listing office and replaced by 'a bloke whose shirt hangs out'. Judges remarked that it seemed to be policy to move people 'as soon as they got the hang of the job'. As we saw in the county court chapter, a CJ took it for granted that a defendant bank *had* sent the evidence it claimed to have sent to the court and the court had lost it. The claimant, unaware of the chaotic state of the court office, was convinced that the bank's solicitors were lying. A fellow judge pointed out that files were a mess, as HM Courts Service did not have 'filing' as one of their performance indicators. Elsewhere, judges passed around a *Telegraph* letter about their court's mismanagement of case files. When judges were not angst-ridden about all this, they could see the funny side and amused themselves by swapping stories on their intranet about court letters sent out in judges' names, containing some gems of malapropism.

At one big court, the listing officer was doubling up as the judges' manager. A judge reckoned that because of the usher shortage, the court wasted a day's working time per week. Lack of ushers and court clerks was ubiquitous. A pair covered two or three courts.

---

[18] The 2009 NAO report said 'The Ministry of Justice's recruitment process is not meeting the needs of court-based staff ... [and] has added to pressures ... and reduced court performance' (para 16).

[19] This was so in London but nationally, HMT Courts Service has a low turnover, according to the NAO report but they had a high sick-leave average of over 11 days a year (para 18).

[20] The NAO said 'Staff ... were critical of the quality and availability of...[training] ... In 2007, the Ministry of Justice concluded that...programmes were uncoordinated and inadequately evaluated' (para 17).

Juries were kept waiting to bring in verdicts until a clerk could be found. A resident judge said 'One judge took the verdict himself and the correct forms didn't get filled in!' In the Principal Registry, Caroline had no clerk. She descended from the bench to call the listings office. Elsewhere, a new circuit judge described staffing levels in the 1970s, 'When I started at the Bar, every single court had its own clerk, two ushers, its own police officer, its own CPS clerk and one or two other ancillary staff'.

One HC judge spent between four and five hours of his reading day on filing—'I bet American judges don't have to do the filing! It's just like doctors. They should be cutting people up, not doing admin'. Many Crown Court judges suffered from files that were a random collection of material:

> The history of a case is supposed to be logged onto the outside of a file so that a judge coming to a case which has had previous hearing can track down what has happened … the file that was put in front of me had been hopelessly maintained so that when the matter came before me for a trial of two people out of four, because the two others pleaded guilty, that was not clear to me at all, so I wasted lots of time putting it together.

A DJMC summed up the result of cutbacks in staffing in the magistrates' courts:

> There are less and less resources for an effective administration. Legal advisors are being asked to do … admin. They might as well tie a broom to their backsides and make them tidy up as well.

IT AND VIDEO LINKS

The state of IT in courts is almost too painful to describe. While 49 of the 77 judges were content with their personal IT provision, this included some who described themselves as barely IT literate and two UK Supreme Court (UKSC) Justices who never used IT. Judges had access to almost every UK law database[21] but seemed not to have been adequately trained to use them. I found most judges appeared to be incapable of using *Lexis* or *Westlaw* and some did not even know they possessed these sophisticated and comprehensive databases. Word-processing facilities were adequate and long-term users of the judicial intranet, Felix (available since the early 1990s and now replaced by ePOC)[22] found it useful for co-ordinating practice countrywide. For instance, a resident judge, in dispute with a chief constable, emailed others to check if they allowed police witnesses to appear in court in body armour.

Keen IT users were frustrated. HC judges pointed out that they had to carry two or three laptops around on circuit because other services could not be accessed from the one laptop linked to secure services. A circuit judge referred to

---

[21] eLIS: see K Davis, The Association of HM District Judges *Law Bulletin*, Vol 20, summer 2009, 4.

[22] P Atkinson, 'The Judicial Portal' *Law Bulletin*, Vol 20, winter 2008–09, 22.

her paper court diary. 'The kind of computer diarising that chambers had fifteen years ago, which is bog-standard, isn't available to the court service. It is just appalling.' While most of us in large organisations take for granted access to an on-site technician, judges call helplines. They were expected to help one another. This normally worked. Self-taught IT literate judges were commissioned to train 'legacy judges' who were not. Recipients of such training praised it. There was heavy reliance on self-education. At one combined court, everyone depended on a member of staff who was a self-taught IT expert. We saw that in the county court chapter, a CJ who was a keen IT user had had software installed on her laptop at the Crown Court and now could not open her civil templates. She was trying to sort it out from instructions, rather than waiting *10* days for someone to come and help her.

During the research, the LINK system was being installed in the Crown Court, to link it to criminal justice agencies and lawyers.[23] Judges were enthusiastic but found their training unhelpful. One CJ said some people walked out because it was 'useless'. 'They learned to paint a steam engine' but no-one knew how to use LINK to get them to their usual databases and he had no CD-drive to use his CD-Rom of *Archbold*, criminal judges' essential encyclopaedia. (He could have found it on *Westlaw* but of course he did not know that.) Another CJ, who travelled a lot, found her LINK password only worked at her base court.

Lord Woolf, devising the current civil justice system in the mid-1990s, assumed that that all civil files would soon be handled electronically but a decade later I observed judges at two courts piloting experimental software that did not work. One said the dream of a paperless back office was 'dead in the water'. It took 40 minutes to handle four files, by which time he could have taken about 10 paper-based case management decisions. The judge at the other court was unable to operate the software for the whole of the research week and no technical help was available. DJs were frustrated that they could not access case management software and had to depend on clerks. A civil DJ had enviously watched an American family judge managing his own court 'dockets' back in 2001.[24]

In 2009, DJ Oldham, President of the Association of HM District Judges, said proposals for e-filing for courts had been shelved, therefore courts worked with paper files. These got lost regularly and there were fewer staff now to manage files and keep them up-to-date. He encouraged parties to email a case summary and draft directions to the court, provided they copied in their opponents. This meant that at least the judge would have the documents before the hearing, but not all judges did this.[25] Over in the magistrates' court, a DJMC said:

---

[23] The NAO found that 20-year-old case management software 'runs on ageing computers' (para 20).

[24] The CaseMan and FamilyMan systems were so old they were, astonishingly, supported on DOS: S Gailey, 'Service Upgrade Projects', *Law Bulletin*, Vol 20, winter 2008–09, 23.

[25] D Oldham, 'Online justice' (2009) 159 *New Law Journal* 615.

> I am looking at a chap who is on bail but I cannot get into any system that tells you he is lying because he says he is not but you know he is. It is a complete mess.

In the High Court, a Commercial Court judge and a chancery judge were embarrassed by the system's inability to email the type of files routinely exchanged by City solicitors. The first, Trollope, explained that there were 25 IT systems in the Royal Courts of Justice, with HM Courts Service and the judiciary locked into a contract with one provider. In the Family Division, Stanford bought her own laptop, as those provided were not sturdy enough. She could not connect hers to the printer at court, or in her circuit lodgings. She sent her clerk out to buy the correct hardware and a phone extension to connect her bed phone to the desk in her room. There was no broadband connection. She could not read her email attachments on circuit. Her clerk could open them but not print them. Stanford resorted to using her private email address, which was against the rules, as it was not secure.

DJs design and swap their own templates for orders and, for the HC masters, one of their staff wrote their software programme. 'If you waited for the Courts Service you'd wait for ever. That's the way we do things!' explained the Senior Master. Judges on the judicial IT working group were very frustrated:

> We have fallen seriously behind other jurisdictions … The promises made to the judges at the time of the introduction of the Woolf reforms have not been met.

> Appalling. I should be linked into high-speed access from my courtroom and my desk. The hardware is very unreliable … the civil side will continue to be the poor relation of the criminal side and I also think there should be a lot more provision for the public to access their resources online in court. It is grotesque. We live in the stone-age compared to large City firms.

Money-wasting and lack of co-ordination were rife. Apart from the doubling of laptops, some had two excellent printers. A circuit judge, whose new kit sat unused most of the time was typical.

> I want someone to explain things to me and have someone around to help me and better training would be a good idea. I had three days' training and they sent me the kit six months later by which time I had forgotten all the things they had told me about it.

Many were cynical: 'I can't think of a single government IT programme that has been on time, on budget and successful'.

At several Crown Courts, judges were concerned about poor quality videos of children's evidence, claiming this caused a high acquittal rate of alleged child abusers who judges were convinced were guilty. At one court, judges were very disappointed when told that experimental digital recording equipment was being removed. It was useful because they could pinpoint items in children's testimony. But as it cost £30,000 per year, HM Courts Service were looking for something more cost-effective.

OTHER AGENCIES AND LAWYERS

The 60 judges who depended on outside agencies for their courts to function smoothly were asked to comment on their adequacy. Of the 24 who were content, most of them qualified the answer, recognising that all agencies were under-funded. As has been seen throughout the book, the delays this caused wasted enormous amounts of court time.

CPS and Prosecution/Youth Sentencing

In the Crown Court chapter, I described how many trials were postponed or prolonged through lack of preparation and this was accompanied by a culture in which advocates did not apologise or accept responsibility. Prosecution barristers would say 'I know nothing of this'. There was a litany of excuses for the most blatant shortcomings, such as failure to produce video evidence to the defence, or a disclosure 15 minutes before a scheduled trial, or a last-minute public interest immunity application, requiring the judge to spend 7.5 hours reading files which could have been delivered three months earlier. At one court, the resident was asked by a junior judge if he could order a fourth trial, the first three having been aborted because of poor video footage. The story in the magistrates' courts was the same. A court clerk of 25 years said things were more frustrating now. There were more instances of cases not ready to go ahead and people happy to admit they were not prepared. Cases had to be adjourned because the 'forensics' weren't ready. Portia knew referral orders would not be carried out before a child had re-offended.

The pilot-study judge disapproved of a move to organise regular meetings between the CPS and the judiciary because he felt the CPS should explain themselves in open court. He persuaded an MP to ask a Parliamentary question about wasted costs. The CPS routinely blamed prosecution failures on the police. Crown Court judges were frustrated by these inefficiencies. Most asked for explanations in open court but one resident said 'It doesn't do to get het up about things not being done by solicitors or CPS because they are all stretched. If they only have incompetent staff then that's that. They can't be blamed'.

The Crown Court chapter contains a litany of stories of poor prosecution barristers. Judges would remark, aside, on the incompetence of prosecutions: why didn't they check the defendant's story that the station loos were locked? Why didn't the prosecution tell us about the handprint on the knife? In their interviews, the CPS was the agency most likely to be criticised by judges. One resident wrote to a chief constable about a case where 15-year-old was beaten by drunken football hooligans. 'The police did not conduct an ID parade for months and were very slow at gathering evidence.' He did not even get a reply. Typically, an HC circuit presider said the CPS was profoundly inadequate and despite the fact that the government are trying to improve it and say how much it has improved, it is a profoundly flawed agency. Funding has been a problem … They can't properly draft an ordinary indictment.

Probation

In interviews, the commonest view was typified by 'under resourced and under-manned. I am full of admiration for their commitment'. Many judges mentioned an excellent local working relationship but said understaffing meant delays in report-writing, a severe handicap in sentencing. One judge had just handled a list of 20 sentencing cases. Reports were missing for 10. Some judges complained that inadequately trained officers made recommendations that were illegal or inappropriate, such as recommending a specific length of sentence—the job of the judge.

Cafcass and Guardians in Children's Cases

A DJ explained that guardians used to be self-employed before Cafcass was created and made them all low-paid employees.

> Now you can't get a guardian sometimes. The situation is dire in London. Big public law cases and no-one to represent the kids—damaged kids. That's why I get so hot under the collar.

In 2003–05, nationwide, judges had to wait 14 weeks for a Cafcass report but some of the research judges waited 18.[26] Almost all family judges expressed concern over the profound delays and distortion this caused, in determining children's futures.

Social Services

As we saw in the family chapter, one judge wasted three days waiting for a care case to commence because social services directed the mother to the wrong court and she was only tracked down on the judge's initiative. Then the case could not be heard because the social worker had a fear of heights and the courtroom was on the first floor. Renewing orders for public funding for the troops of lawyers, the judge remarked on what a waste of money it was. Elsewhere, a judge was angry with local authority social worker who had done nothing when a baby born to two child abusers needed taking into care and adopting. In another case, a child was born to a mother who was known to be vulnerable. The local

---

[26] Delays were much worse by July 2010, when the NAO reported in *Cafcass's response to increased demand for its services*, 'By June 2010 Cafcass was working on more than 4,600 (44 per cent) more open public law cases than in November 2008', summary, para 23.

authority did nothing for month and had done nothing to initiate full proceedings two months later.

Secure Prison Escort Services

Delays in security companies delivering prisoners were costly. I was forewarned before the research, by the Chief Clerk at the Old Bailey, who said that he was sometimes 'hard pressed' to start any courts before noon. Mortimer made an official complaint about Group 4 causing delay. Another resident told me Monday mornings were unpredictable. Prisoners did not appear. He laughed at the explanation given by security firm that they have to collect from several locations, saying 'well you should have set off earlier then!' As one HC judge put it:

> The private companies that now run most of the prisons, or the business of conveying prisoners from A to B, are totally incompetent and they waste millions of pounds worth of time and money.

Lawyers

As can be seen from the substantive chapters, the quality varied. The better and more trustworthy the lawyer, the easier the judge's job. Judges had to trust that lawyers had prepared thoroughly, or they were left to research the law themselves, in a lunchtime panic. This applied in the Court of Appeal just as much as the Crown or county court. Judges needed to trust lawyers' stories on case progression and applied their experiences in practice to understanding how lawyers worked. For instance, a DJMC was kept waiting from 2.00 pm while a solicitor interviewed a defendant. She explained it would be inappropriate to 'have a go' at the lawyer, as the child had only just been delivered from custody at 2.30 pm. Judges could not give a proper sentence indication unless they could trust the advocate to have provided all relevant information. A London judge said, typically, 'You get a lot of inexperienced counsel. You ask them how they wish to proceed and get a blank look'.

POLICY INITIATIVES

As has been seen from the criminal courts chapters, judges suffered from very frequent changes in policy and layer upon layer of unworkable legislation, produced by cost-cutting or vote-catching soundbites, meant to symbolise 'tough on crime'. Judges, all ex-practitioners, had an acute sense of fairness, and resisted the executive's punitive and bureaucratic demands where these conflicted. While Portia found her youth sentencing powers 'useless', and felt she could not secure executive attention on this, her court was bombarded with new procedural experiments, like 'simple, speedy, summary justice', whose bureaucratic demands for immediate defence disclosure she felt conflicted with adversarial due process. She silently cheered defendants who retorted 'prove it' to the prosecution, when they were expected to disclose their defence before receiving full prosecution disclosure. She was cynical about defendants 'appearing' in her court from their police cell on TV. How were lay justices meant to handle 50 a day? Portia's cynicism was summed up in her recent comment 'Everything is to save money'.

At one county court, the judges had repeatedly requested another part-timer. At a second, the lone rural DJ was coping with a backlog because his retired colleague had not been replaced. In central London, a retired CJ had not been replaced. At a fourth, both CJs wanted a third or even a DJ to man an unused courtroom. It was a struggle even to get a recorder (part-timer) occasionally. In an important London Crown Court, there was a shortage of HC judges to try serious frauds because they were all tied up in terrorist trials. At another, a shortage of four CJs meant that in February 2007, trial dates were being fixed for the following September. In the East Midlands, the lack of two judges meant some trials could not proceed. Two lawyers had been told they were to be appointed as judges but were kept in suspense. One judge complained that all some judges did was sex offences. There were cases which needed trying by a senior CJ which could not proceed. Two judges were there from the West Midlands to help out. We saw in the family chapter that CJs on three different circuits were barely coping, because of a judge shortage. By 2009, it had become normal to delay the replacement of retired judges for months or years, while, as we saw from the recruitment chapters, lawyers who succeeded as applicants were kept waiting for years before being given posts.

JOB CONDITIONS

Hazards

When advocates are appointed as full-time judges, they switch from travelling around and jumping up and down in court to sitting in one chair all day. Judges saw gaining weight and a bad back as occupational hazards. One new judge had put on half a stone, 'You spend a fortune at the gym'. Another had put on two stones. Another put on 1.5 stones then bought a multi-track exerciser and tried swimming 40 lengths a day. Three were being treated for bad backs (one was off sick then worked half-time for years); two did medical Pilates. One heavy laptop-user started to get RSI (repetitive strain injury). Judges are not provided with private health insurance so all these judges waited in NHS queues while off sick—a wasted resource, again. Though lower court judges in this research did not complain of emotional strain, HC judges handling grisly murder trials did. As we have seen, HC, CA and family judges suffered enormous workloads. In 2007, judges gained an advice line to help on emotional needs and stress.[27]

Pay, Pensions and Perks

Judges' salaries are transparent—displayed on the Judiciary website. It is well-known by lawyers but apparently an alien concept to some newspapers that senior judges and many circuit judges take a massive pay cut on appointment. In 2011, the top judge, the Lord Chief Justice, is paid less than a quarter of a million pounds, and CJs under £130,000, when 11 London headteachers earned over £150,000 in 2010 and one primary school head received £200,000.[28] In practice as QCs, senior judges would have been earning at least £250,000. Top silks earn £6 million per year, even those dependent on legal aid. Ironically, HC judges make very little money compared with the organised criminals they try. No research judge complained about pay, though. Occasionally, judges remarked, 'I hope you realise we do this as a public service'. Some were embarrassed by some CJs' demands for higher pay.

> There are some greedy judges who think they should be paid lots more. They don't see it is a privilege to do the job. They are very selfish … and appear to lack the public service drive which is a precondition to doing this job.

Judges enjoyed long holidays but, as we saw, many family and senior judges worked very long hours, including evenings and weekends, and many senior judges spent vacation time writing judgments.

Judges enjoyed no perks whatsoever, in the nature of, for example, MPs' gifts and expenses. They are banned from accepting gifts and fees so the judge who was a consultant on this project, Sedley LJ, gave his fee to charity. Unlike MPs, they do not have any second home allowance so HC judges appointed from the provinces were classified as based in London and they used taxed income to pay for their London accommodation and travel home at weekends. This included circuit presiders so a presider in say, the West, might spend a lot of time there but was not provided with a second home allowance, although they would be permitted to stay in judges' lodgings. There was no guarantee that their family could be accommodated.

---

[27]   F Gibb, 'Advice line is set up for lonely judges', *The Times*, 26 March 2007. Few in this research suffered the isolation of Australian judges discussed in this article.

[28]   'Union 'outraged at head teacher £200,000 pay package', 13 July 2010, BBC News website.

Mobility

Unlike veteran judges, new circuit judges were often appointed to circuits other than where they had practised so their commute might take several hours. I met more than one new judge who was expected to serve on two circuits and one who served about five courts in an eight-week cycle. Judges were paid for travel from their base court but not for overnight accommodation. Some judges commented that this work pattern was not 'family friendly'. One new judge dropped her children at school, then drove 1.5 hours to work. Her family court went on until 5.55 pm one day and 7.00 pm the next, in order to fulfil her week's list and for the convenience of the parties but in doing so, she relied on her husband, a barrister, to look after the children.

One HC presider, who had been a resident CJ had strong opinions that judges ought to move around though, and managing judges should be in fixed-term posts.

> There is a danger in sitting in one court all the time. I draw on my own experience ... If you are running a court as a resident judge ... you have two functions ... running the court ... getting the work through the mill as quickly, efficiently and as justly as possible [and] being a judge and deciding the case. They impact one upon the other ... You have to impress your stamp on the court, the court officials and the people who appear before you. You also have your own personal likes and dislikes and ... you may have a particular bête noir about something and they are not going to tell you that you are wrong. No-one is going to come into your room and say 'Look that was a bloody awful summing-up or that was bloody unfair the way you dealt with so-and-so'. I have seen other judges who have been in post ... for a long time and their influence on everything is great. In some respects it can be benign; in other respects [malignant], in particular, if they are in a position to influence people's career ... it is a good idea to move judges around ... and ... ensure that people in charge of the court get the opportunity to go out and sit elsewhere ... and remain in charge of that court for only a finite period.

> There is another advantage to that ... There is no point in the resident judge alone attacking the CPS because of their inadequacies and inefficiencies. You have to interest other judges...If the others think 'Well he is going to be doing this job for the next 15 or 20 years. I am just quite happily pootling along and doing my own thing', they may not take an interest in ensuring the ... court works efficiently but ... if they think 'in five years' time this job is going to become vacant' ... they will show an interest ... and *getting involved* is the important thing. Many circuit judges regard appointment as semi-retirement. They think a nice easy job, gentleman farmer approach. Well, that is no longer acceptable. People have to *work* ... the approach to the work has to be proactive.

CONCLUSION

Some of the stories in this book, especially those of the pilot-study judges here, look as if I have made them up. However, anyone can replicate these aspects of this research, by sitting in a variety of courtrooms as an observer. The budget problem is exacerbated by the fact that the courts have not been well run. The National Audit Office was critical of court administration in the 2009 report cited here. They found no staffing model, no satisfactory training regime or central property inventory, and ancient IT. Were I to replicate the fieldwork today, the picture would be much worse, because the fieldwork reported here was executed before the Labour Government announced a massive budget cut for the Ministry of Justice, which was followed by the Coalition's announcement of another cut and the threat of closure of hundreds of county and magistrates' courts. Although the study demonstrated that London fared worst in the provision of courts, equipment, staffing and support agencies, there were some striking inadequacies outside London, and it must be remembered that 40 per cent of district and circuit judges sit in London and the South East. Money was wasted everywhere, though, whether in a northern court waiting for a 'witness stuck in traffic' or a Midlands court where police witnesses hung around waiting for two days for a trial. The Resident sent them back to work—'They won't thank me, though!'

Court buildings were variable. The Royal Courts of Justice building is spectacular but in some respects unsuitable for modern life. Unbeknown to the public, behind its splendid courtrooms, it has no retiring rooms and no communal or dining facilities. Most county, Crown or combined courts were adequately equipped but many new ones and new conversions and some RCJ courtrooms were constructed without consulting the judiciary, which one would have assumed to be a prerequisite. Building or courtroom layout created problems or rendered them unusable. It is unforgivable that a blueprint for court design has only been established as recently as 2004. Some judges still worked in old courthouses without dining rooms and with inadequate facilities for court users. Some architecturally important old buildings had been sold off for incongruous uses or left to rot, while courts were shifted into unprepossessing office blocks. Judges explained the unco-ordinated use of the court estate. Courtrooms often suffered freezing air conditioning, even in midsummer. There were false economies on building repairs and heating. Security was ineffective. Of course, as we have seen throughout the book, false economies were not confined to the failure to repair buildings. We have seen that while judge time and court time was meant to be at a premium, judges could not proceed with their work while they waited for such fundamentals as prisoners, (ill-prepared) lawyers, document bundles, a client directed to the wrong court by social workers, and so on.

Remarkably poor staff pay caused a very high turnover, especially in London, and consequent unreliable support for the judiciary in the lower courts. Understaffing and the failure to establish satisfactory IT systems caused chaotic case 'filing' and lost paperwork and wasted more judge time and court time. Returning incorrectly completed forms to the court office or solicitors was yet another waste of public money.

Provision of IT hardware, software and training was inconsistent, unco-ordinated and wasteful and, in the civil courts, Lord Woolf's 1996 vision of computerised case management appears to have been abandoned. Judges trained one another and developed their own software but provision of IT and technical support was unacceptable in any modern organisation. Judges were provided with sophisticated law databases but were not trained how to use them. Failures in other equipment wasted yet more time. High Court judges were embarrassed by the lack of basic businesslike IT provision and many judges and other court users were inconvenienced.

All agencies serving the courts were underfunded, causing poor or incompetent case preparation or presentation, with consequent lack of readiness, adjournments and thus a cumulative waste of resources. A number of courts were short of judges and suffered a case backlog, while successful lawyers waited for months, for their judicial appointments to become effective. Violent offenders had to be released because custody time limits were exceeded.

Contrary to their public image as privileged, senior judges and some lower court judges took a thumping pay cut from practice but none complained of poor pay, seeing judicial work as public service. Judges were sympathetic with their staff. Most judges are paid less than some London headteachers. Further, they are not allowed to accept gifts and have no second home allowance so High Court judges appointed from the provinces had to pay for a London flat out of taxed income. New circuit judges were often appointed to different circuits and expected to move around.

Remarkably, judges very seldom complained about their chaotic working environment and if they did, it was not usually on their own behalf but in sympathy with the court user, court staff and the taxpayer.

18

The World of Judges from 2011

I EMBARKED ON this research because it seemed there was mis-match between the folk-devil and the real judge. Judges are acutely aware of their image as old, white, male, privileged, out-of-touch and generally pompous and unpleasant Nevertheless, as judges nowadays all have to apply for the post, it is feasible that they want to do a good job, not just shake off the bad image.

The composition of the judiciary remains an international embarrassment. Thanks to the pre-2006 old-boy recruitment network explored here, the UK's unusual passion for buying private education and the hierarchical legal profession from which judges are recruited, the judiciary *is* disproportionately male[1] and the *senior* judiciary (161 of 3,598 judges)[2] are mostly privately educated. Like any judiciary recruited from practising lawyers, judges are older than lawyers on average, unlike, say, French judges, who are recruited straight from college and where women dominate the ranks of trainees and ordinary judges. A wig adds 10 years to a male judge's appearance and fossilises him into a Dickensian character. Judges speak with patrician accents acquired at public school or the Bar.

This book has shown, however, that the rest of the image is unfair, anachronistic, and a product of lazy journalism, where wig-wearers are soft targets. A few judges' inappropriate comments lodge in the collective memory for decades, fuelling the stereotype so then 'all judges are like this'. People visualise Crown Court judges, because they feature in the news. District judges (DJs) in the county court are regularly asked 'how many people have you sent to prison this week?' Like DJs in the magistrates' court and all family and most civil judges, no-one ever watches them. None wears a wig. They are entirely missing from the public image but for most people who are affected by a court decision, it is these judges, alongside lay magistrates, who will touch their lives. Academics, like journalists, have concentrated on the senior judiciary, on judgments, but this book is about all types of judge in their working world.

Although the judiciary over-represents the happily marrieds, the judges here included the disabled, the divorced, the widowed and the children of widows and

---

[1] Eight per cent of LJs are women, as are 15 per cent of HC judges and CJs and 25 per cent of DJs and DJMCs. Baroness Hale is one female of 11 UKSC Justices: 2010 statistics, Judiciary website.

[2] Excluding tribunal judges.

divorcees. Seven of the 77 had suffered the death of a child. Three were carers. Judges were kept grounded in domestic life by their families and friends. Their hobbies were prosaic and middle class: walking, gardening, music, travel, family and football. Some said they had become more compassionate and less judgmental. Being on the bench, or practising law, had broadened their outlook, making them more aware of social problems, or more critical of government policy. Their experiences had radicalised some. As one said, 'I used to be a Tory'.

In court, judges donned a 'working personality' and were much more similar than they thought, because of training and socialisation into the judicial culture, where 'judgitis' is derided and discourtesy castigated by the Court of Appeal (CA). Obviously, there are some pompous judges. Anyone can test this by watching the courts but judges generally manifested the qualities they prioritised: patience, fairness, sympathy, good listening skills, decisiveness and courtesy. They put jurors, witnesses and litigants in person (LIPs) at ease. Judges' patience and listening skills were striking. They tolerated behaviour that would have been regarded as contempt in the 1970s. Court users and lawyers have become far less deferential in court. Judges were sometimes too tolerant of inefficient, unapologetic professionals who failed to take responsibility for their lack of readiness and the consequent waste of public money.

They are not all from privileged backgrounds. Today's baby boomer judges were far more socially mobile than their predecessors. They do not lead privileged lives. They eat packed lunches. They travel to work by tube or bike or motorbike or car or foot. Some have breeze block cells for 'chambers'. Many *top* judges are educated at elite universities, as they are elsewhere in the world, but criticising this is silly. We need the cleverest, workaholic judges to handle the hardest cases. The senior judges all had stellar CVs. They had earned their places at the top. Their salaries, much less than their earnings as lawyers, were not more than some headteachers. They called judging 'payback-time', a 'public service'. The state had its pound of flesh. As one DJ said, 'they work them to death'.

The most inaccurate element of judges' image is 'out-of-touch'. Through the people they meet in court and the stories they hear, judges are far, *far* more in touch with the range of human experiences that any non-judge. Consider the DJ struggling through her crowded lists in the magistrates' court, often in the unseen youth court, judging in junior gangland, where mothers inject their children with heroin, and there have been murders on the court house steps. Consider the Crown Court resident, dealing out the murder files to his judges, 'the steak knife murder, the single-blow murder, the chopped-up prostitutes in plastic bags'. From his Crown Court window, another resident had an overhead view of glue-sniffers and heroin addicts shooting-up. The county courts, one of which had been fire-bombed, shared the same clientele. County courts are not full of rich people, asserting their civil rights, but the debtors, the dispossessed, the disadvantaged and the disorganised. The DJs there know all about immigrants and the homeless and state benefits and drug and alcohol addiction. In the Crown Court, I was given photos of bodies kicked to death in crack-houses. In the family courts, I saw photos of filthy, beaten babies in maggoty, soaked cots. I read the judges' fat files in children's care cases, tales of cyclical family violence and depravity and deprivation. I watched Stanford in the Family Division, gently coaxing a mother to a confession of murder. In the 'privileged' judges' lodgings, Karen told me of the grey-faced High Court (HC) judge who could not eat after a day's hearing of a multiple child murder.

Judges are not out of touch but journalists and academics are out of touch with this real world of judging because most never go there: the magistrates' court, the family courts, the county courts and indeed most HC and CA cases are completely off their radar. Journalists watch the Crown Court or report on celebrity cases in the Royal Courts of Justice (RCJ). Academics sit at their desks writing about law reports.

REPEATING THEMES AND THE STATE OF THE COURTS IN 2011

Lawyers

Most of the 77 judges here had practised law. They understood lawyers. Sometimes they accommodated them. This did not mean judges were tolerant of sloppy lawyers. They applied the standards they themselves had met as lawyers. This research demonstrated the heavy dependence of the common law judge on thorough preparation by the lawyer. As an HC judge explained 'We do depend…on high quality advocacy. We don't have time to conduct research'. At every level of court, judges valued 'lawyers you can trust'. One HC judge wondered what life would be like in a country where you could not trust the lawyers.

The Lawyer Hierarchy and the Barrister/Solicitor Divide

This work included some solicitor-judges with chips on their shoulders. They were brought up in the hierarchical profession described by Hazell in 1978. The practice rules, etiquette and language emphasised barristers as their superiors, 'my learned friend' instead of 'my friend', yet there is and was nothing in barristers' exams or education to make them better lawyers than the nine-tenths of practising lawyers called solicitors. Barristers are still complaining of the poor advocacy of solicitor-advocates yet this book is full of examples of incompetent barristers, including silks. Solicitors have been eligible to sit as recorders since 1972, yet they have not made inroads into the ranks above DJ. Before 2006, recruitment was by nepotism. Existing judges were 'consulted' about applicants. People will favour those of their own group, even where they are placed in meaningless groups by experimental psychologists.[3] Solicitors aspiring to be judges know this. This book shows the lengths some went to in order to become known to the 'right' judges to support an application. Some still felt like outsiders on the circuit bench. Decades of campaigning to diversify the judiciary by attracting solicitors to the circuit bench and above have not worked. In March 2011, the Judicial Appointments Commission (JAC), whose statutory duty is diversifying the judiciary, is advertising for 98 recorders, yet in the last recruitment drive in 2008, solicitors represented only 20 per cent of applicants. In January 2011 they published a *Statistical digest of judicial appointments of Solicitors in England and Wales from 1998–99 to 2008–09*, containing some depressing statistics. No practising solicitors were appointed to the High Court in 1999–2009. The number of solicitors applying to the circuit bench remained constant at 12 per cent but appointees declined from 10 to six per cent, since the creation of the JAC. On three circuits, while the number of recorder applicants had increased to 20 per cent, only nine per cent of appointees were solicitors. The proportion of solicitor DJ appointees *declined* from 89 per cent to 68 per cent in the post-JAC period. Their 2009 report *Barriers to Application for Judicial Appointment Research*, found (at page 1):

> for barristers and solicitors there was a massive aspiration gap in terms of how likely they were to apply in the future. Whereas half of the barristers surveyed (49%) expected to apply for judicial office (20% are 'very likely'), this fell to only one in five solicitors (22% with only 6% 'very' likely).

This book exposed more problems wrought by the UK's unusual, divided legal profession. It confirmed previous research on the Crown Court Bar culture of last-minute preparation (or non-preparation) and the system of late briefs and northern courthouse plea bargaining. In family cases and many others, the split profession meant double lawyers. The more professionals there were in a complex child case, the more difficult it was to make progress. In his 2010 consultation on legal aid, below, the Minister of Justice reiterated the complaint that we have the world's most expensive legal aid system. He did not mention that we continue to pay for double lawyers. Practising lawyers, as he was, take the spilt profession for granted, because most have no experience of normal legal systems. Some commentators predict that the Legal Services Act 2007, further dismantling lawyers' monopolies, will see the death of the Bar as a separate profession but the same comment was made about the Courts and Legal Services Act 1990 and the Access to Justice Act 1999 and yet both sides continued to grow.[4]

---

[3] *Mind Changers: Henry Tajfel's Minimal Groups*, 27 February 2011, BBC Radio 4. Group identity is 'immensely powerful'.

[4] P Darbyshire, *Darbyshire on the English Legal System* (London, Sweet & Maxwell, 2011) ch 13.

The Judicial Hierarchy

Judges are not homogeneous. There is no sign of a career judiciary developing. The judiciary reflects the lawyers' hierarchy. One district judge (magistrates' court) DJMC was generally right when he said there was a chasm between the senior judiciary and the rest. Very few leap the divide. They were all part of the same group, marked out by their intellect, exceptional achievements and workload. The HC and CA only function thanks to the recruitment of workaholics, with people in their seventh decade doing night shifts. They thrive on challenging points of law and travelling on circuit. London's Commercial Court depends on some of the world's most brilliant judges. States litigate for the right to bring cases within its jurisdiction. It is a loss leader for the UK economy.

Judges pointed out that the circuit bench was the broadest in terms of ability. Some circuit judges (CJs) were like senior judges and many did High Court work but CJs wanted to sleep in their own beds at night. County court DJs were mostly solicitors and their resentment of CJs only became apparent in their interviews. It did not help that some were excluded from CJs' dining rooms till 1996 and the dining room saga, embarrassing to modern managing judges, rumbled on. The DJMCs were unconnected with the rest of the judiciary at the time of the research. Indeed, CJs were so oblivious of them that they could not imagine how a solitary judge could try a criminal case without a jury, despite the fact that they are handling the same cases. High Court DJs were a mystery to all.

Inquisitorial Procedure and Law Free Zones

Procedure in common law countries is described as adversarial, with the judge as neutral umpire. Law students spend years learning the law, in the expectation that in courts of law, disputes are resolved by the law. This study confirmed that magistrates' courts are generally 'law free zones'. The law seldom arises because common offences—theft, criminal damage and so on, are well-known and undisputed. Judges took what one described as a 'hands-on approach...some adversarial, some inquisitorial'. The family courts are also a law free zone. Indeed family procedure, especially in children's cases, was unique—multi-party, multi-court, multi-lawyer, and multi-issued, trundling on for years, with the children as both the parties and objects of the dispute.

Litigants in Person

Self-help works in small claims because they are geared for the unrepresented and this is another law free zone. The rules permit judicial flexibility and an inquisitorial approach. But LIPs were prevalent in all civil courts. Our adversarial system is predicated on the expectation that the parties bring to the court everything the judge needs: evidence, witness testimony, the law and legal argument. D-I-Y representation does not work in bigger cases. LIPs slow proceedings. They cannot sift the wheat from the chaff. LIPs can make mistakes and waste court time and that of the professionals and other parties because they do not understand procedure. When legal aid is cut, the number of LIPs increases. In the past, judges have been left to find their own solutions to the problem. As one CJ said, 'You've got to look after their interests'. They invented judicial assistants in the Royal Courts of Justice and one disgusted DJ devised the new 'judgecraft' training but that came too late for all the judges here. There is advice and support in the Royal Courts of Justice but inadequate services elsewhere. Some become obsessive. They and aggressive McKenzie friends can be a nuisance and the courts have been remarkably tolerant. At last, in Practice Guidance issued in July 2010, judges have reminded McKenzie friends that they have 'no independent right to provide assistance' and 'no right to act as advocates or to carry out litigation'. Courts should be 'slow to grant' applications for audience rights.[5]

In November 2010, to the horror of judges, the Government proposed more deep cuts in legal aid. In February 2011, the Judges' Council, chaired by the Lord Chief Justice, predicted:

> The proposals would lead to a huge increase in the incidence of unrepresented litigants, with serious implications for the quality of justice … at a time when courts are having to cope in any event with closures, budgetary cut-backs and reductions in staff numbers.[6]

Legal aid money saved would be offset by extra costs in the courts. They said the problem would be acute in the family courts, already struggling under the workload. They estimated a further 50,000 unrepresented parties per year. Backlogs would occur. In other courts, people would be bringing cases with no prospect of success, because they had not been filtered out by good advice.

Resources and the Threat to Independence

Spending money on justice does not attract votes. The courts are out of sight and out of mind. Many judges work in straightened circumstances. Buildings are badly designed or crumbling; lodgings are shabby; IT systems unco-ordinated and decades behind the outside world, with a lack of support. In the county courts, paper files are lost and in the Crown Court, and sometimes the magistrates' courts, cases just do not progress, because the police or forensics or lawyers or other professionals are not prepared, or, in London, the probation service has run out of money. All this, yet the Judicial and Court Statistics 2009 showed the

---

[5] Judiciary website, July 2010.
[6] Judiciary press notice, 'Judges' Council Co-ordinated Response', 24 February 2011 and A Hirsch 'Legal aid cuts will cost more in the long run, say judges', *Guardian*, 24 February 2011.

number of Crown Court defendants has gone from 78,000 to 101,000 in 2005–08. In the family courts, the 56-week average delay in saving children who need to be taken into care or adopted is beyond a scandal. This book shows the system is shot through with false economies and that was supported by the Audit Commission in 2009 and now the Interim Family Justice Review in 2011.

Judges do not complain of their own conditions because they know their staff are paid a pittance and public agencies are underfunded. Family and senior judges work so hard that do not have the time to complain. Conditions can only get worse. In October 2010, the Chancellor announced the Ministry of Justice must face a target budget reduction of 23 per cent, plus a 50 per cent cut in capital spending, plus a 33 per cent cut in the administration budget. The Ministry had already reduced its budget by £1 billion under the previous Labour administration. In December 2010, the Ministry announced the closure of 49 county courts and 93 magistrates' courts, on the grounds that some lacked appropriate modern facilities but these courts were meant to provide easily accessible, local justice, a concept that in some towns will now be gone forever. In October 2010, the Senior Presiding Judge, Goldring LJ, drew attention to a series of 'significant errors' in the proposal.[7] He said poor public transport meant many court users would not be able to get to their local courts before 10.00 am.

In February 2011, Lord Phillips, President of the UKSC, gave a speech expressing concern over a more sinister outcome of budget cuts: the danger to the UKSC's independence. In planning the Court, Lord Falconer had assured Parliament that it would be paid direct by the Treasury but the Constitutional Reform Act 2005 did not provide for that. Instead, the cost was to be borne by the civil courts of the three jurisdictions. This had not worked out. There was no money from England and Wales so the Lord Chancellor made up the difference. Thus, the Court was not independent. The budget was cut. Lord Phillips said they did not mind cutting back. They had managed with 11 judges for years and could shrink permanently but the lack of independence from government funding was the real concern. Half the Court's cases related to public law. Human rights cases like the *Belmarsh* case irritate governments and he cited instances of Labour and Conservative politicians criticising judges as 'unelected and unaccountable'.

Is the English Legal System a System?

In the *Family Justice Review*, Interim Report, March 2011, David Norgrove said (at page 3 and paras 13 and 14):

> The lack of IT and management information is astonishing, with the result—among other things—that little is known about performance and what things cost. The system, in short, is not a system. … There is an almost unbelievable lack of management

---

[7] For instance, Abergavenny MC was listed for closure, because it was said not to have been used since 1999 but it was refurbished and re-opened in 2010.

information at a system-wide level, with little data on performance, flows, costs or efficiency available to support the operation of the system ... These are the symptoms of a situation that simply cannot be allowed to continue.

Like any piece of empirical research, this study identified some elements of the system that were not working as intended. It used to be said that a premium was set on the judge's time and others organised themselves around this schedule. Doubtless, this was the case before 1972, when judges travelled on assize, and sessions were conducted quarterly, but now the judge was at the mercy of everyone else. Every trial was delayed or abortive. The judge provided a service to be called on as and when everyone else was ready. Criminal case management rules introduced in 2005 did not appear to have shifted Crown Court business forward as intended. Demanding a 'change of culture' will not bring it about. The national cracked trial rate has steadily increased since 2005 to 42 per cent. The research confirmed the strong plea bargaining culture of some northern courts, with judges waiting outside the courtroom and the assumption that plea negotiations would start once the defendant reached the court house. In November 2010, the Minister of Justice published a detailed consultation called *Proposals for the Reform of Legal Aid in England and Wales.*[8] Among other things, he said advocates and litigators are paid more for a cracked trial than an early guilty plea, sometimes double, regardless of whether extra work has been done. He proposes increasing guilty plea fees by 25 per cent, to encourage early guilty pleas. The problem is, though, this will place more pressure on defendants to plead guilty. An experienced lawyer, C Yarnley, said in a letter to *The Times*, on 14 June 2010, 'A great many defendants can be described as of limited intellect and strength of character. The temptation to yield to the offer "plead now and you can go home and we promise you lenient sentencing" could be overwhelming'.

Money is wasted everywhere. In 2001, Lord Justice Auld pointed out that lawyers are rewarded not for preparation but for long trials and there is an imbalance between prosecution and defence remuneration and consequently the quality of their work. In this research, Crown Court days were wasted by ill-prepared and disorganised lawyers, and shambolic prosecutions. In a 2010 consultation called *Legal Aid: Reforming Advocates' Graduated Fees*, the Ministry consulted (yet again) on aligning defence fees with (lower) prosecution fees. In the 2010 *Legal Aid Reform* paper, they said litigators and advocates are paid according to the number of pages of prosecution evidence. That problem was clear in chapter nine of this book. Juries were swamped with pages of unedited prosecution transcripts. The paper said that in 2008–09, payments to QCs and leading juniors cost £52 million. The average number of prosecution pages has increased by 65 per cent since 2004–05. The Ministry proposes to replace this system with a 'better indicator of complexity'.

[8]   (CP12/10) Cm 7967.

Every resident Crown Court judge routinely approved last-minute applications by defendants to sack their legal teams, sometimes more than once, wasting legal aid money and successfully delaying the trial for a month.

This research showed that simple solutions could have saved shocking amounts of money, like the aborted Crown Court trial, where the protected witness blurted out details of the accused because no-one had thought to instruct him to stick to answering the questions, or, in the family courts, ensuring that a mother with special needs attended the correct court so that a care hearing could proceed.

In the family courts, procedure was not working as intended. Time limits were a fiction. Paternal contact with small children was suspended for years because of the difficulty of preparing and convening multiple experts and multiple lawyers. The outsider was left to wonder that there must be a better way to determine the futures of children than a system that disrupts their entire childhood.

Over in the county court, where the Civil Procedure Rules 1998 (CPR) tasked judges with promoting alternative dispute resolution (ADR), I never heard a district judge trying to persuade lawyers or parties that they would be better off using it. Sir Rupert Jackson in his 2010 review of costs considered ADR to be under-used. He said all litigation lawyers and judges, the public and small businesses should be informed about the benefits of ADR. The President of HM Association of District Judges called for all DJs to be trained in mediation, in 2010[9] and he was supported in a speech by Lord Neuberger MR. Judicial training on ADR is only now being introduced, 12 years after the CPR required them to promote it.

The study showed the costs in some cases were remarkably disproportionate. Judges and lawyers were tasked by the CPR with keeping costs proportionate. That has not happened so in March 2011, the Minister was consulting on a range of radical options to get a grip on civil justice[10] in preparation for the Legal Aid, Sentencing and Punishment Offenders Bill.

Law books describe the disclosure rules and the rules on the right of silence as if they work as intended but at the time of this research, a normal defence statement amounted to a few unhelpful sentences and judges routinely chose not to act where a defendant did not produce a statement, with at least one Crown Court judge not understanding that he had such a power. Though the rules have been reformed a number of times since the early 1990s, the Ministry's 2010 paper on legal aid said that the disclosure rules are under review once again.

The study shows the value of observational research over purely statistical research. Whereas case progression statistics show that the 2005 management

<hr>

[9]   *New Law Journal* news, April 2010.
[10]   *Solving disputes in the county courts: creating a simpler, quicker and more proportionate system—A consultation on reforming civil justice in England and Wales* CP6/2011.

system appears to have improved matters in the Crown Court, the judges showed me how they fiddled the statistics and said they knew that sanctions could not work.

WHY DO JUDGES GO ON?

Despite relentless hard work and long hours for some, and the impoverished state of the courts, which caused Genn to call judges 'heroic', all but three judges of these 77 loved the job. A DJMC called himself 'the luckiest man in the world'; CJs said they had 'one of the best jobs in England', 'the best job in the Principality'. Judges loved 'being able to make a difference—show the public the system isn't necessarily against them' (DJMC); 'playing my part in trying to ensure a just outcome' (CJ); 'making a huge difference to children's lives' (HC). An HC judge said 'It's a fantastic job, hugely rewarding' and, in the Commercial Court, another said 'hopefully, we're contributing to certainty in international trade'.

We are indeed lucky to live in a country where we take the integrity, independence and intellect of our judges for granted but there lies the problem. We take them for granted.

Index